IT Interview Questions

A Primer For The IT Job Interviews

By

Narasimha Karumanchi

CONCEPTS PROBLEMS INTERVIEW QUESTIONS

Designed by *Narasimha Karumanchi*

Acknowledgements

Mother and *father*, it is impossible to thank you adequately for everything you have done, from loving me unconditionally to raising me in a stable household, where you persistent efforts traditional values and taught your children to celebrate and embrace life. I could not have asked for better parents or role-models. You showed me that anything is possible with faith, hard work and determination.

This book would not have been possible without the help of many people. I would like to thank them for their efforts in improving the end result. Before we do so, however, I should mention that I have done my best to correct the mistakes that the reviewers have pointed out and to accurately describe the protocols and mechanisms. I alone am responsible for any remaining errors.

First and foremost, I would like to express my gratitude to many people who saw me through this book, to all those who provided support, talked things over, read, wrote, offered comments, allowed me to quote their remarks and assisted in the editing, proofreading and design. In particular, I would like to thank the following individuals.

- *Mohan Mullapudi*, IIT Bombay, Architect, dataRPM Pvt. Ltd.
- *Navin Kumar Jaiswal*, Senior Consultant, Juniper Networks Inc.
- *A.Vamshi Krishna*, IIT Kanpur, Mentor Graphics Inc.
- *Kiran Kumar Pasupuleti*, IISc, Bangalore
- *Hirak Chatterjee*, Yahoo Inc.
- *Suresh Kodati*, Development Manager, IBM Software Labs
- *Balakrishna Veerala*, *M-Tech.*, *Factuly*, *GATE* Subjects.
- *Kondrakunta Murali Krishna,* B-Tech., Technical Lead, HCL
- *Kota Veeraiah*, Head Master, Obulasuni Palle, Z. P. H. School
- *Potla Venkateswarlu*, Teacher, Kambhampadu, Z. P. H. School
- *Muralidhar*, Teacher, Durgi
- *Chaganti Siva Rama Krishna Prasad*, Founder, StockMonks Pvt. Ltd.
- *Naveen Valsakumar*, Co-Founder, NotionPress Pvt. Ltd.
- *Ramanaiah*, Lecturer, Nagarjuna Institute of Technology and Sciences, MLG

-Narasimha Karumanchi
M. Tech, *IIT Bombay*
Founder, *CareerMonk.com*

Dedicated to my soulmate & love of my life
-Late Sri Sailaja

Preface

Dear Reader,

Please Hold on! I know many people do not read the preface. But I would strongly recommend that you go through the preface of this book at least.

India has many of the key ingredients for making this transition. It has a critical mass of skilled, English-speaking knowledge workers, especially in the sciences. It has a well-functioning democracy. Its domestic market is one of the world's largest. It has a large and impressive scattering, creating valuable knowledge linkages and networks. In addition, the development of the IT sector in recent years has been remarkable. India has created profitable niches in information technology (IT) and is becoming a global provider of software services.

Many software companies hire graduates with different backgrounds computer science, electrical, civil, mechanical, B.E., B. Tech., MCAs, MBAs etc. The year 2013-14 characterizes a landmark year as aggregate revenue for the Indian IT-BPO sector is estimated to cross USD 120 billion.

India currently produces a solid core of knowledge workers in tertiary and scientific and technical education, although the country needs to do more to create a larger cadre of educated and agile workers who can adapt and use knowledge. Efforts have been put into establishing a top-quality university system that includes many world-class institutions of higher learning that are competitive and meritocratic, such as Indian Institute of Technology (IIT), International Institute of Information Technology (IIIT), Indian Institutes of Management, Indian Institute of Science, National Institute of Technology (NIT), and the Birla Institute of Technology & Science (BITS). Despite these efforts, not all publicly funded universities or other educational institutions in India have been able to maintain high-quality standards or keep pace with developments in knowledge and technology.

IT Interview Questions try to facilitate pupils who arrive from colleges where they could not find proper assistance for career counseling.

There are hundreds of books on IT interviews already flooding the market. You may naturally wonder what the need of writing another book on IT interviews is! This book assumes you have basic knowledge about computer science. Main objective of the book is *not* to provide you the *catalog* of *IT interview questions* and *their answers*. Before writing the book, I set myself the following *goals*:

- The book be written in *such a way* that students from non-IT branches should be able to understand it *easily* and *completely*.
- The book should present the concepts in *simple* and straightforward manner with a *clear – cut* explanation.
- The book should provide enough *realtime* examples so that students get better understanding of the *IT interview questions* and also useful for the *campus/off-campus* interviews.
- It should challenge you to look at the small but significant changes you need to make to improve your impact at interviews.
- In this book you will learn all the secrets you need to know to help nail your job interview and get the job.

Please remember, the books which are available in the market are lacking one or many of these goals. This book is different from other books available on the market. The main goals of this book are to provide students with a good knowledge base, and to offer a better understanding to those new to IT. Based on my experience, I thought of writing this book aiming at achieving these goals in a simple way. A 3-stage formula is used in writing this book, i.e.

Concepts + Problems + Interview Questions

I used very simple language such that a school going student can also understand the concepts easily. Once the concept is discussed, it is then interlaced into problems. The solutions of each and every problem are well explained. Finally, interview questions with answers on every concept are covered. All the interview questions in this book are collected from various interviews conducted by top software development companies.

Interviewing is all about research, confidence and creating a good rapport. Everyone is nervous on interviews. If you simply allow yourself to feel nervous, you'll do much better. Remember also that it's difficult for the interviewer as well. In general, be upbeat and positive. Never be negative. As a job seeker if you read complete book with good understanding, I am sure you will challenge the interviewers and that is the objective of this book.

It is *recommended* that, at least *one complete* reading of this book is required to get full understanding of all the topics. In the *subsequent* readings, you can directly go to any chapter and refer. Even though, enough readings were given for correcting the errors, due to human tendency there could be some minor typos in the book. If any such typos found, they will be updated at *CareerMonk.com*. I request you to constantly monitor this site for any corrections, new problems and solutions. Also, please provide your valuable suggestions at: *Info@CareerMonk.com*.

Wish you all the best! I am certain that you will discover this volume useful.

-Narasimha Karumanchi
M. Tech, *IIT Bombay*
Founder, *CareerMonk.com*

Table of Contents

CHAPTER

Organization of Chapters

1

1.1 Why Separate Book on IT Interviews?

Computer science is one of the most exciting and important technical fields of our time. *Necessity* is the mother of invention, and whenever we really need something, humans will find a way to get it.

I saw many students, who graduated two years ago and couldn't get a suitable job, decided he would sit for the civil services exam instead. In many Indian colleges, the faculty and infrastructure is not good or it is simply not there at all. According to a study, hardly 30 to 35% colleges have the basic facilities and students from there do fine. For the rest, even getting a job that will earn them 5,000 rupees is very difficult. Remember, even the daily wage workers are making more than 10,000 rupees a month.

In our anxiety to expand technical education in the country, we have started a large number of institutes, but unfortunately, we don't have technically qualified people to teach our engineering students. What people are saying is that there is a requirement, a demand, but your students coming out of engineering colleges are not employable.

Technical jobs are not shrinking. There is still a growing demand, but engineers here are unable to get those jobs because they lack subject and technical knowledge as well as analytical ability, communication and social skills.

The aim of this book is to assist those pupils who could not take proper direction for campus preparation, including career guidance, technical and non-technical help, hints for successful long IT career. A successful job search requires a careful, thoughtful plan. This book reviews all of the steps involved in getting a job in today's market. It serves as a comprehensive guide to finding the perfect career.

1.2 What Is this Book About?

A unique feature of this book that is missing in most of the available books on IT interviews is to offer a balance between theoretical, practical concepts, problems and interview questions.

Concepts + Problems + Interview Questions

This text provides graduate students in computer science, IT, and electrical engineering, as well as practitioners in industry with an understanding of the specific interview questions and solutions for them.

The book offers a large number of questions to practice each exam objective and will help you assess your knowledge before you take the real interview. The detailed answers to every question will help reinforce your knowledge.

The work of engineers is everywhere—online ticket reservation, online retain, the bathroom, bedroom, kitchen, and living room. We see results of engineering when we travel—trains, buses, traffic lights, railroads, buildings, etc.—and when we go to work—computers, paper, books, furniture, clocks, pens, etc. Grocery stores, restaurants and hospitals all house the work of engineers. Considering all of this, it is essential that students continue to be encouraged to enter this creative and challenging field. This book provides the aspiring engineer with an overview of the profession. It reveals the pros and cons encountered by the author in his long, successful career as a software engineer. Other topics include job security, the importance of keeping track of goals, maintaining the network, tips for writing good resume, and many more. Hopefully, reading this book will help to answer all relevant questions.

Salient features of the book are:

- While some of the technical expertise you gain in college is essential to your career as an engineer or scientist, much of it will never be used. Your success may depend on other factors all together. This book discusses these factors, passes along some true examples, and gives some real-world advice on how to avoid most of the pitfalls associated with your chosen career.
- This is primarily for college graduates who, upon receiving their degree, are not sure of what they truly want to do with their lives.
- An easy-to-use guide to writing the resume and cover letter that will help two year college students land the job best suited to their interests and experience.
- Useful for anyone preparing for interviews (campus/off-campus interviews, walk-in interview and company internal interviews for transferring to other teams).
- This book is unique in that it helps you master the most commonly asked questions, instilling you with the confidence that you need to endure the most difficult of interviews.

1.3 Should I Take this Book?

This book is for those who are preparing for campus placements. Although this book is more precise and analytical than many other interview books, it rarely uses any mathematical concepts that are not taught in high school.

I have made an effort to avoid using any advanced calculus, probability, or stochastic process concepts. The book is therefore appropriate for undergraduate students for their interview preparation.

This book is for students (irrespective of branch) who *want* to learn IT interview questions. This covers all probable domains of questions during the technical interviews in your campus/off-campus placements.

I have identified the major areas where a student should prepare himself for an aptitude test or a technical interview so as to get placed into an IT company. The technical fields are: C, C++, Java, DBMS, JDBC, operating system concepts, data structures, algorithms, basics of design patterns, scripting languages, basics of web development, and networking. Similarly, amongst the non-technical fields a student needs to mentally prepare himself for an aptitude test, resume writing skills, brain teasers, and a HR interview. All the basic study material required to prepare concerning the above related fields are deployed in this book. In addition, this book includes latest buzzwords like cloud computing, big data etc...

1.4 Organization of Chapters

The *second* chapter of this text book focus on designing resume and best ways to get an interview call along with dos and don'ts of that process.

After completion of *second* chapter, I recommend reading remaining chapters in sequence. Each of these chapters leverages material from the preceding chapters. There are no major interdependencies among the chapters, so they can be read in any order.

The chapters are arranged in the following way:

3. *Group Discussions*: Group discussions (GDs) have become an integral part of the selection process. It is being used as a selection tool not only by business schools but also by core and software companies. GD is a forum where people sit together to discuss a topic with the common objective of finding a solution for a problem or an issue that is given. GD is conducted to measure certain attributes in a candidate such as content, communication skills, group behaviour and leadership skills. This chapter provides detailed overview of GDs.
4. *Operating System Concepts*: The operating system is an example of system software. The primary role of an operating system is to manage the computer's resources. This includes both physical (hardware) resources, and abstract resources. For every computer science and IT student, it is very important to have basics of operating system concepts. This chapter discusses about basics of process management, memory management, and all interview questions related to different areas of the OS.
5. *C/C++/Java Interview Questions*: If you're interviewing at the fast-moving end of companies like the typical startup, the choice of programming language matters, and most candidates prefer C, C++, or Java. Languages like C, C++, or Java tends to be significantly more verbose than more productive languages like Python or Ruby that come with more powerful built-in primitives like list comprehensions, functional arguments, destructuring assignment, etc. This chapter covers most of the common interview questions in this space and is one of the biggest chapters of this book.
6. *Scripting Languages*: These types of questions would help interviewers to determine if the candidate for the position has spent any time actually writing shell scripts, either on the job or as part of a shell scripting course or training class, or has just read about them in books or online. If you don't know a scripting language well, it's better to use a language you're proficient at, though it'd be even better to just get proficient at a scripting language. If you are a fresh graduate, having knowledge of scripting languages will give you an edge over others. This chapter focuses on the basics of Shell, Python, and Perl scripting.
7. *Bitwise Hacking*: The commonality or applicability depends on the problem in hand. Some real-life projects do benefit from bit-wise operations.

   Some examples:
   - You're setting individual pixels on the screen by directly manipulating the video memory, in which every pixel's color is represented by 1 or 4 bits. So, in every byte you can have packed 8 or 2 pixels and you need to separate them. Basically, your hardware dictates the use of bit-wise operations.
   - You're dealing with some kind of file format (e.g. GIF) or network protocol that uses individual bits or groups of bits to represent pieces of information.
   - Your data dictates the use of bit-wise operations. You need to compute some kind of checksum (possibly, parity or CRC) or hash value and some of the most applicable algorithms do this by manipulating with bits.

   In this chapter, we discuss few tips and tricks with focus on interviews.
8. *Concepts of Computer Networking*: This chapter provides computer networking fundamentals. They include, OSI and TCP models, IP addressing, UDP, Client/Server Models, Wireless networking, DNS, FTP, DHCP, routing protocols etc...
9. *Database Management Systems*: A database is a collection of data organized in a particular way. In other words, it is a collection of information that is organized

so that it can easily be accessed, managed, and updated. Databases can store information about people, products, orders, or anything else. Many databases start as a list in a word-processing program or spreadsheet. As the list grows bigger, redundancies and inconsistencies begin to appear in the data. The data becomes hard to understand in list form, and there are limited ways of searching or pulling subsets of data out for review.

A database is a structure that can store information about multiple types of things (or entities), the characteristics (or attributes) of those entities, and the relationships among the entities. It also contains data types for attributes and indexes.

Databases can be of many types such as Flat File Databases, Relational Databases, Distributed Databases etc. A relational database uses the concept of linked two-dimensional tables which comprise of rows and columns. A user can draw relationships between multiple tables and present the output as a table again. A user of a relational database need not understand the representation of data in order to retrieve it. This chapter focuses on DBMS advantages, database normalization, SQL queries, and interview questions on them.

10. *Brain Teasers*: There were huge numbers of brain teasers and it is very difficult to cover all of them in a technical book. This chapter covers a few sample questions.

Chapters 11 *to* 26: *Data Structures and Algorithms*

Data Structures and Algorithms are important parts of computer science in an interview. They form the fundamental building blocks of developing logical solutions to problems. They help in creating efficient programs that perform tasks optimally. Data Structure refers to the principles of storing and organizing data. The algorithm is the set of logical steps involved in solving a problem.

It focuses on giving solutions for complex problems in data structures and algorithm. It even provides multiple smart solutions for a single problem, thus familiarizing readers with different possible approaches to the same situation. The book comprehensively covers the topics required for a thorough understanding of the subjects. It focuses on concepts like Linked Lists, Stacks, Queues, Trees, Priority Queues, Searching, Sorting, Hashing, Algorithm Design Techniques, Greedy, Divide and Conquer, Dynamic Programming and Symbol Tables.

27. *Basics of Design Patterns*: A design pattern is a defined, used and tested solution for a known problem. Design patterns got popularity after the evolution of object oriented programming. Object oriented programming and design patterns became inseparable. In software engineering, a design pattern is a general reusable solution to a commonly occurring problem within a given context in software design. A design pattern is not a finished design that can be transformed directly into code. It is a description for how to solve a problem that can be used in many different situations. This chapter does not cover design patterns in depth, but focuses on interviews. Design patterns deal with an efficient way of creating classes, objects and interconnecting them.
28. *Non – Technical Help*: This chapter gives tips on non-technical areas. Few sample questions are:
    - What do you like and/or dislike most about your current and/or last position?
    - Why are you leaving your current position?
    - How do you handle pressure? Do you like or dislike these situations?
    - What are your strengths and weaknesses?
29. *Quantitative Aptitude Concepts*: Every placement test paper on quantitative aptitude will contain at least 30% of questions on numbers and series. Aptitude questions on numbers form the backbone for placement preparation. You can score easily on quantitative aptitude section if you understand the basics of number system. Since the questions are simple, importance lies in acquiring the

right skills to tackle these problems with speed. This chapter presents the list of important formulae and tips to help you understand and prepare for the quantitative aptitude section.

30. *Basics of Cloud Computing*: Cloud Computing is a new concept which was recently came popular in computer industry. The main idea of cloud computing is the sharing of computing recourses among a community of users. Cloud computing is a term you can see being used a lot, but there is a lack of clarity about what cloud computing is. However, most of us are probably making use of the cloud without realizing that this is the case; whenever we access our Gmail, Hotmail, or Yahoo mail accounts, or upload a photo to Facebook, we are using the cloud. The potential benefits and risks, however, are more apparent. In this chapter, we will try to shed some focus on defining cloud computing and other latest buzz words.
31. *Miscellaneous Concepts*: This chapter covers other important topics of IT interviews (such as HTML, CSS, Javascript, Ruby on Rails, Google Search Tips, Web Crawling, XML etc.) even though they are out of scope of this book.
32. *Career Options*: You must have asked yourself this question a lot of times at some or the other point in your life. The society is more concerned about the job and pay you get after education and not the intellectual property you have earned. Don't leave an option straight forward because it is too mediocre. You don't need to follow others but to follow your heart. It's okay if a million other people like you are preparing for an entrance exam, including your friends! If you believe you can crack the exam, trust me YOU CAN. Do whatever you want with 100% dedication. In this chapter, we explore list of those options.

At the end of each chapter, a set of problems/questions are provided for you to improve/check your understanding of the concepts. The examples in this book are kept simple for easy understanding. The objective is to enhance the explanation of each concept with examples for a better understanding.

CHAPTER

Getting Ready 2

In this chapter, we focus on designing resume and best ways to get an interview call along with dos and don'ts of that process.

2.1 Best Ways to Get an Interview Call

Knowing that you are likely one of many applicants, how do you get *noticed*? There are a few steps that you can follow to greatly increase your odds of landing that interview.

Be Specific

Develop a list of specific target companies that you can identify to those with whom you are networking. For example, if you say, "I want to work in engineering," that doesn't really get my brain working.

However, if you say, " I want to work for ABC company in an engineering capacity, namely leading a team of hardware engineers," that helps me to

a) Understand what you are looking for and
b) Start thinking about who I may know at ABC Company.

Know Your Strengths

Knowing what you bring to the table and clearly expressing it sets you apart from the masses right away. Often, people are not clear on what they can do to specifically help a company. Hiring companies want to know what you can do for them; it helps to answer that question well.

Research Your Target Companies

Know those companies that appeal to you and appear to be a great fit. If you don't know about the company or if you don't really want to work there, it typically shows in a conversation.

If you are excited about the potential of working for the company and you have clearly done your research that will make you extremely appealing and different from the rest. In simple terms, know the history of all your target companies.

Develop a Resume That Stands Out From the Rest

I have seen great resumes and terrible resumes. What makes a great resume? Clearly defining what problems you will solve for the company and adjusting the resume based on the job available are two important factors.

Develop Marketing Material

What can you leave with a new contact that sets you apart from the other people they have talked with? Professional business cards are a must but what about a biographic? This doesn't replace a resume but is rather a marketing piece that visually tells the story of your job history.

Don't Be Afraid To Call the Hiring Manager

Be assertive. If you know who the hiring manager is, call him/her and briefly state that you have applied for the position. Take the opportunity to alert them to this and let them know that if they took ten minutes to meet with you, they would find you a viable candidate. The worst thing that can happen is that you get turned down.

Don't Rely On Job Boards

Not that you cannot find a job utilizing a job board but statistics show that 90% of jobs are never posted and those that are posted are swamped with job seekers taking the traditional, ineffective route.

Create Your Brand Utilizing Social Media

Develop your brand as an industry expert using *LinkedIn* and, if you're brave, *Twitter*. Post professional, relevant articles that are pertinent to the type of jobs in which you are interested.

Network

I can't say this strongly enough. The best way to make it to the top of the resume pile is to *network*. Your goal is to have someone hand the resume to the appropriate person and say, "I think we need to look at this person."

Follow Up

Networking and all the other steps are worthless without following up. Be persistent without being obnoxious. Ask your contact how best he/she likes to be communicated with and how often. Respect that they have their own priorities but don't give up if they don't respond immediately. While nothing can guarantee an interview, taking a proactive, professional approach will certainly increase your odds. What are some tips I may have missed? I would love to hear from you!

2.2 Reasons Why You Are Not Getting Interview Calls

No matter how strong your skills or experience are, you won't land a new job without first securing an interview with a prospective employer. Job seekers often consider this step of the hiring process the most difficult.

After all, how many times have you considered your qualifications ideal for an open position only to never hear from the hiring manager about the resume and cover letter you submitted? You are putting a lot of time and effort into applying for jobs, you have perfected your CV and covering letter are applying stealthily but somehow never seem to get called for an interview?

Always check that you are not making any of the following common mistakes:

You have not considered enough potential employers

Companies that continually grab headlines and are highly recognizable can be exciting places to work. But so are many companies you've never heard of. Keep in mind those organizations that are household names often receive thousands of resumes for each opening. Consider exploring opportunities with small and midsize companies. Some people have a tendency to only apply for jobs in well-established multinational companies who are very well marketed.

While you may think this will be a very exciting place to work so too are up and coming companies who may not currently have the same market exposure. Smaller companies will not have as many applications and are always a great stepping stone to gaining experience in and may grow with you as you work there.

You don't follow directions [You didn't use the application method specified]

Each company has a different procedure it asks applicants to follow for submitting employment applications. Some ask that you use a form on their Web sites while others prefer traditional phone calls or faxes. Make sure you understand what the prospective employer seeks by carefully reading the job listing.

Then, follow the directions to the letter. If you don't, your application may never reach the hiring manager.

Sometimes job applicants make the mistake of using the same method of application for every job even though this may not be the one specified by the potential employer. For example if an employer wants you to apply in writing posting your application then do this and don't send an email. Follow application instructions very carefully.

You need to improve your resume

Sending out the same cover letter and resume to all companies isn't likely to capture the attention of prospective employers. Hiring managers want to know why you're a good match for their specific business needs. So take the time to research employers and customize your job search materials by explaining why you're interested in a particular position and how you could make a contribution to the company.

You must tailor fit every CV and cover letter to that specific job description and sending out a copy of the same one will leave many job recruiters unimpressed as they can see that no specific input or research has been undertaken. Always use specific examples on your CV by matching your skills to what they are looking for.

Your cover letter isn't enticing

Your cover letter is your opportunity to sell yourself to the potential employer. Is it dynamic? What have you got to put you above the other couple of hundred applicants? Why are your skills more suited to the job than anyone else? The best cover letters take select details from the resume and expand upon them, explaining in depth how your talents and experience can benefit the prospective employer.

You don't reference keywords [Your CV isn't Keyword Rich]

Companies that receive a high volume of resumes often use scanning software that looks for certain keywords to determine which candidates to call for interviews. More often than not, keywords come directly from the job description. It could be any terms of their choosing e.g. 'Cisco Certified Network Administrator,' or 'Accounts Payable experience.' So include as many keywords as possible in both your CV and Covering letter.

There are Mistakes on your CV and Cover letter

Submitting an application that contains typos and grammatical goofs is perhaps the quickest way to foil your chances of securing an interview. In fact, 84 percent of executives polled in a recent survey by our company said it takes just one or two errors to remove a candidate from consideration. The reason: These types of mistakes show a lack of professionalism and attention to detail. Make sure to carefully proofread your resume prior to submitting it and ask a friend or family member to do the same.

You don't know who to send your resume to

Though it's fine to start your cover letter with the generic salutation "To Whom It May Concern," hiring managers pay special attention to applications that are addressed directly to them. While this may not be specified on the Job Advert and often isn't do everything within your power to find out this information.

Call the company and ask the receptionist, explain your situation more often than not you will get the information you require. That means, if the job advertisement doesn't include the hiring manager's name, call the company and speak to the receptionist or a member of the person's department. More often than not, you can obtain the information fairly easily if you're candid about your reason for wanting it.

You don't have an 'in' with the company [Try to have an inside Contact]

Using the name of a common contact to make the connection between you and the hiring manager is by far the best way to ensure your cover letter and resume get optimal attention. So, keep in touch with members of your professional network; you never know who has a contact at the company you hope to work for.

If you know anyone in the organization then by all means use this contact name on your covering letter. This is where Networking comes in and having a name to use really does out your application to the top of the pile.

You don't follow up [You don't follow up on every Job Application]

One way to improve the odds a hiring manager gives consideration to your resume is to follow up with him or her. According to a survey by our company, 86 percent of executives said job seekers should contact a hiring manager within two weeks of sending a resume and cover letter.

It is surprising how many people never pick up the phone and follow up on jobs they have applied for. Employers generally say that job applicants should follow up on their application within two weeks of submitting it. In many instances just a brief phone call reminding them about you or a quick email can get you an interview.

Your skills might not match the job requirements

The bottom line may be that you're simply not as perfect for the job as you think. Before submitting your resume, take a close look at the job description and compare your skills and experience with those required for the position. Always compare your skills and experience with what is listed on the Job Advert.

If it calls for six years' experience in a certain field and you only have three you may be less qualified than the other applicants. While you may still be called for interview bear in mind that you will probably be up against others who do have more experience.

By avoiding common pitfalls, you can improve your chances of landing a job interview. Often something small -- fixing a typo, for example -- makes all the difference.

2.3 Does Your GPA (or Percentage) Really Matter?

As students and post graduates begin preparing their resumes, the importance of a grade point average (GPA) may differ depending on the position, but the general consensus is while work experience is more important, a good GPA doesn't hurt one's chances of landing a job in a competitive labor market.

Where it really counts

Keeping your GPA or percentage up can be important to your academic success. For higher studies, having low GPA could land you on academic probation, or the university could stop your scholarship. Also, according to a report, maintaining a high GPA is crucial to those who dream of attending top colleges.

Also, some employers and even internships require GPA in order to apply for positions, and those with lower GPA's may have an issue. If you are applying for a job in biochemistry and your major was biochemistry, they are probably going to ask for your GPA.

If your major is similar to the job you are applying to, it might be more important to include it. Also, the importance of GPA depends on the employer. If you have a low GPA, you should probably explain in their cover letter why you had a lower GPA and why you should still be a good candidate for the job. A decent GPA matters mainly because it shows the candidate is a hard worker.

The realities of the job market

Thankfully, most employers don't enforce these same academic standards on their job applicants. According to the "Job Outlook 2005" survey, 70 percent of hiring managers do report screening applicants based on their GPA (or Percentage). But, maintaining a GPA of 6.5 or more (or Percentage 65%) would be good as few employer's use that as their cutoff.

All other factors being equal, an employer is more likely to choose the candidate with stellar grades, but that doesn't mean a so-so student can't land a competitive job with a prestigious company.

Employers understand that students have different circumstances. Employers do take a university's reputation into consideration, but they also understand working to pay your way through school, extracurricular involvement and extenuating circumstances can lower your academic marks.

Having relevant experience like internships is the key to getting ahead in today's cutthroat job market. Luckily, a superior GPA from a top-ranked university isn't required to get an internship. Internship coordinators look for candidates with a go-getter attitude, something that can be expressed in a cover letter and interview? Not a resume or transcript.

Don't be deceptive

Although employers may not automatically cut you for your low grades, leaving your GPA off of your resume completely may do you more harm than good. If you're a new grad and omit your GPA from your resume, you might find employers warily wondering how terrible your grades really are.

One career adviser even said if there's no GPA on a resume, he automatically assumes it's under a 3.0. And it should go without saying that you should never lie and tell an employer you have better grades than you really do.

Resume remedies for mediocre students

If your GPA falls below your dream employer's minimum standards, you do have options. Again, leaving the figure out isn't wise, but you should emphasize your academic strengths as much as possible.

Luckily, some business schools and other graduate programs pay closer attention to the grades you earned during your junior and senior years than to your overall transcript. This can really help out people who are struggling to raise their averages after a rough transition into college life. Another option is to list your major GPA, or your average grades for only the classes taken in your major.

2.4 Hot Tips on Resume Writing

Having a solid and effective resume can greatly improve your chances of getting an interview call. You might be wondering how make resume top notch and bullet proof?

There are several websites with tips around the web, but most bring just a handful of them. I wanted to put them all together in a single place, and that is what you will find below: 44 resume writing tips.

1. Know the purpose of your resume

Some people write a resume as if the purpose of the document was to land a job. As a result they end up with a really long and boring piece that makes them look like desperate job hunters. The objective of your resume is to land an interview, and the interview will land you the job (hopefully!).

2. Back up your qualities and strengths

Instead of creating a long (and boring) list with all your qualities (e.g., disciplined, creative, problem solver), try to connect them with real life and work experiences. In other words, you need to back these qualities and strengths up; else it will appear that you are just trying to inflate things.

3. Make sure to use the right keywords

Most companies (even smaller ones) are already using digital databases to search for candidates. This means that the HR department will run search queries based on specific keywords. Guess what, if your resume doesn't have the keywords related to the job you are applying for, you will be out even before the game starts.

These keywords will usually be nouns. Check the job description and related job ads for a clue on what the employer might be looking for.

4. Use effective titles

Like it or not, employers will usually make a judgment about your resume in 5 seconds. Under this time frame the most important aspect will be the titles that you listed on the resume, so make sure they grab the attention. Try to be as descriptive as possible, giving the employer a good idea about the nature of your past work experiences.
For example:

Bad title:	Accounting
Good title:	Management of A/R and A/P and Recordkeeping

5. Proofread it twice

It would be difficult to emphasize the importance of proofreading your resume. One small typo and your chances of getting hired could slip. Proofreading it once is not enough, so do it twice, three times or as many as necessary. If you don't know how to proofread effectively, here are 8 tips that you can use.

6. Use bullet points

No employer will have the time (or patience) to read long paragraphs of text. Make sure, therefore, to use bullet points and short sentences to describe your experiences, educational background and professional objectives.

7. Where are you going?

Including professional goals can help you by giving employers an idea of where you are going, and how you want to arrive there. You don't need to have a special section devoted to your professional objectives, but overall the resume must communicate it.

The question of whether or not to highlight your career objectives on the resume is a polemic one among HR managers, so go with your feeling. If you decide to list them, make sure they are not generic.

8. Put the most important information first

This point is valid both to the overall order of your resume, as well as to the individual sections. Most of the times your previous work experience will be the most important part of the resume, so put it at the top. When describing your experiences or skills, list the most important ones first.

9. Attention to the typography

First of all make sure that your fonts are big enough. The smaller you should go is 11 points, but 12 is probably safer. Do not use capital letters all over the place; remember that your goal is to communicate a message as fast and as clearly as possible. Arial and Times are good choices.

10. Do not include "no kidding" information

There are many people that like to include statements like "Available for interview" or "References available upon request." If you are sending a resume to a company, it should be a given that you are available for an interview and that you will provide references if requested. Just avoid items that will make the employer think "no kidding!"

11. Explain the benefits of your skills

Merely stating that you can do something will not catch the attention of the employer. If you manage to explain how it will benefit his company, and to connect it to tangible results, then you will greatly improve your chances.

12. Avoid negativity

Do not include information that might sound negative in the eyes of the employer. This is valid both to your resume and to interviews. You don't need to include, for instance, things that you hated about your last company.

13. Achievements instead of responsibilities

Resumes that include a long list of "responsibilities included..." are plain boring, and not efficient in selling yourself. Instead of listing responsibilities, therefore, describe your professional achievements.

14. No pictures

Sure, we know that you are good looking, but unless you are applying for a job where the physical traits are very important (e.g., modeling, acting and so on), and unless the employer specifically requested it, you should avoid attaching your picture to the resume.

15. Use numbers

This tip is a complement to the 13th one. If you are going to describe your past professional achievements, it would be a good idea to make them as solid as possible. Numbers are your friends here.

Doesn't merely mention that you increased the annual revenues of your division, say that you increased them by $100,000, by 78%, and so on.

16. One resume for each employer

One of the most common mistakes that people make is to create a standard resume and send it to all the job openings that they can find. Sure it will save you time, but it will also greatly decrease the chances of landing an interview (so in reality it could even represent a waste of time). Tailor your resume for each employer. The same point applies to your cover letters.

17. Identify the problems of the employer

A good starting point to tailor your resume for a specific employer is to identify what possible problems he might have at hand. Try to understand the market of the company you are applying for a job, and identify what kind of difficulties they might be going through.

After that illustrate on your resume how you and your skills would help to solve those problems.

18. Avoid age discrimination

It is illegal to discriminate people because of their age, but some employers do these considerations nonetheless. Why risk the trouble? Unless specifically requested, do not include your age on your resume.

19. You don't need to list all your work experiences

If you have job experiences that you are not proud of, or that are not relevant to the current opportunity, you should just omit them. Mentioning that you used to sell hamburgers when you were 17 is probably not going to help you land that executive position.

20. Go with what you got

If you never had any real working experience, just include your summer jobs or volunteer work. If you don't have a degree yet, mention the title and the estimated date for completion. As long as those points are relevant to the job in question; it does not matter if they are official or not.

21. Sell your fish

Remember that you are trying to sell yourself. As long as you don't go over the edge, all the marketing efforts that you can put in your resume (in its content, design, delivery method and so on) will give you an advantage over the other candidates.

22. Don't include irrelevant information

Irrelevant information such as political affiliation, religion and sexual preference will not help you. In fact it might even hurt your chances of landing an interview. Just skip it.

23. Use Mr. and Ms. If appropriate

If you have a gender neutral name like Alex or Ryan make sure to include the Mr. or Ms. prefix, so that employers will not get confused about your gender.

24. No lies, please

Seems like a no brainer, but you would be amused to discover the amount of people that lie in their resumes. Even small lies should be avoided. Apart from being wrong, most HR departments do background checks these days, and if you are buster it might ruin your credibility for good.

25. Keep the salary in mind

The image you will create with your resume must match the salary and responsibility level that you are aiming for.

26. Analyze job ads

You will find plenty of useful information on job ads. Analyze no only the ad that you will be applying for, but also those from companies on the same segment or offering related positions.

You should be able to identify what profile they are looking for and how the information should be presented.

27. Get someone else to review your resume

Even if you think you resume is looking kinky, it would be a good idea to get a second and third opinion about it. We usually become blind to our own mistakes or way of reasoning, so another people will be in a good position to evaluate the overall quality of your resume and make appropriate suggestions.

28. One or two pages

The ideal length for a resume is a polemic subject. Most employers and recruiting specialists, however, say that it should contain one or two pages at maximum. Just keep in mind that, provided all the necessary information is there, the shorter your resume, the better.

29. Use action verbs

A very common advice to job seekers is to use action verbs. But what are they? Action verbs are basically verbs that will get noticed more easily, and that will clearly communicate what your experience or achievement were.

Examples include managed, coached, enforced and planned. Here you can find a complete list of action verbs divided by skill category.

30. Use a good printer

If you are going to use a paper version of your resume, make sure to use a decent printer. Laser printers usually get the job done. Plain white paper is the preferred one as well.

31. No hobbies

Unless you are 100% sure that some of your hobbies will support you candidacy, avoid mentioning them. I know you are proud of your swimming team, but share it with your friends and not with potential employers.

32. Update your resume regularly

It is a good idea to update your resume on a regular basis. Add all the new information that you think is relevant, as well as courses, training programs and other academic qualifications that you might receive along the way. This is the best way to keep track of everything and to make sure that you will not end up sending an obsolete document to the employer.

33. Mention who you worked with

If you have reported or worked with someone that is well known in your industry, it could be a good idea to mention it on the resume. The same thing applies to presidents and CEOs. If you reported to or worked directly with highly ranked executives, add it to the resume.

34. No scattered information

Your resume must have a clear focus. If would cause a negative impression if you mentioned that one year you were studying drama, and the next you were working as an accountant. Make sure that all the information you will include will work towards a unified image. Employers like decided people.

35. Make the design flow with white space

Do not jam your resume with text. Sure we said that you should make your resume as short and concise as possible, but that refers to the overall amount of information and not to how much text you can pack in a single sheet of paper. White space between the words, lines and paragraphs can improve the legibility of your resume.

36. Lists all your positions

If you have worked a long time for the same company (over 10 years) it could be a good idea to list all the different positions and roles that you had during this time separately.

You probably had different responsibilities and developed different skills on each role, so the employer will like to know it.

37. No jargon or slang

It should be common sense, but believe me, it is not. Slang should never be present in a resume. As for technical jargon, do not assume that the employer will know what you are talking about.

Even if you are sending your resume to a company in the same segment, the person who will read it for the first time might not have any technical expertise.

38. Careful with sample resume templates

There are many websites that offer free resume templates. While they can help you to get an idea of what you are looking for, do not just copy and paste one of the most used ones. You certainly don't want to look just like any other candidate, do you?

39. Create an email proof formatting

It is very likely that you will end up sending your resume via email to most companies. Apart from having a Word document ready to go as an attachment, you should also have a text version of your resume that does not look disfigured in the body of the email or in online forms.

Attachments might get blocked by spam filters, and many people just prefer having the resume on the body of the email itself.

40. Remove your older work experiences

If you have been working for 20 years or more, there is no need to have 2 pages of your resume listing all your work experiences, starting with the job at the local coffee shop at the age of 17! Most experts agree that the last 15 years of your career are enough.

41. No fancy design details

Do not use a colored background, fancy fonts or images on your resume. Sure, you might think that the little flowers will cheer up the document, but other people might just throw it away at the sight.

42. No pronouns

You resume should not contain the pronouns "I" or "me." That is how we normally structure sentences, but since your resume is a document about your person, using these pronouns is actually redundant.

43. Don't forget the basics

The first thing on your resume should be your name. It should be bold and with a larger font than the rest of the text. Make sure that your contact details are clearly listed. Secondly, both the name and contact details should be included on all the pages of the resume (if you have more than one).

44. Consider getting professional help

If you are having a hard time to create your resume, or if you are receiving no response whatsoever from companies, you could consider hiring a professional resume writing service. There are both local and online options are available, and usually the investment will be worth the money.

2.5 Designing the Resume

The following page includes a general outline of a standard resume with major headings. Since the purpose of the resume is to get you an interview, the document needs to announce to the reader that your candidacy should be seriously considered. Study resumes format which are related to your career field. Seek advice from different resources.

In the end, however, you will have to decide which style best fits your needs. Make it easy to read and understand, free of errors, and targeted for the type of positions you are seeking. Be prepared to do several drafts and revisions before you are satisfied. The time spent is well worth the effort in the long run.

Here are a few tips:

- "OnE sIzE dOeS nOt FiT aLl". Tailor your resume to the position, the company, and the industry.
- Research the type of job or company you are aiming for. Try to find out what resume or format style they prefer, if possible.
- Know your audience. Selectively include or exclude information depending on who your audience is.
- Use a simple readable font and font size at least 12 point
- Bolding is acceptable if used moderately. Italicizing is not, especially if your resume will be scanned or faxed.
- Avoid condensing spacing between letters of a word.
- Leave spaces between lines for better readability.
- Avoid underlining and use bullets sparingly.
- Avoid graphics, ornaments, fancy paper, outlining, boxing or shadowing text.
- Be careful about abbreviations which may have more than one meaning or unclear meanings.
- Use keywords, "buzzwords", acronyms which are related to your field and will help if your resume is scanned by a computerized resume bank doing a keyword search.

- Work the resume so that it includes the exact words and phrases from the job advertisement or job description.
- KISS! Keep it short and simple. Can it pass the "30 second" test?

SAMPLE- BASIC RESUME OUTLINE

NAME
Mailing Address
City, State, Zip
Phone number with area code
E-mail address or website address

Job/ Career Objective:	Use exact job titles or statement indicating the type of position desired and name of organization selected, if possible.
Highlights of Qualifications:	Summarize abilities, responsibilities, skills, qualifications, and achievements
Related Skills:	Use action verbs when listing skills and accomplishments. Relate and transfer current skills to the preferred position. Draw from all volunteer and paid experience. Group skills under subheadings (e.g., technical, computer, language)
Employment History:	Begin with most recent paid or unpaid work or activity. List history and dates in reverse chronological order. Briefly list primary/significant duties not usually associated with the position (e.g., cashier—most readers know what the basic duties of a cashier are. However, if the cashier is responsible for closing out her cash bank daily and for preparing bank deposits, those duties could be included).
Education:	List most recent first, including name of school, degree or certificate earned or pursuing, major area of study, or relevant coursework. List relevant workshops or seminars or continuing education in your field. List any licenses or teaching credentials.
Membership in Professional Organizations or Service to Community or College:	List any memberships in business, educational, professional, or technical associations, and offices/ jobs/ you held, such as president, membership chair, conference chairperson, and speaker.
References or Career Portfolio:	Available upon request (you may exclude this if there is insufficient space or it is not applicable to you.)

[Writer may select other category titles depending on their experience, type of profession, focus of the position sought, and / or the minimum and desirable qualifications requested by the employer. Writer may also vary the order of the categories.]

COVER LETTER OR LETTER OF APPLICATION

KISS: Keep it short and simple! One page is sufficient.

- Remember who your audience is – who will be reviewing the letter and resume?

- Write to a specific person rather than "To whom it may concern".
- Most cover letters and resumes are given all of 2 minutes to make an impression.
- Tailor your letter to the company receiving it.
- Show that you know something about the company.
- Be positive in your approach.
- Correct grammar, punctuation, and spelling are absolutely essential- strive for perfection!

Three BASIC SECTIONS:

First Paragraph: INTRODUCTION – TO STATE YOUR PURPOSE

- Have a businesslike but attention-getting beginning.
- State how you heard about the job.
- State the specific job for which you are applying.
- Let the employer know that you are qualified for the position.

Middle Paragraphs: TEXT- GIVING YOUR SUPPORTING DATA

- Discuss in a personalized manner the qualifications that you listed on your resume. Describe your education and training related to the job for which you are applying.
- Describe experiences related to the job.
- Make one reference to your enclosed resume.
- Limit it to one or two paragraphs only.

Last Paragraph: CONCLUSION- REQUESTING ACTION

- Pave the way for an interview appointment.
- Request an interview at the prospective employer's convenience.
- Suggest times you are available.
- Make it easy for the employer to get in touch with you. Including your phone number is best.
- Thank the person for his/her consideration of your application and resume.

2.6 Sample Resume

Aryan Babu

Address: 1-3-132,Hinjewadi, Pune (MH) -411036

Mobile: <Mobile Number>
Email: <email ID>

CAREER OBJECTIVE

Always seeking innovative and challenging career in the professionally managed and dynamic organization, which provides the best opportunities for the development and greater responsibilities to contribute towards organization.

EDUCATIONAL QUALIFICATION

- B. Tech* (Electronics and Communication Engineering) with aggregate 7.8 CGPA (scale of 10.0) in 2006-2010 from Bharath University, Chennai.
- 12th with aggregate 74% from Chakdwipa high school in 2006.
- 10th with aggregate 80% from Chakdwipa high school in 2004.

SOFTWARE SKILLS

Languages & Skills	:	*C, C++*
Operating Systems	:	Windows 9x/2000/XP
Softwares	:	*Microsoft Word, Powerpoint and Excel*

HARDWARE SKILLS

- Assembling of PC
- Networking & Troubleshooting PC

PROJECTS UNDERTAKEN

Efficient Algorithm for Terrain Simplification for Fast Rendering

Improves the state of the art in occlusion plane detection given terrain data. My implementation showed a user controlled drive-through of a complex scene with real-time rendering of 3 million polygons using a 16 node Beowulf cluster. A paper was published in IEEE '04.

TRAININGS UNDERWENT

Summer Training at Bharath Sanchar Nigam Limited, India (June 2006, 4 weeks) on modern telecommunication switch systems.

FIELDS OF INTEREST

Digital Signal Processing & Embedded systems.

ACHIEVEMENTS

- Best B.Tech project – 2004. Dept. of Computer Science, Bharath University.
- Scored 1150 in GRE test.
- Won many prizes in quiz and elocution in College.

EXTRA CURRICULAR ACTIVITIES

- Served as joint secretary of student body. Won first prize in school Drama
- Organized various cultural programs in a club
- Won prizes in quiz competition

STRENGTHS

- Determined to learn with practical approach
- Good communication skills
- Enthusiastic and can produce results under deadline constraints

PERSONAL DETAILS

Father's Name	Arun Kumar
Date of Birth	27-02-1988
Sex	Male
Marital Status	Single
Languages known	English, Hindi, Bengali, Oriya and Tamil
Permanent Address	B 33/29, Lanka, Hyderabad -500045
Hobbies	Listening to music, drawing, playing cricket.

REFERENCES

1. Prof. R. K. Ravindra,
   Dept. of Computer Science, Bharath University,

<Mobile>, <Mail ID>

2. Prof. Janaki Rajagopalan,
   Dept. of Computer Science, Bharath University,
   <Mobile>, <Mail ID>

DECLARATION

I hereby declare that all the above facts are true to best of my knowledge.

Aryan Babu
21st March, 2014
Pune

CHAPTER

Group Discussions 3

3.1 What is Group Discussion?

The definition of group discussion is, "it is an informal way gathering of individuals (in *person*, through a *conference* call, or *website*) to exchange ideas, information, and suggestions on needs, problems, subjects, etc., of mutual interest".

It is a generic type of qualitative research in which a small group of people provides information by discussing a topic. In other terms, it is a methodology where exchange of ideas and opinions are debated upon.

Group discussion is an integral part of any personality development program. Also, it is a very good exercise to improve spoken English, and to build confidence in the speaker. It's tough if you have fear within you, but easy if you believe in yourself.

Few advantages of group discussions are:

- Ideas can be *generated*
- Ideas can be *shared*
- Ideas can be *tried out*
- Ideas can be *responded* to by others
- When the *dynamics* (selection of members for the group) are right, every group member will contribute to the best of their ability
- Working in groups is fun
- It helps us to understand a subject more deeply

3.2 Group Discussions in Interviews

Group Discussion (GD) is used as a tool to select the prospective candidates in a comparative perspective. GDs may be used by an interviewer at an organization, colleges or even at different types of management competitions.

A GD is a methodology used by an organization to check whether the candidate has certain personality distinguishing feature and/or skills that it desires in its members. In this methodology, the group of candidates is given a topic or a situation, given a few minutes to think about the same, and then asked to discuss the topic among themselves for 15-20 minutes. It is a very useful tool to screen the candidate's potential as well as their skills.

GD evaluation is done by the subject experts based on the discussions. A report will be prepared on analyzing the facts at the end of the discussion.

Organizations use GDs to make the students discuss topics in English, and gain confidence in speaking. Also the exercise will be helpful in overcoming public speaking fear and develop a great personality for the individual.

3.3 Group Discussions at Universities/Colleges

Assignments at many universities (and colleges) involve group-work. Working in a group can be challenging, especially where the members are very diverse in age, cultural background, linguistic and academic ability, and preferred learning styles. However, when well-managed, groups can provide a valuable experience of the kind of collaboration required in the professional workplace.

A useful way for developing effective working relationships in a discussion group is to identify enterprise and development roles that members can take up. Well-managed groups have clear rules agreed on by all members at the beginning of the group assignment. A few examples of these rules might be:

- Group members will treat each other with respect.
- Every group member will contribute to the best of their ability.
- Timelines for assignments will be followed properly.
- Everyone is encouraged to express their own opinion and to seriously consider the opinions of others.
- A timetable for out-of-class meetings will take into consideration the preferences and other commitments of all members.
- All members will attend out-of-class meetings.
- Cultural differences will be respected and members will make the effort to understand the cultural conventions of others.

By discussing and setting ground-rules early in the assignment process, groups save time and avoid misunderstandings later.

Note: Our remaining discussion focuses on *GDs in Interviews*.

3.4 How to Face Group Discussion in Interviews?

A group discussion consists of following components.

1. Display of communication skills
2. Thorough knowledge of ideas regarding the subject
3. Exhibiting leadership qualities
4. Positive and cooperative approach towards other candidates in the group
5. Addressing the group as a whole
6. Ability to stand up to physical and mental stresses and difficulties
7. Maintain Relationship with Group Members

3.4.1 Display of Communication Skills

The basic requirement to fulfill in order to perform well in any group discussion is the power of expression. In a group discussion, a candidate has to talk effectively so that he is able to convince others. For convincing, one has to speak forcefully and at the same time create an impact by his knowledge of the subject. A candidate who is successful in holding the attention of the audience creates a positive impact.

You should be able to talk effectively and impressively so as to convince others. You will have to speak forcefully to put your idea across and create an impact by your knowledge regarding the subject. Be very precise and clear in your expression.

It is necessary that you should be precise and clear. As a rule evaluators do not look for the wordage produced. Your knowledge on a given subject, your precision and clarity of thought are the things that are evaluated. Irrelevant talks lead you nowhere. You should speak as much as necessary, neither more nor less. Group discussions are not debating stages.

Ability to listen is also what evaluator's judge. They look for your ability to react on what other participants say. Hence, it is necessary that you listen carefully to others and then react or proceed to add some more points. Your behaviour in the group is also put to test to judge whether you are a loner or can work in a group.

3.4.2 Thorough Knowledge of the Subject

Knowledge of the subject under discussion and clarity of ideas are important. Knowledge comes from consistent reading on various topics. You can use online resources for gaining knowledge on few selected topics for preparation.

3.4.3 Exhibiting Leadership Qualities

The basic aim of a group discussion is to judge a candidate's leadership qualities. That means; group discussion is used to evaluate your ability to fit yourself in the group and lead it towards its goal. The moderator withdraws and watches silently once the discussion starts.

You need to display tactfulness, understanding and knowledge on various topics, enterprise, assertiveness and other leadership qualities to motivate and influence other candidates who are equally competitive.

3.4.4 Exchange of Thoughts with Group Members

A group discussion is an exchange of thoughts and ideas among members of a group. These discussions are held for selecting personnel in organisations where there is a high level of competition. Generally, the moderator asks the group of students to choose a topic from a list of 3 to 5 topics. Once the topic is finalized, they give the group 15 min to prepare, and then 20 min to discuss it among them. The number of participants in a group can vary between 8 and 15.

The purpose is to get an idea about candidates in a short time and make assessments about their skills, which normally cannot be evaluated in an interview. These skills may be team membership, leadership skills, listening and articulation skills.

A note is made of your contributions to the discussion, comprehension of the main idea, the rapport you strike, patience, assertion, accommodation, amenability, etc. *Body language* and *eye contact* too are important points which are to be considered.

3.4.5 Addressing the Group as a Whole

While addressing the group as a whole, you need to be very specific and focused. The language used should also be formal, not the language used in normal conversations. For example, words and phrases like *yar*, *chalta hai*, *I donno*, etc. should not be used. This is not to say you should use a high sounding, pedantic language. Avoiding both, just use formal, plain and simple language.

Mixing of *multiple languages* should be discarded. In a group discussion it is not necessary to address anyone by name. Rather than addressing persons by name, it is better to address the group as a whole.

Needless to say, for the interview, attend the group discussion in *normal dress*. Confidence and coolness while presenting your points are of help. See that you do not keep repeating a point. Do not use more words than necessary. Do not be superfluous. Try to be specific. Do not *exaggerate*.

3.4.6 Ability to Stand up to Physical and Mental

To be successful in a group discussion, you need to be very sound, emotionally and physically. You should not display any nervousness. Be sure of yourself and let others know the same.

3.4.7 Relationship with Group Members

A good *support* always results in a good *relationship* with others, which eventually brings success. Rapport building starts from the very first step. But there must be conflicting opinions which alone will help to look at a problem from various angles and come up with alternatives. As such when conflicting viewpoints arise, they should be resolved by active participation and a positive attitude.

3.5 Points to Remember

In interviews, knowledge is strength. A candidate with good reading habits has more chances of success. In other words, sound knowledge on different topics like politics, finance, economy, science and technology is helpful. The power of convincing effectively is another quality that makes you stand out among others.

- Clarity in talk and expression is yet another essential quality.
- If you are not sure about the topic of discussion, it is better not to initiate. Lack of knowledge or wrong approach creates a bad impression. Instead, you might adopt the wait and watch attitude. Listen attentively to others, may be you would be able to come up with a point or two later.
- A group discussion is a formal occasion where slang is to be avoided.
- A group discussion is not a debating stage. Participants should confine themselves to expressing their viewpoints. In the second part of the discussion candidates can exercise their choice in agreeing, disagreeing or remaining neutral.
- Language should be simple, direct and straight forward.
- Don't interrupt a speaker when the session is on. Try to score by increasing your size, not by cutting others short.
- Maintain rapport with group members.
- Eye contact plays a major role.
- Non-verbal gestures, such as *listening* and *nodding* while appreciating someone's viewpoint speak of you positively.
- Communicate with each and every candidate present. While speaking don't keep looking at a single member. Address the entire group in such a way that everyone feels you are speaking to him or her.

3.6 Tips for Group Discussion

TIP 1: Initiation Techniques

Initiating a GD is a high profit-high loss strategy. When you initiate a GD, you not only grab the opportunity to speak, you also grab the attention of the moderator/examiner and your group members.

If you can make a good first impression with your knowledge and communication skills, it will help you keep going through the discussion. But if you initiate a GD with wrong facts and figures, the damage might not be possible to repair.

If you initiate a GD with *no fault* but don't speak much after that, it gives the impression that you started the GD for the sake of starting it or getting those initial positive points as an *initiator*.

When you start a GD, you are responsible for putting it into the right perspective or framework. So initiate one only if you have in-depth knowledge about the topic at hand.

TIP 2: During The Discussion

Different techniques to initiate a GD and make a good first impressions are:

1. Quotes
2. Definition
3. Question
4. Shock statement
5. Facts, figures and statistics
6. Short story
7. General statement

3.6.1 Quotes

Quotes are an effective way of starting a GD. For example, if the topic of a GD *Customer is King*, you could quote IBM CEO's quote saying, "There is only one boss: the customer."

3.6.2 Definition

Start a GD by defining the topic or an important term in the topic. For example, if the topic of the GD is Advertising is a Diplomatic Way of Telling a Lie, why not start the GD by defining advertising as, 'Any paid form of non-personal presentation and promotion of ideas, goods or services through mass media like newspapers, magazines, television or radio by an identified sponsor'?

3.6.3 Question

Asking a question is an impact way of starting a GD. It does not signify asking a question to any of the candidates in a GD so as to disrupt the flow. It implies asking a question, and answering it yourself. Any question that might disrupt the flow of a GD or insult a participant or play devil's advocate must be discouraged.

Questions that promote a flow of ideas are always appreciated. For a topic like, Should India go to war with Pakistan and China, you could start by asking, 'What does war bring to the people of a nation? We have had four clashes with Pakistan and China. The important question in relation for this case would be: what have we achieved?

3.6.4 Shock Statement

Initiating a GD with a shocking statement is the best way to grab immediate attention and put forth your point. For example, if a GD topic is “The Impact of Population on the Indian Economy” then you could start with, 'At the center of the Indian capital stands a population clock that ticks away relentlessly.

It tracks 29 births a minute, 1,768 an hour, 42,434 a day. It calculates to about 15 million every year. That is roughly the size of Australia. As a current political slogan puts it, “Nothing's impossible when 1 billion Indians work together.”

3.6.5 Facts, Figures and Statistics

If you decide to start your GD with facts, figure and statistics then make sure to quote them accurately. Approximation is allowed in macro level figures, but micro level figures need to be correct and accurate.

For example, you can say, approximately 70 per cent of the Indian population stays in rural areas (macro figures, approximation allowed), but you cannot say 30 states of India instead of 28 (micro figures, no approximations).

Stating wrong facts works to your disadvantage. For a GD topic like, China, a Rising Tiger, you could start with, 'In 1983, when China was still in its initial stages of reform and opening up, China's real use of Foreign Direct Investment only stood at $636 million. China actually utilized $110 billion of FID in 2013, which is almost 200 times that of its 1983 statistics."

3.6.6 Short Story

Use a short story in a GD topic like ”Attitude is Everything”. For example, this can be initiated with, 'A child once asked a balloon vendor, who was selling helium gas-filled balloons, whether a blue-colored balloon will go as high in the sky as a green-colored balloon. The balloon vendor told the child, it is not the color of the balloon but what is inside it that makes it go high.

3.6.7 General Statement

Use a general statement to put the GD in proper perspective. For example, if the topic is “Should *Narendra Modi* be the prime minister of India?” You could start by saying, 'Before jumping to conclusions like, 'Yes, *Narendra Modi* should be', or 'No, *Narendra Modi* should not be', let's first find out the qualities one needs to be a good prime minister of India.

Then we can compare these qualities with those that *Narendra Modi* possesses. This will help us reach the conclusion in a more objective and effective manner.

TIP 3: Summarizing or Concluding

Most GD's don't really have conclusions. A conclusion is where the whole group decides in favor or against the topic, but every GD is summarized. You can take the opportunity to summaries what the group has discussed in the GD in a nutshell. Keep the following points in mind while summarizing a discussion:

- Avoid raising new points.
- Avoid stating only your viewpoint.
- Avoid dwelling only on one aspect of the GD.
- Keep it brief and concise.
- It must incorporate all the important points that came out during the GD.
- If the examiner asks you to summaries a GD, it means the GD has come to an end.
- Do not add anything once the GD has been summarized.

3.7 Do's of a Group Discussion

Here are some do's; if implemented may help you be a successful participant at a GD.

Apart from the below points, the panel will also judge group members for their alertness and presence of mind, problem-solving abilities, ability to work as a team without alienating certain members, and creativity.

3.7.1 Be Yourself

You should try to be as natural as possible. Do not try and be someone you are not.

3.7.2 Speak Out

Make the best of this opportunity, the panel wants to hear you speak. A GD is a chance to be more vocal.

3.7.3 Think Before You Speak

Take time to organize your thoughts. Think of what you are going to say.

3.7.4 Seek Clarification

If you are not clear and you have doubts regarding the subject, ask for clarification before the GD begins.

3.7.5 Be Confident Before You Speak

Don't start speaking until you have clearly understood and analyzed the subject.

3.7.6 Begin Smartly

Work out various strategies to help you make an entry, initiate the discussion or agree with someone else's point and then move onto express your views.

3.7.7 Adding Valuable Thoughts

Opening the discussion is not the only way of gaining attention and recognition. If you do not give valuable insights during the discussion, all your efforts of initiating the discussion will be in vain.

3.7.8 Good Body Language

Your body language says a lot about you. Your gestures and mannerisms are more likely to reflect your attitude than what you say.

3.7.9 Usage Of Effective Language

Language skills are important only to the effect as to how you get your points across clearly and fluently.

3.7.10 Maintain Your Pitch While Communicating

Be assertive not dominating; try to maintain a balanced tone in your discussion and analysis.

3.7.11 Be Patience

Don't lose your cool if anyone says anything you object to. The key is to stay objective: Don't take the discussion personally.

3.7.12 Be Polite

Try to avoid using extreme phrases like: `I strongly object' or `I disagree'. Instead try phrases like: `I would like to share my views on...' or `One difference between your point and mine...' or "I beg to differ with you".

3.7.13 Motivating Others To Speak

This will demonstrate your leadership skills. You may motivate the other team members to speak but you need to identify the right time to do that. Also, don't keep repeating the same thing as you may lose your time to speak and this may show too much of leadership.

Be receptive to others opinions and do not be abrasive or aggressive.

3.7.14 Practice

If you have a group of like-minded friends, you can have a mock group discussion where you can learn from each other through giving and receiving feedback.

3.8 Topics for Practicing Group DIscussions

Below are the commonly used list of topics for group discussions:

- Stop importing China manufactured items
- Is Foreign Direct Investment (FDI) in retail sector good for India?
- How to deal with high oil Prices?
- Are Indians less quality conscious?
- Is the consumer really the king in India?
- Commercialization of health care: Good or Bad?
- Is there any point in having a business strategy when the world changes from month to month?
- Is the patents bill good for India?
- Public sector being a guarantor of job security is a myth
- How can a business get rid of the bad name that it has earned?

- Government pumping money into the economy is not the solution for our economic problems
- Is the budgeting exercise of any use?
- Should agricultural subsidies be stopped?
- Is MNCs superior to Indian companies?
- Advertising is a waste of resources
- Should India break diplomatic ties with Pakistan?
- Skilled manpower shortage in India
- Technology creates income disparities
- Government should clean its own hands before pointing finger at the private sector for corruption.
- Globalization vs. Nationalism
- Economic freedom not old fashioned theories of development will lead to growth and prosperity
- Should businessmen run the finance ministry?
- What we need to reduce scams is better regulatory bodies.
- Water resources should be nationalised
- Indian villages - our strength or our weakness?
- Space missions are a wastage of resources for a resource-starved nation like India
- Satyam Scandal would impact foreign investments in India
- Private participation in infrastructure is highly desirable
- Poverty in third world countries is due to prosperity in first world countries
- Indian economy: Old Wine in New Bottle!
- Is Globalization really necessary?
- What shall we do about our Ever-Increasing Population?
- Banning of trade unions will be beneficial in growth of the economy
- Why can't India be a World-Class Player in Manufacturing Industry as it is in IT & BPO Sectors?
- We need drinking water and not Coke & Pepsi in rural India
- Rise of regional issues threatens independent nations like India
- Should the public sector be privatized?
- Business and ethics cannot go together
- Is India better than China in software?
- Should there be limits on artistic freedom
- Should India sign the Comprehensive Nuclear-Test-Ban Treaty (CTBT)?
- Is there any point in having a business strategy?
- Women make good managers than men
- Influence of social media on youth
- Why skilled manpower leaving to USA and other countires?
- Which one do you prefer arranged marriages or love marriages?
- Should there be private universities?
- Civil society and individual freedom
- Discuss Lokpal bill
- Internet/Mobile Phones – a boon or nuisance
- Corruption is the price we pay for Democracy
- Skilled manpower shortage in India
- Balance between professional and family
- Internet censorship
- Are Indians less quality conscious?

- Value based politics
- Is India strong enough to fight with China in Military?
- Nothing succeeds like success
- Eating non-vegetarian good is a crime
- Should the public sector be privatized?
- Stock trading can help the poor?
- India is a soft nation
- Religion should not be mixed with politics
- Cricketers are not to blame for match fixing
- Success is all about human relations
- Is dependency on computers a good thing?
- Should businessmen run the finance ministry?
- Privatization will lead to Less Corruption
- Is bullet-to-bullet the right policy?

3.9 Mock Group Discussions

Typically, members are divided in groups of 8 to 10 and each group is tested by a panel of judges. Usually topics of general interest are given by the panel to the group and the group is asked to proceed with discussion.

Every candidate is supposed to express his/her opinion and views on the topic given. The time for discussion is approximately 20 minutes. During the discussion, the panel of interviewers quietly observes the performance and behavior of the members and makes their assessment.

Mock Discussion-1: Multinationals → Bane or Boon

For our discussion, assume that we have interviewers and the group members are named *A, B, C, D, E, and F*.

Judge/Moderator: Good morning. You can choose any topic you like or take a slip from that box. You are given 10 minutes to think to start with the discussion. The observers will not interfere in your discussion. If no conclusion is reached, we may ask each of you to speak for a minute on the topic at the end of the discussion. The topic on the slip is *Multinationals: Bane or Boon*. I suggest you should start the discussion.

Mr. A: This is a good topic. I am against multinationals. We have *Coca – Cola, Sprite* and *Pepsi*. Do we need them? We can manufacture our own soft drinks. Multinationals destroy the local industry and sell non-essential products.

Mr. B: I agree with you. What is the fun of having *Coca – Cola, Sprite* and *Pepsi*? We have our own *Gold Spot*.

Mr. C: I think water is good enough.

Mr. D: We are not here to discuss soft drinks. The topic given to us is a much larger one. First, let us define multinational companies. They are merely large companies which operate in a number of countries.

There could be some Indian multinationals also. So there is nothing wrong with them. The point is whether they have a good or bad impact on the host countries. We have to discuss their business practices and find out whether they are desirable or not.

Mr. E: That is a very good introduction to the topic. Multinational companies do serve an important function that they bring new products and technologies in countries which do not have them. And it is not just *Coca – Cola, Sprite* and *Pepsi*. They set up power plants and build roads and bridges, which really help in the development of host countries.

Mr.F: But are they all that good? We have seen that they destroy local industry. In India they just took over existing companies. They came in areas of low technology. Moreover, we have to see why they come at all. They come for earning profits and often remit more money abroad than they bring in.

Mr.A: I agree with you. I am against multinationals. We can produce everything ourselves. We should be *swadeshi* in our approach. Why do we need multinational companies?

Mr.E: We may not need multinational companies but then it also means that our companies should not do business abroad. Can we live in an isolated world? The fact is that we are moving towards becoming a global village.

The world is interconnected. Then we have also seen that foreign companies bring in business practices that we are impressed with. Look at *foreign banks*. They are so efficient and friendly that the nationalized banks look pathetic in comparison. I think we can learn a lot from multinationals if we keep our eyes and mind open.

Mr.B: Take a look at *McDonald's*. They are providing quality meals at affordable prices. One does not have to wait at their restaurants.

Mr.C: How do you account for the fact that they take out more than they put in and thus lead to impoverishing the country?

Mr.D: The fact is that every poor country needs foreign investment. Poor countries often lack resources of their own. That is why they have to invite foreign companies in. There is nothing wrong in this because then products like cars, air conditioners and so on can be made in poor countries. Often multinationals source products from different countries which helps boost their export earnings.

Mr.E: We have been talking about *Coca – Cola, Sprite* and *Pepsi*. It is well known that *Pepsi* is in the foods business also and has helped farmers in *Punjab* by setting up modern farms to grow potatoes and tomatoes. Modern practices have helped the people in that area.

Mr.A: I still feel that multinationals are harmful for the country.

Mr.D: Well, there could be negative things associated with such companies. They may not be very good in their practices. But can we do without them? I think the best way is to invite them but also impose some controls so that they follow the laws of the country and do not indulge in unfair practices.

Mr.E: I think laws are applicable to everyone. Very often officials in poor countries take bribes. The fault lies not with the company which gives a bribe but the person who actually demands one. Why blame the companies for our own ills?

Mr.A: What about the money they take out?

Mr.D: We have had a good discussion and I think it is time to sum up. Multinationals may have good points and some bad ones too, but competition is never harmful for anyone. We cannot live in a protected economy any longer.

We have been protected for many years and the results are there for everyone to see. Rather than be close about multinationals, let us invite them in selected areas so that we get foreign investment in areas which we are lacking. Laws can be strictly enforced that companies operate within limits and do not start meddling in political affairs.

Analysis: From the above discussion it is clear that; though *Mr.A* started the discussion, he could not make any good points. Later, he could not give any points about why multinationals are bad. It is also a bad strategy to say at the outset whether you are for or against the topic.

Remember, it is not a debate but a discussion. The first step should always be to introduce the topic without taking sides. See the way in which the discussion is proceeding and give arguments for or against. The observer is more interested in what you saying than knowing what you belief.

The participation of *Mr. B and C* is below average. A candidate must make 3-4 interventions. Their arguments are also not well thought out and add nothing to the argument. It is important to say relevant things make an impact.

Mock Discussion-2: How to Succeed in Group Discussions

Mr. A, Mr. B, Mr. C, Mr. D and Mr. E are waiting for their group discussion to start. They do not have a topic yet and are waiting for the moderator to make everybody comfortable. There, the moderator looks at the clock and announces: You have 5 minutes for this group discussion. And your topic is *'How to Succeed in Group Discussions.'* Please start.

Mr. B: This should be interesting. A GD on GD! I suggest we should discuss the importance of a GD first. I mean, why have a GD at all?

Mr. C: I find this very strange. How can you have a GD on GD? We should be discussing some current topic to test our knowledge.

Mr. E: I agree that this is rather unusual. At the same time, our job is to conduct a meaningful discussion regardless of the topic. *Mr. B* has suggested we start with the importance of GD. Today, GD is a very important part of various selection procedures.

Mr. A: GD is all about teamwork. That's all.

Mr. B: Management is all about working with people. I suppose GD is one way of establishing one's ability to work with others. How we are able to lead and be led.

Mr. C: (Laughs) You are using some impressive management jargon, my friend! I don't think GD has anything to do with leading or being led. At the most, a GD may give an idea about how a business meeting is held. Otherwise it is only about sharing your knowledge with others.

Mr. B: (Visibly irritated) Looks like you are very sure about your knowledge. Perhaps there is no need for a group or even a discussion?

Mr. E: We have some interesting points here, *leadership* and sharing knowledge. Perhaps, a GD is a good tool to assess how well you are able to function within a group.

Mr. D: I want to...

Mr. A: I don't think any discussion is meaningful unless everyone has the same level of knowledge.

Mr. D: I want to say something. Pardon if I make any wrong. I am from vernacular medium...

Mr. A: Don't waste our time talking about your background. The topic is GD. Talk about that.

Mr. B: Every subject has various angles. So, many heads can raise many ideas.

Mr. C: Also, too many cooks spoil the broth (laughs).

Mr. E: Yes, a group makes it possible to brainstorm any issue. Perhaps *Mr. D* has something to add to this thought ...

Mr. D: Thanks for giving me chance. A GD is good for *consensus*. It is always better everybody agree. Otherwise only one person is there.

Mr. C: (Leaning forward and pointing to *Mr. D*) I think the correct word is *consensus*. Don't use a word unless you know what you are talking about.

Mr. B: Consensus is fine. But is it necessary that everyone should have the same viewpoint?

Mr. E: That is an interesting thought. Yes, *Mr. D* is right that a GD is about consensus but there can still be differences. A GD provides an opportunity to discuss various aspects of an issue and weigh merits and demerits of different approaches.

Mr. C: Agree to disagree.

Mr. B: But the question is how to succeed in GD's. I think the first prerequisite is patience. Some of us must learn to shut up and let others talk (looks directly at *Mr. C*).

Mr. A: If everyone follows that we will only have silence and no discussion.

Mr. E: I suppose the point is to participate and give others also a chance to participate.

Mr. D: Please can I speak?

Mr. A: Come on! You don't have to beg for permission to speak!

Mr. D: I said that because I thought someone might have wanted to speak before me. Anyway, is it not possible to only listen?

Mr. C: (Smirks) I don't know how the moderator will rate your profound silence!

Mr. B: But *Mr. D*, no one can read your mind. Unless you speak, how do you contribute?

Mr. E: I think a GD is very much like a business meeting. Every participant may present an individual point of view but the thinking about that point of view is collective.

Mr. A: I don't think you can compare a GD to a business meeting. In a meeting, there is usually a chairman whose job is to control the meeting.

Mr. B: A GD may not have a chairman but I suppose one person usually emerges as the leader and guides the discussion.

Mr. C: I suppose someone fancies himself to be a leader. This is so boring!

Moderator: Your time is up. Thank you everyone. Moderator's notes: *Mr. E* shows leadership skills and the ability to hold a group together. He appears to have a good grasp of the subject though on the whole the GD failed to do justice to the core subject of how to succeed. *Mr. B* also has some interesting ideas but is prone to being provoked easily. *Mr. C* is too sure and too full of himself to be able to contribute to a group. *Mr. A* is guilty of intolerance and rude interruptions. *Mr. D* needs to work on his language and his confidence, though he may have the right concepts.

Mock Discussion-3: Cricket has Spoiled Other Streams of Sports

Names of participants: *Mr. A, Mr. B, Mr. C, Mr. D, and Mr. E*
Time: 20 Minutes

Mr. A: Hi all, I think it is not correct to consider cricket as a *national obsession*. It is one game due to which all Indians are proud about. We have won 2 world cups. We should appreciate the efforts of the name of the country high.

In other sports as well, like Abhinav Bindra winning gold medal in Olympics, Indian hockey team winning 8 gold medals in past, are also highly appreciated. In 1983, when India won the world cup, the TV's were just becoming popular.

Cricket fever was high on everyone's head. That made it more popular than any other sport. Every Indian wants to play cricket in streets. It is in Indian blood and no media is required for cricket. Cricket is, and will be the most popular sport in India although I hope other sports also will do well.

Mr. B: Hi Friends, I do agree with *Mr. A*. Even I think alike that cricket hasn't hurt any other sports. If cricket is more interesting, full of excitement, inculcating a nation *patriotism* feeling, then it is not the *sport's* fault. I think it is just because cricket has a very interesting format and that is why it has become so popular and loved by all. It is followed as a religion and the cricketers are worshiped as *god* in our country. But also the fame that cricket has given to India, cannot be ignored.

Also, I would like to say that other sports have not lost their importance. Whether it is tennis, badminton or hockey they are still very popular. But yes, it is a fact that cricket is the most popular and followed by more people.

Mr. C: Hi! Thank you for the opportunity. I don't think cricket as a national obsession is a deterrent to other sports. Cricket has got popularity because of the legends cricket has given to us like *Sunil Gavaskar, Kapil Dev, Sachin Tendulkar*, etc. Due to the achievement of these people it has become the most appreciated sports in India.

If we take an example, recently when *Rajyawardhan Singh Rathore* won silver in Olympics, just after that we won lots of medals in shooting. So, if we want other games to be equally appreciated, then we need some great legends in other games too.

As a whole I believe that if other sports will also produce great players then definitely they will get as much appreciation as cricket in this country.

Mr. D: Hi Friends, as the topic suggests, that cricket is detriment to other sports, I quite agree with it. It is because:

1. This game is promoted by different ways of advertisements
2. Cricket sport stars are seen in most of the advertisements related to cricket or promotion of any product.
3. One of the main reasons for the game of cricket being preferred is when there is a match between India and Pakistan. And the way it is advertised on the news make cricket not only detriment to other sports but to national peace.
4. In newspapers, most of the sports page is filled with cricket news, wherever it is held.

To summarize along with cricket the Indian media too is playing the role of detriment to other sports of India. As we all know media has the highest power today in our country, it they wish they can change the shape of sports too.

Mr. E: Hi Everyone, I don't think that cricket is a detriment to other sports. It is our people in the country who have a supportive spirit towards cricket and this is what is destructing other sports. Most people do not even know that India has teams in *Hockey, Rugby, Soccer, Basketball* etc.

It feels affronted extremely, to know that a huge nation like India does not support its athletes. I hope that we will recognize our athletes of all games and support them in their respective sports.

Mr. A: As I said mentioned earlier, according to me cricket is not at all detrimental to any other sports, it is suppressed by ourselves, we the people of the country are to be blamed. According to me there cannot be a comparison between 2 sports. Each has its own existence, so how can cricket suppress the other sports?

It is just the matter of fact that Indian people are crazy about the cricket. So the comparison lies not in sports but in our thinking only. Few days ago, the Economic Times conducted a survey to find out who inspires the people in the field of sports and the results announced that almost:

43% people inspires with S R Tendulkar
35% people inspires with M S Dhoni
11% people inspires with S. Nehwal
04% people inspires with Vijendra Singh
04% people inspires with A. Bindra

This survey observed that a total of 78% people inspired by the cricketers, that shows the craziness of the people towards cricket.

Mr. D: Well, I personally feel that obsession with cricket is a detriment to other sports. It is all because of the way it is promoted. It is just like in the case of a movie, if a movie is hyped about, all of us go to watch it. But on the same time some epic movie just gets neglected because of poor advertisement. Also, it is not the case that there is less talent in other sports. If other sports are unable to match up to the expectations, it is only because of improper training due to lack of finances.

Mr. B: Well friends, I am a cricket fan & support cricket a lot but I too feel that it has come to a point where it has become detrimental to other sports. The best can check with ourselves, how many of us watch other sports played by Indian sportsmen? Of course there are few but why so few?

One strong reason could be the support & hype cricket gets through media. People not only watch the match with shear attention but also the pre and post-match shows.

The other strong reason is the investment of money either by the Government and/or, now as we can see, by the business individuals which lures young minds to have a great profession in cricket.

Lastly, I would say that the Government should definitely see to this and take necessary measures to allow other sports perpetuate.

Mr. E - Concludes

To conclude the discussion, I would highlight the main points that were discussed.

First: most of us agreed that the game Cricket itself is not spoiling other streams of sports bit it's the people of our country who go crazy for its favorite sport.

Second: Media should give the similar level of exposure to other sports, as it does for cricket.

Third: Government and other sponsors, who fund Cricket big time, should do the same for other sports as well, so that they get trained and bring the same popularity as it does for cricket.

Mr. A

Confident and aware of his stance
Knows how to take leadership
Started the discussion and paved the way throughout
Aware of current happenings
Believes in producing proper data
Strong chances of getting selected

Mr. B

Confident but loses his stance
Gets drifted by others persuasive arguments
Believes in accepting what comes along
Strong analyzing power
Does stand a chance to get selected

Mr. C

Not very confident
Spoke only once in 20 mins
Believes in joining the bandwagon
Not in a habit of going through newspapers and thus not updated about sport stars.
Does not stand chance of selection

Mr. D

Extremely confident
Believes in walking down his own path
Very clear on his stance
Knows how to put across his points and views
High chance of selection

Mr. E

Confident
Aware of current happenings
Patriotic
Analytical mind
Does stand a chance of selection

Mock Discussion-4: Voting Should Be Made Compulsory

Assume that we have five participants and a moderator.

Names of participants: *Mr. A, Mr. B, Mr. C, Mr. D, and Mr. E*
Time: 20 Minutes

Mr. A: I think low voter turnouts in parliamentary as well as assembly elections are good enough reasons for making voting compulsory. On the face of it, this may seem like a violation of democratic rights. The idea to force people to come out and vote mat appear a bit harsh.

But the idea of making voting compulsory has its merits. Elections are perhaps the most important component of a democratic system. It is where people exercise their franchise and choose their government. They entrust the running of their country to the representatives they select by casting a vote. If a significant number of voters abstain then the elected candidate can be scarcely representative of the electorate of his constituency.

Mr. B: I fully agree with him. Making voting compulsory means, in essence, that the electorate must go to the polling booths and have their attendance marked. It does not prevent them from exercising their right to not express an opinion by deliberately casting an invalid vote. It does not prevent them from expressing their displeasure with the candidates by scribbling any manner of graffiti they deem necessary.

All it does is ensure that a minority government is not left in charge. The percentage of invalid votes cast may be a little higher when voting is compulsory, but the difference between that number and the voter turnout is still significant. For example, in the last general election, India's voter turnout decreased to 57.7% from 59.7% but only 0.1 per cent of the votes cast were invalid.

Mr. C: I believe that compulsory voting is essential as voluntary voting does not motivate people to come out and cast their votes. A voluntary vote makes people believe that the chance of their vote influencing the final outcome is negligible. They feel that the time and effort they put into voting - however small this may be - is not worth it. But if too many people follow this line of reasoning and do not vote, there is a significant possibility that a minority will determine who forms government, leaving a majority of the population discontented.

People vote for many reasons, from wanting to exercise their democratic rights to having nothing better to do. But if these considerations are not enough to get people to vote, as our declining voter turnout indicates, compulsory voting ensures that the responsibility of maintaining democracy is at least brought home to each and every citizen.

Mr. C: I disagree with the concept of compulsory voting. I don't think it is an appropriate response to low turnouts. Such a solution is flawed for a variety of reasons. It is undemocratic to force a citizen to vote. The right not to vote is implicit in the right to vote. Not to exercise the right to vote can also be a democratic way of expressing dissent. Democracy is about choice. However, a citizen can't be forced to make his choice. He has every right to reject the candidates before him. He may do so by abstaining from the vote.

And, that's certainly a legal way of participating in a democracy. A law that forces citizen to vote fetters his freedom to exercise his democratic will. It is against the spirit of democracy.

Democracy should not be evaluated solely by voter participation in elections.

Mr. D: I don’t think compulsory voting is a good idea as a high voter turnout does not necessarily ensure a better government. A number of states report heavy polling during elections. However, that's hardly a reason to assume that people are happy with the state of affairs.
%In many cases, voters are merely herded to the polling station by threat of violence or are induced to support a particular political party by promising sops. A government formed by such a majority is in any case a sham. The point is to enable citizens to make an informed choice. After all, mobs don't make for a democracy.

Legislations can ensure the freedom of the citizen to make an informed choice. And that's all these laws ought to do. The rest should be left to the individual citizen to decide. Let him have the freedom to choose a candidate, cast an invalid vote or even abstain from the electoral process. The state should not interfere in his right to exercise any one of these choices.

CHAPTER

Operating System Concepts

4

4.1 What is an Operating System?

An OS is a program which acts as an interface between computer system users and the computer hardware. It provides a user-friendly environment in which a user may easily develop and execute programs. Otherwise, hardware knowledge would be mandatory for computer programming. So, it can be said that an OS hides the complexity of hardware from uninterested users.

System software is any computer software which manages and controls computer hardware so that application software can perform a task. Operating systems, such as Microsoft Windows, Mac OS X, Linux or AIX, are examples of system software. System software contrasts with application software, which are programs that enable the end-user to perform specific, productive tasks, such as word processing (Microsoft Office Word).

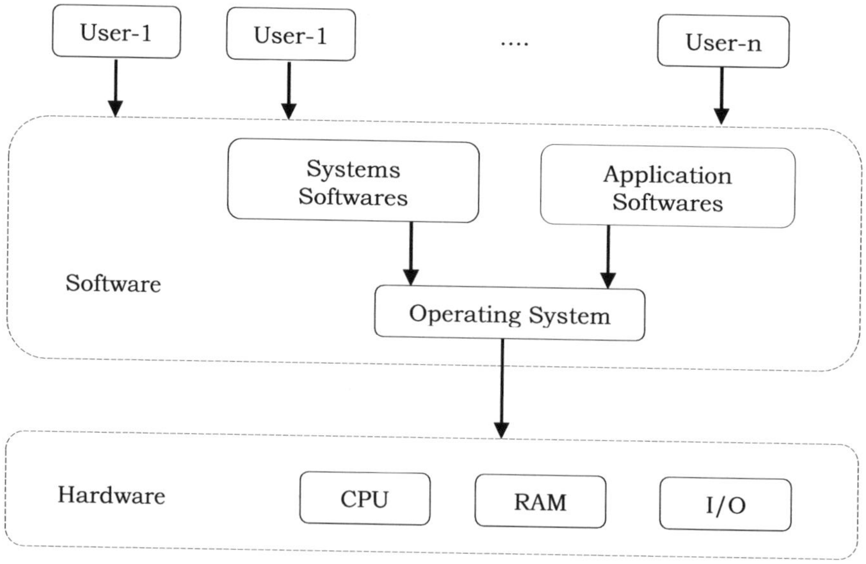

The operating system is a *program* which controls the software and hardware so that the device behaves in a flexible and also in predictable way. The main operating system components are:

- Memory management
- Process management
- File management
- Device management

4.2 Types of Operating Systems

There are different types of operating systems.

4.2.1 Batched Operating Systems

In batched operating systems users give their jobs to the operator. Operator sorts the programs based on their requirements and executes them. This is time consuming but makes the CPU busy all the time.

4.2.2 Multi-programmed operating systems

These operating systems can execute a number of programs concurrently. They fetch a group of programs from the secondary memory and place them in the main memory. Then it selects a program from the ready queue and gives them to CPU for execution.

While an executing program, if they needs some I/O operation then the operating system fetches another program and gives it to the CPU for execution and makes CPU busy all the time.

4.2.3 Timesharing operating systems

In these operating systems, CPU executes multiple jobs by switching between them, but the switches occur so frequently that the user feels as if the operating system is running only one (his) program.

4.2.4 Multi-processor systems or Parallel systems

They contain a number of processors to increase the speed of execution, and reliability, and economy. They are of two types:

- *Symmetric multiprocessing*: Each processor runs an identical copy of the OS and they communicate with each other as and when needed.
- *Asymmetric multiprocessing*: Each processor is assigned a specific task.

4.2.5 Distributed Operating Systems

Distributed systems work in a network. They can share the network resources, communicate with each other.

4.2.6 Real-time Operating Systems

These are used when rigid time requirement have been placed on the operation of a processor or on the flow of data. They are used as a control device in a dedicated application. They are of two types:

- *Hard real time OS*: It has a well-defined fixed time constraint.
- *Soft real time OS*: It has less stringent timing constraints.

4.3 Memory Management

Memory management is the management of main memory. Main memory is a large array of words or bytes where each word or byte has its own address. Main memory provides a fast storage that can be access directly by the CPU. So for a program to be executed, it must in the main memory. Operating System does the following activities for memory management.

1. Keeps tracks of primary memory i.e. what part of it are in use by whom, what part are not in use.

2. In multiprogramming, OS decides which process will get memory when and how much.
3. Allocates the memory when the process requests it to do so.
4. De-allocates the memory when the process no longer needs it or has been terminated.

4.3.1 Primary and Secondary Memory

The memory hierarchy is very crucial operation functionality in the computer and can be categorized into primary and secondary memory. Both these memories vary in the speed, cost and capacity.

Primary memory is considered as a main memory that is accessed directly by the computer, so as to store and retrieve information. Secondary memory is considered as an external or additional memory, this memory is not directly accessed by the CPU because the secondary memory is an external storage device. It can be used as a permanent memory; because even the computer is turned off we can retrieve the information.

- Processor access the primary memory in a random fashion. Unlike primary memory, secondary memory is not directly accessed through CPU. The accessing of the primary memory through CPU is done by making use of address and data buses, whereas input/ output channels are used to access the secondary memory.
- The primary memory is embedded with two types of memory technologies; they are the RAM (Random Access Memory) and ROM (Read Only Memory). The secondary memory is accessible in the form of Mass storage devices such as hard disk, memory chips, Pen drive, floppy disk storage media, CD and DVD.
- Primary memory is volatile in nature, while secondary memory is nonvolatile. The information that is stored in the primary memory cannot be retained when the power is turned off. In case of secondary memory, the information can be retrieved even if the power is turned off because the data will not be destructed until and unless the user erases it.
- When the data processing speed is compared between the primary and secondary memory, the primary memory is much faster than the secondary memory.
- In the cost perspective, the primary memory is costlier than the secondary memory devices. Because of this reasons most of the computer users install smaller primary memory and larger secondary memory.
- As the secondary memory is permanent, all the files and programs are stored in the secondary memory most and as the primary memory interacts very fast with the microprocessor, when the computer needs to access the files that are stored in the secondary memory, then such files are first loaded into the primary memory and then accessed by the computer.

4.3.2 Cache memory

Cache memory is random access memory (RAM) that a computer microprocessor can access more quickly than it can access regular RAM. As the microprocessor processes data, it looks first in the cache memory and if it finds the data there (from a previous reading of data), it does not have to do the more time-consuming reading of data.

4.3.3 Virtual Memory

A virtual memory is hardware technique where the system appears to have more memory that it actually does. This is done by time-sharing, the physical memory and storage parts of the memory one disk when they are not actively being used.

4.3.4 Memory Partitioning

In a multiprogramming system, in order to share the processor, a number of processes must be kept in memory. Memory management is achieved through memory management algorithms. Each memory management algorithm requires its own hardware support. In this section, we shall see the memory partitioning, paging and segmentation methods.

In order to be able to load programs at anywhere in memory, the compiler must generate relocatable object code. Also we must make it sure that a program in memory, addresses only its own area, and no other program's area. Therefore, some protection mechanism is also needed.

4.3.4.1 Fixed Partitioning

In this method, memory is divided into partitions whose sizes are fixed. Operating system is placed into the lowest bytes of memory. Getting back to the issue of loading multiple processes into memory at the same time, we can divide memory into multiple fixed partitions (segments).

The partitions could be of varying sizes and they would be defined by the system administrator when the system starts up. A new program gets placed on a queue for the smallest partition that can hold it. Any unused space within a partition remains unused. This is called *internal fragmentation.*

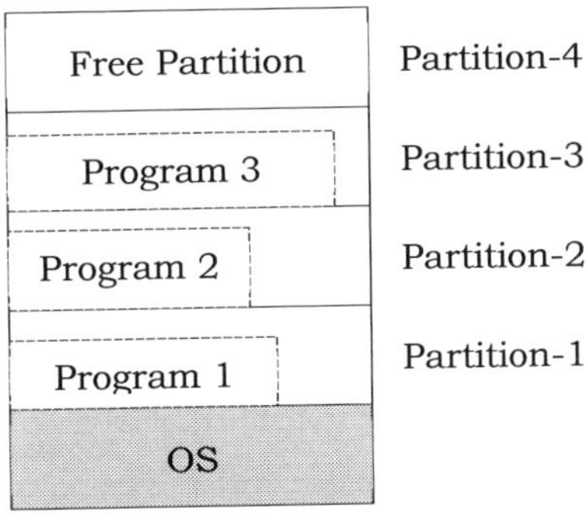

If any partitions have no programs to run then the memory in that partition is always wasted. This is called *external* fragmentation. External fragmentation refers to areas of storage that are not allocated and are therefore unused. A modification of the multiple queue approach is to use a single queue. All incoming jobs go on this queue. When a partition is free, the memory manager searches the entire queue for the biggest job for that available partition. This gives small jobs poor service, a problem that can be partially remedied by defining more small partitions when the partitions are configured.

Overall, a system using multiple fixed partitions is simple to implement but does not make good use of memory. It also messes up the scheduler's decision of what processes should run since partitions dictate which processes could be loaded into the system in the first place.

Finally, this method of allocation requires knowing just how big the process will get. If there isn't enough room in the partition, then the operating system will have to move the memory contents into a larger partition (if available) or, if no partition is available, then save the partition contents and processor register state onto some temporary storage on the disk and queue the process until a larger partition becomes available.

4.3.4.1.1 Fixed Partitioning with Swapping

This is a version of fixed partitioning that uses RRS with some time quantum. When time quantum for a process expires, it is swapped out of memory to disk and the next process in the corresponding process queue is swapped into the memory. Normally, a process swapped out will eventually be swapped back into the same partition. But this restriction can be relaxed with dynamic relocation.

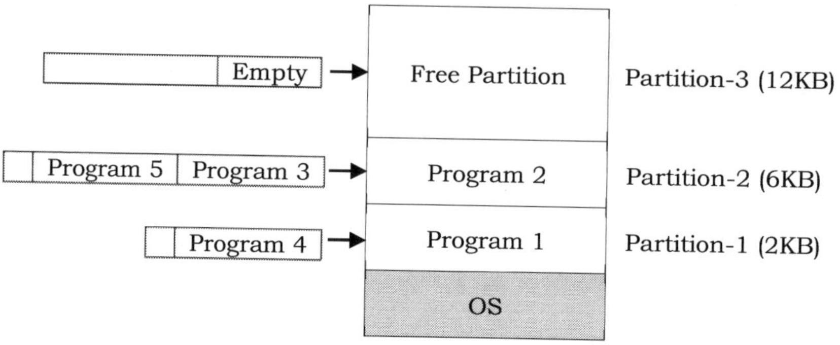

In some cases, a process executing may request more memory than its partition size. Say we have a 6 KB process running in 6 KB partition and it now requires a more memory of 1 KB. Then, the following policies are possible:

- Return control to the user program. Let the program decide either quit or modify its operation so that it can run (possibly slow) in less space.
- Abort the process. (The user states the maximum amount of memory that the process will need, so it is the user's responsibility to stick to that limit)
- If dynamic relocation is being used, swap the process out to the next largest PQ and locate into that partition when its turn comes.

The main problem with the fixed partitioning method is how to determine the number of partitions, and how to determine their sizes. If a whole partition is currently not being used, then it is called an external fragmentation. And if a partition is being used by a process requiring some memory smaller than the partition size, then it is called an internal fragmentation.

In this composition of memory, if a new process, Program 3, requiring 8 KB of memory comes, although there is enough total space in memory, it cannot be loaded because fragmentation.

4.3.4.2 Variable Partitioning

With fixed partitions we have to deal with the problem of determining the number and sizes of partitions to minimize internal and external fragmentation. If we use variable partitioning instead, then partition sizes may vary dynamically. In the variable partitioning method, we keep a table (linked list) indicating used/free areas in memory. Initially, the whole memory is free and it is considered as one large block.

When a new process arrives, the OS searches for a block of free memory large enough for that process. We keep the rest available (free) for the future processes. If a block becomes free, then the OS tries to merge it with its neighbors if they are also free.

There are three algorithms for searching the list of free blocks for a specific amount of memory.

- First Fit: Allocate the first free block that is large enough for the new process. This is a fast algorithm.
- Best Fit: Allocate the smallest block among those that are large enough for the new process. In this method, the OS has to search the entire list, or it can keep it sorted and stop when it hits an entry which has a size larger than the size of new process. This algorithm produces the smallest left over block. However, it requires more time for searching the entire list or sorting it.
- Worst Fit: Allocate the largest block among those that are large enough for the new process. Again a search of the entire list or sorting it is needed. This algorithm produces the largest over block.

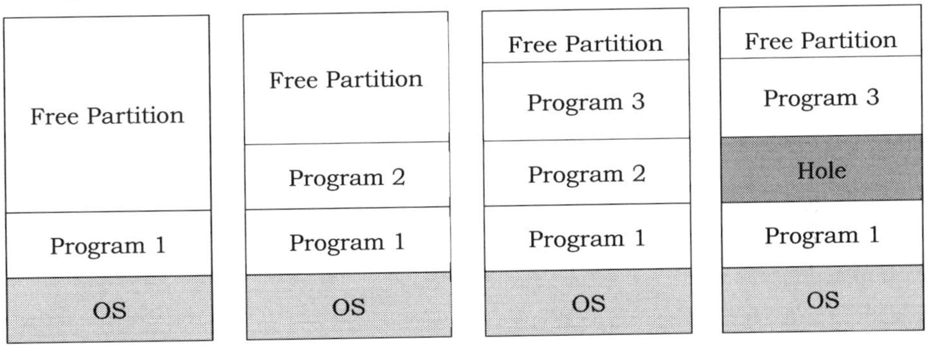

4.3.4.2.1 Compaction

Compaction is a method to overcome the external fragmentation problem. All free blocks are brought together as one large block of free space. Compaction requires dynamic relocation. Certainly, compaction has a cost and selection of an optimal compaction strategy is difficult. One method for compaction is swapping out those processes that are to be moved within the memory, and swapping them into different memory locations.

4.3.5 Paging

Paging is a solution to external fragmentation problem which is to permit the logical address space of a process to be noncontiguous, thus allowing a process to be allocating physical memory wherever the latter is available. Paging permits a program to allocate noncontiguous blocks of memory.

The OS divide programs into pages which are blocks of small and fixed size. Then, it divides the physical memory into frames which are blocks of size equal to page size. The OS uses a page table to map program pages to memory frames. Page size (S) is defined by the hardware. Generally page size is chosen as a power of 2 such as 512 words/page or 4096 words/page etc.

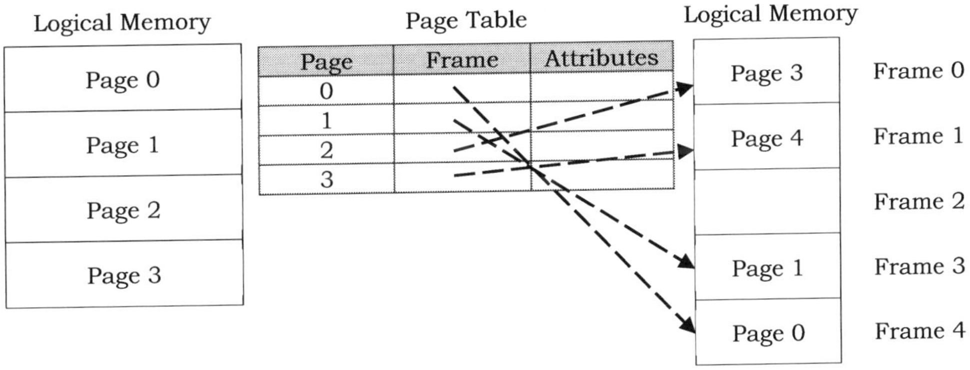

With this arrangement, the words in the program have an address called as *logical address*.

Every logical address is formed of

- A page number p where p = logical address div S
- An offset d where d = logical address mod S

When a logical address $<p, d>$ is generated by the processor, first the frame number f corresponding to page p is determined by using the page table and then the physical address is calculated as $(f * S + d)$ and the memory is accessed.

4.3.6 Segmentation

In segmentation, programs are divided into variable size segments, instead of fixed size pages. Every logical address is formed of a segment name and an offset within that segment. In practice, segments are numbered. Programs are segmented automatically by the compiler or assembler. For example, a C compiler will create separate segments for:

1. The code of each function
2. The local variables for each function
3. The global variables.

For logical to physical address mapping, a *segment table* is used. When a logical address <s, d> is generated by the processor:

1. Base and limit values corresponding to segment s are determined using the segment table.
2. The OS checks whether d is in the limit. (0 = d < limit).
3. If so, then the physical address is calculated as (base + d), and the memory is accessed.

4.4 What is Job Scheduling and a Process?

The process of fetching a program from the secondary memory and placing it in main memory is called *job scheduling*.

The current program which is running in main memory is called *process*. In the OS, each process is represented by its PCB (Process Control Block). The PCB generally contains the following information:

- Process State
- Process ID
- Program Counter (PC) value
- Register values
- Memory Management Information (page tables, base/bound registers etc.)
- Processor Scheduling Information (priority, last processor burst time etc.)
- I/O Status Info (outstanding I/O requests, I/O devices held, etc.)
- List of Open Files
- Accounting Info

4.4.1 Process States

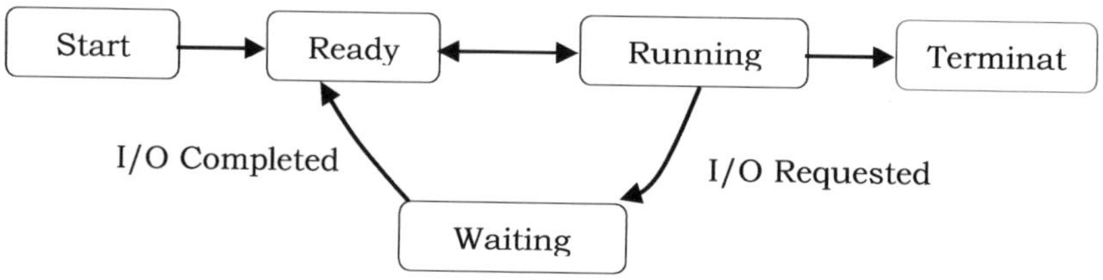

- Start: The process has just arrived.
- Ready: The process is waiting to grab the processor.
- Running: The process has been allocated by the processor.
- Waiting: The process is doing I/O work or blocked.
- Halted: The process has finished and is about to leave the system.

4.4.2 Preemptive and non-preemptive Scheduling

Consider any system where people use some kind of resources and compete for them. The non-computer examples for preemptive scheduling the traffic on the single lane road if there is emergency or there is an ambulance on the road the other vehicles give path to the vehicles that are in need. The example for preemptive scheduling is people standing in queue for tickets.

4.4.3 System Call

A System call is a mechanism used by applications for requesting a service from the OS. For example, allocation and deallocation of memory, reporting of current date and time etc. These services can be used by an application with the help of system calls.

4.4.4 Kernel

An operating system kernel is the piece or pieces of software that is responsible for servicing resource requests from applications and the management of resources. Kernels use system calls to handshake with applications.

4.4.5 Context Switching

Transferring the control from one process to other process requires saving the state of the old process and loading the saved state for new process. This task is called *context switching*. Context-switch time is overhead, because the system does no useful work while switching. Its speed varies from machine to machine, depending on the memory speed, the number of registers which must be copied, the existed of special instructions (such as a single instruction to load or store all registers).

4.4.6 Co-operating Processes

The processes which share system resources as data among each other. Also the processes can communicate with each other via inter-process communication facility (generally used in distributed systems). Example: chat programs.

4.4.7 Thread

A thread is a program line under execution. Thread sometimes called a light-weight process, is a basic unit of CPU utilization; it comprises a thread id, a program counter, a register set, and a stack.

4.4.7.1 User thread

User threads are easy to create and use but the disadvantage is that if they perform a blocking system calls the kernel is engaged completely to the single user thread blocking other processes. They are created in user space.

4.4.7.2 Kernel thread

Kernel threads are supported directly by the operating system. They are slower to create and manage.

4.5 Processor Scheduling Algorithms

Now, let's discuss some processor scheduling algorithms again stating that the goal is to select the most appropriate process in the ready queue. For the sake of simplicity, we will assume that we have a single I/O server and a single device queue, and we will assume our device queue always implemented with FIFO method. We will also neglect the switching time between processors (context switching).

4.5.1 First-Come-First-Served (FCFS)

In this algorithm, the process to be selected is the process which requests the processor first. This is the process whose PCB is at the head of the ready queue. Contrary to its simplicity, its performance may often be poor compared to other algorithms.

FCFS may cause processes with short processor bursts to wait for a long time. If one process with a long processor burst gets the processor, all the others will wait for it to release it and the ready queue will be filled very much. This is called the convoy effect.

4.5.2 Shortest-Process-First (SPF)

In this method, the processor is assigned to the process with the smallest execution (processor burst) time. This requires the knowledge of execution time. In our examples, it is given as a table but actually these burst times are not known by the OS. So it makes prediction. One approach for this prediction is using the previous processor burst times for the processes in the ready queue and then the algorithm selects the shortest predicted next processor burst time.

4.5.3 Shortest-Remaining-Time-First (SRTF)

The scheduling algorithms we discussed so far are all non-preemptive algorithms. That is, once a process grabs the processor, it keeps the processor until it terminates or it requests I/O. To deal with this problem (if so), preemptive algorithms are developed. In this type of algorithms, at some time instant, the process being executed may be preempted to execute a new selected process. The preemption conditions are up to the algorithm design.

SPF algorithm can be modified to be preemptive. Assume while one process is executing on the processor, another process arrives. The new process may have a predicted next processor burst time shorter than what is left of the currently executing process. If the SPF algorithm is preemptive, the currently executing process will be preempted from the processor and the new process will start executing. The modified SPF algorithm is named as Shortest-Remaining-Time-First (SRTF) algorithm.

4.5.4 Round-Robin Scheduling (RRS)

In RRS algorithm the ready queue is treated as a FIFO circular queue. The RRS traces the ready queue allocating the processor to each process for a time interval which is smaller than or equal to a predefined time called time quantum (slice).

The OS using RRS, takes the first process from the ready queue, sets a timer to interrupt after one time quantum and gives the processor to that process. If the process has a processor burst time smaller than the time quantum, then it releases the processor voluntarily, either by terminating or by issuing an I/O request. The OS then proceed with the next process in the ready queue.

On the other hand, if the process has a processor burst time greater than the time quantum, then the timer will go off after one time quantum expires, and it interrupts (preempts) the current process and puts its PCB to the end of the ready queue.

The performance of RRS depends heavily on the selected time quantum.

- Time quantum → ∞ ➔ RRS becomes FCFS
- Time quantum → 0 ➔ RRS becomes processor sharing (It acts as if each of the n processes has its own processor running at processor speed divided by *n*)

For an optimum time quantum, it can be selected to be greater than 80 % of processor bursts and to be greater than the context switching time.

4.5.5 Priority Scheduling

In this type of algorithms a priority is associated with each process and the processor is given to the process with the highest priority. Equal priority processes are scheduled with FCFS method. To illustrate, SPF is a special case of priority scheduling algorithm where

Priority(i) = 1 / next processor burst time of process i

Priorities can be fixed externally or they may be calculated by the OS from time to time. Externally, if all users have to code time limits and maximum memory for their programs, priorities are known before execution. Internally, a next processor burst time prediction such as that of SPF can be used to determine priorities dynamically.

A priority scheduling algorithm can leave some low-priority processes in the ready queue indefinitely. If the system is heavily loaded, it is a great probability that there is a higher priority process to grab the processor. This is called the starvation problem. One solution for the starvation problem might be to gradually increase the priority of processes that stay in the system for a long time.

4.6 Process Synchronization

Process synchronization is required when several processes access and manipulate the same data concurrently and the outcome of the execution depends on the particular order in which the access takes place (is called *race condition*).

To guard against the race condition we need to ensure that only one process at a time can be manipulating the same data. The technique used for this is called process synchronization.

4.6.1 Critical Section Problem

Critical section is the code segment of a process in which the process may be changing common variables, updating tables, writing a file and so on. Only one process is allowed to go into critical section at any given time (*mutually exclusive*). The critical section problem is to design a protocol that the processes can use to co-operate. The three basic requirements of critical section are:

- Mutual exclusion
- Progress
- Bounded waiting

Note: Bakery algorithm is one of the solutions to CS problem.

4.6.2 Deadlocks

Suppose a process request resources, if the resources are not available at that time the process enters into a wait state. A waiting process may never again change state, because the resources they have requested are held by some other waiting processes. This situation is called *deadlock*.

In a multiprogramming system, processes request resources. If those resources are being used by other processes then the process enters a waiting state. However, if other processes are also in a waiting state, we have deadlock. The formal definition of deadlock is as follows:

Definition: A set of processes is in a deadlock state if every process in the set is waiting for an event (release) that can only be caused by some other process in the same set.

Example: Process-1 requests the printer, gets it
Process-2 requests the tape unit, gets it
Process-1 requests the tape unit, waits
Process-2 requests the printer, waits
Process-1 and Process-2 are deadlocked!

In this chapter, we shall analyze deadlocks with the following assumptions:

- A process must request a resource before using it. It must release the resource after using it. (request→use→release)
- A process cannot request a number more than the total number of resources available in the system.

For the resources of the system, a resource table shall be kept, which shows whether each process is free or if occupied, by which process it is occupied. For every resource, queues shall be kept, indicating the names of processes waiting for that resource.

A deadlock occurs if and only if the following four conditions hold in a system simultaneously:

1. Mutual Exclusion: At least one of the resources is non-sharable (that is; only a limited number of processes can use it at a time and if it is requested by a process while it is being used by another one, the requesting process has to wait until the resource is released.).
2. Hold and Wait: There must be at least one process that is holding at least one resource and waiting for other resources that are being hold by other processes.
3. No Preemption: No resource can be preempted before the holding process completes its task with that resource.
4. Circular Wait: There exists a set of processes: $\{P_1, P_2, ..., P_n\}$ such that
   P_1 is waiting for a resource held by P_2
   P_2 is waiting for a resource held by P_3
   ...
   P_{n-1} is waiting for a resource held by P_n
   P_n is waiting for a resource held by P_1

Methods for handling deadlocks are:

- Deadlock prevention
- Deadlock avoidance
- Deadlock detection and recovery

4.6.2.1 Deadlock Prevention

To prevent the system from deadlocks, one of the four discussed conditions that may create a deadlock should be discarded. The methods for those conditions are as follows:

4.6.2.1.1 Mutual Exclusion

In general, we do not have systems with all resources being sharable. Some resources like printers, processing units are *non-sharable*. So it is not possible to prevent deadlocks by denying mutual exclusion.

4.6.2.1.2 Hold and Wait

One protocol to ensure that hold-and-wait condition never occurs says each process must request and get all of its resources before it begins execution.

Another protocol is "Each process can request resources only when it does not occupy any resources."

The second protocol is better. However, both protocols cause low resource utilization and starvation. Many resources are allocated but most of them are unused for a long period of time. A process that requests several commonly used resources causes many others to wait indefinitely.

4.6.2.1.3 No Preemption

One protocol is "If a process that is holding some resources requests another resource and that resource cannot be allocated to it, then it must release all resources that are currently allocated to it."

Another protocol is "When a process requests some resources, if they are available, allocate them. If a resource it requested is not available, then we check whether it is being used or it is allocated to some other process waiting for other resources. If that resource is not being used, then the OS preempts it from the waiting process and allocate it to the requesting process.

If that resource is used, the requesting process must wait." This protocol can be applied to resources whose states can easily be saved and restored (registers, memory space). It cannot be applied to resources like printers.

4.6.2.1.4 Circular Wait

One protocol to ensure that the circular wait condition never holds is "Impose a linear ordering of all resource types." Then, each process can only request resources in an increasing order of priority. Another protocol is "Whenever a process requests a resource r_j, it must have released all resources r_k with priority(r_k) = priority (r_j).

4.6.2.2 Deadlock Avoidance

Given some additional information on how each process will request resources, it is possible to construct an algorithm that will avoid deadlock states. The algorithm will dynamically examine the resource allocation operations to ensure that there won't be a circular wait on resources.

When a process requests a resource that is already available, the system must decide whether that resource can immediately be allocated or not. The resource is immediately allocated only if it leaves the system in a safe state.

A state is safe if the system can allocate resources to each process in some order avoiding a deadlock. A deadlock state is an unsafe state.

4.6.2.3 Deadlock Detection

If a system has no deadlock prevention and no deadlock avoidance scheme, then it needs a deadlock detection scheme with recovery from deadlock capability. For this, information should be kept on the allocation of resources to processes, and on outstanding allocation requests.

Then, an algorithm is needed which will determine whether the system has entered a deadlock state. This algorithm must be invoked periodically.

4.6.3 Semaphore

It is a synchronization tool used to solve complex *critical section problems*. A semaphore is an integer variable that, apart from initialization, is accessed only through two standard atomic operations: *Wait* and *Signal*.

4.7 Interprocess Communication [IPC]

4.7 Interprocess Communication [IPC]

Interprocess communication is the term which describes how two processes may exchange information with each other. In general, the two processes may be running on the same machine or on different machines.

The processes can exchange information by passing *open files* across a *fork* or an *exec*, or through the file system. But there are different types of interprocess communication (IPC), such as

1. Pipes (Half Duplex)
2. Named Pipes [FIFOs]
3. Stream Pipes (Full Duplex)
4. Message Queues
5. Semaphores
6. Shared memory
7. Mapped Memory
8. Sockets

4.7.1 Pipes

A pipe is a communication device that allows one-way communication. Data written to the *write end* of the pipe is read back from the *read end*. Pipes are serial devices; the data is always read from the pipe in the same order it was written. Typically, a pipe is used to communicate between two threads in a single process or between parent and child processes.

In shell programming, the symbol | creates a pipe. For example, this shell command causes the shell to produce two child processes, one for *ls* and one for *less*:

```
% ls | less
```

The shell also creates a pipe connecting the standard output of the *ls* subprocess with the standard input of the *less* process. The filenames listed by *ls* are sent to *less* in exactly the same order as if they were sent directly to the terminal.

A pipe's data capacity is limited. If the writer process writes faster than the reader process consumes the data, and if the pipe cannot store more data, the writer process blocks until more capacity becomes available. If the reader tries to read but no data is available, it blocks until data becomes available. Thus, the pipe automatically synchronizes the two processes.

Pipes are the oldest form of IPC and are provided by all Unix systems. They have two limitations:

- They are half-duplex data flows only in one direction.
- They can be used only between processes that have a common ancestor.

4.7.2 Named Pipes [FIFOs]

Named pipes allow two unrelated processes to communicate with each other. They are also known as FIFOs (First-In, First-Out) and can be used to establish a one-way (half-duplex) flow of data.

Named pipes are identified by their *access point*, which is basically in a file kept on the file system. Because named pipes have the pathname of a file associated with them, it is possible for unrelated processes to communicate with each other. In other words, two unrelated processes can open the file associated with the named pipe and begin communication.

Unlike anonymous pipes, which are process-persistent objects, named pipes are file system-persistent objects, that is, they exist beyond the life of the process. They have to be explicitly deleted by one of the processes by calling *unlink* or else deleted from the file system via the command line.

In order to communicate by means of a named pipe, the processes have to open the file associated with the named pipe. By opening the file for reading, the process has access to the reading end of the pipe, and by opening the file for writing, the process has access to the writing end of the pipe.

A named pipe supports blocked read and write operations by default: if a process opens the file for reading, it is blocked until another process opens the file for writing, and vice versa. However, it is possible to make named pipes support non-blocking operations by specifying the O_NONBLOCK flag while opening them. A named pipe must be opened either read-only or write-only. It must not be opened for read-write because it is half-duplex, that is, a one-way channel.

Shells make extensive use of pipes; for example, we use pipes to send the output of one command as the input of the other command. In real-life UNIX® applications, named pipes are used for communication, when the two processes need a simple method for synchronous communication.

4.7.3 Stream Pipes (Full Duplex)

A *stream* based pipe is a bidirectional (full-duplex) pipe. To obtain bidirectional data flow between a parent and a child, only a single stream pipe is required. If we look inside a stream pipe, we see that it is simply two stream heads, with each write queue (WQ) pointing at the other's read queue (RQ). Data written to one end of the pipe is placed in messages on the other's read queue.

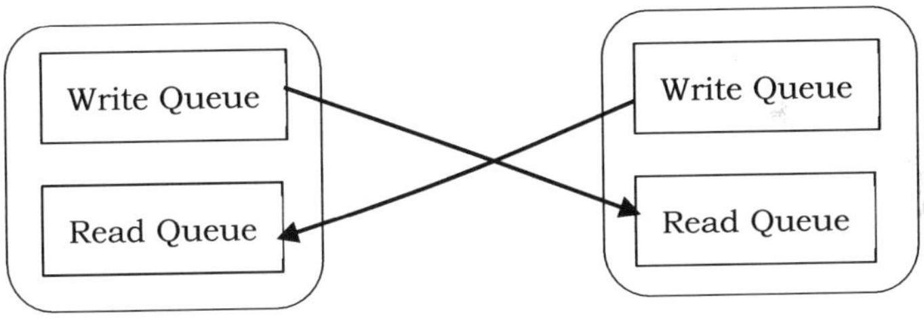

Stream pipes have the following *advantages*:

- Unlike shared-memory connections, stream pipes do not pose the security risk of being overwritten or read by other programs that explicitly access the same portion of shared memory.
- Unlike shared-memory connections, stream-pipe connections allow distributed transactions between database servers that are on the same computer.

Stream pipes have the following *disadvantages*:

- Stream pipes might be slower than shared-memory connections on some computers.
- Stream pipes are not available on all platforms.
- When you use shared memory or stream pipes for client/server communications, the hostname is ignored.

4.7.4 Message Queues

Message queues allow one or more processes to write messages, which will be read by one or more reading processes. Message queuing has been used in data processing for many years. It is most commonly used today in electronic mail. Without queuing, sending an electronic message over long distances requires every node on the route to be available for forwarding messages, and the addressees to be logged on and conscious of the fact that you are trying to send them a message. In a queuing system, messages are stored at intermediate nodes until the system is ready to forward them. At their final destination they are stored in an electronic mailbox until the addressee is ready to read them.

Two (or more) processes can exchange information via access to a common system message queue. The sending process places via some (OS) message-passing module a message onto a queue which can be read by another process. Each message is given an identification or type so that processes can select the appropriate message. Process must share a common key in order to gain access to the queue in the first place

The message type of IPC allows processes (executing programs) to communicate through the exchange of data stored in buffers. This data is transmitted between processes in discrete portions called messages. Processes using this type of IPC can send and receive messages.

We can think of message queuing as being electronic mail for programs. In a message queuing environment, each program from the set that makes up an application suite is designed to perform a well-defined, self-contained function in response to a specific request. To communicate with another program, a program must put a message on a predefined queue. The other program retrieves the message from the queue, and processes the requests and information contained in the message. So message queuing is a style of program-to-program communication.

Queuing is the mechanism by which messages are held until an application is ready to process them. Queuing allows you to:

- Communicate between programs (which might each be running in different environments) without having to write the communication code.
- Select the order in which a program processes messages.
- Balance loads on a system by arranging for more than one program to service a queue when the number of messages exceeds a threshold.
- Increase the availability of your applications by arranging for an alternative system to service the queues if your primary system is unavailable.

4.7.5 Semaphores

In its simplest form a semaphore is a location in memory whose value can be tested and set by more than one process. The test and set operation is, so far as each process is concerned, uninterruptible or atomic; once started nothing can stop it. The result of the test and set operation is the addition of the current value of the semaphore and the set value, which can be positive or negative. Depending on the result of the test and set operation one process may have to sleep until the semaphore's value is changed by another process. Semaphores can be used to implement critical regions, areas of critical code that only one process at a time should be executing.

Say you had many cooperating processes reading records from and writing records to a single data file. You would want that file access to be strictly coordinated. You could use a semaphore with an initial value of 1 and, around the file operating code, put two semaphore operations, the first to test and decrement the semaphore's value and the second to test and increment it.

The first process to access the file would try to decrement the semaphore's value and it would succeed, the semaphore's value now being 0. This process can now go ahead and use the data file but if another process wishing to use it now tries to decrement the semaphore's value it would fail as the result would be -1. That process will be suspended until the first process has finished with the data file. When the first process has finished with the data file it will increment the semaphore's value, making it 1 again. Now the waiting process can be woken and this time its attempt to increment the semaphore will succeed.

4.7.6 Shared memory

One of the simplest interprocess communication methods is using shared memory. Shared memory allows two or more processes to access the same memory as if they all called *malloc* and were returned pointers to the same actual memory. When one process changes the memory, all the other processes see the modification.

Shared memory allows one or more processes to communicate via memory that appears in all of their virtual address spaces. The pages of the virtual memory is referenced by page table entries in each of the sharing processes' page tables. It does not have to be at the same address in all of the processes' virtual memory. Access to shared memory areas is controlled via keys and access rights checking. Once the memory is being shared, there are no checks on how the processes are using it. They must rely on other mechanisms to synchronize access to the memory.

Shared memory is the fastest form of interprocess communication because all processes share the same piece of memory. Access to this shared memory is as fast as accessing a process's nonshared memory, and it does not require a system call or entry to the kernel. It also avoids copying data unnecessarily.

Because the kernel does not synchronize accesses to shared memory, you must provide your own synchronization. For example, a process should not read from the memory until after data is written there, and two processes must not write to the same memory location at the same time. A common strategy to avoid these race conditions is to use semaphores.

4.7.7 Mapped Memory

Mapped memory permits different processes to communicate using a shared file. Although you can think of mapped memory as using a shared memory segment with a name, you should be aware that there are technical differences. Mapped memory can be used for interprocess communication or as an easy way to access the contents of a file.

Mapped memory forms an association between a file and a process's memory. Linux splits the file into page-sized chunks and then copies them into virtual memory pages so that they can be made available in a process's address space. Thus, the process can read the file's contents with ordinary memory access. It can also modify the file's contents by writing to memory. This permits fast access to files.

You can think of mapped memory as allocating a buffer to hold a file's entire contents, and then reading the file into the buffer and (if the buffer is modified) writing the buffer back out to the file afterward. Linux handles the file reading and writing operations for you.

4.7.8 Sockets

A socket is a *bidirectional* communication device that can be used to communicate with another process on the same machine or with a process running on other machines. Sockets are the only interprocess communication we'll discuss in this section that permit communication between processes on different computers. Internet programs such as Telnet, rlogin, FTP, talk, and the World Wide Web use sockets.

For example, you can obtain the *www* page from a Web server using the Telnet program because they both use sockets for network communications. To open a connection to a *www* server at *www.CareerMonk.com*, use telnet www.CareerMonk.com 80. The magic constant 80 specifies a connection to the Web server programming running *www.CareerMonk.com* instead of some other process.

Try typing GET / after the connection is established. This sends a message through the socket to the Web server, which replies by sending the home page's HTML source and then closing the connection—for example:

```
% telnet www.CareerMonk.com 80
Trying 178.79.184.217...
Connected to merlin.CareerMonk.com (178.79.184.217).
Escape character is '^]'.
GET /
<html>
<head>
<meta http-equiv="Content-Type" content="text/html; charset=iso-8859-1">
...
```

When you create a socket, you must specify three parameters: communication style, namespace, and protocol.

A communication style controls how the socket treats transmitted data and specifies the number of communication partners. When data is sent through a socket, it is packaged into chunks called packets. The communication style determines how these packets are handled and how they are addressed from the sender to the receiver. In Connection styles guarantee delivery of all packets in the order they were sent. If packets are lost or reordered by problems in the network, the receiver automatically requests their retransmission from the sender.

A connection-style socket is like a telephone call: The addresses of the sender and receiver are fixed at the beginning of the communication when the connection is established. In datagram styles do not guarantee delivery or arrival order. Packets may be lost or reordered in transit due to network errors or other conditions. Each packet must be labeled with its destination and is not guaranteed to be delivered. The system guarantees only best effort, so packets may disappear or arrive in a different order than shipping.

A datagram-style socket behaves more like postal mail. The sender specifies the receiver's address for each individual message. A socket namespace specifies how socket addresses are written. A socket address identifies one end of a socket connection. For example, socket addresses in the *local namespace* are ordinary filenames. In *Internet namespace*, a socket address is composed of the Internet address (also called an Internet Protocol address or IP address) of a host attached to the network and a port number. The port number distinguishes among multiple sockets on the same host.

A protocol specifies how data is transmitted. Some protocols are TCP/IP, the primary networking protocols used by the Internet; the AppleTalk network protocol; and the UNIX local communication protocol. Not all combinations of styles, namespaces, and protocols are supported.

4.8 Starvation and Aging

4.8.1 Starvation

Starvation is a resource management problem where a process does not get the resources it needs for a long time because the resources are being allocated to other processes.

4.8.2 Aging

Aging is a technique to avoid starvation in a scheduling system. It works by adding an aging factor to the priority of each request. The aging factor must increase the request's priority as time passes and must ensure that a request will eventually be the highest priority request (after it has waited long enough).

4.9 Complier and Interpreter

An interpreter reads one instruction at a time and executes that instruction. It does not perform any translation. But a compiler translates the entire instructions.

Note: for detailed review refer *Scripting Languages* chapter.

4.10 Process Loading and Linking

4.10.1 Load Modules and Address Binding

A load module is a compiled and possibly linked (see below) version of the source code. The processing of the source code is done with no knowledge of where the resulting load module is put in memory.

Thus the *process* when loaded into memory, must ultimately have all addresses *mapped* into the *process address space* in real memory before it can execute. This is called *address binding*. Address binding can be done at:

- Compile time
- Load time
- Execution (run) time

4.10.2 Loading and linking

A program (load module) may be made up from a number of *object* module files. To be executable in memory, a program must map all relative internal addresses in the load module(s) to memory addresses (binding), and in addition any references made to other modules must also be resolved (linking).

Thus to create an active process in memory, the modules must be both linked (resolve references among modules) and loaded into memory.

We distinguish between loading a single load module which requires only binding of the relative addresses (already linked), and the loading of multiple modules which requires also linking (at load or run time). The next three items assumes a single load module.

4.10.3 Absolute loading

The references in the program load module are already resolved into specific physical memory addresses.

- Programmer must know where the process would be loaded in memory (or the strategy for assigning processes to memory)
- Modifications made to the process may require changing all addresses in the module (recompile)
- Absolute address assignment can be done either by the programmer or the compiler/assembler. The latter means that the programmer uses symbolic references to be later filled in by the compiler or assembler.

4.10.4 Relocatable Loading (bind to real addresses at load time)

Assume a *single linked* load module that can be located anywhere in memory. It is not desirable to decide in advance into which region of memory s load module must be loaded, so we now defer that decision to load time. The module does not have absolute addresses, but addresses that are relative to some known point, such as the start of the program module.

The loader places the module at location x, by adding x to each memory reference in the module as it loads the module into memory. In order to do this the module needs a relocation dictionary which tells where the addresses are, and how to translate them at load time.

If a process image is swapped out to disk, and then brought back into memory, it would have to be loaded into the same location it was before (x), since it already has its memory references resolved to absolute values because it was previously resolved at load time.

The "process image" swapped to disk generally retains the resolved absolute addresses in the memory image that were created at initial load tine. Comment: resetting the module addresses to their pre-loaded relative (re-locatable) addresses would probably involve too much overhead for swapping.

4.10.5 Dynamic Run-time Real Address Binding

Assumes this is a single linked load module. This would allow the swapping mechanism to restore a swapped process to an arbitrary location in memory, not necessarily its old location and maximizes memory utilization. Defer the calculation of absolute addresses until it is actually needed at run time. Thus, the load module is loaded into main memory with all memory references in relative form (unresolved to real). For example the references would be offsets from the beginning of the process.

It is not until an instruction is actually executed that the absolute address is calculated. Because these actions are at run time, hardware assistance is needed for the dynamic address translation in order to have good performance. The hardware adds a base address value to each address in real time.

4.10.6 Linking

The function of the linker is to take a collection of object modules and produce a load module. Address references to other modules must be expressed symbolically in an unlinked object module.

Linker may produce a single load module where all references are resolved relative to some point in the module, if done before loading. If linking is deferred to later (loading or run time), then the references to other modules (only) are left as symbolic with local references being resolved to relative addresses.

4.10.7 Linkage Editor

The nature of the address linkage depends on the type of load module to be created and when the linkage occurs. If (usual case), a relocatable load module is needed, then the link is done follows:

Each compiled object module is created with references relative to the beginning of the beginning of the object module. All modules linked are put together in a single load module with all references relative the origin of the load module. A linker that produces a relocatable load module is often referred to as a linkage editor.

Note: distinguish between linking and logical to physical address binding

4.10.8 Dynamic Linking

Meaning of "dynamic": Defer linkage of external modules until after the load module has been created: at load time or run time. Load module contains unresolved references to other modules (symbolic) – these references can be resolved either at load time or run time.

4.10.8.1 Load-time Dynamic Linking

Like relocatable loading above, except multiple modules are involved. This is the "DLL" (Dynamic Link Library) concept in Windows or OS/2. The load module is read into main memory. Any reference to an external module causes the ***loader*** to find this module, load it, and alter the reference to a relative address in memory from the beginning of the application. Several advantages to this approach over static loading:

- Easier to incorporate changes – no need to relink the entire application.
- Automatic code sharing – OS will load a single copy of a routine for multiple applications referencing it.
- Easier for independent software developers to extend the function a widely used software package such as an operating system- extension packages as a dynamic link module.

4.10.8.2 Run-time Dynamic Linking (Dynamic/Run-time Loading)

Like dynamic runtime address binding for a single load module above, except multiple modules involved which must be loaded at run time when referenced. This is the "DLL" (Dynamic Link Library) concept in Windows or OS/2

Some of the linking is postponed until execution time. External references to target modules remain in the loaded module (in memory). When a call is made to the absent module, the OS locates the module, loads it, and links it to the calling module

4.10.8.3 Dynamic Address Binding versus Dynamic Linking

Dynamic address binding (single load module) allows an entire module to be moved around – however, the structure of the module is static, being unchanged throughout the execution of the process and from one execution to the next.

In some cases it is not possible to determine prior to execution which module will be required thus dynamic linking will be required. The advantage of dynamic linking is that it is not necessary to allocate memory for program units unless those units are actually referenced.

4.10.9 Dynamic-Link Libraries (DLL's)

The following are some concepts on Dynamic-Link Libraries on the familiar DLL's you see in many Windows applications and in Windows system folders. They are taken from the book: "Advanced Windows", 3rd Ed., pp. 529-533, by Jeffrey Richter

A DLL is a set of modules, with each module containing a set of functions. These functions are written with the expectation that an application (.exe file) or another DLL will call them. The source code files will be compiled and linked just as an exe file would be. The linker when used in creating a DLL, results in a (DLL) file such that the Operating System loader will recognize this file as a DLL rather than an exe file.

For an application or another DLL to call functions contained within a DLL, the DLL's file image must first be mapped into the calling processes addresses space. This can be accomplished using one of two methods:

4.10.9.1 Implicit Load-Time Linking or Explicit Runtime Linking

Once the DLL's file image is mapped into the calling processes' address space, the DLL's functions are available to all **threads in the processes.** After this mapping, the DLL code becomes completely integrated into the process and the threads cannot distinguish the DLL code and data from other code and data in the process address space.

4.10.9.2 Mapping a DLL into a Process's Address Space

4.10.9.2.1 Implicit Linking (Load Time)

When the OS loads an exe file, the system examines the contents of the exe file image to see which DLLs must be loaded for the application to run. The linker of the "base" exe file embeds information in the exe modules which tells the loader which additional DLL's must be linked at load time. The loader/linker then links the specified DLL's to the exe file during load time.

4.10.9.2.2 Explicit Linking (Run Time)

A DLL's file image can be explicitly mapped into a process's address space when one of the processes threads calls a function in one of the DLL's associated with the exe application. The called DLL file images are then located, loaded, and mapped into the calling process's address space (dynamically at run time).

Problems and Questions with Answers

Question 1: What is marshaling?

Answer: Marshaling is the process of gathering data from one or more applications (or sources) in computer storage, putting them into a message buffer, and converting it into a format that is prescribed for a particular receiver or programming interface. Marshaling is usually required when passing the output parameters of a program written in one language as input to a program written in another language.

Question 2: What are the basic functions of an operating system?

Answer: Operating system controls and coordinates the use of the hardware among the various applications programs for various uses. Operating system acts as resource allocator and manager. Since there are many possibly conflicting requests for resources the operating system must decide which requests are allocated resources to operating the computer system efficiently and fairly.

Also operating system is a control program which controls the user programs to prevent errors and improper use of the computer. It is especially concerned with the operation and control of I/O devices.

Question 3: Why paging is used?

Answer: Paging is solution to external fragmentation problem which is to permit the logical address space of a process to be noncontiguous, thus allowing a process to be allocating physical memory wherever the latter is available.

Question 4: What resources are used when a thread created? How they differ when a process is created?

Answer: When a thread is created the threads does not require any new resources to execute the thread shares the resources like memory of the process to which they belong to. The benefit of code sharing is that it allows an application to have several different threads of activity all within the same address space. Whereas if a new process creation is very heavyweight because it always requires new address space to be created and even if they share the memory then the inter process communication is expensive when compared to the communication between the threads.

Question 5: What is virtual memory?

Answer: Virtual memory is hardware technique where the system appears to have more memory that it actually does. This is done by time-sharing, the physical memory and storage parts of the memory one disk when they are not actively being used.

Question 6: What is Throughput, Turnaround time, Waiting time and Response time?

Answer: *Throughput*: number of processes that complete their execution per time unit. *Turnaround* time: amount of time to execute a particular process. *Waiting* time: amount of time a process has been waiting in the ready queue. *Response* time: amount of time it takes from when a request was submitted until the first response is produced, not output (for time-sharing environment).

Question 7: What is the important aspect of a real-time system or mission critical systems?

Answer: A real time operating system has well defined fixed time constraints. Process must be done within the defined constraints or the system will fail. An example is the operating system for a flight control computer or an advanced jet airplane. Often used as a control device in a dedicated application such as controlling scientific experiments, medical imaging systems, industrial control systems, and some display systems. Real-Time systems may be either hard or soft real-time.

Hard real-time: Secondary storage limited or absent, data stored in short term memory, or read-only memory (ROM), Conflicts with time-sharing systems, not supported by general-purpose operating systems. *Soft* real-time: Limited utility in industrial control of robotics, Useful in applications (multimedia, virtual reality) requiring advanced operating-system features.

Question 8: What is the difference between Hard and Soft real-time systems?

Answer: A hard real-time system guarantees that critical tasks complete on time. This goal requires that all delays in the system be bounded from the retrieval of the stored data to the time that it takes the operating system to finish any request made of it. A soft real time system where a critical real-time task gets priority over other tasks and retains that priority until it completes. As in hard real time systems kernel delays need to be bounded.

Question 9: What is the cause of thrashing? How does the system detect thrashing? Once it detects thrashing, what can the system do to eliminate this problem?

Answer: Thrashing is caused by under allocation of the minimum number of pages required by a process, forcing it to continuously page fault. The system can detect thrashing by evaluating the level of CPU utilization as compared to the level of *multiprogramming*. It can be eliminated by reducing the level of *multiprogramming*.

Question 10: What is multi-tasking, multi programming, multi-threading?

Answer: Multi programming: Multiprogramming is the technique of running several programs at a time using timesharing. It allows a computer to do several things at the same time. Multiprogramming creates logical parallelism. The concept of multiprogramming is that the operating system keeps several jobs in memory simultaneously. The operating system selects a job from the job pool and starts executing a job, when that job needs to wait for any I/O operations the CPU is switched to another job. So the main idea here is that the CPU is never idle. Multi-tasking: Multitasking is the logical extension of multiprogramming.

The concept of multitasking is quite similar to multiprogramming but difference is that the switching between jobs occurs so frequently that the users can interact with each program while it is running. This concept is also known as time-sharing systems. A time-shared operating system uses CPU scheduling and multiprogramming to provide each user with a small portion of time-shared system. Multi-threading: An application typically is implemented as a separate process with several threads of control.

In some situations a single application may be required to perform several similar tasks for example a web server accepts client requests for web pages, images, sound, and so forth. A busy web server may have several of clients concurrently accessing it. If the web server ran as a traditional single-threaded process, it would be able to service only one client at a time. The amount of time that a client might have to wait for its request to be serviced could be enormous.

So it is efficient to have one process that contains multiple threads to serve the same purpose. This approach would multithread the web-server process, the server would create a separate thread that would listen for client requests when a request was made rather than creating another process it would create another thread to service the request. To get the advantages like responsiveness, Resource sharing economy and utilization of multiprocessor architectures multithreading concept can be used.

Question 11: What is fragmentation? Different types of fragmentation?

Answer: Fragmentation occurs in a dynamic memory allocation system when many of the free blocks are too small to satisfy any request. External Fragmentation: External Fragmentation happens when a dynamic memory allocation algorithm allocates some memory and a small piece is left over that cannot be effectively used.

If too much external fragmentation occurs, the amount of usable memory is drastically reduced. Total memory space exists to satisfy a request, but it is not contiguous. Internal Fragmentation: Internal fragmentation is the space wasted inside of allocated memory blocks because of restriction on the allowed sizes of allocated blocks. Allocated memory may be slightly larger than requested memory; this size difference is memory internal to a partition, but not being used.

Question 12: Solve producer/consumer problem using *Java* threads.

Answer: The use of the implicit monitors in Java objects is powerful, but we can achieve a more subtle level of control through inter-process communication. Multithreading replaces event loop programming by dividing the tasks into discrete and logical units. Threads also provide a secondary benefit: they do away with polling. *Polling* is usually implemented by a loop that is used to check some condition repeatedly. Once the condition is true, appropriate action is taken. This wastes CPU time.

For example, consider the classic queuing problem, where one thread is producing some data and another is consuming it. To make the problem more interesting, suppose that the producer has to wait until the consumer is finished before it generates more data. In a polling system, the consumer would waste many CPU cycles while it waited for the producer to produce. Once the producer was finished, it would start polling, wasting more CPU cycles waiting for the consumer to finish, and so on. Clearly, this situation is undesirable.

To avoid polling, Java includes an elegant inter-process communication mechanism via the wait( ), notify( ), and notifyAll( ) methods. These methods are implemented as final methods in Object, so all classes have them. All three methods can be called only from within a synchronized method. Although conceptually advanced from a computer science perspective, the rules for using these methods are actually quite simple:

- wait( ) tells the calling thread to give up the monitor and go to sleep until some other thread enters the same monitor and calls notify( ).
- notify( ) wakes up the first thread that called wait( ) on the same object.
- notifyAll( ) wakes up all the threads that called wait( ) on the same object. The highest priority thread will run first.

These methods are declared within Object, as shown here:

```
final void wait( ) throws InterruptedException
final void notify( )
final void notifyAll( )
```

Additional forms of wait( ) exist that allow you to specify a period of time to wait. The following sample program incorrectly implements a simple form of the producer-consumer problem. It consists of four classes: Q, the queue that you're trying to synchronize; Producer, the threaded object that is producing queue entries; Consumer, the threaded object that is consuming queue entries; and PC, the tiny class that creates the single Q, Producer, and Consumer.

```
import java.util.*;
import java.io.*;
public class ProdCons {
  protected LinkedList list = new LinkedList();
  protected int MAX = 10;
  protected boolean done = false; // Also protected by lock on list.
  /** Inner class representing the Producer side */
  class Producer extends Thread {
    public void run() {
      while (true) {
        synchronized(list) {
            while (list.size() == MAX) // queue "full"
            try {       System.out.println("Producer WAITING");
              list.wait();   // Limit the size
            } catch (InterruptedException ex) {
              System.out.println("Producer INTERRUPTED");
            }
          list.addFirst(justProduced);
          list.notifyAll();  // must own the lock
          System.out.println("Produced 1; List size now " + list.size());
        }
      }
    }
  }
  class Consumer extends Thread {
    public void run() {
      while (true) {
        Object obj = null;
        synchronized(list) {
          while (list.size() == 0) {
            try {
              System.out.println("CONSUMER WAITING");
              list.wait();  // must own the lock
            } catch (InterruptedException ex) {
              System.out.println("CONSUMER INTERRUPTED");
            }
          }
          obj = list.removeLast();
          list.notifyAll();
          int len = list.size();
          System.out.println("List size now " + len);
        }
      }
    }
  }
  ProdCons(int nP, int nC) {
    for (int i=0; i<nP; i++)
      new Producer().start();
    for (int i=0; i<nC; i++)
      new Consumer().start();
  }
  public static void main(String[] args) throws IOException, InterruptedException {
    // Start producers and consumers
    int numProducers = 4;
```

```
    int numConsumers = 3;
    ProdCons pc = new ProdCons(numProducers, numConsumers);
    Thread.sleep(10*1000); // Let it run for, say, 10 seconds
    // End of simulation - shut down gracefully
    synchronized(pc.list) {
      pc.done = true;
      pc.list.notifyAll();
    }
  }
}
```

Question 13: What is stack unwinding?

Answer: When an exception is thrown and control passes from a try block to a handler, the *C++* run time calls destructors for all automatic objects constructed since the beginning of the try block. This process is called *stack unwinding*. The automatic objects are destroyed in reverse order of their construction. Automatic objects are local objects that have been declared auto or register, or not declared static or extern. An automatic object *x* is deleted whenever the program exits the block in which *x* is declared.

If an exception is thrown during construction of an object consisting of subobjects or array elements, destructors are only called for those subobjects or array elements successfully constructed before the exception was thrown. A *destructor* for a local static object will only be called if the object was *successfully constructed*.

As you create objects statically (on the stack as opposed to allocating them in the heap memory) and perform function calls, they are *stacked up*. When a scope (anything delimited by { and }) is exited (by using *return XXX;*, reaching the end of the scope or throwing an exception) everything within that scope is destroyed (destructors are called for everything). This process of destroying local objects and calling destructors is called stack unwinding. (Exiting a code block using *goto* will not unwind the stack which is one of the reasons you should never use *goto* in *C++*).

If any destructor throws an *exception* during stack unwinding we end up in the land of *undefined behavior* which could cause your program to *terminate* unexpectedly.

Question 14: What are signals?

Answer: *signals* is an useful method for one process to disturb another process. Basically, one process can *raise* a signal and deliver it to another process. The destination process's signal handler (just a function) is invoked and the process can handle it.

Signals provide a useful service. For example, one process might want to stop another one, and this can be done by sending the signal SIGSTOP to that process. To continue, the process has to receive signal SIGCONT. How does the process know to do this when it receives a certain signal? Well, many signals are predefined and the process has a default signal handler to deal with it.

A default handler? Yes. Take SIGINT for example. This is the interrupt signal that a process receives when the user hits *^C*. The default signal handler for SIGINT causes the process to exit! Sound familiar? Well, as you can imagine, you can override the SIGINT to do whatever you want (or nothing at all!) You could have your process printf() "Interrupt?! No way, Man!" and continue.

So now you know that you can have your process respond to just about any signal in just about any way you want. Naturally, there are exceptions because otherwise it would be too easy to understand. Take the ever popular SIGKILL, signal #9. Have you ever typed "kill -9 <process ID>" to kill a running process? You were sending it SIGKILL. Now you might also remember that no process can get out of a "kill -9", and you would be correct. SIGKILL is one of the signals you can't add your own signal handler for. The aforementioned SIGSTOP is also in this category.

There are a set of defined signals that the kernel can generate or that can be generated by other processes in the system, provided that they have the correct privileges.

Signal	D escription
SIGABRT	Process abort signal.
SIGALRM	Alarm clock.
SIGFPE	Erroneous arithmetic operation.
SIGHUP	Hangup.
SIGILL	Illegal instruction.
SIGINT	Terminal interrupt signal.
SIGKILL	Kill (cannot be caught or ignored).
SIGPIPE	Write on a pipe with no one to read it.
SIGQUIT	Terminal quit signal.
SIGSEGV	Invalid memory reference.
SIGTERM	Termination signal.
SIGUSR1	User-defined signal 1.
SIGUSR2	User-defined signal 2.
SIGCHLD	Child process terminated or stopped.
SIGCONT	Continue executing, if stopped.
SIGSTOP	Stop executing (cannot be caught or ignored).
SIGTSTP	Terminal stop signal.
SIGTTIN	Background process attempting read.
SIGTTOU	Background process attempting write.
SIGBUS	Bus error.
SIGPOLL	Pollable event.
SIGPROF	Profiling timer expired.
SIGSYS	Bad system call.
SIGTRAP	Trace/breakpoint trap.
SIGURG	High bandwidth data is available at a socket.
SIGVTALRM	Virtual timer expired.
SIGXCPU	CPU time limit exceeded.
SIGXFSZ	File size limit exceeded.

Example: Here's one that handled SIGINT, which can be delivered by hitting ^C.

```
#include <stdio.h>
#include <stdlib.h>
#include <unistd.h>
#include <errno.h>
#include <signal.h>
void sigint_handler(int sig){
   write(0, "Testing! SIGINT!\n", 14);
}
int main(void){
   void sigint_handler(int sig);
   char str[200];
   struct sigaction sa;
   sa.sa_handler = sigint_handler;
   sa.sa_flags = 0; // or SA_RESTART
   sigemptyset(&sa.sa_mask);
   if (sigaction(SIGINT, &sa, NULL) == -1) {
      perror("sigaction");
      exit(1);
```

```
    }
    printf("Enter a test string:\n");
    if (fgets(str, sizeof str, stdin) == NULL)
        perror("fgets");
    else
        printf("We entered: %s\n", str);
    return 0;
}
```

This program has two functions: main() which sets up the signal handler (using the sigaction() call), and sigint_handler() which is the signal handler, itself.

What happens when you run it? If you are in the midst of entering a string and you hit ^C, the call to gets() fails and sets the global variable errno to EINTR. Additionally, sigint_handler() is called and does its routine, so you actually see:

```
Enter a string:
I am testing the signals of ^CAhhh! SIGINT!
fgets: Interrupted system call
And then it exits. Hey—what kind of handler is this, if it just exits anyway?
```

Well, we have a couple things at play, here. First, you'll notice that the signal handler was called, because it printed "Testing! SIGINT!" But then fgets() returns an error, namely EINTR, or "Interrupted system call". See, some system calls can be interrupted by signals, and when this happens, they return an error. You might see code like this (sometimes cited as an excusable use of goto):

```
restart:
    if (some_system_call() == -1) {
        if (errno == EINTR) goto restart;
        perror("some_system_call");
        exit(1);
    }
```

Instead of using goto like that, you might be able to set your sa_flags to include SA_RESTART. For example, if we change our SIGINT handler code to look like this:

```
    sa.sa_flags = SA_RESTART;
```

Then our run looks more like this:

```
Enter a string:
Hello^CTesting! SIGINT!
Er, hello!^CTesting! SIGINT!
This time for sure!
You entered: This time for sure!
```

Some system calls are interruptible, and some can be restarted. It's system dependent.

C/C++/Java Interview Questions

CHAPTER

5

The objective of this chapter is to explain the basics of programming. In this chapter you will know about data types, pointers, scoping rules, memory layout of program, parameter passing techniques, types of languages and problems related to them.

5.1 Variables

Before getting in to the definition of variables, let us relate them to an old mathematical equation. Many of us would have solved many mathematical equations since childhood. As an example, consider the equation below:

$$x^2 + 2y - 2 = 1$$

We don't have to worry about the use of this equation. The important thing that we need to understand is, the equation has some names (x and y), which hold values (data). That means, the *names* (x and y) are placeholders for representing data. Similarly, in computer science we need something for holding data, and *variables* is the way to do that.

5.2 Data types

In the above-mentioned equation, the variables x and y can take any values such as integral numbers (10, 20.), real numbers (0.23, 5.5) or just 0 and 1. To solve the equation, we need to relate them to kind of values they can take and *data type* is the name used in computer science for this purpose. A *data type* in a programming language is a set of data with predefined values. Examples of data types are: integer, floating point unit number, character, string, etc.

Computer memory is all filled with zeros and ones. If we have a problem and wanted to code it, it's very difficult to provide the solution in terms of zeros and ones. To help users, programming languages and compilers provide us with data types. For example, *integer* takes 2 bytes (actual value depends on compiler), *float* takes 4 bytes, etc. This says that, in memory we are combining 2 bytes (16 bits) and calling it as *integer*. Similarly, combining 4 bytes (32 bits) and calling it as *float*. A data type reduces the coding effort. At the top level, there are two types of data types:

- System-defined data types (also called *Primitive* data types)
- User-defined data types

System-defined data types (Primitive data types): Data types that are defined by system are called *primitive* data types. The primitive data types provided by many programming languages are: int, float, char, double, bool, etc. The number of bits allocated for each primitive data type depends on the programming languages, compiler and operating system. For the same primitive data type, different languages may use different sizes. Depending on the size of the data types the total available values (domain) will also changes.

For example, "*int*" may take 2 bytes or 4 bytes. If it takes 2 bytes (16 bits) then the total possible values are -32,768 to +32,767 (-2^{15} *to* $2^{15}-1$). If it takes, 4 bytes (32 bits), then the possible values are between −2,147,483,648 and +2,147,483,648 (-2^{31} *to* $2^{31}-1$). Same is the case with remaining data types too.

User defined data types: If the system defined data types is not enough then most programming languages allow the users to define their own data types called as user defined data types. Good example of user defined data types are: structures in $C/C++$ and classes in *Java*.

For example, in the snippet below, we are combining many system-defined data types and call it as user-defined data type with name "*newType*". This gives more flexibility and comfort in dealing with computer memory.

```
struct newType {
        int data1;
        float data 2;
        ...
        char data;
};
```

5.3 Data Structure

Based on the discussion above, once we have data in variables, we need some mechanism for manipulating that data to solve problems. *Data structure* is a particular way of storing and organizing data in a computer so that it can be used efficiently. A *data structure* is a special format for organizing and storing data. General data structure types include arrays, files, linked lists, stacks, queues, trees, graphs and so on.

Depending on the organization of the elements, data structures are classified into two types:

1) *Linear data structures*: Elements are accessed in a sequential order but it is not compulsory to store all elements sequentially (say, Linked Lists). *Examples*: Linked Lists, Stacks and Queues.
2) *Non – linear data structures*: Elements of this data structure are stored / accessed in a non-linear order. *Examples*: Trees and graphs.

5.4 Abstract Data Types (ADTs)

Before defining abstract data types, let us consider the different view of system-defined data types. We all know that, by default, all primitive data types (int, float, etc.) support basic operations such as addition and subtraction. The system provides the implementations for the primitive data types. For user-defined data types also we need to define operations. The implementation for these operations can be done when we want to actually use them. That means, in general user defined data types are defined along with their operations.

To simplify the process of solving the problems, we combine the data structures along with their operations and call it as *Abstract Data Types* (ADTs). An ADT consists of *two* parts:

1. Declaration of data
2. Declaration of operations

Commonly used ADTs *include*: Linked Lists, Stacks, Queues, Priority Queues, Binary Trees, Dictionaries, Disjoint Sets (Union and Find), Hash Tables, Graphs, and many other. For example, stack uses LIFO (Last-In-First-Out) mechanism while storing the data in data structures. The last element inserted into the stack is the first element that gets deleted. Common operations of it are: creating the stack, pushing an element onto the stack, popping an element from stack, finding the current top of the stack, finding number of elements in the stack, etc.

While defining the ADTs do not worry about the implementation details. They come into picture only when we want to use them. Different kinds of ADTs are suited to different kinds of applications, and some are highly specialized to specific tasks.

By the end of this book, we will go through many of them and you will be in a position to relate the data structures to the kind of problems they solve.

5.5 Memory and Variables

First let's understand the way memory is organized in a computer. We can treat the memory as an array of bytes. Each location is identified by an address (index to array). In general, the address 0 is not a valid memory location. It is important to understand that the address of any byte (location) in memory is an integer. In the diagram below n value depends on the main memory size of the system.

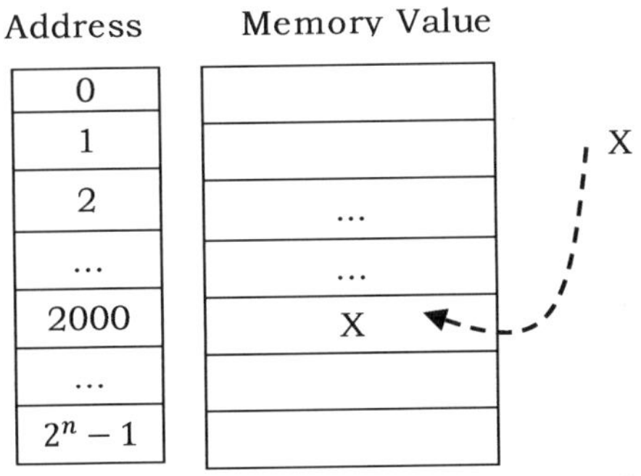

To read or write any location, CPU accesses it by sending its address to the memory controller. When we create a variable (for example, in C: $int\ X$), the compiler allocates a block of contiguous memory locations and its size depends on the size of the variable.

The compiler also keeps an internal tag that associates the variable name X with the address of the first byte allocated to it (sometimes called *symbol table*). So when we want to access that variable like this: $X = 10$, the compiler knows where that variable is located and it writes the value 10.

Size of a Variable: $Sizeof$ operator is used to find size of the variable (how much memory a variable occupies). For example, on some computers, $sizeof(X)$ gives the value 4. This means an integer needs 4 contiguous bytes in memory. If the address of X is 2000, then the actual memory locations used by X are: 2001, 2002, 2003, and 2004.

Address of a Variable: In C language, we can get the address of a variable using $address - of$ operator (&). The code below prints the address of X variable. In general, addresses are printed in hexadecimal as they are compact and also easy to understand if the addresses are big.

```
int X;
printf("The address is: %u\n", &X);
```

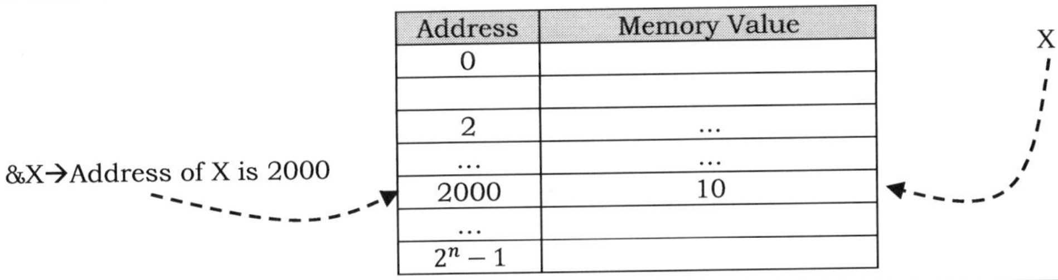

5.6 Pointers

Pointers are also variables which can hold the address of another variable.

5.6.1 Declaration of Pointers

To declare a pointer, we have to specify the type of the variable it will point to. That means we need to specify the type of the variable whose address it is going to hold. The declaration is very simple. Let us see some examples of pointer declarations below:

```
int *ptr1;
float *ptr2;
unsigned int *ptr3;
char *ptr4; void *ptr5;
```

Here *ptr*1 is a pointer that can point to an *int* variable, *ptr*2 can point to a *float*, *ptr*3 to an *unsigned int*, and *ptr*4 to a *char*. Finally *ptr*5 is a pointer that can point to anything.

These pointers are called *void* pointers, and there are some restrictions on what we can do with void pointers.

5.6.2 Pointers Usage

As we said, pointers hold addresses. That means we can assign the address of a variable to it. Let us consider the sample code below:

```
int X = 10;
int *ptr = &X;
```

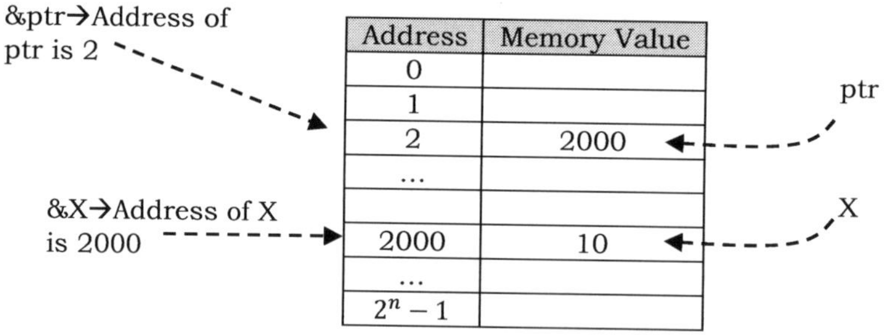

Here, we first declare an integer named *X* and initialize it to the value 10. Then we create a pointer to *int* named *ptr* and assign the address of *X* to it. This is called, "*making the pointer ptr point to X.*" A common operation is done with a pointer and is called *indirection.*

It is a way to access the contents of the memory that it points to. The indirection operator is represented by the asterisk symbol. Do not confuse this operator with the use of the same asterisk symbol in the declaration of pointers. They are not the same thing.

If we would like to access the contents of the memory where *ptr* points to, we will do it like this: $*ptr$. Let's see a small code that shows pointer indirections.

```
int X = 10;
int *ptr = &X;
printf("X contains the value %d\n", X);
printf("ptr points to %p\n", ptr);
printf("there lies the value %d\n", *ptr);
*ptr = 25;
printf("now X contains the value %d\n", X);
```

Here we first declare X and *ptr* just like before. Then we print X (which is10), followed by *ptr*, i.e., the contents of the variable *ptr* which is an address; the address of X. And finally we print $*ptr$, which is the value of the memory location where *ptr* points to (again 10, since it points to the location occupied by the variable X in memory).

Finally we change the contents of the location where *ptr* points to by writing $*ptr = 25$. This means assign the value 25 to wherever *ptr* is pointing to. Note that when we do that, what is actually happening is that the value of X is being modified. This is because, *ptr* holds the address of X, and changing the contents of the memory at that address changes the value of X.

One limitation of *void* pointers, i.e. pointers that can point to any type, is that they cannot be *dereferenced*. This is because each variable type takes different amount of memory. On a 32-bit computer for example usually an int needs 4 bytes, while a *short* 2 bytes. So in order to read the actual value stored there, the compiler has to know how many consecutive memory locations to read in order to get the full value.

5.6.3 Pointer Manipulation

Pointers are useful as they allow us to perform arithmetic operations on them. This might be obvious to the careful reader, since we said that pointers are just integers. However, there are a few small differences on pointer arithmetic that make their use even more intuitive and easy. Try the following code:

```
char *cptr = (char*)2;
printf("cptr before: %p ", cptr);

cptr++;
printf("and after: %p\n", cptr);
```

We declare a pointer named *cptr* and assign the address 2 to it. We print the contents of the pointer (i.e. the address 2), increment it, and print again. Sure enough the first time it prints 2 and then 3, and that was exactly what we expected. However try this one as well:

```
int *iptr = (int*)2;
printf("iptr before: %p ", iptr);

iptr++;
printf("and after: %p\n", iptr);
```

Now the output, on my computer, is *iptr* before: 2 and after: 6! Why does this pointer point to the address 6 after it is incremented by one and not to 3 as the previous pointer? The answer lies with what we said about the *size of* variables. An int is 4 bytes on my computer. This means that if we have an int at address 2, then that int occupies the memory locations 2, 3, 4 and 5.

In order to access the next int we have to look at the address 6, 7, 8 and 9. Thus when we add one to a pointer, it is not the same as adding one to any integer; it means give me a pointer to the next variable which for variables of type int, in this case, is 4 bytes ahead.

The reason that in the first example with the char pointer, the actual address after incrementing, was one more than the previous address is because the size of char is exactly 1. So the next char can indeed be found on the next address.

Another limitation of void pointers is that we cannot perform arithmetic on them, since the compiler cannot know how many bytes ahead the next variable is located. So void pointers can only be used to keep addresses that we have to convert later on to a specific pointer type, before using them.

5.6.4 Arrays and Pointers

There is a strong connection between arrays and pointers. So strong in fact, that most of the time we can treat them as one and the same. The name of an array can be considered just as a pointer to the beginning of a memory block as big as the array. So for example, making a pointer point to the beginning of an array is done in exactly the same way as assigning the contents of a pointer to another:

```
short *ptr;
short array[10];
ptr = array;
```

And then we can access the contents of the array through the pointer as if the pointer itself was that array. For example this: $ptr[2] = 25$ is perfectly legal. Furthermore, we can treat the array itself as a pointer, for example, $*array = 4$ is equivalent to $array[0] = 4$. In general $*(array + n)$ is equivalent to $array[n]$.

The only difference between an array, and a pointer to the beginning of an array, is that the compiler keeps some extra information for the arrays, to keep track of their storage requirements.

For example if we get the size of both an array and a pointer using the *sizeof* operator, sizeof(ptr) will give us how much space does the pointer itself occupies (4 on my computer), while sizeof array will give us, the amount of space occupied by the whole array (on my computer $20, 10$ elements of 2 bytes each).

5.6.5 Dynamic Memory Allocation

In the earlier sections, we have seen that pointers can hold addresses of other variables. There is another use of pointers: pointers can hold addresses of memory locations that do not have a specific compile-time variable name, but are allocated dynamically while the program runs (sometimes such memory is called *heap*).

To allocate memory during runtime, *C* language provides us the facility interms of *malloc* function. This function allocates the requested amount of memory, and returns a pointer to that memory. To deallocate that block of memory, *C* supports it by providing *free* function.

This function takes the pointer as an argument. For example, in the code below, an array of 5 integers is allocated dynamically, and then deleted.

```
int count = 5;
int *A = malloc(count * sizeof(int));
.........
free(arr);
```

In this example, the $count * sizeof(int)$ calculates the amount of bytes we need to allocate for the array, by multiplying the number of elements, to the size of each element (i.e. the size of one integer).

5.6.6 Function Pointers

Like data, executable code (including functions) is also stored in memory. We can get the address of a function. But the question is what type of pointers do we use for that purpose?

In general, we use function pointers and they store the address of functions. Using function pointers we can call the function indirectly. But, function pointers manipulation has its limitation: it is limited to assignment and indirection and cannot do arithmetic on function pointers. Because for function pointers there is no ordering (functions can be stored anywhere in memory). The following example illustrates how to create and use function pointers.

```
int (*fptr)(int);
fptr = function1;
printf("function1of 0 is: %d\n", fptr(5));
fptr = function2;
printf("function2 of 0 is: %d\n", fptr(10));
```

First we create a pointer that can point to functions accepting an *int* as an argument and returning int, named *fptr*. Then we make *fptr* point to the *function*1, and proceed to call it through the *fptr* pointer, to print the *function*1 of 5. Finally, we change *fptr* to point to *function*2, and call it again in exactly the same manner, to print the *function*2 of 10.

5.7 Techniques of Parameter Passing

Before starting our discussion on parameter passing techniques, let us concentrate on the terminology we use.

5.7.1 Actual and Formal Parameters

Let us assume that a function *B*() is called from another function *A*(). In this case, *A* is called the *caller function* and *B* is called the *called function* or *callee function*. Also, the arguments which *A* sends to *B* are called actual arguments and the parameters of *B* function are called formal arguments.

In the example below, the *func* is called from *main* function. *main* is the caller function and *func* is the called function. Also, the *func* arguments *param*1 and *param*2 are formal arguments and *i*, *j* of *main* function are actual arguments.

```
int main() {
    long i = 1;
    double j = 2;
    func( i, j ); // Call func with actual arguments i and j.
}
// func with formal parameters param1 and param2.
void func( long param1, double param2 ){
}
```

5.7.2 Semantics of Parameter Passing

Logically, parameter passing uses the following semantics:

- IN: Passes info from caller to *callee*. Formal arguments can take values from actual arguments, but cannot send values to actual arguments.
- OUT: Callee writes values in the caller. Formal arguments can send values from actual arguments, but cannot take values from actual arguments.
- IN/OUT: Caller tells callee value of variable, which may be updated by callee. Formal arguments can send values from actual arguments, and can also take values from actual arguments.

5.7.3 Language Support for Parameter Passing Techniques

Passing Technique	Supported by Languages
Pass by value	*C*, *Pascal*, *Ada*, *Scheme*, *Algol*68
Pass by result	*Ada*
Pass by value-result	*Fortran*, sometimes *Ada*
Pass by reference	*C* (achieves through pointers), *Fortran*, *Pascal var params*, *Cobol*
Pass by name	*Algol*60

5.7.4 Pass by Value

This method uses in-mode semantics. A formal parameter is like a new local variable that exists within the scope of the procedure/function/subprogram. Value of actual parameter is used to initialize the formal parameter. Changes made to formal parameter *do not* get transmitted back to the caller.

If pass by value is used then the formal parameters will be allocated on stack like a normal local variable. This method is sometimes called *call by value*. Advantage of this method is that, it allows the actual arguments not to modify.

In general the pass by value technique is implemented by copy and it has the following disadvantages:

- Inefficiency in storage allocation
- Inefficiency in copying value
- Costly copy semantics for objects and arrays

Example: In the following example, main passes func two values: 5 and 7. The function func receives copies of these values and accesses them by the identifiers a and b. The function func changes the value of a. When control passes back to main, the actual values of x and y are not changed.

```
void func (int a, int b) {
    a += b;
    printf("In func, a = %d   b = %d\n", a, b);
}
int main(void) {
    int x = 5, y = 7;
    func(x, y);
    printf("In main, x = %d   y = %d\n", x, y);
    return 0;
}
```

The output of the program is: In func, a = 12 b = 7. In main, x = 5 y = 7

5.7.5 Pass by Result

This method uses out-mode semantics. A formal parameter is a new local variable that exists within the scope of the function. No value is transmitted from actual arguments to formal arguments. Just before control is transferred back to the caller, the value of the formal parameter is transmitted back to the actual parameter.

This method is sometimes called *call by result*. Actual parameter *must* be a variable. $foo(x)$ and $foo(a[1])$ are fine but not $foo(3)$ or $foo(x * y)$.

5.7.6 Parameter collisions can occur

Let us assume that there is a function $write(p1, p1)$. If the two formal parameters in write had different names, which value should go into $p1$? Order in which actual parameters are copied determines their value. In general the pass by result technique is implemented by copy and it has the following disadvantages:

- Inefficiency in storage allocation
- Inefficiency in copying value
- For objects and arrays, the copy semantics are costly
- We cannot use the value of actual argument for initializing the formal argument

Example: Since C does not support this technique, let us assume that the syntax below is not specific to any language.

In the following example, main uses two variables x and y. They both were passed to $func$. Since this is pass by result technique, the values of x and y will not be copied to formal arguments. As a result, the variables *a* and *b* of *func* should be initialized. But in the function only *b* is initialized. For this reason, the value of a is unknown, whereas the value of *b* is 5. After the function execution, the values of a and b will be copied to *x* and *y*.

```
void func (int a, int b) {
    b = 5;
   a += b;
   printf("In func, a = %d    b = %d\n", a, b);
}
int main(void) {
     int x = 5, y = 7;
     func(x, y);
    printf("In main, x = %d    y = %d\n", x, y);
    return 0;
}
```

The output of the program is: In func, a = garbage value b = 5. In main, x = garbage value y = 5.

5.7.7 Pass by Value-Result

This method uses inout-mode semantics. It is a combination of Pass-by-Value and Pass-by-Result. Formal parameter is a new local variable that exists within the scope of the function. Value of actual parameter is used to initialize the formal parameter. Just before control is transferred back to the caller, the value of the formal parameter is transmitted back to the actual parameter. This method is sometimes called *call by value − result*.

Pass by Value − Result shares with *Pass − by − Value* and *Pass − by − Result*. The disadvantage is that it requires multiple storage parameters and time for copying values. Shares with Pass-by-Result the problem associated with the order in which actual parameters are assigned. So this technique has some advantages and some disadvantages.

Example: Since *C* does not support this technique, let us assume that the syntax below is not specific to any language.

In the following example, *main* uses two variable *x* and *y*. They both were passed to *func*. Since this is pass by value-result technique, the values of *x* and *y* will be copied to formal arguments. As a result, the variables *a* and *b* of *func* will get 5 and 7 respectively.

In the *func,* the values a and b are modified to 10 and 5 respectively. After the function execution, the values of *a* and *b* will be copied to *x* and *y*. The disadvantage of this method is that, for each argument a new allocation is created.

```
void func (int a, int b) {
    b = 5;
    a += b;
    printf("In func, a = %d    b = %d\n", a, b);
}
int main(void) {
    int x = 5, y = 7;
    func(x, y);
    printf("In main, x = %d    y = %d\n", x, y);
   return 0;
}
```

The output of the program is: In *func*, $a = 10$ $b = 5$. In *main*, $x = 10$ $y = 5$

5.7.8 Pass by Reference (aliasing)

This technique uses inout-mode semantics. Formal parameter is an alias for the actual parameter. Changes made to formal parameter *do* get transmitted back to the caller through parameter passing. This method is sometimes called *call by reference* or *aliasing*. This method is efficient in both time and space. Disadvantages of *aliasing* are:

- Many potential scenarios can occur
- Programs are not readable

Example: In *C*, the pointer parameters are initialized with pointer values when the function is called. When the function *swapnum*() is called, the actual values of the variables *a* and *b* are exchanged because they are passed by reference.

```
void swapnum(int *i, int *j) {
   int temp = i;
   i = j;
   j = temp;
}
int main(void) {
    int a = 10, b = 20;
    swapnum(&a, &b);
    printf("A is %d and B is %d\n", a, b);
    return 0;
}
```

The output is: A is 20 and B is 10

5.7.9 Pass by Name

Rather than using pass-by-reference for input/output parameters, *Algol* used the more powerful mechanism of *Pass – by – Name*. In essence, you can pass in the symbolic "*name*", of a variable, which allows it both to be accessed and updated. For example, to double the value of *C*[*j*], you can pass its name (not its value) into the following procedure.

```
procedure double(x);
    real x;
begin
    x := x * 2
end;
```

In general, the effect of pass-by-name is to textually substitute the argument expressions in a procedure call for the corresponding parameters in the body of the procedure, e.g., double($C[j]$) is interpreted as $C[j] := C[j] * 2$.

Technically, if any of the variables in the called procedure clash with the caller's variables, they must be renamed uniquely before substitution. Implications of the *Pass – by – Name* mechanism:

1. The argument expression is re-evaluated each time the formal parameter is accessed.
2. The procedure can change the values of variables used in the argument expression and hence change the expression's value.

5.8 Binding

In the earlier sections we have seen that every variable is associated with a memory location. At the top level, *binding* is the process of associating the *name* and the thing it contains. For example, association of variable names to values they contain.

Binding Times: Based on the time at which association happens, binding times can be one of the following:

Static

- *Language design time*: Binding operators to operations (for example, " + " to addition of numbers).
- *Language implementation time*: Binding data types to possible values (for example, "*int*" to its range of values).
- *Program writing time*: Associating algorithms and data structures to problem.
- *Compile time*: Binding a variable to data type.
- *Link time*: Layout of whole program in memory (names of separate modules (libraries) are finalized.
- *Load time*: Choice of physical addresses (e.g. static variables in *C* are bound to memory cells at load time).
- *Run time*: Binding variables to values in memory locations.

Dynamic

Basically there are *two* types of bindings: *static* binding and *dynamic* binding.

5.8.1 Static Binding (Early binding)

Static binding occurs before runtime and doesn't change during execution. This is sometimes called *early binding*.

Examples:
- Bindings of values to constants in *C*
- Bindings of function calls to function definitions in *C*

5.8.2 Dynamic Binding (Late binding)

Dynamic binding occurs or changes at runtime. This is sometimes called late binding.

Examples:
- Bindings of pointer variables to locations
- Bindings of member function calls to virtual member function definitions in *C++*

5.9 Scope

A scope is a program section of maximal size in which no bindings change, or at least in which no redeclarations are permitted. The scope rules of a language determine how references to names are associated with variables. Basically there are *two* types of scoping techniques: *static* scoping and *dynamic* scoping.

5.9.1 Static Scope

Static scope is defined in terms of the physical structure of the program. The determination of scopes can be made by the compiler. That means, bindings are resolved by examining the program text. Enclosing static scopes (to a specific scope) are called its *static ancestors* and the nearest static ancestor is called a *static parent*.

Variables can be hidden from a unit by having a "*closer*" variable with the same name. Ada and *C++* allow access to these (e.g. class_name:: name). Most compiled languages, *C* and *Pascal* included, use static scope rules.

Example-1: Static scope rules: Most closest nested rule used in blocks

```
for (...){
    int i;
    {...
        {
```

```
            i = 5;
            }
        }
        ...
    }
```

To resolve a reference, we examine the local scope and statically enclosing scopes until a binding is found.

Example-2: Static scope in nested function calls. In the code below, with static scoping, the *count* variable of *func2* takes the value of global variable value (10).

```
int count=10;
void func2() {
    printf("In func2=%d", count);
}
void func1(in) {
    int count = 20;
    func2();
}
int main(void) {
  funct1();
   return 0;
}
```

5.9.2 Dynamic Scope

Dynamic scope rules are usually encountered in interpreted languages. Such languages do not normally have type checking at compile time because type determination isn't always possible when dynamic scope rules are in effect.

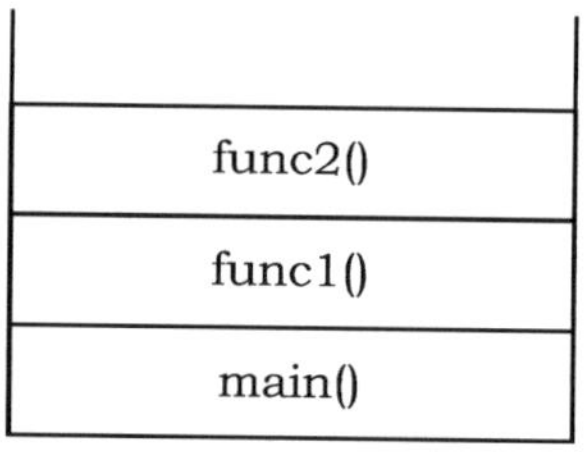

In dynamic scoping, binding depends on the flow of control at run time and the order in which functions are called, refers to the closest active binding. If we look at the second example of static scoping, the *count* variable of *func2* takes the value of *func1* variable value (20). This is because, during runtime the *func2* is called from *func1* which in turn called from main. That means *func2* looks at the stack and starts searching in the back ward direction.

Let us take another example. In the code below, the *count* variable of *func3* takes the *count* value of *funct1*().

```
int count=10;
void func3() {
    printf("In func3=%d", count);
}
void func2() {
    func3();
}
void func1(in) {
    int count = 30;
    func2();
```

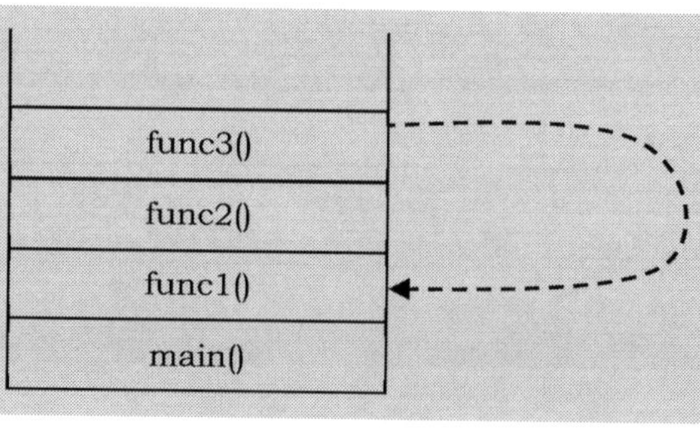

```
}
int main(void) {
    funct1();          func3 searches the stack in reverse direction
    return 0;          and find the count in funct1().
}
```

Note: For the above example, if we use *static* scope then the *count* variable of *func3* takes the value of global *count* variable (10).

5.10 Storage Classes

Let us now consider the storage classes in *C*. The storage class determines the part of memory where storage is allocated for the variable or object and how long the storage allocation continues to exist. It also determines the scope which specifies the part of the program over which a variable name is visible, i.e. the variable is accessible by name. There are four storage classes in *C* are automatic, register, external, and static.

5.10.1 Auto Storage Class

This is the default storage class in *C*. Auto variables are declared inside a function in which they are to be utilized. Also, keyword *auto* (e.g. auto int number;) is used for declaring the auto variables. These are created when the function is called and destroyed automatically when the function is exited. This variable is therefore private(local) to the function in which it is declared. Variables declared inside a function without storage class specification is, by default, an automatic variable.

Any variable local to main will normally live throughout the whole program, although it is active only in main. During recursion, the nested variables are unique auto variables. Automatic variables can also be defined within blocks. In that case they are meaningful only inside the blocks where they are declared. If automatic variables are not initialized they will contain garbage.

Example:

```
int main() {
    int m=1000;
    function2();
    printf("%d\n",m);
}                                          Output:
                                                10
void function1() {                              100
    int m = 10;                                 1000
    printf("%d\n",m);
}
void function2() {
    int m = 100;
    function1();
    printf("%d\n",m);
}
```

5.10.2 Extern storage class

These variables are declared outside any function. These variables are active and alive throughout the entire program. Also known as global variables and default value is zero. Unlike local variables they are accessed by any function in the program. In case local variable and global variable have the same name, the local variable will have precedence over the global one.

Sometimes the keyword *extern* is used to declare this variable. It is visible only from the point of declaration to the end of the program.

Example-1: The variable *number* and *length* are available for use in all three functions

```
int number;
float length=7.5;
main() {
    . . .
}
funtion1() {
    . . .
}
funtion1() {
    . . .
}
```

Example-2: When the function references the variable *count*, it will be referencing only its local variable, not the global one.

```
int count;
main() {
    count=10;
    .....
}
funtion() {
    int count=0;
    .....
    count=count+1;
}
```

Example-3: On global variables: Once a variable has been declared global any function can use it and change its value. The subsequent functions can then reference only that new value.

```
int x;
int main() {
    x=10;
    printf("x=%d\n",x);
    printf("x=%d\n",fun1());
    printf("x=%d\n",fun2());
    printf("x=%d\n",fun3());
}
int fun1() {
    x=x+10;
    return(x);
}
int fun2() {
    int x;
    x=1;
    return(x);
}
int fun3() {
    x=x+10;
    return(x);
}
```

```
Output:
    x=10
    x=20
    x=1
    x=30
```

Example-4: External declaration: As far as main is concerned, *y* is not defined. So compiler will issue an error message. There are two ways to solve this issue:

1 Define *y* before main.
2 Declare *y* with the storage class extern in main before using it.

```
int main() {
    y=5;
    . . .
}
int y;
func1() {
    y=y+1;
}
```

Example-5: External declaration: Note that extern declaration does not allocate storage space for variables

```
int main() {
    extern int y;
    . . .
}
func1() {
    extern int y;
    . . .
}
int y;
```

Example-6: If we declare any variable as extern variable then it searches that variable either it has been initialized or not. If it has been initialized which may be either extern or static* then it is ok otherwise compiler will show an error. For example:

```
int main() {
    extern int i;  //It will search the initialization of variable i.
    printf("%d",i);
    return 0;
}
int i=2;           //Initialization of variable i.
Output: 2
```

Example-7: It will search any initialized variable *i* which may be static or extern.

```
int main() {
    extern int i;
    printf("%d",i);
    return 0;
}
extern int i=2;      //Initialization of extern variable i.
Output: 2
```

Example-8: It will search any initialized variable *i* which may be static or extern.

```
int main() {
  extern int i;
  printf("%d",i);
  return 0;
}
static int i=2;      //Initialization of static variable i.
Output: 2
```

Example-9: Variable *i* has been declared but not initialized.

```
int main() {
    extern int i;
    printf("%d",i);
    return 0;
}
Output: Compilation error: Unknown symbol i.
```

Example-10: A particular extern variable can be declared many times but we can initialize at only one time. For example:

```
extern int i;      //Declaring the variable i.
int i=5;           //Initializing the variable.
extern int i;      //Again declaring the variable i.
int main() {
 extern int i; //Again declaring the variable i.
    printf("%d",i);
    return 0;
}
Output: 5
```

Example-11:

```
extern int i;      //Declaring the variable
int i=5;       //Initializing the variable
int main() {
   printf("%d",i);
   return 0;
}
int i=2; //Initializing the variable
Output: Compilation error: Multiple initialization variable i.
```

Example-12: We cannot write any assignment statement globally.

```
extern int i;
int i=10;          //Initialization statement
i=5;               //Assignment statement
int main() {
   printf("%d",i);
   return 0;
}
Output: Compilation error
```

Note: Assigning any value to the variable at the time of declaration is known as *initialization* while assigning any value to variable not at the time of declaration is known as *assignment*.

Example-13:

```
extern int i;
int main() {
    i=5;      //Assignment statement
    printf("%d",i);
    return 0;
}
int i=10;  //Initialization statement
Output: 5
```

5.10.3 Register Storage Class

These variables are stored in one of the machine's registers and are declared using *register* keyword. e.g. register int count;

Since register access is much faster than a memory access, keeping frequently accessed variables in the register leads to faster execution of program. Since only few variables can be placed in the register, it is important to carefully select the variables for this purpose. However, *C* will automatically convert register variables into non-register variables once the limit is reached. Don't try to declare a global variable as register because the register will be occupied during the lifetime of the program.

5.10.4 Static Storage Class

The value of static variables persists until the end of the program. It is declared using the keyword static like:

```
static int x;
static float y;
```

It may be of external or internal type depending on the place of their declaration. Static variables are initialized only once, when the program is compiled.

5.10.4.1 Internal Static Variables

Are those which are declared inside a function? Scope of Internal static variables extends up to the end of the program in which they are defined. Internal static variables are almost same as auto variable except they remain in existence (alive) throughout the remainder of the program. Internal static variables can be used to retain values between function calls. *Example*: Internal static variable can be used to count the number of calls made to function.

```
int main() {
    for(int i=1; i<=3; i++)
        stat();
}                                    Output:
                                         x = 1
void stat() {                            x = 2
    static int x=0;                      x = 3
    x = x+1;
    printf("x= %d\n",x);
}
```

5.10.4.2 External Static Variables

An external static variable is declared outside of all functions and is available to all the functions in the program. An external static variable is similar to simple external variable except that the former is available only within the file where it is defined whereas simple external variable can be accessed by other files.

5.10.4.3 Static Function

Static declaration can also be used to control the scope of a function. If you want a particular function to be accessible only to the functions in the file in which it is defined and not to any function in other files, declare the function to be static.

```
static int power(int x, int y) {
    . . .
}
```

5.11 Storage Organization

When we write a program and execute it, lot of things happen. Now, let us try to understand what happens internally. Any program we run has some memory associated with it. That memory is divided into 3 parts as shown below. Storage organization is the process of binding values to memory locations.

Static Segment: As shown above, the static storage is divided into two parts:

- *Code segment*: In this part, the programs code is stored. This will not change throughout the execution of the program. In general, this part is made read-only and protected. Constants may also be placed in the static area depending on their type.
- *Data segment*: In simple terms, this part holds the global data. In this part, the program's static data (except code) is stored. In general, this part is editable

(like global variables and static variables come under this category). These includes the following:

- o Global variables
- o Numeric and string-valued constant literals
- o Local variables that retain value between calls (e.g., static variables)

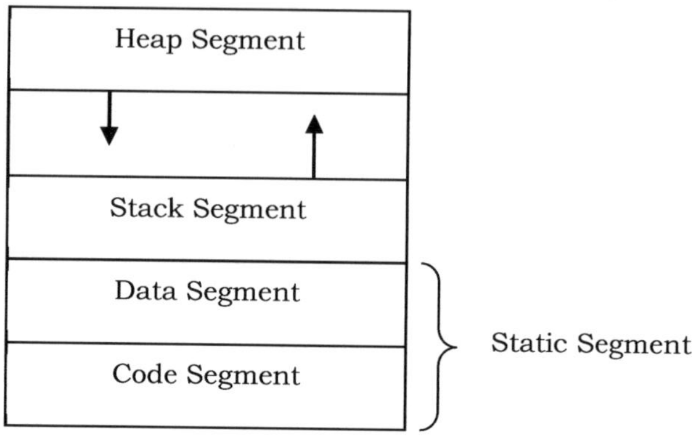

Stack Segment: If a language supports recursion, then the number of instances of a variable that may exist at any time is unlimited (at least theoretically). In this case, static allocation is not useful.

As an example, let us assume that a function *B*() is called from another function *A*(). In the code below, the *A*() has a local variable *count*. After executing *B*(), if *A*() tries to get *count,* then it should be able to get its old value. That means, it needs a mechanism for storing the current state of the function, so that once it comes back from calling function it restores that context and uses its variables.

```
A() {
    int count=10;
    function();
    count=20;
    . . .. . .
}
B() {
    int b=0;
    . . .. . .
}
```

To solve these kinds of issues, stack allocation is used. When we call a *function*, push a new activation record (also called a frame) onto the run-time stack, which is particular to the *function*.

Each frame can occupy many consecutive bytes in the stack and may not be of a fixed size. When the *callee* function returns to the *caller*, the activation record of the callee is popped out. In general the activation record stores the following information:

- Local variables
- Formal parameters
- Any additional information needed for activation
- Temporary variables
- Return address

Heap Segment: If we want to dynamically increase the temporary space (say, through pointers in *C*), then the *static* and *stack* allocation methods are not enough. We need a separate allocation method for dealing with these kinds of requests. *Heap allocation* strategy addresses this issue.

Heap allocation method is required for dynamically allocated pieces of linked data structures and for dynamically resized objects. Heap is an area of memory which is dynamically allocated. Like a stack, it may grow and shrinks during runtime.

But unlike a stack it is not a *LIFO* (Last In First Out) which is more complicated to manage. In general, all programming languages implementation we will have both heap-allocated and stack allocated memory.

5.11.1 How do we allocate Memory for both?

One simple approach is to divide the available memory at the start of the program into two areas: stack and heap.

5.11.1.1 Heap Allocation Methods

Heap allocation is performed by searching the heap for available free space. Basically there are two types of heap allocations.

- *Implicit heap allocation*: Allocations are done automatically. For example, *Java/C#* class instances are placed on the heap. Scripting languages and functional languages make extensive use of the heap for storing objects.
- *Explicit heap allocation*: In this method, we need to explicitly tell the system to allocate the memory from heap. Examples include:
  - statements and/or functions for allocation and deallocation
  - malloc/free, new/delete

5.11.1.2 Fragmentations

Sometimes the small free blocks will get wasted without allocating to any process and we call this *fragmentation*. Basically there are two types of fragmentations:

- *Internal heap fragmentation*: If the block allocated is larger than required to hold a given object and the extra space is unused.
- *External heap fragmentation*: If the unused space is composed of multiple blocks. No one piece may be large enough to satisfy some future request. That means, multiple unused blocks, but not one is large enough to be used.

5.11.1.3 Heap Allocation Algorithms

In general, a linked list of free heap blocks is maintained and when a request is made for memory, then it uses one of the techniques below and allocates the memory.

- *First − fit*: select the first block in the list that is large enough to satisfy the given request
- *Best − fit*: search the entire list for the smallest free block that is large enough to hold the object

If an object is smaller than the block, the extra space can be added to the list of free blocks. When a block is freed, adjacent free blocks are merged.

5.12 Programming Techniques

5.12.1 Unstructured Programming

Generally, people start programming by writing small programs consisting only of one *main* program. This programming technique runs into problems once the program becomes large. For example, if the same statement sequence is needed at different locations within the program, the sequence must be copied.

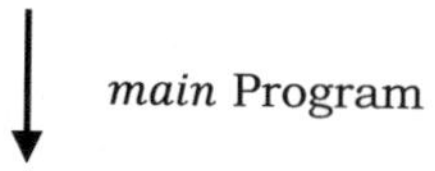

5.12.2 Procedural Programming

n this method, we combine sequences of statements into one single place. A procedure call is used to invoke the procedure. After the sequence is processed, flow of control proceeds right after the position where the call was made. By introducing parameters as well as procedures of procedures (subprocedures) programs can now be written that are more structured and error free.

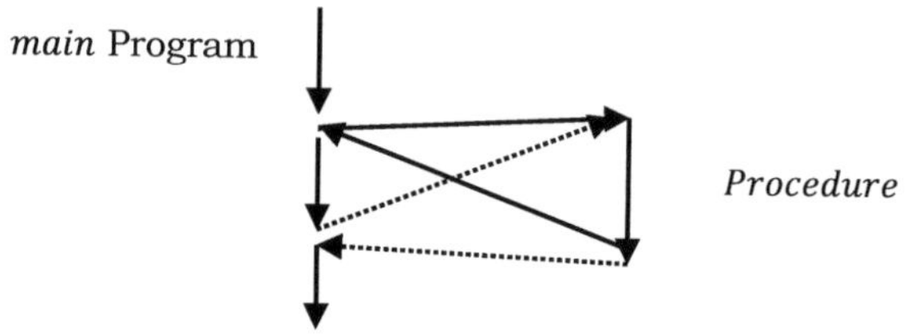

5.12.3 Modular Programming

With modular programming, procedures of a common functionality are grouped together into separate modules. It is now divided into several smaller parts which interact through procedure calls and which form the whole program. Each module can have its own data.

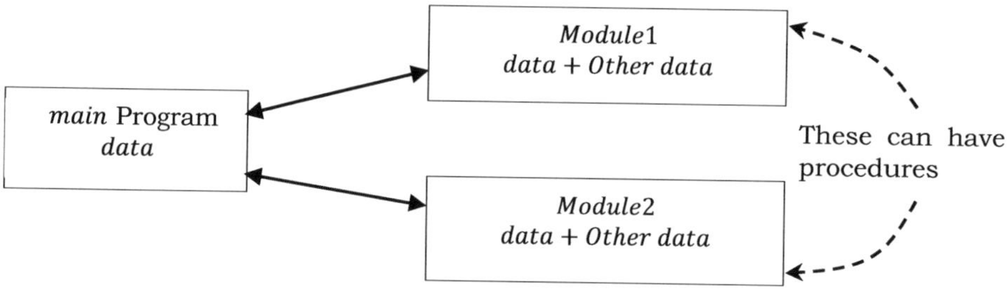

5.12.4 Object-oriented Programming

It is programming language model organized around *objects* instead of functions and *data* rather than logic. Object-oriented programming views the problem as objects we want to manipulate instead of logic required to manipulate them. The first step in OOP is to identify all the objects we want to manipulate and how they relate to each other (called *data modeling*). Once we have identified an object, we generalize it as a class of objects and define the kind of data it contains and any functions (also called *methods*) that can manipulate it.

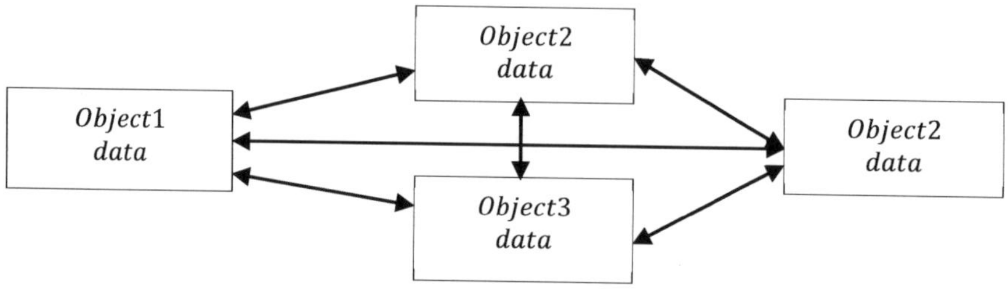

The idea behind object-oriented programming is that a computer program may be seen as a collection of objects that act on each other. In traditional view, a program can be seen as a collection of functions or simply as a list of instruction to the computer. Each object is capable of receiving messages, processing data and sending messages to other objects. Each object can be viewed as an independent little machine or actor with a distinct role or responsibility.

In order to act as an object-oriented programming language, a language must support three object-oriented features:

1. Polymorphism
2. Inheritance
3. Encapsulation

5.13 Basic Concepts of OOPS

The following are the basic of object-oriented programming languages.

1. Class and object
2. Encapsulation
3. Abstraction
4. Data hiding
5. Polymorphism
6. Inheritance
7. Dynamic binding
8. Message passing

5.13.1 Class and Object

Object is the basic unit of object-oriented programming. Objects are identified by its unique name. An object represents a particular instance of a class. There can be more than one instance of an object. Each instance of an object can hold its own relevant data.

An Object is a collection of data members and associated member functions (also called *methods*). For example whenever a class name is created according to the class an object should be created without creating object can't able to use class.

A class is a basic unit of encapsulation. It is a collection of function code and data, which forms the basis of object-oriented programming. A class is an abstract data type (ADT), i.e., the class definition only provides the logical abstraction. The data and function defined within the class, spring to life only when a variable of type class is created.

The variable of type class is called an object which has a physical existence and also known as instance of class. From one class, several objects can be created. Each object has similar set of data defined in the class and it can use functions defined in the class for the manipulation of data. For example, the class of *Cat* defines all possible cats by listing the characteristics and behaviors they can have; the object *Abyssinian* is one particular cat, with particular versions of the characteristics. A *Cat* has hair; *Abyssinian* has *ruddy* hair.

All objects are instances of a class. Depending upon the type of class, an object may represent anything such as a person, mobile, chair, student, employee, book, lecturer, speaker, car, vehicle or anything which we see in our daily life. The state of an object is determined by the data values they are having at a particular instance.

Objects occupy space in memory, and all objects share same set of data items which are defined when class is created. Two objects may communicate with each other through functions by passing messages.

Examples:

- Animal can be stated as a class and lion, tiger, elephant, wolf, cow , etc., are its objects.
- Bird can be stated as class and sparrow, eagle, hawk, pigeon, etc., are its objects.

- Musician can be stated as a class and Himesh Reshmia, Anu Malik, Jatin-Lalit are its objects.

5.13.2 Encapsulation

Encapsulation is the mechanism that binds together function and data in one compact form, called *class*.

The data and function may be private or public. Private data/function can be accessed only within the class. Public data/code can be accessed outside the class. The use of encapsulation hides complexity from the implementation. Linking of function code and data together gives rise to objects which are variables of type class.

5.13.3 Abstraction

Abstraction is a mechanism to represent only essential features which are of significance and hides the unimportant details. To make a good abstraction we require a sound knowledge of the problem domain, which we are going to implement using OOP principle. As an example of the abstraction consider a class *Vehicle* .

When we create the *Vehicle* class, we can decide what function code and data to put in the class such as vehicle name, number of wheels, fuel type, vehicle type, etc., and functions such as changing the gear, accelerating/decelerating the vehicle. At this time we are not interested in vehicle works such as how acceleration, changing gear takes place. We are also not interested in making other parts of the vehicle to be part of the class such as model number, vehicle color, etc.

5.13.4 Data Hiding

Data hiding hides the data from external access by the user. In OOP language, we have special keywords such as public, private, protected, etc., which hides the data. There are *three* types of access specifier. They are

- Within a class members can be declared as either *public protected* or *private* in order to explicitly enforce encapsulation.
- The elements placed after the *public* keyword is accessible to all the user of the class.
- The elements placed after the *protected* keyword is accessible only to the methods of the class.
- The elements placed after the *private* keyword are accessible only to the methods of the class.
- The data is hidden inside the class by declaring it as *private* inside the class. Thus private data cannot be directly accessed by the object.

5.13.5 Polymorphism

If we divide the word polymorphism we get *'poly'*, which means many and *'morphism'*, which means form. Thus, polymorphism means more than one form.

Polymorphism provides a way for an entity to behave in several forms. In simple terms an excellent example of polymorphism is *Lord Krishna* in *Hindu* mythology. From programmers' point of view polymorphism means one interface, many methods.'

It is an attribute that allows one interface to control access to a general class of actions. For example, we want to find out addition of three numbers; no matter what type of input we pass, i.e., integer, float, etc. Because of polymorphism we can define three versions of the same function with the name *addition*3. Each version of this function takes three parameters of the same time, i.e., one version of *addition*3takes three arguments of type integer, another takes three arguments of type double and so on. The compiler automatically selects the right version of the function depending upon the type of data passed to the function *addition3*. This is also called as *function polymorphism* or *function overloading*.

The two types of polymorphism are the following:

- Compile time polymorphism
- Run time polymorphism

5.13.6 Inheritance

Inheritance is the mechanism of deriving a new class from the earlier existing class. The inheritance provides the basic idea of reusability in object-oriented programming. The new class inherits the features of the old class. The old class and new class is called (given as pair) base-derived, parent-child, super-sub.

The inheritance supports the idea of classification. In classification we can form hierarchies of different classes each of which having some special characteristics besides some common properties. Through classification, a class needs only definition of those qualities that make it unique within its class.

Examples:

1. In the example given below, we have a vehicle class at the top in hierarchy. All the common features of a vehicle can be put in this class. From this, we can derive a new class, i.e., two wheeler, which contains features specific to two-wheeler vehicles only.
2. As another example we can take an engineering college as the top class and its various departments such as computer, electronics, electrical , etc., as the sub classes. The university to which the engineering college is affiliated may be its parent class.

5.13.7 Types of Inheritances

There are five different types inheritances.

1. Single Inheritance
2. Hierarchical Inheritance
3. Multi-Level Inheritance
4. Hybrid Inheritance
5. Multiple Inheritance

5.13.7.1 Single Inheritance

Single inheritance is the simplest form of inheritance. When a class extends another one class only then we call it a single inheritance. The below flow diagram shows that class B extends only one class which is A. Here A is a parent class of B and B would be a child class of A.

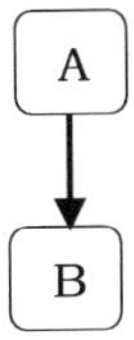

When a single derived class is created from a single base class then the inheritance is called as single inheritance.

5.13.7.2 Hierarchical Inheritance

When more than one derived class are created from a single base class, then that inheritance is called as hierarchical inheritance. In such kind of inheritance one class is inherited by many sub classes. In the example, class B, C and D inherits the same class A. A is parent class (or base class) of B, C, and D.

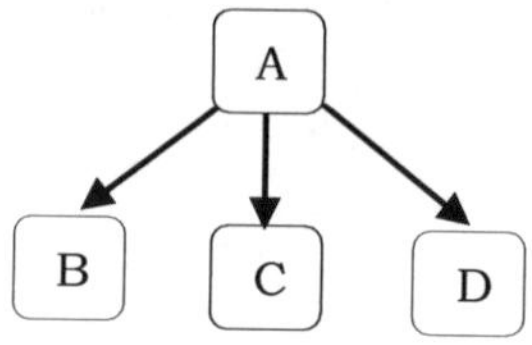

5.13.7.3 Multi-Level Inheritance

When a derived class is created from another derived class, then that inheritance is called as multi level inheritance.

Multilevel inheritance refers to a mechanism in object oriented technology where one can inherit from a derived class, thereby making this derived class the base class for the new class. As you can see in figure C is subclass or child class of B and B is a child class of A.

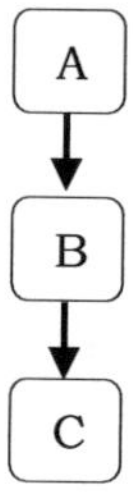

5.13.7.4 Hybrid Inheritance

Any combination of single, hierarchical and multi level inheritances is called as hybrid inheritance. In simple terms we can say that Hybrid inheritance is a combination of Single and Multiple inheritance. A hybrid inheritance can be achieved in the Java using interfaces.

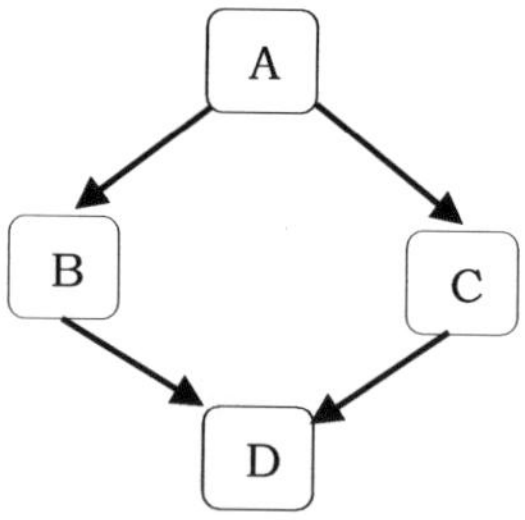

5.13.7.5 Multiple Inheritance

When a derived class is created from more than one base class then that inheritance is called as multiple inheritance. But multiple inheritance is not supported by Java using classes and can be done using interfaces.

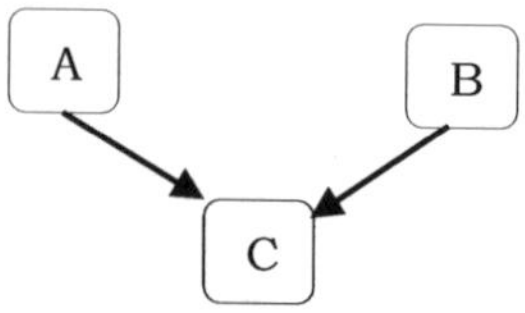

Handling the complexity that causes due to multiple inheritance is very complex. Hence it was not supported in Java with class and it can be done with interfaces.

Note: Refer *Problems* section for more details.

5.13.8 Dynamic Binding

Binding means *linking*. It involves linking of function definition to a function call.

1. If linking of function call to function definition, i.e., a place where control has to be transferred is done at compile time, it is known as *static* binding.
2. When linking is delayed till run time or done during the execution of the program then this type of linking is known as *dynamic* binding. Which function will be called in response to a function call is find out when program executes.

5.13.9 Message Passing

In C++ and Java, objects communicate each other by passing messages to each other. A message contains the name of the member function and arguments to pass. The message passing is shown below:

```
object. method (parameters);
```

Message passing here means object calling the method and passing parameters. Message passing is nothing but calling the method of the class and sending parameters. The method in turn executes in response to a message.

Problems and Questions with Answers

Question 1: What is the output of following code snippet?

```
#include<stdio.h>
int main(){
    printf("%d\t",sizeof(9.75));
    printf("%d\t",sizeof(60000));
    printf("%d",sizeof('D'));
    return 0;
}
```

Answer: 8 4 4 [assuming Linux GCC Compiler]. As you know size of data types is compiler dependent in c. On other compilers:

Compiler	Expected Output		
Turbo C++ 3.0	8	4	2
Turbo C ++4.5	8	4	2
Linux GCC	8	4	4
Visual C++	8	4	4

Question 2: What is the output of following code snippet?

```
#include<stdio.h>
int main(){
    double number=7.2;
    int variable =7;
    printf("%d\t",sizeof(!number));
    printf("%d\t",sizeof(variable=25/2));
    printf("%d", variable);
    return 0;
}
```

Answer: 4 4 7 [assuming Linux GCC Compiler]. *sizeof(Expr)* operator always returns the an integer value which represents the size of the final value of the expression expr. Consider on the following expression:

```
!number = !7.2 = 0
```

0 is int type integer constant and it size is 4 by in Linux GCC compiler. Consider on the following expression:

```
variable = 25/2 => var = 12 => 12 and 12 is int type integer constant.
```

Any expression which is evaluated inside the *sizeof* operator its *scope* always will be within the sizeof operator. So value of variable var will remain 7 in the *printf* statement.

Question 3: What is name mangling?

Answer: *C* compiler links a function or symbol by *prepending* with under score. For example, *main*() function links to symbol name *_main*() and a variable *counter* (int *counter*;) will link to *_count*. For *C++* compiler this will not work. *C++* has function overloading mechanism. If *C++* uses only under score before function name to link its symbol the purpose of overloading will not be resolved. For example, we have a function *test*() and overloaded as:

```
int test(int a, int b)
int test(int a, int b, int c)
```

Now if *C++* uses *_test*() as symbol name then the two function body can never be linked. To solve this, *C++* linker uses *me mangling*. Name mangling is the mechanism of *C++* compiler to link functions and variables of same names to resolve them to some unique symbol names by altering the names with some extra information line index, argument size etc.. Function name mangling is done as

```
<function index><function name>@<argument size>
```

and variable name mangling is done as

```
?<variable name>@@<UNIQUE ID>.
```

For the above example,

```
int test(int a, int b) links to _1test@8
int test(int a, int b, int c) links to _2test@12
```

Question 4: Explain preprocessor directives and macros in C/C++.

Answer: When we write a C program, first we compile the program and then run the program. The compiler is a program that converts the source code into machine code. We can imagine the compiler as having two parts: the preprocessor and the rest of the compiler. To understand the preprocessor, let us take an example. Generally, we write an include statement in the beginning of a C program as:

```
#include<stdio.h>
```

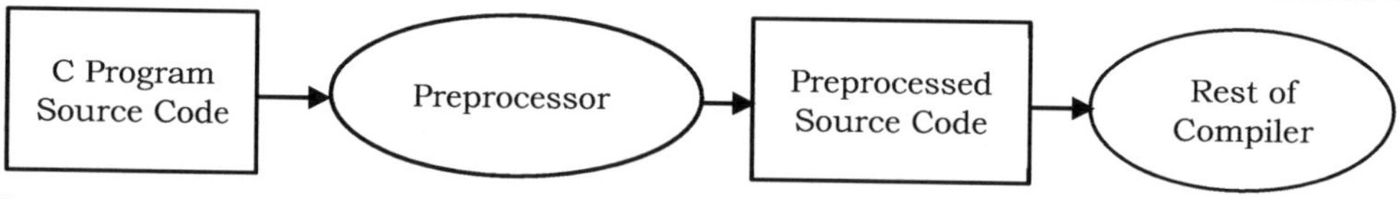

The preprocessor sees this statement and includes all function prototypes available in stdio.h file into the actual C program source code. The resultant source code is called 'preprocessed source code' which is given as input to the rest of the compiler. In the next step, the compiler converts this source code into machine code. This machine code is run during the time of running the program.

The preprocessor is a program inside the C compiler that does some activities like including the header files or macros before the actual compilation takes place.

The preprocessor provides the following facilities:

- Inclusion of header file code into our C program. For example, we write

  ```
  #include<stdio.h>
  ```

  In this case, all the function prototypes which are available in the header file <stdio.h> will be physically copied into the C program by the preprocessor.
- *Macro expansion*: We can define macros which represent some fixed set of statements. Whenever the macro is used in the program, it is replaced by the

corresponding set of statements by the preprocessor. For example, we can write a macro, as:

```
#define MAX 100
```

Where ever we use MAX in the rest of the program, its value 100 is substituted in the place of MAX. This type of macro is called 'constant' since the value of PI is fixed.

- *Conditional compilation*: Using special preprocessing directives, we can include or exclude parts of the program according to various conditions. For example, we can write a statement which looks like if...else:

```
#ifdef AIX
    Code suitable for AIX
#else
   Code suitable for LINUX
#endif
    Code common to both the types
```

This is called conditional compilation because depending upon the type of the computer, certain code will be included. For example, before main() function, if we write

```
#define AIX
```

Then, the code suitable for AIX will be included into the program. If the #define statement is not included, then the code related to Linux will be included.

The preprocessor is also called 'macro processor' since it allows us to define macros and helps to resolve them. Let us understand that the preprocessor statements will start with a hash symbol (#). These preprocessor statements are also called 'directives' as they are instructions (directions) to the preprocessor.

Question 5: What is the output of following code snippet?

```
#include<stdio.h>
void main(){
  printf("%s",__DATE__);
}
```

Answer: Feb 17 2014.

In C/C++, the following predefined macro names shall be defined by the implementation:

__LINE__	The line number of the current source line (a decimal constant).
__FILE__	The presumed name of the source file (a character string literal).
__DATE__	The date of translation of the source file.
__TIME__	The time of translation of the source file.

Question 6: What is the output of following code snippet?

```
#include <stdio.h>
int main(){
    int a=43;
    printf("%d\n",printf("%d",printf("%d",a)));
    return 0;
}
```

Answer: 4321.

The *printf*() function will return the number of characters printed. For example, the code below prints 10005 (4 characters in 1000 plus *n* character).

```
int a=1000;
```

```
printf("%d",printf("\n%d",a));
```

Question 7: What is the output of following code snippet?

```
#include<stdio.h>
#define ABC   30
#define XYZ   10
#define XXX   ABC - XYZ
void main(){
    int    a;
    a = XXX * 10;
    printf("%d ", a);
}
```

Answer: -70. Expression XXX * 10 would be converted to ABC – XYZ * 10 = 30 – 10 * 10 = -70.

Question 8: What is the output of following code snippet?

```
#include<stdio.h>
#define  calculator(A, B)     (A * B) / (A - B)
void main(){
   int A = 20, B = 10;
   printf("%d ", calculator(A + 4, B -2));
}
```

Answer: 4. calculator(A + 4, B -2)) would be converted to (A + 4 * B - 2) / (A + 4 - B -2) = (20 + 4 * 10 - 2) / (20 + 4 - 10 -2) = 58 /12 = 4.

Question 9: What is the output of following code snippet?

```
#include<stdio.h>
#define  calculator(A, B)     (A * B) / (A - B)
int main(){
   int k = 5;
   if (++k < 5 && k++/5 || ++k <= 8);
   printf("%d ", k);
   return 0;
}
```

Answer: 7. The first condition ++k < 5 is checked and it is false (Now k = 6). So, it checks the third condition (or condition ++k <= 8) and (now k = 7) it is true. At this point k value is incremented by twice, hence the value of k becomes 7.

Question 10: What is the output of following code snippet?

```
#include<stdio.h>
void func(int, int);
main(){
   int    a = 5;
   printf("Main:  %d  %d ", a++, ++a);
   func(a, a++);
}
void func(int a, int b){
   printf("\nFunc: a = %d  b = %d ", a, b);
}
```

Answer: Main : 6 7 Func : a = 8 b = 7 [based on Linux GCC]

The solution depends on the implementation of stack. In some machines the arguments are passed from left to right to the stack. In this case the result will be

```
Main:  5  7    Func: a = 7  b = 7
```

Other machines the arguments may be passed from right to left to the stack. In that case the result will be

```
Main: 6 7   Func: a = 8  b = 7
```

Question 11: What is the output of following code snippet?

```
#include<stdio.h>
int main(){
    int *temp, *ptr, i;
    ptr = temp = (int *) malloc( 4 * sizeof(int));
    for (i=0; i<4; i++)
        *(temp+i) = i * 10;
    printf("%d\n", *ptr++);
    printf("%d\n", (*ptr)++);
    printf("%d\n", *ptr);
    printf("%d\n", *++ptr);
    printf("%d\n", ++*ptr);
    return 0;
}
```

Answer: 0   10   11   20   21

Based on operator precedence the expressions would be converted as shown below.

```
*ptr++   → *(ptr++)
*++ptr   → *(++ptr)
++*ptr   → ++(*ptr)
```

Question 12: What is the output of following code snippet?

```
#include<stdio.h>
void func(int);
static int value = 5;
int main(){
    while (value --) func(value);
    printf("%d\n", value);
    return 0;
}
void func(int val){
    static int value = 0;
    for (; value < 5; value ++)
        printf("%d\n", value);
}
```

Answer: 0   1   2   3   4   -1

Question 13: What is the output of following code snippet?

```
int main(){
  typedef struct {
        int   a;
        int   b;
        int   c;
        char  ch;
        int   d;
  }xyz;
  typedef union {
        xyz X;
        char y[100];
  }abc;
  printf("sizeof xyz = %d sizeof abc = %d\n",sizeof(xyz), sizeof(abc));
  return 0;
```

```
}
```

Answer: Size of xyz = 20 Size of abc = 100

This is the problem about Unions. Unions are similar to structures but it differs in some ways. Unions can be assigned only with one field at any time. In this case, unions x and y can be assigned with any of the one field a or b or c at one time. During initialisation of unions it takes the value (whatever assigned) only for the first field. So, The statement $y = \{100\}$ intialises the union y with field $a = 100$.

In this example, all fields of union x are assigned with some values. But at any time only one of the union field can be assigned. So, for the union x the field c is assigned as 21.50. Thus, The output will be

```
Union 2 : 22 22 21.50
Union Y : 100 22 22 ( 22 refers unpredictable results )
```

Question 14: What are the similarities and differences between $C++$ and $Java$?

Answer: There are many similarities and differences between $C++$ and $Java$.

- *Java* does not support *typedefs*, *defines*, or a *preprocessor*. *Java* supports *classes*, but does not support *structures* or *unions*.
- All $C++$ programs require a function named *main*.
- All classes in *Java* inherit from the *Object* class.
- All function or method definitions in *Java* are contained within the class definition.
- Both $C++$ and *Java* support *class* (*static*) methods or functions that can be called without the requirement to instantiate an object of the class.
- The *interface* keyword in *Java* is used to create the equivalence of an abstract base class containing only method declarations and constants. No variable data members or method definitions are allowed. (True abstract base classes can also be created in *Java*). The *interface* concept is not supported by $C++$.
- *Java* does not support *multiple inheritance*. To some extent, the *interface* feature provides the desirable features of multiple inheritance to a *Java* program without some of the underlying problems.
- *Java* does not support *automatic type conversions*.
- Unlike $C++$, *Java* has a *String* type, and objects of this type are immutable (cannot be modified). Quoted strings are automatically converted into *String* objects. *Java* also has a *StringBuffer* type. Objects of this type can be modified.
- Unlike $C++$, *Java* provides arrays as objects with *length* member, which tells how big the array is. An exception is thrown if you attempt to access an array out of bounds.
- *Java* does not support *pointers* (at least it does not allow you to modify the address contained in a pointer or to perform pointer arithmetic). Much of the need for pointers was eliminated by providing types for arrays and strings. For example, the oft-used $C++$ declaration $char * ptr$ needed to point to the first character in a $C++$ null-terminated "string" is not required in *Java*, because a string is a true object in *Java*.
- The scope resolution operator (::) required in $C++$ is not used in *Java*. The dot is used to construct all fully-qualified references. Also, since there are no pointers, the pointer operator (→) used in $C++$ is not required in *Java*.
- In $C++$, *static* data members and functions are called using the name of the class and the name of the static member connected by the scope resolution operator. In *Java*, the dot is used for this purpose.
- Like $C++$, *Java* has primitive types such as *int, float*, etc. Unlike $C++$, the size of each primitive type is the same regardless of the platform. There is no unsigned integer type in *Java*. Type checking and type requirements are much tighter in *Java* than in $C++$.
- Unlike $C++$, *Java* provides a true *boolean* type.

- Conditional expressions in *Java* must evaluate to *boolean* rather than to integer, as is the case in *C++*. Statements such as *if(x + y)...* are not allowed in *Java* because the conditional expression doesn't evaluate to a *boolean*.
- The *char* type in *C++* is an 8-bit type that maps to the ASCII (or extended ASCII) character set. The *char* type in *Java* is a 16-bit type.
- *C++* allows the instantiation of variables or objects of all types either at compile time in static memory or at run time using dynamic memory. However, *Java* requires all variables of primitive types to be instantiated at compile time, and requires all objects to be instantiated in dynamic memory at runtime. Wrapper classes are provided for all primitive types except *byte* and *short* to allow them to be instantiated as objects in dynamic memory at runtime if needed.
- In *C++*, unless you specifically initialize variables of primitive types, they will contain garbage. Although local variables of primitive types can be initialized in the declaration, primitive data members of a class cannot be initialized in the class definition in *C++*.
- In *Java*, you can initialize primitive data members in the class definition. You can also initialize them in the constructor. If you fail to initialize them, they will be initialized to zero (or equivalent) automatically.
- Like *C++*, *Java* supports constructors that may be overloaded. As in *C++*, if you fail to provide a constructor, a default constructor will be provided for you. If you provide a constructor, the default constructor is not provided automatically.
- All objects in *Java* are passed by reference, eliminating the need for the *copy constructor* used in *C++*. (In reality, all parameters are passed by value in *Java*. However, passing a copy of a reference variable makes it possible for code in the receiving method to access the object referred to by the variable, and possibly to modify the contents of that object. However, code in the receiving method cannot cause the original reference variable to refer to a different object.)
- There are no destructors in *Java*. Unused memory is returned to the operating system by way of a *garbage collector*, which runs in a different thread from the main program. This leads to a whole host of subtle and extremely important differences between *Java* and *C++*.
- Like *C++*, *Java* allows you to overload functions. However, default arguments are not supported by *Java*.
- Unlike *C++*, *Java* does not support *templates*. Thus, there are no *generic* functions or classes.
- Unlike *C++*, several *data structure* classes are contained in the "standard" version of *Java*.
- *Multithreading* is a standard feature of the *Java* language.
- Although *Java* uses the same keywords as *C++* for access control: *private*, *public*, and *protected*, the interpretation of these keywords is significantly different between *Java* and *C++*.
- There is no *virtual* keyword in *Java*. All non-static methods always use dynamic binding, so the *virtual* keyword isn't needed for the same purpose that it is used in *C++*.
- *Java* provides the *final* keyword that can be used to specify that a method cannot be overridden and that it can be statically bound. (The compiler *may* elect to make it *inline* in this case.)
- The detailed implementation of the *exception handling* system in *Java* is significantly different from that in *C++*.
- Unlike *C++*, *Java* does not support *operator overloading*. However, the (+) and (+=) operators are automatically overloaded to concatenate strings, and to convert other types to *string* in the process.

- As in *C++*, *Java* applications can call functions written in another language. This is commonly referred to as *native methods*. However, applets cannot call native methods.

Question 15: What is the difference between assignment and initialization in C++?

Answer: Consider the following code snippet:

```
MyTempClass one;
MyTempClass two = one;
```

Here, the variable two is initialized to one because it is created as a copy of another variable. When two is created, it will go from containing garbage data directly to holding a copy of the value of one with no intermediate step. However, if we rewrite the code as

```
MyTempClass one, two;
two = one;
```

Then two is assigned the value of one. Note that before we reach the line two = one, two already contains a value. This is the difference between assignment and initialization – when a variable is created to hold a specified value, it is being initialized, whereas when an existing variable is set to hold a new value, it is being assigned.

If you're ever confused about when variables are assigned and when they're initialized, you can check by sticking a const declaration in front of the variable. If the code still compiles, the object is being initialized. Otherwise, it's being assigned a new value.

Question 16: Explain overloading in C++.

Answer: C++ allows you to specify more than one definition for a function name or an operator in the same scope, which is called function overloading and operator overloading respectively. An overloaded declaration is a declaration that had been declared with the same name as a previously declared declaration in the same scope, except that both declarations have different arguments and obviously different definition (implementation).

When you call an overloaded function or operator, the compiler determines the most appropriate definition to use by comparing the argument types you used to call the function or operator with the parameter types specified in the definitions. The process of selecting the most appropriate overloaded function or operator is called overload resolution.

Function overloading in C++

You can have multiple definitions for the same function name in the same scope. The definition of the function must differ from each other by the types and/or the number of arguments in the argument list. You cannot overload function declarations that differ only by return type. Following is the example where same function print() is being used to print different data types:

```
#include <iostream>
using namespace std;

class printData {
   public:
   void print(int i) {
      cout << "Printing int: " << i << endl;
   }
   void print(double f) {
      cout << "Printing float: " << f << endl;
   }
   void print(char* c) {
      cout << "Printing character: " << c << endl;
   }
```

```
};
int main(void){
    printData pd;
    // Call print to print integer
    pd.print(5);
    // Call print to print float
    pd.print(500.263);
    // Call print to print character
    pd.print("Hello C++ Programmer");

    return 0;
}
```

When the above code is compiled and executed, it produces the following result:

```
Printing int: 5
Printing float: 500.263
Printing character: Hello C++
```

Operator overloading in C++

We can redefine or overload most of the built-in operators available in C++. Thus a programmer can use operators with user-defined types as well. Overloaded operators are functions with special names the keyword operator followed by the symbol for the operator being defined. Like any other function, an overloaded operator has a return type and a parameter list.

```
Box operator+(const Box&);
```

declares the addition operator that can be used to add two Box objects and returns final Box object. Most overloaded operators may be defined as ordinary non-member functions or as class member functions. In case we define above function as non-member function of a class then we would have to pass two arguments for each operand as follows:

```
Box operator+(const Box&, const Box&);
```

Following is the example to show the concept of operator over loading using a member function. Here an object is passed as an argument whose properties will be accessed using this object, the object which will call this operator can be accessed using this operator as explained below:

```
#include <iostream>
using namespace std;
class Box{
    public:
    double getVolume(void) {
        return length * breadth * height;
    }
    void setLength( double len ) {
        length = len;
    }
    void setBreadth( double bre ) {
        breadth = bre;
    }
    void setHeight( double hei ) {
        height = hei;
    }
    // Overload + operator to add two Box objects.
    Box operator+(const Box& b) {
        Box box;
```

```
        box.length = this->length + b.length;
        box.breadth = this->breadth + b.breadth;
        box.height = this->height + b.height;
        return box;
    }
    private:
        double length; // Length of a box
        double breadth; // Breadth of a box
        double height; // Height of a box
};
// Main function for the program
int main( ){
    Box Box1;        // Declare Box1 of type Box
    Box Box2;        // Declare Box2 of type Box
    Box Box3;        // Declare Box3 of type Box
    double volume = 0.0; // Store the volume of a box here
    // box 1 specification
    Box1.setLength(6.0);
    Box1.setBreadth(7.0);
    Box1.setHeight(5.0);
    // box 2 specification
    Box2.setLength(12.0);
    Box2.setBreadth(13.0);
    Box2.setHeight(10.0);
    // volume of box 1
    volume = Box1.getVolume();
    cout << "Volume of Box1 : " << volume <<endl;
    // volume of box 2
    volume = Box2.getVolume();
    cout << "Volume of Box2 : " << volume <<endl;
    // Add two object as follows:
    Box3 = Box1 + Box2;
    // volume of box 3
    volume = Box3.getVolume();
    cout << "Volume of Box3 : " << volume <<endl;
    return 0;
}
```

When the above code is compiled and executed, it produces the following result:

```
Volume of Box1 : 210
Volume of Box2 : 1560
Volume of Box3 : 5400
```

Question 17: What is the difference between overloading and overriding?

Answer:

	Method Overloading	Method Overriding
Definition	Methods of the same class share the same name but each method must have different number of parameters or parameters having different types and order.	Sub class have the same method with same name and exactly the same number and type of parameters and same return type as a super class.
Meaning	Method Overloading means more than one method shares the same name in the class but having different signature.	Method Overriding means method of base class is redefined in the derived class having same signature.

Behavior	Method Overloading is to "add" or "extend" more to method's behavior.	Method Overriding is to "Change" existing behavior of method.
	Overloading and Overriding is a kind of polymorphism. Polymorphism means "one name, many forms".	
Polymorphism	It is a compile time polymorphism.	It is a run time polymorphism.
Inheritance	It may or may not need inheritance in Method Overloading.	It always requires inheritance in Method Overriding.
Signature	Methods must have different signature.	Methods must have same signature.
Relationship of Methods	Relationship is there between methods of same class.	Relationship is there between methods of super class and sub class.
Criteria	In Method Overloading, methods have same name different signatures but in the same class.	In Method Overriding, methods have same name and same signature but in the different class.
Number of Classes	Method Overloading does not require more than one class for overloading.	Method Overriding requires at least two classes for overriding.

Example	Class Addition {
	int add(int a, int b) {
	return a + b;
	}
	int add(int a) {
	return a + 20;
	}
	}
		Class A { // Super Class
		void display(int num) {
		print num ;
		}
		}
		//Class B inherits Class A
		Class B { //Sub Class
		void display(int num) {
		print num ;
		}
		}

Question 18: Explain copy constructor in C++.

Answer: The copy constructor is a constructor which creates an object by initializing it with an object of the same class, which has been created previously. The copy constructor is used to:

- Initialize one object from another of the same type.
- Copy an object to pass it as an argument to a function.
- Copy an object to return it from a function.

If a copy constructor is not defined in a class, the compiler itself defines one. If the class has pointer variables and has some dynamic memory allocations, then it is a must to have a copy constructor. The most common form of copy constructor is shown here:

```
classname (const classname &obj) {
 // body of constructor
}
```

Here, obj is a reference to an object that is being used to initialize another object.

```
#include <iostream>
using namespace std;
class Line{
    public:
    int getLength( void );
    Line( int len );            // simple constructor
    Line( const Line &obj); // copy constructor
```

```
    ~Line();                // destructor
    private:
    int *ptr;
};
// Member functions definitions including constructor
Line::Line(int len){
    cout << "Normal constructor allocating ptr" << endl;
    // allocate memory for the pointer;
    ptr = new int;
    *ptr = len;
}
Line::Line(const Line &obj){
    cout << "Copy constructor allocating ptr." << endl;
    ptr = new int;
    *ptr = *obj.ptr; // copy the value
}
Line::~Line(void){
    cout << "Releasing memory!" << endl;
    delete ptr;
}
int Line::getLength( void ){
    return *ptr;
}
void display(Line obj){
    cout << "Length of line : " << obj.getLength() <<endl;
}
// Main function for the program
int main( ){
    Line line(10);
    display(line);
    return 0;
}
```

When the above code is compiled and executed, it produces the following result:

```
Normal constructor allocating ptr
Copy constructor allocating ptr.
Length of line : 10
Releasing memory!
Releasing memory!
```

Let us see the same example but with a small change to create another object using existing object of the same type:

```
#include <iostream>
using namespace std;
class Line{
    public:
    int getLength( void );
    Line( int len );            // simple constructor
    Line( const Line &obj); // copy constructor
    ~Line();                // destructor
    private:
    int *ptr;
};
// Member functions definitions including constructor
Line::Line(int len){
    cout << "Normal constructor allocating ptr" << endl;
    // allocate memory for the pointer;
```

```
    ptr = new int;
    *ptr = len;
}
Line::Line(const Line &obj){
    cout << "Copy constructor allocating ptr." << endl;
    ptr = new int;
    *ptr = *obj.ptr; // copy the value
}
Line::~Line(void){
    cout << "Releasing memory!" << endl;
    delete ptr;
}
int Line::getLength( void ){
    return *ptr;
}
void display(Line obj){
    cout << "Length of line : " << obj.getLength() <<endl;
}
// Main function for the program
int main( ){
    Line line1(10);
    Line line2 = line1; // This also calls copy constructor
    display(line1);
    display(line2);
    return 0;
}
```

When the above code is compiled and executed, it produces the following result:

```
Normal constructor allocating ptr
Copy constructor allocating ptr.
Copy constructor allocating ptr.
Length of line : 10
Releasing memory!
Copy constructor allocating ptr.
Length of line : 10
Releasing memory!
Releasing memory!
Releasing memory!
```

Question 19: What is shallow and deep copy in $C++$?

Answer: A *shallow copy* of an object copies all of the member field values. This works well if the fields are values, but may not be what we want for fields that point to dynamically allocated memory (pointers). The pointer will be copied. But the memory it points to will not be copied. The field in both the original object and the copy will then point to the same dynamically allocated memory, which is not usually what we want. The default copy constructor and assignment operator make shallow copies.

Deep copy copies all fields, and makes copies of dynamically allocated memory pointed to by the fields. To make a deep copy, we need to write a copy constructor and overload the assignment operator, otherwise the copy will point to the original.

Question 20: What is object slicing in $C++$?

Answer: When a derived class object is assigned to base class, the base class contents in the derived object are copied to the base class leaving behind the derived class specific contents. This is referred as *object Slicing*. That is, the base class object can access only the base class members. This also implies that the separation of base class members from derived class members has happened.

```
class base{
    public:
        int i, j;
};
class derived : public base{
     public:
         int k;
};
```

```
int main(){
    base b;
    derived d;
    b=d;
    return 0;
}
```

Here *b* contains *i* and *j* whereas *d* contains *i*, *j* & *k*. On assignment only *i* and *j* of the *d* get copied into *i* and *j* of *b*, *k* does not get copied and on the effect object *d* gets sliced.

Question 21: Are there copy constructor and assignment constructor in java?

Answer: There is such a thing as a copy constructor in Java, but it does not play the special role that such constructors do in C++. A copy constructor in Java is just like any other constructor: we call it with new.

```
public class A {
private int x;
public A(int x) { this.x = v; }
public A(A that) { this.x = that.x; }
}
...
A temp1 = new A(5);
A temp2;
temp2 = new A(temp1);
...
```

There are no assignment constructors, or anything much like them, in Java. That is because Java does *not* have operator overloading. The assignment operation (=) is always a shallow copy.

Java does have the notion of a *clone* (copy) method. Any object can support the clone() method; by convention the method implementation is supposed to perform a deep copy of the object on which it is called, and return the copy.

Question 22: Explain templates concept in C++.

Answer: C++ templates are the foundation of generic programming, which involves writing code in a way that is *independent* of any particular *type*. A template is a formula for creating a generic class or a function. The library containers like iterators and algorithms are examples of generic programming and have been developed using template concept.

There is a single definition of each container, such as vector, but we can define many different kinds of vectors for example, *vector < int >* or *vector < string >*. You can use templates to define functions as well as classes, let us see how do they work:

Function Template

The general form of a template function definition is shown here:

```
template <class type> ret-type func-name(parameter list){
  // body of function
}
```

Here, type is a placeholder name for a data type used by the function. This name can be used within the function definition.

The following is the example of a function template that returns the maximum of two values:

```
#include <iostream>
```

```
#include <string>
using namespace std;
template <typename T>
inline T const& Max (T const& a, T const& b) {
   return a < b ? b:a;
}
int main (){
   int i = 49;
   int j = 10;
   cout << "Max(i, j): " << Max(i, j) << endl;
   double f1 = 23.5;
   double f2 = 10.7;
   cout << "Max(f1, f2): " << Max(f1, f2) << endl;
   string s1 = "Hello";
   string s2 = "World";
   cout << "Max(s1, s2): " << Max(s1, s2) << endl;
  return 0;
}
```

If we compile and run above code, this would produce the following result:

```
Max(i, j): 49
Max(f1, f2): 23.5
Max(s1, s2): World
```

Class Template

Just as we can define function templates, we can also define class templates. The general form of a generic class declaration is shown here:

```
template <class type> class class-name {
.
.
.
}
```

Here, type is the placeholder type name, which will be specified when a class is instantiated. You can define more than one generic data type by using a comma-separated list.

Following is the example to define class Stack<> and implement generic methods to push and pop the elements from the stack:

```
#include <iostream>
#include <vector>
#include <cstdlib>
#include <string>
#include <stdexcept>
using namespace std;
template <class T>
class Stack {
 private:
   vector<T> elems;     // elements
 public:
   void push(T const&);  // push element
   void pop();            // pop element
   T top() const;          // return top element
   bool empty() const{      // return true if empty.
       return elems.empty();
```

```
    }
};
template <class T>
void Stack<T>::push (T const& elem) {
    // append copy of passed element
    elems.push_back(elem);
}
template <class T>
void Stack<T>::pop () {
    if (elems.empty()) {
        throw out_of_range("Stack<>::pop(): empty stack");
    }
    // remove last element
    elems.pop_back();
}
template <class T>
T Stack<T>::top () const {
    if (elems.empty()) {
        throw out_of_range("Stack<>::top(): empty stack");
    }
    // return copy of last element
    return elems.back();
}
int main() {
    try {
        Stack<int>         intStack;  // stack of ints
        Stack<string> stringStack;    // stack of strings
        // Update int stack
        intStack.push(7);
        cout << intStack.top() <<endl;
        // Update string stack
        stringStack.push("hello");
        cout << stringStack.top() << std::endl;
        stringStack.pop();
        stringStack.pop();
    }
    catch (exception const& ex) {
        cerr << "Exception: " << ex.what() <<endl;
        return -1;
    }
}
```

If we compile and run above code, this would produce the following result:

```
7
hello
Exception: Stack<>::pop(): empty stack
```

Question 23: Explain *vitual* functions in $C++$.

Answer: When a function call is made, $C++$ matches a function call with the correct function definition at compile time. This is called *static binding*. We can specify that the compiler match a function call with the correct function definition at run time and this is called *dynamic binding*. We declare a function with the keyword *virtual* if we want the compiler to use dynamic binding for that specific function. The following example demonstrates static binding:

```
class A {
  void f() {
```

```
void g(A& arg) {
  arg.f();
```

```
        cout << "Base Class A" << endl;
    }
};

class B: A {
    void f() {
        cout << "Derived Class B" << endl;
    }
};
}
int main() {
    B x;
    g(x);
}
Output of the example: Class A
```

When function $g()$ is called, function $A::f()$ is called, although the argument refers to an object of type B. At compile time, the compiler knows only that the argument of function $g()$ will be a reference to an object derived from A, it cannot determine whether the argument will be a reference to an object of type A or type B. However, this can be determined at run time. The following example is the same as the previous example, except that A::f() is declared with the *virtual* keyword:

```
class A {
    virtual void f() {
        cout << "Base Class A" << endl;
    }
};
class B: A {
    void f() {
        cout << "Derived Class B" << endl;
    }
};
void g(A& arg) {
    arg.f();
}
int main() {
    B x;
    g(x);
}
Output of the example: Class B
```

Question 24: What are *abstract* classes and *interfaces*? What is the difference between them?

Answer: An *abstract* class is a class that cannot be instantiated and is usually implemented as a class that has one or more *pure virtual* (abstract) functions.

A *pure virtual* function is one which must be overridden by any concrete (i.e., non-abstract) derived class. This is indicated in the declaration with the syntax "= 0" in the member function's declaration.

```
class AbstractClass {
public:
    //pure virtual function makes this class Abstract class
    virtual void AbstractMemberFunction() = 0;
    virtual void NonAbstractVirtualMemberFunction(); //virtual function
    void NonAbstractMemberFunction();
};
```

In general an abstract class is used to define an implementation and is intended to be inherited from concrete classes. If a class has *only* pure virtual functions then we call it *pure abstract* class or an *interface*. The concept of interface is mapped to pure abstract classes in $C++$, as there is no keyword *interface* in $C++$ the same way that there is in *Java*. That means, in *Java* we can use an *interface* keyword to define pure abstract classes as shown below.

```
interface InterfaceClass {
    void function1(int value);
    void function2(int newValue);
    void function3(int someValue);
}
```

In object-oriented programming, a *virtual* function is a method whose behaviour can be overridden within an inheriting class by a function with the same signature to provide the polymorphic behavior. Therefore according to definition, every non-static method in

Java is by *default* virtual method except *final* and *private* methods. The method which cannot be inherited for polymorphic behavior is not a virtual method.

In design, we want the base class to present only an interface for its derived classes. This means, we don't want anyone to actually instantiate an object of the base class. We only want to upcast it, so that its interface can be used. This is accomplished by making that class abstract using the *abstract* keyword. If anyone tries to make an object of an abstract class, the compiler prevents it. An abstract class can have executable methods and abstract methods can only subclass one abstract class.

The *interface* keyword takes this concept of an abstract class a step further by preventing any method or function implementation at all. We can only declare a method or function but not provide the implementation. The class, which is implementing the interface, should provide the actual implementation. In interface, all methods are abstract. A class can implement any number of interfaces.

Difference between *abstract* and *interface* classes in *Java*:

- Main difference in methods of a *Java interface* are implicitly abstract and cannot have implementations. A *Java abstract* class can have instance methods that implement a default behavior.
- Variables declared in *Java* interface are by default final. An abstract class may contain non-final variables.
- Members of *Java* interface are *public* by default. A *Java* abstract class can have the usual flavors of class members like private, protected, etc..
- *Java* interface should be implemented using keyword *implements* and a *Java* abstract class should be extended using keyword *extends*.
- An interface can extend another *Java* interface only, an abstract class can extend another *Java* class and implement multiple *Java* interfaces.
- A *Java* class can implement multiple interfaces but it can extend only one abstract class.
- Interface is absolutely abstract and cannot be instantiated, a *Java* abstract class also cannot be instantiated, but can be invoked if a main() exists.

Question 25: What's the difference between *memcpy* and *memmove*?

Answer: *memmove* gives guaranteed behavior if the memory regions pointed to by the source and destination arguments overlap. *memcpy* makes no such guarantee, and may therefore be more efficiently implementable. When in doubt, it's safer to use memmove. It seems simple enough to implement *memmove*; the overlap guarantee apparently requires only an additional test:

```
void *memmove(void *destination, void const *source, int size){
    register char *dptr = destination;
    register char const *sptr = source;
    if(dptr < sptr) {
        while(size-- > 0)
            *dptr++ = *sptr++;
    } else {
        dptr += size;
        sptr += size;
        while(size-- > 0)
            *--dptr = *--sptr;
    }
    return destination;
}
```

The problem with this code is in that additional test: the comparison (dptr < sptr) is not quite portable (it compares two pointers which do not necessarily point within the same object) and may not be as cheap as it looks.

With *memcpy*, the destination cannot overlap the source at all. With *memmove* copying takes place as if an intermediate buffer was used, allowing the destination and source to overlap. This means that *memmove* might be very slightly slower than *memcpy*, as it cannot make the same assumptions. In other words, *memcpy* copies source to destination without checking for overlapping of source and destination memory areas. *memmove* copies source to destination carefully by checking for overlapping of source and destination memory areas.

Question 26: What is the output of following code snippet?

```
#include <stdio.h>
int main(void){
   int a = 3;
   int b;
   b = sizeof(++a + ++a);
   printf("a=%d   b=%d\n", a, b);
   return 0;
}
```

Answer: a=3 b=4

sizeof gives the number of bytes allocated for an operand. Hence, the evaluation of ++a will get cancelled and *a*'s value remains unchanged.

Question 27: Compare C++ and Java performance.

Amswer: In addition to running a compiled Java program, computers running Java applications generally must also run the Java virtual machine (JVM), while compiled C++ programs can be run without external applications. Early versions of Java were significantly outperformed by statically compiled languages such as C++. This is because the program statements of these two closely related languages may compile to a few machine instructions with C++, while compiling into several byte codes involving several machine instructions each when interpreted by a JVM.

Since performance optimization is a very complex issue, it is very difficult to say in numbers the performance difference between C++ and Java in general terms. And given the very different natures of the languages, definitive qualitative differences are also difficult to draw. There are inherent inefficiencies as well as hard limitations on optimizations in Java given that it heavily relies on flexible high-level abstractions, however, the use of a powerful JIT compiler (as in modern JVM implementations) can resolve some issues.

Certain inefficiencies that are inherent to the Java language:

- All objects are allocated on the heap. For functions using small objects this can result in performance degradation and heap fragmentation, while stack allocation, in contrast, costs essentially zero. However, modern JIT compilers mitigate this problem to some extent with escape analysis or escape detection to allocate objects on the stack.
- Lack of access to low-level details prevents the developer from improving the program where the compiler is unable to do so.

Benefits of Java's design:

- Java garbage collection may have better cache coherence than the usual usage of malloc/new for memory allocation.
- In Java, thread synchronization is built into the language.

Also, some performance problems exist in C++ as well:

- Allowing pointers to point to any address can make optimization difficult due to the possibility of interference between pointers that alias each other. However, the introduction of strict-aliasing rules largely solves this problem.

- Because dynamic linking is performed after code generation and optimization in C++, function calls spanning different dynamic modules cannot be inlined.
- Because thread support is generally provided by libraries in C++, C++ compilers cannot perform thread-related optimizations.

Question 28: Explain *virtual tables* in *C + +*.

Answer: To implement virtual functions, *C + +* uses a special form of late binding known as *virtual table*. The virtual table is a lookup table of functions used to resolve function calls in a *dynamic/late* binding manner. The virtual table is also called *vtable*, *virtual function table* or *virtual method table*.

The virtual table is actually quite simple, though it's a little complex to describe in words. First, every class that uses virtual functions (or is derived from a class that uses virtual functions) is given its own virtual table. This table is simply a static array that the compiler sets up at compile time.

A virtual table contains one entry for each virtual function that can be called by objects of the class. Each entry in this table is simply a function pointer that points to the most-derived function accessible by that class.

Second, the compiler also adds a hidden pointer to the base class, which we will call *__vptr. *__vptr is set (automatically) when a class instance is created so that it points to the virtual table for that class. Unlike the *this pointer, which is actually a function parameter used by the compiler to resolve self-references, *__vptr is a real pointer.

That means, it makes each class object allocated bigger by the size of one pointer. It also means that *__vptr is inherited by derived classes. Let's take a look at a simple example:

```
class Base{
public:
   virtual void
        function1() {};
   virtual void
        function2() {};
};
```

```
class D1: public Base{
   public:
     virtual void
           function1() {};
};
```

```
class D2: public Base{
   public:
     virtual void
           function2() {};
};
```

Since there are 3 classes here, the compiler will set up 3 virtual tables: one for Base, one for D1, and one for D2. The compiler also adds a hidden pointer to the most base class that uses virtual functions. Although the compiler does this automatically, we'll put it in the next example just to show where it's added:

```
class Base{
public:
   FunctionPointer *__vptr;
   virtual void function1() {};
   virtual void function2() {};
};
```

```
class D1: public Base {
   public:
     virtual void
           function1() {};
};
```

```
class D2: public
Base{
   public:
   virtual void
           function2() {};
};
```

When a class object is created, *__vptr is set to point to the virtual table for that class. For example, when an object of type Base is created, *__vptr is set to point to the virtual table for Base. When objects of type D1 or D2 are constructed, *__vptr is set to point to the virtual table for D1 or D2 respectively.

Now, let's see how these virtual tables are filled out. Because there are only two virtual functions here, each virtual table will have two entries (one for function1(), and one for function2()). Remember that when these virtual tables are filled, each entry is filled out with the most-derived function an object of that class type can call.

Base's virtual table is simple. An object of type Base can only access the members of Base. Base has no access to D1 or D2 functions. Consequently, the entry for function1 points to Base::function1(), and the entry for function2 points to Base::function2().

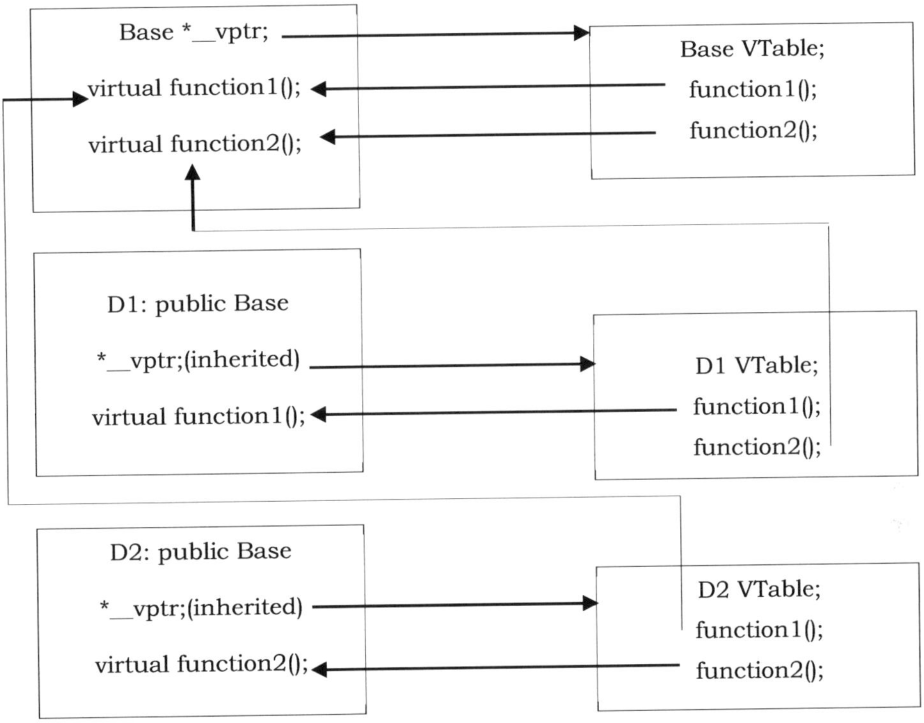

D1's virtual table is slightly more complex. An object of type D1 can access members of both D1 and Base. However, D1 has overridden function1(), making D1::function1() more derived than Base::function1(). Consequently, the entry for function1 points to D1::function1(). D1 hasn't overridden function2(), so the entry for function2 will point to Base::function2(). D2's virtual table is similar to D1, except the entry for function1 points to Base::function1(), and the entry for function2 points to D2::function2().

In the diagram: the *__vptr in each class points to the virtual table for that class. The entries in the virtual table point to the most-derived version of the function objects of that class are allowed to call. So consider what happens when we create an object of type D1:

```
int main(){
    D1 cClass;
}
```

Because cClass is a D1 object, cClass has it's *__vptr set to the D1 virtual table. Now, let's set a base pointer to D1:

```
int main() {
    D1 cClass;
    Base *pClass = &cClass;
}
```

Note that because pClass is a base pointer, it only points to the Base portion of cClass. However, also note that *__vptr is in the Base portion of the class, so pClass has access to this pointer. Finally, note that pClass→__vptr points to the D1 virtual table! Consequently, even though pClass is of type Base, it still has access to D1's virtual table. So what happens when we call pClass→function1()?

```
int main() {
    D1 cClass;
    Base *pClass = &cClass;
    pClass→function1();
```

```
}
```

First, the program recognizes that function1() is a virtual function. Second, uses pClass→__vptr to get to D1's virtual table. Third, it looks up which version of function1() to call in D1's virtual table. This has been set to D1::function1(). Therefore, pClass→function1() resolves to D1::function1()!

Now, you might be saying, "But what if Base really pointed to a Base object instead of a D1 object. Would it still be called D1::function1()?". The answer is no.

```
int main() {
    Base cClass;
    Base *pClass = &cClass;
    pClass→function1();
}
```

In this case, when cClass is created, __vptr points to Base's virtual table, not D1's virtual table. Consequently, pClass→__vptr will also point to Base's virtual table. Base's virtual table entry for function1() points to Base::function1(). Thus, pClass→function1() resolves to Base::function1(), which is the most-derived version of function1() that a Base object should be able to call.

By using these tables, the compiler and program are able to ensure function calls resolve to the appropriate virtual function, even if you're only using a pointer or reference to a base class!

Calling a virtual function is slower than calling a non-virtual function for a couple of reasons: First, we have to use the *__vptr to get to the appropriate virtual table. Second, we have to index the virtual table to find the correct function to call. Only then can we call the function. As a result, we have to do 3 operations to find the function to call, as opposed to 2 operations for a normal indirect function call, or one operation for a direct function call. However, with modern computers, this added time is insignificant.

Question 29: Write a function for swapping two integers without using third integer (ie. without using any temporary variable).

Answer: There are multiple solutions for this problem. The code snippet below exploits those.

```
#include<stdio.h>
int main(){
    int a=15,b=25;
    //Method one
    a=b+a;
    b=a-b;
    a=a-b;
    printf("a= %d  b= %d",a,b);
    //Method two
    a=a+b-(b=a);
    printf("\na= %d  b= %d",a,b);
    //Method three
    a=a^b;
    b=a^b;
    a=b^a;
    printf("\na= %d  b= %d",a,b);
    //Method four
    a=b-~a-1;
    b=a+~b+1;
    a=a+~b+1;
    printf("\na= %d  b= %d",a,b);
```

```
    //Method five
    a=b+a,b=a-b,a=a-b;
    printf("\na= %d  b=  %d",a,b);
    return 0;
}
```

Question 30: What does *'public static void'* mean in Java?

Answer: The *public* keyword is an access specifier, which allows the programmer to control the visibility of class members. When a class member is preceded by public, then that member may be accessed by code outside the class in which it is declared. (The opposite of public is private, which prevents a member from being used by code defined outside of its class.) In other words, public means that the method is visible and can be called from other objects of other types.

In this case, main( ) must be declared as *public*, since it must be called by code outside of its class when the program is started.

The keyword *static* allows main( ) to be called without having to instantiate a particular instance of the class. This is necessary since main( ) is called by the Java interpreter before any objects are made.

The keyword *void* simply tells the compiler that main( ) does not return a value. As you will see, methods may also return values.

Question 31: What if the *main* method is declared as *private*?

Answer: The program compiles properly but at runtime it will give "Main method not public." message.

Question 32: What if the *static* modifier is removed from the signature of the main method?

Answer: Program compiles. But at runtime throws an error "NoSuchMethodError".

Question 33: What if I write *static public void* instead of *public static void*?

Answer: Program compiles and runs properly.

Question 34: What if I do not provide the *String* array as the argument to the method?

Answer: Program compiles but throws a runtime error "NoSuchMethodError".

Question 35: What is the first argument of the *String* array in main method?

Answer: The String array is empty. It does not have any element. This is unlike C/C++ where the first element by default is the program name.

Question 36: If I do not provide any arguments on the command line, then the *String* array of Main method will be empty or null?

Answer: It is empty. But not null.

Question 37: What is the main difference between an *ArrayList* and a *Vector* in *Java*?

Answer: *Java* arrays are faster than an ArrayList/Vector and therefore it may be preferable if we know the size of the array upfront (because arrays cannot grow as Lists do).

ArrayList/Vector are specialized data structures that internally use an array with some convenient methods like add(..), remove(...), etc. so that they can grow and shrink from their initial size. ArrayList also supports index based searches with indexOf(Object obj) and lastIndexOf(Object obj) methods.

Question 38: Discuss about constructors, destructors and their order of execution in inheritance.

Answer: The process of creating and deleting objects in C++ is not a trivial task. Every time an instance of a class is created the constructor method is called. The constructor has the same name as the class and it doesn't return any type, while the destructor's name it's defined in the same way, but with a '~' in front:

```
class Base{
  public:
  Base ( ) {
    cout << "Base constructor" << endl;
  }
  ~Base ( ){
    cout << "Base destructor" << endl;
  }
};
```

Base class constructors are always called in the derived class constructors. Whenever you create derived class object, first the base class default constructor is executed and then the derived class's constructor finishes execution.

1. Important Notes

1. Whether derived class's default constructor is called or parameterized is called, base class's default constructor is always called inside them.
2. To call base class's parameterized constructor inside derived class's parameterized constructor, we must mention it explicitly while declaring derived class's parameterized constructor.

2. Base class Default Constructor in Derived class Constructors

```
class Base{
    int a;
    public:
        Base() { cout << "Default base constructor"<<endl; }
};
class Derived : public Base{
    int b;
    public:
        Derived() { cout << "Default derived constructor"<<endl; }
        Derived(int i) { cout << "Parameterized derived constructor"<<endl; }
};
int main(){
    Base b;
    Derived d1;
    Derived d2(20);
}
```

Expected Output:

```
Default base constructor
Default base constructor
Default derived constructor
Default base constructor
Parameterized derived constructor
```

You will see in the above example that with both the object creation of the Derived class, Base class's default constructor is called.

3. Base class Parameterized Constructor in Derived class Constructor

We can explicitly mention to call the Base class's parameterized constructor when Derived class's parameterized constructor is called.

```
class Base {
    public: int x;
    public:
        Base(int i){
            x = i;
            cout << "Base Parameterized Constructor"<<endl;
        }
};
class Derived : public Base{
    public: int y;
    public:
    Derived(int j) : Base(j){
        y = j;
        cout << "Derived Parameterized Constructor"<<endl;
    }
};
int main(){
    Derived d(20) ;
    cout << d.x <<endl; // Output will be 20
    cout << d.y <<endl; // Output will be 20
}
```

Expected Output:

```
Base Parameterized Constructor
Derived Parameterized Constructor
20
20
```

4. Why is Base class Constructor called inside Derived class ?

Constructors have a special job of initializing the object properly. A Derived class constructor has access only to its own class members, but a Derived class object also have inherited property of Base class, and only base class constructor can properly initialize base class members. Hence all the constructors are called, else object wouldn't be constructed properly.

5. Constructor call in Multiple Inheritance

It's almost the same, all the Base class's constructors are called inside derived class's constructor, in the same order in which they are inherited.

```
class A : public B, public C ;
```

In this case, first class B constructor will be executed, then class C constructor and then class A constructor.

6. Upcasting in C++

Upcasting is using the Super class's reference or pointer to refer to a Sub class's object. Or we can say that, the act of converting a Sub class's reference or pointer into its Super class's reference or pointer is called Upcasting.

```
class Super{
    int x;
    public:
    void funBase() { cout << "Super function"; }
};
class Sub : public Super{
    int y;
};
int main(){
```

```
    Super* ptr; // Super class pointer
    Sub obj;
    ptr = &obj;
    Super &ref; // Super class's reference
    ref=obj;
}
```

The opposite of *Upcasting* is *Downcasting*, in which we convert Super class's reference or pointer into derived class's reference or pointer. We will study more about *Downcasting* later

7. Functions that are never Inherited

Constructors and Destructors are never inherited and hence never overrided. Also, assignment operator = is never inherited. It can be overloaded but can't be inherited by sub class.

8. Inheritance and Static Functions

1. They are inherited into the derived class.
2. If you redefine a static member function in derived class, all the other overloaded functions in base class are hidden.
3. Static Member functions can never be virtual.

9. Hybrid Inheritance and Virtual Class

In Multiple Inheritance, the derived class inherits from more than one base class. Hence, in Multiple Inheritance there are a lot chances of ambiguity.

```
class A{   void show(); };
class B:public A {};
class C:public A {};
class D:public B, public C {};
int main(){
    D obj;
    obj.show();
}
```

In this case both class B and C inherits function show() from class A. Hence class D has two inherited copies of function show(). In main() function when we call function show(), then ambiguity arises, because compiler doesn't know which show() function to call. Hence we use Virtual keyword while inheriting class.

```
class B : virtual public A {};
class C : virtual public A {};
class D : public B, public C {};
```

Now by adding virtual keyword, we tell compiler to call any one out of the two show() functions.

10. Hybrid Inheritance and Constructor call

As we all know that whenever a derived class object is instantiated, the base class constructor is always called. But in case of Hybrid Inheritance, as discussed in above example, if we create an instance of class D, then following constructors will be called : before class D's constructor, constructors of its super classes will be called, hence constructors of class B, class C and class A will be called. when constructors of class B and class C are called, they will again make a call to their super class's constructor. This will result in multiple calls to the constructor of class A, which is undesirable. As there is a single instance of virtual base class which is shared by multiple classes that inherit from it, hence the constructor of the base class is only called once by the constructor of concrete class, which in our case is class D.

Question 39: Explain how HashMap works in *Java*.

Answer: HashMap works on principle of hashing, we have *put*() and *get*() methods for storing and retrieving data from HashMap. When we pass an object to *put*() method to store it on HashMap, HashMap implementation calls *hashcode*() method HashMap key object and by applying that hashcode on its own hashing funtion it identifies a bucket location for storing value object.

The important part here is HashMap stores both *key + value* in bucket, which is essential to understand the retrieving logic. If we fail to recognize this and assume it only stores value in the bucket they will fail to explain the retrieving logic of any object stored in HashMap.

What will happen if two different objects have same hashcode?

Now the confusion starts. The interviewer may say that since Hashcodes are equal, objects are equal and HashMap will throw exception or not store it again, etc. Then you might want to remind them about equals and hashCode() contract that two unequal objects in *Java* can have equal hashcode. Some will give up at this point and some will move ahead and say "since hashcode() is same, bucket location is the same and collision occurs in hashMap. Since HashMap uses a linked list to store in bucket, value object will be stored in next node of linked list.

How will you retrieve if two different objects have same hashcode?

After finding bucket location, we will call keys.equals() method to identify correct node in linked list and return associated value object for that key in *Java* HashMap.

What happens On HashMap in *Java* if the size of the Hashmap exceeds a given threshold defined by load factor?

Until we know how hashmap works we won't be able to answer this question. If the size of the map exceeds a given threshold defined by load-factor e.g. if load factor is .75 it will act to re-size the map once it fills 75%. *Java Hashmap* does that by creating another new bucket array twice the size of previous hashmap, and then starts putting every old element into that new bucket array. This process is called rehashing, because it also applies hash function to find new bucket location.

Question 40: What is the difference between *HashMap* and *HashTable* in *Java*?

Answer:

1. The HashMap class is roughly equivalent to Hashtable, except that it is non-synchronized and permits nulls. (HashMap allows null values as key and value whereas Hashtable doesn't allow nulls).
2. HashMap does not guarantee that the order of the map will remain constant over time.
3. HashMap is non-synchronized whereas Hashtable is synchronized.
4. Iterator in the HashMap is fail-fast while the enumerator for the Hashtable is not and throw ConcurrentModificationException if any other Thread modifies the map structurally by adding or removing any element except Iterator's own remove() method. But this is not a guaranteed behavior and will be done by JVM on best effort.

Question 41: Explain *Java* threads.

Answer: Java provides has support for multithreaded programming. A multithreaded program contains two or more parts that can run concurrently. Each part of such a program is called a thread, and each thread defines a separate path of execution.

As discussed earlier, a process consists of the memory space allocated by the operating system that can contain one or more threads. A thread cannot exist on its own; it must be a part of a process. A process remains running until all of the non-daemon threads are done executing. Multithreading enables us to write very efficient programs that make maximum use of the CPU, because idle time can be kept to a minimum.

Creating a Thread

In Java, we have two ways in which this can be accomplished:

- We can implement the Runnable interface.
- We can extend the Thread class itself.

Create Thread by Implementing Runnable

The simplest way to create a thread is to create a class that implements the *Runnable* interface. To implement Runnable, a class needs to only implement a single method called run( ), which is declared like this:

```
public void run( )
```

We will define the code that constitutes the new thread inside run() method. It is important to understand that run() can call other methods, use other classes, and declare variables, just like the main thread can.

After we create a class that implements *Runnable*, we will instantiate an object of type Thread from within that class. Thread defines several constructors. The one that we will use is shown here:

```
Thread(Runnable threadObject, String threadName);
```

Here, *threadObject* is an instance of a class that implements the *Runnable* interface and the name of the new thread is specified by threadName.

After the new thread is created, it will not start running until you call its start( ) method, which is declared within Thread. The start( ) method is shown here:

```
void start( );
```

Example

Here is an example that creates a new thread and starts it running:

```
// create a new thread.
class NewThread implements Runnable {
  Thread t;
  NewThread() {
    // create a new, second thread
    t = new Thread(this, "Demo Thread");
    System.out.println("Child thread: " + t);
    t.start(); // Start the thread
  }
  // Entry point for the second thread.
  public void run() {
    try {
      for(int i = 5; i > 0; i--) {
        System.out.println("Child Thread: " + i);
        Thread.sleep(50);  // sleep for a while.
      }
    } catch (InterruptedException e) {
      System.out.println("Child interrupted.");
    }
    System.out.println("Terminating child thread.");
  }
}
public class ThreadDemo {
  public static void main(String args[]) {
```

```
    new NewThread(); // create a new thread
    try {
      for(int i = 5; i > 0; i--) {
        System.out.println("Main Thread: " + i);
        Thread.sleep(100);
      }
    } catch (InterruptedException e) {
      System.out.println("Main thread interrupted.");
    }
    System.out.println("Main thread terminating.");
  }
}
```

This would produce the following result:

```
Child thread: Thread[Demo Thread,5,main]
Main Thread: 5
Child Thread: 5
Child Thread: 4
Main Thread: 4
Child Thread: 3
Child Thread: 2
Main Thread: 3
Child Thread: 1
Terminating child thread.
Main Thread: 2
Main Thread: 1
Main thread terminating.
```

Create Thread by Extending Thread

The second way to create a thread is to create a new class that extends Thread, and then to create an instance of that class. The extending class must override the run( ) method, which is the entry point for the new thread. It must also call start( ) to begin execution of the new thread.

Example

Here is the preceding program rewritten to extend Thread:

```
// Create a second thread by extending Thread
class NewThread extends Thread {
  NewThread() {
    // Create a new, second thread
    super("Demo Thread");
    System.out.println("Child thread: " + this);
    start(); // Start the thread
  }
  // This is the entry point for the second thread.
  public void run() {
    try {
      for(int i = 5; i > 0; i--) {
        System.out.println("Child Thread: " + i);
        // Let the thread sleep for a while.
        Thread.sleep(50);
      }
    } catch (InterruptedException e) {
      System.out.println("Child interrupted.");
    }
    System.out.println("Terminating child thread.");
```

```
    }
}
public class ExtendThread {
  public static void main(String args[]) {
    new NewThread(); // create a new thread
    try {
      for(int i = 5; i > 0; i--) {
        System.out.println("Main Thread: " + i);
        Thread.sleep(100);
      }
    } catch (InterruptedException e) {
      System.out.println("Main thread interrupted.");
    }
    System.out.println("Main thread terminating.");
  }
}
```

This would produce the following result:

```
Child thread: Thread[Demo Thread,5,main]
Main Thread: 5
Child Thread: 5
Child Thread: 4
Main Thread: 4
Child Thread: 3
Child Thread: 2
Main Thread: 3
Child Thread: 1
Terminating child thread.
Main Thread: 2
Main Thread: 1
Main thread terminating.
Thread Methods:
```

Following is the list of important methods available in the Thread class.

Function	Description
public void start()	Starts the thread in a separate path of execution, then invokes the run() method on this Thread object.
public void run()	If this Thread object was instantiated using a separate Runnable target, the run() method is invoked on that Runnable object.
public final void setName(String name)	Changes the name of the Thread object. There is also a getName() method for retrieving the name.
public final void setPriority(int priority)	Sets the priority of this Thread object. The possible values are between 1 and 10.
public final void setDaemon(boolean on)	A parameter of true denotes this Thread as a daemon thread.
public final void join(long millisec)	The current thread invokes this method on a second thread, causing the current thread to block until the second thread terminates or the specified number of milliseconds passes.
public void interrupt()	Interrupts this thread, causing it to continue execution if it was blocked for any reason.
public final boolean isAlive()	Returns true if the thread is alive, which is any time after the thread has been started but before it runs to completion.

The previous methods are invoked on a particular Thread object. The following methods in the Thread class are static. Invoking one of the static methods performs the operation on the currently running thread.

Function	Description
public static void yield()	Causes the currently running thread to yield to any other threads of the same priority that are waiting to be scheduled.
public static void sleep(long millisec)	Causes the currently running thread to block for at least the specified number of milliseconds.
public static boolean holdsLock(Object x)	Returns true if the current thread holds the lock on the given Object.
public static Thread currentThread()	Returns a reference to the currently running thread, which is the thread that invokes this method.
public static void dumpStack())	Prints the stack trace for the currently running thread, which is useful when debugging a multithreaded application.

Example

The following SampleThreadClassDemo program demonstrates some of these methods of the Thread class. Consider a class PrintMessage which implements Runnable:

```
// File Name: PrintMessage.java
// create a thread by implementing Runnable
public class PrintMessage implements Runnable{
  private String message;
  public PrintMessage(String message){
    this.message = message;
  }
  public void run(){
    while(true){
      System.out.println(message);
    }
  }
}
```

Following is another class which extends Thread class:

```
// File Name: GuessingANumber.java
// Create a thread to extend Thread
public class GuessingANumber extends Thread{
  private int number;
  public GuessingANumber(int number){
    this.number = number;
  }
  public void run(){
    int counter = 0, guess = 0;
    do{
       guess = (int) (Math.random() * 100 + 1);
       System.out.println(this.getName() + " guesses " + guess);
       counter++;
    }while(guess != number);
    System.out.println("** Guess Correct! " + this.getName() +
                                           " in " + counter + " guesses.**");
  }
}
```

Following is the main program which makes use of above defined classes:

```
// File Name: SampleThreadClassDemo.java
public class SampleThreadClassDemo{
  public static void main(String [] args){
    Runnable hello = new PrintMessage("Hello");
    Thread th1 = new Thread(hello);
```

```
        th1.setDaemon(true);
        th1.setName("hello");
        System.out.println("Starting hello thread...");
        th1.start();
        Runnable bye = new PrintMessage("Bye Bye");
        Thread th2= new Thread(bye);
        th2.setPriority(Thread.MIN_PRIORITY);
        th2.setDaemon(true);
        System.out.println("Starting Bye thread...");
        th2.start();
        System.out.println("Starting thread3...");
        Thread th3= new GuessingANumber(27);
        th3.start();
        try{
          th3.join();
        }catch(InterruptedException e){
          System.out.println("Thread interrupted.");
        }
        System.out.println("Starting Thread 4...");
        Thread th4 = new GuessingANumber(75);
        th4.start();
        System.out.println("main() is ending...");
    }
}
```

This would produce the following result. You can try this example again and again and you would get different result every time.

```
Starting hello thread...
Starting Bye thread...
Hello
Hello
Hello
Hello
Hello
Hello
Bye Bye
Bye Bye
Bye Bye
Bye Bye
Bye Bye
.......
```

Question 42: Explain how synchronization works in *Java*.

Answer: Synchronization in *Java* is an important concept since *Java* is multi-threaded language where multiple threads run parallel to complete program execution. Synchronization in *Java* is possible by using java keyword "synchronized" and "volatile". In Summary *Java synchronized* keyword provides following functionality essential for concurrent programming:

- *synchronized* keyword in *Java* provides locking which ensures mutual exclusive access of shared resource and prevents data race.
- *synchronized* keyword also prevents reordering of code statement by compiler which can cause subtle concurrent issue if we don't use synchronized or volatile keyword.
- *synchronized* keyword involves locking and unlocking. Before entering into synchronized method or block thread needs to acquire the lock at this point it reads data from main memory than cache and when it releases the lock it

flushes write operation into main memory which eliminates memory inconsistency errors.

Synchronized keyword in *Java*: Any code written in synchronized block in *Java* will be mutually exclusive and can only be executed by one thread at a time. We can have both static synchronized method and non-static synchronized method and synchronized blocks in *Java* but we cannot have synchronized variable in *Java*. Using *synchronized* keyword with variable is illegal and will result in compilation error.

Instead of *Java* synchronized variable we can have *Java* volatile variable, which will instruct JVM threads to read value of volatile variable from main memory and don't cache it locally. Block synchronization in *Java* is preferred over method synchronization in *Java* because by using block synchronization we only need to lock the critical section of code instead of whole method. Since *Java* synchronization comes with cost of performance we need to synchronize only part of code, which absolutely needs to be synchronized.

Example of synchronized method in *Java*: Using synchronized keyword along with method is easy. It can be done by applying synchronized keyword in front of method. What we need to be vigilant about is that static synchronized method locks on class object lock and non-static synchronized method locks on current object (this).

So it's possible that both static and non-static *Java* synchronized methods run in parallel. This is the common mistake a naive developer does while writing *Java* synchronized code.

```
public class Counter{
  private static int count = 0;
  public static synchronized int getCount(){
    return count;
  }
  public synchoronized setCount(int count){
    this.count = count;
  }
}
```

In this example of *Java* synchronization code is not properly synchronized because both getCount() and setCount() are not locked on same object and can run in parallel. This results in incorrect count. Here getCount() will lock in Counter.class object while setCount() will lock on current object (this). To properly synchronize this code in *Java* you need to either make both methods static or non-static or use *Java* synchronized block instead of *Java* synchronized method.

Example of synchronized block in Java: Using synchronized block in *Java* is also similar to using synchronized keyword in methods. Only important thing to note here is that if object used to lock synchronized block of code, Singleton.class in the example below is null then *Java* synchronized block will throw a NullPointerException.

```
public class Singleton{
  private static volatile Singleton _instance;
  public static Singleton getInstance(){
    if(_instance == null){
      synchronized(Singleton.class){
        if(_instance == null)
          _instance = new Singleton();
      }
    }
    return _instance;
}
```

This is a classic example of double checked locking in Singleton [refer *Design Interview Questions* chapter for more details]. In this example of *Java* synchronized code we have synchronized only critical section (part of code which is creating instance of singleton) and saved some performance because if we synchronize the whole method every call of this method will be blocked while you only need to create instance on first call.

Important points of synchronized keyword in Java:

1. Synchronized keyword in *Java* is used to provide mutual exclusive access of a shared resource with multiple threads in *Java*. Synchronization in *Java* guarantees that no two threads can execute a synchronized method which requires same lock simultaneously or concurrently.
2. You can use *Java* synchronized keyword only on synchronized method or synchronized block.
3. Whenever a thread enters a *Java* synchronized method or block it acquires a lock and whenever it leaves *Java* synchronized method or block it releases the lock. Lock is released even if thread leaves synchronized method after completion or due to any *Error* or *Exception*.
4. *Java* Thread acquires an object level lock when it enters an instance synchronized java method and acquires a class level lock when it enters static synchronized *Java* method.
5. *Java* synchronized keyword is re-entrant in nature. It means if a *Java* synchronized method calls another synchronized method, which requires same lock then current thread which is holding lock can enter that method without acquiring lock.
6. *Java* Synchronization will throw NullPointerException if object used in *Java* synchronized block is null e.g. synchronized (myInstance) will throws NullPointerException if myInstance is null.
7. One Major disadvantage of *Java* synchronized keyword is that it doesn't allow concurrent read which you can implement using

   java.util.concurrent.locks.ReentrantLock.

8. One limitation of *Java* synchronized keyword is that it can only be used to control access of shared object within the same JVM. If we have more than one JVM and need to synchronize access to a shared file system or database, the *Java* synchronized keyword is not adequate. We need to implement a kind of global lock for that.
9. Java synchronized keyword incurs performance cost. Synchronized method in Java is very slow and can degrade performance. So use synchronization in java when it is absolutely required and consider using java synchronized block for synchronizing critical section only.
10. Java synchronized block is better than java synchronized method in java because by using synchronized block you can only lock critical section of code and avoid locking whole method, which can possibly degrade performance. A good example of java synchronization around this concept is *getInstance*() method Singleton class.
11. It's possible that both static synchronized and non-static synchronized method can run simultaneously or concurrently because they lock on different object.
12. *Java synchronized* code could result in deadlock or starvation while accessing by multiple thread if synchronization is not implemented correctly. To know how to avoid deadlock in java see here.
13. According to the *Java* language specification you cannot use java synchronized keyword with constructor. It's illegal and results in compilation errors. So you cannot synchronize constructor in Java, which seems logical because other threads cannot see the object being created until the thread creating it has finished it.
14. You cannot apply java synchronized keyword with variables and cannot use Java volatile keyword with method.

15. Java.util.concurrent.locks extends capability provided by java synchronized keyword for writing more sophisticated programs since they offer more capabilities e.g. Reentrancy and interruptible locks.
16. *Java synchronized* keyword also synchronizes memory.
17. Important method related to synchronization in Java are wait(), notify() and notifyAll() which is defined in Object class.
18. Do not synchronize on non-final field on synchronized block in *Java* because reference of non final field may change any time and then different threads might synchronize on different objects i.e. no synchronization at all. example of synchronizing on non-final fields:

```
private String lock = new String("lock");
synchronized(lock){
   System.out.println("locking on :" + lock);
}
```

If you write synchronized code like above in *Java* you may get a warning "Synchronization on non-final field" in IDE like Netbeans and InteliJ.
19. It's not recommended to use String object as lock in Java synchronized block because string is immutable object and literal string and interned string get stored in String pool. So by any chance if any other part of code or any third party library uses same String as it's lock then they both will be locked on same object despite being completely unrelated which could result in unexpected behavior and bad performance. Instead of String object it is advised to use new Object() for Synchronization in Java on synchronized block.

```
private static final String LOCK = "lock";   //not recommended
private static final Object OBJ_LOCK = new Object(); //better
public void process() {
  synchronized(LOCK) {
    ........
  }
}
```

20. From *Java* library Calendar and SimpleDateFormat classes are not thread-safe and requires external synchronization in Java to be used in multi-threaded environment.

Question 43: Solve producer/consumer problem using *Java* threads.

Answer: refer *Operating System Concepts* chapter.

Question 44: What is the size of empty class in $C++$, *Java*?

Answer: Since each object needs to have a unique address (also defined in the standard) we can't really have zero sized objects. Imagine an array of zero sized objects. Because they have zero size they all line up on the same address location. So, it is easier to say that objects cannot have zero size. Even though an object has a non-zero size, if it actually takes up zero room it does not need to increase the size of derived class.

```
#include <iostream>
class A {};
class B {};
class C: public A, B {};
int main() {
    std::cout << sizeof(A) << "\n"; //Prints 1
    std::cout << sizeof(B) << "\n"; //Prints 1
    std::cout << sizeof(C) << "\n"; //Prints 1
}
```

Question 45: What's the value of i++ + i++ in C and $C++$?

Answer: It's undefined. Basically, in C and $C++$, if we read a variable twice in an expression where you also write it, the result is undefined. Don't do that. Another example is: v[i] = i++; Related example: func(v[i],i++);

Here, the result is undefined because the order of evaluation of function arguments is undefined. Having the order of evaluation *undefined* is claimed to yield better performing code.

Question 46: What is the difference between *int main*() and *int main(void)* in C and C++?

Answer: In C++, there is no difference. In C++ having a function func(void) and func() is the same thing. In C, in a prototype (not in C++ though) an empty argument list means that the function could take any number of arguments (in the definition of a function, it means no arguments). In C++, an empty parameter list means no arguments. In C, to get no arguments, you have to use void.

```
void foo(void);
```

That is the correct way to say *no parameters* in C, and it also works in C++. But:

```
void foo();
```

Means different things in C and C++! In C it means "could take any number of parameters of unknown types", and in C++ it means the same as foo(void).

Question 47: What is the difference between *String* and *StringBuffer* classes in *Java*?

Answer: *Java* provides the StringBuffer and String classes, and the String class is used to manipulate character strings that cannot be changed. Simply stated, objects of type String are read only and immutable. The *StringBuffer* class is used to represent characters that can be modified.

The significant performance difference between these two classes is that *StringBuffer* is faster than *String* when performing simple concatenations. In *String* manipulation code, character strings are routinely concatenated. Using the *String* class, concatenations are typically performed as follows:

```
String str = new String ("Testing the ");
str += "strings!!";
```

If we were to use *StringBuffer* to perform the same concatenation, we would need code that looks like this:

```
StringBuffer str = new StringBuffer ("Testing the ");
str.append("strings!!");
```

Developers usually assume that the first example above is more efficient because they think that the second example, which uses the append method for concatenation, is more costly than the first example, which uses the + operator to concatenate two *String* objects.

Question 48: What is the difference between "==" and *equals*(...) method in *Java*? What is the difference between shallow comparison and deep comparison of objects?

Answer: The == returns true, if the variable reference points to the same object in memory. This is a "shallow comparison". The *equals*() - returns the results of running the *equals*() method of a user supplied class, which compares the attribute values.

The *equals*() method provides "deep comparison" by checking if two objects are logically equal as opposed to the shallow comparison provided by the operator ==. If *equals*() method does not exist in a user supplied class than the inherited Object class's *equals*() method is run which evaluates if the references point to the same object in memory. The object.equals() works just like the "==" operator (i.e. shallow comparison).

Question 49: What is serialization? How would you exclude a field of a class from serialization or what is a transient variable?

Answer: Serialization is a process of reading or writing an object. It is a process of saving an object's state to a sequence of bytes, as well as a process of rebuilding those bytes back into a live object at some future time. An object is marked serializable by implementing the *java.io.Serializable* interface, which is only a marker interface -- it simply allows the serialization mechanism to verify that the class can be persisted, typically to a file.

Transient variables cannot be serialized. The fields marked transient in a serializable object will not be transmitted in the byte stream. An example would be a file handle, a database connection, a system thread etc. Such objects are only meaningful locally. So they should be marked as transient in a serializable class.

Question 50: What is the difference between *final*, *finally* and *finalize*() in *Java*?

Answer: *final* - constant declaration. *Final* class cannot be inherited and final mehod cannot be overridden. *finally* handles exception. The finally block is optional and provides a mechanism to clean up regardless of what happens within the try block (except *System.exit*(0) call). Use the *finally* block to close files or to release other system resources like database connections, statements etc.

finalize() - method helps in garbage collection. A method that is invoked before an object is discarded by the garbage collector, allowing it to clean up its state. Should not be used to release non-memory resources like file handles, sockets, database connections etc. because Java has only a finite number of these resources and you do not know when the garbage collection is going to kick in to release these non-memory resources through the finalize() method.

Question 51: What do you know about the *Java garbage collector*?

Answer: Each time an object is created in Java, it goes into the area of memory known as heap. The Java heap is called the *garbage collectable heap*. The garbage collection cannot be forced. The garbage collector runs in low memory situations. When it runs, it releases the memory allocated by an unreachable object. The garbage collector runs on a low priority daemon (i.e. background) thread. We can nicely ask the garbage collector to collect garbage by calling *System.gc*() but we can't force it.

An object's life has no meaning unless something has reference to it. If we can't reach it then we can't ask it to do anything. Then the object becomes unreachable and the garbage collector will figure it out. Java automatically collects all the unreachable objects periodically and releases the memory consumed by those unreachable objects to be used by the future reachable objects.

Question 52: What is the diamond problem? Does it exist in Java? If so, how can it be avoided?

Answer: Taking a look at the figure below helps in explaining the diamond problem. In the diagram above, we have 2 classes B and C that derive from the same class – which would be class A in the diagram above. We also have class D that derives from both B and C by using multiple inheritance. You can see in the figure above that the classes essentially form the shape of a diamond – which is why this problem is called the diamond problem.

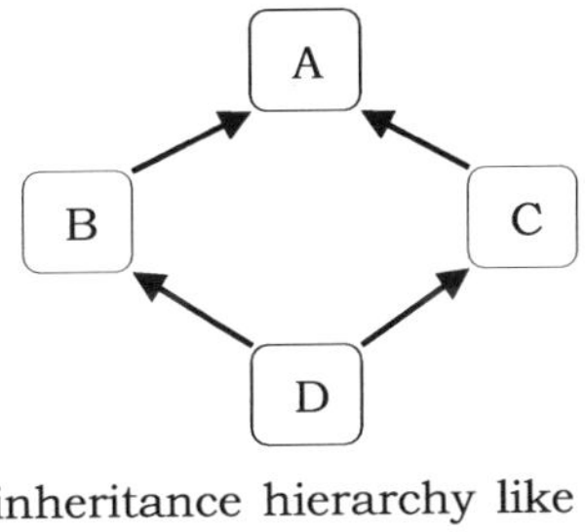

The problem with having an inheritance hierarchy like the one shown in the diagram above is that when we instantiate an object of class D, any calls to method definitions in class A will be ambiguous – because it's not sure whether to call the version of the method derived from class B or class C.

Java does not have multiple inheritance

But, wait one second. Java does not have multiple inheritance! This means that Java is not at risk of suffering the consequences of the diamond problem. However, C++ does have multiple inheritance, and if you want to read more about the diamond problem in C++, check this out: Diamond problem in C++.

Java uses interfaces to support multiple inheritance

Java has interfaces which do allow it to mimic multiple inheritance. Although interfaces give us something similar to multiple inheritance, the implementation of those interfaces is singly (as opposed to multiple) inherited. This means that problems like the diamond problem – in which the compiler is confused as to which method to use – will not occur in Java.

Question 53: What is the difference between declaring a variable and defining a variable?

Answer: In declaration we just mention the type of the variable and its name. We do not initialize it. But defining means declaration and initialization. For example, *String s;* is just a declaration while *String s = new String ("abcd");* and *String s = "abcd";* are both definitions.

Question 54: What is serialization?

Answer: Serialization is a mechanism by which you can save the state of an object by converting it to a byte stream.

Question 55: How do we serialize an object to a file?

Answer: The class whose instances are to be serialized should implement an interface *Serializable*. Then you pass the instance to the *ObjectOutputStream* which is connected to a *fileoutputstream*. This will save the object to a file.

Question 56: Explain JDBC.

Answer: JDBC is the short for Java Database Connectivity. It is a Java API that enables Java programs to execute SQL statements. This allows Java programs to interact with any SQL-compliant database. Since nearly all relational database management systems (DBMSs) support SQL, and because Java itself runs on most platforms, JDBC makes it possible to write a single database application that can run on different platforms and interact with different DBMSs.

JDBC is similar to ODBC (Open DataBase Connectivity), but is designed specifically for Java programs, whereas ODBC is language-independent. ODBC a standard database access method developed by the SQL Access group in 1992. The goal of ODBC is to make it possible to access any data from any application, regardless of which database management system (DBMS) is handling the data.

ODBC manages this by inserting a middle layer, called a *database driver*, between an application and the DBMS. The purpose of this layer is to translate the application's data queries into commands that the DBMS understands. For this to work, both the application and the DBMS must be ODBC-compliant -- that is, the application must be capable of issuing ODBC commands and the DBMS must be capable of responding to them.

Creating JDBC Application

There are six steps involved in building a JDBC application which we are going to discuss in this section:

Step 1: Import The Packages

This requires that you include the packages containing the JDBC classes needed for database programming. Most often, using import java.sql.* will suffice as follows:

```
import java.sql.*;
```

Step 2: Register The JDBC Driver

This requires that you initialize a driver so you can open a communications channel with the database. Following is the code snippet to achieve this:

```
Class.forName("com.mysql.jdbc.Driver");
```

Step 3: Open a Connection

This requires using the DriverManager.getConnection() method to create a Connection object, which represents a physical connection with the database as follows:

```
// Privide authentication parameters
static final String USER = "username";
static final String PASS = "password";
System.out.println("Connecting to database...");
conn = DriverManager.getConnection(DB_URL,USER,PASS);
```

Step 4: Execute a Query

This requires using an object of type Statement or PreparedStatement for building and submitting an SQL statement to the database as follows:

```
System.out.println("Creating statement...");
stmt = conn.createStatement();
String sql;
sql = "SELECT id, firstName, lastName, age FROM Students";
ResultSet rs = stmt.executeQuery(sql);
```

If there is an SQL UPDATE,INSERT or DELETE statement required, then following code snippet would be required:

```
System.out.println("Creating statement...");
stmt = conn.createStatement();
String sql;
sql = "DELETE FROM Students";
ResultSet rs = stmt.executeUpdate(sql);
```

Step 5: Extract Data From Result Set

This step is required in case you are fetching data from the database. You can use the appropriate ResultSet.getXXX() method to retrieve the data from the result set as follows:

```
while(rs.next()){
   //Retrieve by column name
   int id  = rs.getInt("id");
   int age = rs.getInt("age");
   String firstName = rs.getString("first");
   String lastName = rs.getString("last");
   //Display values
   System.out.print("ID: " + id);
   System.out.print(", Age: " + age);
   System.out.print(", First Name: " + firstName);
   System.out.println(", Last Name: " + lastName);
}
```

Step 6: Clean Up The Environment

You should explicitly close all database resources versus relying on the JVM's garbage collection as follows:

```
//Step 6: Clean-up environment
rs.close();
stmt.close();
conn.close();
```

Sample JDBC Program

Based on the above steps, we can have following consolidated sample code which we can use as a template while writing our JDBC code:

```
//Step 1. Import required packages
import java.sql.*;
public class FirstExample {
  // JDBC driver name and database URL
  static final String JDBC_DRIVER = "com.mysql.jdbc.Driver";
  static final String DB_URL = "jdbc:mysql://localhost/EMP";
  //  Database credentials
  static final String USER = "username";
  static final String PASS = "password";
  public static void main(String[] args) {
  Connection conn = null;
  Statement stmt = null;
  try{
      //Step 2: Register JDBC driver
      Class.forName("com.mysql.jdbc.Driver");
      //Step 3: Open a connection
      System.out.println("Connecting to database...");
      conn = DriverManager.getConnection(DB_URL,USER,PASS);
      //Step 4: Execute a query
      System.out.println("Creating statement...");
      stmt = conn.createStatement();
      String sql;
      sql = "SELECT id, first, last, age FROM Students";
      ResultSet rs = stmt.executeQuery(sql);
      //Step 5: Extract data from result set
      while(rs.next()){
        //Retrieve by column name
        int id  = rs.getInt("id");
        int age = rs.getInt("age");
        String firstName = rs.getString("firstName");
        String lastName = rs.getString("lastName");
        //Displaying values
        System.out.print("ID: " + id);
        System.out.print(", Age: " + age);
        System.out.print(", First Name: " + firstName);
        System.out.println(", Last Name: " + lastName);
      }
      //Step 6: Clean-up environment
      rs.close();
      stmt.close();
      conn.close();
    }catch(SQLException se){
      //Handle errors for JDBC
      se.printStackTrace();
    }catch(Exception e){
      //Handle errors for Class.forName
      e.printStackTrace();
```

```
    }finally{
      //finally block used to close resources
      try{
        if(stmt!=null)
          stmt.close();
      }catch(SQLException se2){
      }
      try{
        if(conn!=null)
          conn.close();
      }catch(SQLException se){
        se.printStackTrace();
      }
    }
  }
}
```

Question 57: What is the difference between const int*, const int * const, int const * in C/C++?

Answer: Read it backwards...

int*	pointer to int
int const *	pointer to const int
int * const	const pointer to int
int const * const	const pointer to const int

For example, consider the following declarations:

"const Item* ptr", "Item* const ptr" and "const Item* const ptr"

We have to read pointer declarations right-to-left.

- *const Item * ptr* means "ptr points to an Item that is const" — that is, the Item object can't be changed via ptr.
- *Item * const ptr* means "ptr is a const pointer to an Item" — that is, you can change the Item object via ptr, but you can't change the pointer ptr itself.
- *const Item * const ptr* means "ptr is a const pointer to a const Item" — that is, you can't change the pointer ptr itself, nor can you change the Item object via ptr.

Now the first const can be on either side of the type so:

```
const int * == int const *
const int * const == int const * const
```

Question 58: What are the differences between .dll and .lib?

Answer: A *dll* is a library of functions that are shared among other executable programs. Just look in your windows/system32 directory and you will find many of them. When your program creates a *dll* it also normally creates a lib file so that the application *.exe program can resolve symbols that are declared in the *dll*.

A .lib is a library of functions that are statically linked to a program. They are not shared by other programs. Each program that links with a *.lib file has all the code in that file. If you have two programs *X.exe* and *Y.exe* that link with *Z.lib* then each *X* and *Y* will both contain the code in *Z.lib*.

How you create dlls and libs depend on the compiler you use. Each compiler does it differently.

Question 59: What is the difference between big and little endian?

Answer: The big-endian and little-endian refer to which bytes are most significant in multi-byte data types and describe the order in which a sequence of bytes is stored in a computer memory.

If the hardware is built so that the lowest, least significant byte of a multi-byte scalar is stored *first*, at the lowest memory address, then the hardware is said to be *little-endian*; the *little* end of the integer gets stored first, and the next bytes get stored in higher (increasing) memory locations. Little-Endian byte order is "littlest end goes first (to the littlest address)".

Machines such as the Intel/AMD x86, Digital VAX, and Digital Alpha, handle scalars in Little-Endian form.

If the hardware is built so that the highest, most significant byte of a multi-byte scalar is stored *first*, at the lowest memory address, then the hardware is said to be *big-endian*; the *big* end of the integer gets stored first, and the next bytes get stored in higher (increasing) memory locations. Big-Endian byte order is "biggest end goes first (to the lowest address)".

Machines such as IBM mainframes, the Motorola 680x0, Sun SPARC, PowerPC, and most RISC machines, handle scalars in Big-Endian form.

Four-byte Integer Example

Consider the four-byte integer 0x44332211. The "*little*" end byte, the lowest or least significant byte, is 0x11, and the "*big*" end byte, the highest or most significant byte, is 0x44. The two memory storage patterns for the four bytes are:

Four-Byte Integer: 0x44332211

Memory address	Big-Endian byte value	Little-Endian byte value
104	11	44
103	22	33
102	33	22
101	44	11

Here is sample code to determine what is the type of your machine

```
#include <stdio.h>
int main(void) {
    int num = 1;
    if(*(char *)&num == 1){
        printf("\nLittle-Endian\n");
    }
    else {
        printf("Big-Endian\n");
    }
    return 0;
}
```

Question 60: Explain the concept of C++ Containers and STL.

Answer: The C++ STL (Standard Template Library) is a set of C++ template classes to provides general-purpose templatized classes and functions that implement many popular and commonly used algorithms and data structures like vectors, lists, queues, and stacks. A container is an object that stores a collection of other objects (its elements). They are implemented as class templates, which allows a great flexibility in the types supported as elements.

The container manages the storage space for its elements and provides member functions to access them, either directly or through iterators (reference objects with similar properties to pointers). Containers replicate structures very commonly used in programming: dynamic arrays (vector), queues (queue), stacks (stack), heaps (priority_queue), linked lists (list), trees (set), associative arrays (map), etc...

Many containers have several member functions in common, and share functionalities. The decision of which type of container to use for a specific need does not generally depend only on the functionality offered by the container, but also on the efficiency of some of its members (complexity). This is especially true for linear containers, which offer different trade-offs in complexity between inserting/removing elements and accessing them.

Container Classes	
Sequences	• *vector*: Vectors are sequence containers representing arrays that can change in size. • *deque*: Array which supports insertion/removal of elements at beginning or end of array. It is a double ended queue with pop and push at both ends. • *list*: Linked list of variables, struct or objects. It is a randomly changing sequence of items.
Associative Containers	• *set* (duplicate data not allowed in set), multiset (duplication allowed): It is an unordered collection of items. • *map* (unique keys), multimap (duplicate keys allowed): Associative key-value pair held in balanced binary tree structure. An collection of pairs of items indexed by the first one.
Container Adapters	• *stack* [LIFO]: A sequence of items with pop and push at one end only. • *queue* [FIFO]: A Sequence of items with pop and push at opposite ends. • $priority_{queue}$: It returns element with highest priority.
String	• *string*: Character strings and manipulation. • *rope*: String storage and manipulation.
Bits	• *bitset*: Contains a more intuitive method of storing and manipulating bits.
Operations/Utilities	• *iterator*: STL class to represent position in an STL container. An iterator is declared to be associated with a single container class type. • *algorithm*: Routines to find, count, sort, search, ... elements in container classes. • *auto_ptr*: Class to manage memory pointers and avoid memory leaks.

Sample Code:

```
#include <iostream>
#include <vector>
#include <string>
using namespace std;
main(){
  vector<string> stk;
  stk.push_back("The number is 100");
  stk.push_back("The number is 200");
  stk.push_back("The number is 300");
  cout << "Loop by index:" << endl;
  int i;
  for(i=0; i < stk.size(); i++){
    cout << stk[i] << endl;
  }
  cout << endl << "Constant Iterator:" << endl;
  vector<string>::const_iterator ci;
  for(ci=stk.begin(); ci!=stk.end(); ci++){
    cout << *ci << endl;
  }
```

```
    cout << endl << "Reverse Iterator:" << endl;
    vector<string>::reverse_iterator ri;
    for(ri=stk.rbegin(); ri!=stk.rend(); ++ri){
        cout << *ri << endl;
    }
    cout << endl << "Output:" << endl;
    cout << stk.size() << endl;
    cout << stk[2] << endl;
    swap(stk[0], stk[2]);
    cout << stk[2] << endl;
}
```

Question 61: Explain the concept of smart pointers in C++.

Answer: The power of C++ comes with pointers and objects. In C++, pointers are very commonly used, but the built-in pointers may give unexpected results if they were not used properly. When a built-in pointer is created, it is not automatically set to NULL. If an uninitialized pointer is then compared to NULL (*pointer == NULL*) the test will pass, and any dereferencing will result in undefined behavior.

It's fairly easy to remember to set a pointer to NULL when you create it, so this issue isn't that important, but what if you call a function that returns a pointer? If the memory was allocated on the heap (i.e. came from a call to *new* or *malloc*) then someone has to delete it, or it will be a memory leak. It's up to the programmer to read the documentation and figure it out.

What about in a multi-threaded environment? It's very easy for two threads to share the same data, but what if both of them are using the same pointer, and one thread calls delete on the pointer while the other thread is still using it?

Finally, if you're using exceptions, you've probably had a pretty hard time making sure that each time an exception is thrown, all of the allocated memory gets freed. Take the following code:

```
    try{
        int* ptr = new int;
        Foo();
        .
        delete ptr;
    }
```

What if *Foo* throws an exception? You have to make sure that each and every exception that *Foo* (or any function called by *Foo*) throws will be caught, in order to *delete ptr*; otherwise you'll have a memory leak. Certainly there must be a better solution than using these built-in pointers. The answer for such problems is smart pointers.

The idea behind this *smart pointer* implementation is to have a set of objects that wrap the functionality of a built-in pointer. These smart pointers either *point* to an object or they equal NULL (they never point to memory that has been deleted and they are always initialized).

- The pointers must always point to valid memory, or be NULL
- The pointers will be reference counted and handle freeing the memory being pointed to (so they can be exception safe while at the same time eliminating memory leaks)
- The pointers should be as similar to the built-in pointers as possible

Also, in order for the *smart pointers* to act like the built-in types, it was necessary for the implementation to be non-intrusive. An intrusive smart pointer is one that requires a common base class be used in any object that will be pointed to. When you create your custom objects, you would have to inherit from a base class the gives reference counting functionality to your object. This approach only works for user defined types, and the *smart pointers* would never be able to point to built-in types (like int and float).

A non-intrusive approach requires no changes to a defined type (whether built-in or user defined) because the pointer has a more intelligent means of keeping track of the reference count.

With smart pointers, the programmer doesn't have to worry about memory management (never see the word *delete* again!), the pointers are copy safe, thread safe, exception safe, and they never point to memory that has already been deleted. If used properly, they avoid circular references, and they work almost identically to the built-in pointers.

Question 62: Explain the concept of auto_ptr in C++.

Answer: The standard C++ library comes with a smart pointer called auto_ptr, for "automatic pointer." The auto_ptr smart pointer owns the object it holds a pointer to. That is, it releases the memory associated to it upon destruction; it does not do any allocation by itself, nor does it keep a reference counter of the memory involved.

The auto_ptr class overloads the * and -> operators so as to allow transparent access to the dynamic object. To access the raw pointer itself, use the get method. Consider a simple example:

```
std::auto_ptr<int> ptr1(new int(5));
*ptr1 = 4;
std::cout << *ptr1 << std::endl;
int* ptr2 = ptr1.get();
*ptr2 = 3;
std::cout << *ptr1 << ", " << *ptr2 << std::endl;
```

It is important to note in the example above that auto_ptr's constructor cannot fail (it is declared as throws()) If it could, the code would need to be more complex in order to catch those failures, defeating in part the purpose of the smart pointer. The automatic pointer also provides the release method, which detaches itself from the memory object, returning a raw pointer to it. This allows the use of an automatic pointer in a critical section only, falling back to manual management once that delicate code is over. As an example, imagine a function that returns a raw pointer to a dynamically allocated object. This function needs to do multiple initialization tasks and has several exit points if errors happen. You can use an automatic pointer to simplify its code:

```
foo * get_new_foo(void){
    std::auto_ptr<foo> obj(new foo);
    // The following two operations can raise an exception.
    // We need not care about it thanks to the smart pointer.
    obj->do_something();
    obj->do_something_else();
    // We are done.  The caller is only interested in the raw
    // pointer, which we can safely return now.
    return obj.release();
}
```

Automatic pointers are not copyable. If the developer attempts to copy an instance of auto_ptr, the object it points to will be transferred to the new smart pointer, invalidating the old one. Therefore, using this class together with STL collections is dangerous; don't do it, because it does not follow the required semantics.

```
std::auto_ptr<int> ptr1(new int(5));
// ptr1 is valid and can be accessed.
*ptr1 = 4;
std::auto_ptr<int> ptr2(ptr1);
// ptr2 now owns the dynamically allocated integer, so we can access it.
*ptr2 = 3;
// However, ptr1 is now longer valid; the following crashes the program.
*ptr1 = 2;
// At last, the following has undefined behavior.
```

```
int* i = new int(1);
std::auto_ptr<int> ptr3(i);
std::auto_ptr<int> ptr4(i);
```

Furthermore, if two automatic pointers hold a reference to the same memory object, the behavior is undefined (but typically the application will simply crash).

Note: In the C++11 standard, *std::unique_ptr* is used instead of *std::auto_ptr*.

Question 63: What is Serialization and Deserialization in Java?

Answer: We can convert a Java object to an Stream that is called *Serialization*. Once an object is converted to Stream, it can be saved to file or send over the network or used in socket connections. The object should implement Serializable interface and we can use java.io.ObjectOutputStream to write object to file or to any OutputStream object. The process of converting stream data created through serialization to Object is called *deserialization*.

Question 64: Why Java is not pure Object Oriented language?

Answer: Java is not said to be pure object oriented because it support primitive types such as int, byte, short, long etc. I believe it brings simplicity to the language while writing our code. Obviously java could have wrapper objects for the primitive types but just for the representation, they would not have provided any benefit.

As we know, for all the primitive types we have wrapper classes such as Integer, Long etc. that provides some additional methods.

Question 65: What is difference between *path* and *classpath* variables?

Answer: PATH is an environment variable used by operating system to locate the executable. That's why when we install Java or want any executable to be found by OS, we need to add the directory location in the PATH variable.

Classpath is specific to java and used by java executables to locate class files. We can provide the classpath location while running java application and it can be a directory, ZIP files, JAR files etc.

Question 66: Can we have multiple public classes in a java source file?

Answer: We can't have more than one public class in a single java source file. A single source file can have multiple classes that are not public.

Question 67: What is final keyword?

Answer: *final* keyword is used with Class to make sure no other class can extend it, for example String class is final and we can't extend it.

We can use *final* keyword with methods to make sure child classes can't override it.

final keyword can be used with variables to make sure that it can be assigned only once. However the state of the variable can be changed, for example we can assign a final variable to an object only once but the object variables can change later on.

Java interface variables are by default *final* and *static*.

Question 68: What is static keyword?

Answer: *static* keyword can be used with class level variables to make it global i.e all the objects will share the same variable.

static keyword can be used with methods also. A *static method* can access only static variables of class and invoke only static methods of the class.

Question 69: What is finally and finalize in Java?

Answer: *finally* block is used with try-catch to put the code that you want to get executed always, even if any exception is thrown by the try-catch block. finally block is mostly used to release resources created in the try block.

finalize() is a special method in Object class that we can override in our classes. This method gets called by garbage collector when the object is getting garbage collected. This method is usually overridden to release system resources when object is garbage collected.

Question 70: Can we declare a class as static?

Answer: We can't declare a top-level class as static however an inner class can be declared as static. If inner class is declared as static, it's called static nested class. Static nested class is same as any other top-level class and is nested for only packaging convenience.

Question 71: What is *static* import?

Answer: If we have to use any static variable or method from other class, usually we import the class and then use the method/variable with class name.

```
import java.lang.Math;
//inside class
double test = Math.PI * 5;
```

We can do the same thing by importing the static method or variable only and then use it in the class as if it belongs to it.

```
import static java.lang.Math.PI;
//no need to refer class now
double test = PI * 5;
```

Use of static import can cause confusion, so it's better to avoid it. Overuse of static import can make your program unreadable and unmaintainable.

Question 72: What is Java *Annotations*?

Answer: Java Annotations provide information about the code and they have no direct effect on the code they annotate. Annotations are introduced in Java 5. Annotation is metadata about the program embedded in the program itself.

It can be parsed by the annotation parsing tool or by compiler. We can also specify annotation availability to either compile time only or till runtime also. Java Built-in annotations are @Override, @Deprecated and @SuppressWarnings.

Question 73: What is *anonymous inner* class?

Answer: A local inner class without name is known as anonymous inner class. An anonymous class is defined and instantiated in a single statement. Anonymous inner class always extend a class or implement an interface. Since an anonymous class has no name, it is not possible to define a constructor for an anonymous class. Anonymous inner classes are accessible only at the point where it is defined.

Question 74: What is *Classloader* in Java?

Answer: Java Classloader is the program that loads byte code program into memory when we want to access any class. We can create our own classloader by extending ClassLoader class and overriding loadClass(String name) method.

Question 75: What is this keyword?

Answer: this keyword provides reference to the current object and it's mostly used to make sure that object variables are used, not the local variables having same name.

```
//constructor
public Point(int x, int y) {
    this.x = x;
    this.y = y;
}
```

We can also use this keyword to invoke other constructors from a constructor.

```
public Rectangle() {
   this(0, 0, 0, 0);
}
public Rectangle(int width, int height) {
   this(0, 0, width, height);
}
public Rectangle(int x, int y, int width, int height) {
   this.x = x;
   this.y = y;
   this.width = width;
   this.height = height;
}
```

Question 76: What is the use of *System* class?

Answer: Java System Class is one of the core classes. One of the easiest way to log information for debugging is System.out.print() method.

System class is final and static so that we can't subclass and override it's behavior through inheritance. System class doesn't provide any public constructors, so we can't instantiate this class and that's why all of its methods are static.

Some of the utility methods of System class are for array copy, get current time, reading environment variables.

Question 77: What is *instanceof* keyword?

Answer: We can use *instanceof* keyword to check if an object belongs to a class or not. We should avoid it's usage as much as possible. Sample usage is:

```
public static void main(String args[]){
   Object str = new String("Test");
   if(str instanceof String){
      System.out.println("String value:"+str);
   }
   if(str instanceof Integer){
      System.out.println("Integer value:"+str);
   }
}
```

Since str is of type String at runtime, first *if* statement evaluates to true and second one to false.

Question 78: Can we have try without catch block in Java?

Answer: Yes, we can have try-finally statement and hence avoiding catch block.

Question 79: What does super keyword do?

Answer: *super* keyword can be used to access *super* class method when you have overridden the method in the child class.

We can use *super* keyword to invoke super class constructor in child class constructor but in this case it should be the first statement in the constructor method.

```
package com.journaldev.access;
public class SuperClass {
   public SuperClass(){
   }
   public SuperClass(int i){}
   public void test(){
      System.out.println("super class test method");
```

```
    }
}
```

Use of super keyword can be seen in below child class implementation.

```
package com.journaldev.access;
public class ChildClass extends SuperClass {
    public ChildClass(String str){
        //access super class constructor with super keyword
        super();
        //access child class method
        test();
        //use super to access super class method
        super.test();
    }
    @Override
    public void test(){
        System.out.println("child class test method");
    }
}
```

Question 80: Explain the concepts of Java Servlets and JavaServer Pages (JSP).

Answer: JavaServer Pages (JSP) is a technology for developing web pages that support dynamic content which helps developers insert java code in HTML pages by making use of special JSP tags, most of which start with <% and end with %>.

A JavaServer Pages component is a type of Java servlet that is designed to fulfill the role of a user interface for a Java web application. Web developers write JSPs as text files that combine HTML or XHTML code, XML elements, and embedded JSP actions and commands.

Using JSP, you can collect input from users through web page forms, present records from a database or another source, and create web pages dynamically.

JSP tags can be used for a variety of purposes, such as retrieving information from a database or registering user preferences, accessing JavaBeans components, passing control between pages and sharing information between requests, pages etc.

JavaServer Pages often serve the same purpose as programs implemented using the Common Gateway Interface (CGI). But JSP offer several advantages in comparison with the CGI.

- Performance is significantly better because JSP allows embedding Dynamic Elements in HTML Pages itself instead of having a separate CGI files.
- JSP are always compiled before it's processed by the server unlike CGI/Perl which requires the server to load an interpreter and the target script each time the page is requested.
- JavaServer Pages are built on top of the Java Servlets API, so like Servlets, JSP also has access to all the powerful Enterprise Java APIs, including JDBC, JNDI, EJB, JAXP etc.
- JSP pages can be used in combination with servlets that handle the business logic, the model supported by Java servlet template engines.

Finally, JSP is an integral part of Java EE, a complete platform for enterprise class applications. This means that JSP can play a part in the simplest applications to the most complex and demanding.

How it works?

The web server (such as Apache) needs a JSP engine ie. container to process JSP pages. The JSP container (such as WebLogic) is responsible for intercepting requests for JSP pages. This tutorial makes use of Apache which has built-in JSP container to support JSP pages development.

A JSP container works with the Web server to provide the runtime environment and other services a JSP needs. It knows how to understand the special elements that are part of JSPs.

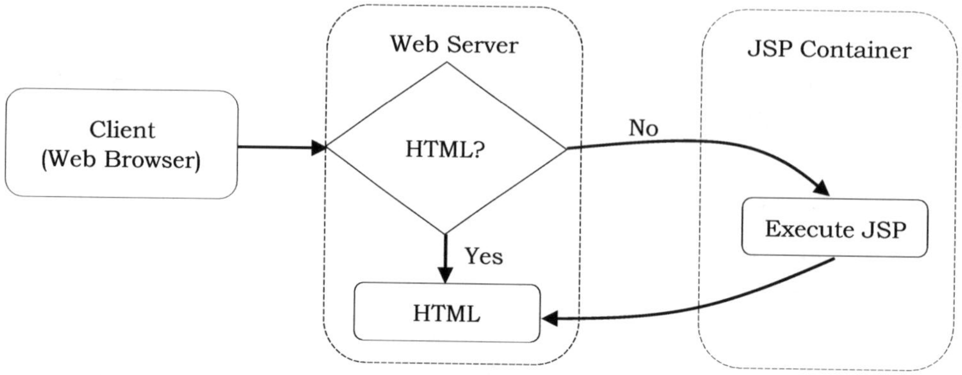

The following steps explain how the web server creates the web page using JSP:

- As with a normal page, your browser sends an HTTP request to the web server.
- The web server recognizes that the HTTP request is for a JSP page and forwards it to a JSP engine. This is done by using the URL or JSP page which ends with .jsp instead of .html.
- The JSP engine loads the JSP page from disk and converts it into a servlet content. This conversion is very simple in which all template text is converted to println( ) statements and all JSP elements are converted to Java code that implements the corresponding dynamic behavior of the page.
- The JSP engine compiles the servlet into an executable class and forwards the original request to a servlet engine.
- A part of the web server called the servlet engine loads the Servlet class and executes it. During execution, the servlet produces an output in HTML format, which the servlet engine passes to the web server inside an HTTP response.
- The web server forwards the HTTP response to your browser in terms of static HTML content.
- Finally web browser handles the dynamically generated HTML page inside the HTTP response exactly as if it were a static page.

JSP Life Cycle

A JSP life cycle can be defined as the entire process from its creation till the destruction which is similar to a servlet life cycle with an additional step which is required to compile a JSP into servlet. The following are the paths followed by a JSP.

1. Compilation
2. Initialization
3. Execution
4. Cleanup

1.*JSP Compilation*: When a browser asks for a JSP, the JSP engine first checks to see whether it needs to compile the page. If the page has never been compiled, or if the JSP has been modified since it was last compiled, the JSP engine compiles the page. The compilation process involves three steps:

1. Parsing the JSP.
2. Turning the JSP into a servlet.
3. Compiling the servlet.

2.*JSP Initialization*: When a container loads a JSP it invokes the jspInit() method before servicing any requests. If you need to perform JSP-specific initialization, override the jspInit() method:

```
public void jspInit(){
  // Initialization code...
}
```

Typically initialization is performed only once and as with the servlet *init* method, you generally initialize database connections, open files, and create lookup tables in the jspInit method.

3.*JSP Execution*: This phase of the JSP life cycle represents all interactions with requests until the JSP is destroyed. Whenever a browser requests a JSP and the page has been loaded and initialized, the JSP engine invokes the _jspService() method in the JSP. The _jspService() method takes an HttpServletRequest and an HttpServletResponse as its parameters as follows:

```
void _jspService(HttpServletRequest request, HttpServletResponse response){
  // Service handling code...
}
```

The _jspService() method of a JSP is invoked once per a request and is responsible for generating the response for that request and this method is also responsible for generating responses to all seven of the HTTP methods ie. GET, POST, DELETE etc.

4.*JSP Cleanup*: The destruction phase of the JSP life cycle represents when a JSP is being removed from use by a container. The jspDestroy() method is the JSP equivalent of the destroy method for servlets. Override jspDestroy when you need to perform any cleanup, such as releasing database connections or closing open files. The jspDestroy() method has the following form:

```
public void jspDestroy(){
  // cleanup code
}
```

jspInit(), _jspService() and jspDestroy() are called the life cycle methods of the JSP.

Question 81: What are Javabeans?

Answer: *super* keyword can be used to access super class method when you have JavaBeans is an object-oriented programming interface from Oracle that lets you build re-useable applications or program building blocks called components that can be deployed in a network on any major operating system platform. Like Java applets, JavaBeans components (or "Beans") can be used to give World Wide Web pages (or other applications) interactive capabilities such as computing interest rates or varying page content based on user or browser characteristics.

From a user's point-of-view, a component can be a button that you interact with or a small calculating program that gets initiated when you press the button. From a developer's point-of-view, the button component and the calculator component are created separately and can then be used together or in different combinations with other components in different applications or situations.

When the components or Beans are in use, the properties of a Bean (for example, the background color of a window) are visible to other Beans and Beans that haven't "met" before can learn each other's properties dynamically and interact accordingly.

Beans are developed with a Beans Development Kit (BDK) from Oracle and can be run on any major operating system platform inside a number of application environments (called *containers*), including browsers, word processors, and other applications.

To build a component with JavaBeans, you write language statements using Oracle's Java programming language and include JavaBeans statements that describe component properties such as user interface characteristics and events that trigger a bean to communicate with other beans in the same container or elsewhere in the network.

The enterprise version of Javabeans are usually called *EJB*.

Question 82: What is Hibernate Framework?

Answer: Hibernate is an object-relational mapping library for the Java language, providing a framework for mapping an object-oriented domain model to a traditional relational database.

Mapping Java classes to database tables is accomplished through the configuration of an XML file or by using Java Annotations.

Hibernate's primary feature is mapping from Java classes to database tables (and from Java data types to SQL data types). Hibernate also provides data query and retrieval facilities. It generates SQL calls and relieves the developer from manual result set handling and object conversion.

Question 83: What are Java Struts?

Answer: Struts is the most popular framework for developing Java based web applications. Struts is being developed as an open source project started by Apache. Struts framework is based on Model View Controller (MVC) architecture.

Question 84: Explain Java Spring Framework.

Answer: Spring is a Framework that provides comprehensive infrastructure support for developing Java applications. Spring handles the infrastructure so we can focus on our application.

Spring enables us to build applications from "plain old Java objects" (POJOs) and to apply enterprise services non-invasively to POJOs. This capability applies to the Java SE programming model and to full and partial Java EE.

Spring framework *advantages*:

- Make a Java method execute in a database transaction without having to deal with transaction APIs.
- Make a local Java method a remote procedure without having to deal with remote APIs.
- Make a local Java method a management operation without having to deal with JMX APIs.
- Make a local Java method a message handler without having to deal with JMS APIs.

CHAPTER 6

Scripting Languages

6.1 Interpreter versus Compiler

By now, you might have understood that, any programming language is essentially a human-friendly formalism for writing instructions for a computer to follow. These instructions are at some point translated into machine language, which is what the computer really *understands*. Let's introduce at this point some concepts of execution of programs written in high level programming languages. As we have already seen, the only language that a computer can understand is the so called *machine language*. These languages are composed of a set of basic operations whose execution is implemented in the hardware of the processor.

A *Compiler* and *Interpreter* both carry out the same purpose – convert a high level language (like C, Java) instructions into the binary form which is understandable by computer hardware. However both compiler and interpreter have the same objective but they differ in the way they accomplish their task.

6.1.1 Compiler

A compiler is defined as a computer program that is used to convert high level instructions or language into a form that can be understood by the computer. Since computer can understand only in binary numbers so a compiler is used to fill the gap otherwise it would have been difficult for a human to find info in the 0 and 1 form.

Earlier the compilers were simple programs which were used to convert symbols into bits. The programs were also very simple and they contained a series of steps translated by hand into the data. However, this was a very time consuming process. So, some parts were programmed or automated. This formed the first compiler.

More sophisticated compliers are created using the simpler ones. With every new version, more rules added to it and a more natural language environment is created for the human programmer. The complier programs are evolving in this way which improves their ease of use.

There are specific compliers for certain specific languages or tasks. Compliers can be multiple or multistage pass. The first pass can convert the high level language into a language that is closer to computer language. Then the further passes can convert it into final stage for the purpose of execution.

6.1.2 Interpreter

The programs created in high level languages can be executed by using two different ways. The first one is the use of compiler and the other method is to use an interpreter. High level instruction or language is converted into intermediate from by an interpreter.

The advantage of using an interpreter is that the high level instruction does not goes through compilation stage which can be a time consuming method. So, by using an interpreter, the high level program is executed directly. That is the reason why some programmers use interpreters while making small sections as this saves time.

Almost all high level programming languages have compilers and interpreters. But some languages like LISP and BASIC are designed in such a way that the programs made using them are executed by an interpreter.

6.1.3 Difference between compiler and interpreter

- A complier converts the high level instruction into machine language while an interpreter converts the high level instruction into an intermediate form.
- Before execution, entire program is executed by the compiler whereas after translating the first line, an interpreter then executes it and so on.
- List of errors is created by the compiler after the compilation process while an interpreter stops translating after the first error.
- An independent executable file is created by the compiler whereas interpreter is required by an interpreted program each time.

6.2 What Are Scripting Languages?

Languages like C and C++ allow a programmer to write code at a very detailed level which has *good execution* speed. But in many applications sometimes we would prefer to write at a higher level. For example, for text processing applications, the basic unit in C/C++ is a character, while for languages like *Perl* and *Python* the basic units are lines of text and words within lines. We can work with lines and words in C/C++, but one must go to greater effort to accomplish the same thing. C/C++ might give better speed, but if speed is *not* an issue, the convenience of a scripting language is very attractive.

The term scripting language has never been formally defined, but here are the typical characteristics:

- Used often for system administration.
- Very casual with regard to typing of variables, e.g. no distinction between integer, floating-point or string variables.
- Lots of high-level operations intrinsic to the language, e.g. stack push/pop.
- *Interpreted*, rather than being compiled to the instruction set of the host machine.

Today many people prefer *Python*, as it is much cleaner and more elegant. Our introduction here assumes knowledge of C/C++ programming. There will be a couple of places in which we describe things briefly in a Unix context, so some Unix knowledge would be helpful.

In this chapter we look at three scripting languages: Shell, PERL and Python.

6.3 Shell Scripting

Steve Bourne wrote the *Bourne* shell that appeared in the Bell Labs research version for Unix. Since then, many other shells have been written. The most commonly used shells are SH(Bourne SHell) CSH(C SHell) and KSH(*Korn* SHell), most of the other shells you encounter will be variants of these shells and will share the same syntax.

The various shells all have built in functions which allow for the creation of shell scripts, that is, the putting together of shell commands and constructs to automate what can be automated in order to make life easier for the user. We can specify the shell we want to interpret our shell script within the script itself by including the following in the first line.

```
#!/path/to/shell
```

Usually anything following (#) is *interpreted* as a comment and ignored but if it occurs on the first line with a (!) following it is treated as being special and the filename following the (!) is considered to point to the location of the shell that should interpret the script. When a script is *executed* it is being interpreted by an invocation of the shell that is running it. Hence the shell is said to be running non-interactively, when the shell is used *normally* it is said to be running interactively.

6.3.1 Command Redirection and Pipelines

By default a normal command accepts input from standard input, which we call *stdin*, standard input is the command line in the form of arguments passed to the command. By default a normal command directs its output to standard output, which we abbreviate to stdout, standard output is usually the console display.

For some commands this may be the desired action but other times we may wish to get our input for a command from somewhere other than stdin and direct our output to somewhere other than stdout. This is done by redirection:

- We use > to *redirect stdout* to a *file*, for instance, if we wanted to redirect a directory listing generated by the ls we could do the following:

  ```
  ls > file
  ```

- We use < to specify that we want the command immediately before the redirection symbol to get its *input* from the source specified immediately after the symbol, for instance, we could redirect the input to grep(which searches for strings within files) so that it comes from a file like this:

  ```
  grep searchterm < file
  ```

- We use >> to *append* stdout to a *file*, for instance, if we wanted to append the date to the end of a file we could redirect the output from date like so:

  ```
  date >> file
  ```

- One can redirect standard *error* (stderr) to a file by using 2>, if we wanted to redirect the standard error from commandA to a file we would use:

  ```
  commmandA 2>
  ```

Pipelines are another form of redirection that are used to chain commands so that powerful composite commands can be constructed, the pipe symbol '|' takes the stdout from the command preceding it and redirects it to the command following it:

```
ls -l | grep searchword | sort -r
```

The example above firsts requests a long (-l directory listing of the current directory using the *ls* command, the output from this is then piped to *grep* which filters out all the listings containing the searchword and then finally pipes this through to sort which then sorts the output in reverse (-r, sort then passes the output on normally to stdout.

6.3.2 Variables

When a script starts, all environment variables are turned into shell variables. New variables can be instantiated like this:

```
name=value
```

You must do it exactly like that, with *no spaces* either side of the equals sign, the name must only be made up of alphabetic characters, numeric characters and underscores, it cannot begin with a numeric character. Variables are referenced like this: $name, here is an example:

```
#!/bin/sh
msg1=Hello
```

```
msg2=World!
echo $msg1 $msg2
```

This would echo "Hello World!" to the console display, if you want to assign a string to a variable and the string contains spaces you should enclose the string in double quotes ("), the double quotes tell the shell to take the contents literally and ignore keywords, however, a few keywords are still processed. You can still use $ within a (") quoted string to include variables:

```
#!/bin/sh
msg1="one"
msg2="$msg1 two"
msg3="$msg2 three"
echo $msg3
```

Would echo "one two three" to the screen. The escape character can also be used within a double quoted section to output special characters, the escape character is "\", it outputs the character immediately following it literally so \\ would output \.

A special case is when the escape character is followed by a newline, the shell ignores the newline character which allows the spreading of long commands that must be executed on a single line in reality over multiple lines within the script. The escape character can be used anywhere else too.

Except within single quotes, surrounding anything within single quotes causes it to be treated as literal text that is it will be passed on exactly as intended; this can be useful for sending command sequences to other files in order to create new scripts because the text between the single quotes will remain untouched. For example:

```
#!/bin/sh
echo 'msg="Hello World!"' > hello
echo 'echo $msg' >> hello
chmod 700 hello
./hello
```

This would cause "msg="Hello World!" to be echoed and redirected to the file hello, "echo $msg" would then be echoed and redirected to the file hello but this time appended to the end. The chmod line changes the file permissions of hello so that we can execute it. The final line executes hello causing it output "Hello World". If we had not used literal quotes we never would have had to use escape characters to ensure that ($) and (") were echoed to the file, this makes the code a little clearer. A variable may be referenced like so ${VARIABLENAME}, this allows one to place characters immediately preceding the variable like ${VARIABLENAME}aaa without the shell interpreting *aaa* as being part of the variable name.

6.3.3 Command Line Arguments

Command line arguments are treated as special variables within the script, the reason I am calling them variables is because they can be changed with the shift command. The command line arguments are enumerated in the following manner $0, $1, $2, $3, $4, $5, $6, $7, $8 and $9. $0 is special in that it corresponds to the name of the script itself. $1 is the first argument; $2 is the second argument and so on.

To reference after the ninth argument you must enclose the number in brackets like this ${nn}. You can use the shift command to shift the arguments 1 variable to the left so that $2 becomes $1, $1 becomes $0 and so on, $0 gets scrapped because it has nowhere to go, this can be useful to process all the arguments using a loop, using one variable to reference the first argument and shifting until you have exhausted the arguments list.

As well as the command-line arguments there are some special built-in variables:

- $# represents the parameter count. Useful for controlling loop constructs that need to process each parameter.
- $@ expands to all the parameters separated by spaces. Useful for passing all the parameters to some other function or program.
- $- expands to the flags (options) the shell was invoked with. Useful for controlling program flow based on the flags set.
- $$ expands to the process id of the shell innovated to run the script. Useful for creating unique temporary filenames relative to this instantiation of the script.

6.3.4 Command Substitution

In the words of the shell manual "Command substitution allows the output of a command to be substituted in place of the command name itself". There are two ways this can be done. The first is to enclose the command like this:

```
$(command)
```

The second is to enclose the command in back quotes like this:

```
`command`
```

The command will be executed in a sub-shell environment and the standard output of the shell will replace the command substitution when the command completes.

6.3.5 Arithmetic Expansion

Arithmetic expansion is also allowed and comes in the form:

```
$((expression))
```

The value of the expression will replace the substitution. Eg:

```
!#/bin/sh
echo $((1 + 3 + 4))
```

Will echo "8" to stdout.

6.3.6 Control Constructs

The flow of control within shell scripts is done via four main constructs; if...then...elif..else, do...while, for and case.

6.3.6.1 If..Then..Elif..Else

This construct takes the following generic form. The parts enclosed within ([) and (]) are optional:

```
if list
then list
[elif list
then list] ...
[else list]
fi
```

When a Unix command exits it exits with what is known as an *exit status*, this indicates to anyone who wants to know the degree of success the command had in performing whatever task it was supposed to do, usually when a command executes without error it terminates with an exit status of zero. An exit status of some other value would indicate that some error had occurred, the details of which would be specific to the command.

The commands' manual pages detail the exit status messages that they produce. A list is defined in the shell as "a sequence of zero or more commands separated by newlines, semicolons, or ampersands, and optionally terminated by one of these three characters.", hence in the generic definition of the if above the list will determine which of the execution paths the script takes.

For example, there is a command called test on UNIX which evaluates an expression and if it evaluates to true will return zero and will return one otherwise, this is how we can test conditions in the list part(s) of the if construct because test is a command.

We do not actually have to type the test command directly into the list to use it, it can be implied by encasing the test case within ([) and (]) characters, as illustrated by the following (silly) example:

```
#!/bin/sh
if [ "$1" = "1" ]
then
    echo "The first option is nice"
elif [ "$1" = "2" ]
then
    echo "The second option is just as nice"
elif [ "$1" = "3" ]
then
    echo "The third option is excellent"
else
    echo "I see you were wise enough not to choose"
    echo "You win"
fi
```

What this example does is compare the first parameter (command line argument in this case) with the strings "1", "2" and "3" using tests' (=) test which compares two strings for equality, if any of them match it prints out the corresponding message. If none of them match it prints out the final case. OK the example is silly and actually flawed (the user still wins even if they type in (4) or something) but it illustrates how the if statement works.

Notice that there are spaces between (if) and ([), ([) and the test and the test and (]), these spaces must be present otherwise the shell will complain. There must also be spaces between the operator and operands of the test otherwise it will not work properly.

Notice how it starts with (if) and ends with (fi), also, notice how (then) is on a separate line to the test above it and that (else) does not require a (then) statement. You must construct this construct exactly like this for it to work properly.

It is also possible to integrate logical AND and OR into the testing, by using two tests separated by either "&&" or "||" respectively. For example we could replace the third test case in the example above with:

```
elif [ "$1" = "3"] || [ "$1" = "4" ]
then echo "The third choi...
```

The script would print out "The third choice is excellent" if the first parameter was either "3" OR "4". To illustrate the use of "&&

```
elif [ "$1" = "3"] || [ "$2" = "4" ]
then echo "The third choi...
```

The script would print out "The third choice is excellent" if and only if the first parameter was "3" AND the second parameter was "4".

"&&" and "||" are both lazily evaluating which means that in the case of "&&", if the first test fails it won't bother evaluating the second because the list will only be true if they BOTH pass and since one has already failed there is no point wasting time evaluating the second. In the case of "||" if the first test passes it won't bother evaluating the second test because we only need ONE of the tests to pass for the whole list to pass.

6.3.6.2 Do...While

The Do...While takes the following generic form:

```
while list
do list
done
```

In the words of the SH manual "The two lists are executed repeatedly while the exit status of the first list is zero." there is a variation on this that uses until in place of while which executes until the exit status of the first list is zero. Here is an example use of the while statement:

```
#!/bin/sh
count=$1                        # Initialize count to first parameter
while [ $count -gt 0 ]           # while count is greater than 10 do
do
    echo $count seconds till supper time!
    count=$(expr $count -1)   # decrement count by 1
    sleep 1                     # sleep for a second using the Unix sleep command
done
echo Supper time!!, YEAH!!      # were finished
```

If called from the commandline with an argument of 4 this script will output

```
4 seconds till supper time!
3 seconds till supper time!
2 seconds till supper time!
1 seconds till supper time!
Supper time!!, YEAH!!
```

You can see that this time we have used the -gt of the test command implicitly called via '[' and ']', which stands for greater than. Pay careful attention to the formatting and spacing.

6.3.6.3 For Loop

The syntax of the *for* command is:

```
for variable in word ...
do list
done
```

The shell manual states "The words are expanded, and then the list is executed repeatedly with the variable set to each word in turn.". A word is essentially some other variable that contains a list of values of some sort, the for construct assigns each of the values in the word to variable and then variable can be used within the body of the construct, upon completion of the body variable will be assigned the next value in word until there are no more values in word. An example should make this clearer:

```
#!/bin/sh
fruitlist="Apple Pear Tomato Peach Grape"
for fruit in $fruitlist
do
    if [ "$fruit" = "Tomato" ] || [ "$fruit" = "Peach" ]
    then
        echo "I like ${fruit}es"
    else
        echo "I like ${fruit}s"
```

```
    fi
done
```

In this example, fruitlist is word, fruit is variable and the body of the statement outputs how much this person loves various fruits but includes an if...then..else statement to deal with the correct addition of letters to describe the plural version of the fruit, notice that the variable fruit was expressed like ${fruit} because otherwise the shell would have interpreted the preceding letter(s) as being part of the variable and echoed nothing because we have not defined the variables fruits and fruites. When executed this script will output:

```
I like Apples
I like Pears
I like Tomatoes
I like Peachs
I like Grapes
```

Within the for construct, do and done may be replaced by '{' and '}'. This is not allowed for while.

6.3.6.4 Case

The case construct has the following syntax:

```
case word in
pattern) list ;;
...
esac
```

An example of this should make things clearer:

```
!#/bin/sh
case $1 in
1) echo 'First Choice';;
2) echo 'Second Choice';;
*) echo 'Other Choice';;
esac
```

"1", "2" and "*" are patterns, word is compared to each pattern and if a match is found the body of the corresponding pattern is executed, we have used "*" to represent everything, since this is checked last we will still catch "1" and "2" because they are checked first.

In our example word is "$1", the first parameter, hence if the script is ran with the argument "1" it will output "First Choice", "2" "Second Choice" and anything else "Other Choice". In this example we compared against numbers (essentially still a string comparison however) but the pattern can be more complex, see the SH man page for more information.

6.3.7 Functions

The syntax of an shell function is defined as follows:

```
name ( ) command
```

It is usually laid out like this:

```
name() {
   commands
}
```

A function will return with a default exit status of zero, one can return different exit statuses by using the notation return exit status. Variables can be defined locally within a function using local name=value. The example below shows the use of a user defined increment function:

Example 1. Increment Function Example

```
#!/bin/sh
inc() {                  # The increment is defined first so we can use it
  echo $(($1 + $2))      # We echo the result of the first
                         # parameter plus the second parameter
}
# We check to see that all the command line arguments are present
if [ "$1" "" ] || [ "$2" = "" ] || [ "$3" = "" ]
then
   echo USAGE:
   echo " counter startvalue incrementvalue endvalue"
else
   count=$1                    # Rename are variables with clearer names
   value=$2
   end=$3
   while [ $count -lt $end ]   # Loop while count is less than end
   do
      echo $count
      count=$(inc $count $value) # Call increment with count and value as parameters
   done   # so that count is incremented by value
fi
inc() {
   echo $(($1 + $2))
}
```

The function is defined and opened with inc() {, the line echo $(($1 + $2)) uses the notation for arithmetic expression substitution which is $((expression)) to enclose the expression, $1 + $2 which adds the first and second parameters passed to the function together, the echo bit at the start echoes them to standard output, we can catch this value by assigning the function call to a variable, as is illustrated by the function call.

```
count=$(inc $count $value)
```

We use command substitution which substitutes the value of a command to substitute the value of the function call whereupon it is assigned to the count variable. The command within the command substitution block is inc $count $value, the last two values being its parameters. Which are then referenced from within the function using $1 and $2. We could have used the other command substitution notation to call the function if we had wanted:

```
count=`inc $count $value`
```

Example 2. Variable Scope, Example

We will show another quick example to illustrate the scope of variables:

```
#!/bin/sh
inc() {
   local value=4
   echo "value is $value within the function\\n"
   echo "\\b\$1 is $1 within the function"
}
value=5
echo value is $value before the function
echo "\$1 is $1 before the function"
echo
echo -e $(inc $value)
```

```
echo
echo value is $value after the function
echo "\$1 is $1 after the function"
inc() {
    local value=4
    echo "value is $value within the function\\n"
    echo "\\b\$1 is $1 within the function"
}
```

We assign a local value to the variable value of 4. The next three lines construct the output we would like, remember that this is being echoed to some buffer and will be replace the function call with all the stuff that was passed to stdout within the function when the function exits. So the calling code will be replaced with whatever we direct to standard output within the function. The function is called like this:

```
echo -e $(inc $value)
```

We have passed the option -e to the echo command which causes it to process C-style backslash escape characters, so we can process any backslash escape characters which the string generated by the function call contains.

If we just echo the lines we want to be returned by the function it will not pass the newline character onto the buffer even if we explicitly include it with an escape character reference so what we do is actually include the sequence of characters that will produce a new line within the string so that when it is echoed by the calling code with the -e the escape characters will be processed and the newlines will be placed where we want them.

```
echo "value is $value within the function\\n"
```

Notice how the newline has been inserted with \\n, the first two backslashes indicate that we want to echo a backslash because within double quotes a backslash indicates to process the next character literally, we have to do this because we are only between double quotes and not the literal-text single quotes.

If we had used single quotes we would had have to echo the bit with the newline in separately from the bit that contains $value otherwise $value would not be expanded.

```
echo "\\b\$1 is $1 within the function"
```

This is our second line, and is contained within double quotes so that the variable $1 will be expanded, \\b is included so that \b will be placed in the echoed line and our calling code will process this as a backspace character. We have to do this because for some reason the shell prefixes a space to the second line if we do not, the backspace removes this space. The output from this script called with 2 as the first argument is:

```
alue is 5 before the function
$1 is 2 before the function
value is 4 within the function
$1 is 5 within the function
value is 5 after the function
$1 is 2 after the function
```

6.4 PERL [Practical Extraction and Report Language]

Perl (or PERL) is an acronym, short for Practical Extraction and Report Language. Perl is a scripting language with powerful text processing capabilities. Because of these, Perl has become a very popular language in the context of web servers.

Perl is an interpreted language. That means, program code is interpreted at run time. Code is compiled by the interpreter before it is actually executed. It was designed By *Larry Wall* as a tool for writing programs in the UNIX environment.

Perl is a very feature-rich language, which clearly cannot be discussed in full detail here. Instead, our goals here are to

- Enable the reader to quickly become proficient at writing simple Perl programs and
- Prepare the reader to consult full Perl books (or Perl tutorials on the Web) for further details of whatever Perl constructs he/she needs for a particular application.

6.4.1 Starting with "Hello world!"

Perl *script* is a text file with default extension *.pl*. As an example let us consider the text of *helloworld.pl* given below:

```
#!/usr/bin/perl
# This is my first Perl program!
print ("Hello World!\n");
print ("This is my first Perl program.\n\n");
```

Perl scripts are interpreted by the Perl interpreter: perl, or perl.exe.

```
perl helloworld.pl [arg0 [arg1 [arg2 ...]]]
```

In the above code, *print*() is a function that displays text to the screen. \n prints a new line to the screen; i.e. it goes to the start of the next line. The symbol # indicates beginning of the comment – everything after it will be ignored. Perl has no block comment syntax. The semicolon (;) separates the Perl statements from one another. Statements do not have to occur on separate lines.

6.4.2 Perl Command Line Arguments

When you run a program, it is often desired to use different data. We will now update the helloworld program to use command line arguments that can be used to set different options for a program. In this specific example, we will allow the user to enter in their name, which then gets printed to the screen.

Edit the hello.pl file so it now looks like the following:

```
#!/usr/bin/perl
use Getopt::Long;
#usage: perl helloCommandLine.pl –name <YourName>
&GetOptions("name=s" => \$Name);
# The above line lets the user enter in their name
print ("Hello $Name \n");
print ("This is a perl program using command line arguments \n\n");
```

Once you have finished, save this file as *helloCommandLine.pl* and then run it by typing:

```
perl helloCommandLine.pl –name <yourname>
```

In the above code, for now assume that *use Getopt::Long*; is used whenever we want to retrieve command line arguments. Basically this line tells the perl interpreter that we are using a function that is already defined in another location. *&GetOptions*() is a function that retrieves the command line options.

In this example, it retrieves the value directly after the *–name* when the program is run. It stores the value entered in in a variable called *$Name*. This value can be retrieved any time in the program. We will talk about variables more in the next perl session.

6.4.3 Perl Datatypes and Variables

Perl is loosely typed language. In Perl, there is no need to specify a type for your data; the Perl interpreter will choose the type based on the context of the data itself. Before we can proceed much further with Perl, we'll need some understanding of variables.

A variable is a container that holds one or more values that can change throughout a program. Perl variables come in three types: *scalars*, *arrays* and *hashes*. Variables in Perl are always preceded with a sign called a *sigil*. These signs are $ for scalars, @ for arrays, and % for hashes.

6.4.3.1 Scalar Variables

Scalars are simple variables. They are preceded by a dollar sign ($). A scalar is either a number, a string, or a reference. A reference is actually an address of a variable. Here is a simple example of using scalar variables:

```
#!/usr/bin/perl
$age = 31;                   # An integer assignment
$name = "Srinivas Mary";     # A string
$salary = 1999.50;           # A floating point
print "Age = $age\n";
print "Name = $name\n";
print "Salary = $salary\n";
```

This will produce following result:

```
Age = 31
Name = Srinivas Mary
Salary = 1999.50
```

The '.' is used to concatenate strings. For example,

```
$x = $x . "abc"
```

would add the string "abc" to $x.

6.4.3.2 Array Variables

An array is a variable that stores an ordered list of scalar values. Array variables are preceded by an "at" (@) sign. To refer to a single element of an array, you will use the dollar sign ($) with the variable name followed by the index of the element in square brackets. Array indices are integers beginning at 0. Here is a simple example of using array variables:

```
#!/usr/bin/perl
@ages = (32, 20, 21);
@names = ("Rama Krishna", "Mary", "Ahmed");
print "\$ages[0] = $ages[0]\n";
print "\$ages[1] = $ages[1]\n";
print "\$ages[2] = $ages[2]\n";
print "\$names[0] = $names[0]\n";
print "\$names[1] = $names[1]\n";
print "\$names[2] = $names[2]\n";
```

Here we used escape sign (\) before $ sign just to print it other Perl will understand it as a variable and will print its value. When exected, this will produce following result:

```
$ages[0] = 32
$ages[1] = 20
$ages[2] = 21
$names[0] = Rama Krishna
```

```
$names[1] = Mary
$names[2] = Ahmed
```

Array elements can only be scalars, and not for instance other arrays. For example

```
@wt = (1,(2,3),4);
```

would have the same effect as

```
@wt = (1,2,3,4);
```

Since array elements are scalars, their names begin with $, not @, e.g.

```
@wt = (1,2,3,4);
print $wt[2]; # prints 3
```

Arrays are referenced for the most part as in C, but in a more flexible manner. Their lengths are not declared, and they grow or shrink dynamically, without "warning," i.e. the programmer does not "ask for permission" in growing an array. For example, if the array x currently has 7 elements, i.e. ends at $x[6], then the statement

```
$x[7] = 12;
```

changes the array length to 8. For that matter, we could have assigned to element 99 instead of to element 7, resulting in an array length of 100.

The programmer can treat an array as a *queue* data structure, using the Perl operations push and shift (usage of the latter is especially common in the Perl idiom), or treat it as a stack by using push and pop. We'll see the details below.

An array without a name is called a *list*. For example, in

```
@x = (88,12,"abc");
```

we assign the array name @x to the list (88,12,"abc"). We will then have $x[0] = 88, etc. One of the big uses of lists and arrays is in loops, e.g.:

```
# prints out 1, 2 and 4
for $i ((1,2,4)) {
   print $i, "\n";
}
```

The length of an array or list is obtained calling scalar() or by simply using the array name (though not a list) in a scalar context.

Operations

```
$x[0] = 15; # don't have to warn Perl that x is an array first
$x[1] = 16;
$y = shift @x; # "output" of shift is the element shifted out
print $y, "\n"; # prints 15
print $x[0], "\n"; # prints 16
push(@x,9); # sets $x[1] to 9
print scalar(@x), "\n"; # prints 2
print @x, "\n"; # prints 169 (16 and 9 with no space)
$k = @x;
print $k, "\n"; # prints 2
@x = (); # @x will now be empty
print scalar(@x), "\n"; # prints 0
@rt = ('abc',15,20,95);
delete $rt[2]; # $rt[2] now = undef
print "scalar(@rt) \n"; # prints 4
print @rt, "\n"; # prints abc1595
```

```
print "@rt\n"; # prints abc 15 95, due to quotes
print "$rt[-1]\n"; # prints 95
$m = @rt;
print $m, "\n"; # prints 4
($m) = @rt; # 4-element array truncated to a 1-element array
print $m, "\n"; # prints abc
```

A useful operation is array slicing. Subsets of arrays may be accessed—"sliced"—via commas and a .. range operator. For example:

```
@z = (5,12,13,125);
@w = @z[1..3];                # @w will be (12,13,125)
@q = @z[0..1];                # @q will be (5,12)
@y = @z[0,2];                 # @y will be (5,13)
@w[0,2] = @w[2,0];            # swaps elements 0 and 2
@g = @z[0,2..3];              # can mix "," and
print "@g\n"                  # prints 0 13 125
```

6.4.3.3 Hash Variables

A hash is a set of key/value pairs. Hash variables are preceded by a percent (%) sign. To refer to a single element of a hash, you will use the hash variable name followed by the *key* associated with the value in curly brackets. Here is a simple example of using hash variables:

```
#!/usr/bin/perl
%data = ('Rama Krishna', 32, 'Mary', 30, 'Ahmed', 40);
print "\$data{'Rama Krishna'} = $data{'Rama Krishna'}\n";
print "\$data{'Mary'} = $data{'Mary'}\n";
print "\$data{'Ahmed'} = $data{'Ahmed'}\n";
```

This will produce following result:

```
$data{'Rama Krishna'} = 32
$data{'Mary'} = 30
$data{'Ahmed'} = 40
```

In the code above, if we add the line

```
print %data, "\n";
```

the output of that statement will be

```
Rama Krishna32Mary30Ahmed40
```

6.4.4 References

References are like C pointers. They are considered scalar variables, and thus have names beginning with $. They are dereferenced by prepending the symbol for the variable type, e.g. prepending a $ for a scalar, a @ for an array, etc.:

```
# set up a reference to a scalar
$r = \3; # \ means "reference to," like & means "pointer to" in C
# now print it; $r is a reference to a scalar, so $$r denotes that scalar
print $$r, "\n"; # prints 3
@x = (1,2,4,8,16);
$s = \@x;
# an array element is a scalar, so prepend a $
print $$s[3], "\n"; # prints 8
# for the whole array, prepend a @
```

```
print scalar(@$s), "\n"; # prints 5
```

In Line 4, for example, you should view $$r as $($r), meaning take the reference $r and dereference it. Since the result of dereferencing is a scalar, we get another dollar sign on the left.

6.4.5 Declaration of Variables

A variable need not be explicitly declared; its *declaration* consists of its first usage. For example, if the statement

```
$var = 5;
```

were the first reference to $var, then this would both declare $var and assign 5 to it. If you wish to make a separate declaration, you can do so, e.g.

```
$var;
...
$var = 5;
```

If you wish to have protection against accidentally using a variable which has not been previously defined, say due to a misspelling, include a line

```
use strict;
```

at the top of your source code.

6.4.6 Scope of Variables

Variables in Perl are global by default. To make a variable local to subroutine or block, the my construct is used. For instance,

```
my $x;
my $y;
```

would make the scope of $x and $y only the subroutine or block in which these statements appear. You can also combine the above two statements, using a list:

```
my ($x,$y);
```

Other than the scope aspect, the effect of my is the same as if this keyword were not there. Thus for example

```
my $z = 3;
```

is the same as

```
my $z;
...
$z = 3;
```

and

```
my($x) = @rt;
```

would assign $rt[0] to $x.

Note that my does apply at the block level. This can lead to subtle bugs if you forget about it. For example,

```
if ($x == 2) {
   my $y = 5;
}
print $y, "\n";
will print 0.
```

There are other scope possibilities, e.g. namespaces of packages and the local keyword.

6.4.7 String Literals

In perl there are two ways to represent string literals: single-quoted strings and double-quoted strings.

.4.7.1 Single-Quoted Strings

Single quoted are a sequence of characters that begin and end with a single quote. These quotes are not a part of the string they just mark the beginning and end for the Perl interpreter. If you want a ' inside of your string you need to preclude it with a \ like this \' as you'll see below. Let's see how this works below.

```
'five'          #has four letters in the string
'can\'t'        #has five characters and represents "can't"
'hi\there'      #has eight characters and represents"hi\\there" (one \ in the string)
'mam\\blah'     #has nine characters and represents "mam\\blah" (one \ in the string)
```

If you want to put a new line in a single-quoted string it goes something like this

```
'line1
line2'     #has eleven characters line1, newline character, and then line2
```

Single-quoted strings don't interpret \n as a newline.

6.4.7.2 Double-Quoted Strings

Double quoted strings act more like strings in C or C++ the backslash allows you to represent control characters. Another nice feature Double-Quoted strings offers is variable interpolation this substitutes the value of a variable into the string. Some examples are below:

```
$word="hello";                #$word becomes hello
$statement="$word world!";    #variable interpolation, $statement becomes "hello world!"
"Hello World!\n";             #"Hello World!" followed by a newline
```

6.4.8 PERL Standard Input

As an example, consider the script below.

```
#!/usr/bin/perl
$title = "PERL Programming";
print "Hello there.  What is your name?\n";
$name = <STDIN>;
chomp($name);
print "Hello, $you. Welcome to $title.\n";
```

The script will prompt you for your name, and read your name using the following line:

```
$name = <STDIN>;
```

STDIN is standard input. This is the default input channel for your script; if you're running your script in the shell, STDIN is whatever you type as the script runs. The program will print "Hello there. What is your name?", then pause and wait for you to type something in. Whatever you typed is stored in the scalar variable $name. Since $name also contains the carriage return itself, we use

```
chomp($name);
```

to remove the carriage return from the end of the string you typed in. The following print statement:

```
print "Hello, $name. Welcome to $classname.\n";
```

substitutes the value of $name that you entered. The "\n" at the end if the line is the perl syntax for a carriage return.

6.4.9 PERL Operators

6.4.9.1 Numeric PERL Operators

6.4.9.1.1 Arithmetic PERL Operators

In the table below you see the Perl operators used in arithmetic operations.

Symbol	Name	Definition
+	addition	It's a binary operator that returns the sum of two operands. Example: $v1 = 22; $v2 = 6; $v = $v1+$v2; print "$v (expected 28)\n";
-	subtraction	It's a binary operator that returns the difference of two operands. Example: $v1 = 12; $v2 = 5; $v = $v1-$v2; print "$v (expected 7)\n";
-	negation	I's a unary operator that performs arithmetic negation. Example: $v1 = 12; $v2 = -$v1; print "$v2 (expected -12)\n";
*	multiplication	It's a binary operator that multiplies two operands. Example: $v1 = 12; $v2 = 5; $v = $v1 * $v2; print "$v (expected 60)\n";
/	division	It's a binary operator that divides left value by right value. Example: $v1 = 12; $v2 = 5; $v = $v1 / $v2; print "$v (expected 2.4)\n";
**	exponentiation	It's a binary operator that raises the left value to the power of the right value. Example: $v1 = 12; $v2 = 2; $v = $v1 ** $v2; print "$v (expected 144)\n";
%	modulus	It's a binary operator that returns the remainder of dividing left value by right value. Example: $v1 = 12; $v2 = 5; $v = $v1 % $v2; print "$v (expected 2)\n";
++	auto increment	If you place this unary operator before/after a variable, the variable will be incremented before/after returning the alue. Example: $v1 = 10; $v2 = ++$v1; print "$v1 $v2(expected 11 11)\n"; $v1 = 10; $v2 = $v1++; print "$v1 $v2(expected 11 10)\n";
--	auto decrement	If you place this unary operator before/after a variable, the variable will be decremented before/after returning the alue. Example: $v1 = 10; $v2 = --$v1; print "$v1 $v2(expected 9 9)\n"; $v1 = 10; $v2 = $v1--; print "$v1 $v2(expected 9 10)\n";

6.4.9.1.2 Numeric Relational PERL Operators

The numeric relational Perl operators compare two numbers and determine the validity of a relationship.

Symbol	Name	Definition

<	less than	The *less than* operator indicates if the value of the left operand is less than the value of the right one.
		
		Example:
		($v1, $v2) = (5, 7);
		if($v1 < $v2){
		print "OK (expected)\n";
		}

<=	less than or equal to	The *less than or equal to* operator indicates if the value of the left operand is less than or equal to the value of the right one.
		
		Example:
		($v1, $v2) = (5, 5);
		if($v1 <= $v2){
		print "OK (expected)\n";
		}

>	greater than	The *greater than* operator indicates if the value of the left operand is greater than the value of the right one.
		
		Example:
		($v1, $v2) = (5, 7);
		if($v2 > $v1){
		print "OK (expected)\n";
		}

>=	greater than or equal to	The *greater than or equal to* operator indicates if the value of the left operand is greater than or equal to the value of the right one.
		
		Example:
		($v1, $v2) = (5, 5);
		if($v2 >= $v1){
		print "OK (expected)\n";
		}

==	equal	The *equal* operator returns true if the left operand is equal to the right one.
		
		Example:
		($v1, $v2) = (5, 5);
		if($v1 == $v2){
		print "OK (expected)\n";
		}

!=	not equal to	The *not equal to* operator returns true if the left operand is not equal to the right one.
		
		Example:
		($v1, $v2) = (5, 7);
		if($v1 != $v2){
		print "OK (expected)\n";
		}

<=>	numeric comparison	This binary operator returns -1, 0, or 1 if the left operand is less than, equal to or greater than the right one. Example: ($v1, $v2) = (5, 7); $v = $v1 <=> $v2; print "$v\n"; # displays -1;

6.4.9.1.3 Numerical Logical PERL Operators

The numeric logical Perl operators are generally derived from boolean algebra and they are mainly used to control program flow, finding them as part of an if, a while or some other control statement. See in the table below the logical numerical Perl operators.

Symbol	Name	Definition
!	negation	This unary operator evaluates an operand and return true if the operand has the false value (0) and false otherwise. Example: $v1 = !25; $v2 = !0; print "v1=$v1,v2=$v2\n"; # displays v1=,v2=1
not	not	It has the same meaning as the "!" operator, described above.

and, &&	and	The *and* operator returns the logical conjunction of two operands.
		Example:
		($v1, $v2) = (5, 7);
		if($v1 == 5 && $v2 == 7) {
		print "OK (expected)\n";
		}

or, ||	or	The *or* operator returns the logical disjunction of two operands.
		Example:
		($v1, $v2) = (5, 7);
		if($v1 == 5 || $v2 == 0) {
		print "OK (expected)\n";
		}

xor	exclusive or	The *exclusive or* operator returns the logical exclusive-or of two operands (the result is true if either but not both of the operands is true). Example: ($v1, $v2) = (5, 7); print ($v1==5 xor $v2==3); # displays 1 print ($v1==5 xor $v2==7); # displays
?	conditional operator	This ternary operator is like the symbolic if ... then ... else clause from the C language. It returns the second operand if the leftmost operand is true and the third operand otherwise. Example: $v = (2 == 2) ? "Equal\n" : "Not equal\n"; print $v; # displays Equal

6.4.9.1.4 Numeric Bitwise PERL Operations

Numeric bitwise Perl operators are similar to the logical operators, but they work on the binary representation of data. They are used to change individual bits in an operand. Please note that both operands associated with bitwise operators are integers.

Symbol	Name	Definition
<<	shift left	The *shift left* << operator is a binary operator that shifts the bits to the left. Its first operand specifies the integer value to be shifted meanwhile the second one specifies the number of position that the bits in the value will be shifted. The rightmost bits of the integer value will be assigned with 0 and the leftmost bits will be discarded. Example: $v = 25 << 3; print "$v (expected 200)\n";
>>	shift right	The *shift right* >> operator is a binary operator that shifts the bits to the right. Its first operand specifies the integer value to be shifted meanwhile the second one specifies the number of position that the bits in the value will be shifted. The leftmost bits of the integer value will be assigned with 0 and the rightmost bits will be discarded. Example: $v = 32 >> 3; print "$v (expected 4)\n";
&	and	The *and* operator sets a bit to 1 if both of the corresponding bits in its operands are 1, and 0 otherwise. Example: $v = 32 & 16; print "$v (expected 0)\n";
|	or	The *or* operator sets a bit to 0 if both of the corresponding bits in its operands are 0, and 1 otherwise. Example:

<table>
<tr><td></td><td></td><td>$v = 32 | 16; print "$v (expected 48)\n";</td></tr>
<tr><td>^</td><td>exclusive or</td><td>The exclusive or operator sets a bit to 1 if the corresponding bits in its operands are different, and 0 otherwise.
Example:
$v = 3 ^ 9; print "$v (expected 10)\n";</td></tr>
<tr><td>~</td><td>not</td><td>The unary not operator inverts each bit in the operand, changing all the ones to zeros and zeros to ones.
Example:
$v = ~1024;</td></tr>
</table>

6.4.9.1.5 Other Numeric PERL Operations

See in the table below other numeric Perl operators:

Symbol	Name	Definition

,	comma	In scalar context this binary operator evaluates its left argument, discards this value, then evaluates its right argument and returns that value. In a list context, it's just a separator and inserts both its arguments into the list.
		Example (in scalar context):
		$v1 = 2; $v2 = 4; $v3 = $v1 == $v2;
		$v = ($v3, 5 == 5);
		print(" $v3(expected)\n");
		print(" $v(expected 1)\n");

=>	comma	It has the same function like the comma operator described above.
..	Range operator	In scalar context, this operator returns false as long as its left operand is false. When the left operand becomes true, the range operator returns true until the right operator remains true, after which it becomes false again. In a list context, this operator will return an array with contiguous sequences of items, beginning with the left operand value and ending with the right operand value (the items can be characters or numbers). Example (in a list context): print ('a'..'zz'); print ('1'..'10');

6.4.9.1.6 Numeric Assignment PERL Operations

Numeric assignment Perl operators perform some type of numeric operation and then assign the value to the existing variable.

Symbol	Name	Definition
=	assignment	This is the ordinary assignment operator. In a scalar context, it assigns the right operand's value to the left operand. In a list context, it assigns multiple values to the left array operand if the right operand is a list. Example: $v = 15; print $v, "\n"; # displays 15 @array = (10, 20, 30); print "@array\n"; # displays 10 20 30
+=	addition	It adds the right operand's value to the left operand. Example: $v = 10; $v += 15; print "$v (expected 25)\n";
-=	subtraction	It subtracts the right operand from the left operand. Example: $v = 25; $v -= 15; print "$v (expected 10)\n";
*=	multiplication	It multiplies the left operand's value by the right operand's value. Example: $v = 10; $v *= 15; print "$v (expected 150)\n";
/=	division	It divides the left operand's value by the right operand's value. Example: $v = 150; $v /= 15; print "$v (expected 10)\n";
**=	exponentiation	It raises the left operand's value to the power of the right operand's value.

		Example: $v = 12; $v **= 2; print "$v (expected 144)\n";
&&=	logical and	It's a combination between the logical "&&" and the assignment operators. Example: $v = 1; $v &&= 7 == 7; print "$v (expected 1)\n";
%=	modulus	It divides the left operand value by the right operand value and assigns the remainder to the left operand. Example: $v = 12; $v %= 5; print "$v (expected 2)\n";
||=	logical or	It's a combination between the logical "||" and the assignment operators. Example: $v = 0; $v \|\|= 7 == 7; print "$v (expected 1)\n";
<<=	bitwise shift left	It's a bitwise left shift assign. example: $v = 25; $v <<= 3; print "$v (expected 200)\n";
>>=	bitwise shift right	It's a bitwise right shift assign. Example: $v = 32; $v >>= 3; print "$v (expected 4)\n";
&=	bitwise and	It's a bitwise AND assign. Example: $v = 32; $v &= 16; print "$v (expected 0)\n";
|=	bitwise or	It's a bitwise OR assign. Example: $v = 32; $v \|= 16; print "$v (expected 48)\n";
^=	bitwise exclusive or	It's a bitwise XOR assign. Example: $v = 3; $v ^= 9; print "$v (expected 10)\n";

6.4.9.2 String PERL Operators

6.4.9.2.1 String Relational PERL Operators

The string relational Perl operators compare two strings and determine the validity of a relationship.

Symbol	Name	Definition

lt	less than	It returns true if the left operand is string wise less then the right one.
		Example:
		($v1, $v2) = ("abc", "abz");
		if($v1 lt $v2){
		print ("$v1 is less than $v2\n");
		}

le	less than or equal to	It returns true if the left operand is string wise less than or equal to the right one.
		Example:
		($v1, $v2) = ("abc", "abc");
		if($v1 le $v2){
		print("$v1 is less than or equal to $v2");
		print "\n";
		}

gt	greater than	It returns true if the left operand is string wise greater then the right one.
		Example:
		($v1, $v2) = ("abc", "abz");
		if($v2 gt $v1){
		print ("$v2 is greater than $v1\n");
		}

<table>
<tr><td></td><td></td><td></td></tr>
<tr><td>ge</td><td>greater than or equal to</td><td>It returns true if the left operand is string wise greater than or equal to the right one.
Example:
($v1, $v2) = ("abc", "abc");
if($v1 ge $v2){
print("$v1 is greater than or equal to $v2");
print "\n";
}</td></tr>
<tr><td>eq</td><td>equality</td><td>It returns true if the left operand is string wise equal to the right one.
Example:
($v1, $v2) = ("abc", "abc");
if($v1 eq $v2){
print ("$v1 is equal to $v2\n");
}</td></tr>
<tr><td>ne</td><td>not equal to</td><td>It returns true if the left operand is string wise not equal to the right one.
Example:
($v1, $v2) = ("abc", "ab1");
if($v1 ne $v2){
print ("$v1 is not equal to $v2\n");
}</td></tr>
<tr><td>cmp</td><td>comparison</td><td>It returns -1, 0, or 1 if the left operand is string wise less than, equal to or greater than the right one.
Example:
($v1, $v2) = ("am", "ak");
$v = $v1 cmp $v2;
print ("$v(expected 1)\n");</td></tr>
</table>

6.4.9.2.2 String Logical PERL Operators

The string logical Perl operators are generally derived from Boolean algebra and they are mainly used to control program flow, finding them as part of an if, a while or some other control statement. See in the table below the logical string Perl operators.

<table>
<tr><th>Symbol</th><th>Name</th><th>Definition</th></tr>
<tr><td>!</td><td>not</td><td>It returns true if the operand is a null string or an undefined value and false otherwise.
Example:
$v1 = !'some string here'; $v2 = !'';
The $v1 variable will return false and the $v2 variable will return true.</td></tr>
<tr><td>not</td><td>not</td><td>The same meaning as above, but it is a lower-precedence version.</td></tr>
<tr><td>&&</td><td>and</td><td>This operator is used to determine if both operands are true.
Example:
($v1, $v2) = ('abc', 'abzu');
$v = $v1 == 'abc' && $v2 == 'abzu';
print "$v (expected 1)";</td></tr>
<tr><td>and</td><td>and</td><td>Same as above.</td></tr>
<tr><td>||</td><td>or</td><td>This operator is used to determine if either of the operands is true.
Example:
($v1, $v2) = ('hello', 'good');
$v = $v1 == 'hello' || $v2 == 'hello';
print "$v (expected 1)";</td></tr>
<tr><td>or</td><td>or</td><td>Same as above.</td></tr>
<tr><td>xor</td><td>exclusive or</td><td>It returns true if either but not both of the operands is true.
Example:
($v1, $v2) = ('hello', 'good');
$v = $v1 == 'hello' xor $v2 == 'world';</td></tr>
</table>

		print "$v (expected 1)";
?	conditional operator	This is a ternary operator and it works like an if ... then ... else clause from the C language. If the left operand is true, it will return the central operand, otherwise the right operand. Example: $v = ("abc" eq "abd") ? "It's equal.\n" : "It's not equal. (expected)\n"; print $v;

6.4.9.2.3 Other String PERL Operations

See in the table below other string Perl operators:

Symbol	Name	Definition
,	comma	In a scalar context, the comma operator evaluates each element from left to right and returns the value of the rightmost element. In a list context, the comma operator separates the elements of a literal list. Example: # scalar context $colors = ('blue', 'red', 'yellow'); print "$colors (expected yellow)\n"; # list context @colors = ('blue', 'red', 'yellow'); print "@colors[1] (expected red)\n";
=>	comma	This operator is a special type of comma, for example ('dog', 'cat') is similar to (dog => 'cat'). Or it can be used to separate key/value pairs in a hash structure: %petColors = (dog => 'brown', cat => 'white');
-	negation	If the string operand begins with a plus or minus sign, the string negation operator returns a string with the opposite sign. Example: $v = "-abcd"; print (-$v, "(expected +abcd)\n");
.	concatenation	This operator joins two or more strings like in the example below. Example: $v = "Hello" . " World" . "!"; print $v, " (expected Hello World!)\n";
..	range operator	The range operator, in a list context, produces the range of values from the left value through the right value in increments of 1. Example: @v = ('ab' .. 'ae'); print @v, " (expected abacadae)\n";
x	repetition	The repetition operator returns the first operand (which is a string) repeated by the number of times specified by the second operand (which is an integer). Example: @v = 'ab' x 3; print @v, " (expected ababab)\n";

6.4.9.2.4 String Assignment PERL Operations

String assignment Perl operators perform some type of string operation and then assign the value to the existing variable.

<table>
<tr><th>Symbol</th><th>Name</th><th>Definition</th></tr>
<tr><td>=</td><td>Assignment</td><td>This is the ordinary assignment operator.
Example:
$v = 'Hello World!'; print $v, " (expected Hello World!)\n";</td></tr>
<tr><td>&&=</td><td>logical and</td><td>It's a combination between the logical "&&" and the assignment operators.
Example:
$v = 1; $v &&= 'abc' eq 'abc';
print $v, " (expected 1)\n";</td></tr>
<tr><td>||=</td><td>logical or</td><td>It's a combination between the logical "||" and the assignment</td></tr>
</table>

<table>
<tr><td></td><td></td><td>operators.
Example:
$v = 0; $v ||= 'abc' eq 'abc'; print $v, " (expected 1)\n";</td></tr>
<tr><td>.=</td><td>concatenation</td><td>It's a combination between the concatenation "." and the assignment operators.
Example:
$v = "Hello "; $v .= 'World!'; print $v, " (expected Hello World!)\n";</td></tr>
<tr><td>x=</td><td>repetition</td><td>It's a repetition assignment operator.
Example:
$v = "true "; $v x= 2; print $v, " (expected true true)\n";</td></tr>
</table>

6.4.9.3 Special PERL Operations

See in the table below the special Perl operators:

Symbol	Name	Definition
\	reference	We call reference the scalar value that contains a memory address. In order to reference a variable, we use the operator. Look at the below snippet code to see how to use it. Example: $v="Hello World!"; $ref_v=\$v; print $$ref_v, " (expected Hello World!)\n";
->	dereference	The dereference operator was used for the first time in the Perl 5 language. This operator let us to access and manipulates the elements of an array, hash, object of a class data structure. If you use the reference operator to reference a scalar variable, before you use it you must dereference the reference variable. Example: @v = ('black', 'white', 'blue', 'orange'); $vRef = \@v; # the reference variable print $v[1], " (expected white)\n"; $vRef->[1] = 'red'; # dereference before use print $v[1], " (expected red)\n";

=~	pattern binding	This binary operator binds a string expression to a pattern match. The string which is intended to bind is put on the left meanwhile the operator itself is put on the right. We use the pattern binding operator in the case we have a string which is not stored in the $_ variable and we need to perform some matches or substitutions of that string.
		Example:
		$v = "black and white";
		if($v =~ m/white/) {
		print "Yes (expected)\n";
		}
		$v =~ s/black and white/red/;
		print $v, " (expected red)\n";

!~	pattern binding (not)	This operator is similar the operator above, but the return value is negated logically.
		Example:
		$v = "black and white";
		if($v =! m/yellow/) {
		print "Yes (expected)\n";
		}

6.4.10 PERL Conditional Statements

In this section, we will see how to use the if statement in Perl scripts. The if statement let you execute a block of statements between two curly braces if a boolean condition is evaluated true, otherwise the execution continues with the following block, either an elsif/else block or after the end of the if statement.

6.4.10.1 if used as a modifier

```
Statement if (Expr)
```

In this first form we used Perl *if* as a modifier of a statement. *Expr* is a condition which must be evaluated in order to execute the Perl *if* statement. By writing code like this, you can put the important part of the statement at the beginning, in order to monitor it. The next code sample shows you how to use it when you need to print the values of certain variables in order to debug your Perl script:

```
$debug = 1;
$a = 1; $b = 2;
# ... some statements here
print "a = $a\n" if $debug;   # check the $a value
# ... other statements
print "b = $b\n" if $debug;   # check the $b value
# the rest of script statements
```

If we want to print the debug messages, at the beginning of the script we set the $debug variable value to 1, otherwise we set it to 0. The next example will show you how to use the regular expressions in the Perl if condition (the =~ operator):

```
$vari = "An example with the if modifier";
print "\$v contains the word \'example\'\n" if ($vari =~ /example/);
# it prints: $v contains the word 'example'
$vari = "";
```

This code will execute the print statement only if the $vari string variable matches the 'example' word. If it doesn't, the script will continue with the next statement (i.e. $v = "").

6.4.10.2 General if statement

The second syntax form is more general:

```
if (Expr) Block elsif (Expr) Block ... else Block
```

where:

- Expr represents a Boolean conditional expression
- the elsif and else clauses are optional and are used if you want to check a certain sequence of conditional expressions and find out which one of them is true
- Block consists of one or more statements enclosed in curly braces; in the construction of a block, the curly braces are always required.

We can split the general conditional Perl if statement as follows:

6.4.10.2.1 A simple if statement

```
if (Expr) Block
```

Perl will evaluate the *Expr* and if it is true, it will execute the code between the curly braces of the block. Otherwise, the script will continue with the next statement after the block. Neither *elsif* nor *else* clauses are used in the above format. See the next snippet code example:

```
$a = -1;
if($a < 0) {
   $a += 2;
}
print "a = $a\n";  # it outputs a = 1
```

The Perl interpreter will check the condition between parentheses and if the result is true, it will increment the $a scalar variable value with 2. It is possible that *Expr* doesn't represent a condition, like in the following example:

```
if(1) {
    $a = 1;
}
```

Because the expression is true, the Perl interpreter will continue with the execution of the block, i.e. it will assign the value 1 to the $a scalar variable. As you guess, in this example you don't need to use the Perl if statement at all, the assign statement $a = 1 is sufficient to do the job.

6.4.10.2.2 if-else

```
if (Expr) Block else Block
```

The Perl interpreter will evaluate the conditional expression and if the result is true, the execution of the script will continue with the block that follows the conditional expression; otherwise, the script execution will skip inside the block that is after the else clause. Let's look at a simple example where we need to find the maximum of two numbers:

```
$a = 15;
$b = 27;
if($a > $b) {
   print "max($a, $b) = $a\n";
} else {
   print "max($a, $b) = $b\n";
}
# it prints: max(15, 27) = 27
```

Well, there is a shorter way to do this by using the ? logical ternary operator - also called the conditional operator. I remind you briefly that the ternary operator (named ternary because it uses three operands) is like an if-else compound statement both included into an expression.

Please note that this operator is an expression that returns a value based on the conditional sentence it evaluates. It can be used by following the syntax:

```
Expr ?  true-value : false-value
```

The logical ternary operator evaluates its first argument (*Expr*) and if this is true, it returns the second argument (true-value), otherwise it returns the third argument (false-value). With the ternary operator, we can rewrite the above code like so:

```
$a = 15; $b = 27;
print "max($a, $b) = ", $a > $b ? $a : $b,"\n";
```

The output obtained after running this code will be the same as in the previous example, where we used Perl if statement. Now I'll discuss a bit about the case when in a Perl *if* statement we have an empty block after the expression, like in the following snippet code example:

```
$a = 12; $b = -25;
if($a*$b >= 0 && $a + $b  >= 0) {
   # do nothing
} else {
   print "at least $a or $b is negative\n";
}
```

There are at least two ways to get rid of the empty if block. One way is to use the Perl unless statement instead of the Perl *if* statement:

```
$a = 12; $b = -25;
unless($a*$b >= 0 && $a + $b  >= 0) {
  print "at least $a or $b is negative\n";
}
```

In writing the conditional statements, you can swap as you wish between Perl *if* and Perl *unless* in order to make your code more readable. Another way is to rewrite the conditional expression enclosed between the parentheses that follow the if keyword: ($a*$b >= 0 && $a + $b >= 0). This is a boolean expression and as you expect Perl provides you with the logical AND operator (&&) and the logical OR operator (||) in order to manipulate the boolean expressions.

When you use the && and || operators be careful not to include any spaces between the symbols ("& &" or "| |" is wrong) because you'll get something you couldn't expect. So than we can rewrite the above condition in order to get rid of the empty block:

```
$a = 12; $b = -25;
if($a*$b < 0) {
    print "at least $a or $b is negative\n";
}
```

6.4.10.2.3 if-elsif-else

```
if (Expr) Block elsif (Expr) Block ... else Block
```

This form uses the elsif clause that allows you to check as many conditional expressions as are required. The else clause from the end of the form is still optional but you can use it at the end of the *if* statement if all other tests fail – with other words, the block of the final else will be executed if none of the conditions are true.

The next snippet code shows you an example about how to use if in connection with the elsif and else clauses:

```
chomp ($line = <STDIN>);
$line = lc($line);
if($line eq "index"){
    print "index function\n";
} elsif ($line eq "chomp") {
    print "chomp function\n";
} elsif ($line eq "hex") {
    print "hex function\n";
} elsif ($line eq "substr") {
    print "substr function\n";
} else {
    print "$line: unknown function\n";
}
```

In this example we read a line from <STDIN>, remove the last newline with the chomp function and convert all the characters in lowercases. Next we check if the text read from <STDIN> is the name of index, chomp, hex or substr functions. If we don't find any occurrence, the script program will execute the block that follows the else clause.

6.4.11 PERL Loops

6.4.11.1 For Loop

A *for* loop goes through the loop a certain number of times. Here is the general form of a for loop:

```
for (starting assignment; test condition; increment){
  code to repeat
```

```
}
```

Well, that's great, but it doesn't tell us much about what happens. Instead, let's use a real example. Let's say we wanted to print the word "Hi" ten times in a row. We could use a for loop like this:

```
for ($count=1; $count<6; $count++){
  print "Hi\n";
}
```

You'll notice above we created a variable named $count to test the condition each time through. In this case, we only used it to test the condition and not inside the loop itself. The first time through $count is 1 since we have that as our starting condition.

The loop will keep repeating until count finishes the 6th time through. When it tries to go through as 6, it is stopped because it fails the test condition— 6 is not less than 6. So, what we get is this repetitive list:

```
Hi
Hi
Hi
Hi
Hi
```

You could also use the $count variable inside the *for* loop to change what is printed. This comes in handy when we get to arrays, but for now we will just print the value of $count each time through. This will print a list of numbers from one to five:

```
for ($count=1; $count<6; $count++){
  print "$count\n";
}
```

Now you will get this:

```
1
2
3
4
5
```

6.4.11.2 While Loop

The *while* loop repeats a portion of code, but it repeats it until the condition you provide comes back *false*. Here is the general syntax for the while loop:

```
while (test condition){
  code to repeat
}
```

So, we could print out that list of numbers from one to ten with the while loop instead. Be sure to define your test variable (in our case $count) before the loop begins. You will also need to be sure to increment the test variable inside the loop. Here is the code for the number list with a while loop:

```
$count=1;
while ($count<6){
  print "$count\n";
  $count++;
}
```

For some things, this is easier to use than the *for* loop. It just depends on what action you wish to perform.

6.4.11.3 Foreach Loop

The *foreach* loop is one that is often used with some sort of array. If you have an understanding of arrays, this will make a bit more sense:

```
foreach variable_name (array_name){
  code to repeat
}
```

An array is a way of storing a group of variables that makes them easy to access and manipulate later. The *foreach* loop takes each element of the array and uses it with your code. Let's say we had an array named @bank (The @ sign signals an array). Using the *foreach* loop, we could print out each element of the array. If we use the variable $dollar to represent an element in the array, we could print out every $dollar we have in the @bank, so to speak!

```
foreach $dollar (@bank){
  print "$dollar\n";
}
```

6.4.12 Subroutines

6.4.12.1 Arguments, Return Values

Arguments for a subroutine are passed via an array @. Note once again that the @ sign tells us this is an array; we can think of the array name as being , with the @ sign then telling us it is an array. Here are some examples:

```
# read in two numbers from the command line (note: the duality of
# numbers and strings in Perl means no need for atoi()!)
$x = $ARGV[0];
$y = $ARGV[1];
# call subroutine which finds the minimum and print the latter
$z = min($x,$y);
print $z, "\n";
sub min {
    if ($_[0] < $_[1]) {return $_[0];}
    else {return $_[1];}
}
```

A common Perl idiom is to have a subroutine use shift on @ to get the arguments and assign them to local variables.

Arguments must be pass-by-value, but this small restriction is more than compensated by the facts that (a) arguments can be references, and (b) the return value can also be a list. Here is an example illustrating all this:

```
$x = $ARGV[0];
$y = $ARGV[1];
($mn,$mx) = minmax($x,$y);
print $mn, " ", $mx, "\n";
sub minmax {
    $s = shift @_; # get first argument
    $t = shift @_; # get second argument
    if ($s < $t) {return ($s,$t);} # return a list
        else {return ($t,$s);}
}
```

Or, one could use array assignment:

```
($s,$t) = @_
```

However, this won't work for subroutines having a variable number of arguments.

Any subroutine, even if it has no return, will return the last value computed. So for instance in the minmax() example above, it would still work even if we were to remove the two return keywords. This is a common aspect of many scripting languages, such as the R data manipulation language and the Yacas symbolic mathematics language.

If any of the arguments in a call are arrays, all of the arguments are flattened into one huge array, @ . For example, in the call to f() here,

```
$n = 10;
@x = (5,12,13);
f($n,@x);
$ [2] would be 12.
```

6.4.12.2 Some Remarks on Notation

Instead of enclosing arguments within parentheses, as in C, one can simply write them in "command-line arguments" fashion. For example, the call

```
($mn,$mx) = minmax($x,$y);
```

can be written as

```
($mn,$mx) = minmax $x,$y;
```

In fact, we've been doing this in all our previous examples, in our calls to print(). This style is often clearer. In any case, you will often encounter this in Perl code, especially in usage of Perl's built-in functions, such as the print() example we just mentioned.

On the other hand, if the subroutine, say x(), has no arguments make sure to use the parentheses in your call:

```
x();
```

rather than

```
x;
```

In the latter case, the Perl interpreter will treat this as the "declaration" of a variable x, not a call to x().

6.4.12.3 Passing Subroutines as Arguments

Older versions of Perl required that subroutines be referenced through an ampersand preceding the name, e.g.

```
($mn,$mx) = &minmax $x,$y;
```

In some cases we must still do so, such as when we need to pass a subroutine name to a subroutine. The reason this need arises is that we may write a packaged program which calls a user-written subroutine. Here is an example of how to do it:

```
sub x {
    print "this is x\n";
}
sub y {
    print "this is y\n";
}
sub w {
    $r = shift;
    &$r();
}
w \&x; # prints "this is x"
```

```
w \&y; # prints "this is y"
```

Here w() calls r(), with the latter actually being either x() or y().

6.4.13 String Manipulation in Perl

One major category of Perl string constructs involves searching and possibly replacing strings. For example, the following program acts like the UNIX *grep* command, reporting all lines found in a given file which contains a given string (the file name and the string are given on the command line):

```
open(INFILE,$ARGV[0]);
while ($line = <INFILE>) {
   if ($line =~ /$ARGV[1]/) {
      print $line;
   }
}
```

Here the Perl expression

```
($line =~ /$ARGV[1]/)
```

checks $line for the given string, resulting in a true value if the string is found. In this string-matching operation Perl allows many different types of regular expression conditions.3 For example,

```
open(INFILE,$ARGV[0]);
while ($line = <INFILE>) {
   if ($line =~ /us[ei]/) {
      print $line;
   }
}
```

would print out all the lines in the file which contain either the string "use" or "usi". Substitution is another common operation. For example, the code

```
open(INFILE,$ARGV[0]);
while ($line = <INFILE>) {
   if ($line =~ s/abc/xyz/) {
      print $line;
   }
}
```

would pull out all lines in the file which contain the string "abc", replace the first instance of that string in each such line by "xyz", and then print out those changed lines. There are many more string operations in the Perl repertoire. As mentioned earlier, Perl uses eq to test string equality; it uses ne to test string inequality.

A popular Perl operator is chop, which removes the last character of a string. This is typically used to remove an end-of-line character. For example,

```
chop $line;
```

removes the last character in $line, and reassigns the result to $line. Since chop is actually a function, and in fact one that has $ as its default argument, if $line had been read in from STDIN, we could write the above code as

```
chop;
```

6.4.14 Perl Packages/Modules

In the spirit of modular programming, it's good to break up our program into separate files, or packages. Perl specialized the packages notion to modules, and it will be the latter that will be our focus here. Except for the top-level file (the one containing the analog of main() in C/C++), a file must have the suffix .pm ("Perl module") in its name and have as its first noncomment/nonblank line a package statement, named after the file name. For example the module X.pm would begin with

```
package X;
```

The files which draw upon X.pm would have a line

```
use X;
```

near the beginning.

The :: symbol is used to denote membership. For example, the expression $X::y refers to the scalar $y in the file X.pm, while @X::z refers to the array @z in that file. The top-level file is referred to as main from within other modules. As you can see, packages give one a separate namespace. Modules which are grouped together as a library are placed in the same directory, or the same directory tree.

6.5 Python

6.5.1 What is Python?

Python is an *interpreted, object-oriented, high-level programming* language with dynamic semantics. Its high-level built in data structures, combined with dynamic typing and dynamic binding, make it very attractive for Rapid Application Development, as well as for use as a scripting or glue language to connect existing components together. Python's simple, easy to learn syntax emphasizes readability and therefore reduces the cost of program maintenance.

Python supports modules and packages, which encourages program modularity and code reuse. The Python interpreter and the extensive standard library are available in source or binary form without charge for all major platforms, and can be freely distributed.

Often, programmers fall in love with Python because of the increased productivity it provides. Since there is no compilation step, the edit-test-debug cycle is incredibly fast. *Debugging Python* programs is easy: a bug or bad input will never cause a segmentation fault. Instead, when the interpreter discovers an error, it raises an exception. When the program doesn't catch the exception, the interpreter prints a stack trace.

A source level debugger allows inspection of local and global variables, evaluation of arbitrary expressions, setting breakpoints, stepping through the code a line at a time, and so on. The debugger is written in Python itself, testifying to Python's introspective power. On the other hand, often the quickest way to debug a program is to add a few print statements to the source: the fast edit-test-debug cycle makes this simple approach very effective.

6.5.2 Booleans

The *Boolean* constants are *True* and *False*, and the six relational operators work on all primitives, including strings. !, ||, and && have been replaced by the more expressive not, or, and and. Also, we can chain relational tests like *min < mean < max* make perfect sense.

```
>>> 4 > 0
True
>>> "apple" == "bear"
False
>>> "apple" < "bear" < "candy cane" < "dill"
True
```

```
>>> x = y = 7
>>> x <= y and y <= x
True
>>> not x >= y
False
```

6.5.3 Whole Numbers

Integers work as you'd expect, though you're insulated almost entirely from the fact that small numbers exist as four-byte figures and super big numbers are managed as longs, without the memory limits:

```
>>> 1 * -2 * 3 * -4 * 5 * -6
-720
>>> factorial(6)
720
>>> factorial(5)
120
>>> factorial(10)
3628800
>>> factorial(15)
1307674368000L
>>> factorial(40)
815915283247897734345611269596115894272000000000L
```

When the number is big, you're reminded how big by the big fat L at the end. Also, assume that we defined the factorial function, because it's not a built-in.

6.5.4 Strings

String constants can be delimited using either double or single quotes. Substring selection, concatenation, and repetition are all supported.

```
>>> interjection = "ohplease"
>>> interjection[2:6]
'plea'
>>> interjection[4:]
'ease'
>>> interjection[:2]
'oh'
>>> interjection[:]
'ohplease'
>>> interjection * 4
'ohpleaseohpleaseohpleaseohplease'
>>> oldmaidsays = "pickme" + interjection * 3
>>> oldmaidsays
'pickmeohpleaseohpleaseohplease'
>>> 'abcdefghijklmnop'[-5:] # negative indices count from the end!
'lmnop'
```

The quirky syntax that's likely new to you is the slicing, ala [start:stop]. The [2:6] identifies the substring of interest: character data from position 2 up through but not including position 6. Leave out the start index and it's taken to be 0.

Leave out the stop index, it's the full string length. Leave them both out, and you get the whole string. (Python doesn't burden us with a separate character type. We just use one-character strings where we'd normally use a character, and everything works just swell.)

Strings are really objects, and there are good number of methods. Rather than exhaustively document them here, I'll just illustrate how some of them work. In general, you should expect the set of methods to more or less imitate what strings in other objectoriented languages do.

You can expect methods like find, startswith, endswith, replace, and so forth, because a string class would be a pretty dumb string class without them. Python's string provides a bunch of additional methods that make it all the more useful in scripting and WWW capacities—methods like capitalize, split, join, expandtabs, and encode. Here's are some examples:

```
>>> 'abcdefghij'.find('ef')
4
>>> 'abcdefghij'.find('ijk')
-1
>>> 'yodelady-yodelo'.count('y')
3
>>> 'google'.endswith('ggle')
False
>>> 'lItTle ThIrTeEn YeAr OlD gIrl'.capitalize()
'Little thirteen year old girl'
>>>
>>> 'Spiderman 3'.istitle()
True
>>> '1234567890'.isdigit()
True
>>> '12345aeiuo'.isdigit()
False
>>> '12345abcde'.isalnum()
True
>>> 'sad'.replace('s', 'gl')
'glad'
>>> 'This is a test.'.split(' ')
['This', 'is', 'a', 'test.']
>>> '-'.join(['ee','eye','ee','eye','oh'])
'ee-eye-ee-eye-oh'
```

6.5.5 Lists and Tuples

Python has two types of sequential containers: lists (which are read-write) and tuples (which are immutable, read-only). Lists are delimited by square brackets, whereas tuples are delimited by parentheses. Here are some examples:

```
>>> streets = ["Castro", "Noe", "Sanchez", "Church",
"Dolores", "Van Ness", "Folsom"]
>>> streets[0]
'Castro'
>>> streets[5]
'Van Ness'
>>> len(streets)
7
>>> streets[len(streets) - 1]
'Folsom'
```

The same slicing that was available to us with strings actually works with lists too:

```
>>> streets[1:6]
['Noe', 'Sanchez', 'Church', 'Dolores', 'Van Ness']
>>> streets[:2]
['Castro', 'Noe']
>>> streets[5:5]
[]
```

Coolest feature ever: you can splice into the middle of a list by identifying the slice that should be replaced:

```
>>> streets
['Castro', 'Noe', 'Sanchez', 'Church', 'Dolores', 'Van Ness', 'Folsom']
>>> streets[5:5] = ["Guerrero", "Valencia", "Mission"]
>>> streets
['Castro', 'Noe', 'Sanchez', 'Church', 'Dolores', 'Guerrero',
'Valencia', 'Mission', 'Van Ness', 'Folsom']
>>> streets[0:1] = ["Eureka", "Collingswood", "Castro"]
>>> streets
['Eureka', 'Collingswood', 'Castro', 'Noe', 'Sanchez', 'Church',
'Dolores', 'Guerrero', 'Valencia', 'Mission', 'Van Ness', 'Folsom']
>>> streets.append("Harrison")
>>> streets
['Eureka', 'Collingswood', 'Castro', 'Noe', 'Sanchez', 'Church',
'Dolores', 'Guerrero', 'Valencia', 'Mission', 'Van Ness', 'Folsom', 'Harrison']
```

The first splice states that the empty region between items 5 and 6—or in [5, 5), in interval notation—should be replaced with the list constant on the right hand side. The second splice states that streets[0:1]—which is the sublist ['Castro']—should be overwritten with the sequence ['Eureka', 'Collingswood', 'Castro']. And naturally there's an append method.

Note: lists need not be homogenous. If you want, you can model a record using a list, provided you remember what slot stores what data.

```
>>> prop = ["355 Noe Street", 3, 1.5, 2460,
[[1988, 385000],[2004, 1380000]]]
>>> print("The house at %s was built in %d." % (prop[0], prop[4][0][0])
```

The house at 355 Noe Street was built in 1988. The list's more conservative brother is the tuple, which is more or less an immutable list constant that's delimited by parentheses instead of square brackets. It's supports readonly slicing, but no clever insertions:

```
>>> cto = ("Will Shulman", 154000, "BSCS Stanford, 1997")
>>> cto[0]
'Will Shulman'
>>> cto[2]
'BSCS Stanford, 1997'
>>> cto[1:2]
(154000,)
>>> cto[0:2]
('Will Shulman', 154000)
>>> cto[1:2] = 158000
Traceback (most recent call last):
File "<stdin>", line 1, in ?
TypeError: object doesn't support slice assignment
```

6.5.6 Functions

In practice, I'd say that Python walks the fence between the procedural and objectoriented paradigms. Here's an implementation of a standalone gatherDivisors function. This illustrates if tests, for-loop iteration, and most importantly, the dependence on white space and indentation to specify block structure:

```
# Function: gatherDivisors
# ------------------------
# Accepts the specified number and produces
```

```
# a list of all numbers that divide evenly
# into it.
def gatherDivisors(num):
    """Synthesizes a list of all the positive numbers
    that evenly divide into the specified num."""
    divisors = []
    for d in xrange(1, num/2 + 1):
        if (num % d == 0):
            divisors.append(d)
    return divisors
```

The syntax takes some getting used to. We don't really miss the semicolons (and they're often ignored if you put them in by mistake). You'll notice that certain parts of the implementation are indented one, two, even three times. The indentation (which comes in the form of either a tab or four space characters) makes it clear who owns whom. You'll notice that def, for, and if statements are punctuated by colons: this means at least one statement and possibly many will fall under the its jurisdiction.

Note the following:

- The # marks everything from it to the end of the line as a comment. I bet you figured that out already.
- None of the variables—neither parameters nor locals—are strongly typed. Of course, Python supports the notion of numbers, floating points, strings, and so forth. But it doesn't require you state why type of data need be stored in any particular variable. Identifiers can be bound to any type of data at any time, and it needn't be associated with the same type of data forever. Although there's rarely a good reason to do this, a variable called data could be set to 5, and reassigned to "five", and later reassigned to [5, "five", 5, [5]] and Python would approve.
- The triply double-quote delimited string is understood to be a string constant that's allowed to span multiple lines. In particular, if a string constant is the first expression within a def, it's taken to be a documentation string explanation the function to the client. It's not designed to be an implementation comment—just a user comment so they know what it does.
- The for loop is different than it is in other language. Rather than counting a specific numbers of times, for loops iterate over what are called iterables. The iterator (which in the gatherDivisors function is d) is bound to each element within the iterable until it's seen every one. Iterables take on several forms, but the list is probably the most common. We can also iterate over strings, over sequences (which are read-only lists, really), and over dictionaries (which are Python's version of the C++ hash_map)

6.5.7 Packaging Code In Modules

Once you're solving a problem that's large enough to require procedural decomposition, you'll want to place the implementations of functions in files—files that operate either as modules (sort of like Java packages, C++ libraries, etc) or as scripts.

This gatherDivisors function above might be packaged up in a file called divisors.py. If so, and you launch python from the directory storing the divisors.py file, then you can import the divisors module, and you can even import actual functions from within the module. Look here:

```
bash-3.2$ python
Python 2.5.1 (r251:54863, Oct 5 2007, 21:08:09)
```

```
[GCC 4.0.1 (Apple Inc. build 5465)] on darwin
Type "help", "copyright", "credits" or "license" for more information.
>>> import divisors
>>> divisors.gatherDivisors(54)
[1, 2, 3, 6, 9, 18, 27]
>>> gatherDivisors(216)
Traceback (most recent call last):
File "<stdin>", line 1, in ?
NameError: name 'gatherDivisors' is not defined
>>> from divisors import gatherDivisors
>>> gatherDivisors(216)
[1, 2, 3, 4, 6, 8, 9, 12, 18, 24, 27, 36, 54, 72, 108]
>>> "neat"
'neat'
```

If everything you write is designed to be run as a standalone script—in other words, an independent interpreted program—then you can bundle the collection of meaningful functions into a single file, save the file, and mark the file as something that's executable (i.e. chmod a+x narcissist.py).

CHAPTER

Bitwise Hacking 7

7.1 Introduction

In this chapter we will cover the bitwise operations topics which are useful for interviews and exams.

7.1 Hacks on Bitwise Programming

In C and $C++$ we can work with bits effectively. First let us see the definitions of each bit operation and then move onto different techniques for solving the problems. Basically, there are six operators that C and $C++$ support for bit manipulation:

Symbol	Operation
&	Bitwise AND
|	Bitwise OR
^	Bitwise Exclusive-OR
≪	Bitwise left shift
≫	Bitwise right shift
~	Bitwise complement

7.2.1 Bitwise AND

The bitwise AND tests two binary numbers and returns bit values of 1 for positions where both numbers had a one, and bit values of 0 where both numbers did not have one:

```
    01001011
&   00010101
    ----------
    00000001
```

7.2.2 Bitwise OR

The bitwise OR tests two binary numbers and returns bit values of 1 for positions where either bit or both bits are one, the result of 0 only happens when both bits are 0:

```
    01001011
|   00010101
    ----------
    01011111
```

7.2.3 Bitwise Exclusive-OR

The bitwise Exclusive-OR tests two binary numbers and returns bit values of 1 for positions where both bits are different, if they are the same then the result is 0:

```
   01001011
^  00010101
  ----------
   01011110
```

7.2.4 Bitwise Left Shift

The bitwise left shift moves all bits in the number to the left and fills vacated bit positions with 0.

```
01001011
    << 2
--------
00101100
```

7.2.5 Bitwise Right Shift

The bitwise right shift moves all bits in the number to the right.

```
01001011
    >> 2
--------
??010010
```

Note the use of ? for the fill bits. Where the left shift filled the vacated positions with 0, a right shift will do the same only when the value is unsigned. If the value is signed then a right shift will fill the vacated bit positions with the sign bit or 0, which is implementation-defined. So the best option is to never right shift signed values.

7.2.6 Bitwise Complement

The bitwise complement inverts the bits in a single binary number.

```
01001011
   ~
---------
10110100
```

7.2.7 Checking whether K-th bit is set or not

Let us assume that the given number is n. Then for checking the Kth bit we can use the expression: $n \,\&\, (1 \ll K - 1)$. If the expression is true then we can say the Kth bit is set (that means, set to 1).

Example:

$n =$	01001011 and $K = 4$
$1 \ll K - 1$	00001000
$n \,\&\, (1 \ll K - 1)$	00001000

7.2.8 Setting K-th bit

For a given number n, to set the Kth bit we can use the expression: $n \mid 1 \ll (K - 1)$

Example:

$n =$	01001011 and $K = 3$
$1 \ll K - 1$	00000100
$n \mid (1 \ll K - 1)$	01001111

7.2.9 Clearing K-th bit

To clear K^{th} bit of a given number n, we can use the expression: $n \,\&\, \sim(1 \ll K - 1)$

Example:

$n =$	01001011 and $K = 4$
$1 \ll K - 1$	00001000

$$\sim(1 \ll K-1) \quad 11110111$$
$$n \,\&\sim(1 \ll K-1) \quad 01000011$$

7.2.10 Toggling K-th bit

For a given number n, for toggling the Kth bit we can use the expression: $n \,\hat{}\,(1 \ll K-1)$

Example: $n = 01001011$ and $K = 3$

$$1 \ll K-1 \quad 00000100$$
$$n \,\hat{}\, (1 \ll K-1) \quad 01001111$$

7.2.11 Toggling Rightmost One bit

For a given number n, for toggling rightmost one bit we can use the expression: $n \,\&\, n-1$

Example: $n = 01001011$

$$n-1 \quad 01001010$$
$$n \,\&\, n-1 \quad 01001010$$

7.2.12 Isolating Rightmost One bit

For a given number n, for isolating rightmost one bit we can use the expression: $n \,\&\, -n$

Example: $n = 01001011$

$$-n \quad 10110101$$
$$n \,\&\, -n \quad 00000001$$

Note: For computing $-n$, use two's complement representation. That means, toggle all bits and add 1.

7.2.13 Isolating Rightmost Zero bit

For a given number n, for isolating rightmost zero bit we can use the expression: $\sim n \,\&\, n+1$

Example: $n = 01001011$

$$\sim n \quad 10110100$$
$$n+1 \quad 01001100$$
$$\sim n \,\&\, n+1 \quad 00000100$$

7.2.14 Checking Whether Number is Power of 2 or not

Given number n, to check whether the number is in 2^n form for not, we can use the expression: $if(n \,\&\, n-1 == 0)$

Example: $n = 01001011$

$$n-1 \quad 01001010$$
$$n \,\&\, n-1 \quad 01001010$$
$$if(n \,\&\, n-1 == 0) \quad 0$$

7.2.15 Multiplying Number by Power of 2

For a given number n, to multiply the number with 2^K we can use the expression: $n \ll K$

Example: $n = 00001011$ and $K = 2$

$$n \ll K \quad 00101100$$

7.2.16 Dividing Number by Power of 2

For a given number n, to divide the number with 2^K we can use the expression: $n \gg K$

Example: $n = 00001011$ and $K = 2$

$n \gg K$ 00010010

7.2.17 Finding Modulo of a Given Number

For a given number n, to find the %8 we can use the expression: $n \,\&\, 0x7$. Similarly, to find %32, use the expression: $n \,\&\, 0x1F$

Note: Similarly, we can find modulo value of any number.

7.2.18 Reversing the Binary Number

For a given number n, to reverse the bits (reverse (mirror) of binary number)we can use the following code snippet:

```
unsigned int n, nReverse = n;
int s = sizeof(n);
for (; n; n >>= 1) {
 nReverse <<= 1;
 nReverse |= n & 1;
 s--;
}
nReverse <<= s;
```

This requires one iteration per bit and the number of iterations depends on the size of the number.

7.2.19 Counting Number of One's in number

For a given number n, to count the number of $1's$ in its binary representation we can use any of the following methods.

*Method*1: Process bit by bit

```
unsigned int n;
unsigned int count=0;
while(n) {
 count += n & 1;
 n >>= 1;
}
```

This approach requires one iteration per bit and the number of iterations depends on system.

*Method*2: Using modulo approach

```
unsigned int n;
unsigned int count=0;
while(n) {
 if(n%2 ==1) count++;
 n = n/2;
}
```

This requires one iteration per bit and the number of iterations depends on system.

*Method*3: Using toggling approach: $n \,\&\, n - 1$

```
unsigned int n;
unsigned int count=0;
while(n) {
   count++;
   n &= n - 1;
}
```

The number of iterations depends on the number of 1 bits in the number.

Method4: Using preprocessing idea. In this method, we process the bits in groups. For example if we process them in groups of 4 bits at a time, we create a table which indicates the number of one's for each of those possibilities (as shown below.)

0000→0	0100→1	1000→1	1100→2
0001→1	0101→2	1001→2	1101→3
0010→1	0110→2	1010→2	1110→3
0011→2	0111→3	1011→3	1111→4

The following code to count the number of 1s in the number with this approach:

```
int Table = {0,1,1,2,1,2,2,3,1,2,2,3,2,3,3,4};
int count = 0;
for(; n; n >>= 4)
   count = count + Table[n & 0xF];
return count;
```

This approach requires one iteration per 4 bits and the number of iterations depends on system.

7.2.20 Creating Mask for Trailing Zero's

For a given number n, to create a mask for trailing zeros, we can use the expression: $(n \,\&\, -n) - 1$

Example:

$n =$	01001011
$-n$	10110101
$n \,\&\, -n$	00000001
$(n \,\&\, -n) - 1$	00000000

Note: In the above case we are getting the mask as all zeros because there are no trailing zeros.

7.2.21 Swap all odd and even bits

Example: $n =$ 01001011

Find even bits of given number (evenN) =	n & 0xAA	00001010
Find odd bits of given number (oddN) =	n & 0x55	01000001
	evenN >>= 1	00000101
	oddN <<= 1	10000010
Final Expression:	evenN | oddN	10000111

7.2.212 Performing Average without Division

Is there a bit-twiddling algorithm to replace $mid = \frac{low + high}{2}$ (used in Binary Search and Merge Sort) with something much faster?

We can use $mid = (low + high) >> 1$. Note that using $\frac{low + high}{2}$ for midpoint calculations won't work correctly when integer overflow becomes an issue. We can use bit shifting and also overcome a possible overflow issue: $low + ((high - low)/\,2)$ and the bit shifting operation for this is $low + ((high - low) >> 1)$.

Problems and Questions with Answers

Question 1: Give an algorithm for printing the matrix elements in spiral order.

Answer: Non-recursive solution involves directions right, left, up, down, and dealing their corresponding indices. Once the first row is printed, direction changes (from right) to down, the row is discarded by incrementing the upper limit. Once the last column is printed, direction changes to left, the column is discarded by decrementing the right hand limit.

```
void Spiral(int **A, int n) {
   int rowStart=0, columnStart=0;
   int rowEnd=n-1, columnEnd=n-1;
   while(rowStart<=rowEnd && columnStart<=columnEnd) {
      int i=rowStart, j=columnStart;
      for(j=columnStart; j<=columnEnd; j++) printf("%d ",A[i][j]);
      for(i=rowStart+1, j--; i<=rowEnd; i++) printf("%d ",A[i][j]);
      for(j=columnEnd-1, i--; j>=columnStart; j--) printf("%d ",A[i][j]);
      for(i=rowEnd-1, j++; i>=rowStart+1; i--) printf("%d ",A[i][j]);
      rowStart++; columnStart++; rowEnd--; columnEnd--;
   }
}
```

Question 2: Give an algorithm for shuffling a deck of cards.

Answer: Assume that we want to shuffle an array of 52 cards, from 0 to 51 with no repeats, such as we might want for a deck of cards. First fill the array with the values in order, then go through the array and exchange each element with a randomly chosen element in the range from itself to the end. It's possible that an element will swap with itself, but there is no problem with that.

```
void Shuffle(int cards[], int n){
     srand(time(0));                        // initialize seed randomly
     for (int i=0; i<n; i++)
        cards[i] = i;                       // filling the array with card number
      for (int i=0; i<n; i++) {
        int r = i + (rand() % (52-i));      // Random remaining position.
        int temp = cards[i]; cards[i] = cards[r]; cards[r] = temp;
     }
     printf("Shuffled Cards:" );
     for (int i=0; i<n; i++)
        printf("%d", cards[i]);
}
```

Question 3: Reversal algorithm for array rotation: Write a function rotate(A[], d, n) that rotates A[] of size n by d elements. For example, the array $1, 2, 3, 4, 5, 6, 7$ becomes $3, 4, 5, 6, 7, 1, 2$ after 2 rotations.

Answer: Consider the following algorithm.

Algorithm:

```
rotate(Array[], d, n)
reverse(Array[], 1, d) ;
reverse(Array[], d + 1, n);
reverse(Array[], l, n);
```

Let AB be the two parts of the input Array where A = Array[0..d-1] and B = Array[d..n-1]. The idea of the algorithm is:

```
Reverse A to get ArB. /* Ar is reverse of A */
Reverse B to get ArBr. /* Br is reverse of B */
Reverse all to get (ArBr) r = BA.
For example, if Array[] = [1, 2, 3, 4, 5, 6, 7], d =2 and n = 7 then,
          A = [1, 2] and B = [3, 4, 5, 6, 7]
Reverse A, we get ArB = [2, 1, 3, 4, 5, 6, 7],
      Reverse B, we get ArBr = [2, 1, 7, 6, 5, 4, 3]
Reverse all, we get (ArBr)r = [3, 4, 5, 6, 7, 1, 2]
```

Implementation:

```
/* Function to left rotate Array[] of size n by d */
void leftRotate(int Array[], int d, int n) {
  rvereseArray(Array, 0, d-1);
  rvereseArray(Array, d, n-1);
  rvereseArray(Array, 0, n-1);
}
/*UTILITY FUNCTIONS: function to print an Array */
void printArray(int Array[], int size){
  for(int i = 0; i < size; i++)
printf("%d ", Array[i]);
  printf("%\n ");
}
/*Function to reverse Array[] from index start to end*/
void rvereseArray(int Array[], int start, int end) {
  int i;
  int temp;
  while(start < end){
    temp = Array[start];
    Array[start] = Array[end];
    Array[end] = temp;
    start++;
    end--;
  }
}
```

Question 4: Suppose you are given an array s[1...n] and a procedure reverse (s,i,j) which reverses the order of elements in between positions i and j (both inclusive). What does the following sequence

do, where 1 < k <= n:

```
reverse (s, 1, k);
reverse (s, k + 1, n);
reverse (s, 1, n);
```

(a) Rotates s left by k positions (b) Leaves s unchanged (c) Reverses all elements of s (d) None of the above

Answer: (b). Effect of the above 3 reversals for any *k* is equivalent to left rotation of the array of size *n* by *k* [refer Question 3:].

Question 5: Given a string that has set of words and spaces, write a program to move the spaces to *front* of string, you need to traverse the array only once and need to adjust the string in place.

Input = "move these spaces to beginning"
Output ="   movethesepacestobeginning"

Answer: Maintain two indices *i* and *j*; traverse from end to beginning. If the current index contains char, swap chars in index *i* with index *j*. This will move all the spaces to beginning of the array.

```
void mySwap(char A[],int i,int j){
   char temp=A[i];
   A[i]=A[j];
   A[j]=temp;
}
void moveSpacesToBegin(char A[]){
   int i=strlen(A)-1;
   int j=i;
   for(; j>=0; j--){
      if(!isspace(A[j]))
         mySwap(A,i--,j);
```

```
void main(int argc, char * argv[]){
   char sparr[]="move these spaces
                                    to beginning";
   printf("Value of A is: %s\n", sparr);
   moveSpacesToBegin(sparr);
   printf("Value of A is: %s", sparr);
}
```

```
    }
}
```

Question 6: For the Question 5, can we improve the complexity?

Answer: We can avoid swap operation with a simple counter. But, it does not reduce the overall complexity.

```
void moveSpacesToBegin(char A[]){
    int n=strlen(A)-1,count=n;
    int i=n;
    for(;i>=0;i--){
        if(A[i]!=' ')
            A[count--]=A[i];
    }
    while(count>=0)
        A[count--]=' ';
}
```

```
int testCode(){
    char sparr[]="move these spaces
                                to beginning";
    printf("Value of A is: %s\n", sparr);
    moveSpacesToBegin(sparr);
    printf("Value of A is: %s", sparr);
}
```

Question 7: Given a string that has set of words and spaces, write a program to move the spaces to *end* of string, you need to traverse the array only once and need to adjust the string in place.

Input = "move these spaces to end" *Output* ="movethesepacestoend   "

Answer: Traverse the array from left to right. While traversing, maintain a counter for non-space elements in array. For every non-space character A[*i*], put the element at A[*count*] and increment *count*. After complete traversal, all non-space elements have already been shifted to front end and *count* is set as index of first 0. Now, all we need to do is that run a loop which fills all elements with spaces from *count* till end of the array.

```
void moveSpacesToEnd(char A[]){
// Count of non-space elements
    int count = 0;
    int n =strlen(A)-1;
    int i =0;
    for (; i <= n; i++)
        if (!isspace(A[i]))
            A[count++] = A[i];

    while (count <= n)
        A[++count] = ' ';
}
```

```
void testCode(int argc, char * argv[]){
    char sparr[]="move these spaces to end";
    printf("Value of A is: %s\n", sparr);
    moveSpacesToEnd(sparr);
    printf("Value of A is: %s", sparr);
}
```

Question 8: Moving Zeros to end: Given an array of n integers, move all the zeros of a given array to the end of the array. For example, if the given arrays is {1, 9, 8, 4, 0, 0, 2, 7, 0, 6, 0}, it should be changed to {1, 9, 8, 4, 2, 7, 6, 0, 0, 0, 0}. The order of all other elements should be same.

Answer: Maintain two variables i and j; and initialize with 0. For each of the array element $A[i]$, if $A[i]$ non-zero element, then replace the element $A[j]$ with element $A[i]$. Variable i will always be incremented till $n - 1$ but we will increment j only when the element pointed by i is non-zero.

```
void moveZerosToEnd(int A[], int size){
    int i=0,j=0;
    while (i <= size - 1){
        if (A[i] != 0){
            A[j++] = A[i];
        }
        i++;
    }
```

```
int testCode(){
    int A[ ] = {1,9,8,4,0,0,2,7,0,6,0};
    int i;
    int size = sizeof(A) / sizeof(A[0]);
    moveZerosToEnd(A, size);
    for (i = 0; i <= size - 1; i++)
        printf("%d ", A[i]);
    return 0;
```

```
    while (j <= size - 1)                    }
        A[j++] = 0;
}
```

Question 9: For the Question 8, can we improve the complexity?

Answer: Using simple swap technique we can avoid the unnecessary second *while* loop from the above code.

```
void mySwap(int A[],int i,int j){
    int temp=A[i];
    A[i]=A[j];
    A[j]=temp;
}
void moveZerosToEnd(int A[], int len){
    int i, j;
    for(i=0,j=0; i<len; i++)   {
        if (A[i] !=0)
            mySwap(A,j++,i);
    }
}
```

Question 10: *Variant* of Question 8 and Question 9: Given an array containing negative and positive numbers; give an algorithm for separating positive and negative numbers in it. Also, maintain the relative order of positive and negative numbers. Input: -5, 3, 2, -1, 4, -8 Output: -5 -1 -8 3 4 2

Answer: In the *moveZerosToEnd* function, just replace the condition $A[i] \, !=0$ with $A[i] < 0$.

Concepts of Computer Networking

CHAPTER 8

8.1 What is a Computer Network?

A computer network is a group of computers that are connected together and communicate with one another. These computers can be connected by the telephone lines, co-axial cable, satellite links or some other communication techniques.

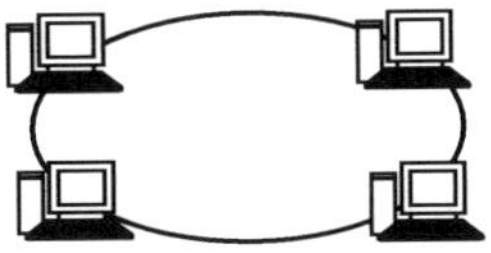

8.2 Basic Elements of Computer Networks

More and more, it is networks that connect us. People communicate online from everywhere. We focus on these aspects of the information network:

- Devices that make up the network (work stations, laptops, file servers, web servers, network printers, VoIP phones, security cameras, PDAs, etc..)
- Media that connect the devices
- Messages that are carried over the network
- Rules (protocols) and processes that control network communications
- Tools and commands for constructing and maintaining networks

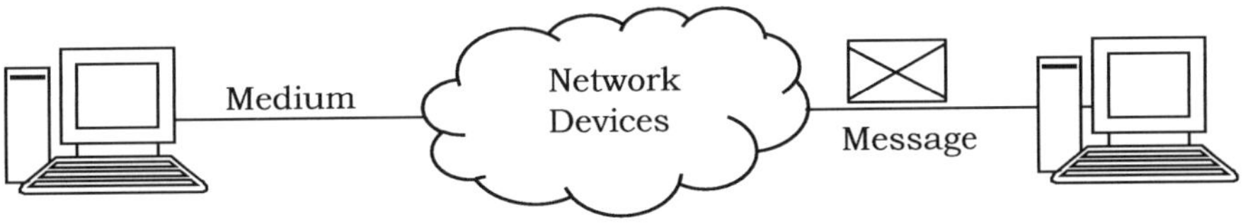

Communication begins with a message that must be sent from one device to another. People exchange ideas using many different communication methods. All of these methods have *three* elements in common.

- The first of these elements is the *message source* (*sender*). Message sources are people, or electronic devices, that need to send a message to other individuals/devices.
- The second element of communication is the *destination*(*receiver*), of the message. The destination receives the message and interprets it.
- A third element, called a *channel*, consists of the media that provides the pathway over which the message can travel from source to destination.

8.3 What is an Internet?

Connecting two or more networks together is called an *Internet*. In other words, an Internet is a network of networks.

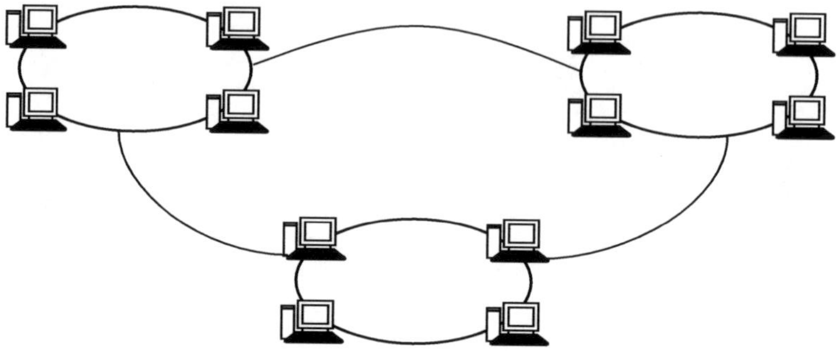

8.4 Fundamentals of Data and Signals

Data and *signals* are two of the basic elements of any computer network. A signal is the transmission of data. Both data and signals can be in either analog or digital form, which gives us *four* possible combinations:

1. Transmitting digital data using digital signals
2. Transmitting digital data using analog signals
3. Transmitting analog data using digital signals
4. Transmitting analog data using analog signals

8.4.1 Analog and Digital Data

Information that is stored within computer systems and transferred over a computer network can be divided into two categories: data and signals. Data are entities that convey meaning within a computer or computer system.

Data refers to information that conveys some meaning based on some mutually agreed up rules or conventions between a sender and a receiver and today it comes in a variety of forms such as text, graphics, audio, video and animation. Data can be of two types:

- *Analog* data
- *Digital* data

Analog data take *continuous* values on some interval. Examples of analog data are voice and video. The data that are collected from the real world with the help of transducers are continuous-valued or analog in nature. On the contrary, digital data take *discrete* values. Text or character strings can be considered as examples of digital data. Characters are represented by suitable codes, e.g. ASCII code, where each character is represented by a 7-bit code.

8.4.2 Analog and Digital Signals

If we want to transfer this data from one point to another, either by using a physical wire or by using radio waves, the data has to be converted into a signal. Signals are the electric or electromagnetic encoding of data and are used to transmit data. Signals (electric signals) which run through conducting wires are divided into the following two categories. Also, a system used when transmitting signals is called a *transmission system*.

8.4.3 Analog Signals

Analog refers to physical quantities that vary continuously instead of discretely. Physical phenomena typically involve analog signals. Examples include temperature, speed, position, pressure, voltage, altitude, etc. To say a signal is analog simply means that the signal is continuous in time and amplitude. Take, for example, your standard mercury glass thermometer. This device is analog because the temperature reading is updated constantly and changes at any time interval.

A new value of temperature can be obtained whether you look at the thermometer one second later, half a second later, or a millionth of a second later, assuming temperature can change that fast.

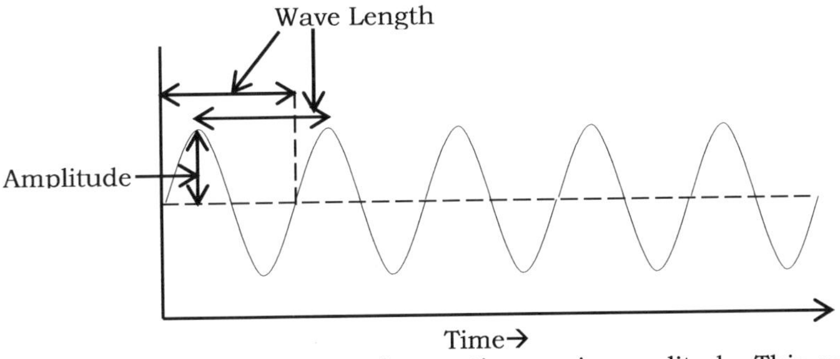

The readings from the thermometer are also continuous in amplitude. This means that assuming your eyes are sensitive enough to read the mercury level, readings of 37, 37.4, or 37.440183432°C are possible. In actuality, most cardiac signals of interest are analog by nature. For example, voltages recorded on the body surface and cardiac motion is continuous functions in time and amplitude. In this, signals 0 and 1 are transmitted as electric waves. A system of transmitting analog signals is called *broadband* system.

8.4.4 Digital Signals

Digital signals consist of patterns of bits of information. These patterns can be generated in many ways, each producing a specific code. Modern digital computers store and process all kinds of information as binary patterns. All the pictures, text, sound and video stored in this computer are held and manipulated as patterns of binary values.

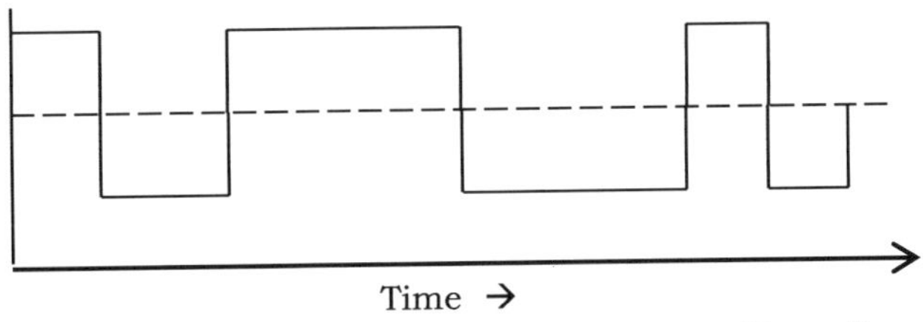

Basically, code 1 is transmitted when applying a specific voltage and code 0 is transmitted in the case of 0 V. A system of transmitting digital signals is called *baseband* system.

8.4.5 Converting Data into Signals

Like data, signals can be analog or digital. Typically, digital signals convey digital data, and analog signals convey analog data. However, we can use analog signals to convey digital data and digital signals to convey analog data. The choice of using either analog or digital signals often depends on the transmission equipment that is used and the environment in which the signals must travel.

8.4.6 Data Codes

One of the most common forms of data transmitted between a sender and a receiver is textual data. This textual information is transmitted as a sequence of characters. To distinguish one character from another, each character is represented by a unique binary pattern of 1s and 0s.

The set of all textual characters or symbols and their corresponding binary patterns is called a *data code*. Three important data codes are EBCDIC, ASCII, and Unicode.

8.4.7 Frequency

Frequency describes the number of waves that pass a fixed place in a given amount of time. So if the time it takes for a wave to pass is 1/2 second, the frequency is 2 per second. If it takes 1/100 of an hour, the frequency is 100 per hour.

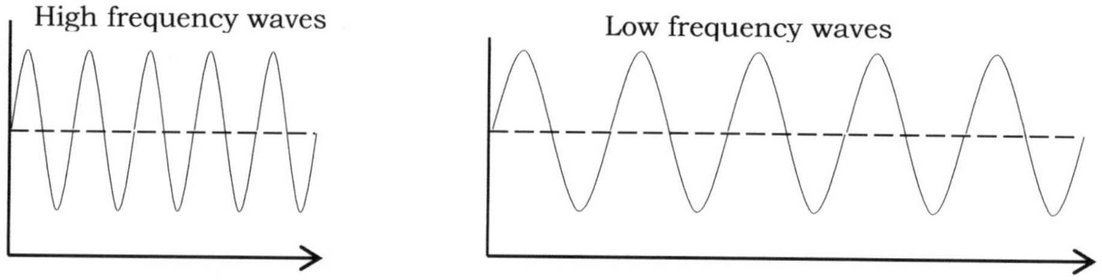

Usually frequency is measured in the *hertz* unit, named in honor of the 19th-century German physicist Heinrich Rudolf Hertz. The hertz measurement, abbreviated Hz, is the number of waves that pass by per second.

8.4.8 Bit Rate

Two new terms, bit interval (instead of period) and bit rate (instead of frequency) are used to describe digital signals. The bit interval is the time required to send one single bit. The bit rate is the number of bit interval per second. This mean that the bit rate is the number of bits send in one second, usually expressed in bits per second (*bps*) as shown in figure.

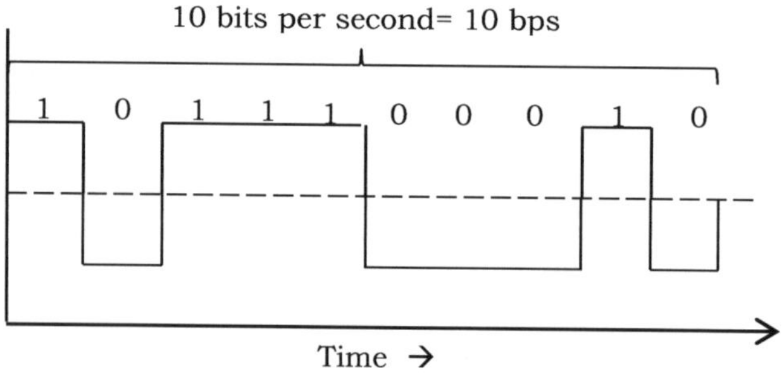

The speed of the data is expressed in bits per second (bits/s, bits per second or bps). The data rate *R* is a function of the duration of the bit or bit time:

$$R = \frac{1}{Bit\ Time}$$

Rate is also called *channel capacity* C. If the bit time is 10 *ns*, the data rate equals:

$$R = \frac{1}{10\times 10^{-9}} = 10^8 \text{ bps or 100 million bits/sec}$$

This is usually expressed as 100 Mbits/s.

8.4.9 Baud Rate

The baud rate of a data communications system is the *number* of *symbols* per *second* transferred. A symbol may have more than two states, so it may represent more than one binary bit (a binary bit always represents exactly two states). Therefore the baud rate may not equal the bit rate, especially in the case of recent modems, which can have (for example) up to nine bits per symbol.

Baud rate is a technical term associated with modems, digital televisions, and other technical devices. It is also called as *symbol rate* and *modulation rate*. The term roughly means the speed that data is transmitted, and it is a derived value based on the number of symbols transmitted per second. The units for this rate are either *symbols per second* or *pulses per second*. Baud can be determined by using the following formula:

$$Baud = \frac{Gross\ Bit\ Rate}{Number\ of\ Bits\ per\ Symbol}$$

This can be used to translate baud into a bit rate using the following formula:

$$Bit\ Rate = Bits\ per\ Symbol \times Symbol\ Rate$$

Baud can be abbreviated using the shortened form *Bd* when being used for technical purposes. The significance of these formulas is that higher baud rates equate to greater amounts of data transmission, as long as the bits per symbol are the same. A system using 4800 baud modems that has 4 bits per symbol will send less data than a system using 9600 baud modems that also has 4 bits per symbol. So, all other things being equal, a higher rate is generally preferred.

8.4.10 Attenuation

Attenuation (also called *loss*) is a general term that refers to any reduction in the strength of a signal. Attenuation occurs with any type of signal, whether digital or analog. It usually occurs while transmitting analog or digital signals over long distances.

8.4.11 Signal to Noise Ratio

Signal to noise ratio measures the level of the audio signal compared to the level of noise present in the signal. Signal to noise ratio specifications are common in many components, including amplifiers, phonograph players, CD/DVD players, tape decks and others. Noise is described as hiss, as in tape deck, or simply general electronic background noise found in all components.

8.5 Network Topologies

In a computer network, the way in which the devices are linked is called *topology*. Topology is the physical layout of computers, cables, and other components on a network. Following are few types of topologies which we will look at:

- Bus topology
- Star topology
- Mesh topology
- Ring topology

8.5.1 Bus Topology

A bus topology uses one cable (also called a *trunk*, a *backbone*, and a *segment*) to connect multiple systems. Most of the time, T-connectors (because they are shaped like the letter T) are used to connect to the cabled segment. Generally, coaxial cable is used in bus topologies.

Another key component of a bus topology is the need for *termination*. To prevent packets from bouncing up and down the cable, devices called *terminators* must be attached to both ends of the cable. A terminator absorbs an electronic signal and clears the cable so that other computers can send packets on the network. If there is no termination, the entire network fails.

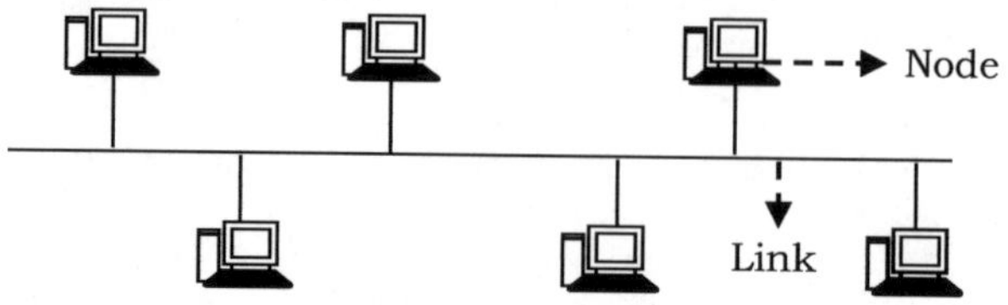

Only one computer at a time can transmit a packet on a bus topology. Systems in a bus topology listen to all traffic on the network but accept only the packets that are addressed to them. Broadcast packets are an exception because all computers on the network accept them. When a computer sends out a packet, it travels in both directions from the computer. This means that the network is occupied until the destination computer accepts the packet.

The number of computers on a bus topology network has a major influence on the performance of the network. A bus is a passive topology. The computers on a bus topology only listen or send data. They do not take data and send it on or regenerate it. So if one computer on the network fails, the network is still up.

Advantages

One advantage of a bus topology is *cost*. The bus topology uses less cable than other topologies. Another advantage is the ease of *installation*. With the bus topology, we simply connect the system to the cable segment. We need only the amount of cable to connect the workstations we have. The ease of working with a bus topology and the minimum amount of cable make this the most economical choice for a network topology. If a computer fails, the network stays up.

Disadvantages

The main disadvantage of the bus topology is the difficulty of *troubleshooting*. When the network goes down, usually it is from a break in the cable segment. With a large network this can be tough to isolate. A cable break between computers on a bus topology would take the entire network down. Another disadvantage of a bus topology is that the *heavier* the traffic, the *slower* the network. Scalability is an important consideration with the dynamic world of networking. Being able to make changes easily within the size and layout of your network can be important in future productivity or downtime. The bus topology is not very scalable.

8.5.2 Star Topology

In star topology, all systems are connected through one central hub or switch, as shown in figure. This is a very common network scenario.

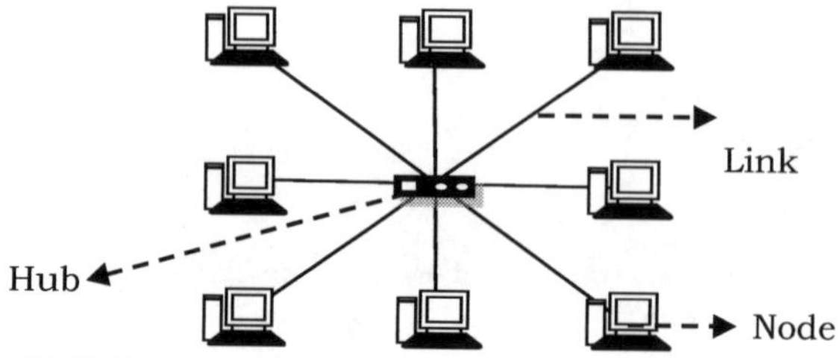

Advantages

One advantage of a start topology is the centralization of cabling. With a hub, if one link fails, the remaining systems are not affected like they are with other topologies. Centralizing network components can make an administrator's life much easier in the long run. Centralized management and monitoring of network traffic can be vital to network success. With this type of configuration, it is also easy to add or change configurations with all the connections coming to a central point.

Disadvantages

On the flip side to this is the fact that if the hub fails, the entire network, or a good portion of the network, comes down. This is, of course, an easier fix than trying to find a break in a cable in a bus topology. Another disadvantage of a star topology is cost: to connect each system to a centralized hub, we have to use much more cable than we do in a bus topology.

8.5.3 Ring Topology

In ring topology each system is attached nearby systems on a point to point basis so that the entire system is in the form of a ring. Signals travel in one direction on a ring topology.

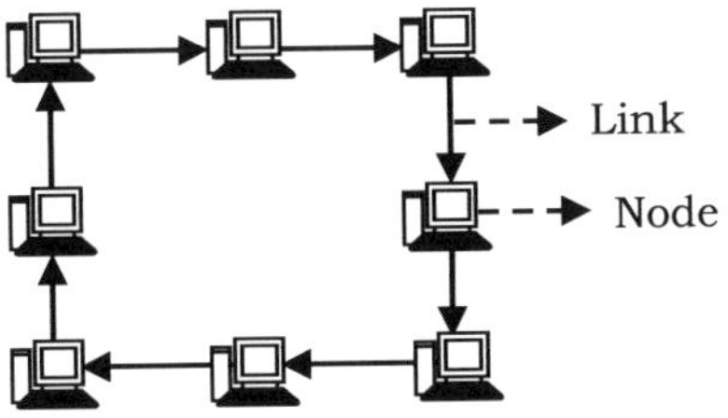

As shown in figure, the ring topology is a circle that has no start and no end. Terminators are not necessary in a ring topology. Signals travel in one direction on a ring while they are passed from one system to the next. Each system checks the packet for its destination and passes it on as a repeater would. If one of the systems fails, the entire ring network goes down.

Advantages

The nice thing about a ring topology is that each computer has equal access to communicate on the network. (With bus and star topologies, only one workstation can communicate on the network at a time.) The ring topology provides good performance for each system. This means that busier systems that send out a lot of information do not inhibit other systems from communicating. Another advantage of the ring topology is that signal degeneration is low.

Disadvantages

The biggest problem with a ring topology is that if one system fails or the cable link is broken the entire network could go down. With newer technology this isn't always the case. The concept of a ring topology is that the ring isn't broken and the signal hops from system to system, connection to connection. Another disadvantage is that if we make a cabling change to the network or a system change, such as a move, the brief disconnection can interrupt or bring down the entire network.

8.5.4 Mesh Topology

A mesh topology is not very common in computer networking. The mesh topology is more commonly seen with something like the national phone network. With the mesh topology, every system has a connection to every other component of the network.

Systems in a mesh topology are all connected to every other component of the network. If we have 4 systems, we must have six cables— three coming from each system to the other systems. Two nodes are connected by dedicated point-point links between them. So the total number of links to connect n nodes would be

$$\frac{n(n-1)}{2} \text{ [Proportional to } n^2\text{]}$$

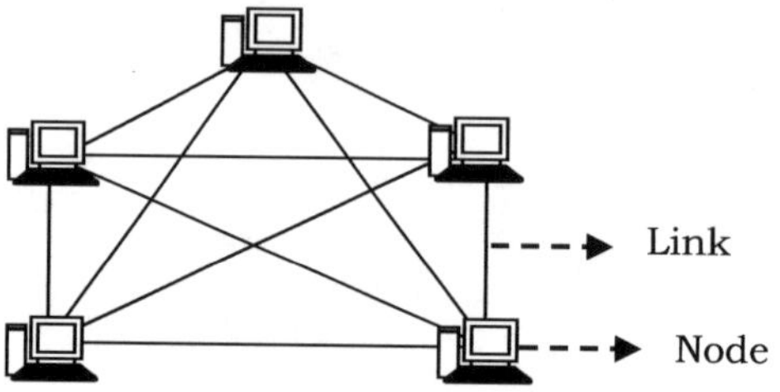

A mesh topology is not very common in computer networking. The mesh topology is more commonly seen with something like the national phone network. With the mesh topology, every system has a connection to every other component of the network. Systems in a mesh topology are all connected to every other component of the network. If we have 4 systems, we must have six cables— three coming from each system to the other systems. Two nodes are connected by dedicated point-point links between them. So the total number of links to connect n nodes would be

$$\frac{n(n-1)}{2} \text{ [Proportional to } n^2\text{]}$$

Advantages

The biggest advantage of a mesh topology is fault tolerance. If there is a break in a cable segment, traffic can be rerouted. This fault tolerance means that the network going down due to a cable fault is almost impossible.

Disadvantages

A mesh topology is very hard to administer and manage because of the numerous connections. Another disadvantage is cost. With a large network, the amount of cable needed to connect and the interfaces on the workstations would be very expensive.

8.5.5 Tree Topology

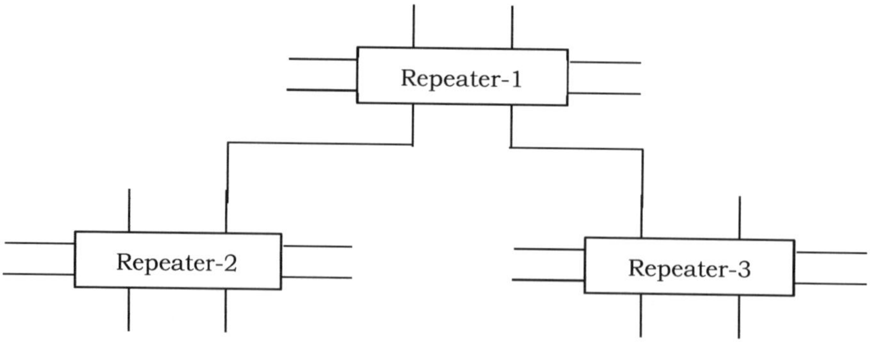

This topology can be considered as an extension to bus topology. It is commonly used in cascading equipment's. For example, we have a repeater box with 8-port, as far as we have eight stations, this can be used in a normal fashion. But if we need to add more stations then we can connect two or more repeaters in a hierarchical format (tree format) and can add more stations. In the figure Repeater-1 refers to repeater one and so on and each repeater is considered to have 8-ports.

8.5.6 Unconstrained Topology

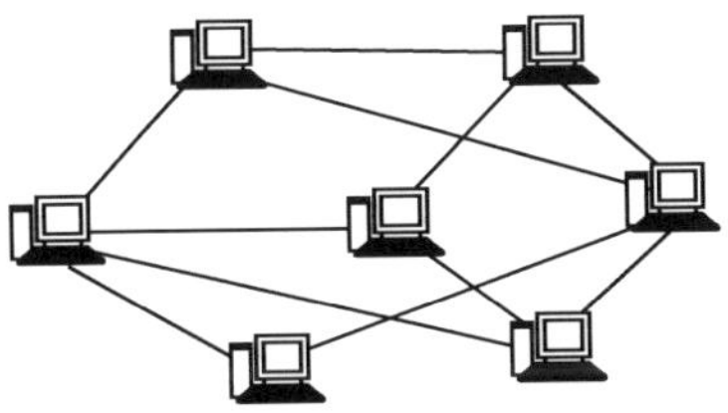

All the topologies discussed so far are symmetric and constrained by well-defined interconnection pattern. However, sometimes no definite pattern is followed and nodes are interconnected in an arbitrary manner using point-to-point links.

Unconstrained topology allows a lot of configuration flexibility but suffers from the complex routing problem. Complex routing involves unwanted overhead and delay.

8.6 Network Operating Systems

Network operating system NOS is an operating system that includes special functions for connecting computers and devices into a local area network (LAN). Few standalone operating systems, such as Microsoft Windows NT, can also act as network operating systems. Some of the most well-known network operating systems include Microsoft Windows Server 2003, Microsoft Windows Server 2008, Linux and Mac OS X.

8.6.1 Peer-to-peer

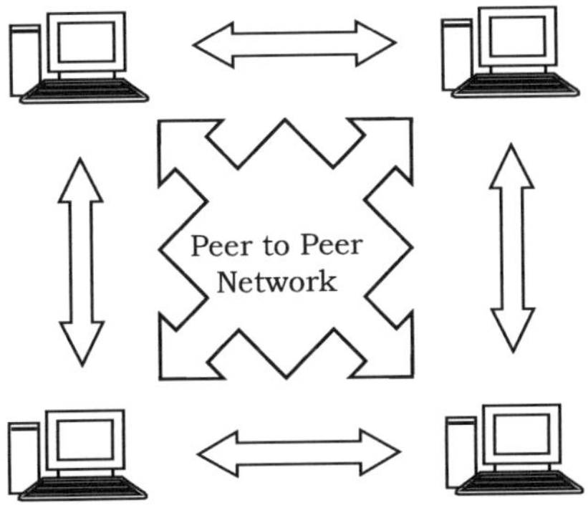

Peer – to – Peer networks are more commonly implemented where less than ten computers are involved and where strict security is not necessary. All computers have the same status, hence the term *peer*, and they communicate with each other on an equal footing. Files, such as word processing or spreadsheet documents, can be shared across the network and all the computers on the network can share devices, such as printers or scanners, which are connected to any one computer.

8.6.2 Client/server networks

Client/Server networks are more suitable for larger networks. A central computer, or *server*, acts as the storage location for files and applications shared on the network. Usually the server is a higher than average performance computer.

The server also controls the network access of the other computers which are referred to as the 'client' computers. Typically, teachers and students in a school will use the client computers for their work and only the network administrator (usually a designated staff member) will have access rights to the server [figure on right side].

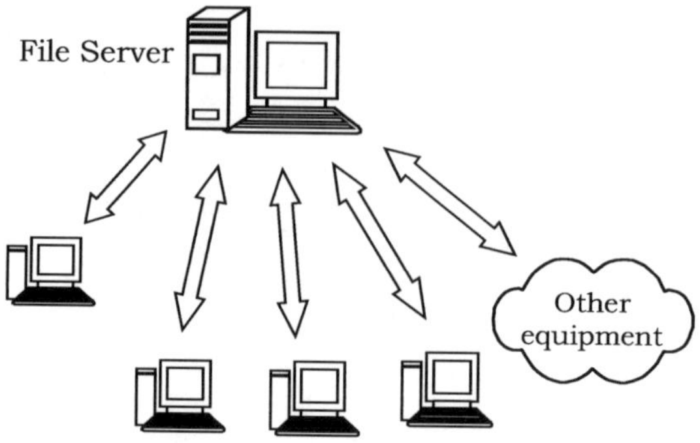

8.7 Transmission Medium

Communication across a network is carried on a *medium*. The medium provides the channel through which the data travels from source to destination. There are several types of media, and the selection of the right media depends on many factors such as cost of transmission media, efficiency of data transmission and the transfer rate. Different types of network media have different features and benefits.

8.7.1 Two wire open line

This is the simplest of all the transmission media. It consists of a simple pair of metallic wires made of copper or sometimes aluminums of between 0.4 and 1mm diameter, and each wire is insulated from the other. There are variations to this simplest form with several pairs of wire covered in a single protected cable called a *multi core cable* or molded in the form of a *flat ribbon*.

Example: Electric power transmission

This line consists of two wires that are generally spaced from 2 to 6 inches apart by insulating spacers. This type of line is most often used for power lines. This type of media is used for communication within a short distance, up to about 50 Meters, and can achieve a transfer rate of up to 19200 bits per second.

8.7.2 Twisted Pair cable

As the name implies, the line consists of two insulated wires twisted together to form a flexible line without the use of spacers. It is not used for transmitting high frequency because of the high dielectric losses that occur in the rubber insulation. When the line is wet, the losses are high. Twisted Pair cable is used for communication up a distance of 1 kilometer and can achieve a transfer rate of up to 1-2 Mbps. But as the speed increased the maximum transmission distances reduced, and may require repeaters.

Twisted pair cables are widely used in telephone network and are increasingly being used for data transmission.

8.7.3 Co-axial Cable

Coaxial cable is the kind of copper cable used by cable TV operators between the antenna and user homes. It is called *coaxial* because it includes one physical channel that carries the signal surrounded (after a layer of insulation) by another concentric physical channel, and both running along the same axis. The outer channel serves as a ground.

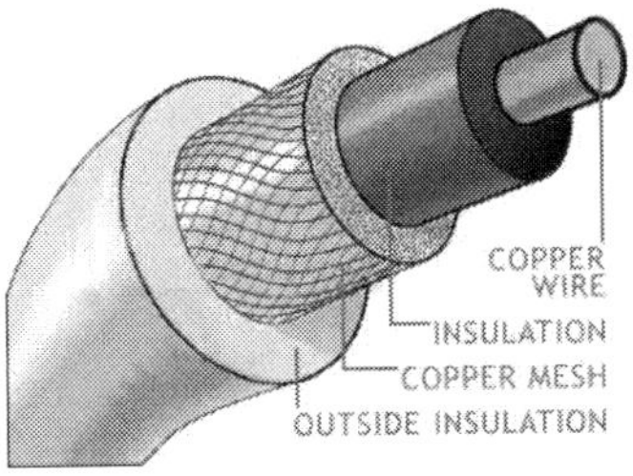

Larger the cable diameter, lower is the transmission loss, and higher transfer speeds can be achieved. A co-axial cable can be used over a distance of about 1 KM and can achieve a transfer rate of up to 100 Mbps.

8.7.4 Fiber Optic Cables

Fiber-based media use light transmissions instead of electronic pulses. Fiber is well suited for the transfer of data, video, and voice transmissions. Also, fiber-optic is the most secure of all cable media. Anyone trying to access data signals on a fiber-optic cable must physically tap into the media and this is a difficult task.

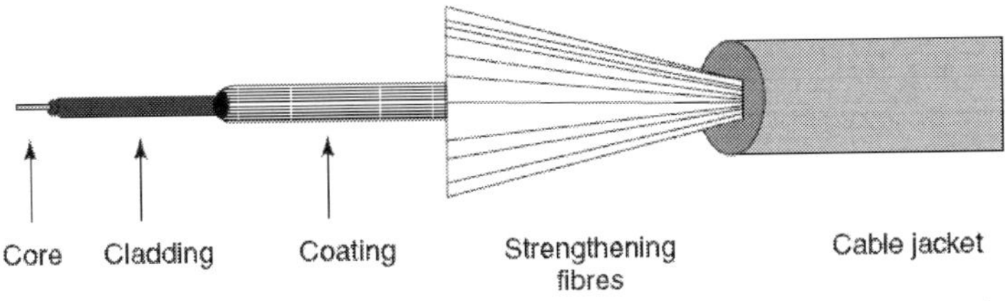

On the flip side, difficult installation and maintenance procedures of fiber require skilled technicians. Also, the cost of a fiber-based solution is more. Another drawback of implementing a fiber solution involves cost for fitting to existing network equipment/hardware. Fiber is incompatible with most electronic network equipment. That means, we have to purchase fiber-compatible network hardware.

Fiber-optic cable is made-up of a core glass fiber surrounded by cladding. An insulated covering then surrounds both of these within an outer protective sheath.

Since light waves give a much high bandwidth than electrical signals, this leads to high data transfer rate of about 1000 Mbps. This can be used for long and medium distance transmission links.

8.7.5 Radio, Microwaves and Satellite Channels

Radio, Microwaves and Satellite Channels use electromagnetic propagation in open space. The advantage of these channels depends on their capability to cove large geographical areas and being inexpensive than the wired installation. The demarcation between radio, Microwave and satellite channels depends on the frequencies in which they operate. Frequencies below 1000 MHZ are radio frequencies and higher are the Microwave frequencies.

The radio frequency transmission may be below 30 MHZ or above 30 MHZ and thus the techniques of transmission are different. Above 30MHz propagation is on *line – of – sight* paths. Antennas are placed in between the line-of- sight paths to increase the distance. Radio frequencies are prone to attenuation and, thus, they require repeaters along the path to enhance the signal. Radio frequencies can achieve data transfer rate of 100 Kbps to 400 Kbps.

Microwave links use *line – of – sight* transmission with repeaters placed every 100-200 KM. Microwave links can achieve data transfer rates of about 1000 Mbps. Satellite links use microwave frequencies in the order of 4-12 GHz with the satellite as a repeater. They can achieve data transfer rates of about 1000 Mbps.

8.8 Types of Networks

8.8.1 Local Area Network [LAN]

A local area network (LAN) is a network confined to one location, one building or a group of buildings. LAN's are composed of various components like desktops, printers, servers and other storage devices. All hosts on a LAN have addresses that fall in a single continuous and contiguous range. LANs usually do not contain routers. LANs have higher communication and data transfer rates. A LAN is usually administered by a single organization.

8.8.2 Metropolitan Area Network (MAN)

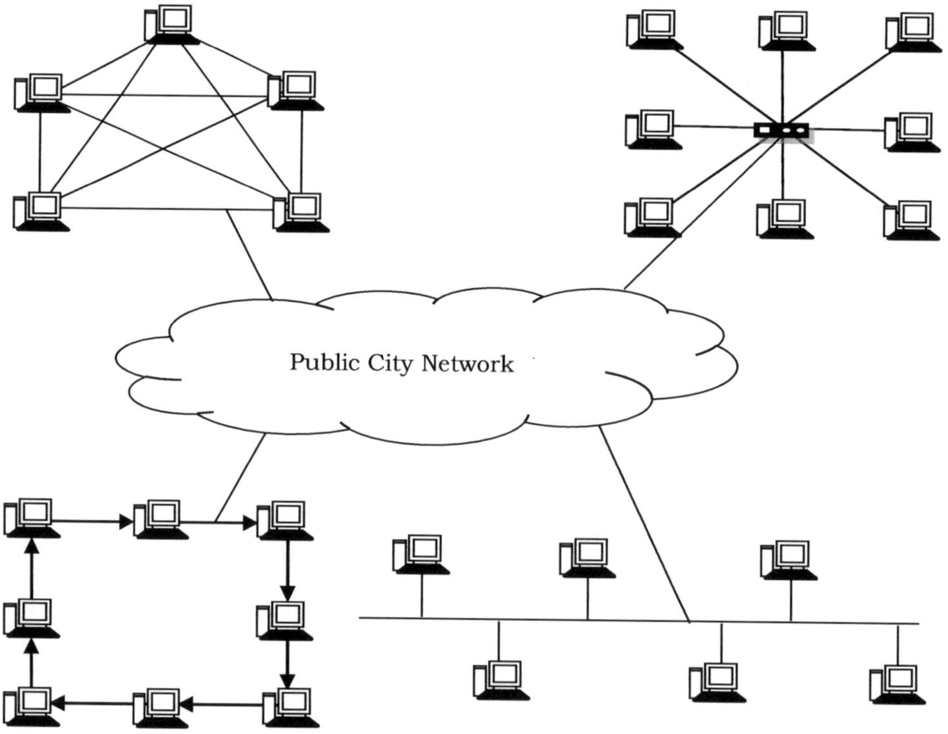

A metropolitan area network (MAN) is a large computer network that usually spans a city or a large campus. Usually a MAN interconnects a number of local area networks (LANs) using a high-capacity backbone technology (fibre-optical links). It is designed to extend over an entire city. That means it can be a single network (for example, cable television network) or connecting a number of LANs into a larger network. A MAN may be fully owned and operated by a private company or be a service provided by a public company.

8.8.3 Wide Area Network [WAN]

A wide area network (WAN) provides long-distance transmission of data, voice, image and video information over large geographical areas that may comprise a country, or even the whole world. WANs may utilize public, leased, or private communication devices, usually in combinations, therefore span an unlimited number of miles.

A WAN that is wholly owned and used by a single company is often referred to as an enterprise network. Maintaining WAN is difficult because of its wider geographical coverage and higher maintenance costs. Internet is the best example of a WAN. WANs have a lower data transfer rate as compared to LANs.

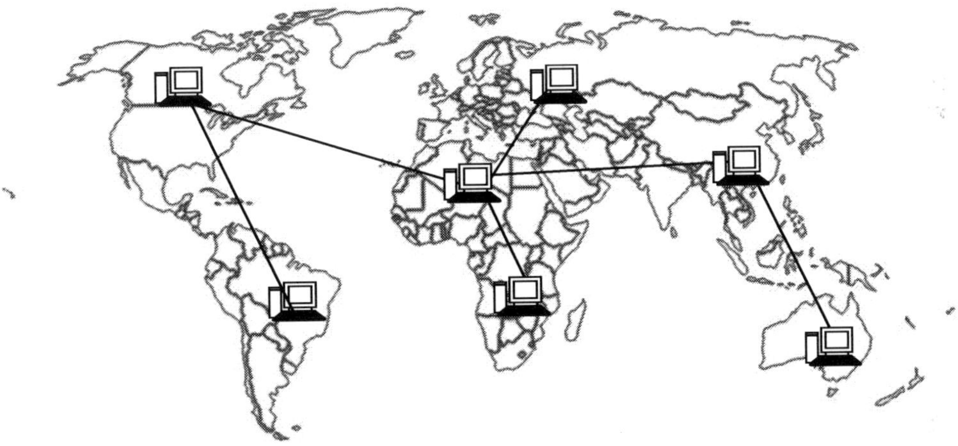

8.8.4 Personal Area Network

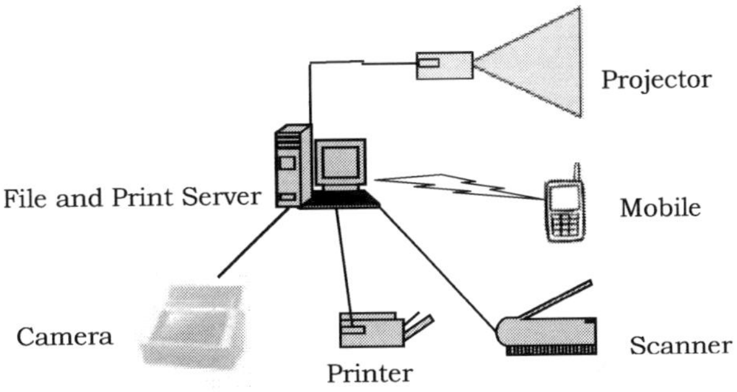

A personal area network (PAN) is a computer network organized around an individual person. PANs usually involve a computer, a cell phone and/or a handheld computing device such as a PDA. We can use these networks to transfer files including email and calendar appointments, digital photos and music. Personal area networks can be constructed with cables [for example, USB] or be wireless [for example, Bluetooth]. Personal area networks generally cover a range of less than 10. PANs can be viewed as a special type LAN that supports one person instead of a group.

8.8.5 LAN vs. WAN

	LAN	WAN
Definition	LAN (Local Area Network) is a	WAN (Wide Area Network) is a

	computer network covering a small geographic area, like a home, office, schools, or group of buildings.	computer network that covers a broad area (e.g., any network whose communications links cross metropolitan, regional, or national boundaries over a long distance
Maintenance costs	Because it covers a relatively small geographical area, LAN is easier to maintain at relatively low costs.	Maintaining WAN is difficult because of its wider geographical coverage and higher maintenance costs.
Fault Tolerance:	LANs tend to have fewer problems associated with them, as there are a smaller number of systems to deal with.	WANs tend to be fewer faults tolerant as it consists of a large number of systems there is a lower amount of fault tolerance.
Example	Network in an organization can be a LAN	Internet is the best example of a WAN
Geographical spread	LANs will have a small geographical range and do not need any leased telecommunication lines	WANs generally spread across boundaries and need leased telecommunication lines
Set-up costs	If there is a need to set-up a couple of extra devices on the network, it is not very expensive to do that	In this case since networks in remote areas have to be connected hence the set-up costs are higher. However WANs using public networks can be setup very cheaply, just software (VPN etc.)
Ownership	Typically owned, controlled, and managed by a single person or organization	WANs (like the Internet) are not owned by any one organization but rather exist under collective or distributed ownership and management over long +distances
Components	Layer 2 devices like switches, bridges. layer1 devices like hubs , repeaters	Layers 3 devices Routers, Multi-layer Switches and Technology specific devices like ATM or Frame-relay Switches etc.
Data transfer rates	LANs have a high data transfer rate	WANs have a lower data transfer rate as compared to LANs
Technology	Tend to use certain connectivity technologies, primarily Ethernet and Token Ring	WANs tend to use technology like MPLS, ATM, Frame Relay and X.25 for connectivity over the longer distances
Connection	One LAN can be connected to other LANs over any distance via telephone lines and radio waves	Computers connected to a WAN are often connected through public networks, such as the telephone system. They can also be connected through leased lines or satellites
Speed	High speed(1000mbps)	Less speed(150mbps)

8.8.6 Wireless Networks

A wireless network is a computer network that uses a wireless network connection such as Wi-Fi. In wireless networks, can have the following types:

- Wireless PAN (WPAN): interconnect devices within a relatively small area that is generally within a person's reach.
- Wireless LAN (WLAN): interconnects two or more devices over a short distance using a wireless distribution method. IEEE 802.11 standard describes about WLAN.
- Wireless MAN (WMAN): connects multiple wireless LANs. IEEE 802.16 standard describes about WMAN.
- Wireless WAN (WWAN): covers large areas, such as between neighboring towns and cities, or city and suburb. The wireless connections between access points are usually point to point microwave links using parabolic dishes, instead of omnidirectional antennas used with smaller networks.

8.9 Connection-oriented and Connectionless services

There are two different techniques for transferring data in computer networks. Both have advantages and disadvantages. They are the connection-oriented method and the connectionless method:

8.9.1 Connection-oriented service

This requires a session connection be established before any data can be sent. This method is often called a reliable network service. It guarantees that data will arrive in the same order. Connection-oriented services set up virtual links between sender and receiver systems through a network. Transmission Control Protocol (TCP) is a connection-oriented protocol. The most common example for the connection oriented service is the telephone system that we use every day. In connection oriented system such as the telephone system, a direct connection is established between you and the person at the other end.

Therefore, if you called from India to United States of America (USA) for 5 minutes, you are in reality actually the owner of that copper wire for the whole 5 minutes. This inefficiency however overcame by the multiple access techniques invented (refer *LAN Technologies* chapter).

Connection-oriented services set up *virtual* path between source and destination systems through a network. Connection-oriented service provides its services with the following three steps:

1. *Handshaking*: This is the process of establishing a connection to the desired destination prior to the transfer of data. During this hand-shaking process, the two end nodes decide the parameters for transferring data.
2. *Data Transfer*: During this step, the actual data is being sent in order. Connection oriented protocol is also known as *reliable* network service as it provides the service of delivering the stream of data in order. It ensures this as most of the connection oriented service tries to resend the lost data packets.
3. *Connection Termination*: This step is taken to release the end nodes and resources after the completion of data transfer.

8.9.2 Connectionless Service

Connectionless service does not require a session connection between sender and receiver. The sender simply starts sending packets (called *datagrams*) to the destination. This service does not have the reliability of the connection-oriented method, but it is useful for periodic burst transfers. Neither system must maintain state information for the systems that they send transmission to or receive transmission from. A connectionless network provides minimal services. User Datagram Protocol (UDP) is a connectionless protocol. Common features of a connectionless service are:

- Data (packets) do not need to arrive in a specific order
- Reassembly of any packet broken into fragments during transmission must be in proper order
- No time is used in creating a session
- No acknowledgement is required.

8.10 Segmentation and Multiplexing

In theory, a single communication, such as a music video or an e-mail message, could be sent across a network from a source to a destination as one massive continuous stream of bits. If messages were actually transmitted in this manner, it would mean that no other device would be able to send or receive messages on the same network while this data transfer was in progress.

These large streams of data would result in significant delays. Further, if a link in the interconnected network infrastructure failed during the transmission, the complete message would be lost and have to be retransmitted in full. A better approach is to divide the data into smaller, more manageable pieces to send over the network. This division of the data stream into smaller pieces is called *segmentation*. Segmenting messages has two primary benefits.

First, by sending smaller individual pieces from source to destination, many different conversations can be interleaved on the network. The process used to interleave the pieces of separate conversations together on the network is called *multiplexing*. *Second*, segmentation can increase the reliability of network communications. The separate pieces of each message need not travel the same pathway across the network from source to destination. If a particular path becomes congested with data traffic or fails, individual pieces of the message can still be directed to the destination using alternate pathways. If part of the message fails to make it to the destination, only the missing parts need to be retransmitted.

8.11 Network Performance

Network performance has been the subject of much research over the past decades. One important issue in networking is the performance of the network—how good is it? Internet data is packaged and transported in *small* pieces of data. The flow of these small pieces of data directly affects a user's internet experience. When data packets arrive in a timely manner the user sees a continuous flow of data; if data packets arrive with *large delays* between packets the user's experience is *degraded*.

8.11.1 Round Trip Time

In TCP, when a host sends a segment (also called packet) into a TCP connection, it starts a timer. If the timer expires before the host receives an acknowledgment for the data in the segment, the host retransmits the segment. The time from when the timer is started until when it expires is called the *timeout* of the timer. What should be the ideal *timeout* be? Clearly, the timeout should be larger than the connection's round-trip time, i.e., the time from when a segment is sent until it is acknowledged.

Otherwise, unnecessary retransmissions would be sent. But the timeout should not be much larger than the *round-trip time*; otherwise, when a segment is lost, TCP would not quickly retransmit the segment, thereby introducing significant data transfer delays into the application. Before discussing the timeout interval in more detail, let us take a closer look at the round-trip time (*RTT*). The round trip time calculation algorithm is used to calculate the average time for data to be acknowledged. When a data packet is sent, the elapsed time for the acknowledgment to arrive is measured and the *Van Jacobean* mean deviation algorithm is applied. This time is used to determine the interval to retransmit data.

8.11.1.1 Estimating the Average Round Trip Time

The sample RTT, denoted with *SampleRTT*, for a segment is the time from when the segment is sent (i.e., passed to IP) until an acknowledgment for the segment is received. Each segment sent will have its own associated *SampleRTT*. Obviously, the *SampleRTT* values will change from segment to segment due to congestion in the routers and to the varying load on the end systems. Because of this fluctuation, any given *SampleRTT* value may be atypical. In order to estimate a typical *RTT*, it is therefore natural to take some sort of average of the *SampleRTT* values.

TCP maintains an average of *SampleRTT* values, denoted with called *EstimatedRTT*. Upon receiving an acknowledgment and obtaining a new *SampleRTT*, TCP updates *EstimatedRTT* according to the following formula:

$$EstimatedRTT = (1-\alpha) * EstimatedRTT + \alpha * SampleRTT$$

The above formula is written in the form of a programming language statement - the new value of *EstimatedRTT* is a weighted combination of the previous value of *EstimatedRTT* and the new value for *SampleRTT*. A typical value of α is $\alpha = .1$, in which case the above formula becomes:

$$EstimatedRTT = .9\ EstimatedRTT + .1\ SampleRTT$$

Note that *EstimatedRTT* is a weighted average of the *SampleRTT* values. This weighted average puts more weight on recent samples than on old samples. This is natural, as the more recent samples better reflect the current congestion in the network. In statistics, such an average is called an *exponential weighted moving average* (*EWMA*). The word *exponential* appears in EWMA because the weight of a given *SampleRTT* decays exponentially fast as the updates proceed.

8.11.2 Causes for Latency?

Regardless of the speed of the processor or the efficiency of the software, it takes a finite amount of time to manipulate and present data. Whether the application is a web page showing the latest news or a live camera shot showing a traffic jam, there are many ways in which an application can be affected by latency. Four key causes of latency are: *propagation delay*, *serialization delay*, *routing* and *switching delay*, and *queuing* and *buffering delay*.

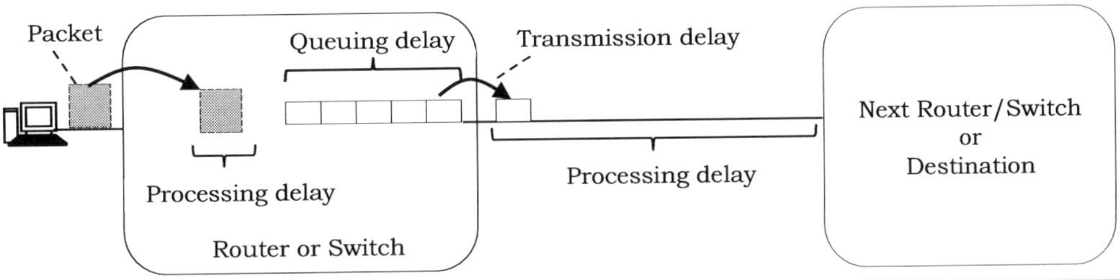

$$Latency = Propagation\ delay + Serialization\ delay + Queuing\ delay + Processing\ delay$$

8.11.2.1 Propagation Delay

Propagation delay is the primary source of latency. It is a function of how long it *takes* information to *travel* at the speed of light in the communications media from source to destination. In free space, the speed of light is approximately 3×10^5 km/sec. The speed of light is lower in other media such as copper wire or fiber optic cable. The amount of slowing caused by this type of transmission is called the *velocity factor* (VF).

Fiber optic cables typically measure around 70% of the speed of light whereas copper cable varies from 40% to 80% depending on the construct. Coaxial cable is commonly used and many types have a VF of 66%.

Satellite communication links use electromagnetic waves to propagate information through the atmosphere and space. The information is converted from electrical signals to radio signals by the transmitter and the antenna. Once these radio signals leave the antenna, they travel approximately at the speed of light for free space.

Let's calculate how long it will take an email to travel from Hyderabad to New York assuming that we are the only user on a private communications channel.

Ignoring the actual routes taken by undersea cables due to the ocean's floor, let's assume the path from Hyderabad to New York is the great circle distance of 5458 km.

$$Propagation\ delay = \frac{Distance\ (or\ length\ of\ physical\ link)}{Propagation\ speed}$$

The email sent using a copper link: $\frac{5458}{197863.022}$ = 23.58 ms

The email sent using a fiber-optic link: $\frac{5458}{209854.720}$ = 26.01 ms

The email sent using a radio link: $\frac{5458}{299792.458}$ = 18.21 ms

These are the latencies caused only by propagation delays in the transmission medium. If you were the only one sending one single data bit and you had unlimited bandwidth available, the speed of the packet would still be delayed by the propagation delay.

This delay happens without regard for the amount of data being transmitted, the transmission rate, the protocol being used or any link impairment.

8.11.2.2 Serialization Delay [Transmission Delay]

Serialization is the conversion of bytes (8 bits) of data stored in a computer's memory into a serial bit stream to be transmitted over the communications media. Serialization delay is also called *transmission delay* or *delay*. Serialization takes a finite amount of time and is calculated as follows:

$$Serialization\ delay = \frac{Packet\ size\ in\ bits}{Transmission\ rate\ in\ bits\ per\ second}$$

For example:

- Serialization of a 1500 byte packet used on a 56K modem link will take 214 milliseconds
- Serialization of the same 1500 byte packet on a 100 Mbps LAN will take 120 microseconds

Serialization can represent a significant delay on links that operate a lower transmission rates, but for most links this delay is a tiny fraction of the overall latency when compared to the other contributors.

Voice and video data streams generally use small packet sizes (~20 ms of data) to minimize the impact of serialization delay.

8.11.2.3 Processing Delay

In IP networks such as the Internet, IP packets are forwarded from source to destination through a series of IP routers or switches that continuously update their decision about which next router is the best one to get the packet to its destination. A router or circuit outage or congestion on a link along the path can change the routing path which in turn can affect the latency.

High performance IP routers and switches add approximately 200 microseconds of latency to the link due to *packet processing*. If we assume that the average IP backbone router spacing is 800 km, the 200 microseconds of routing/switching delay is equivalent to the amount of latency induced by 40km of fiber; routing/switching latency contributes to only 5% of the end to end delay for the average internet link.

8.11.2.4 Queuing and Buffer Management

Another issue which occurs within the transport layers is called *queuing latency*. This refers to the amount of time an IP packet spends sitting in a queue awaiting transmission due to over-utilization of the outgoing link after the routing/switching delay has been accounted for. This can add up to an additional 20 ms of latency.

8.11.3 Transmission Rate and Bandwidth

Transmission rate is a term used to describe the number of bits which can be extracted from the medium. Transmission rate is commonly measured as the number of bits measured over a period of one second. The *maximum transmission rate* describes the fundamental limitation of a network medium: If the medium is a copper Local Area Network, maximum transmission rates are commonly 10, 100, or 1000 Megabits per second. These rates are primarily limited by the properties of the copper wires and the capabilities of the network interface card are also a factor.

Fiber-optic the transmission rates range from around 50 Mbps up to 100 Gbps. Unlike copper networks, the primary factor limiting fiber-optic transmission rates is the electronics which operates at each end of the fiber. Wireless local area networks (LANs) and satellite links use modems (modulator/demodulator) to convert digital bits into an analog modulated waveform at the transmitter end of a link, and then at the receive end a demodulator will then convert the analog signal back into digital bits.

The limiting factor in transmitting information over radio-based channels is the bandwidth of the channel that is available to a particular signal and the noise that is present that will corrupt the signal waveform.

8.11.3.1 Radio Channel Bandwidth and Noise

Signals transmitted using radio waves occupy radio spectrum. Radio spectrum is not an unlimited resource and must be shared. To prevent radio interference between users the use of radio spectrum is controlled by nearly every government on the planet. The amount of radio spectrum occupied by any given radio signal is called its bandwidth.

The nature of radio spectrum use is beyond this paper but it's important to understand that generally the occupied radio spectrum of a modem signal will increase with the data rate:

- Higher modem data rates cause the modem to occupy more radio bandwidth
- Lower modem data rates will let the modem occupy less radio bandwidth

Since radio spectrum is a limited resource, the occupied radio bandwidth is an important limiting factor in wireless and satellite links.

Noise in the radio channel will perturb the analog signal waveform and can cause the demodulator at the receiver to change a digital one into a zero or vice versus. The effect of noise can be overcome by increasing the power level of the transmitted signal, or by adding a few extra error correcting bits to the data that is being transmitted. These error correcting bits help the receiver correct bit errors. However, the error correction bits increase the bandwidth that is required.

8.11.3.2 Data Bandwidth

In data transmission, the *data bandwidth* is synonymous to the transmission rate being used. Bandwidth is important because it defines the maximum capacity of a data link.

- A 10 Mbps copper LAN cannot sustain traffic flowing at a higher rate than 10 megabits every second.
- A satellite link using modems operating at a 600 Mbps rate cannot flow any more than 600 megabits every second.

It's very important to understand that data bandwidth is a maximum data flow obtainable over a given transportation segment over a given period of time.

8.11.6 Throughput versus Bandwidth

Even though widely used in the field of networking, bandwidth and throughput are two commonly misunderstood concepts. When planning and building new networks, network administrators widely use these two concepts. Bandwidth is the maximum amount of data that can be transferred through a network for a specified period of time while throughput is the actual amount of data that can be transferred through a network during a specified time period.

Bandwidth can be defined as the amount of information that can flow through a network at a given period of time. Bandwidth actually gives the maximum amount of data that can be transmitted through a channel in theory. When you say that you have a 100 Mbps broadband line you are actually referring to the maximum amount of data that can travel through your line per second, which is the bandwidth.

Even though the basic measurement for bandwidth is bits per second (bps), since it is a relatively small measurement, we widely use kilobits per second (kbps), megabits bits per second (Mbps), and gigabits per second (Gbps).

Most of us know from experience that the actual network speed is much slower than what is specified. Throughput is the actual amount of data that could be transferred through the network. That is the actual amount of data that gets transmitted back and forth from your computer, through the Internet to the web server in a single unit of time. When downloading a file you will see a window with a progress bar and a number. This number is actually the throughput and you must have noticed that it is not constant and almost always has a value lower than specified bandwidth for your connection.

Several factors like the number of users accessing the network, network topology, physical media and hardware capabilities can effect this reduction in the bandwidth. As you can imagine, throughput is also measured using the same units used to measure the bandwidth.

As you have seen, bandwidth and throughput seems to give a similar measurement about a network, at the first glance. They are also measured using the same units of measurement. Despite all these similarities they are actually different. We can simply say that the bandwidth is the maximum throughput you can ever achieve while the actual speed that we experience while surfing is the throughput.

To simplify further, you can think of the bandwidth as the width of a highway. As we increase the width of the highway more vehicles can move through a specified period of time. But when we consider the road conditions (craters or construction work in the highway) the number of vehicles that can actually pass through the specified period of time could be less than the above.

This is actually analogous to the throughput. So it is clear that bandwidth and throughput gives two different measurements about a network.

8.12 Network Switching

The purpose of a communication system is to exchange information between two or more devices. Such system can be optimized for voice, data, or both.

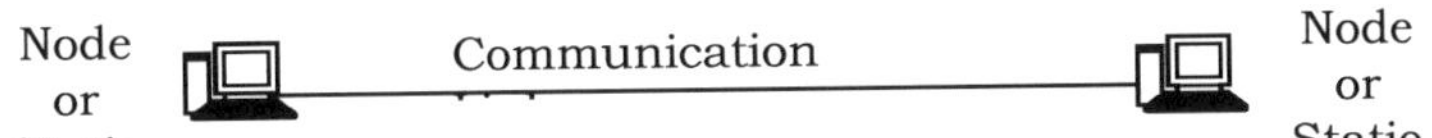

Point-to-Point Network

In its simplest form, a communication system can be established between two nodes (or stations) that are directly connected by some form of *point-to-point* transmission medium. A station may be a PC, telephone, fax machine, mainframe, or any other communicating device. This may, however, be impractical, if there are many geographically dispersed nodes or the communication requires dynamic connection between different nodes at various times.

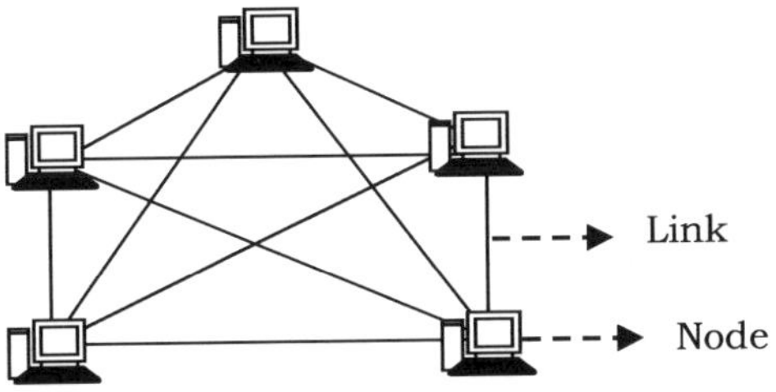

It is not efficient to build a physically separate path for each pair of communicating end systems. An alternative method to a *point-to-point* connection is *establishing* a *communication* network. In a communication network, each communicating *device* (or *station* or *node* or *host*) is connected to a network node. The interconnected nodes are capable of transferring data between stations.

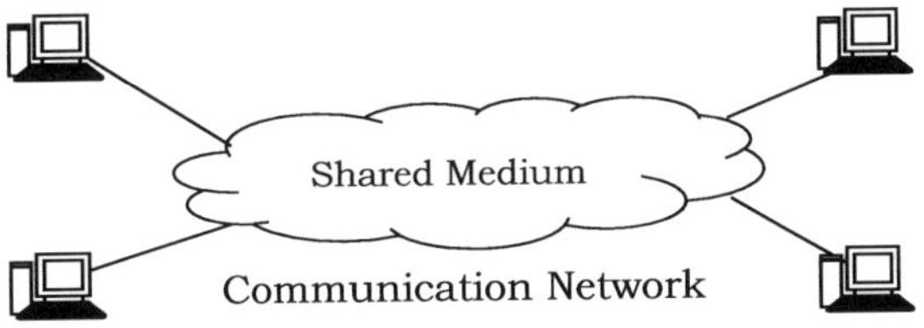

Depending on the architecture and techniques used to transfer data, two basic categories of communication networks are broadcast networks and switched networks.

- Broadcast Networks
- Switched Networks

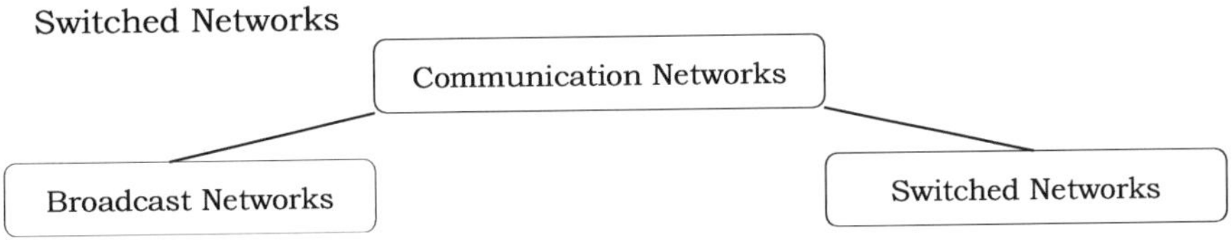

8.12.1 Broadcast Networks

In *broadcast* networks, a single node transmits the information to all other nodes and hence, all stations will receive the data. A simple example of such network is a simple radio system, in which all users tuned to the same channel can communicate with each other. Other examples of broadcast networks are satellite networks and Ethernet-based local area networks, where transmission by any station will propagates through the network and all other stations will receive the information.

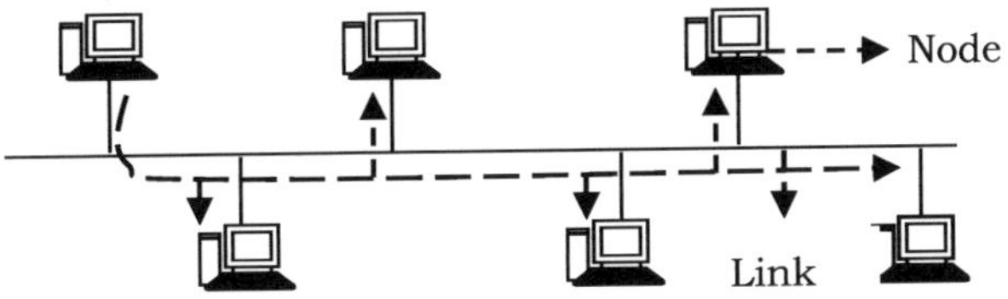

Broadcast is a method of sending a signal where multiple nodes may hear a single sender node. As an example, consider a conference room with full of people. In this conference room, a single person starts saying some information loudly.

During that time, some people may be sleeping, and may not hear what person is saying. Some people may not be sleeping, but not paying attention (they are able to hear the person, but choose to ignore). Another group of people may not only be awake, but be interested in what is being said.

This last group is not only able to hear the person speaking, but is also listening to what is being said. In this example, we can see that a single person is broadcasting a message to all others that may or may not be able to hear it, and if they are able to hear it, may choose to listen or not.

8.12.2 Switched Networks

A network is a series of connected devices. Whenever we have many devices, the interconnection between them becomes more difficult as the number of devices increases. Some of the conventional ways of interconnecting devices are

a. Point to point connection between devices as in *mesh* topology.
b. Connection between a central device and every other device as in *star* topology.
c. Bus topology is not practical if the devices are at greater distances.

The solution to this interconnectivity problem is *switching*. A switched network consists of a series of interlinked nodes called *switches*. A switch is a device that creates temporary connections between two or more systems. Some of the switches are connected to end systems (computers and telephones) and others are used only for routing.

In a switched network, the transmitted data is not passed on to the entire medium. Instead, data are transferred from source to destination through a series of *intermediate* nodes, called *switchingnodes*. Such nodes are only concerned about how to move the data from one node to another until the data reaches its destination node.

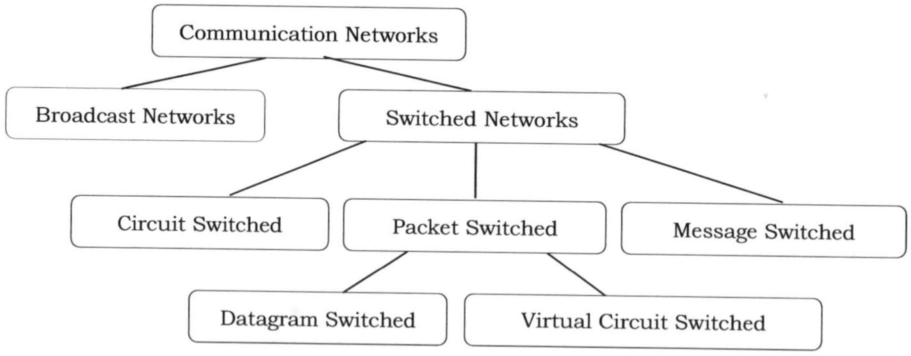

Switched communication networks can be categorized into different types as shown above.

8.12.2.1 Circuit Switched Networks

The term circuit switching refers to a communication mechanism that establishes a path between a sender and receiver with guaranteed isolation from paths used by other pairs of senders and receivers. Circuit switching is usually associated with telephone technology because a telephone system provides a dedicated connection between two telephones. In fact, the term originated with early dialup telephone networks that used electromechanical switching devices to form a physical circuit.

In a circuit-switched network, also called *line-switched* network, a dedicated physical communication path is established between two stations through the switching nodes in the network. Hence, the end-to-end path from source to destination is a connected sequence of physical links between nodes and at each switching node the incoming data is switched to the appropriate outgoing link.

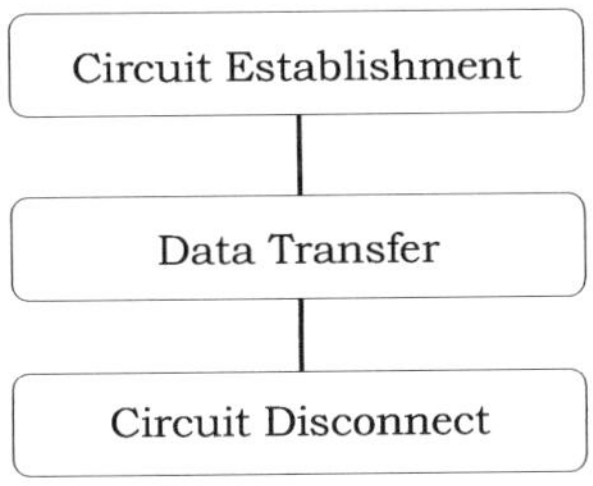

A circuit-switched communication system involves *three* phases: circuit establishment (setting up dedicated links between the source and destination); *data transfer* (transmitting the data between the source and destination); and *circuit disconnect* (removing the dedicated links). In circuit switching the connection path is established before data transmission begins (*on-demand*).

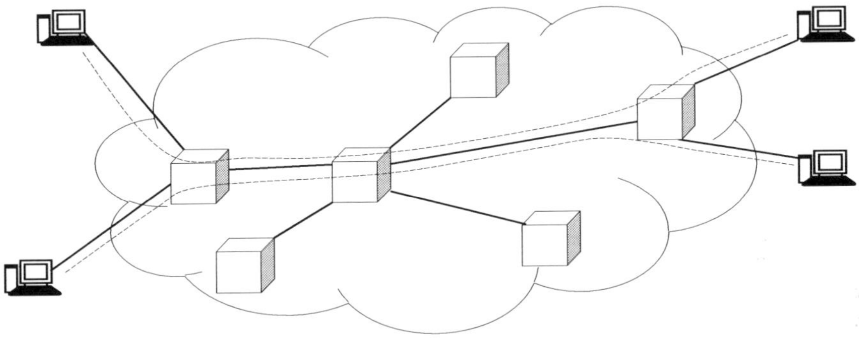

Therefore, the channel capacity must be reserved between the source and destination throughout the network and each node must have available internal switching capacity to handle the requested connection. Clearly, the switching nodes must have the intelligence to make proper allocations and to establish a route through the network.

The most common example of a circuit-switched network can be found in public telephone network supporting services such as POTS (plain old telephone systems) and long-distance calls.

8.12.2.2 Packet Switched Networks

The main alternative to circuit switching is packet switching which forms the basis for the Internet. A packet switching system uses statistical multiplexing in which communication from multiple sources competes for the use of shared media.

The main difference between packet switching and other forms of statistical multiplexing arises because a packet switching system requires a sender to divide each message into blocks of data that are known as packets. The size of a packet varies; each packet switching technology defines a maximum packet size.

Three general properties define a packet switched paradigm:

1. Arbitrary, asynchronous communication
2. No set-up required before communication begins
3. Performance varies due to statistical multiplexing among packets

The first property means that packet switching can allow a sender to communicate with one recipient or multiple recipients, and a given recipient can receive messages from one sender or multiple senders. Furthermore, communication can occur at any time, and a sender can delay arbitrarily long between successive communications.

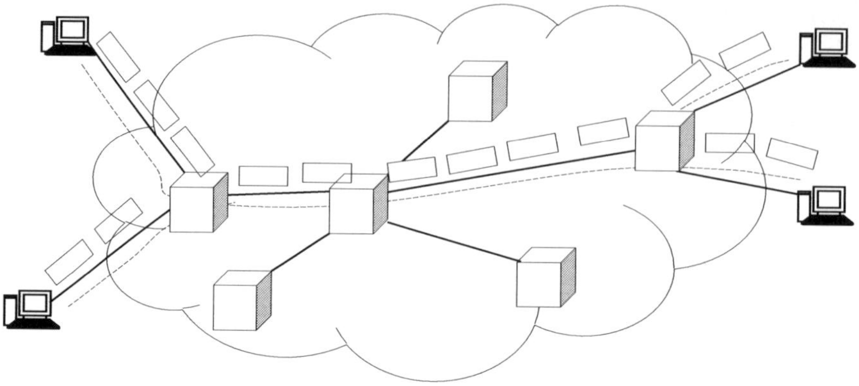

The second property means that, unlike a circuit switched system, a packet switched system remains ready to deliver a packet to any destination at any time. Thus, a sender does not need to perform initialization before communicating, and does not need to notify the underlying system when communication terminates.

The third property means that multiplexing occurs among packets rather than among bits or bytes. That is, once a sender gains access to the underlying channel, the sender transmits an entire packet, and then allows other senders to transmit a packet. When no other senders are ready to transmit a packet, a single sender can transmit repeatedly.

However, if n senders each have a packet to send, a given sender will transmit approximately $\frac{1}{n}$ of all packets.

In packet switching, packets can be handled in two ways:

1. Datagram
2. Virtual Circuit

8.12.2.2.1 Datagram Packet Switching

Datagram packet-switching is a *packet* switching technology. Each packet is routed independently through the network. Each packet can take any practical route to the desired destination. Therefore packets contain a header with the full information about the destination. The intermediate nodes examine the header of a packet and select an appropriate link to another node which is nearer to the destination. In this system, the packets do not follow a pre-established route, and the intermediate nodes do not require prior knowledge of the routes that will be used.

The packets may arrive out of order and they may go missing. The receiver will take care of re-ordering the packets and recover from missing packets.

In this technique, there is no need for setting up a connection. We just need to make sure each packet contains enough information to get it to destination. To give importance to critical packets, priorities can be attached to each packet.

The individual packets which form a data stream may follow different paths between the source and the destination. As a result, the packets may arrive at the destination out of order. When this occurs, the packets will have to be reassembled to form the original message. Because each packet is switched independently, there is no need for connection setup and no need to dedicate bandwidth in the form of a circuit.

Datagram packet switches use a variety of techniques to forward traffic; they are differentiated by how long it takes the packet to pass through the switch and their ability to filter out corrupted packets.

The most common datagram network is the Internet, which uses the IP network protocol. Applications which do not require more than a best effort service can be supported by direct use of packets in a datagram network, using the User Datagram Protocol (UDP) transport protocol. Applications like voice and video communications and notifying messages to alert a user that she/he has received new email are using UDP. Applications like e-mail, web browsing and file upload and download need reliable communications, such as guaranteed delivery, error control and sequence control. This reliability ensures that all the data is received in the correct order without errors. It is provided by a protocol such as the Transmission Control Protocol (TCP) or the File Transfer Protocol (FTP).

To forward the packets, each switch creates a table (maps destinations to output port). When a packet with a destination address in the table arrives, it pushes it out on the appropriate output port. When a packet with a destination address not in the table arrives, it will find the optimal route based on routing algorithms.

8.12.2.2.2 Virtual Circuit Packet Switching

Virtual circuit switching is a packet switching methodology whereby a path is established between the source and the final destination through which all the packets will be routed during a call. This path is called a virtual circuit because to the user, the connection appears to be a dedicated physical circuit. However, other communications may also be sharing the parts of the same path.

The idea of virtual circuit switching is to combine the advantages of circuit switching with the advantages of datagram switching. In virtual circuit packet switching, after a small connection setup phase only short (compared to full addresses) connection identifier are used per packet; this reduces the addressing overhead per packet.

Before the data transfer begins, the source and destination identify a suitable path for the virtual circuit. All intermediate nodes between the two points put an entry of the routing in their routing table for the call. Additional parameters, such as the maximum packet size, are also exchanged between the source and the destination during call setup. The virtual circuit is cleared after the data transfer is completed.

Virtual circuit packet switching is connection orientated. This is in contrast to datagram switching, which is a connection less packet switching methodology.

8.12.2.2.2.1 Advantages of Virtual Circuit Switching

Advantages of virtual circuit switching are:

- Packets are delivered in order, since they all take the same route;
- The overhead in the packets is smaller, since there is no need for each packet to contain the full address;
- The connection is more reliable, network resources are allocated at call setup so that even during times of congestion, provided that a call has been setup, the subsequent packets should get through;
- Billing is easier, since billing records need only be generated per call and not per packet.

8.12.2.2.2.2 Disadvantages of Virtual Circuit Switching

Disadvantages of a virtual circuit switched network are:

- The switching equipment needs to be more powerful, since each switch needs to store details of all the calls that are passing through it and to allocate capacity for any traffic that each call could generate;
- Resilience to the loss of a trunk is more difficult, since if there is a failure all the calls must be dynamically re-established over a different route.

8.12.2.3 Message Switched Networks

Prior to advances in packet switching, message switching was introduced as an effective alternative to circuit switching. In message switching, end-users communicate by sending each other a message, which contains the entire data being delivered from the source to destination node.

As a message is routed from its source to its destination, each intermediate switch within the network stores the entire message, providing a very reliable service. In fact, when congestion occurs or all network resources are occupied, rather than discarding the traffic, the message-switched network will store and delay the traffic until sufficient resources are available for successful delivery of the message.

The message storing capability can also lead to reducing the cost of transmission; for example, messages can be delivered at night when transmission costs are typically lower.

Message switching techniques were originally used in data communications. Early examples of message switching applications are Electronic mail (E-mail) and voice mail. Today, message switching is used in many networks, including adhoc sensor networks, satellite communications networks, and military networks.

Message-switched data networks are hop-by-hop systems that support two distinct characteristics: *store-and-forward* and *message delivery*.

In a message-switched network, there is no direct connection between the source and destination nodes. In such networks, the intermediary nodes (switches) have the responsibility of conveying the received message from one node to another in the network. Therefore, each intermediary node within the network must store all messages before retransmitting them one at a time as proper resources become available. This characteristic is called *store-and-forward*. In message switching systems (also called *store-and-forward* systems), the responsibility of the message delivery is on the next hop, as the message travels through the path toward its destination. Hence, to ensure proper delivery, each intermediate switch may maintain a copy of the message until its delivery to the next hop is guaranteed.

In case of message broadcasting, multiple copies may be stored for each individual destination node. The store-and-forward property of message-switched networks is different from queuing , in which messages are simply stored until their preceding messages are processed. With store-and-forward capability, a message will only be delivered if the next hop and the link connecting to it are both available. Otherwise, the message is stored indefinitely. For example, consider a mail server that is disconnected from the network and cannot receive the messages directed to it. In this case, the intermediary server must store all messages until the mail server is connected and receives the e-mails.

The store-and-forward technology is also different from admission control techniques implemented in packet-switched or circuit switched networks. Using admission control, the data transmission can temporarily be delayed to avoid overprovisioning the resources. Hence, a message-switched network can also implement an admission control mechanism to reduce network's peak load.

The message delivery in message-switched networks includes wrapping the entire information in a single message and transferring it from the source to the destination node. The message size has no upper bound; although some messages can be as small as a simple database query, others can be very large. For example, messages obtained from a meteorological database center can contain several million bytes of binary data. Practical limitations in storage devices and switches, however, can enforce limits on message length.

Each message must be delivered with a header. The header often contains the message routing information, including the source and destination, priority level, expiration time. It is worth mentioning that while a message is being stored at the source or any other intermediary node in the network, it can be bundled or aggregated with other messages going to the next node. This is called *message interleaving*. One important advantage of message interleaving is that it can reduce the amount of overhead generated in the network, resulting in higher link utilization.

8.13 Why OSI Model?

During the initial days of computer networks, they usually used proprietary solutions, i.e., technologies manufactured one company were used in the computer networks. And, that manufacturer was in-charge of all systems present on the network. There is no option to use equipment's from different vendors.

In order to help the interconnection of different networks, ISO (*International Standards Organization*) developed a reference model called OSI (*Open Systems Interconnection*) and this allowed manufacturers to create protocols using this model. Some people get confused with these two acronyms, as they use the same letters. ISO is the name of the organization, while OSI is the name of the reference model for developing protocols.

ISO is the organization; OSI is the model.

8.14 What is a Protocol-Stack?

Before understanding what a protocol is, let us take an example. In some cultures shaking head *up* and *down* means *yes*, in other cultures it means *no*. If we don't ensure correct communication, we will soon have a war on our hands! Protocols are the rules developed for communicating. In simple terms, a protocol is a standard set of rules and regulations that allow two electronic devices to connect to and exchange information with one another.

All of us are familiar with protocols for human communication. We have rules for speaking, appearance, listening and understanding. These rules govern different layers of communication. They help us in successful communication. Similarly, in computer networks, a protocol is a set of rules that govern communications between the computers. A protocol stack is a complete *set* of network protocol layers that work together to provide *networking* capabilities. It is called a *stack* because it is typically designed as a hierarchy of layers, each supporting the one above it and using those below it.

The number of layers can vary between models. For example, TCP/IP (transmission control protocol/Internet protocol) has five layers (application, transport, network, data link and physical) and the OSI (open systems interconnect) model has seven layers (application, presentation, session, transport, network, data link and physical).

In order for two devices to communicate, they both must be using the same protocol stack. Each protocol in a stack on one device must communicate with its equivalent stack, or peer, on the other device. This allows computers running different operating systems to communicate with each other easily.

8.15 OSI Model

The OSI model divides the problem of moving data between computers into seven smaller tasks and they equate to the seven layers of the OSI reference model.
The OSI model deals with the following issues:

- How a device on a network sends its data, and how it knows when and where to send it.
- How a device on a network receives its data, and how to know where to look for it.
- How devices using different languages communicate with each other.

- How devices on a network are physically connected to each other.
- How protocols work with devices on a network to arrange data.

7	Application	***Network Processes to Applications*** Provides network services to application processes (such as e-mail, file transfer [FTP], and web browsing)
6	Presentation	***Data Representation*** This layer ensures data is readable by receiving system; formats data; negotiates data transfer syntax for application layer. *Examples*: ASCII, EBCDIC, Encryption, GIF, JPEG, PICT, and mp3.
5	Session	***Interhost Communication*** This layer establishes, manages, and terminates sessions between applications. *Examples*: NFS, SQL, and X Windows.
4	Transport	***End-to-end connections*** Deals with data transport issues between systems. It offers reliability, establishes virtual circuits, detects/recovers from errors, and provides flow control. *Examples*: TCP and UDP.
3	Network	***Addresses and Best Path Determination*** Provides connectivity and path selection between two end systems. Routers live here. *Examples*: IP, IPX, RIP, IGRP, and OSPF.
2	Data link	***Access to Media*** Provides reliable transfer of data across media. Responsible for physical addressing, network topology, error notification, and flow control. *Examples*: NIC, Ethernet, and IEEE 802.3.
1	Physical	***Binary Transmission*** Uses signaling to transmit bits (0s and 1s). *Examples*: UTP, coaxial cable, fiber optic cable, hubs, and repeaters.

8.15.1 The Application Layer

The top layer of the OSI model is the Application layer. The first thing that we need to understand about the application layer is that it does not refer to the actual applications that users run. Instead, it provides the framework that the actual applications run on top of.

To understand what the application layer does, suppose for a moment that a user wanted to use *Google Chrome* to open an FTP session and transfer a file. In this particular case, the application layer would define the file transfer protocol. This protocol is not directly accessible to the end user.

The end user must still use an application that is designed to interact with the file transfer protocol. In this case, *Google Chrome* would be that application.

8.15.2 The Presentation Layer

The presentation layer does some rather complex things, but everything that the presentation layer does can be summed up in one sentence. The presentation layer takes the data that is provided by the application layer, and converts it into a standard format that the other below layers can understand. Likewise, this layer converts the inbound data that is received from the session layer into something that the application layer can understand. The reason why this layer is necessary is because applications handle data differently from one another. In order for network communications to function properly, the data needs to be structured in a standard way.

8.15.3 The Session Layer

Once the data has been put into the correct format, the sending host must establish a session with the receiving host. This is where the session layer comes into play. It is responsible for establishing, maintaining, and eventually terminating the session with the remote host.

The interesting thing about the session layer is that it is more closely related to the application layer than it is to the physical layer. It is easy to think of connecting a network session as being a hardware function, but in actuality, sessions are usually established between applications. If a user is running multiple applications, several of those applications may have established sessions with remote resources at any time.

8.15.4 The Transport Layer

Transport layer is responsible for maintaining flow control. As you are no doubt aware, the Windows operating system allows users to run multiple applications simultaneously. It is therefore possible that multiple applications, and the operating system itself, may need to communicate over the network simultaneously. The Transport Layer takes the data from each application, and integrates it all into a single stream.

This layer is also responsible for providing error checking and performing data recovery when necessary. In essence, the Transport Layer is responsible for ensuring that all of the data makes it from the sending host to the receiving host.

8.15.5 The Network Layer

The Network Layer is responsible for determining how the data will reach the recipient. This layer handles things like addressing, routing, and logical protocols. Since this series is geared toward beginners, I do not want to get too technical, but The Network Layer creates logical paths, known as virtual circuits, between the source and destination hosts.

This circuit provides the individual packets with a way to reach their destination. The Network Layer is also responsible for its own error handling, and for packet sequencing and congestion control. Packet sequencing is necessary because each protocol limits the maximum size of a packet. The amount of data that must be transmitted often exceeds the maximum packet size. Therefore, the data is fragmented into multiple packets. When this happens, the Network Layer assigns each packet a sequence number.

When the data is received by the remote host, that device's Network layer examines the sequence numbers of the inbound packets, and uses the sequence number to reassemble the data and to figure out if any packets are missing.

If you are having trouble understanding this concept, then imagine that you need to mail a large document to a friend, but do not have a big enough envelope. You could put a few pages into several small envelopes, and then label the envelopes so that your friend knows what order the pages go in. This is exactly the same thing that the Network Layer does.

8.15.6 The Data Link Layer

The data link layer can be sub divided into two other layers; the Media Access Control (MAC) layer, and the Logical Link Control (LLC) layer. The MAC layer basically establishes the computer's identity on the network, via its MAC address. A MAC address is the address that is assigned to a network adapter at the hardware level. This is the address that is ultimately used when sending and receiving packets. The LLC layer controls frame synchronization and provides a degree of error checking.

8.15.7 The Physical Layer

The physical layer of the OSI model refers to the actual hardware specifications. The Physical Layer defines characteristics such as timing and voltage. The physical layer defines the hardware specifications used by network adapters and by the network cables (assuming that the connection is not wireless).

To put it simply, the physical layer defines what it means to transmit and to receive data.

8.15.8 How OSI Model Works? [Communications between Stacks]

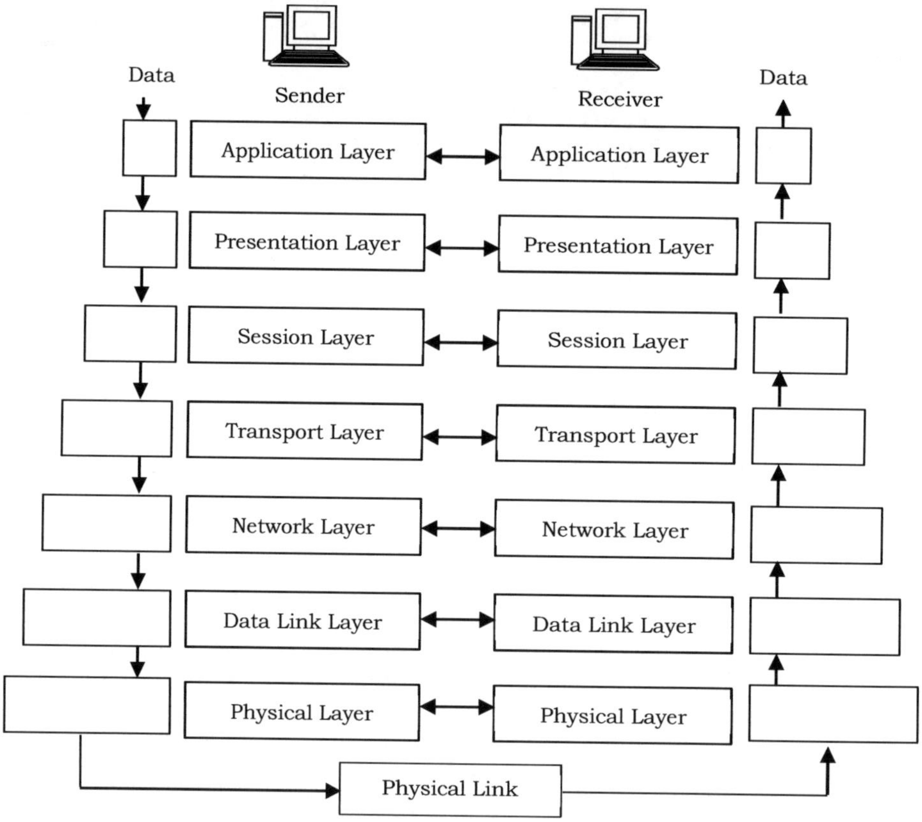

The OSI reference model is actually used to describe how data that is generated by a user, such as an email message, moves through a number of intermediary forms until it is converted into a stream of data that can actually be placed on the network media and sent out over the network. The model also describes how a communication session is established between two devices, such as two computers, on the network.

Since other types of devices, such as printers and routers, can be involved in network communication, devices (including computers) on the network are actually referred to as *nodes*. Therefore, a client computer on the network or a server on the network would each be *referred* to as a *node*.

While sending data over a network, it moves down through the OSI stack and is transmitted over the transmission media. When the data is received by a node, such as another computer on the network, it moves up through the OSI stack until it is again in a form that can be accessed by a user on that computer.

Layer #	Name	Encapsulation Units	Devices	Keywords/Description
7	Application	data	PC	Network services for application processes, such as file, print, messaging, database services
6	Presentation	data		Standard interface to data for the application layer. MIME encoding, data encryption, conversion, formatting, compression
5	Session	data		Inter host communication. Establishes, manages and terminates connection between applications
4	Transport	segments		Provides end-to-end message delivery and error recovery (reliability). Segmentation/desegmentation of data in proper sequence (flow control).
3	Network	packets	router	Logical addressing and path determination. Routing. Reporting delivery errors
2	Data Link	frames	bridge, switch, NIC	Physical addressing and access to media. Two sublayers: Logical Link Control (LLC) and Media Access Control (MAC)
1	Physical	bits	repeater, hub, transceiver	Binary transmission signals and encoding. Layout of pins, voltages, cable specifications, modulation

Each of the layers in the OSI model is responsible for certain aspects of getting user data into a format that can be transmitted on the network. Some layers are for establishing and maintaining the connection between the communicating nodes, and other layers are responsible for the addressing of the data so that it can be determined where the data originated (on which node) and where the data's destination is. An important aspect of the OSI model is that each layer in the stack provides services to the layer directly above it. Only the *Application* layer, which is at the top of the stack, would not provide services to a higher-level layer.

The process of moving user data down the OSI stack on a sending node (again, such as a computer) is called *encapsulation*. The process of moving raw data received by a node up the OSI stack is referred to as *de-encapsulation*. To encapsulate means to enclose or surround, and this is what happens to data that is created at the Application layer and then moves down through the other layers of the OSI model. A header, which is a segment of information affixed to the beginning of the data, is generated at each layer of the OSI model, except for the Physical layer.

This means that the data is encapsulated in a succession of headers—first the *Application* layer header, then the *Presentation* layer header, and so on. When the data reaches the *Physical* layer, it is like a candy bar that has been enclosed in several different wrappers. When the data is transmitted to a receiving node, such as a computer, the data travels up the OSI stack and each header is stripped off of the data. First, the *Data Link* layer header is removed, then the *Network* layer header, and so on. Also, the headers are not just removed by the receiving computer; the header information is read and used to determine what the receiving computer should do with the received data at each layer of the OSI model.

In OSI model, the sending computer uses these headers to communicate with the receiving computer and provide the receiving computer with useful. As the data travels up the levels of the peer computer, each header is removed by its equivalent protocol. These headers contain different information depending on the layer they receive the header from, but tell the peer layer important information, including packet size, frames, and datagrams.

Control is passed from one layer to the next, starting at the application layer in one station, and proceeding to the bottom layer, over the channel to the next station and back up the hierarchy. Each layer's header and data are called *packages*. Although it may seem confusing, each layer has a different name for its service data unit. Here are the common names for service data units at each level of the OSI model.

8.16 TCP/IP Model

The TCP/IP model is a networking model with a set of communication protocols for the Internet and similar networks. It is commonly known as TCP/IP, because its *Transmission Control Protocol* (TCP) and *Internet Protocol* (IP) were the first networking protocols defined in this model.

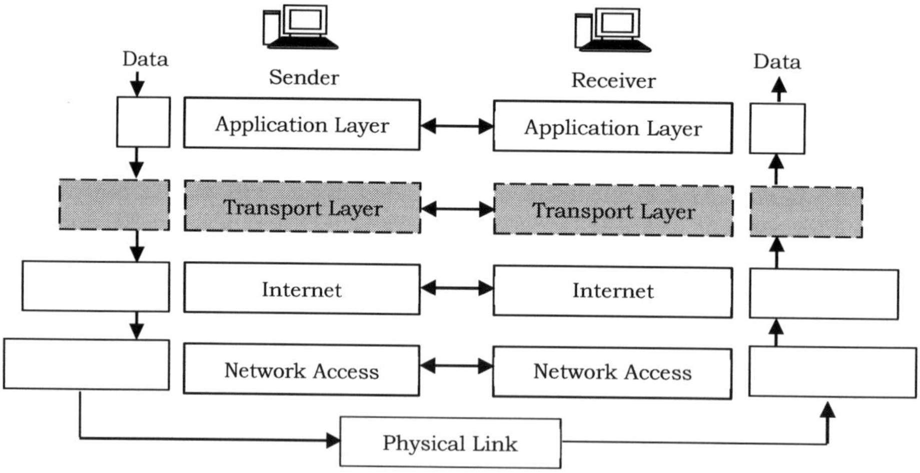

The TCP/IP model, similar to the OSI model, has a set of layers. The OSI has seven layers and the TCP/IP model has *four* or *five* layers depending on different preferences. Some people use the Application, Transport, Internet and Network Access layers. Others split the *Network Access* layer into the Physical and Data Link components.

The OSI model and the TCP/IP models were both created independently. The TCP/IP network model represents reality in the world, whereas the OSI mode represents an ideal.

Layer #	Description	Protocols
Application	Defines TCP/IP application protocols and how host programs interface with transport layer services to use the network.	HTTP, Telnet, FTP, TFTP, SNMP, DNS, SMTP, X Windows, other application protocols

Transport	Provides communication session management between the nodes/computers. Defines the level of service and status of the connection used when transporting data.	TCP, UDP, RTP
Internet	Packages data into IP datagrams, which contain source and destination address information that is used to forward the datagrams between hosts and networks. Performs routing of IP datagrams.	IP, ICMP, ARP, RARP
Network Access	Specifies details of how data is physically sent through the network, including how bits are electrically signaled by hardware devices that interface directly with a network medium, such as coaxial cable, optical fiber, or twisted-pair copper wire.	Ethernet, Token Ring, FDDI, X.25, Frame Relay, RS-2

8.16.1 Application Layer

Application layer is the top most layer of four layer TCP/IP model. Application layer is present on the top of the Transport layer. Application layer defines TCP/IP application protocols and how host programs interface with transport layer services to use the network. This layer is comparable to the application, presentation, and session layers of the OSI model all combined into one.

Application layer includes all the higher-level protocols like DNS (Domain Naming System), HTTP (Hypertext Transfer Protocol), Telnet, FTP (File Transfer Protocol), SNMP (Simple Network Management Protocol), SMTP (Simple Mail Transfer Protocol), DHCP (Dynamic Host Configuration Protocol), RDP (Remote Desktop Protocol) etc.

8.16.2 Transport Layer

Transport Layer is the third layer of the four layer TCP/IP model. The position of the Transport layer is between Application layer and Internet layer. Transport layer (also called *Host-to-Host* protocol) in the TCP/IP model provides more or less the same services with its equivalent Transport layer in the OSI model. This layer acts as the delivery service used by the application layer. Again the two protocols used are TCP and UDP. The choice is made based on the application's transmission reliability requirements.

It also ensures that data arrives at the application on the host for which it is targeted. Transport layer manages the flow of traffic between two hosts or devices. The transport layer also handles all error detection and recovery. It uses checksums, acknowledgements, and timeouts to control transmissions and end to end verification.

8.16.3 Internet Layer

Internet layer in TCP/IP model provides same services as the OSI model Network layer. Their purpose is to route packets to destination independent of the path taken. The routing and delivery of data is the responsibility of this layer and is the key component of this architecture. It allows communication across networks of the same and different types, and performs translations to deal with dissimilar data addressing schemes. It injects packets into any network and delivers them to the destination independently to one another.

Since the path through the network is not predetermined, the packets may be received out of order. The upper layers are responsible for the reordering of the data. This layer can be compared to the network layer of the OSI model. The main protocols included at Internet layer are IP (Internet Protocol), ICMP (Internet Control Message Protocol), ARP (Address Resolution Protocol), RARP (Reverse Address Resolution Protocol) and IGMP (Internet Group Management Protocol).

8.16.4 Network Access Layer

Network Access Layer is the first layer of the four layer TCP/IP model. Network Access layer defines details of how data is physically sent through the network. That means how bits are electrically or optically sent by hardware devices that interface directly with a network medium (such as coaxial cable, optical fiber, or twisted pair copper wire). The protocols included in Network Access layer are Ethernet, Token Ring, FDDI, X.25, Frame Relay etc.

The most popular LAN architecture among those listed above is Ethernet. Ethernet uses an *access method* called *CSMA/CD* (Carrier Sense Multiple Access/Collision Detection) to access the media. An access method determines how a host will place data on the medium. In CSMA/CD access method, every host has equal access to the medium and can place data on the wire when the wire is free from network traffic. When a host wants to place data on the wire, it will check the wire to find whether another host is already using the medium.

If there is traffic already in the medium, the host will wait and if there is no traffic, it will place the data in the medium. But, if two systems place data on the medium at the same instance, they will collide with each other, destroying the data. If the data is destroyed during transmission, the data will need to be retransmitted. After collision, each host will wait for a small interval of time and again the data will be retransmitted.

This is a combination of the Data Link and Physical layers of the OSI model which consists of the actual hardware.

8.17 Difference between OSI and TCP/IP models

The OSI model describes computer networking in seven layers. The TCP/IP model uses four layers to perform the functions of the seven-layer OSI model. The network access layer is functionally equal to a combination of OSI physical and data link layers.

The Internet layer performs the same functions as the OSI network layer. Things get a bit more complicated at the host-to-host layer of the TCP/IP model. If the host-to-host protocol is TCP, the matching functionality is found in the OSI transport and session layers. Using UDP equates to the functions of only the transport layer of the OSI model. The TCP/IP process layer, when used with TCP, provides the functions of the OSI model's presentation and application layers. When the TCP/IP transport layer protocol is UDP, the process layer's functions are equivalent to OSI session, presentation, and application layers.

8.17.1 OSI comparison with TCP/IP Protocol Stack

The main differences between the two models are as follows:

- OSI is a reference model and TCP/IP is an implementation of OSI model.
- TCP/IP protocols are considered to be standards around which the internet has developed. The OSI model however is a *generic, protocol-independent* standard.
- TCP/IP combines the presentation and session layer issues into its application layer.
- TCP/IP combines the OSI data link and physical layers into the network access layer.
- TCP/IP appears to be a simpler model and this is mainly due to the fact that it has fewer layers.

- TCP/IP is considered to be a more credible model- This is mainly due to the fact because TCP/IP protocols are the standards around which the internet was developed therefore it mainly gains creditability due to this reason. Where as in contrast networks are not usually built around the OSI model as it is merely used as a guidance tool.
- The OSI model consists of 7 architectural layers whereas the TCP/IP only has 4 layers.

OSI #	OSI Layer Name	TCP/IP #	TCP/IP Layer Name	Encapsulation Units	TCP/IP Protocols
7	Application	4	Application	data	FTP, HTTP, POP3, IMAP, telnet, SMTP, DNS, TFTP
6	Presentation			data	
5	Session			data	
4	Transport	3	Transport	segments	TCP, UDP
3	Network	2	Internet	packets	IP
2	Data Link	1	Network Access	frames	
1	Physical			bits	

8.18 How does TCP/IP Model (Internet) work?

As we have seen, there are a set of protocols that support computer networks. Computers on the Internet communicate by exchanging packets of data, called Internet Protocol (IP) *packets*. IP is the network protocol used to send information from one computer to another over the Internet. All computers on the Internet communicate using IP. IP moves information contained in IP packets. The IP packets are routed via special routing algorithms from a source to destination. The routing algorithms figure out the best way to send the packets from source to destination.

In order for IP to send packets from a source computer to a destination computer, it must have some way of identifying these computers. All computers on the Internet are identified using one or more IP addresses. A computer may have more than one IP address if it has more than one interface to computers that are connected to the Internet.

IP addresses are 32-bit numbers. They may be written in decimal, hexadecimal, or other formats, but the most common format is dotted decimal notation. This format breaks the 32-bit address up into four bytes and writes each byte of the address as unsigned decimal integers separated by dots. For example, one of *CareerMonk.com* IP addresses is $0xccD499C1$. Since, $0xcc = 204$, $0xD4 = 212$, $0x99 = 153$, and $0xC1 = 193$, *CareerMonk.com* IP address in dotted decimal form is 204.212.153.193.

8.18.1 Domain Name System (DNS)

IP addresses are not easy to remember, even using dotted decimal notation. The Internet has adopted a mechanism, referred to as the *Domain Name System* (DNS), whereby computer names can be associated with IP addresses. These computer names are called *domain names*. The DNS has several rules that determine how domain names are constructed and how they relate to one another. The mapping of domain names to IP addresses is maintained by a system of *domain name servers*. These servers are able to look up the IP address corresponding to a domain name. They also provide the capability to look up the domain name associated with a particular IP address, if one exists.

8.18.2 TCP and UDP

Computers running on the Internet communicate to each other using either the Transmission Control Protocol (TCP) or the User Datagram Protocol (UDP). When we write *Java* programs that communicate over the network, we are programming at the application layer. Typically, we don't need to concern with the TCP and UDP layers. Instead, we can use the classes in the java.net package. These classes provide system-independent network communication. However, to decide which *Java* classes our programs should use, we do need to understand how TCP and UDP differ.

8.18.2.1 TCP [Transmission Control Protocol]

When two applications want to communicate to each other reliably, they establish a connection and send data back and forth over that connection. This is analogous to making a telephone call. If we want to speak to a person who is in another country, a connection is established when we dial the phone number and the other party answers.

We send data back and forth over the connection by speaking to one another over the phone lines. Like the phone company, TCP guarantees that data sent from one end of the connection actually gets to the other end and in the same order it was sent. Otherwise, an error is reported.

TCP provides a point-to-point channel for applications that require reliable communications. The Hypertext Transfer Protocol (HTTP), File Transfer Protocol (FTP), and Telnet are all examples of applications that require a reliable communication channel. The order in which the data is sent and received over the network is critical to the success of these applications. When HTTP is used to read from a URL, the data must be received in the order in which it was sent. Otherwise, we end up with a jumbled HTML file, a corrupt zip file, or some other invalid information.

Application: HTTP, ftp, telnet, SMTP,...
Transport: TCP, UDP,...
Network: IP,...
Link: Device driver,...

Definition: TCP is a connection-based protocol that provides a reliable flow of data between two computers.

Transport protocols are used to deliver information from one port to another and thereby enable communication between application programs. They use either a connection-oriented or connectionless method of communication. TCP is a connection-oriented protocol and UDP is a connectionless transport protocol.

The reliability of the communication between the source and destination programs is ensured through error-detection and error-correction mechanisms that are implemented within TCP. TCP implements the connection as a stream of bytes from source to destination. This feature allows the use of the stream I/O classes provided by java.io.

8.18.2.2 UDP [User Datagram Protocol]

The UDP protocol provides for communication that is not guaranteed between two applications on the network. UDP is not connection-based like TCP. But, it sends independent packets of data (called datagrams) from one application to another. Sending datagrams is much like sending a letter through the postal service: The order of delivery is not important and is not guaranteed, and each message is independent of any other.

Definition: UDP is a protocol that sends independent packets of data, called *datagrams*, from one computer to another with no guarantees about arrival. UDP is not connection-based.

For many applications, the guarantee of reliability is critical to the success of the transfer of information from one end of the connection to the other. However, other forms of communication don't require such strict standards. In fact, they may be slowed down by the extra overhead or the reliable connection may invalidate the service altogether.

Consider, for example, a clock server that sends the current time to its client when requested to do so. If the client misses a packet, it doesn't really make sense to resend it because the time will be incorrect when the client receives it on the second try.

If the client makes two requests and receives packets from the server out of order, it doesn't really matter because the client can figure out that the packets are out of order and make another request. The reliability of TCP is unnecessary in this instance because it causes performance degradation and may hinder the usefulness of the service.

Another example of a service that doesn't need the guarantee of a reliable channel is the ping command. The purpose of the ping command is to test the communication between two programs over the network. In fact, ping needs to know about dropped or out-of-order packets to determine how good or bad the connection is. A reliable channel would invalidate this service altogether.

The UDP protocol provides for communication that is not guaranteed between two applications on the network. UDP is not connection-based like TCP. Rather, it sends independent packets of data from one application to another. Sending datagrams is much like sending a letter through the mail service: The order of delivery is not important and is not guaranteed, and each message is independent of any others.

The UDP connectionless protocol differs from the TCP connection-oriented protocol in that it does not establish a link for the duration of the connection. An example of a connectionless protocol is postal mail. To mail something, you just write down a destination address (and an optional return address) on the envelope of the item you're sending and drop it in a mailbox.

When using UDP, an application program writes the destination port and IP address on a datagram and then sends the datagram to its destination. UDP is less reliable than TCP because there are no delivery-assurance or error-detection and error-correction mechanisms built into the protocol.

Application protocols such as FTP, SMTP, and HTTP use TCP to provide reliable, stream-based communication between client and server programs. Other protocols, such as the Time Protocol, use UDP because speed of delivery is more important than end-to-end reliability.

8.19 Understanding Ports

Generally speaking, a computer has a single physical connection to the network. All data destined for a particular computer arrives through that connection. However, the data may be intended for different applications running on the computer. So, how does the computer know to which application to forward the data? Through the use of ports.

Data transmitted over the Internet is accompanied by addressing information that identifies the computer and the port for which it is destined. The computer is identified by its 32-bit IP address, which IP uses to deliver data to the right computer on the network. Ports are identified by a 16-bit number, which TCP and UDP use to deliver the data to the right application.

In connection-based communication such as TCP, a server application binds a socket to a specific port number. This has the effect of registering the server with the system to receive all data destined for that port. A client can then rendezvous with the server at the server's port, as illustrated here:

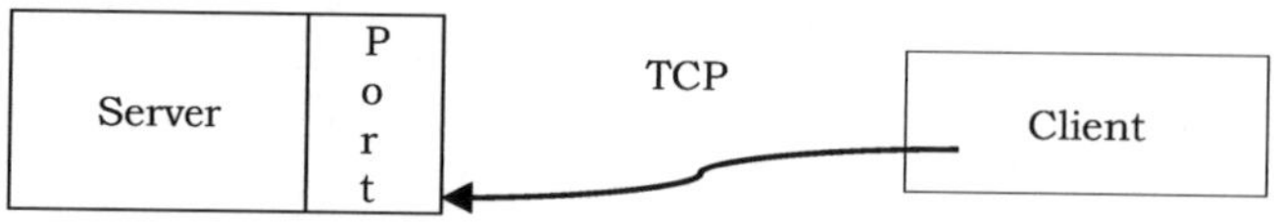

Definition: The TCP and UDP protocols use ports to map incoming data to a particular process running on a computer.

In datagram-based communication such as UDP, the datagram packet contains the port number of its destination and UDP routes the packet to the appropriate application, as illustrated in this figure:

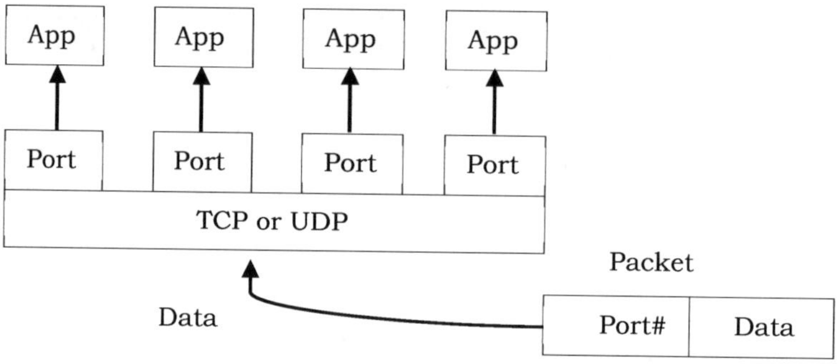

Port numbers range from 0 to 65,535 because ports are represented by 16-bit numbers. The port numbers ranging from 0 - 1023 are restricted; they are reserved for use by well-known services such as HTTP and FTP and other system services. These ports are called well – known ports. Your applications should not attempt to bind to them.

Port	Protocol
21	File Transfer Protocol
23	Telnet Protocol
25	Simple Mail Transfer Protocol
80	Hypertext Transfer Protocol

8.20 Hypertext Transfer Protocol [HTTP]

8.20.1 What is HTTP?

HTTP (Hypertext Transfer Protocol) is the set of rules for transferring files on the World Wide Web. The files can be text files, graphic images, sound, video, or other multimedia files. As soon as a Web user opens their Web browser, the user is indirectly making use of HTTP. HTTP is an application protocol that runs on top of the TCP/IP suite of protocols (the foundation protocols for the Internet).

Hypertext means an electronic document text that is connected (hyperlinked) to the other chunks of text. HTTP concepts include (as the Hypertext part of the name implies) the idea that files can contain references to other files whose selection will need additional transfer requests. Any Web server machine contains, in addition to the Web page files it can serve, an HTTP daemon, a program that is designed to wait for HTTP requests and handle them when they arrive.

Web browser is an HTTP client, sending requests to server machines. When the browser user enters file requests by either "opening" a Web file (typing in a Uniform Resource

Locator or URL) or clicking on a hypertext link, the browser builds an HTTP request and sends it to the Internet Protocol address (IP address) indicated by the URL. The HTTP daemon in the destination server machine receives the request and sends back the requested file or files associated with the request. A Web page generally consists of more than one file.

8.20.2 Why HTTP?

When you browse the web the situation is basically this: you sit at your computer and want to see a document somewhere on the web, to which you have the URL.

Since the document you want to read is somewhere else in the world and probably very far away from you some more details are needed to make it available to you. The first detail is your browser. You start it up and type the URL into it (at least you tell the browser somehow where you want to go, perhaps by clicking on a link).

However, the picture is still not complete, as the browser can't read the document directly from the disk where it's stored if that disk is on another continent. So for you to be able to read the document the computer that contains the document must run a web server. A web server is a just a computer program that listens for requests from browsers and then execute them.

The browser will display HTML documents directly, and if there are references to images, video clips etc. in it and the browser has been set up to display these it will request these also from the servers on which they reside. It's worth noting that these will be separate requests, and add additional load to the server and network. When the user follows another link the whole sequence starts anew.

These requests and responses are issued in a special language called HTTP, which is short for Hypertext Transfer Protocol.

It's worth noting that HTTP only defines what the browser and web server say to each other, not how they communicate. The actual work of moving bits and bytes back and forth across the network is done by TCP and IP.

When you continue, note that any software program that does the same as a web browser (ie: retrieve documents from servers) is called a client in network terminology and a user agent in web terminology. Also note that the server is properly the server program, and not the computer on which the server is an application program.

8.20.3 How does HTTP work?

Step 1: Parsing the URL

The first thing the browser has to do is to look at the URL of the new document to find out how to get hold of the new document. Most URLs have this basic form: "protocol://server/request-URI". The protocol part describes how to tell the server which document we want and how to retrieve it.

The server part tells the browser which server to contact, and the request-URI is the name used by the web server to identify the document (term request URI means uniform resource identifier defined by HTTP standard).

Step 2: Sending the request

Usually, the protocol is *http*. To retrieve a document via *http* the browser transmits the following request to the server: "GET /request-URI HTTP/version", where version tells the server which HTTP version is used.

One important point here is that this request string is all the server ever sees. So the server doesn't care if the request came from a browser, a link checker, a validator, a search engine robot (web-crawler) or if we typed it in manually. It just performs the request and returns the result.

Step 3: The server response

When the server receives the HTTP request it locates the appropriate document and returns it. However, an HTTP response is required to have a particular form. It must look like this:

```
HTTP/[VER] [CODE] [TEXT]
Field1: Value1
Field2: Value2

...Web page content here...
```

The first line shows the HTTP version used, followed by a three-digit number (the HTTP status code) and a reason phrase meant for humans. Usually the code is 200 (which mean that all is well) and the phrase *OK*. The first line is followed by some lines called the header, which contains information about the document. The header ends with a blank line, followed by the document content. This is a typical header:

```
HTTP/1.0 200 OK
Server: CareerMonk-Communications/1.1
Date: Tuesday, 25-Nov-97 01:22:04 GMT
Last-modified: Thursday, 20-Nov-97 10:44:53 GMT
Content-length: 6372
Content-type: text/html

<!DOCTYPE HTML PUBLIC "-//W3C//DTD HTML 3.2 Final//EN">
<HTML>
...followed by document content...
```

We see from the first line that the request was successful. The second line is optional and tells us that the server runs the CareerMonk Communications web server, version 1.1. We then get what the server thinks is the current date and when the document was modified last, followed by the size of the document in bytes and the most important field: *Content – type*.

The content-type field is used by the browser to tell which format the document it receives is in. HTML is identified with *text/html*, ordinary text with *text/plain*, a GIF is *image/gif* and so on. The advantage of this is that the URL can have any ending and the browser will still get it right.

An important concept here is that to the browser, the server works as a black box. The browser requests a specific document and the document is either returned or an error message is returned. How the server produces the document remains unknown to the browser. This means that the server can read it from a file, run a program to generate it, or compile it by parsing some kind of command file. It is decided by the server administrator.

What the server does

While setting up the server, it is usually configured to use a directory somewhere on disk as its root directory and that there be a default file name (say, *index.html*) for each directory. This means that if we ask the server for the file "/" (as in *http://www.CareerMonk.com*) we'll get the file *index.html* in the server root directory.

Usually, asking for */foo/bar.html* will give us the *bar.html* file from the *foo* directory directly beneath the server root. The server can be set up to map */foo/* into some other directory elsewhere on disk or even to use server-side programs to answer all requests that ask for that directory.

8.20.4 What is HTTPS?

Hyper Text Transfer Protocol Secure (https or HTTPS) is a secure version of the http. https allows secure ecommerce transactions, such as online banking.

Web browsers such as Google Chrome, Internet Explorer, and Firefox display a padlock icon to indicate that the website is secure, as it also displays https:// in the address bar. When a user connects to a website via https, the website encrypts the session with a Digital Certificate. A user can tell if they are connected to a secure website if the website URL begins with https:// instead of http://.

8.21 Simple Mail Transfer Protocol [SMTP]

8.21.1 What is SMTP?

SMTP stands for Simple Mail Transfer Protocol and is a TCP/IP protocol used in sending and receiving e-mail. It's a set of communication rules that allow software to send email over the Internet. Most email software is designed to use SMTP for communication for sending email, and it only works for outgoing messages.

8.21.2 Why SMTP?

Email is very similar to sending a letter in the mail. We have a mailbox, and a number of post offices. The SMTP servers act like post offices that handle the routing of the messages. When we put a letter in our mailbox the post office picks it up then routes it to the appropriate post office for delivery. Email is the same way. When we send an email to SMTP server; it is routed to the appropriate receiving server for delivery.

8.21.3 How does SMTP work?

SMTP provides a set of codes that simplify the communication of email messages between servers. It is a kind of shorthand that allows a server to break up different parts of a message into categories the other server can understand.

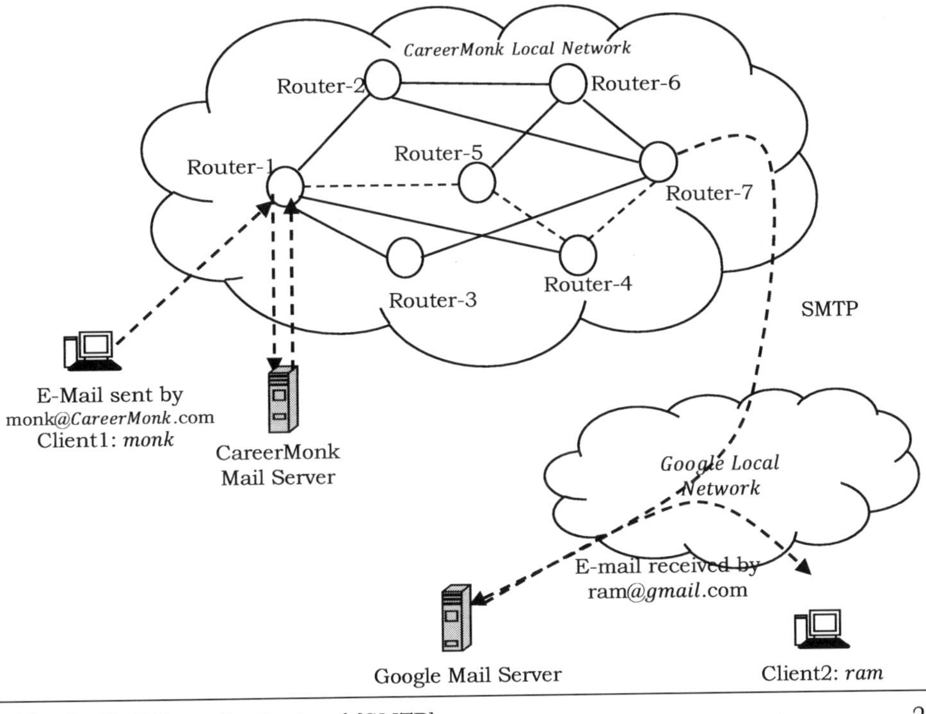

Any email message has a sender, a recipient (sometimes multiple recipients), a message body, and usually a title heading (subject). From users perspective, when they write an email message, they see the graphical user interface of their email software (for example, Outlook), but once that message goes out on the Internet, everything is converted into strings of text. This text is separated by code words or numbers that identify the purpose of each section. SMTP provides those codes, and email server software is designed to understand what they mean. The most common commands are:

HELO	Introduce yourself
EHLO	Introduce yourself and request extended mode
MAIL ROM	Specify the sender
RCPT TO	Specify the recipient
DATA	Specify the body of the message (To, From and Subject should be the first three lines)
RSET	Reset
QUIT	Quit the session
HELP	Get help on commands
VRFY	Verify an address
EXPN	Expand an address
VERB	Verbose

The other purpose of SMTP is to set up communication rules between servers. For example, servers have a way of identifying themselves and announcing what kind of communication they are trying to perform. There are also ways to handle errors, including common things like incorrect email addresses.

In a typical SMTP transaction, a server will identify itself, and announce the kind of operation it is trying to perform. The other server will authorize the operation, and the message will be sent. If the recipient address is wrong, or if there is some other problem, the receiving server may reply with an error message of some kind.

8.22 File Transfer Protocol [FTP]

8.22.1 What is FTP?

FTP is particularly useful for transferring *larger* files. FTP is a more robust and more capable protocol than the HTTP. Since no special browser is required, FTP is also more universal than HTTP. All major operating systems, including Mac OS, Windows and Linux allow FTP file transfers directly from the command line.

File Transfer Protocol (FTP) is an Internet protocol for transferring files between nodes on the Internet. FTP is used for connecting to a remote machine; send or fetch an arbitrary file. Like HTTP (which transfers displayable Web pages and related files), and the SMTP (transfers e-mail), FTP is an application protocol that uses the Internet's TCP/IP protocols. It is also commonly used to download programs and other files to a computer from other servers.

8.22.2 Why FTP?

If we want to copy files between two computers that are on the same local network (LAN), we can simply share a drive or folder, and copy the files the same way we would copy files from one place to another on our own PC.

What if we want to copy files from one computer to another that is far away (around the world)? One possibility could be, using Internet connection and sharing folders over the Internet. But, this way of transferring the files is not secure. To address this *issue*, FTP was invented. File transfers over the Internet use special technique called FTP.

8.22.3 How does FTP work?

In order to transfer a file from a client to a server (or to download a file from a server to a computer), a user must authenticate to an FTP server. By authenticating, the user creates a session on the server during which he can transfer or modify as many files as necessary. The authentication process also allows remote hosts to set proper file permissions, keeping users from viewing files or directories to which they do not have access, and allowing an individual user to set read, write, and execute permissions on his own files or subdirectories.

When the user session is complete, the user simply disconnects from the server and the session is closed. Some FTP servers also allow anonymous connections, where members of the public can connect anonymously to the FTP server and initiate file transfers; these settings are generally used when publicly available information--like program files released for free--needs to be available for download by knowledgeable users.

As a user, we can use FTP with a simple command line interface or with a commercial program (for example, FileZilla) that offers a graphical user interface. Web browser can also make FTP requests to download programs we select from a Web page. Using FTP, we can also update (delete, rename, move, and copy) files on a server. We need to logon to an FTP server. However, publicly available files are easily accessed using anonymous FTP.

8.23 Domain Name Server [DNS]

8.23.1 What is DNS?

Domain name server (DNS) is a protocol with a set of standards for how computers exchange data on the Internet and it is an application protocol that runs on top of the TCP/IP suite of protocols.

A domain name locates an organization or other entity on the Internet. For example, the domain name

www.CareerMonk.com

locates an Internet address for *CareerMonk.com* at IP address199.5.10.2 and a particular host server named *www*. The *com* part of the domain name reflects the purpose of the organization or entity (in this example, *commercial*) and is called the top-level domain name.

The *CareerMonk* part of the domain name defines the organization and together with the top-level is called the *second-level* domain name. The second-level domain name maps to and can be thought of as the *readable* version of the Internet address (IP address).

A third level can be defined to identify a particular host server at the Internet address. In our example, *www* is the name of the server which handles Internet requests (a second server might be called *www*2.) A third level of domain name is not required. For example, the fully-qualified domain name (FQDN) could have been *CareerMonk.com* and the server assumed.

Subdomain levels can also be used for modularity and ease of maintenance. For example, we could have *www.TechnicalServer.CareerMonk.com*. Together, *www.CareerMonk.com* constitutes a fully-qualified domain name.

Second-level domain names must be unique on the Internet and registered for the *com*, *net*, and *org* top-level domains. Where appropriate, a top-level domain name can be geographic. Currently, most non-U.S. domain names use a top-level domain name based on the country the server is in (for example, India uses *.in*).

On the Web, the domain name is that part of the Uniform Resource Locator (URL) that tells a domain name server using the domain name system (DNS) whether and where to forward a request for a Web page. The domain name is mapped to an IP address.

More than one domain name can be mapped to the same Internet address. This allows multiple individuals, businesses, and organizations to have separate Internet identities while sharing the same Internet server.

8.23.2 Hierarchy of domain names

Domain Names are hierarchical and each part of a domain name is referred to as the root, top level, and second level or as a sub-domain. To allow computers to properly recognize a fully qualified domain name, dots are placed between each part of the name. All resolvers treat dots as separators between the parts of the domain name.

The fully qualified domain name is split into pieces at the dots and the tree is searched starting from the root of the hierarchical tree structure. All resolvers start their lookups at the root; therefore the root is represented by a dot and is often assumed to be there, even when not shown.

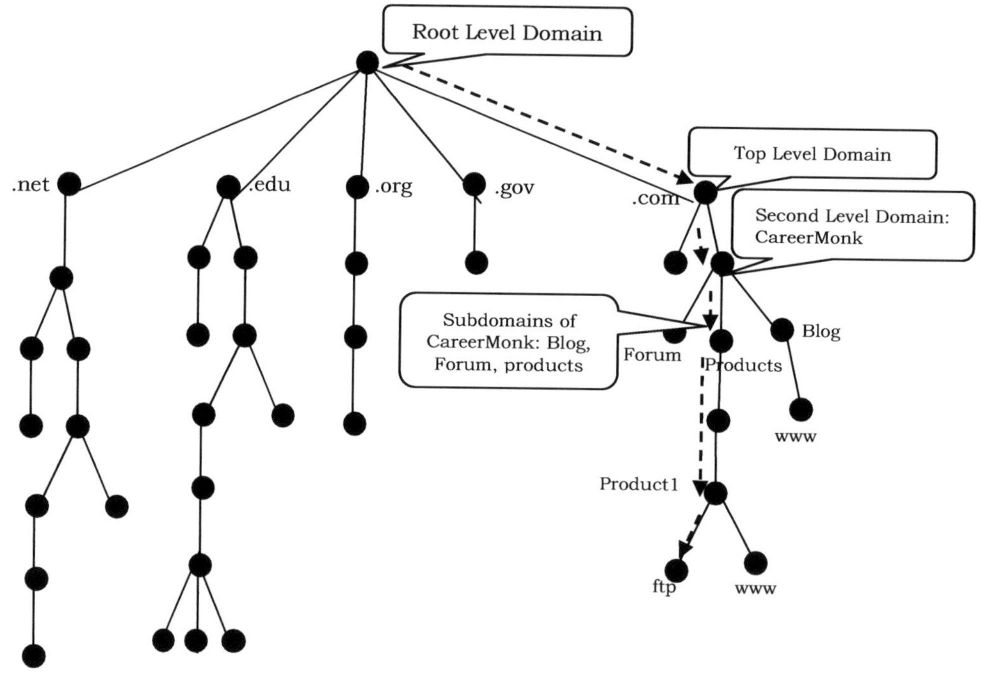

The resolver navigates its way down the tree until it gets to the last, left-most part of the domain name and then looks within that location for the information it needs. Information about a host such as its name, its IP address and occasionally even its function are stored in one or more zone files which together compose a larger zone often referred to as a domain.

- Top Level Domains (TLD's)
- Second Level Domains
- Sub-Domains
- Host Name (a resource record)

Within the hierarchy, we will start resolution at the top level domain, work our way down to the second-level domain, then through zero, one or more sub-domains until we get to the actual host name we want to resolve into an IP address. It is traditional to use different DNS servers for each level of the DNS hierarchy.

A domain is a label of the DNS tree. Each node on the DNS tree represents a domain. Domains under the top-level domains represent individual organizations or entities. These domains can be further divided into subdomains to ease administration of an organization's host computers.

For example, company *CareerMonk* creates a domain called *CareerMonk.com* under the .com top-level domain. *CareerMonk* has separate LANs for its *Forum*, *Blog*, and *Products*. Therefore, the network administrator for *CareerMonk* decides to create a separate subdomain for each division, as shown in figure. Any domain in a subtree is considered part of all domains above it. Therefore, *Forum.CareerMonk.com* is part of the *CareerMonk*.com domain, and both are part of the *.com* domain.

8.23.3 Understanding zones

DNS data is divided into manageable sets of data called *zones*. Zones contain name and IP address information about one or more parts of a DNS domain. A server that contains all of the information for a zone is the authoritative server for the domain. Sometimes it may make sense to *delegate* the authority for answering DNS queries for a particular subdomain to another DNS server.

In this case, the DNS server for the domain can be configured to refer the *subdomain* queries to the appropriate server. For *backup* and *redundancy*, zone data is often stored on servers other than the authoritative DNS server. These other servers are called *secondary* servers, which load zone data from the authoritative server.

Configuring secondary servers allows us to balance the demand on servers and also provides a backup in case the primary server goes down.

Secondary servers obtain zone data by doing zone transfers from the authoritative server. When a secondary server is initialized, it loads a complete copy of the zone data from the primary server. The secondary server also reloads zone data from the primary server or from other secondary's for that domain when zone data changes.

8.23.3 Why DNS is needed?

Computers and other network devices on the Internet use an IP address to route our request to the site we are trying to reach. This is similar to dialling a mobile number to connect to the person we are trying to call. DNS makes our life easy. We don't have to keep our own address book of IP addresses. Instead, we just connect through a domain name server, also called a DNS server or name server, which manages a massive database that maps domain names to IP addresses.

8.23.4 How does DNS work?

A DNS program works like this - every time a domain name is typed in a browser it is automatically passed on to a DNS server, which translates the name into its corresponding IP address. When we visit a domain such as *CareerMonk.com*, our computer follows a series of steps to turn the human-readable web address into a machine-readable IP address. This happens every time we use a domain name, whether we are viewing websites or sending email.

For example, the name specified could be the FQDN for a computer, such as *development.CareerMonk.com*, and the query type specified to look for an address (A) resource record by that name. Think of a DNS query as a client asking a server a two-part question, such as "Do you have any address (A) resource records for a computer named *development.CareerMonk.com*? When the client receives an answer from the server, it reads and interprets the answered A resource record, learning the IP address for the computer it asked for by name.

DNS queries resolve in a number of different ways. Client can sometimes answer a query locally using cached information obtained from a previous query. The DNS server can use its own cache of resource record information to answer a query.

A DNS server can also query or contact other DNS servers on behalf of the requesting client to fully resolve the name, and then send an answer back to the client. This process is known as *recursion*.

Also, the client itself can attempt to contact additional DNS servers to resolve a name. When a client does so, it uses separate and additional non-recursive queries based on referral answers from servers. This process is known as *iteration*.

In general, the DNS query process occurs in two parts:

- A name query begins at a client computer and is passed to a resolver, the DNS Client service, for resolution.
- When the query cannot be resolved locally, DNS servers can be queried as needed to resolve the name.

Both of these processes are explained in more detail in the following sections.

Part 1: The local resolver

The following figure shows an overview of the complete DNS query process.

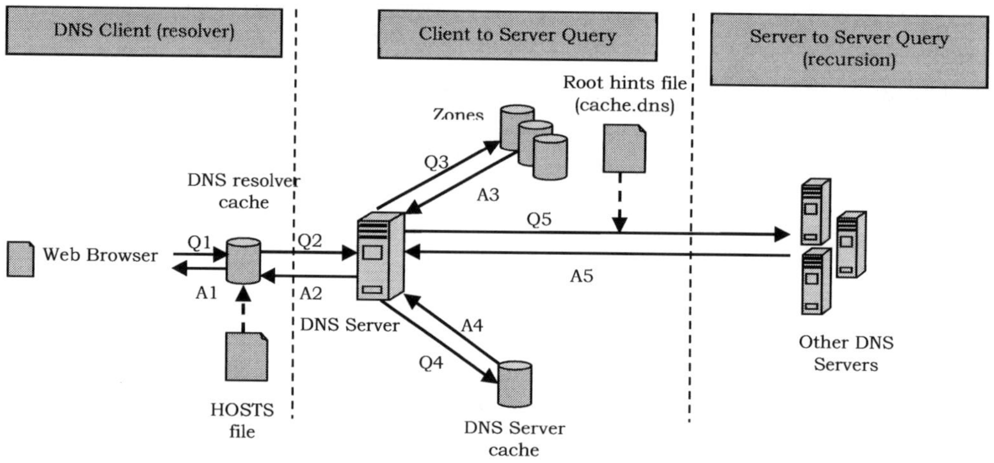

As shown in the initial steps of the query process, a DNS domain name is used in a program on the local computer. The request is then passed to the DNS Client service for resolution using locally cached information. If the queried name can be resolved, the query is answered and the process is completed.

The local resolver cache can include name information obtained from two possible sources:

- If a Hosts file is configured locally, any host name-to-address mappings from that file are preloaded into the cache when the DNS Client service is started.
- Resource records obtained in answered responses from previous DNS queries are added to the cache and kept for a period of time.

If the query does not match an entry in the cache, the resolution process continues with the client querying a DNS server to resolve the name.

Part 2: Querying a DNS server

As indicated in the previous figure, the client queries a preferred DNS server. The actual server used during the initial client/server query part of the process is selected from a global list. For more information about how this global list is compiled and updated.

When the DNS server receives a query, it first checks to see if it can answer the query authoritatively based on resource record information contained in a locally configured zone on the server. If the queried name matches a corresponding resource record in local zone information, the server answers authoritatively, using this information to resolve the queried name.

If no zone information exists for the queried name, the server then checks to see if it can resolve the name using locally cached information from previous queries. If a match is found here, the server answers with this information. Again, if the preferred server can answer with a positive matched response from its cache to the requesting client, the query is completed.

If the queried name does not find a matched answer at its preferred server -- either from its cache or zone information -- the query process can continue, using recursion to fully resolve the name. This involves assistance from other DNS servers to help resolve the name. By default, the DNS Client service asks the server to use a process of recursion to fully resolve names on behalf of the client before returning an answer. In most cases, the DNS server is configured, by default, to support the recursion process as shown in the following figure.

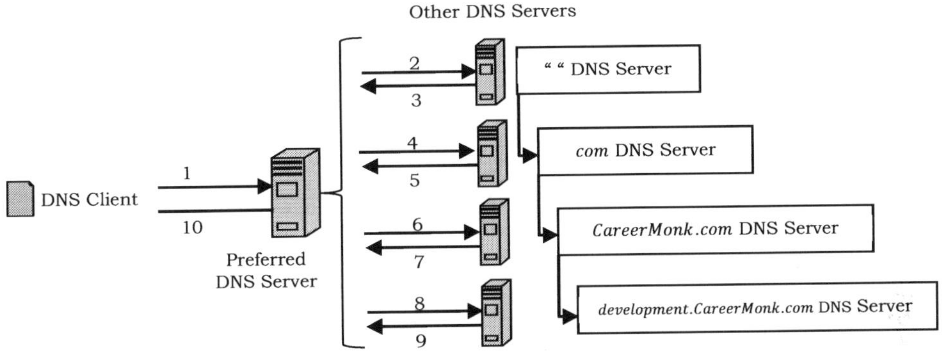

In order for the DNS server to do recursion properly, it first needs some helpful contact information about other DNS servers in the DNS domain namespace. This information is provided in the form of *root hints*, a list of preliminary resource records that can be used by the DNS service to locate other DNS servers that are authoritative for the root of the DNS domain namespace tree. Root servers are authoritative for the domain root and top-level domains in the DNS domain namespace tree.

By using root hints to find root servers, a DNS server is able to complete the use of recursion. In theory, this process enables any DNS server to locate the servers that are authoritative for any other DNS domain name used at any level in the namespace tree.

For example, consider the use of the recursion process to locate the name *development.CareerMonk*.com when the client queries a single DNS server. The process occurs when a DNS server and client are first started and have no locally cached information available to help resolve a name query. It assumes that the name queried by the client is for a domain name of which the server has no local knowledge, based on its configured zones.

First, the preferred server parses the full name and determines that it needs the location of the server that is authoritative for the top-level domain, *com*. It then uses an iterative (that is, a nonrecursive) query to the *com* DNS server to obtain a referral to the *CareerMonk.com* server. Next, a referral answer comes from the *CareerMonk.com* server to the DNS server for *development.CareerMonk.com*.

Finally, the *development.CareerMonk.com* server is contacted. Because this server contains the queried name as part of its configured zones, it responds authoritatively back to the original server that initiated recursion. When the original server receives the response indicating that an authoritative answer was obtained to the requested query, it forwards this answer back to the requesting client and the recursive query process is completed.

Although the recursive query process can be resource-intensive when performed as described above, it has some performance advantages for the DNS server. For example, during the recursion process, the DNS server performing the recursive lookup obtains information about the DNS domain namespace.

This information is cached by the server and can be used again to help speed the answering of subsequent queries that use or match it. Over time, this cached information can grow to occupy a significant portion of server memory resources, although it is cleared whenever the DNS service is cycled on and off.

8.24 Dynamic Host Configuration Protocol [DHCP]

DHCP protocol was introduced in 1993. The standard supports a mix of static and dynamic IP addressing.

The Dynamic Host Configuration Protocol (DHCP) provides a method for passing configuration information to hosts on a TCP/IP network. DHCP is based on its predecessor Bootstrap Protocol (BOOTP), but adds automatic allocation of reusable network addresses and additional configuration options.

8.24.1 What is DHCP?

Dynamic Host Configuration Protocol (DHCP) is a protocol for *automatically* assigning IP addresses to devices throughout a network, and of re-assigning those addresses as they are no longer needed by the device that used them. It provides an effective alternative to manually assigning IP addresses to every client, server, and printer.

Apart from *eliminating* the manual effort of creating and maintaining a list of IP address assignments for network devices, DHCP also provides a measure of *protection* against the *mistakes* that can arise when the process of IP addressing is manual.

For example, when two devices are mistakenly given duplicate IP addresses, only one of them—the first to boot—will be able to communicate on the network at any given time. Finally, DHCP makes it unnecessary to manually re-assign IP addresses when a computer is moved from one subnet to another.

8.24.2 History of DHCP

Historically, the assignment of Internet addresses to host machines required administrators to manually configure each machine and manually keep track of IP address assignments. While this is sufficient for small networks with a few systems, the overhead of manually managing a site's address name space becomes prohibitively expensive as the number of hosts increases.

DHCP was developed from an earlier protocol called *Bootstrap Protocol* (BOOTP), which was used to pass information during initial booting to client systems. The BOOTP standard was originally released in 1985 based on work by *John Gilmore* of Sun Microsystems and *Bill Croft* of Stanford University. It allowed diskless clients (systems without any disk) to store configuration data in a centralized server.

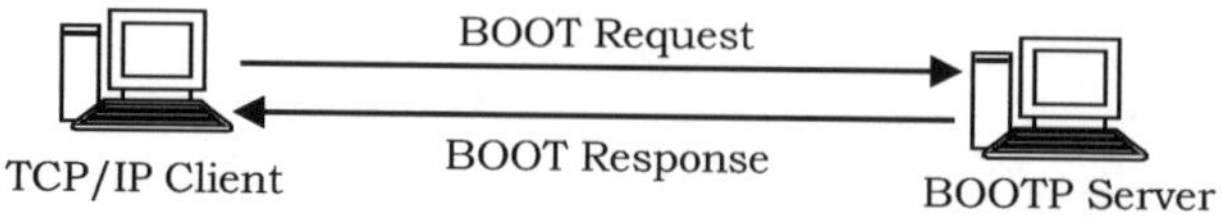

The BOOTP standard was designed to store and update static information for clients, including IP addresses. The BOOTP server always issued the same IP address to the same client. As a result, while BOOTP addressed the need for central management, it did not address the problem of managing IP addresses as a dynamic resource.

To address the need to manage dynamic configuration information in general, and dynamic IP addresses specifically, the IETF standardized a new extension to BOOTP called Dynamic Host Configuration Protocol, or DHCP. DHCP servers utilize BOOTP packets, with DHCP-specific flags and data, to convey information to the DHCP clients.

To standardize the DHCP environment, the IETF issued a series of RFCs focused on DHCP extensions to the BOOTP technology in 1997. DHCP is still an area of active development and it is reasonable to assume that there will be additional RFCs related to the DHCP environment. Sun is working with other vendors to ensure that DHCP continues to be a standard supported by a large number of vendors.

8.24.3 Why DHCP Is Important?

For enterprise clients, the best way to reduce the cost of distributed computing is to move the administration of their client systems to centralized management servers.

DHCP can reduce the cost of ownership for large organizations by shifting the job of managing network configuration information from client systems to remote management by a small pool of system and network managers. It is difficult for organizations to acquire additional Internet addresses.

Corporations must often justify the requirement for these additional addresses through a long and sometimes difficult process of needs definition. DHCP helps reduce the impact of the increasing scarcity of available IP addresses in two ways.

First, DHCP can be used to manage the limited number of standard, routable IP addresses that are available to an organization. It does this by issuing the addresses to clients on an as needed basis and reclaiming them when the addresses are no longer required.

When a client needs an IP address, the DHCP server will issue an available address, along with a lease period during which the client may use the address. When the client is done with the address (or when the lease on the address expires), the address is put back in a pool and is available for the next client seeking an address.

Second, DHCP can be used in conjunction with Network Address Translation (NAT) to issue private network addresses to connect clients (through a NAT system) to the Internet. The DHCP server will issue an address to the client that will not route, such as 192.169.*.* or 10.*.*.*4. The client will use a NAT system as the gateway machine, which packages up the request with the permanent address of the NAT system.

When the response comes back from the Internet, the NAT server will forward the packet back to the client. DHCP enables this to be done without taking up valuable routable addresses and makes certain that all clients use consistent parameters, such as subnet masks, routers, and DNS servers.

8.24.4 Where DHCP Is Useful?

The most common usage of DHCP is to move the management of IP addresses away from the distributed client systems and onto one or more centrally managed servers. These central servers maintain databases of parameter information (addresses, netmasks, etc.), eliminating the need for clients to store static network information on their machines. This specifically obviates the need to configure TCP/IP parameters into client machines.

Since most client systems now ship from the factory with dynamically assigned IP addresses as the default configuration, the user need only boot the machine to be up and running with the TCP/IP protocol. This approach saves time configuring or debugging the network environment, thereby reducing the cost of ownership for client systems.

DHCP is particularly useful in the following environments:

- Sites that have many more TCP/IP clients than network administrators. By using DHCP, managers can more effectively manage a large community of client systems.
- Sites where laptops commonly move among networks within the site. By using DHCP, laptop users can plug into the network at any location and use a local DHCP-assigned IP address to communicate with the local systems.
- Sites that have fewer available TCP/IP addresses than they have clients that need them. Typically, this occurs in dial-up situations, such as an Internet service provider (ISP) environment, where there is a large community of potential users, but only a small percentage of them are online at any given time.

  Here, DHCP is used to issue the IP address to a client machine at the connection time, allowing the DHCP server to reuse the same address once the current client has logged off. Most ISPs have moved to this approach to reduce their need for scarce Internet addresses.
- Sites that frequently need to move the location of services from host to host. Since DHCP delivers the location of services, moving services from one machine to another and changing the appropriate DHCP configuration information means that any DHCP client will automatically pick up the change (without the administrator having to make a trip to the user's machine).
- Sites that support diskless clients. More details on this use of DHCP are provided in the Client Implementation section.
- Any combination of the above.

8.25 How traceroute (or tracert) works?

Tracert (and ping) are both command line utilities that are built into Windows (traceroute and ping for Linux operating systems) computer systems. The basic tracert command syntax is "tracert hostname". For example, "tracert CareerMonk.com" and the output might look like:

```
1 51 ms 59 ms 49 ms 10.176.119.1
2 66 ms 50 ms 38 ms 172.31.242.57
3 54 ms 69 ms 60 ms 172.31.78.130
```

Discover the path: Tracert sends an ICMP echo packet, but it takes advantage of the fact that most Internet routers will send back an ICMP *'TTL expired in transit'* message if the TTL field is ever decremented to zero by a router. Using this knowledge, we can discover the path taken by IP Packets.

How tracert works: Tracert sends out an ICMP echo packet to the named host, but with a TTL of 1; then with a TTL of 2; then with a TTL of 3 and so on. Tracert will then get *'TTL expired in transit'* message back from routers until the destination host computer finally is reached and it responds with the standard ICMP *'echo reply'* packet.

Round Trip Times: Each millisecond (ms) time in the table is the round-trip time that it took (to send the ICMP packet and to get the ICMP reply packet). The faster (smaller) the times the better. *ms* times of 0 mean that the reply was faster than the computers timer of 10 milliseconds, so the time is actually somewhere between 0 and 10 milliseconds.

Packet Loss: Packet loss kills throughput. So, having no packet loss is critical to having a connection to the Internet that responds well. A slower connection with zero packet loss can easily outperform a faster connection with some packet loss. Also, packet loss on the last hop, the destination, is what is most important. Sometimes routers in-between will not send ICMP *'TTL expired in transit'* messages, causing what looks to be high packet loss at a particular hop, but all it means is that the particular router is not responding to ICMP echo.

8.26 How ping works?

The basic ping command syntax is "*ping hostname*". For example, "ping visualroute.com" and the output might look like:

```
Pinging careermonk.com [182.50.143.69] with 32 bytes of data:
Reply from 182.50.143.69: bytes=32 time=130ms TTL=116
Reply from 182.50.143.69: bytes=32 time=130ms TTL=116
Reply from 182.50.143.69: bytes=32 time=137ms TTL=116
```

1. The source host generates an ICMP protocol data unit.
2. The ICMP PDU is encapsulated in an IP datagram, with the source and destination IP addresses in the IP header. At this point the datagram is most properly referred to as an ICMP ECHO datagram, but we will call it an IP datagram from here on since that's what it looks like to the networks it is sent over.
3. The source host notes the local time on its clock as it transmits the IP datagram towards the destination. Each host that receives the IP datagram checks the destination address to see if it matches their own address or is the all hosts address (all 1's in the host field of the IP address).
4. If the destination IP address in the IP datagram does not match the local host's address, the IP datagram is forwarded to the network where the IP address resides.
5. The destination host receives the IP datagram, finds a match between itself and the destination address in the IP datagram.
6. The destination host notes the ICMP ECHO information in the IP datagram performs any necessary work then destroys the original IP/ICMP ECHO datagram.
7. The destination host creates an ICMP ECHO REPLY, encapsulates it in an IP datagram placing its own IP address in the source IP address field, and the original sender's IP address in the destination field of the IP datagram.
8. The new IP datagram is routed back to the originator of the PING. The host receives it, notes the time on the clock and finally prints PING output information, including the elapsed time
9. The process above is repeated until all requested ICMP ECHO packets have been sent and their responses have been received or the default 2-second timeout expired. The default 2-second timeout is local to the host initiating the PING and is NOT the Time-To-Live value in the datagram.

8.27 What is QoS?

QoS (Quality of Service) refers to a broad collection of networking technologies and techniques. The goal of QoS is to provide guarantees on the ability of a network to deliver predictable results. Elements of network performance within the scope of QoS generally includes availability (uptime), bandwidth (throughput), latency (delay), and error rate.

QoS involves prioritization of network traffic. QoS can be targeted at a network interface, toward a given server or router's performance, or in terms of specific applications. A network monitoring system must typically be deployed as part of QoS, to insure that networks are performing at the desired level.

QoS is especially important for the new generation of Internet applications such as VoIP, video-on-demand and other consumer services. Some core networking technologies like Ethernet were not designed to support prioritized traffic or guaranteed performance levels, making it much more difficult to implement QoS solutions across the Internet.

8.28 Wireless Networking

8.28.1 What Is a Wireless Network?

A wireless local-area network (LAN) uses radio waves to connect devices such as laptops to the Internet and to your business network and its applications. When we connect a laptop to a WiFi hotspot at a cafe, hotel, airport lounge, or other public place, we are connecting to that business's wireless network.

8.28.2 Wireless Networks versus Wired Networks

A wired network connects devices to the Internet or other network using cables. The most common wired networks use cables connected to Ethernet ports on the network router on one end and to a computer or other device on the cable's opposite end.

In the past, some believed wired networks were faster and more secure than wireless networks. But continual enhancements to wireless networking standards and technologies have eroded those speed and security differences.

8.28.3 Advantages of Wireless Networks

Wireless LANs offer the following productivity, convenience, and cost advantages over wired networks:

- *Mobility*: Wireless LAN systems can provide LAN users with access to real-time information anywhere in their organization. This mobility supports productivity and service opportunities not possible with wired networks.
  There are now thousands of universities, hotels and public places with public wireless connection. These free you from having to be at home or at work to access the Internet.
- *Installation Speed* and *Simplicity*: Installing a wireless LAN system can be fast and easy and can eliminate the need to pull cable through walls and ceilings.
- *Reduced Cost-of-Ownership*: While the initial investment required for wireless LAN hardware can be higher than the cost of wired LAN hardware, overall installation expenses and life-cycle costs can be significantly lower. Long-term cost benefits are greatest in dynamic environments requiring frequent moves and changes.
- *Scalability*: Wireless LAN systems can be configured in a variety of topologies to meet the needs of specific applications and installations. Configurations are easily changed and range from peer-to-peer networks suitable for a small number of users to full infrastructure networks of thousands of users that enable roaming over a broad area.

8.28.4 Disadvantages of Wireless Networks

Despite these benefits, the wireless network is not without some problems, perhaps the most important:

- *Compatibility issues*: Products made by different companies may not be able to communicate with each other or we may need to extra effort to overcome these problems.
- Traditionally, the wireless networks are often slower than networks.

- Wireless networks the weakest in terms of privacy protection as any person within the scope of coverage of a wireless network can attempt to penetrate this network In order to solve this problem, there are several programs provide protection for wireless networks such as Equivalent Privacy wired networks Wired Equivalent Private (WAP), which did not provide adequate protection for wireless networks and the Wi-Fi Protected Access (WPA), which showed greater success in preventing breaches of its predecessor.

Problems and Questions with Answers

Question 1: Which one of the following is not a client-server application?
A) Internet chat B) Web browsing C) E-mail D) Ping

Answer: D. Internet- Chat is maintained by chat servers, web browsing is sustained by web servers, E-mails are stored at mail servers, but ping is an utility which is used to identify connection between any two computer. One can be client, other can be client or server anything but aim is to identify whether connection exists or not between the two.

Question 2: What is the port number used by Ping command?

Answer: The answer is none. No ports required for Ping as it uses ICMP packets. The ICMP packet does not have source and destination port numbers because it was designed to communicate network-layer information between hosts and routers, not between application layer processes. Each ICMP packet has a "Type" and a "Code". The Type/Code combination identifies the specific message being received. Since the network software itself interprets all ICMP messages, no port numbers are needed to direct the ICMP message to an application layer process.

Database Management Systems

CHAPTER 9

9.1 What is a Database?

A database is a collection of data *organized* in a particular way. In other words, it is a collection of information that is organized so that it can easily be accessed, managed, and updated. Databases can *store* information about people, products, orders, or *anything else*.

Many databases start as a list in a word-processing program or spreadsheet. As the list grows bigger, redundancies and inconsistencies begin to appear in the data. The data becomes hard to understand in list form, and there are limited ways of searching or pulling subsets of data out for review.

A *database* is a structure that can store information about multiple types of things (or entities), the characteristics (or attributes) of those entities, and the relationships among the entities. It also contains data types for attributes and indexes.

Databases can be of many types such as Flat File Databases, Relational Databases, Distributed Databases etc. A relational database uses the concept of linked two-dimensional tables which comprise of rows and columns. A user can draw relationships between multiple tables and present the output as a table again. A user of a relational database need not understand the representation of data in order to retrieve it.

9.2 Database Management System [DBMS]

DBMS is a collection of programs that enables us to store, modify, and extract information from a database efficiently. There are many different types of DBMSs, ranging from small systems that run on personal computers to huge systems that run on mainframes. The DBMS manages incoming data, organizes it, and provides ways for the data to be modified or extracted by users or other programs.

Some DBMS examples include MySQL, PostgreSQL, Microsoft Access, SQL Server, FileMaker, Oracle, RDBMS, dBASE, Clipper, and FoxPro. These software packages are used to manipulate a database. All DBMSs use their own implementation of SQL. Since there are so many database management systems available, it is important for there to be a way for them to communicate with each other.

For this reason, most database software comes with an Open Database Connectivity (ODBC) driver that allows the database to integrate with other databases. For example, common SQL statements such as SELECT and INSERT are translated from a program's proprietary syntax into a syntax other databases can understand.

9.3 Procedural and Non-Procedural

Programming languages are procedural if they use programming elements such as conditional statements (if-then-else, do-while etc.). SQL (Structured Query Language) has none of these types of statements and is an example for non-procedural.

9.4 What is SQL?

SQL (Structured Query Language) is the language used to query all databases. It's simple to learn and appears to do very little but is the heart of a successful database application. Understanding SQL and using it efficiently is highly imperative in designing an efficient database application. The better our understanding of SQL the more versatile we'll be in getting information out of databases.

9.5 Data Definition and Manipulation

DBMS makes use of a Data Definition Language (DDL) and a Data Manipulation Language (DML). The DML enables the specification of data types, structures and constraints that should be part of the database. All specifications defined by the DDL are stored in the database. The DML enables those with access to the database to insert, update, delete and retrieve data from it. Structured Query Language (SQL) is the standard DML used today. SQL is a non-procedural language.

9.6 What is RDBMS?

RDBMS stands for Relational Database Management System. RDBMS is the basis for SQL, and for all modern database systems like MS SQL Server, IBM DB2, Oracle, MySQL, and Microsoft Access. A Relational database management system (RDBMS) is a database management system (DBMS) that is based on the relational model as introduced by E. F. Codd.

Formal Name	Common Name	Also called as
Relation	Table	Entity
Tuple	Row	Record
Attribute	Column	Field

9.7 What is Table?

The data in RDBMS is stored in database objects called *tables*. The table is a collection of related data entries and it consists of columns and rows.

Remember, a table is the most common and simplest form of data storage in a relational database. Following is the example of a CUSTOMERS table:

ID	NAME	AGE	ADDRESS	SALARY
1	Aryan	32	London	2000.00
2	Mary	25	Texas	1500.00
3	Ahmed	23	Abu	2000.00
4	Chaitanya	25	Mumbai	6500.00
5	Rama	27	Hyderabad	8500.00
6	Kishore	22	Chennai	4500.00
7	Richard	24	Delhi	10000.00

9.8 What is Field?

Every table is broken up into smaller entities called *fields*. The fields in the CUSTOMERS table consist of ID, NAME, AGE, ADDRESS and SALARY. A field is a column in a table that is designed to maintain specific information about every record in the table.

9.9 What is Record or Row?

A record, also called a row of data, is each individual entry that exists in a table. For example there are 7 records in the above CUSTOMERS table. Following is a sing le row of data or record in the CUSTOMERS table:

1	Ramesh	32	Ahmedabad	2000.00

A record is a horizontal entity in a table.

9.10 What is Column?

A column is a vertical entity in a table that contains all information associated with a specific field in a table. For example, a column in the CUSTOMERS table is ADDRESS, which represents location description and would consist of the following:

ADDRESS
London
Texas
Abu
Mumbai
Hyderabad
Chennai
Delhi

9.11 What is NULL value?

A NULL value in a table is a value in a field that appears to be blank, which means a field with a NULL value is a field with no value. It is very important to understand that a NULL value is different than a zero value or a field that contains spaces. A field with a NULL value is one that has been left blank during record creation.

9.12 SQL Constraints

Constraints are the rules enforced on data columns on table. These are used to limit the type of data that can go into a table. This ensures the accuracy and reliability of the data in the database. Constraints could be column level or table level. Column level constraints are applied only to one column whereas table level constraints are applied to the whole table. Following are commonly used constraints available in SQL:

- NOT NULL Constraint: Ensures that a column cannot have NULL value.
- DEFAULT Constraint: Provides a default value for a column when none is specified.
- UNIQUE Constraint: Ensures that all values in a column are different.
- PRIMARY Key: Uniquely identified each rows/records in a database table.
- FOREIGN Key: Uniquely identified a rows/records in any another database table.
- CHECK Constraint: The CHECK constraint ensures that all values in a column satisfy certain conditions.
- INDEX: Use to create and retrieve data from the database very quickly.

9.13 Data Integrity

The following categories of the data integrity exist with each RDBMS:

- Entity Integrity: There are no duplicate rows in a table.
- Domain Integrity: Enforces valid entries for a given column by restricting the type, the format, or the range of values.
- Referential integrity: Rows cannot be deleted, which are used by other records.
- User-Defined Integrity: Enforces some specific business rules that do not fall into entity, domain or referential integrity.

9.14 Database Keys

Each database table is consists of rows and columns. Some columns are special columns because they identify a particular record in a table. The special columns are called keys. The 2 most common keys are *primary* keys and *foreign* keys.

In a database table, the column that uniquely identifies each record in the table is called a *primary* key. It is almost always good design to define a primary key for all tables. In some cases, it is not possible to identify a column to be used as the primary key. In such cases, most designers create a dummy column which simply contains a running number to make each and every record in the table unique - for example, the AutoNumber data type in a Microsoft Access database.

Primary keys are also sometimes created from a combination of 2 or more columns. Such primary keys are called *composite* keys. Each column may not be unique by itself within the database table but when combined with the other column(s) in the composite key, the combination is unique.

When a database table is normalized to create an efficient and compact design, multiple tables are created that are linked together using *foreign* keys. Foreign keys are not necessarily unique in the table that stores them but they point to unique values in the referenced table. To understand the concepts of the primary key and the foreign key, consider the sample table design below:

Product table

Column	
product_id	primary key
description	
category_id	foreign key

Category table

Column	
category_id	primary key
description	

Let's assume that the above tables contain the following data:

product_id	description	category_id
0001	table	0001
0002	chair	0001
0003	fan	0002

category_id	description
0001	furniture
0002	electrical

Notice that in both the product table and the category table, the values in the product_id column and the category_id are never repeated. Both the product_id and the category_id columns are primary keys within their respective tables.

Also, notice that although the category_id column in the product table contains duplicate values, they point to records in the category table defined by unique category_id columns. The *category_id* column is a primary key in the category table but is a foreign key in the product table.

9.15 Normalization

Depending on the design of a database, the database may contain redundant data. Such a database becomes:

- Inefficient - the database engine will need to process more data for each query or update
- Bloated - storage requirements increase due to the redundant data
- Error-prone - someone needs to input the redundant data into the database. The more times the same data is input into the database, the more chances there are for errors to occur.

In order to remove redundancy in database, normalization is applied. Normalization is the process of eliminating redundant data from database tables. In other words, database normalization is the process of efficiently organizing data in a database.

A database is designed in a way that removes redundancies, and increases the clarity in organizing data in a database. It means taking similar stuff out of a collection of data and placing them into tables. Keep doing this for each new table recursively and we will have a *normalized* database. There are two reasons of the normalization process:

- Eliminating redundant data, for example, storing the same data in more than one table.
- Ensuring data dependencies make sense.

The important thing here is to know when to normalize and when to be practical. That will come with experience. Normalization of a database helps in modifying the design at later times and helps in being prepared if a change is required in the database design. Normalization raises the efficiency of the database in terms of management, data storage and scalability.

Now normalization of a Database is achieved by following a set of rules called *normal forms* (NFs) in creating the database. These rules are 5 in number (with one extra one stuck in-between 3 & 4) and they are:

First Normal Form or 1NF	Each Column Type is Unique (atomic)
Second Normal Form or 2NF	The entity under consideration should already be in the 1NF and all attributes within the entity should depend solely on the entity's unique identifier.
Third Normal Form or 3NF	The entity should already be in the 2NF and no column entry should be dependent on any other entry (value) other than the key for the table. If such an entity exists, move it outside into a new table. Now if these 3NF are achieved, the database is considered normalized.
BC (Boyce & Codd) Normal Form	The database should be in 3NF and all tables can have only one primary key.
4NF	Tables cannot have multi-valued dependencies on a Primary Key.
5NF	There should be no cyclic dependencies in a composite key.

Well this is a highly simplified explanation for database normalization. After working with databases for some time we'll automatically create normalized databases. For now, don't worry too much about above definitions. Much of database design depends on how we want to keep the data. In real life situations often you may find it more convenient to store data in tables designed in a way that does fall a bit short of keeping all the NFs happy. But that's what databases are all about.

Traditional normalization methods define several different "normal" forms of data. If you consider all possible all relations, only a subset of those are said to be in first normal form , only a subset of those is in second normal form, only a subset of those are in 3NF, and so on. Pictorially, this can be represented as follows.

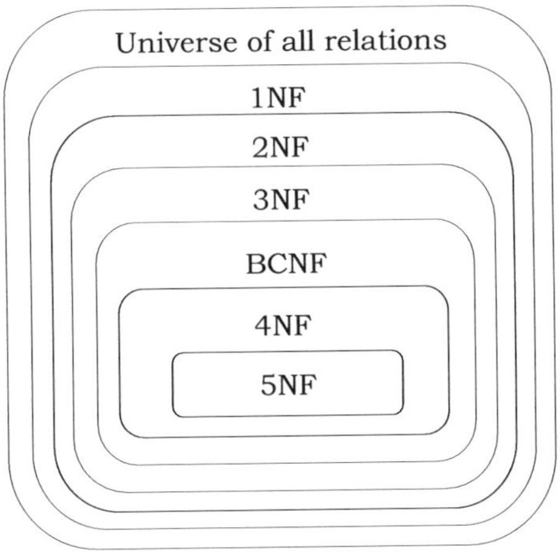

9.15.1 Pros and Cons of a Normalized Database Design

Normalized databases fair very well under conditions where the applications are write-intensive and the write-load is more than the read-load. This is because of the following reasons:

- Normalized tables are generally smaller in size and have a smaller foot-print as the data is divided vertically among many tables. This allows them to perform better as they are small enough to get fit into the buffer.
- The updates are very fast as the data to be updated is located at a single place and there are no duplicates.
- Similarly the inserts are very fast as the data has to be inserted at a single place and does not have to be duplicated.
- The selects are fast in cases where data has to be fetched from a single table, because normally normalized tables are small enough to get fit into the buffer.
- Because the data is not duplicated so there is less need for heavy duty group by or distinct queries.

Although there seems to be much in favor of normalized tables, with all the pros outlined above, but the main cause of concern with fully normalized tables is that normalized data means *joins* between tables. And this joining means that read operations have to suffer because indexing strategies do not go well with table joins.

9.15.2 Pros and Cons of a Denormalized Database Design

Denormalized databases fair well under heavy read-load and when the application is read intensive. This is because of the following reasons:

- The data is present in the same table so there is *no* need for any joins; hence the selects are very fast.
- A single table with all the required data allows much more efficient index usage. If the columns are indexed properly, then results can be filtered and sorted by utilizing the same index. While in the case of a normalized table, since the data would be spread out in different tables, this would not be possible.

Although for reasons mentioned above selects can be very fast on denormalized tables, but because the data is duplicated, the updates and inserts become complex and costly.

Having said that neither one of the approach can be entirely neglected, because a real world application is going to have both read-loads and write-loads. Hence the correct way would be to utilize both the normalized and denormalized approaches depending on situations.

9.16 Functional Dependencies

Functional Dependency (FD) is the starting point for the process of normalization. Functional dependency exists when a relationship between two attributes (columns) allows us to uniquely determine the corresponding attribute's value. If 'X' is known, and as a result you are able to uniquely identify 'Y', there is functional dependency. Combined with keys, normal forms are defined for relations. Consider the relation below:

STUDENTS = {Student_ID, First_Name, Last_Name}

We can state that the set of attributes/columns {First_Name, Last_Name} is functionally dependent on the attribute set {Student_ID}. This means that, given a value for Student_ID, we can always uniquely determine the value of First_Name and the value of Last_Name. Note that, for this relation, the opposite would not be true. For example, if here are three students with the same first and last name we will get a list of three student IDs. That is we cannot uniquely determine a value for Student_ID given values of the attributes {First_Name, Last_Name}.

Student_ID determines {First_Name, Last_Name} but {First_Name, Last_Name} does not determine Student_ID.

We define functional dependency more *formally*:

A set of attributes Y is functionally dependent on a set of attributes X if a given set of values for each attribute in X determines unique values for the set of attributes in Y.

We use the notation:

$$X \rightarrow Y$$

to denote that Y is functionally dependent on X. The set of attributes X is known as the determinant of the FD $X \rightarrow Y$.

.1 Armstrong's Axioms

William W. Armstrong established a set of rules which can be sued to infer the functional dependencies in a relational database.

- Reflexivity rule: If A is a set of attributes, and B is a set of attributes that are completely contained in A, the A implies B.
- Augmentation rule: If A implies B, and C is a set of attributes, then if A implies B, then AC implies BC.
- Transitivity rule: If A implies B and B implies C, then A implies C.

These can be simplified if we also use:

- Union rule: If A implies B and A implies C, the A implies BC.
- Decomposition rule: If A implies BC then A implies B and A implies C.
- Pseudo transitivity rule: If A implies B and CB implies D, then AC implies D.

9.17 First Normal Form or 1NF

First normal form (1NF) sets the very basic rules for an organized database:

1. Define the data items required, because they become the columns in a table. Place related data items in a table.
2. Ensure that there are no repeating groups of data. That means, the table cells must be of single value.
3. Ensure that there is a primary key.

A relation is in first normal form if every attribute in every row can contain only one single (*atomic*) value. A row of data cannot contain repeating group of data i.e each column must have a unique value. Each row of data must have a unique identifier i.e Primary key. For example consider a table which is not in First normal form.

Student Table:

S_ID	S_Name	Subject
401	Ram	Biology, Physics
402	Mary	Maths, Chemistry
403	Raheem	Maths, English, Chemistry

You can clearly see here that student name *Ram* has two subjects Biology and Physics. Similarly, *Mary* has two subjects and *Raheem* has three subjects. This violates the First Normal form. To fix the issue, let us repeat the rows for each of the subject as shown below.

Student Table:

S_ID	S_Name	Subject
401	Ram	Biology
401	Ram	Physics
402	Mary	Maths
402	Mary	Chemistry
403	Raheem	Maths
403	Raheem	English
403	Raheem	Chemistry

In Student table concatenation of *S_ID, S_Name*, and *Subject* is the *primary* key.

9.18 Second Normal Form or 2NF

A relation is in second normal form if it satisfies the following conditions:

- It is in first normal form
- All non-key attributes are fully functional dependent on the primary key

In a table, if attribute B is functionally dependent on A, but is not functionally dependent on a proper subset of A, then B is considered fully functional dependent on A. Hence, in a 2NF table, all non-key attributes cannot be dependent on a subset of the primary key. Note that if the primary key is not a composite key, all non-key attributes are always fully functional dependent on the primary key. A table that is in 1st normal form and contains only a single key as the primary key is automatically in 2nd normal form. Consider the following example, Purchase Table:

Customer_ID	Store_ID	Purchase Location
1	1	Hyderabad
1	3	New York
2	1	New York
3	2	Delhi
4	4	Chennai

This table has a composite primary key [Customer ID, Store ID]. The non-key attribute is [Purchase Location]. In this case, [Purchase Location] only depends on [Store ID], which is only part of the primary key. Therefore, this table does not satisfy second normal form. To bring this table to second normal form, we break the table into two tables, and now we have the following:

Purchase Table

Customer_ID	Store_ID
1	1
1	3
2	1
3	2
4	3

Store Table

Store_ID	Purchase Location
1	Hyderabad
2	Delhi
3	New York
4	Chennai

What we have done is to remove the partial functional dependency that we initially had. Now, in the table *Store*, the column [Purchase Location] is fully dependent on the primary key of that table, which is [Store_ID].

As another example, when we look closely at the ShipmentEquipment table we can see that SizeTypeCode does not depend entirely on ContractID and EquipmentID (our two keys). We can say that the size and type of a container depends on the EquipmentID. Every container has one EquipmentID and one size and type. "PONL34567" is a 40 foot container of standard features. If the EquipmentID value changed (ie a different container was used), then we could not be sure the SizeTypeCode would remain the same. SizeTypeCode is dependent on the EquipmentID.

The same cannot be said for ContractID. The value of ContractID can change without affecting the SizeTypeCode. For example, when the container is transferred to the truck for road haulage – its size and type do not change. Second Normal Form tells us to separate these attributes that don't depend on the entire key. In this case it is the SizeTypeCode and its dependent foreign key, EquipmentID that form a new Equipment table.

ContractID	EquipmentID
PONL40078678	PONL12345
PONL40078678	PONL34567
TNT9439287-5	PONL34567
180-1234567	KAL12345

EquipmentID	SizeTypeCode
PONL12345	4040
PONL34567	4020
KAL12345	747-K10

9.19 Third Normal Form or 3NF

A database is in third normal form if it satisfies the following conditions:

- It is in second normal form
- There is no transitive functional dependency

By transitive functional dependency, we mean we have the following relationships in the table: A is functionally dependent on B, and B is functionally dependent on C. In this case, C is transitively dependent on A via B.

This is similar to Second Normal Form, but now we focus on the non-key dependencies. Consider the following example: Book Detail Table

Book_ID	Genre_ID	Genre_Type	Price
1	1	Gardening	100
2	2	Sports	400
3	1	Gardening	450
4	3	Technical	510
5	2	Sports	600

In the table able, [Book_ID] determines [Genre_ID], and [Genre_ID] determines [Genre Type]. Therefore, [Book_ID] determines [Genre_Type] via [Genre_ID] and we have transitive functional dependency, and this structure does not satisfy third normal form. To bring this table to third normal form, we split the table into two as follows:

Book Table

Book_ID	Genre_ID	Price
1	1	100
2	2	400
3	1	450
4	3	510
5	2	600

Genre Table

Genre_ID	Purchase Location
1	Gardening
2	Sports
3	Technical

Now all non-key attributes are fully functional dependent only on the primary key. In [Book Table], both [Genre_ID] and [Price] are only dependent on [Book_ID]. In [Gen], [Genre Table] is only dependent on [Genre ID].

Let us consider another example. If we look at the ShipmentSeal table, we see that SealNumber and SealIssuer are not independent of each other. Neither are keys values, but there is a dependent relationship between them, for example if the SealIssuer where to change then the SealNumber would presumably change as well. So we must move SealIssuer and its dependant foreign key, SealNumber into a new table. In this case we shall call it the Seal table.

ContractID	EquipmentID	SealNumber
PONL40078678	PONL12345	*ABX123456*
PONL40078678	PONL34567	*ABX123457*
TNT9439287-5	PONL34567	*ABX123457*
TNT9439287-5	PONL34567	*GGDFG99*
180-1234567	KAL12345	*XXX664*

SealNumber	SealIssuer
ABX123456	ABC
ABX123457	ABC
GGDFG99	Customs
XXX664	

9.20 Other Normal Forms

There are many other normal forms, most of which are variations of 3NF, such as 4NF, 5NF, and Boyce Codd Normal Form (BCNF). A few years ago mathematicians showed that the highest form of a set of relations is Domain Key Normal Form (DKNF). In simple terms, a table is in DKNF if the data in each row of each table depends on the primary key, the whole primary key, and nothing but the primary key.

Many databases are not in DKNF, but they still work. Theoretically, they would be more efficient for all operations, including updating data, if they were in DKNF. Practically, in many databases the number of queries that simply retrieve data is often far more than the number of queries that update data, so 3NF is often good enough for most databases. It isn't a theoretically perfect design, but it works and is reasonably efficient. A relation is in BCNF if "every determinant is a candidate key." For example, consider the following relation:

Table(A, B, C, D) where the only FD is B → C .

If B is a candidate key, the table is in BCNF, and hence also in 1, 2 and 3NF. If B is not a candidate key, the table is not in BCNF and must be fixed.

9.21 Transaction Management

A *transaction* is a logical unit of work that contains one or more SQL statements. A transaction is an atomic unit. The effects of all the SQL statements in a transaction can be either all committed (applied to the database) or all rolled back (undone from the database). To describe the concept of a transaction, consider a banking database. When a bank customer transfers money from a savings account to a checking account, the transaction can consist of three separate operations:

- Decrement the savings account
- Increment the checking account
- Record the transaction in the transaction journal

Any Database must allow for two situations. If all three SQL statements can be performed to maintain the accounts in proper balance, the effects of the transaction can be applied to the database. However, if a problem such as insufficient funds, invalid account number, or a hardware failure prevents one or two of the statements in the transaction from completing, the entire transaction must be rolled back so that the balance of all accounts is correct.

Transaction management ensures that the database remains in a consistent (correct) state despite system failures (e.g., power failures and operating system crashes) and transaction failures.

9.21.1 ACID Properties of Transactions

ACID is a set of properties that you would like to apply when modifying a database.

Atomicity: All changes to data are performed as if they are a single operation. That is, all the changes are performed, or none of them are. For example, in an application that transfers funds from one account to another, the atomicity property ensures that, if a debit is made successfully from one account, the corresponding credit is made to the other account.

Consistency: Data is in a consistent state when a transaction starts and when it ends. For example, in an application that transfers funds from one account to another, the consistency property ensures that the total value of funds in both the accounts is the same at the start and end of each transaction.

Isolation: The intermediate state of a transaction is invisible to other transactions. As a result, transactions that run concurrently appear to be serialized. For example, in an application that transfers funds from one account to another, the isolation property ensures that another transaction sees the transferred funds in one account or the other, but not in both, nor in neither.

Durability: After a transaction successfully completes, changes to data persist and are not undone, even in the event of a system failure.

For example, in an application that transfers funds from one account to another, the durability property ensures that the changes made to each account will not be reversed.

Problems and Questions with Answers

Question 1: What is SELECT statement?

Answer: The SELECT statement lets users to select a set of values from a table in a database. The values selected from the database table would depend on the various conditions that are specified in the SQL query.

Question 2: How can we compare a part of the name rather than the entire name?

Answer: SELECT * FROM people WHERE empname LIKE '%na%'; This would return a recordset with records consisting empname the sequence *'na'* in empname.

Question 3: What is the INSERT statement?

Answer: The INSERT statement lets users to insert information into a database.

Question 4: How do you delete a record from a database?

Answer: Use the DELETE statement to remove records or any particular column values from a database.

Question 5: How could we get distinct entries from a table?

Answer: The SELECT statement in conjunction with DISTINCT lets users to select a set of distinct values from a table in a database. The values selected from the database table would of course depend on the various conditions that are specified in the SQL query. Example: SELECT DISTINCT empname FROM emptable

Question 6: How to get the results of a Query sorted in any order?

Answer: We can sort the results and return the sorted results to our program by using ORDER BY keyword thus saving us the pain of carrying out the sorting. The ORDER BY keyword is used for sorting.

```
SELECT empname, age, city FROM emptable ORDER BY empname
```

Question 7: How can we find the total number of records in a table?

Answer: We could use the COUNT keyword , example: SELECT COUNT(*) FROM emp WHERE age > 40

Question 8: What is GROUP BY?

Answer: The GROUP BY keywords has been added to SQL because aggregate functions (like SUM) return the aggregate of all column values every time they are called. Without the GROUP BY functionality, finding the sum for each individual group of column values was not possible.

Question 9: What is the difference "dropping a table", "truncating a table" and "deleting all records" from a table.

Answer: DELETE TABLE is a logged operation, so the deletion of each row gets logged in the transaction log, which makes it slow. TRUNCATE TABLE also deletes all the rows in a table, but it will not log the deletion of each row, instead it logs the de-allocation of the data pages of the table, which makes it faster. Of course, TRUNCATE TABLE can be rolled back.

Question 10: Difference between a *where* clause and a *having* clause.

Answer: *Having* clause is used only with group functions whereas *Where* is not used with.

Question 11: What's the difference between a primary key and a unique key?

Answer: Both *primary key* and *unique* enforce uniqueness of the column on which they are defined. But by default primary key creates a clustered index on the column, whereas unique creates a nonclustered index by default. Another major difference is that, primary key doesn't allow NULLs, but unique key allows one NULL only.

Question 12: What are cursors? Explain different types of cursors. What are the disadvantages of cursors? How can you avoid cursors?

Answer: Cursors allow row-by-row processing of the result sets. Types of cursors: Static, Dynamic, Forward-only, Keyset-driven. *Disadvantages* of cursors: Each time you fetch a row from the cursor, it results in a network roundtrip, where as a normal SELECT query makes only one round trip, however large the result set is. Cursors are also costly because they require more resources and temporary storage (results in more IO operations).

Further, there are restrictions on the SELECT statements that can be used with some types of cursors. Most of the times, set based operations can be used instead of cursors. Here is an example: If you have to give a flat hike to your employees using the following criteria:

```
Salary between 30000 and 40000 -- 5000 hike
Salary between 40000 and 55000 -- 7000 hike
Salary between 55000 and 65000 -- 9000 hike
```

In this situation many developers tend to use a cursor, determine each employee's salary and update his salary according to the above formula. But the same can be achieved by multiple update statements or can be combined in a single UPDATE statement as shown below:

```
UPDATE tbl_emp SET salary =
CASE WHEN salary BETWEEN 30000 AND 40000 THEN salary + 5000
WHEN salary BETWEEN 40000 AND 55000 THEN salary + 7000
WHEN salary BETWEEN 55000 AND 65000 THEN salary + 10000
END
```

Another situation in which developers tend to use cursors: We need to call a stored procedure when a column in a particular row meets certain condition. We don't have to use cursors for this. This can be achieved using WHILE loop, as long as there is a unique key to identify each row.

Question 13: What are triggers? How to invoke a trigger on demand?

Answer: Triggers are special kind of stored procedures that get executed automatically when an INSERT, UPDATE or DELETE operation takes place on a table. Triggers can't be invoked on demand. They get triggered only when an associated action (INSERT, UPDATE, DELETE) happens on the table on which they are defined.

Triggers are generally used to implement business rules, auditing. Triggers can also be used to extend the referential integrity checks, but wherever possible, use constraints for this purpose, instead of triggers, as constraints are much faster.

Question 14: What is a join and explain different types of joins.

Answer: Joins are used in queries to explain how different tables are related. Joins also let you select data from a table depending upon data from another table. *Types* of joins: INNER JOINs, OUTER JOINs, CROSS JOINs. OUTER JOINs are further classified as LEFT OUTER JOINS, RIGHT OUTER JOINS and FULL OUTER JOINS.

Question 15: What is a self-join?

Answer: Self join is just like any other join, except that two instances of the same table will be joined in the query.

Question 16: What is de-normalization and when would you go for it?

Answer: As the name indicates, de-normalization is the reverse process of normalization. It is the controlled introduction of redundancy in to the database design. It helps improve the query performance as the number of joins could be reduced.

Question 17: How to implement one-to-one, one-to-many & many-to-many relationships while designing tables?

Answer: One-to-One relationship can be implemented as a single table and rarely as two tables with primary and foreign key relationships. One-to-Many relationships are implemented by splitting the data into two tables with primary key and foreign key relationships. Many-to-Many relationships are implemented using a junction table with the keys from both the tables forming the composite primary key of the junction table.

Question 18: What's the difference between a primary key and a unique key?

Answer: Both primary key and unique enforce uniqueness of the column on which they are defined. But by default primary key creates a clustered index on the column, where are unique creates a non-clustered index by default. Another major difference is that, primary key does not allow NULLs, but unique key allows one NULL only.

Question 19: What are user defined data types and when you should go for them?

Answer: User defined data types let you extend the base SQL Server data types by providing a descriptive name, and format to the database.

Question 20: Define candidate key, alternate key, and composite key.

Answer: A candidate key is one that can identify each row of a table uniquely. Generally a candidate key becomes the primary key of the table. If the table has more than one candidate key, one of them will become the primary key, and the rest are called alternate keys. A key formed by combining at least two or more columns is called composite key.

Question 21: What are defaults? Is there a column to which a default cannot be bound?

Answer: A default is a value that will be used by a column, if no value is supplied to that column while inserting data. IDENTITY columns and timestamp columns can't have defaults bound to them.

Question 22: What is a transaction and what are ACID properties?

Answer: A transaction is a logical unit of work in which, all the steps must be performed or none. ACID stands for Atomicity, Consistency, Isolation, and Durability. These are the properties of a transaction.

Question 23: What is Lock Escalation?

Answer: Lock escalation is the process of converting a lot of low level locks (like row locks, page locks) into higher level locks (like table locks). Every lock is a memory structure too many locks would mean, more memory being occupied by locks. To prevent this from happening, SQL Server escalates the many fine-grain locks to fewer coarse-grain locks.

Question 24: What are constraints? Explain different types of constraints.

Answer: Constraints enable the RDBMS enforce the integrity of the database automatically, without needing us to create triggers, rule or defaults. *Types* of constraints: NOT NULL, CHECK, UNIQUE, PRIMARY KEY, FOREIGN KEY

Question 25: What is an index? What are the types of indexes? How many clustered indexes can be created on a table? If we create a separate index on each column of a table, what are the advantages and disadvantages?

Answer: Indexes in SQL Server are similar to the indexes in books. They help SQL Server retrieve the data quicker. Indexes are of two types: Clustered indexes and non-clustered indexes. When you create a clustered index on a table, all the rows in the table are stored in the order of the clustered index key. So, there can be only one clustered index per table.

Non-clustered indexes have their own storage separate from the table data storage. Non-clustered indexes are stored as B-tree structures (so do clustered indexes), with the leaf level nodes having the index key and it's row locater. The row located could be the RID or the Clustered index key, depending up on the absence or presence of clustered index on the table.

If you create an index on each column of a table, it improves the query performance, as the query optimizer can choose from all the existing indexes to come up with an efficient execution plan. At the same time, data modification operations (such as INSERT, UPDATE, DELETE) will become slow, as every time data changes in the table, all the indexes need to be updated. Another disadvantage is that, indexes need disk space, the more indexes you have, more disk space is used.

Question 26: What is a join and explain different types of joins?

Answer:

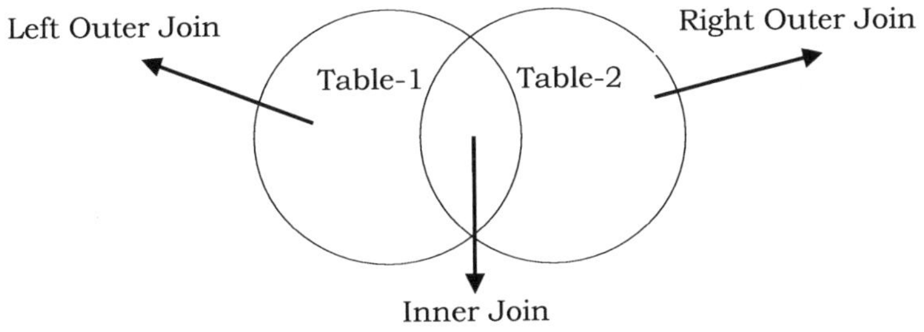

Let us assume that we are joining on columns with no duplicates:

- An inner join of Table-1 and Table-2 gives the result of Table-1 intersect Table-2, i.e. the inner part of a Venn diagram intersection.
- An outer join of Table-1 and Table-2 gives the results of Table-1 union Table-2, i.e. the outer parts of a Venn diagram union.

Suppose we have two tables, with a single column each, and data as follows: note that (1,2) are unique to Table-1, (3,4) are common, and (5,6) are unique to Table-2.

Table-1, Column:A
1
2
3
4

Table-2, Column: B
3
4
5
6

Inner join: An inner join using either of the equivalent queries gives the intersection of the two tables, i.e. the two rows they have in common.

```
select * from Table-1 INNER JOIN Table-2 on Table-1.A = Table-1.B;
```

A	B
3	3
4	4

Left outer join: A left outer join will give all rows in Table-1, plus any common rows in Table-2.

```
select * from Table-1 LEFT OUTER JOIN Table-2 on Table-1.A = Table-1.B;
```

A	B
1	null
2	null
3	3
4	4

Right outer join: A right outer join will give all rows in Table-2, plus any common rows in Table-1.

```
select * from Table-1 RIGHT OUTER JOIN Table-2 on Table-1.A = Table-1.B;
```

A	B
3	3
4	4
null	5
null	6

Full outer join: A full outer join will give you the union of Table-1 and Table-2, i.e. All the rows in Table-1 and all the rows in Table-2. If something in Table-1 doesn't have a corresponding datum in Table-2, then the Table-2 portion is null, and vice versa.

```
select * from Table-1 FULL OUTER JOIN Table-2 on Table-1.A = Table-2.B;
```

A	B
1	null
2	null
3	3
4	4
null	5
null	6

Question 27: What is RAID and what are different types of RAID configurations?

Answer: RAID stands for Redundant Array of Inexpensive Disks, used to provide fault tolerance to database servers. There are six RAID levels 0 through 5 offering different levels of performance, fault tolerance.

Question 28: What is a deadlock and what is a live lock? How will you go about resolving deadlocks?

Answer: Deadlock is a situation when two processes, each having a lock on one piece of data, attempt to acquire a lock on the other's piece. Each process would wait indefinitely for the other to release the lock, unless one of the user processes is terminated. SQL Server detects deadlocks and terminates one user's process. A livelock is one, where a request for an exclusive lock is repeatedly denied because a series of overlapping shared locks keeps interfering. SQL Server detects the situation after four denials and refuses further shared locks. A livelock also occurs when read transactions monopolize a table or page, forcing a write transaction to wait indefinitely.

Question 29: What is blocking?

Answer: Blocking happens when one connection from an application holds a lock and a second connection requires a conflicting lock type. This forces the second connection to wait, blocked on the first.

CHAPTER

Brain Teasers 10

Problems and Questions with Answers

Question 1: **Hats Problem:** Three wise men are told to stand in a straight line, one in front of the other. A hat is put on each of their heads. They are told that each of these hats was selected from a group of five hats: two black hats and three white hats. The first man, standing at the front of the line, can't see either of the men behind him or their hats. The second man, in the middle, can see only the first man and his hat. The last man, at the rear, can see both other men and their hats.

None of the men can see the hat on their own head. They are asked to deduce its color. Some time goes by as the wise men ponder the puzzle in silence. Finally the first one, at the front of the line, makes an announcement: "My hat is white." He is correct. How did he come to this conclusion?

Answer: If the two front hats were black, the third wise man would have called out the color of his hat as white immediately. If the first hat was black, and the third man did not call out any color, the second wise man could deduce that his hat was white. Since neither man called out a color, the first wise man would know that his hat is white, which is the only color that does not allow either the second or third man to guess the color of their own hat.

Question 2: **Weighing:** You have got a 4 liter jug and a 9 liter jug and got a pool of water. What is the fewest number of steps it takes to come up with exactly 6 liters of water? You cannot pour some water into the 9 liter jug and then guess. Nor can you fill each jug up half way or something. You have to be exact. A step is defined as pouring water into or out of a jug. For instance, filling the 4 liter jug and then pouring it into the 9 liter jug, and emptying the 9 liter into the pool is 3 steps.

*Answer***:** One possible full answer is as follows:

1. Fill up the 9 liter jug from the pool.
2. Fill up the 4 liter jug from the 9 liter jug (leaving 5 liters in the 9 liter jug).
3. Empty the 4 liter jug into the pool.
4. Fill the 4 liter jug again from the 9 liter jug (leaving 1 liter in the 9 liter jug).
5. Empty the 4 liter jug into the pool.
6. Put the 1 liter from the 9 liter jug into the 4 liter.
7. Fill the 9 liter jug from the pool.
8. Fill up the 4 liter jug from the 9 liter jug. There was 1 liter in the 4 liter jug, so 3 liters will fill it. This leaves, in the 9 liter jug, exactly 6 *liters*.

Question 3: **Careful Farmer:** A farmer returns from the market, where he bought a goat, a cabbage and a wolf. On the way home he must cross a river. His boat is small and won't fit more than one of his purchases. He cannot leave the goat alone with the cabbage (because the goat would eat it), nor he can leave the goat alone with the wolf (because the goat would be eaten). How can the farmer get everything on the other side in this river crossing puzzle?

Answer: Take the goat to the other side. Go back, take cabbage, and unload it on the other side where you load the goat, go back and unload it. Take the wolf to the other side where you unload it. Go back for the goat.

Question 4: **Algorithmic Weighing:** Weighing in a Harder Way: You've got 27 coin, each of them is 10 g, except for 1. The 1 different coin is 9 g or 11 g (heavier, or lighter by 1 g). You should use balance scale that compares what's in the two pans. You can get the answer by just comparing groups of coins. What is the minimum number weighing's that can always guarantee to determine the different coin.

Answer: Separate the coins into 3 stacks of 9 (A, B, C). Weigh stack A against B and then A against C. Take the stack with the different weight (note lighter or heavier) and break it into 3 stacks of 3 (D, E, F). Weigh stack D against E. If D and E are equal, then F is the odd stack. If D and E are not equal, the lighter or heavier (based on the A, B, C comparison) is the odd stack. You now have three coins (G, H, I). Weigh G and H. If G equals H, then I is the odd and is lighter or heavier (based on the A, B, C comparison). If G and H are not equal, then the lighter or heavier (based on the A, B, C comparison) is the odd coin.

Note: for algorithmic solution refer *Divide* and *Conquer* chapter.

Question 5: Having 2 sandglasses: one 7-minute and the second one 4-minute, how can you correctly time 9 minutes?

Answer: Turn both sand-glasses. After 4 minutes turn upside down the 4-min sand-glass. When the 7-min sand-glass spills the last grain, turn the 7-min upside down. Then you have 1 minute in the 4-min sand-glass left and after spilling everything, in the 7-min sand-glass there will be 1 minute of sand down (already spilt). Turn the 7-min sand-glass upside down and let the 1 minute go back. And that's it. 4 + 3 + 1 + 1 = 9.

Question 6: You are travelling down a country lane to a distant village. You reach a fork in the road and find a pair of identical twin sisters standing there.

- Fork in the road riddle One standing on the road to village and the other standing on the road to neverland (of course, you don't know or see where each road leads).
- One of the sisters always tells the truth and the other always lies (of course, you don't know who is lying).
- Both sisters know where the roads go.

If you are allowed to ask only one question to one of the sisters to find the correct road to the village, what is your question?

Answer: This is one of the most famous logic problems which can be solved by using classic logic operations. You may have heard a few variations of this puzzle before but still, it's one of the best brain teasers. There are a few types of logic questions:

- Indirect question: "Hello there beauty, what would your sister say, if I asked her where this road leads?" The answer is always negated.
- Tricky question: "Excuse me lady, does a truth telling person stand on the road to the village?" The answer will be YES, if I am asking a truth teller who is standing at the road to village, or if I am asking a liar standing again on the same road. So I can go that way. A similar deduction can be made for negative answer.
- Complicated question: "Hey you, what would you say, if I asked you ...?" A truth teller is clear, but a liar should lie. However, she is forced by the question to lie two times and thus speak the truth.

Question 7: **Super Observer**: There are three switches in a room on the first floor and a lamp on the third floor. Each one is labeled On and Off. One (and only one) of the switches controls the lamp. There is no possible way for you to see whether the light is on or off from the first floor. You are alone in the house.

- You are allowed to turn on and off the switches as often and as long as you'd like.
- However, you can only go upstairs once to check on the status of the lamp.
- Determine which switch controls the lamp.

Answer: If the lamp contains a normal bulb that produces heat when turned on, you can turn on the 1st switch for 5 minutes or so then turn it off. Immediately turn on the 2nd light switch and run upstairs to check the light. If the light is on then it is the 2nd switch which controls the light. If it is off but the bulb is still hot/warm then it is the 1st switch. If it is off but cool then it is the 3rd. If the bulb is a fluorescent or LED bulb which gives off less heat then you may not be able to tell.

Question 8: Ten Stacks of Coins: You have ten stacks of ten coins. 9 of the 10 stacks contain coins that weigh 1.0 grams each. The 10th stack contains 1.1 grams. You also have a scale which returns the number of grams of the weighed items. Using the scale once, locate the stack with the 1.1 gram coins.

Answer: Take 1 coin from the first stack, 2 from the second, 3 from the third, ..., and 10 from the tenth stack and weigh them all together. If the weight of these coins is 55.1 grams then you know it is the 1st stack since 1.1 + 2 + 3 + 4 + 5 + 6 + 7 + 8 + 9 + 10 = 55.1. If it is 55.2 then it is the second stack, 55.3 is the third, etc.. If the coins weigh 56 grams then it is the tenth stack which holds the 1.1g coins.

Note: There were huge number of brainteasers and it is very difficult to cover all of them in a technical book. I would suggest you to refer other books specifically designed for those kinds of questions.

CHAPTER

Algorithms Introduction

11

The objective of this chapter is to explain the importance of analysis of algorithms, their notations, relationships and solving as many problems as possible. Let us first focus on understanding the basic elements of algorithms, importance of analysis and then slowly move toward the other topics as mentioned above. After completing this chapter you should be able to find the complexity of any given algorithm (especially recursive functions).

11.1 What is an Algorithm?

Let us consider the problem of preparing an omelette. For preparing omelette, we follow the steps as given below:

1) Get the frying pan.
2) Get the oil.
    a. Do we have oil?
        i. If yes, put it in the pan.
        ii. If no, do we want to buy oil?
            1. If yes, then go out and buy.
            2. If no, we can terminate.
3) Turn on the stove, etc...

What we are doing is, for a given problem (preparing an omelette), giving step by step procedure for solving it. Formal definition of an algorithm can be given as:

An algorithm is the step-by-step instructions to solve a given problem.

Note: we do not have to prove each step of the algorithm.

11.2 Why Analysis of Algorithms?

To go from city *"A"* to city *"B"*, there can be many ways of accomplishing this: by flight, by bus, by train and also by bicycle. Depending on the availability and convenience we choose the one that suits us. Similarly, in computer science multiple algorithms are available for solving the same problem (for example, sorting problem has many algorithms like insertion sort, selection sort, quick sort and many more). Algorithm analysis helps us determining which of them is efficient in terms of time and space consumed.

11.3 Goal of Analysis of Algorithms

The goal of *analysis of algorithms* is to compare algorithms (or solutions) mainly in terms of running time but also in terms of other factors (e.g., memory, developers effort etc.)

11.4 What is Running Time Analysis?

It is the process of determining how processing time increases as the size of the problem (input size) increases. Input size is the number of elements in the input and depending on the problem type the input may be of different types. The following are the common types of inputs.

- Size of an array
- Polynomial degree
- Number of elements in a matrix
- Number of bits in binary representation of the input
- Vertices and edges in a graph

11.5 How to Compare Algorithms?

To compare algorithms, let us define few *objective measures*:

Execution times? *Not a good measure* as execution times are specific to a particular computer.

Number of statements executed? *Not a good measure*, since the number of statements varies with the programming language as well as the style of the individual programmer.

Ideal Solution? Let us assume that we expressed running time of given algorithm as a function of the input size n (i.e., $f(n)$) and compare these different functions corresponding to running times. This kind of comparison is independent of machine time, programming style, etc.

11.6 What is Rate of Growth?

The rate at which the running time increases as a function of input is called *rate of growth*. Let us assume that you went to a shop to buy a car and a cycle. If your friend sees you there and asks what you are buying then in general you say *buying a car*. This is because, cost of car is too big compared to cost of cycle (approximating the cost of cycle to cost of car).

$$Total\ Cost = cost\_of\_car + cost\_of\_cycle$$
$$Total\ Cost \approx cost\_of\_car\ (approximation)$$

For the above-mentioned example, we can represent the cost of car and cost of cycle in terms of function and for a given function ignore the low order terms that are relatively insignificant (for large value of input size, n). As an example in the case below, n^4, $2n^2$, $100n$ and 500 are the individual costs of some function and approximate it to n^4. Since, n^4 is the highest rate of growth.

$$n^4 + 2n^2 + 100n + 500 \approx n^4$$

11.7 Commonly used Rate of Growths

Below diagram shows the relationship between different rates of growth.

Given below is the list of rate of growths which come across in remaining chapters.

Time complexity	Name	Example
1	Constant	Adding an element to the front of a linked list
$logn$	Logarithmic	Finding an element in a sorted array
n	Linear	Finding an element in an unsorted array
$nlogn$	Linear	Sorting n items by 'divide-and-conquer'-

	Logarithmic	Mergesort
n^2	Quadratic	Shortest path between two nodes in a graph
n^3	Cubic	Matrix Multiplication
2^n	Exponential	The Towers of Hanoi problem

11.8 Types of Analysis

To analyze the given algorithm we need to know on what inputs the algorithm takes less time (performing well) and on what inputs the algorithm takes long time. We have already seen that an algorithm can be represented in the form of an expression. That means we represent the algorithm with multiple expressions: one for the case where it takes less time and other for the case where it takes the more time.

In general the first case is called the *best case* and second case is called the *worst case* of the algorithm. To analyze an algorithm we need some kind of syntax and that forms the base for asymptotic analysis/notation. There are three types of analysis:

- **Worst case**
  - Defines the input for which the algorithm takes long time.
  - Input is the one for which the algorithm runs the slower.
- **Best case**
  - Defines the input for which the algorithm takes lowest time.
  - Input is the one for which the algorithm runs the fastest.
- **Average case**
  - Provides a prediction about the running time of the algorithm
  - Assumes that the input is random

$$\text{Lower Bound} <= \text{Average Time} <= \text{Upper Bound}$$

For a given algorithm, we can represent the best, worst and average cases in the form of expressions. As an example, let $f(n)$ be the function, which represents the given algorithm.

$$f(n) = n^2 + 500, \text{ for worst case}$$
$$f(n) = n + 100n + 500, \text{ for best case}$$

Similarly, for average case too. The expression defines the inputs with which the algorithm takes the average running time (or memory).

11.9 Asymptotic Notation and Big-O Notation

Having the expressions for the best, average case and worst cases, for all the three cases we need to identify the upper and lower bounds. To represent these upper and lower bounds we need some kind of syntax and that is the subject of the following discussion. Let us assume that the given algorithm is represented in the form of function $f(n)$.

Big-O notation gives the *tight* upper bound of the given function. Generally, it is represented as $f(n) = O(g(n))$. That means, at larger values of n, the upper bound of $f(n)$ is $g(n)$. For example, if $f(n) = n^4 + 100n^2 + 10n + 50$ is the given algorithm, then n^4 is $g(n)$. That means, $g(n)$ gives the maximum rate of growth for $f(n)$ at larger values of n.

Let us see the O–notation with little more detail. O–notation defined as $O(g(n)) = \{f(n)$: there exist positive constants c and n_0 such that $0 \leq f(n) \leq cg(n)$ for all $n \geq n_0\}$. $g(n)$ is an asymptotic tight upper bound for $f(n)$. Our objective is to give smallest rate of growth $g(n)$ which is greater than or equal to given algorithms rate of growth $f(n)$.

Generally we discard lower values of n. That means the rate of growth at lower values of n is not important. In the figure below, n_0 is the point from which we need to consider the rate of growths for a given algorithm. Below n_0 the rate of growths could be different.

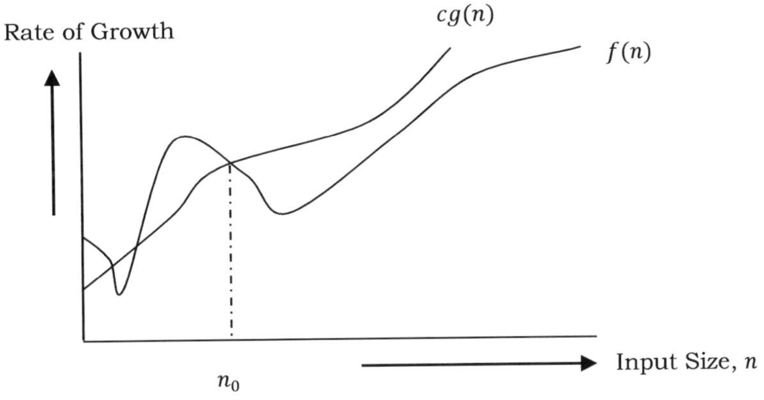

Big-O Visualization

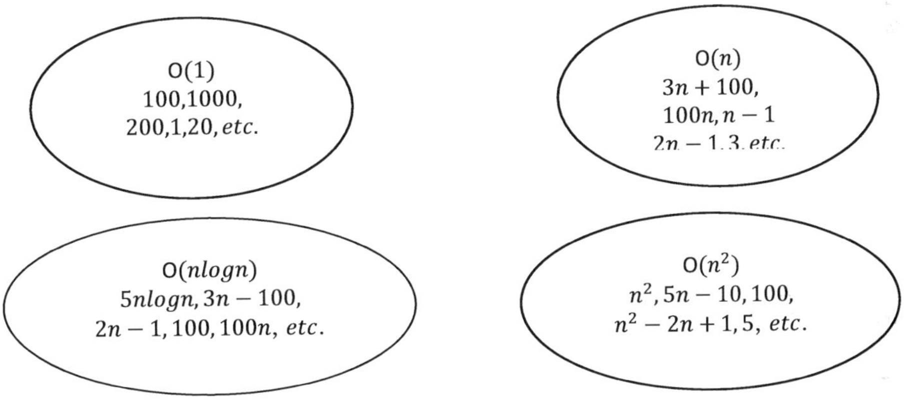

$O(g(n))$ is the set of functions with smaller or same order of growth as $g(n)$. For example; $O(n^2)$ includes $O(1), O(n), O(nlogn)$ etc.

Note: Analyze the algorithms at larger values of n only. What this means is, below n_0 we do not care for rate of growth.

Big-O Examples

Example-1 Find upper bound for $f(n) = 3n + 8$

Solution: $3n + 8 \leq 4n$, for all $n \geq 8$
$\therefore 3n + 8 = O(n)$ with c = 4 and $n_0 = 8$

Example-2 Find upper bound for $f(n) = n^2 + 1$

Solution: $n^2 + 1 \leq 2n^2$, for all $n \geq 1$
$\therefore n^2 + 1 = O(n^2)$ with $c = 2$ and $n_0 = 1$

Example-3 Find upper bound for $f(n) = n^4 + 100n^2 + 50$

Solution: $n^4 + 100n^2 + 50 \leq 2n^4$, for all $n \geq 11$
$\therefore n^4 + 100n^2 + 50 = O(n^4)$ with $c = 2$ and $n_0 = 11$

Example-4 Find upper bound for $f(n) = 2n^3 - 2n^2$

Solution: $2n^3 - 2n^2 \leq 2n^3$, for all $n \geq 1$
$\therefore 2n^3 - 2n^2 = O(2n^3)$ with $c = 2$ and $n_0 = 1$

Example-5 Find upper bound for $f(n) = n$

Solution: $n \leq n$, for all $n \geq 1$
$\therefore n = O(n)$ with $c = 1$ and $n_0 = 1$

Example-6 Find upper bound for $f(n) = 410$

Solution: $410 \leq 410$, for all $n \geq 1$
$\therefore 410 = O(1)$ with $c = 1$ and $n_0 = 1$

No Uniqueness?

There are no unique set of values for n_0 and c in proving the asymptotic bounds. Let us consider, $100n + 5 = O(n)$. For this function there are multiple n_0 and c values possible.

Solution1: $100n + 5 \leq 100n + n = 101n \leq 101n$, for all $n \geq 5$, $n_0 = 5$ and $c = 101$ is a solution.

Solution2: $100n + 5 \leq 100n + 5n = 105n \leq 105n$, for all $n \geq 1$, $n_0 = 1$ and $c = 105$ is also a solution.

11.10 Why is it called Asymptotic Analysis?

From the discussion above (for all the three notations: worst case, best case and average case), we can easily understand that, in every case for a given function $f(n)$ we are trying to find other function $g(n)$ which approximates $f(n)$ at higher values of n. That means, $g(n)$ is also a curve which approximates $f(n)$ at higher values of n.

In mathematics we call such curve *asymptotic curve*. In other terms, $g(n)$ is the asymptotic curve for $f(n)$. For this reason, we call algorithm analysis *asymptotic analysis*.

11.11 Guidelines for Asymptotic Analysis

There are some general rules to help us determine the running time of an algorithm.

1) **Loops**: The running time of a loop is, at most, the running time of the statements inside the loop (including tests) multiplied by the number of iterations.

```
// executes n times
for (i=1; i<=n; i++)
    m = m + 2; // constant time, c
```

Total time = a constant $c \times n = c\,n = O(n)$.

2) **Nested loops:** Analyze from inside out. Total running time is the product of the sizes of all the loops.

```
//outer loop executed n times
for (i=1; i<=n; i++) {
    // inner loop executed n times
    for (j=1; j<=n; j++)
        k = k+1; //constant time
}
```

Total time $= c \times n \times n = cn^2 = O(n^2)$.

3) **Consecutive statements:** Add the time complexities of each statement.

```
x = x +1; //constant time
// executed n times
for (i=1; i<=n; i++)
```

```
    m = m + 2; //constant time
//outer loop executed n times
for (i=1; i<=n; i++) {
    //inner loop executed n times
    for (j=1; j<=n; j++)
        k = k+1; //constant time
}
```

Total time $= c_0 + c_1 n + c_2 n^2 = O(n^2)$.

4) **If-then-else statements:** Worst-case running time: the test, plus *either* the *then* part *or* the *else* part (whichever is the larger).

```
//test: constant
if(length( ) == 0 ) {
    return false; //then part: constant
}
else {// else part: (constant + constant) * n
    for (int n = 0; n < length( ); n++) {
      // another if : constant + constant (no else part)
      if(!list[n].equals(otherList.list[n]))
          //constant
        return false;
    }
}
```

Total time $= c_0 + c_1 + (c_2 + c_3) * n = O(n)$.

5) **Logarithmic complexity:** An algorithm is $O(logn)$ if it takes a constant time to cut the problem size by a fraction (usually by ½). As an example let us consider the following program:

```
for (i=1; i<=n;)
    i = i*2;
```

If we observe carefully, the value of i is doubling every time. Initially $i = 1$, in next step $i = 2$, and in subsequent steps $i = 4, 8$ and so on. Let us assume that the loop is executing some k times. At k^{th} step $2^k = n$ and we come out of loop. Taking logarithm on both sides, gives

$log(2^k) = logn$
$klog2 = logn$
$k = logn$ //if we assume base-2

Total time $= O(logn)$.

Note: Similarly, for the case below also, worst case rate of growth is $O(logn)$. The same discussion holds good for decreasing sequence as well.

```
for (i=n; i>=1;)
    i = i/2;
```

Another example: binary search (finding a word in a dictionary of n pages)

- Look at the center point in the dictionary
- Is word towards left or right of center?
- Repeat process with left or right part of dictionary until the word is found

11.12 Amortized Analysis

Amortized analysis refers to determining the time-averaged running time for a sequence of operations. It is different from average case analysis, because amortized analysis does not make any assumption about the distribution of the data values, whereas average case analysis assumes the data are not "bad" (e.g., some sorting algorithms do well on "average" over all input orderings but very badly on certain input orderings). That is, amortized analysis is a worst-case analysis, but for a sequence of operations, rather than for individual operations.

The motivation for amortized analysis is to better understand the running time of certain techniques, where standard worst case analysis provides an overly pessimistic bound. Amortized analysis generally applies to a method that consists of a sequence of operations, where the vast majority of the operations are cheap, but some of the operations are expensive. If we can show that the expensive operations are particularly rare we can "charge them" to the cheap operations, and only bound the cheap operations.

The general approach is to assign an artificial cost to each operation in the sequence, such that the total of the artificial costs for the sequence of operations bounds total of the real costs for the sequence. This artificial cost is called the amortized cost of an operation. To analyze the running time, the amortized cost thus is a correct way of understanding the overall running time — but note that particular operations can still take longer so it is not a way of bounding the running time of any individual operation in the sequence.

When one event in a sequence affects the cost of later events:

- One particular task may be expensive.
- But it may leave data structure in a state that next few operations become easier.

Example: Let us consider an array of elements from which we want to find k^{th} smallest element. We can solve this problem using sorting. After sorting the given array, we just need to return the kth element from it. Cost of performing sort (assuming comparison based sorting algorithm) is $O(nlogn)$. If we perform n such selections then the average cost of each selection is $O(nlogn/n) = O(logn)$. This clearly indicates that sorting once is reducing the complexity of subsequent operations.

Problems and Questions with Answers

Note: From the following problems, try to understand the cases which give different complexities ($O(n), O(logn), O(loglogn)$ etc...).

Question 1: What is the running time of the following function?

```
void Function(int n) {
        int i=1, s=1;
        while( s <= n) {
                i++;
                s= s+i;
                printf("*");
        }
}
```

Answer: Consider the comments in below function:

```
void Function (int n) {
        int i=1, s=1;
        // s is increasing not at rate 1 but i
        while( s <= n) {
                i++;
                s= s+i;
                printf("*");
        }
}
```

We can define the terms '*s*' according to the relation $s_i = s_{i-1} + i$. The value of '*i*' increases by 1 for each iteration. The value contained in '*s*' at the ith iteration is the sum of the first '*i*' positive integers. If k is the total number of iterations taken by the program, then *while* loop terminates if:

$$1 + 2 + \ldots + k = \frac{k(k+1)}{2} > n \Rightarrow k = O(\sqrt{n}).$$

Question 2: Find the complexity of the function given below.

```
void Function(int n) {
    int i, count =0;
    for(i=1; i*i<=n; i++)
        count++;
}
```

Answer:

```
void Function(int n) {
    int i, count =0;
    for(i=1; i*i<=n; i++)
        count++;
}
```

In the above-mentioned function the loop will end, if $i^2 \le n \Rightarrow T(n) = O(\sqrt{n})$. The reasoning is same as that of Question 1:.

Question 3: What is the complexity of the program given below:

```
void function(int n) {
    int i, j, k , count =0;
    for(i=n/2; i<=n; i++)
        for(j=1; j + n/2<=n; j= j++)
            for(k=1; k<=n; k= k * 2)
                count++;
}
```

Answer: Consider the comments in the following function.

```
void function(int n) {
    int i, j, k , count =0;
            //outer loop execute n/2 times
    for(i=n/2; i<=n; i++)
        //Middle loop executes n/2 times
        for(j=1; j + n/2<=n; j= j++)
            //outer loop execute logn times
            for(k=1; k<=n; k= k * 2)
                count++;
}
```

The complexity of the above function is $O(n^2 logn)$.

Question 4: What is the complexity of the program given below:

```
void function(int n) {
    int i, j, k , count =0;
    for(i=n/2; i<=n; i++)
        for(j=1; j<=n; j= 2 * j)
            for(k=1; k<=n; k= k * 2)
                count++;
}
```

Answer: Consider the comments in the following function.

```
void function(int n) {
  int i, j, k , count =0;
        //outer loop execute n/2 times
  for(i=n/2; i<=n; i++)
      //Middle loop executes logn times
      for(j=1; j<=n; j= 2 * j)
```

```
        //outer loop execute logn times
        for(k=1; k<=n; k= k*2)
            count++;
}
```

The complexity of the above function is O($nlog^2n$).

Question 5: Find the complexity of the program below.

```
function( int n ) {
  if(n == 1) return;
  for(int i = 1 ; i <= n ; i + + ) {
     for(int j= 1 ; j <= n ; j + + ) {
        printf("*" );
        break;
     }
  }
}
```

Answer: Consider the comments in the function below.

```
function( int n ) {
  //constant time
  if( n == 1 ) return;
  //outer loop execute n times
  for(int i = 1 ; i <= n ; i + + ) {
     // inner loop executes only time due to break statement.
     for(int j= 1 ; j <= n ; j + + ) {
        printf("*" );
        break;
     }
  }
}
```

The complexity of the above function is O(n). Even though the inner loop is bounded by n, but due to the break statement it is executing only once.

Question 6: Prove that the running time of the code below is $\Omega(logn)$.

```
void Read(int n) {
        int k = 1;
        while( k < n )
                k = 3*k;
}
```

Answer: The *while* loop will terminate once the value of '*k*' is greater than or equal to the value of '*n*'. In each iteration the value of '*k*' is multiplied by 3. If i is the number of iterations, then '*k*' has the value of $3i$ after i iterations. The loop is terminated upon reaching i iterations when $3^i \geq n \leftrightarrow i \geq \log_3 n$, which shows that $i = \Omega\ (logn)$.

Question 7: Consider the following program:

```
Fib[n]
if(n==0) then return 0
else if(n==1) then return 1
else return Fib[n-1]+Fib[n-2]
```

Answer: The recurrence relation for running time of this program is: $T(n) = T(n-1) + T(n-2) + c$. Note $T(n)$ has two recurrence calls indicating a binary tree. Each step recursively calls the program for n reduced by 1 and 2, so the depth of the recurrence tree is O(n). The number of leaves at depth n is 2^n since this is a full binary tree, and each leaf takes at least O(1) computation for the constant factor. Running time is clearly exponential in n and it is O(2^n).

Question 8: Running time of following program?

```
function(n) {
```

```
            for(int i = 1; i <= n ; i + + )
                    for(int j = 1 ; j <= n ; j+ = i )
                            printf(" * ");
}
```

Answer: Consider the comments in the function below:

```
function (n) {
  //this loop executes n times
        for(int i = 1;  i <= n ; i + + )
     //this loop executes j times with j increase by the rate of i
                for(int j = 1 ; j <= n ; j+ = i )
                        printf( " * " );
}
```

In the above code, inner loop executes n/i times for each value of i. Its running time is $n \times (\sum_{i=1}^{n} n/i) = O(nlogn)$.

Question 9: Running time of following program?

```
function(int n) {
            for(int i = 1 ; i <= n ; i + + )
                    for(int j = 1 ; j <= n ; j * = 2 )
                            printf( " * " );
}
```

Answer: Consider the comments in below function:

```
function(int n) {
  for(int i = 1 ; i <= n ; i + + ) // this loops executes n times
     // this loops executes logn times from our logarithms guideline
     for(int j = 1 ; j <= n ; j * = 2 )
        printf( " * " );
}
```

Complexity of above program is: $O(nlogn)$.

Question 10: Running time of following program?

```
function(int n) {
            for(int i = 1 ; i <= n/3 ; i + + )
                    for(int j = 1 ; j <= n ; j += 4 )
                            printf( " * " );
}
```

Answer: Consider the comments in below function:

```
function(int n) {  // this loops executes n/3 times
  for(int i = 1 ; i <= n/3 ; i + + )
     // this loops executes n/4 times
     for(int j = 1 ; j <= n ; j += 4)
        printf( " * " );
}
```

The time complexity of this program is: $O(n^2)$.

Question 11: Find the complexity of the below function.

```
function(int n) {
  int i=1;
  while (i < n) {
     int j=n;
     while(j > 0)
        j = j/2;
     i=2*i;
  } // i
}
```

Answer:

```
function(int n) {
```

```
        int i=1;
        while (i < n) {
            int j=n;
            while(j > 0)
                j = j/2;   //logn code
            i=2*i;         //logn times
        } // i
    }
```

Time Complexity: $O(logn * logn) = O(log^2 n)$.

Question 12: Find the complexity of the below function.

```
function(int n) {
    int sum = 0;
    for (int i = 0; i<n; i++)
        if (i>j)
            sum = sum +1;
        else {
            for (int k = 0; k < n; k++)
                sum = sum -1;
        }
    }
}
```

Answer: Consider the worst-case.

```
function(int n) {
    int sum = 0;
    for (int i = 0; i<n; i++)              // Executes n times
        if (i>j)
            sum = sum +1;                  // Executes n times
        else {
            for (int k = 0; k < n; k++)    // Executes n times
                sum = sum -1;
        }
    }
}
```

Time Complexity: $O(n^2)$.

CHAPTER

Recursion and Backtracking

12

12.1 Introduction

In this chapter, we will look at one of the important topics *"recursion"*, which will be used in almost every chapter and also its relative *"backtracking"*.

12.2 What is Recursion?

Any function which calls itself is called *recursive*. A recursive method solves a problem by calling a copy of itself to work on a smaller problem. This is called the recursion step. The recursion step can result in many more such recursive calls.

It is important to ensure that the recursion terminates. Each time the function calls itself with a slightly simpler version of the original problem. The sequence of smaller problems must eventually converge on the base case.

12.3 Why Recursion?

Recursion is a useful technique borrowed from mathematics. Recursive code is generally shorter and easier to write than iterative code. Generally, loops are turned into recursive functions when they are compiled or interpreted.

Recursion is most useful for tasks that can be defined in terms of similar subtasks. For example, sort, search, and traversal problems often have simple recursive solutions.

12.4 Format of a Recursive Function

A recursive function performs a task in part by calling itself to perform the subtasks. At some point, the function encounters a subtask that it can perform without calling itself. This case, where the function does not recur, is called the *base case,* the former, where the function calls itself to perform a subtask, is referred to as the *recursive case*.

We can write all recursive functions using the format:

```
if(test for the base case)
   return some base case value
else if(test for another base case)
   return some other base case value
// the recursive case
else
   return (some work and then a recursive call)
```

As an example consider the factorial function: $n!$ is the product of all integers between n and 1. Definition of recursive factorial looks like:

$$n! = 1, \quad \text{if } n = 0$$
$$n! = n * (n-1)! \quad \text{if } n > 0$$

This definition can easily be converted to recursive implementation. Here the problem is determining the value of $n!$, and the subproblem is determining the value of $(n - l)!$. In the recursive case, when n is greater than 1, the function calls itself to determine the value of $(n - l)!$ and multiplies that with n.

In the base case, when n is 0 or 1, the function simply returns 1. This looks like the following:

```
// calculates factorial of a positive integer
int Fact(int n) {
   // base cases: fact of 0 or 1 is 1
   if(n == 1)
      return 1;
   else if(n == 0)
      return 1;
   // recursive case: multiply n by (n – 1) factorial
   else  return n*Fact(n-1);
}
```

12.5 Recursion and Memory (Visualization)

Each recursive call makes a new copy of that method (actually only the variables) in memory. Once a method ends (that is, returns some data), the copy of that returning method is removed from memory. The recursive solutions look simple but visualization and tracing takes times. For better understanding, let us consider the following example.

```
//print numbers 1 to n backward
int Print(int n) {
    // this is the terminating base case
    if( n = = 0)
         return 0;
    else {
        printf ("%d",n);
        return Print(n-1); // recursive call to itself again
    }
}
```

For this example, if we call the print function with n=4, visually our memory assignments may look like:

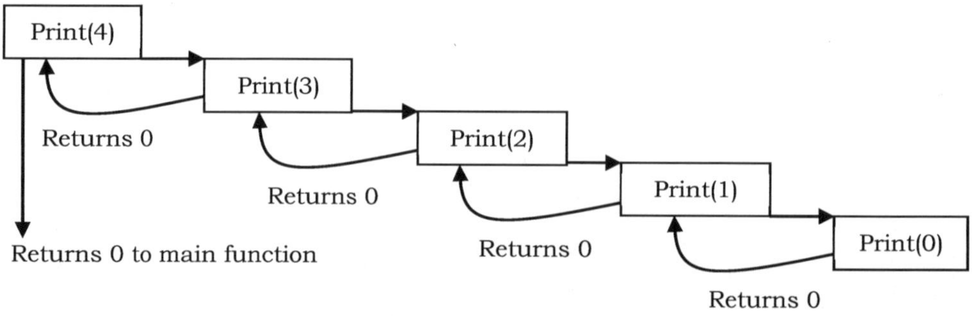

Now, let us consider our factorial function. The visualization of factorial function with n=4 will look like:

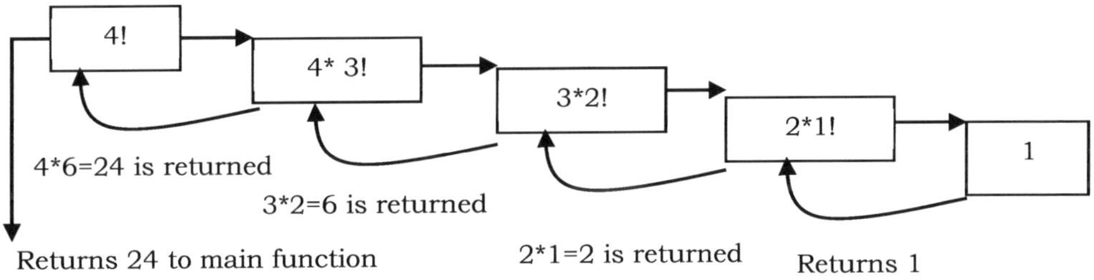

12.6 Recursion versus Iteration

While discussing recursion the basic question that comes in mind is, which way is better? – Iteration or recursion? Answer to this question depends on what we are trying to do. A recursive approach mirrors the problem that we are trying to solve. A recursive approach makes it simpler to solve a problem, which may not have the most obvious of answers. But, recursion adds overhead for each recursive call (needs space on the stack frame).

Recursion

- Terminates when a base case is reached.
- Each recursive call requires extra space on the stack frame (memory).
- If we get infinite recursion, the program may run out of memory and gives stack overflow.
- Solutions to some problems are easier to formulate recursively.

Iteration

- Terminates when a condition is proven to be false.
- Each iteration does not require extra space.
- An infinite loop could loop forever since there is no extra memory being created.
- Iterative solutions to a problem may not always be as obvious as a recursive solution.

12.7 Notes on Recursion

- Recursive algorithms have two types of cases, recursive and base cases.
- Every recursive function case must terminate at base case.
- Generally iterative solutions are more efficient than recursive solutions [due to the overhead of function calls].
- A recursive algorithm can be implemented without recursive function calls using a stack, but it's usually more trouble than its worth. That means any problem that can be solved recursively can also be solved iteratively.
- For some problems, there are no obvious iterative algorithms.
- Some problems are best suited for recursive solutions while others are not.

12.8 Example Algorithms of Recursion

- Fibonacci Series, Factorial Finding
- Merge Sort, Quick Sort
- Binary Search
- Tree Traversals and many Tree Problems: InOrder, PreOrder PostOrder

- Graph Traversals: DFS [Depth First Search] and BFS [Breadth First Search]
- Dynamic Programming Examples
- Divide and Conquer Algorithms
- Towers of Hanoi
- Backtracking algorithms [we will discuss in next section]

Problems and Questions with Answers

In this chapter we cover few problems on recursion and will discuss the rest in other chapters. By the time you complete the reading of entire book you will encounter many problems on recursion.

Question 1: Discuss Towers of Hanoi puzzle.

Answer: The Tower of Hanoi is a mathematical puzzle. It consists of three rods (or pegs or towers), and a number of disks of different sizes which can slide onto any rod. The puzzle starts with the disks on one rod in ascending order of size, the smallest at the top, thus making a conical shape. The objective of the puzzle is to move the entire stack to another rod, satisfying the following rules:

- Only one disk may be moved at a time.
- Each move consists of taking the upper disk from one of the rods and sliding it onto another rod, on top of the other disks that may already be present on that rod.
- No disk may be placed on top of a smaller disk.

Algorithm:

- Move the top $n-1$ disks from *Source* to *Auxiliary* tower,
- Move the nth disk from *Source* to *Destination* tower,
- Move the $n-1$disks from Auxiliary tower to *Destination* tower.
- Transferring the top $n-1$ disks from *Source* to *Auxiliary* tower can again be thought as a fresh problem and can be solved in the same manner. Once we solve *Tower of Hanoi* with three disks, we can solve it with any number of disks with the above algorithm.

```
void TowersOfHanoi(int n, char frompeg, char topeg, char auxpeg) {
    /* If only 1 disk, make the move and return */
    if(n==1) {
        printf("Move disk 1 from peg %c to peg %c",frompeg, topeg);
        return;
    }
    /* Move top n-1 disks from A to B, using C as auxiliary */
    TowersOfHanoi(n-1, frompeg, auxpeg, topeg);
    /* Move remaining disks from A to C */
    printf("\nMove disk %d from peg %c to peg %c", n, frompeg, topeg);
    /* Move n-1 disks from B to C using A as auxiliary */
    TowersOfHanoi(n-1, auxpeg, topeg, frompeg);
}
```

Question 2: Given an array, check whether the array is in sorted order with recursion.

Answer:

```
int isArrayInSortedOrder(int A[],int n){
    if(n == 1)
        return 1;
    return (A[n-1] <= A[n-2])?0:isArrayInSortedOrder(A,n-1);
}
```

Time Complexity: O(n). Space Complexity: O(n) for stack space.

12.9 What is Backtracking?

Backtracking is a method of exhaustive search using divide and conquer.

- Sometimes the best algorithm for a problem is to try all possibilities.
- This is always slow, but there are standard tools that can be used to help.
- Tools: algorithms for generating basic objects, such as binary strings [2^n possibilities for n-bit string], permutations [$n!$], combinations [$n!/r!\,(n-r)!$], general strings [k –ary strings of length n has k^n possibilities], etc...
- Backtracking speeds the exhaustive search by pruning.

12.10 Example Algorithms of Backtracking

- Binary Strings: generating all binary strings
- Generating k –ary Strings
- The Knapsack Problem
- Generalized Strings
- Hamiltonian Cycles [refer *Graphs* chapter]
- Graph Coloring Problem

Problems and Questions with Answers

Question 3: Generate all the strings of n bits. Assume $A[0..n-1]$ is an array of size n.

Answer:

```
void Binary(int n) {
   if(n < 1 )
      printf("%s", A);          //Assume array A is a global variable
   else {
      A[n-1] = 0;
       Binary(n - 1);
       A[n-1] = 1;
       Binary(n - 1);
   }
}
```

Question 4: Generate all the strings of length n drawn from $0...k-1$.

Answer: Let us assume we keep current k-ary string in an array $A[0..n-1]$. Call function *k-string*(n, k):

```
void k-string(int n, int k) {
   //process all k-ary strings of length m
   if(n < 1 )
            printf("%s",A);      //Assume array A is a global variable
   else {
            for (int j = 0 ; j < k ; j++) {
                  A[n-1] = j;
                  k-string(n- 1, k);
      }
   }
}
```

CHAPTER

Linked Lists 13

13.1 What is a Linked List?

Linked list is a data structure used for storing collections of data. Linked list has the following properties.

- Successive elements are connected by pointers
- Last element points to NULL
- Can grow or shrink in size during execution of a program
- Can be made just as long as required (until systems memory exhausts)
- It does not waste memory space (but takes some extra memory for pointers)

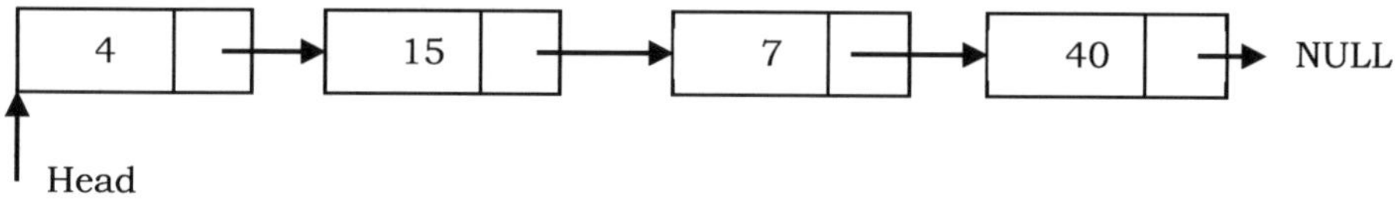

13.2 Linked Lists ADT

The following operations make linked lists an ADT:

Main Linked Lists Operations

- Insert: inserts an element into the list
- Delete: removes and returns the specified position element from the list

Auxiliary Linked Lists Operations

- Delete List: removes all elements of the list (disposes the list)
- Count: returns the number of elements in the list
- Find n^{th} node from the end of the list

13.3 Why Linked Lists?

There are many other data structures that do the same thing as that of linked lists. Before discussing linked lists it is important to understand the difference between linked lists and arrays.

Both linked lists and arrays are used to store collections of data. Since both are used for the same purpose, we need to differentiate their usage. That means in which cases *arrays* are suitable and in which cases *linked lists* are suitable.

13.4 Arrays Overview

One memory block is allocated for the entire array to hold the elements of the array. The array elements can be accessed in a constant time by using the index of the particular element as the subscript.

	3	2	1	2	2	3
Index →	0	1	2	3	4	5

Why Constant Time for Accessing Array Elements?

To access an array element, address of an element is computed as an offset from the base address of the array and one multiplication is needed to compute what is supposed to be added to the base address to get the memory address of the element. First the size of an element of that data type is calculated and then it is multiplied with the index of the element to get the value to be added to the base address.

This process takes one multiplication and one addition. Since these two operations take constant time, we can say the array access can be performed in constant time.

Advantages of Arrays

- Simple and easy to use
- Faster access to the elements (constant access)

Disadvantages of Arrays

- **Fixed size:** The size of the array is static (specify the array size before using it).
- **One block allocation**: To allocate the array at the beginning itself, sometimes it may not be possible to get the memory for the complete array (if the array size is big).
- **Complex position-based insertion**: To insert an element at a given position we may need to shift the existing elements. This will create a position for us to insert the new element at the desired position. If the position at which we want to add an element is at the beginning then the shifting operation is more expensive.

Dynamic Arrays

Dynamic array (also called as *growable array*, *resizable array*, *dynamic table*, or *array list*) is a random access, variable-size list data structure that allows elements to be added or removed.

One simple way of implementing dynamic arrays is, initially start with some fixed size array. As soon as that array becomes full, create the new array of size double than the original array. Similarly, reduce the array size to half if the elements in the array are less than half.

Advantages of Linked Lists

Linked lists have both advantages and disadvantages. The advantage of linked lists is that they can be *expanded* in constant time. To create an array we must allocate memory for a certain number of elements.

To add more elements to the array then we must create a new array and copy the old array into the new array. This can take lot of time.

We can prevent this by allocating lots of space initially but then you might allocate more than you need and wasting memory. With a linked list we can start with space for just one element allocated and *add* on new elements easily without the need to do any copying and reallocating.

Issues with Linked Lists (Disadvantages)

There are a number of issues in linked lists. The main disadvantage of linked lists is *access time* to individual elements. Array is random-access, which means it takes $O(1)$ to access any element in the array. Linked lists takes $O(n)$ for access to an element in the list in the worst case. Another advantage of arrays in access time is special *locality* in memory. Arrays are defined as contiguous blocks of memory, and so any array element will be physically near its neighbors. This greatly benefits from modern CPU caching methods.

Although the dynamic allocation of storage is a great advantage, the *overhead* with storing and retrieving data can make a big difference. Sometimes linked lists are *hard* to *manipulate*. If the last item is deleted, the last but one must now have its pointer changed to hold a NULL reference. This requires that the list is traversed to find the last but one link, and its pointer set to a NULL reference.

Finally, linked lists wastes memory in terms of extra reference points.

13.5 Linked Lists Versus Arrays and Dynamic Arrays

Parameter	Linked list	Array	Dynamic array
Indexing	$O(n)$	$O(1)$	$O(1)$
Insertion/deletion at beginning	$O(1)$	$O(n)$, if array is not full (for shifting the elements)	$O(n)$
Insertion at ending	$O(n)$	$O(1)$, if array is not full	$O(1)$, if array is not full $O(n)$, if array is full
Deletion at ending	$O(n)$	$O(1)$	$O(n)$
Insertion in middle	$O(n)$	$O(n)$, if array is not full (for shifting the elements)	$O(n)$
Deletion in middle	$O(n)$	$O(n)$, if array is not full (for shifting the elements)	$O(n)$
Wasted space	$O(n)$	0	$O(n)$

13.6 Singly Linked Lists

Generally "linked list" means a singly linked list. This list consists of a number of nodes in which each node has a *next* pointer to the following element. The link of the last node in the list is NULL, which indicates end of the list.

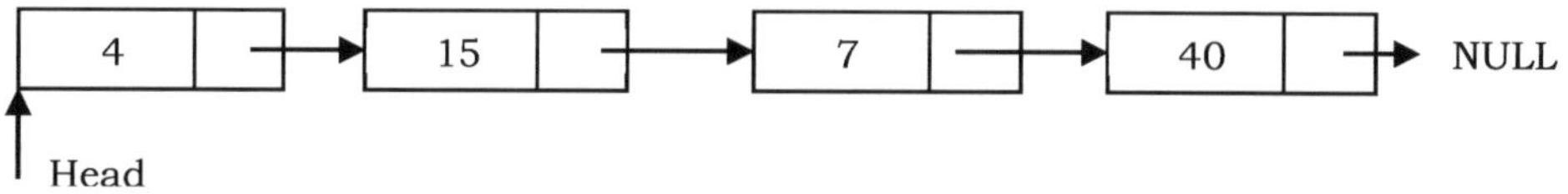

Following is a type declaration for a linked list of integers:

```
struct ListNode {
   int data;
   struct ListNode *next;
};
```

Basic Operations on a List

- Traversing the list
- Inserting an item in the list
- Deleting an item from the list

Traversing the Linked List

Let us assume that the *head* points to the first node of the list. To traverse the list we do the following.

- Follow the pointers.
- Display the contents of the nodes (or count) as they are traversed.
- Stop when the next pointer points to NULL.

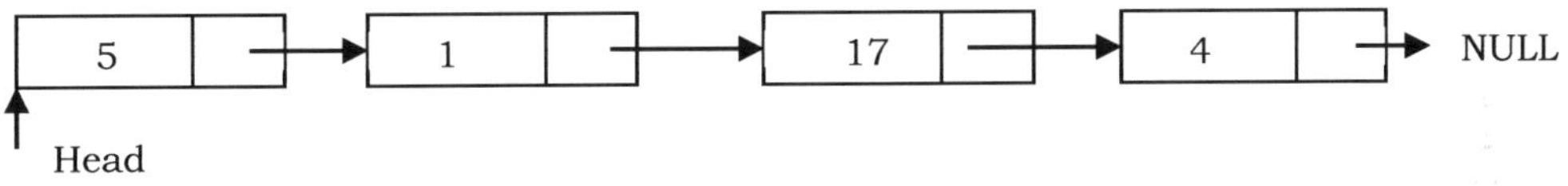

The ListLength() function takes a linked list as input and counts the number of nodes in the list. The function given below can be used for printing the list data with extra print function.

```
int ListLength(struct ListNode *head) {
   struct ListNode *current = head;
   int count = 0;
   while (current != NULL) {
      count++;
      current = current→next;
   }
   return count;
}
```

Singly Linked List Insertion

Insertion into a singly-linked list has three cases:

- Inserting a new node before the head (at the beginning)
- Inserting a new node after the tail (at the end of the list)
- Inserting a new node at the middle of the list (random location)

Note: To insert an element in the linked list at some position p, assume that after inserting the element the position of this new node is p.

Inserting a Node in Singly Linked List at the Beginning

In this case, a new node is inserted before the current head node. *Only one next pointer* needs to be modified (new node's next pointer) and it can be done in two steps:

- Update the next pointer of new node, to point to the current head.

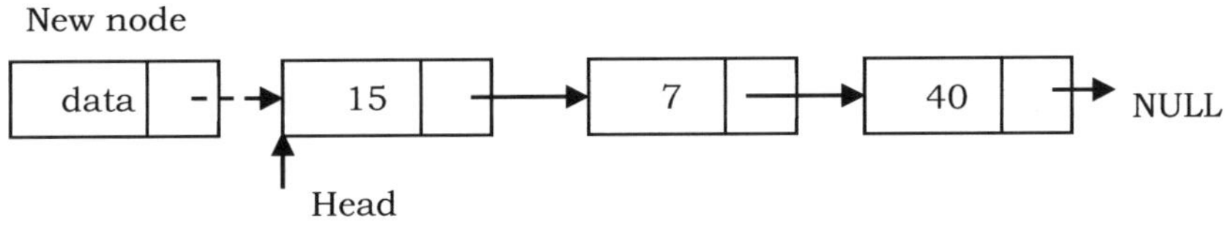

- Update head pointer to point to the new node.

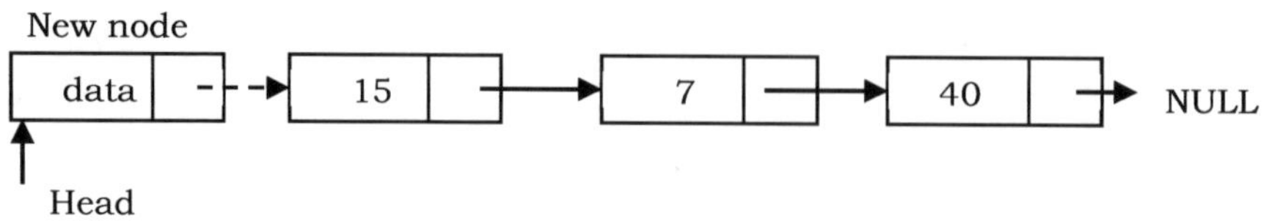

Inserting a Node in Singly Linked List at the Ending

In this case, we need to modify *two next pointers* (last nodes next pointer and new nodes next pointer).

- New nodes next pointer points to NULL.

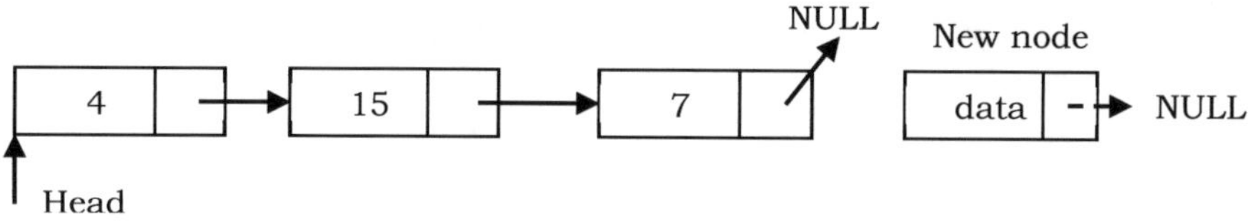

- Last nodes next pointer points to the new node.

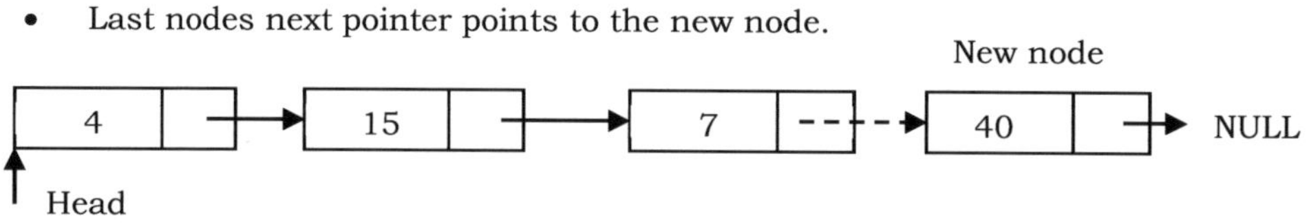

Inserting a Node in Singly Linked List at the Middle

Let us assume that we are given a position where we want to insert the new node. In this case also, we need to modify two next pointers.

- If we want to add an element at position 3 then we stop at position 2. That means we traverse 2 nodes and insert the new node. For simplicity let us assume that second node is called *position* node. New node points to the next node of the position where we want to add this node.

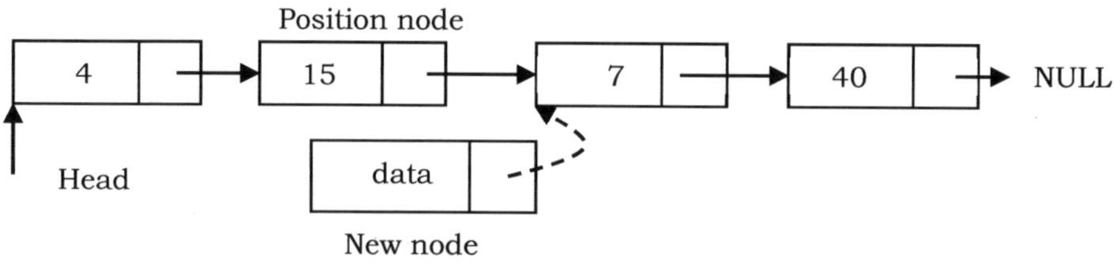

- Position nodes next pointer now points to the new node.

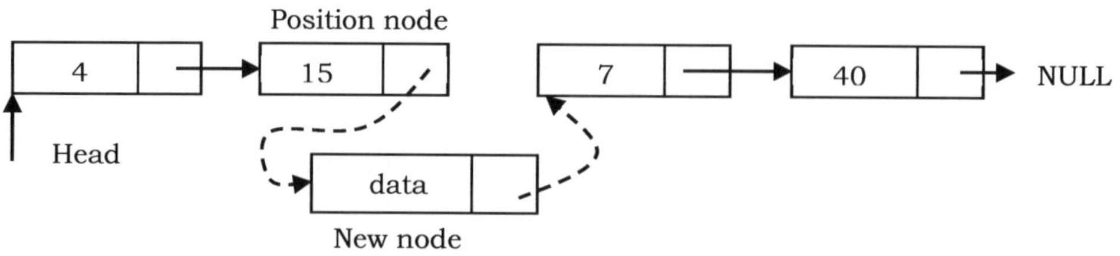

Let us write the code for all these three cases. We must update the first element pointer in the calling function, not just in the called function. For this reason we need to send double pointer. The following code inserts a node in the singly linked list.

```
void InsertInLinkedList(struct ListNode **head,int data,int position) {
    int k=1;
    struct ListNode *p,*q,*newNode;
```

```
    newNode = (ListNode *)malloc(sizeof(struct ListNode));
    if(!newNode){
        printf("Memory Error");
        return;
    }
    newNode→data=data;
    p=*head;
    //Inserting at the beginning
    if(position == 1){
        newNode→next=p;
        *head=newNode;
    }
    else{
        //Traverse the list until the position where we want to insert
        while((p!=NULL) && (k<position)){
            k++;
            q=p;
            p=p→next;
        }
        q→next=newNode;   //more optimum way to do this
        newNode→next=p;
    }
}
```

Note: We can implement the three variations of the *insert* operation separately.

Singly Linked List Deletion

As similar to insertion here also we have three cases.

- Deleting the first node
- Deleting the last node
- Deleting an intermediate node

Deleting the First Node in Singly Linked List

First node (current head node) is removed from the list. It can be done in two steps:

- Create a temporary node which will point to same node as that of head.

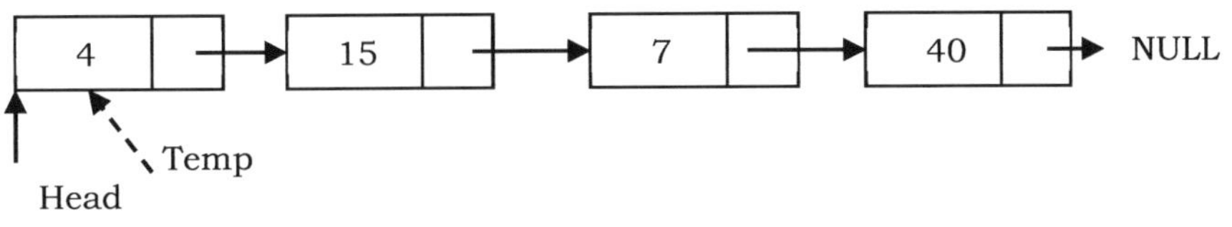

- Now, move the head nodes pointer to the next node and dispose the temporary node.

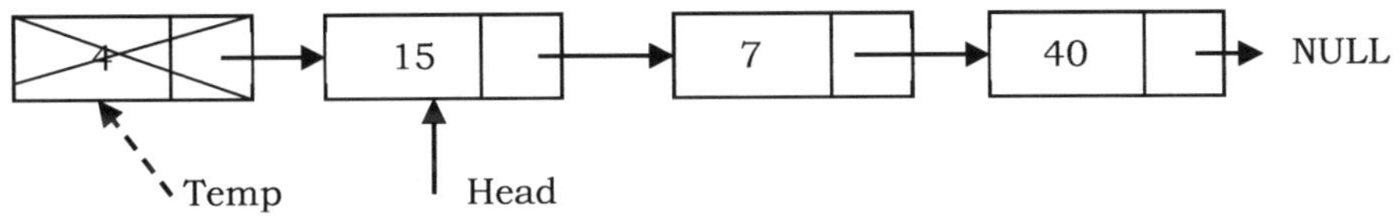

Deleting the last node in Singly Linked List

In this case, last node is removed from the list. This operation is a bit trickier than removing the first node, because algorithm should find a node, which is previous to the tail first. It can be done in three steps:

- Traverse the list and while traversing maintain the previous node address also. By the time we reach the end of list, we will have two pointers one pointing to the *tail* node and other pointing to the node *before* tail node.

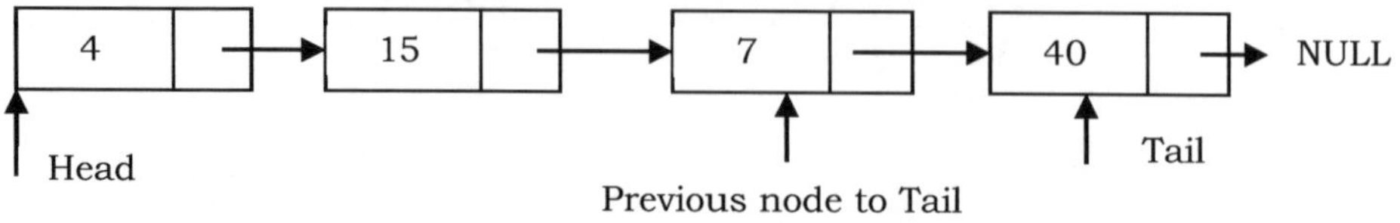

- Update previous nodes next pointer with NULL.

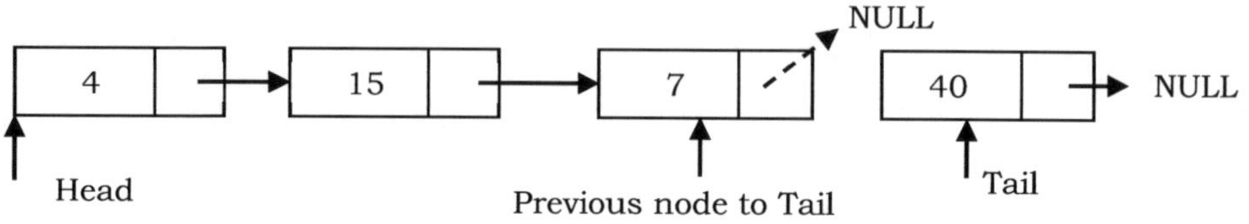

- Dispose the tail node.

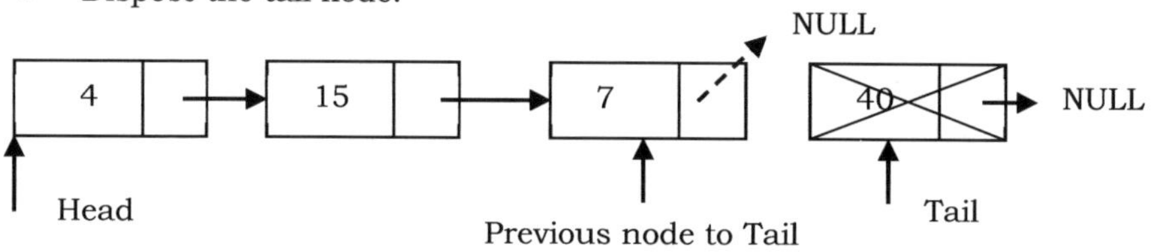

Deleting an Intermediate Node in Singly Linked List

In this case, node to be removed is *always located between* two nodes. Head and tail links are not updated in this case. Such a removal can be done in two steps:

- As similar to previous case, maintain previous node while traversing the list. Once we found the node to be deleted, change the previous nodes next pointer to next pointer of the node to be deleted.

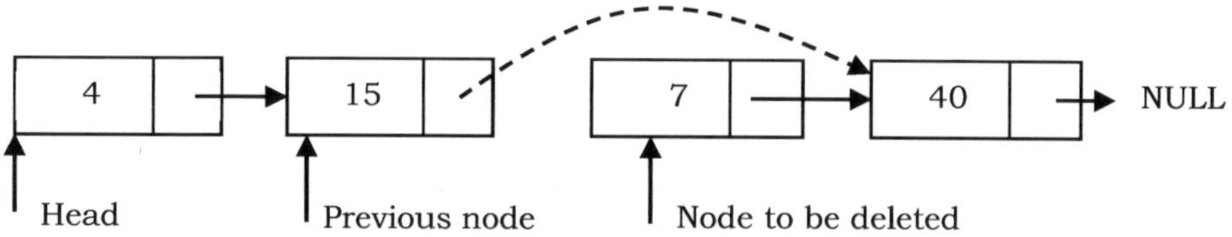

- Dispose the current node to be deleted.

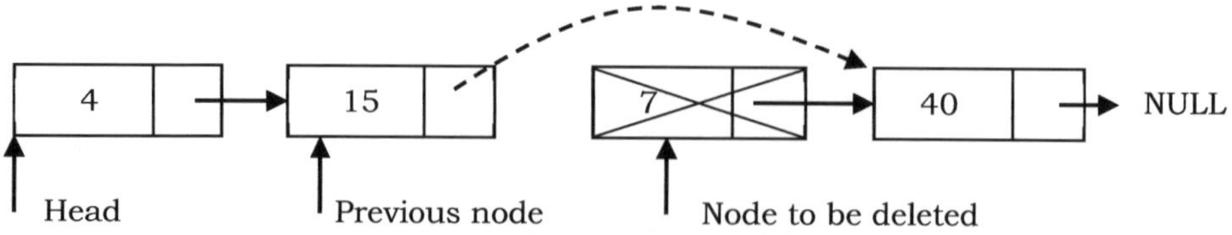


```
void DeleteNodeFromLinkedList (struct ListNode **head, int position) {
   int k = 1;
   struct ListNode *p, *q;
   if(*head == NULL) {
      printf ("List Empty");
      return;
   }
   p = *head;
   /* from the beginning */
```

```
    if(position == 1) {
        *head = (*head)→next;
        free (p);
        return;
    }
    else {
        //Traverse the list until the position from which we want to delete
        while ((p != NULL) && (k < position )) {
            k++;
            q = p;
            p = p→next;
        }
        if(p == NULL)           /* At the end */
            printf ("Position does not exist.");
        else {                  /* From the middle */
            q→next = p→next;
            free(p);
        }
    }
}
```

Deleting Singly Linked List

This works by storing the current node in some temporary variable and freeing the current node. After freeing the current node go to next node with temporary variable and repeat this process for all nodes.

```
void DeleteLinkedList(struct ListNode **head) {
    struct ListNode *auxilaryNode, *iterator;
    iterator = *head;
    while (iterator) {
        auxilaryNode = iterator→next;
        free(iterator);
        iterator = auxilaryNode;
    }
    *head = NULL;           // to affect the real head back in the caller.
}
```

13.7 Doubly Linked Lists

The *advantage* of a doubly linked list (also called *two – way linked list*) is that given a node in the list, we can navigate in both directions. A node in a singly linked list cannot be removed unless we have the pointer to its predecessor.

But in doubly linked list we can delete a node even if we don't have previous nodes address (since, each node has left pointer pointing to previous node and can move backward). The primary *disadvantages* of doubly linked lists are:

- Each node requires an extra pointer, requiring more space.
- The insertion or deletion of a node takes a bit longer (more pointer operations).

As similar to singly linked list, let us implement the operations of doubly linked lists. If you understand the singly linked list operations then doubly linked list operations are very obvious.

Following is a type declaration for a doubly linked list of integers:

```
struct DLLNode {
```

```
    int data;
    struct DLLNode *next;
    struct DLLNode *prev;
};
```

Doubly Linked List Insertion

Insertion into a doubly-linked list has three cases (same as singly linked list):

- Inserting a new node before the head.
- Inserting a new node after the tail (at the end of the list).
- Inserting a new node at the middle of the list.

Inserting a Node in Doubly Linked List at the Beginning

In this case, new node is inserted before the head node. Previous and next pointers need to be modified and it can be done in two steps:

- Update the right pointer of new node to point to the current head node (dotted link in below figure) and also make left pointer of new node as NULL.

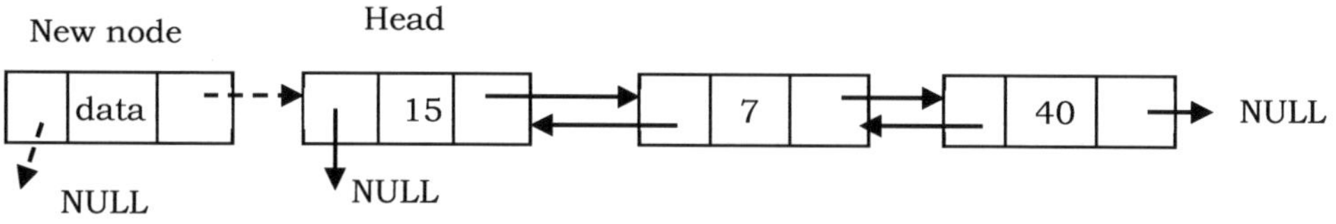

- Update head nodes left pointer to point to the new node and make new node as head.

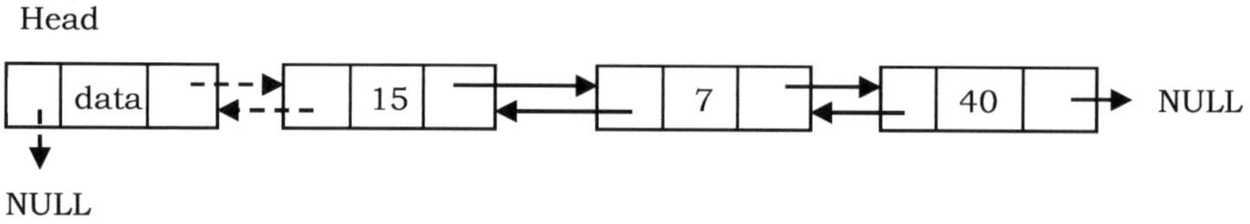

Inserting a Node in Doubly Linked List at the Ending

In this case, traverse the list till the end and insert the new node.

- New node right pointer points to NULL and left pointer points to the end of the list.

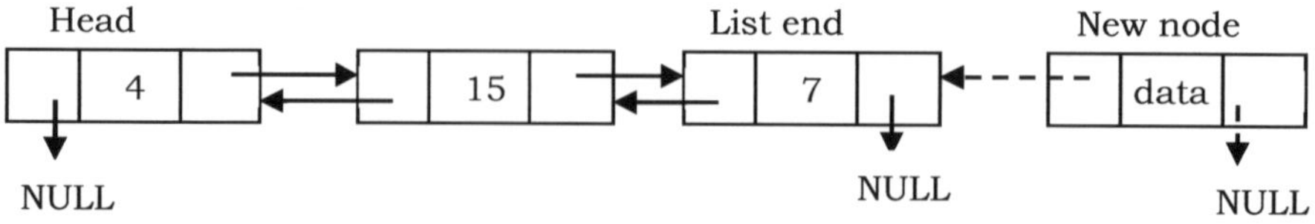

- Update right of pointer of last node to point to new node.

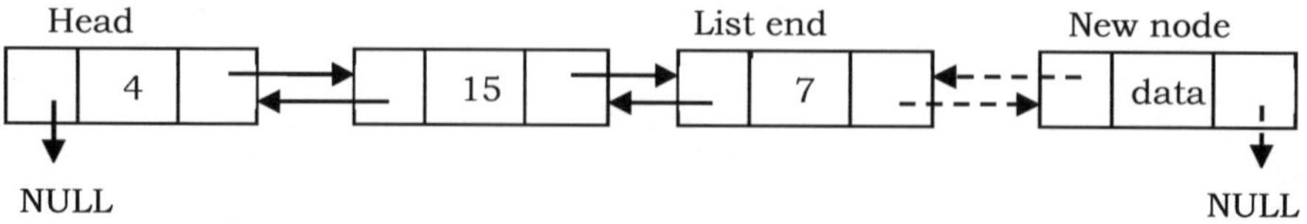

Inserting a Node in Doubly Linked List at the Middle

As discussed in singly linked lists, traverse the list till the position node and insert the new node.

- *New node* right pointer points to the next node of the *position node* where we want to insert the new node. Also, *new node* left pointer points to the *position node.*

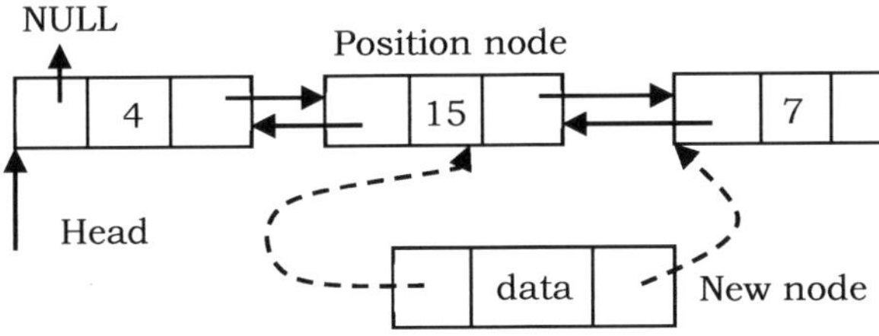

- Position node right pointer points to the new node and the *next node* of position nodes left pointer points to new node.

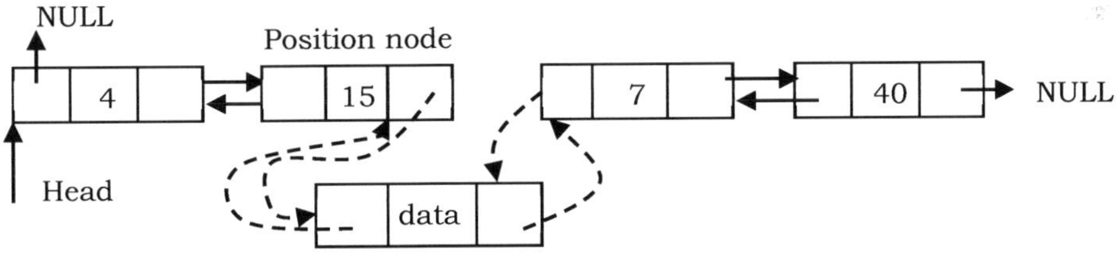

Now, let us write the code for all these three cases. We must update the first element pointer in the calling function, not just in the called function. For this reason we need to send double pointer. The following code inserts a node in the doubly linked list.

```
void DLLInsert(struct DLLNode **head, int data, int position) {
    int k = 1;
    struct DLLNode *temp, *newNode;
    newNode = (struct DLLNode *) malloc(sizeof ( struct DLLNode ));
    if(!newNode) {                  //Always check for memory errors
        printf ("Memory Error");
        return;
    }
    newNode→data = data;
    if(position == 1) {             //Inserting a node at the beginning
        newNode→next = *head;
        newNode→prev = NULL;

        if(*head)
            (*head)→prev = newNode;

        *head = newNode;
        return;
    }
    temp = *head;
    while ( (k < position - 1) && temp→next!=NULL) {
        temp = temp→next;
        k++;
    }
    if(k!=position){
```

```
    printf("Desired position does not exist\n");
  }
  newNode→next=temp→next;
  newNode→prev=temp;
  if(temp→next)
    temp→next→prev=newNode;
  temp→next=newNode;
  return;
}
```

Doubly Linked List Deletion

As similar to singly linked list deletion, here also we have three cases:

- Deleting the first node
- Deleting the last node
- Deleting an intermediate node

Deleting the First Node in Doubly Linked List

In this case, first node (current head node) is removed from the list. It can be done in two steps:

- Create a temporary node which will point to same node as that of head.

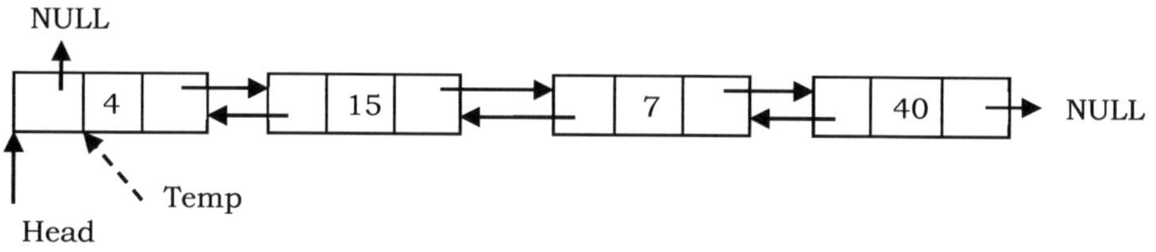

- Now, move the head nodes pointer to the next node and change the heads left pointer to NULL. Then, dispose the temporary node.

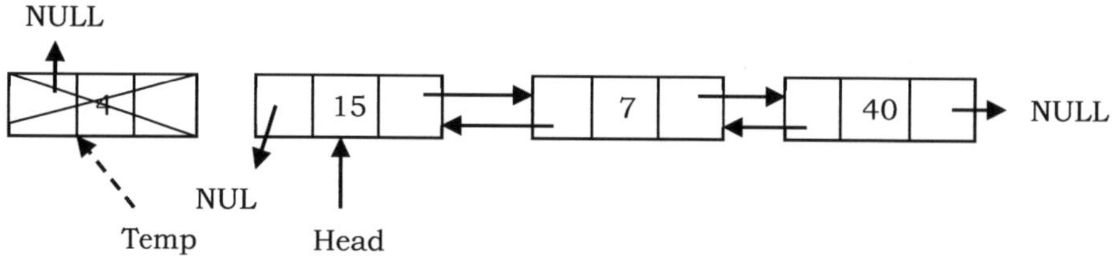

Deleting the Last Node in Doubly Linked List

This operation is a bit trickier, than removing the first node, because algorithm should find a node, which is previous to the tail first. This can be done in three steps:

- Traverse the list and while traversing maintain the previous node address also. By the time we reach the end of list, we will have two pointers one pointing to the tail and other pointing to the node before tail node.

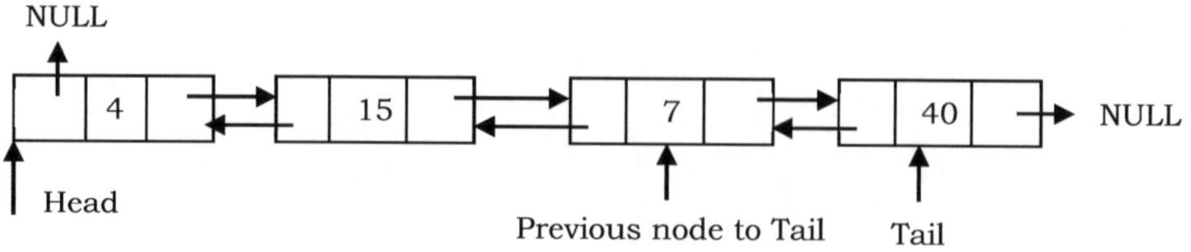

- Update tail nodes previous nodes next pointer with NULL.

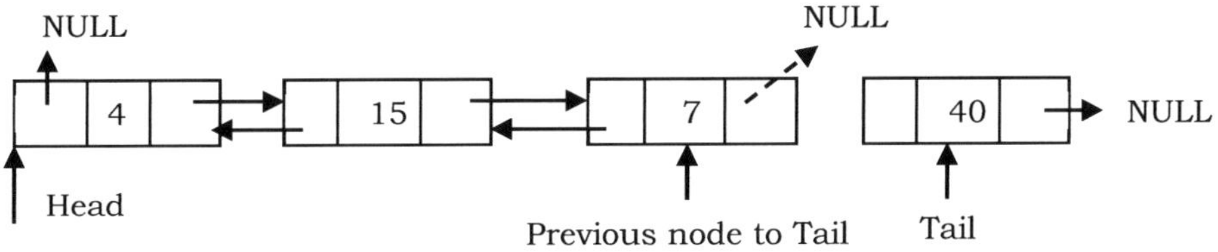

- Dispose the tail node.

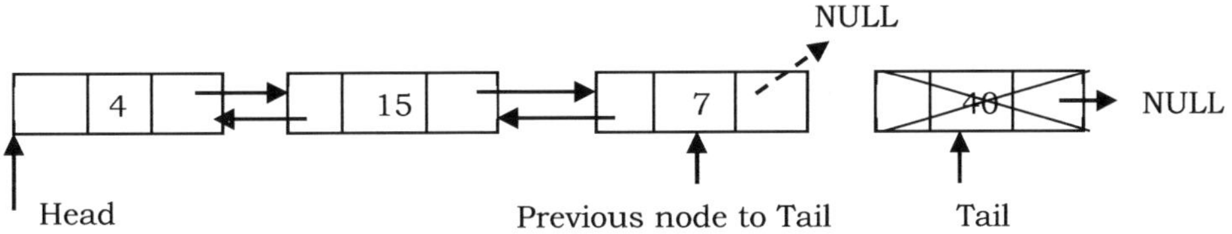

Deleting an Intermediate Node in Doubly Linked List

In this case, node to be removed is *always located between* two nodes. Head and tail links are not updated in this case. Such a removal can be done in two steps:

- Similar to previous case, maintain previous node also while traversing the list. Once we found the node to be deleted, change the previous nodes next pointer to the next node of the node to be deleted.

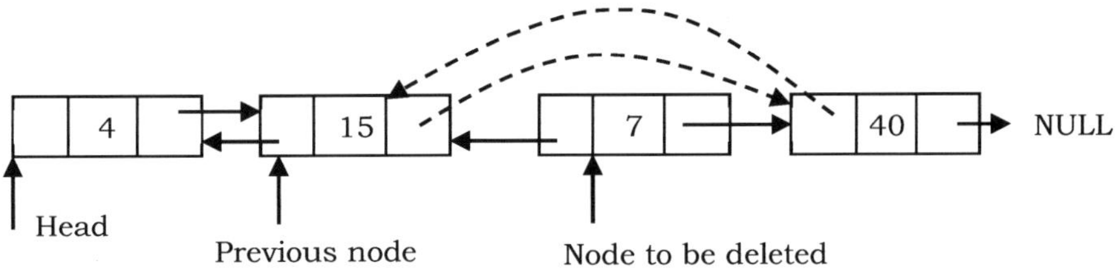

- Dispose the current node to be deleted.

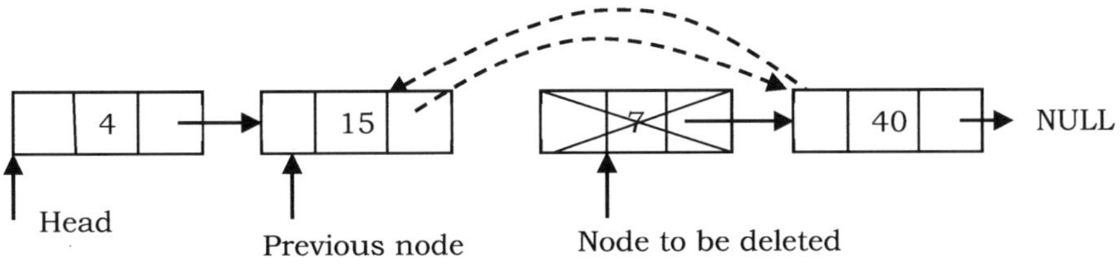


```
void DLLDelete(struct DLLNode **head, int position) {
    struct DLLNode *temp, *temp2, temp = *head;
    int k = 1;
    if(*head == NULL) {
        printf("List is empty");
        return;
    }
    if(position == 1) {
        *head = (*head)→next;
    if(*head != NULL)
        (*head)→prev = NULL;
        free(temp);
        return;
    }
    while((k < position) && temp→next!=NULL) {
```

```
        temp = temp→next;
        k++;
    }
    if(k!=position-1){
        printf("Desired position does not exist\n");
    }
    temp2=temp→prev;
    temp2→next=temp→next;
    if(temp→next) // Deletion from Intermediate Node
        temp→next→prev=temp2;
    free(temp);
    return;
}
```

13.8 Circular Linked Lists

In singly linked lists and doubly linked lists the end of lists are indicated with NULL value. But circular linked lists do not have ends. While traversing the circular linked lists we should be careful otherwise we will be traversing the list infinitely. In circular linked lists each node has a successor. Note that unlike singly linked lists, there is no node with NULL pointer in a circularly linked list. In some situations, circular linked lists are useful.

For example, when several processes are using the same computer resource (CPU) for the same amount of time, we have to assure that no process accesses the resource before all other processes did (round robin algorithm). The following is a type declaration for a circular linked list of integers:

```
typedef struct CLLNode {
    int data;
    struct ListNode *next;
};
```

In circular linked list we access the elements using the *head* node (similar to *head* node in singly linked list and doubly linked lists).

Counting Nodes in a Circular List

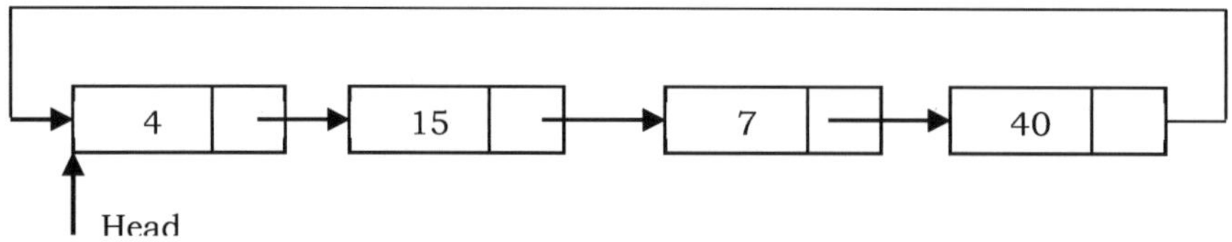

The circular list is accessible through the node marked *head*. To count the nodes, the list has to be traversed from node marked *head*, with the help of a dummy node *current* and stop the counting when *current* reaches the starting node *head*.

If the list is empty, *head* will be NULL, and in that case set *count* = 0. Otherwise, set the current pointer to the first node, and keep on counting till the current pointer reaches the starting node.

```
int CircularListLength(struct CLLNode *head) {
    struct CLLNode *current = head;
    int count = 0;
    if(head == NULL)
        return 0;
    do {
        current = current→next;
```

```
        count++;
    } while (current != head);
    return count;
}
```

Printing the contents of a Circular List

We assume here that the list is being accessed by its *head* node. Since all the nodes are arranged in a circular fashion, the *tail* node of the list will be the node previous to the *head* node. Let us assume we want to print the contents of the nodes starting with the *head* node. Print its contents, move to the next node and continue printing till we reach the *head* node again.

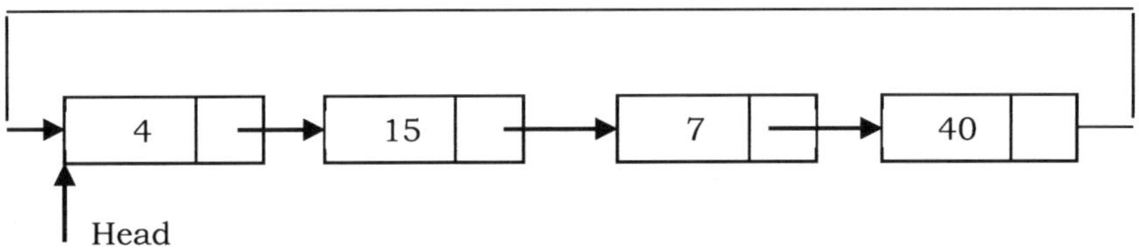


```
void PrintCircularListData(struct CLLNode *head) {
    struct CLLNode *current = head;
    if(head == NULL)
        return;
    do {
        printf ("%d", current→data);
        current = current→next;
    } while (current != head);
}
```

Inserting a node at the end of a Circular Linked List

Let us add a node containing *data*, at the end of a list (circular list) headed by *head*. The new node will be placed just after the tail node (which is the last node of the list), which means it will have to be inserted in between the tail node and the first node.

- Create a new node and initially keep its next pointer points to itself.

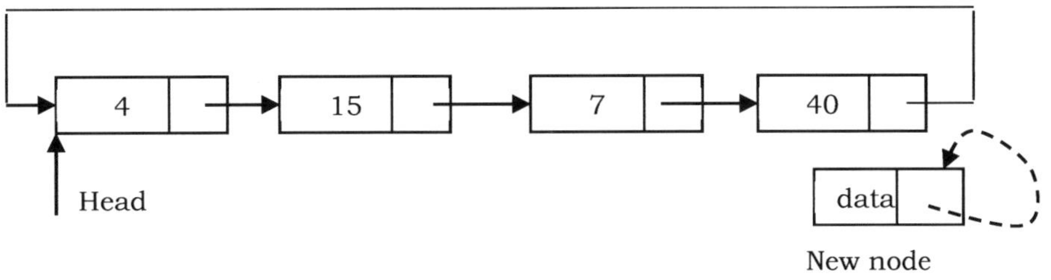

- Update the next pointer of new node with head node and also traverse the list until the tail. That means in circular list we should stop at a node whose next node is head.

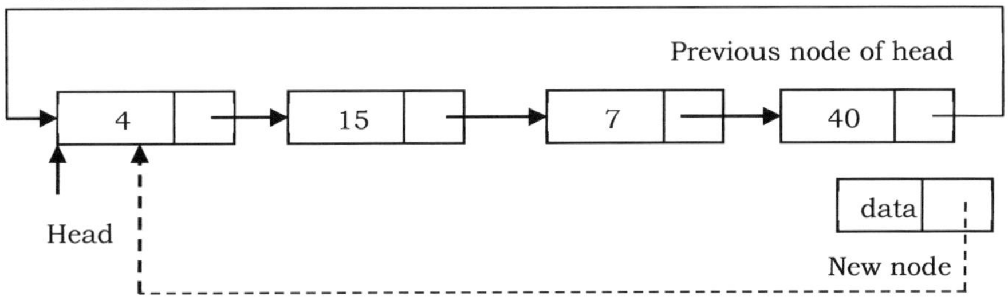

- Update the next pointer of previous node to point to new node and we get the list as shown below.

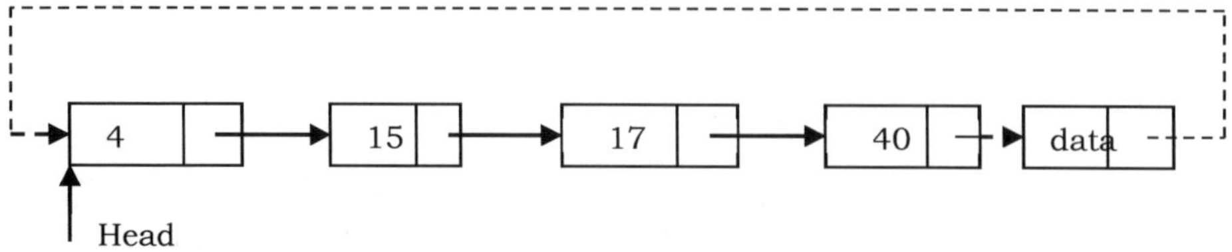


```
void InsertAtEndInCLL (struct CLLNode **head, int data) {
    struct CLLNode *current = *head;
    struct CLLNode *newNode = (struct CLLNode *) (malloc(sizeof(struct CLLNode)));
    if(!newNode) {
        printf("Memory Error");
        return;
    }
    newNode→data = data;
    while (current→next != *head)
        current = current→next;
    newNode→next = newNode;
    if(*head ==NULL)
        *head = newNode;
    else {
        newNode→next = *head;
        current→next = newNode;
    }
}
```

Inserting a node at front of a Circular Linked List

The only difference between inserting a node at the beginning and at the ending is that, after inserting the new node we just need to update the pointer. The steps for doing this are given below:

- Create a new node and initially keep its next pointer points to itself.

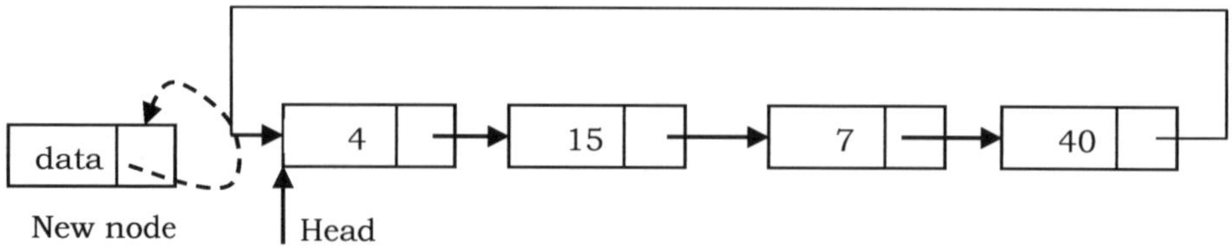

- Update the next pointer of new node with head node and also traverse the list until the tail. That means in circular list we should stop at the node which is its previous node in the list.

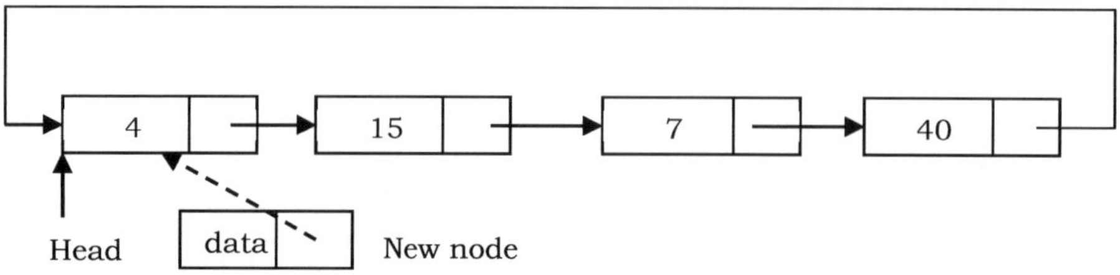

- Update the previous node of head in the list to point to new node.

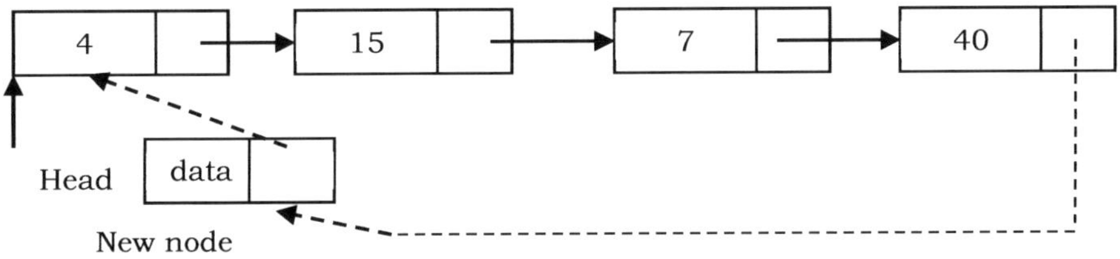

- Make new node as head.

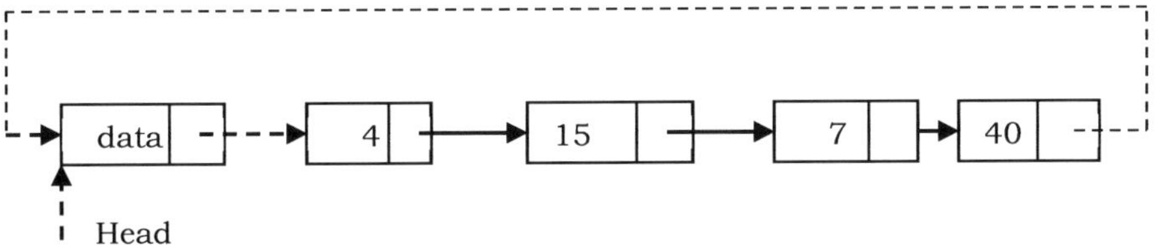


```
void InsertAtBeginInCLL (struct CLLNode **head, int data) {
  struct CLLNode *current = *head;
  struct CLLNode * newNode = (struct CLLNode *) (malloc(sizeof(struct CLLNode)));
  if(!newNode) {
    printf("Memory Error");
    return;
  }
  newNode→data = data;
  while (current→next != *head)
    current = current→next;
  newNode→next = newNode;
  if(*head ==NULL)
    *head = newNode;
  else {
    newNode→next = *head;
    current→next = newNode;
    *head = newNode;
  }
  return;
}
```

Deleting the last node in a Circular List

The list has to be traversed to reach the last but one node. This has to be named as the tail node, and its next field has to point to the first node. Consider the following list.

To delete the last node 40, the list has to be traversed till you reach 7. The next field of 7 has to be changed to point to 60, and this node must be renamed *pTail*.

- Traverse the list and find the tail node and its previous node.

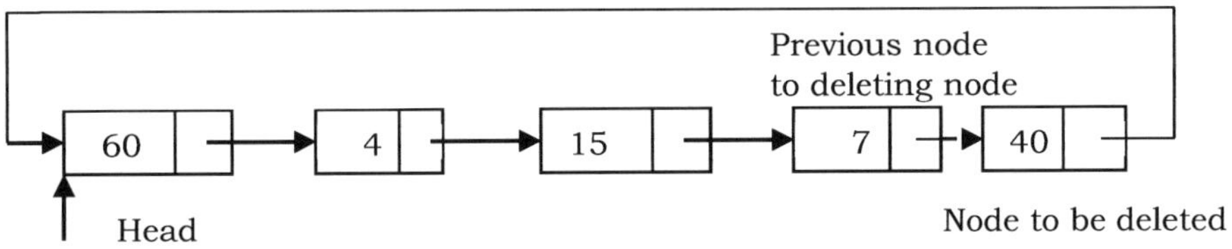

- Update the tail nodes previous node next pointer to point to head.

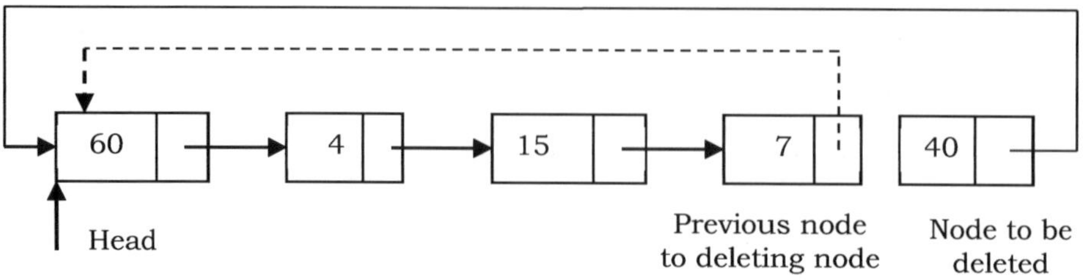

- Dispose the tail node.

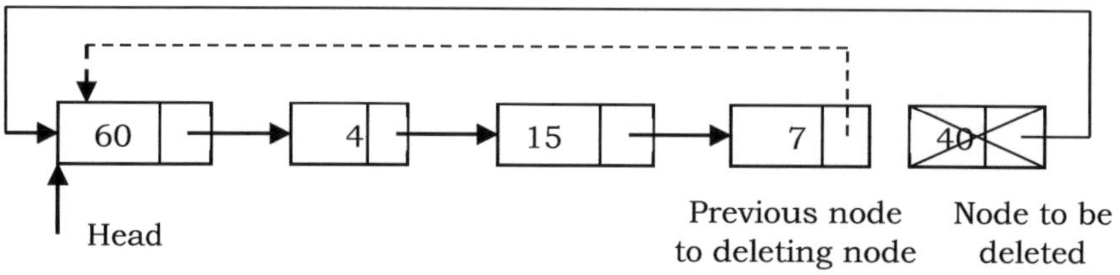


```
void DeleteLastNodeFromCLL (struct CLLNode **head) {
    struct CLLNode *temp = *head, *current = *head;
    if(*head == NULL) {
        printf( "List Empty");
        return;
    }
    while (current→next != *head) {
       temp = current;
       current = current→next;
    }
    temp→next = current→next;
    free(current);
    return;
}
```

Deleting the first node in a Circular List

The first node can be deleted by simply replacing the next field of tail node with the next field of the first node.

- Find the tail node of the linked list by traversing the list. Tail node is the previous node to the head node which we want to delete.

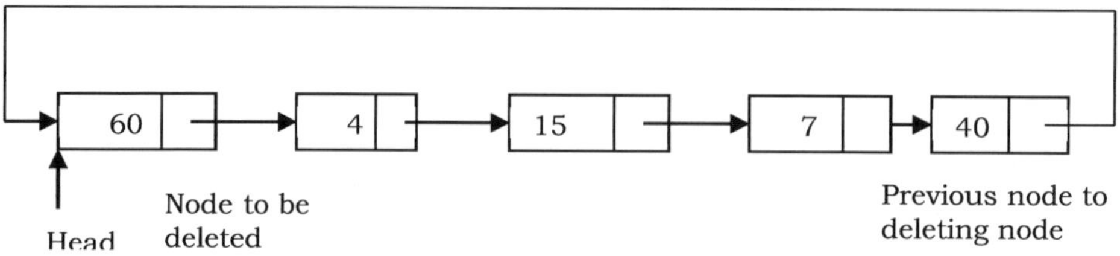

- Create a temporary node which will point to head. Also, update the tail nodes next pointer to point to next node of head (as shown below).

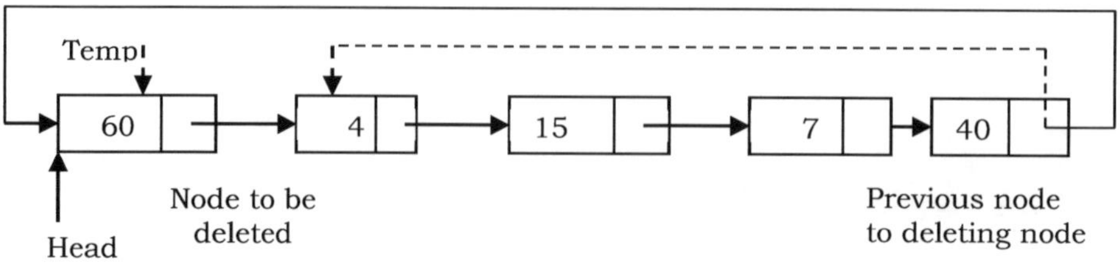

- Now, move the head pointer to next node. Create a temporary node which will point to head. Also, update the tail nodes next pointer to point to next node of head (as shown below).

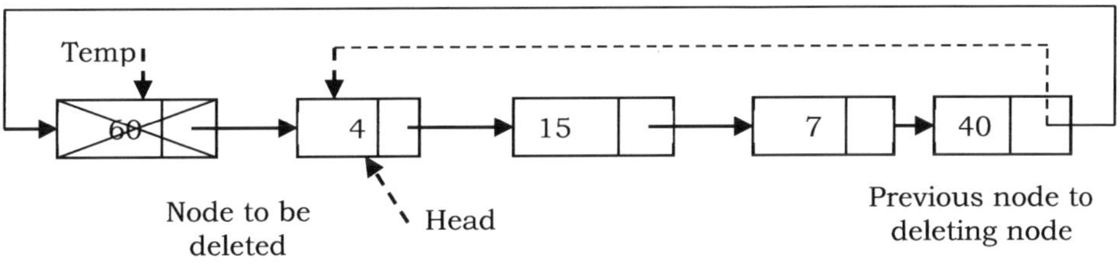


```
void DeleteFrontNodeFromCLL (struct CLLNode **head) {
    struct CLLNode *temp = *head;
    struct CLLNode *current = *head;
    if(*head == NULL) {
        printf("List Empty");
        return;
    }
    while (current→next != *head)
        current = current→next;
    current→ next = *head→next;
    *head = *head→next;
    free(temp);
    return;
}
```

Applications of Circular List

Circular linked lists are used in managing the computing resources of a computer. We can use circular lists for implementing stacks and queues.

13.9 A Memory-Efficient Doubly Linked List

In conventional implementation, we need to keep a forward pointer to the next item on the list and a backward pointer to the previous item. That means, elements in doubly linked list implementations consist of data, a pointer to the next node and a pointer to the previous node in the list as shown below.

Conventional Node Definition

```
typedef struct ListNode {
    int data;
    struct ListNode * prev;
    struct ListNode * next;
};
```

Recently a journal (Sinha) presented an alternative implementation of the doubly linked list ADT, with insertion, traversal and deletion operations. This implementation is based on pointer difference. Each node uses only one pointer field to traverse the list back and forth.

New Node Definition

```
typedef struct ListNode {
    int data;
    struct ListNode * ptrdiff;
};
```

The *ptrdiff* pointer field contains the difference between the pointer to the next node and the pointer to the previous node. The pointer difference is calculated by using exclusive-or (⊕) operation.

$$ptrdiff = pointer\ to\ previous\ node \oplus pointer\ to\ next\ node.$$

The *ptrdiff* of the start node (head node) is the ⊕ of NULL and *next* node (next node to head). Similarly, the *ptrdiff* of end node is the ⊕ of *previous* node (previous to end node) and NULL. As an example, consider the following linked list.

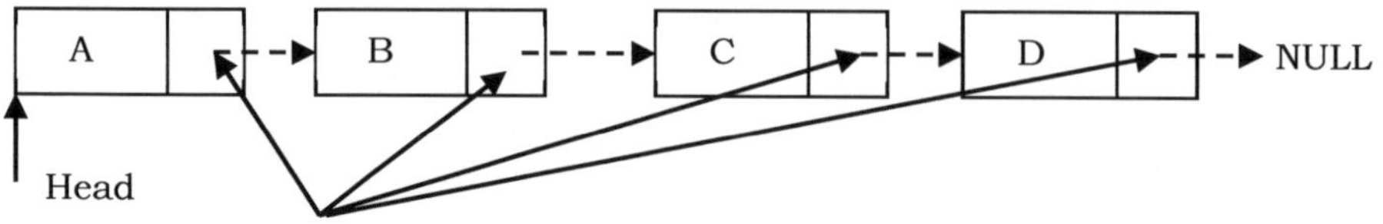

In the example above,

- The next pointer of A is: NULL ⊕ *B*
- The next pointer of B is: A ⊕ *C*
- The next pointer of C is: B ⊕ *D*
- The next pointer of D is: C ⊕ *NULL*

Why does it work?

To have answer for this question let us consider the properties of ⊕:

$X \oplus X = 0$
$X \oplus 0 = X$
$X \oplus Y = Y \oplus X$ (symmetric)
$(X \oplus Y) \oplus Z = X \oplus (Y \oplus Z)$ (transitive)

For the example above, let us assume that we are at C node and want to move to B. We know that Cs *ptrdiff* is defined as B ⊕ *D. If we want to move to B, performing ⊕ on Cs* *ptrdiff* with D would give B. This is due to fact that,

$$(B \oplus D) \oplus D = B \text{ (since, } D \oplus D=0)$$

Similarly, if we want to move to D, then we have to apply ⊕ *to Cs ptrdiff* with B would give D.

$$(B \oplus D) \oplus B = D \text{ (since, } B \oplus B=0)$$

From the above discussion we can see that just by using single pointer, we can move back and forth. A memory-efficient implementation of a doubly linked list is possible without compromising much timing efficiency.

Problems and Questions with Answers

Question 1: Implement Stack using Linked List.

Answer: Refer *Stacks* chapter.

Question 2: Find n^{th} node from the end of a Linked List.

Answer: *Brute – Force Method*: Start with the first node and count the number of nodes present after that node. If the number of nodes are $< n-1$ then return saying "fewer number of nodes in the list". If the number of nodes are $> n-1$ then go to next node. Continue this until the numbers of nodes after current node are $n-1$.

Question 3: Can we improve the complexity of Question-2?

Answer: **Yes**, using hash table. As an example consider the following list.

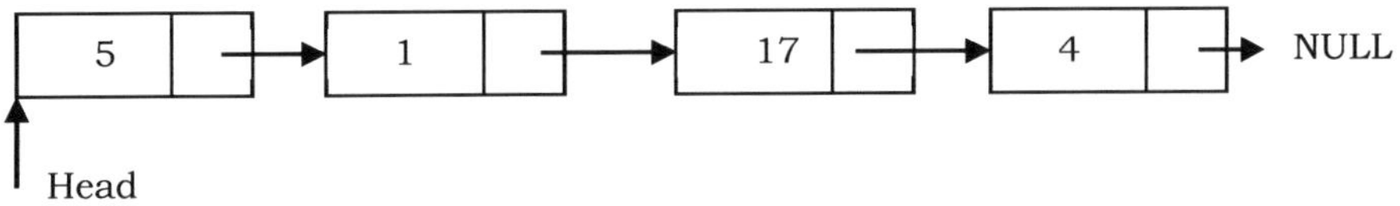

In this approach, create a hash table whose entries are $<$ *position of node, node address* $>$. That means, key is the position of the node in the list and value is the address of that node.

Position in List	Address of Node
1	Address of 5 node
2	Address of 1 node
3	Address of 17 node
4	Address of 4 node

By the time we traverse the complete list (for creating hash table), we can find the list length. Let us say, the list length is M. To find n^{th} from end of linked list, we can convert this to $M\text{-}n+1^{th}$ from the beginning. Since we already know the length of the list, it is just a matter of returning $M\text{-}n+1^{th}$ key value from the hash table.

Time Complexity: Time for creating the hash table, $T(m) = O(m)$.
Space Complexity: Since we need to create a hash table of size m, $O(m)$.

Question 4: Can we use Question 3: approach for solving Question-2 without creating the hash table?

Answer: Yes. If we observe the Question 3: solution, what actually we are doing is finding the size of the linked list. That means, we are using hash table to find the size of the linked list. We can find the length of the linked list just by starting at the head node and traversing the list. So, we can find the length of the list without creating the hash table. After finding the length, compute $M - n + 1$ and with one more scan we can get the $M - n + 1^{th}$ node from the beginning. This solution needs two scans: one for finding the length of list and other for finding $M - n + 1^{th}$ node from the beginning.

Time Complexity: Time for finding the length + Time for finding the $M\text{-}n+1^{th}$ node from the beginning. Therefore, $T(n = O(n) + O(n) \approx O(n)$.
Space Complexity: O(1). Since, no need of creating the hash table.

Question 5: Can we solve Question-2 in one scan?

Answer: Yes. *Efficient Approach*: Use two pointers *pNthNode* and *pTemp*. Initially, both points to head node of the list. *pNthNode* starts moving only after *pTemp* made n moves.

From there both moves forward until *pTemp* reaches end of the list. As a result *pNthNode* points to n^{th} node from end of the linked list.

Note: at any point of time both moves one node at time.

```
struct ListNode *NthNodeFromEnd(struct ListNode *head, int NthNode){
    struct ListNode *pNthNode = NULL, *pTemp = head;
    for(int count =1; count< NthNode;count++) {
        if(pTemp)
            pTemp = pTemp→next;
    }
    while(pTemp) {
        if(pNthNode == NULL)
            pNthNode = head;
        else
            pNthNode = pNthNode→next;
        pTemp = pTemp→next;
```

```
    }
    if(pNthNode)
        return pNthNode;
    return NULL;
}
```

Time Complexity: O(n). Space Complexity: O(1).

Question 6: Check whether the given linked list is either NULL-terminated or ends in a cycle (cyclic).

Answer: *Brute – Force Approach*: As an example consider the following linked list which has a loop in it. The difference between this list and the regular list is that, in this list there are two nodes whose next pointers are same. In regular singly linked lists (without loop) each nodes next pointer is unique. That means, the repetition of next pointers indicates the existence of loop.

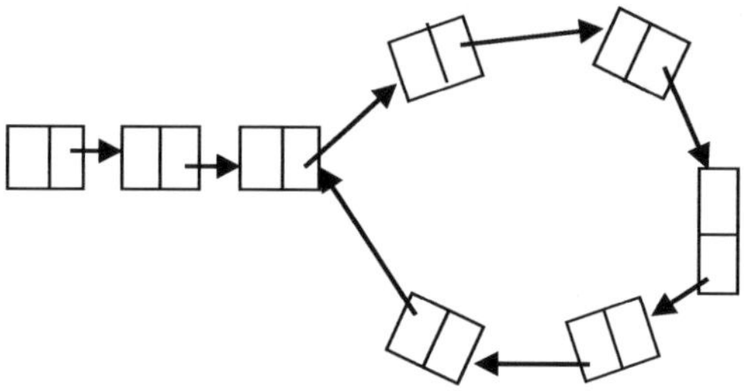

One simple and brute force way of solving this is, start with the first node and see whether there is any node whose next pointer is current node's address. If there is a node with same address then that indicates that some other node is pointing to the current node and we can say loops exists. Continue this process for all the nodes of the linked list.

Does this method works? As per the algorithm we are checking for the next pointer addresses, but how do we find the end of the linked list (otherwise we will end up in infinite loop)?

Note: If we start with a node in loop, this method may work depending on the size of the loop.

Question 7: Can we use hashing technique for solving Question-6?

Answer: Yes. Using Hash Tables we can solve this problem.

Algorithm:

- Traverse the linked list nodes one by one.
- Check if the address of the node is available in the hash table or not.
- If it is already available in the hash table then that indicates that we are visiting the node that was already visited. This is possible only if the given linked list has a loop in it.
- If the address of the node is not available in the hash table then insert that nodes address into the hash table.
- Continue this process until we reach end of the linked list *or* we find loop.

Time Complexity*:* O(n) for scanning the linked list. Note that we are doing only scan of the input.
Space Complexity*:* O(n) for hash table.

Question 8: Can we solve the Question-6 using sorting technique?

Answer: No. Consider the following algorithm which is based on sorting. And then, we see why this algorithm fails.

Algorithm:

- Traverse the linked list nodes one by one and take all the next pointer values into some array.
- Sort the array that has next node pointers.
- If there is a loop in the linked list, definitely two nodes next pointers will pointing to the same node.
- After sorting if there is a loop in the list, the nodes whose next pointers are same will come adjacent in the sorted list.
- If any such pair exists in the sorted list then we say the linked list has loop in it.

Time Complexity*:* $O(nlogn)$ for sorting the next pointers array.
Space Complexity*:* $O(n)$ for the next pointers array.

Problem with above algorithm: The above algorithm works only if we can find the length of the list. But if the list is having loop then we may end up in infinite loop. Due to this reason the algorithm fails.

Question 9: Can we solve the Question-6 in $O(n)$?

Answer: Yes. *Efficient Approach* (*Memory less Approach*): This problem was solved by *Floyd*. The solution is named as Floyd cycle finding algorithm. It uses 2 pointers moving at different speeds to walk the linked list. Once they enter the loop they are expected to meet, which denotes that there is a loop.

This works because the only way a faster moving pointer would point to the same location as a slower moving pointer is, if somehow the entire list or a part of it is circular. Think of a tortoise and a hare running on a track. The faster running hare will catch up with the tortoise if they are running in a loop.

As an example, consider the following example and trace out the Floyd algorithm. From the diagrams below we can see that after the final step they are meeting at some point in the loop which may not be the starting of the loop.

Note: *slowPtr* (*tortoise*) moves one pointer at a time and *fastPtr* (*hare*) moves two pointers at a time.

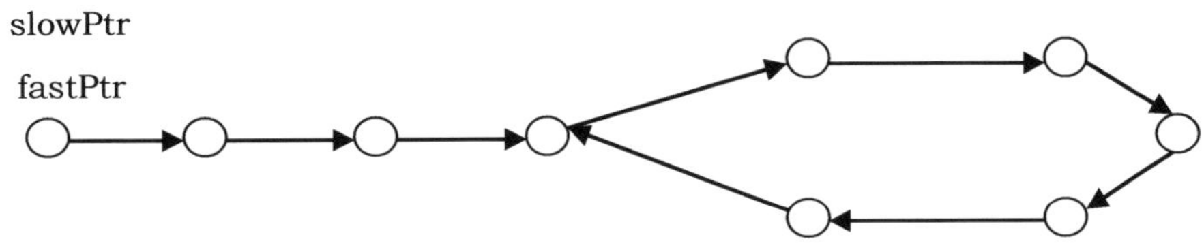

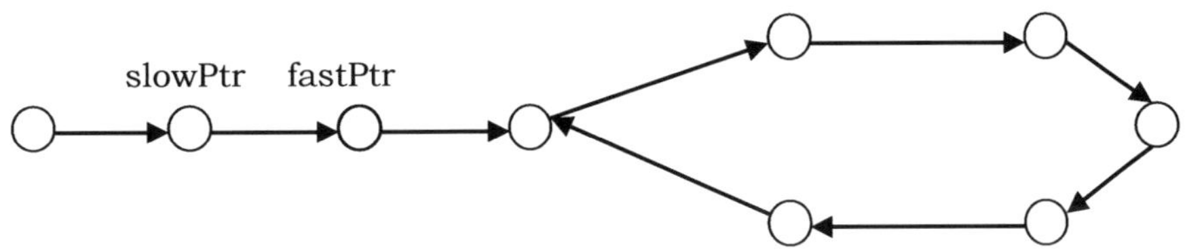

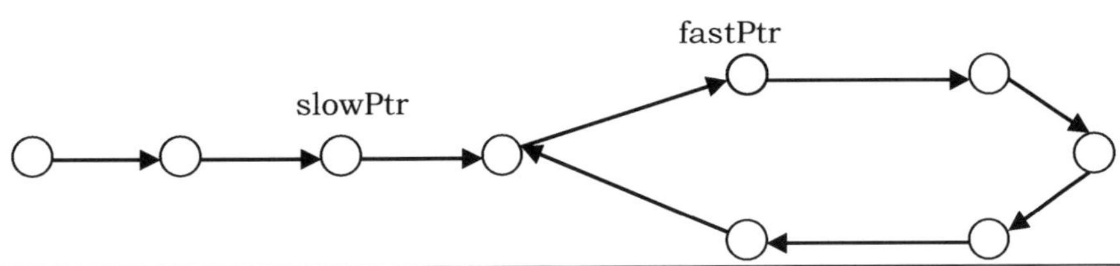

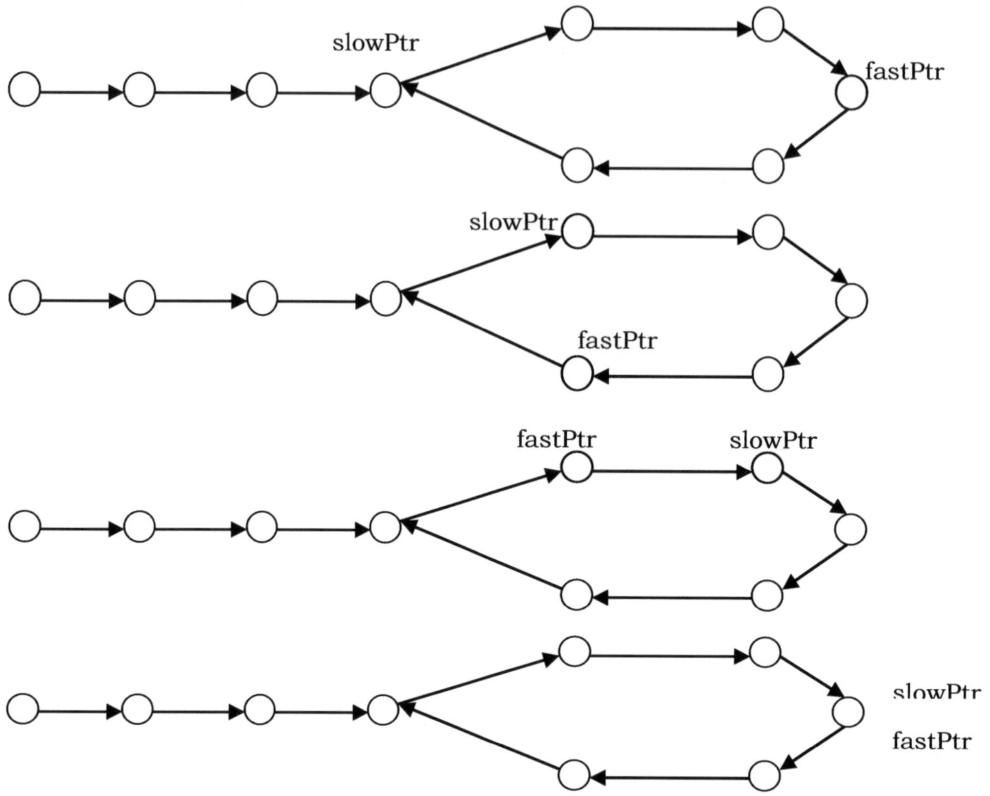


```
int IsLinkedListContainsLoop(struct ListNode * head) {
    struct ListNode *slowPtr = head, *fastPtr = head;
    while(slowPtr && fastPtr) {
        fastPtr = fastPtr→next;
        if(fastPtr == slowPtr)
            return 1;
        if(fastPtr == NULL)
            return 0;
                else fastPtr = fastPtr→next;
        if(fastPtr == slowPtr)
            return 1;
        slowPtr = slowPtr→next;
    }
    return 0;
}
```

Time Complexity: $O(n)$. Space Complexity: O(1).

Question 10: We are given a pointer to the first element of a linked list L. There are two possibilities for L, it either ends (snake) or its last element points back to one of the earlier elements in the list (snail). Give an algorithm that tests whether a given list L is a snake or a snail.

Answer: It is same as Question-6.

Question 11: Check whether the given linked list is either NULL-terminated or not. If there is a cycle find the start node of the loop.

Answer: The solution is an extension to the previous solution (Question-9). After finding the loop in the linked list, we initialize the *slowPtr* to head of the linked list. From that point onwards both *slowPtr* and *fastPtr* moves only one node at a time. The point at which they meet is the start of the loop. Generally we use this method for removing the loops.

```
int FindBeginofLoop(struct ListNode * head) {
    struct ListNode *slowPtr = head, *fastPtr = head;
    int loopExists = 0;
    while(slowPtr && fastPtr) {
        fastPtr = fastPtr→next;
        if(fastPtr == slowPtr) {
            loopExists = 1;
            break;
        }
       if(fastPtr == NULL)
           loopExists = 0;
      else fastPtr = fastPtr→next;
        if(fastPtr == slowPtr) {
            loopExists = 1;
            break;
        }
        slowPtr = slowPtr→next;
    }
    if(loopExists) {
        slowPtr = head;
        while(slowPtr != fastPtr) {
            fastPtr = fastPtr→next;
            slowPtr = slowPtr→next;
        }
        return slowPtr;
    }
    return NULL;
}
```

Time Complexity: $O(n)$. Space Complexity: $O(1)$.

Question 12: From the previous discussion and problems we understand that the meeting of tortoise and hare meeting concludes the existence of loop, but how does moving tortoise to beginning of linked list while keeping the hare at meeting place, followed by moving both one step at a time make them meet at starting point of cycle?

Answer: This problem is the heart of number theory. In Floyd cycle finding algorithm, notice that the tortoise and the hare will meet when they are $n \times L$, where L is the loop length. Furthermore, the tortoise is at the midpoint between the hare and the beginning of the sequence, because of the way they move. Therefore the tortoise is $n \times L$ away from the beginning of the sequence as well.

If we move both one step at a time, from the position of tortoise and from the start of the sequence, we know that they will meet as soon as both are in the loop, since they are $n \times L$, a multiple of the loop length, apart. One of them is already in the loop, so we just move the other one in single step until it enters the loop, keeping the other $n \times L$ away from it at all times.

Question 13: In Floyd cycle finding algorithm, does it work if we use the steps 2 and 3 instead of 1 and 2?

Answer: Yes, but the complexity might be high. Trace out some example.

Question 14: Check whether the given linked list is NULL-terminated. If there is a cycle find the length of the loop.

Answer: This solution is also an extension to the basic cycle detection problem. After finding the loop in the linked list, keep the *slowPtr* as it is. *fastPtr* keeps on moving until it again comes back to *slowPtr*. While moving *fastPtr*, use a counter variable which increments at the rate of 1.

```
int FindLoopLength(struct ListNode * head) {
    struct ListNode *slowPtr = head, *fastPtr = head;
    int loopExists = 0, counter = 0;
    while(slowPtr && fastPtr) {
        fastPtr = fastPtr→next;
        if(fastPtr == slowPtr)  {
            loopExists = 1;
            break;
        }
        if(fastPtr == NULL)  loopExists = 0;
        else fastPtr = fastPtr→next;
        if(fastPtr == slowPtr) {
            loopExists = 1;
            break;
        }
        slowPtr = slowPtr→next;
    }
    if(loopExists) {
        fastPtr = fastPtr→next;
        while(slowPtr  != fastPtr) {
        fastPtr = fastPtr→next;
        counter++;
    }
    return counter;
    }
    return 0;               //If no loops exists
}
```

Time Complexity: $O(n)$. Space Complexity: $O(1)$.

Question 15: Insert a node in a sorted linked list

Answer: Traverse the list and find a position for the element and insert it.

```
struct ListNode *InsertInSortedList(struct ListNode * head,
                                                        struct ListNode * newNode) {
    struct ListNode *current = head, temp;
    if(!head)
        return newNode;
    // traverse the list until you find item bigger the new node value
    while (current != NULL && current→data <  newNode→data){
        temp = current;
        current = current→next;
    }
    //insert the new node before the big item
    newNode→next = current;
    temp→next = newNode;
    return head;
}
```

Time Complexity: $O(n)$. Space Complexity: $O(1)$.

Question 16: Reverse a singly linked list

Answer:

```
// Iterative version
struct ListNode *ReverseList(struct ListNode *head) {
    struct ListNode *temp = NULL, *nextNode = NULL;
  while (head) {
    nextNode = head→next;
    head→next = temp;
    temp = head;
    head = nextNode;
  }
  return temp;
}
```

Time Complexity: O(n). Space Complexity: O(1).

Recursive version: We can find it easier to start from the bottom up, by asking and answering tiny questions (this is the approach in The Little Lisper):

- What is the reverse of NULL (the empty list)? NULL.
- What is the reverse of a one element list? The element itself.
- What is the reverse of an n element list? The reverse of the second element on followed by the first element.

```
struct ListNode * RecursiveReverse(struct ListNode *head) {
   if (head == NULL)
            return NULL;
   if (head→next == NULL)
            return list;
   struct ListNode *secondElem = head→next;
   // Need to unlink list from the rest or you will get a cycle
   head→next = NULL;
  // reverse everything from the second element on
   struct ListNode *reverseRest = RecursiveReverse(secondElem);
   secondElem→next = head;          // then we join the two lists
   return reverseRest;
}
```

Time Complexity: O(n). Space Complexity: O(n), for recursive stack.

Question 17: Suppose there are two singly linked lists both of which intersect at some point and become a single linked list. The head or start pointers of both the lists are known, but the intersecting node is not known. Also, the number of nodes in each of the list before they intersect are unknown and both list may have it different. $List1$ may have n nodes before it reaches intersection point and $List2$ might have m nodes before it reaches intersection point where m and n may be $m = n, m < n$ or $m > n$. Give an algorithm for finding the merging point.

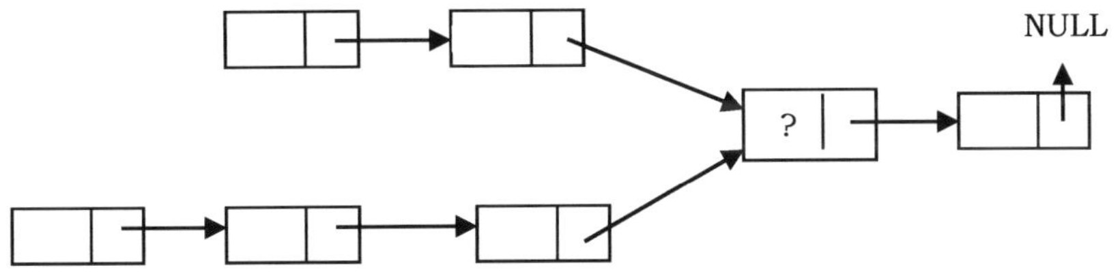

Answer: *Brute – Force Approach*: One easy solution is to compare every node pointer in the first list with every other node pointer in the second list by which the matching node pointers will lead us to the intersecting node. But, the time complexity in this case will $O(mn)$ which will be high.

Time Complexity: $O(mn)$. Space Complexity: $O(1)$.

Question 18: Can we solve Question-17 using sorting technique?

Answer: No. Consider the following algorithm which is based on sorting and see why this algorithm fails.

Algorithm:

- Take first list node pointers and keep in some array and sort them.
- Take second list node pointers and keep in some array and sort them.
- After sorting, use two indexes: one for first sorted array and other for second sorted array.
- Start comparing values at the indexes and increment the index whichever has lower value (increment only if the values are not equal).
- At any point, if we were able to find two indexes whose values are same then that indicates that those two nodes are pointing to the same node and we return that node.

Time Complexity: Time for sorting lists + Time for scanning (for comparing)
$= O(mlogm) + O(nlogn) + O(m + n)$.
We need to consider the one that gives the maximum value.

Space Complexity: $O(1)$.

Any problem with the above algorithm? Yes. In the algorithm, we are storing all the node pointers of both the lists and sorting. But we are forgetting the fact that, there can be many repeated elements. This is because after the merging point all node pointers are same for both the lists. The algorithm works fine only in one case and it is when both lists have ending node at their merge point.

Question 19: Can we solve Question-17 using hash tables?

Answer: Yes.

Algorithm:

- Select a list which has less number of nodes (If we do not know the lengths beforehand then select one list randomly).
- Now, traverse the other list and for each node pointer of this list check whether the same node pointer exists in the hash table.
- If there is a merge point for the given lists then we will definitely encounter the node pointer in the hash table.

Time Complexity: Time for creating the hash table + Time for scanning the second list = $O(m) + O(n)$ (or $O(n) + O(m)$, depends on which list we select for creating the hash table). But in both cases the time complexity is same.
Space Complexity: $O(n)$ or $O(m)$.

Question 20: Can we use stacks for solving the Question-17?

Answer: Yes.

Algorithm:

- Create two stacks: one for the first list and one for the second list.
- Traverse the first list and push all the node address on to the first stack.
- Traverse the second list and push all the node address on to the second stack.
- Now both stacks contain the node address of the corresponding lists.
- Now, compare the top node address of both stacks.
- If they are same, then pop the top elements from both the stacks and keep in some temporary variable (since both node addresses are node, it is enough if we use one temporary variable).

- Continue this process until top node addresses of the stacks are not same.
- This point is the one where the lists merge into single list.
- Return the value of the temporary variable.

Time Complexity: $O(m + n)$, for scanning both the lists.
Space Complexity: $O(m + n)$, for creating two stacks for both the lists.

Question 21: Is there any other way of solving the Question-17?

Answer: Yes. Using "finding the first repeating number" approach in an array (for algorithm refer *Searching* chapter).

Algorithm:

- Create an array A and keep all the next pointers of both the lists in the array.
- In the array find the first repeating element in the array [Refer *Searching* chapter for algorithm].
- The first repeating number indicates the merging point of the both lists.

Time Complexity: $O(m + n)$. Space Complexity: $O(m + n)$.

Question 22: Can we still think of finding an alternative solution for the Question-17?

Answer: **Yes**. By combining sorting and search techniques we can reduce the complexity.

Algorithm:

- Create an array A and keep all the next pointers of the first list in the array.
- Sort these array elements.
- Then, for each of the second list element, search in the sorted array (let us assume that we are using binary search which gives $O(logn)$).
- Since we are scanning the second list one by one, the first repeating element that appears in the array is nothing but the merging point.

Time Complexity: Time for sorting + Time for searching = $O(Max(mlogm, nlogn))$.
Space Complexity: $O(Max(m, n))$.

Question 23: Can we improve the complexity for the Question-17?

Answer: Yes.

Efficient Approach:

- Find lengths (L1 and L2) of both list -- $O(n) + O(m) = O(max(m, n))$.
- Take the difference d of the lengths -- $O(1)$.
- Make d steps in longer list -- $O(d)$.
- Step in both lists in parallel until links to next node match -- $O(min(m, n))$.
- Total time complexity = $O(max(m, n))$.
- Space Complexity = $O(1)$.

```
struct ListNode* FindIntersectingNode(struct ListNode* list1, struct ListNode* list2) {
   int L1=0, L2=0, diff=0;
   struct ListNode *head1 = list1, *head2 = list2;
   while(head1!= NULL) {
      L1++;
      head1 = head1→next;
   }
   while(head2!= NULL) {
      L2++;
      head2 = head2→next;
   }
   if(L1 < L2) {
      head1 = list2;   head2 = list1;   diff = L2 - L1;
```

```
    }else{
        head1 = list1;   head2 = list2;  diff = L1 – L2;
    }
    for(int i = 0; i < diff; i++)
        head1 = head1→next;
    while(head1 !=  NULL && head2 != NULL) {
        if(head1 == head2)
            return head1→data;
        head1= head1→next;
        head2= head2→next;
    }
    return NULL;
}
```

Question 24: How will you find the middle of the linked list?

Answer: Brute-Force Approach: For each of the node count how many nodes are there in the list and see whether it is the middle.

Time Complexity: $O(n^2)$. Space Complexity: O(1).

Question 25: Can we improve the complexity of Question-23?

Answer: Yes.

Algorithm:

- Traverse the list and find the length of the list.
- After finding the length, again scan the list and locate $n/2$ node from the beginning.

Time Complexity: Time for finding the length of the list + Time for locating middle node = $O(n) + O(n) \approx O(n)$.
Space Complexity: O(1).

Question 26: Can we use hash table for solving Question-23?

Answer: Yes. The reasoning is same as that of Question-3.

Time Complexity: Time for creating the hash table. Therefore, $T(n) = O(n)$.
Space Complexity: $O(n)$. Since, we need to create a hash table of size n.

Question 27: Can we solve Question-23 just in one scan?

Answer: Efficient Approach: Use two pointers. Move one pointer at twice the speed of the second. When the first pointer reaches end of the list, the second pointer will be pointing to the middle node.

Note: If the list has even number of nodes, the middle node will be of $\lfloor n/2 \rfloor$.

```
struct ListNode * FindMiddle(struct ListNode *head) {
    struct ListNode *ptr1x, *ptr2x;
    ptr1x = ptr2x = head;
    int i=0;
    // keep looping until we reach the tail (next will be NULL for the last node)
    while(ptr1x→next != NULL) {
        if(i == 0) {
            ptr1x = ptr1x→next; //increment only the 1st pointer
            i=1;
        }
        else if( i == 1) {
            ptr1x = ptr1x→next; //increment both pointers
            ptr2x = ptr2x→next;
            i = 0;
```

```
        }
    }
    return ptr2x;        //now return the ptr2 which points to the middle node
}
```

Time Complexity: $O(n)$. Space Complexity: $O(1)$.

Question 28: How will you display a linked list from the end?

Answer: Traverse recursively till end of the linked list. While coming back, start printing the elements.

```
//This Function will print the linked list from end
void PrintListFromEnd(struct ListNode *head) {
  if(!head)
     return;
  PrintListFromEnd(head→next);
  printf("%d ",head→data);
}
```

Time Complexity: $O(n)$. Space Complexity: $O(n)\rightarrow$ for Stack.

Question 29: Check whether the given Linked List length is even or odd?

Answer: Use a $2x$ pointer. Take a pointer that moves at $2x$ [two nodes at a time]. At the end, if the length is even then pointer will be NULL otherwise it will point to last node.

```
int IsLinkedListLengthEven(struct ListNode * listHead) {
 while(listHead && listHead→next)
    listHead = listHead→next→next;
 if(!listHead)
   return 0;
 return 1;
}
```

Time Complexity: $O(\lfloor n/2 \rfloor) \approx O(n)$. Space Complexity: $O(1)$.

Question 30: If we want to concatenate two linked lists which of the following gives O(1) complexity?

1) Singly linked lists
2) Doubly linked lists
3) Circular doubly linked lists

Answer: Circular Doubly Linked Lists. This is because for singly and doubly linked lists, we need to traverse the first list till the end and append the second list. But in case of circular doubly linked lists we don't have to traverse the lists.

Question 31: Find modular node: Given a singly linked list, write a function to find the last element from the beginning whose $n\%k == 0$, where n is the number of elements in the list and k is an integer constant. For example, if $n = 19$ and $k = 3$ then we should return 18^{th}node.

Answer: For this problem the value of n is not known in advance.

```
struct ListNode *modularNodeFromBegin(struct ListNode *head, int k){
    struct ListNode * modularNode;
    int i=0;
    if(k<=0)
        return NULL;
    for (;head != NULL; head = head→next){
        if(i%k == 0){
```

```
            modularNode = head;
        }
        i++;
    }
    return modularNode;
}
```

Time Complexity: O(n). Space Complexity: O(1).

Question 32: Find modular node from end: Given a singly linked list, write a function to find the first from the end whose $n\%k == 0$, where n is the number of elements in the list and k is an integer constant. If $n = 19$ and $k = 3$ then we should return 16th node.

Answer: For this problem the value of n is not known in advance and it is same as finding the k^{th}element from end of the linked list.

```
struct ListNode *modularNodeFromEnd(struct ListNode *head, int k){
    struct ListNode *modularNode=NULL;
    int i=0;
    if(k<=0)
        return NULL;
    for (i=0; i < k; i++){
        if(head)
            head = head→next;
        else
            return NULL;
    }
    while(head != NULL)
        modularNode = modularNode→next;
        head = head→next;
    }
    return modularNode;
}
```

Time Complexity: O(n). Space Complexity: O(1).

Question 33: Find fractional node: Given a singly linked list, write a function to find the $\frac{n}{k}th$ element, where n is the number of elements in the list.

Answer: For this problem the value of n is not known in advance.

```
struct ListNode *fractionalNodes(struct ListNode *head, int k){
    struct ListNode *fractionalNode = NULL;
    int i=0;
    if(k<=0)
        return NULL;
    for (;head != NULL; head = head→next){
        if(i%k == 0){
            if(fractionalNode == NULL)
                fractionalNode = head;
            else fractionalNode = fractionalNode→next;
        }
        i++;
    }
    return fractionalNode;
}
```

Time Complexity: O(n). Space Complexity: O(1).

Question 34: Find $\sqrt{n}^{th}$ node: Given a singly linked list, write a function to find the $\sqrt{n}^{th}$ element, where n is the number of elements in the list. Assume the value of n is not known in advance.

Answer: For this problem the value of n is not known in advance.

```
struct ListNode *sqrtNode(struct ListNode *head){
    struct ListNode *sqrtN = NULL;
    int i=1, j=1;
    for (;head != NULL; head = head→next){
        if(i == j*j){
            if(sqrtN == NULL)
                sqrtN = head;
            else
                sqrtN = sqrtN→next;

            j++;
        }
        i++;
    }
    return sqrtN;
}
```

Time Complexity: O(n). Space Complexity: O(1).

CHAPTER 14

Stacks

14.1 What is a Stack?

A stack is a simple data structure used for storing data (similar to Linked Lists). In stack, the order in which the data arrives is important. The pile of plates of a cafeteria is a good example of stack. The plates are added to the stack as they are cleaned. They are placed on the top. When a plate is required it is taken from the top of the stack. The first plate placed on the stack is the last one to be used.

Definition: A *stack* is an ordered list in which insertion and deletion are done at one end, called *top*. The last element inserted is the first one to be deleted. Hence, it is called Last in First out (LIFO) or First in Last out (FILO) list.

Special names are given to the two changes that can be made to a stack. When an element is inserted in a stack, the concept is called *push*, and when an element is removed from the stack, the concept is called as *pop*. Trying to pop out an empty stack is called *underflow* and trying to push an element in a full stack is called *overflow*. Generally, we treat them as exceptions. As an example, consider the snapshots of the stack.

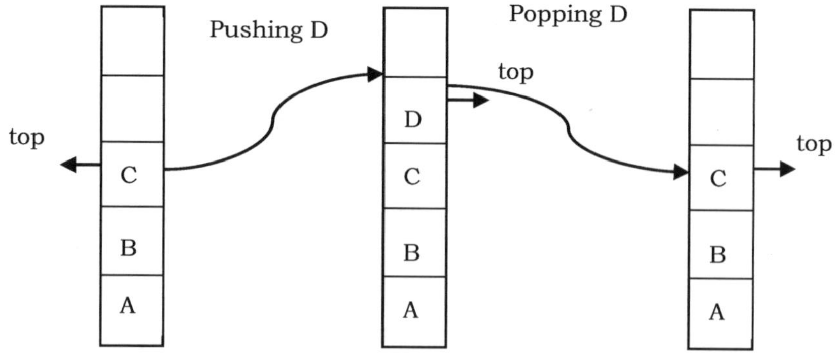

14.2 How Stacks are used?

Consider a working day in the office. Let us assume a developer is working on a long-term project. The manager then gives the developer a new task, which is more important. The developer places the long-term project aside and begins work on the new task. The phone rings, this is the highest priority, as it must be answered immediately. The developer pushes the present task into the pending tray and answers the phone.

When the call is complete the task abandoned to answer the phone is retrieved from the pending tray and work progresses. To take another call, it may have to be handled in the same manner, but eventually the new task will be finished, and the developer can draw the long-term project from the pending tray and continue with that.

14.3 Stack ADT

The following operations make a stack an ADT. For simplicity, assume the data is of integer type.

Main stack operations

- Push (int data): Inserts *data* onto stack.
- int Pop(): Removes and returns the last inserted element from the stack.

Auxiliary stack operations

- int Top(): Returns the last inserted element without removing it.
- int Size(): Returns the number of elements stored in stack.
- int IsEmptyStack(): Indicates whether any elements are stored in stack or not.
- int IsFullStack(): Indicates whether the stack is full or not.

Exceptions

Attempting the execution of an operation may sometimes cause an error condition, called an exception. Exceptions are said to be "thrown" by an operation that cannot be executed. In the Stack ADT, operations pop and top cannot be performed if the stack is empty. Attempting the execution of pop (top) on an empty stack throws an exception. Trying to push an element in a full stack throws an exception.

14.4 Applications

Following are some of the applications in which stacks plays an important role.

Direct applications

- Balancing of symbols
- Infix-to-postfix conversion
- Evaluation of postfix expression
- Implementing function calls (including recursion)
- Finding of spans (finding spans in stock markets, refer *Problems* section)
- Page-visited history in a Web browser [Back Buttons]
- Undo sequence in a text editor
- Matching Tags in HTML and XML

Indirect applications

- Auxiliary data structure for other algorithms (Example: Tree traversal algorithms)
- Component of other data structures (Example: Simulating queues, refer *Queues* chapter)

14.5 Implementation

There are many ways of implementing stack ADT, given below are the commonly used methods.

- Simple array based implementation
- Dynamic array based implementation
- Linked lists implementation

Simple Array Implementation

This implementation of stack ADT uses an array. In the array, we add elements from left to right and use a variable to keep track of the index of the top element.

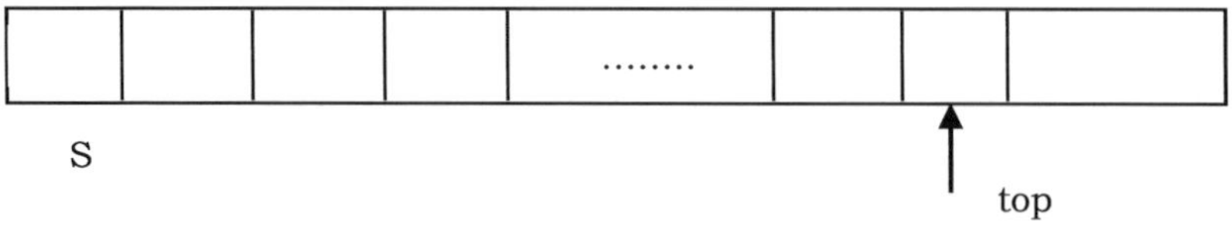

The array storing the stack elements may become full. A push operation will then throw a *full stack exception*. Similarly, if we try deleting an element from empty stack then it will throw *stack empty exception*.

```
struct ArrayStack {
    int top;
    int capacity;
    int *array;
};
struct ArrayStack *CreateStack() {
    struct ArrayStack *S = malloc(sizeof(struct ArrayStack));
    if(!S)
      return NULL;
    S→capacity = 1;
    S→top = -1;
    S→array= malloc(S→capacity * sizeof(int));
    if(!S→array)
      return NULL;
    return S;
}
int IsEmptyStack(struct ArrayStack *S) {
    return (S→top == -1); // if the condition is true then 1 is returned else 0 is
returned
}
int IsFullStack(struct ArrayStack *S){
    //if the condition is true then 1 is returned else 0 is returned
    return (S→top == S→capacity - 1);
}
void Push(struct ArrayStack *S, int data){
    /* S→top == capacity -1 indicates that the stack is full*/
    if(IsFullStack(S))
     printf( “Stack Overflow”);
    else    /*Increasing the ‘top’ by 1 and storing the value at ‘top’ position*/
        S→ array[++S→top]= data;
}
int Pop(struct ArrayStack *S){
        /* S→top == - 1 indicates empty stack*/
    if(IsEmptyStack(S)){
       printf("Stack is Empty");
       return 0;
    }
    else /* Removing element from  ‘top’ of the array and reducing  ‘top’ by 1*/
       return (S→ array[S→top--]);
}
void DeleteStack(struct DynArrayStack *S){
   if(S) {
      if(S→array)
```

```
        free(S→array);
        free(S);
    }
}
```

Limitations

The maximum size of the stack must be defined in prior and cannot be changed. Trying to push a new element into a full stack causes an implementation-specific exception.

Dynamic Array Implementation

First, let's consider how we implemented a simple array based stack. We took one index variable *top* which points to the index of the most recently inserted element in the stack. To insert (or push) an element, we increment *top* index and then place the new element at that index.

Similarly, to delete (or pop) an element we take the element at *top* index and then decrement the *top* index. We represent empty queue with *top* value equal to -1. The issue still need to be resolved is that what we do when all the slots in fixed size array stack are occupied?

First try: What if we increment the size of the array by 1 every time the stack is full?

- Push(): increase size of S[] by 1
- Pop(): decrease size of S[] by 1

Problems with this approach?

This way of incrementing the array size is too expensive. Let us a see the reason for this. For example, at $n = 1$, to push an element create a new array of size 2 and copy all the old array elements to new array and at the end add the new element. At $n = 2$, to push an element create a new array of size 3 and copy all the old array elements to new array and at the end add the new element.

Similarly, at $n = n - 1$, if we want to push an element create a new array of size n and copy all the old array elements to new array and at the end add the new element. After n push operations the total time $T(n)$ (number of copy operations) is proportional to $1 + 2 + \ldots + n \approx O(n^2)$.

Alternative Approach: Repeated Doubling

Let us improve the complexity by using array *doubling* technique. If the array is full, create a new array of twice the size, and copy items. With this approach, pushing n items takes time proportional to n (not n^2).

For simplicity, let us assume that initially we started with $n = 1$ and moved till $n = 32$. That means, we do the doubling at $1, 2, 4, 8, 16$. The other way of analyzing the same is, at $n = 1$, if we want to add (push) an element then double the current size of array and copy all the elements of old array to new array.

At, $n = 1$, we do 1 copy operation, at $n = 2$, we do 2 copy operations, and $n = 4$, we do 4 copy operations and so on. By the time we reach $n = 32$, the total number of copy operations is $1 + 2 + 4 + 8 + 16 = 31$ which is approximately equal to $2n$ value (32). If we observe carefully, we are doing the doubling operation $logn$ times.

Now, let us generalize the discussion. For n push operations we double the array size $logn$ times. That means, we will have $logn$ terms in the expression below. The total time $T(n)$ of a series of n push operations is proportional to

$$1 + 2 + 4 + 8 \ldots + \frac{n}{4} + \frac{n}{2} + n = n + \frac{n}{2} + \frac{n}{4} + \frac{n}{8} \ldots + 4 + 2 + 1$$

$$= n\left(1 + \frac{1}{2} + \frac{1}{4} + \frac{1}{8} \dots + \frac{4}{n} + \frac{2}{n} + \frac{1}{n}\right)$$
$$= n(2) \approx 2n = O(n)$$

T(n) is O(n) and the amortized time of a push operation is O(1).

```
struct DynArrayStack {
int top;
int capacity;
int *array;
};
struct DynArrayStack *CreateStack(){
    struct DynArrayStack *S = malloc(sizeof(struct DynArrayStack));
    if(!S)
        return NULL;
    S→capacity = 1;
    S→top = -1;
    S→array = malloc(S→capacity * sizeof(int));     // allocate an array of size 1 initially
    if(!S→array)
        return NULL;
    return S;
}
int IsFullStack(struct DynArrayStack *S){
    return (S→top == S→capacity-1);
}
void DoubleStack(struct DynArrayStack *S){
    S→capacity *= 2;
    S→array = realloc(S→array, S→capacity);
}
void Push(struct DynArrayStack *S, int x){
    // No overflow in this implementation
     if(IsFullStack(S))
        DoubleStack(S);
    S→array[++S→top] = x;
}
int IsEmptyStack(struct DynArrayStack *S){
    return S→top == -1;
}
int Top(struct DynArrayStack *S){
    if(IsEmptyStack(S))
        return INT_MIN;
    return S→array[S→top];
}
int Pop(struct DynArrayStack *S){
    if(IsEmptyStack(S))
        return INT_MIN;
    return S→array[S→top--];
}
void DeleteStack(struct DynArrayStack *S){
    if(S) {
        if(S→array)
            free(S→array);
        free(S);
    }
}
```

Note: Too many doublings may cause memory overflow exception.

Linked List Implementation

The other way of implementing stacks is by using Linked lists. Push operation is implemented by inserting element at the beginning of the list. Pop operation is implemented by deleting the node from the beginning (the header/top node).

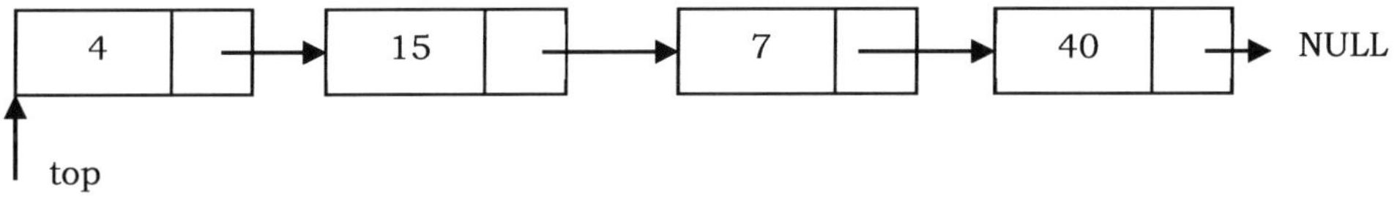


```
struct ListNode{
    int data;
    struct ListNode *next;
};
struct Stack *CreateStack(){
    return NULL;
}
void Push(struct Stack **top, int data){
    struct Stack *temp;
    temp = malloc(sizeof(struct Stack));
    if(!temp)
        return NULL;
    temp→data = data;
    temp→next = *top;
    *top = temp;
}
int IsEmptyStack(struct Stack *top){
    return top == NULL;
}
int Pop(struct Stack **top){
    int data;
    struct Stack *temp;
    if(IsEmptyStack(top))
        return INT_MIN;
    temp = *top;
    *top = *top→next;
    data = temp→data;
    free(temp);
    return data;
}
int Top(struct Stack * top){
    if(IsEmptyStack(top))
        return INT_MIN;
    return top→next→data;
}
void DeleteStack(struct Stack **top){
    struct Stack *temp, *p;
    p = *top;
    while( p→next) {
        temp = p→next;
        p→next = temp→next;
        free(temp);
    }
    free(p);
}
```

14.6 Comparison of Implementations

Comparing Incremental Strategy and Doubling Strategy

We compare the incremental strategy and doubling strategy by analyzing the total time $T(n)$ needed to perform a series of n push operations. We start with an empty stack represented by an array of size 1.

We call *amortized* time of a push operation is the average time taken by a push over the series of operations, that is, $T(n)/n$.

Incremental Strategy

The amortized time (average time per operation) of a push operation is $O(n)$ $[O(n^2)/ n]$.

Doubling Strategy

In this method, the amortized time of a push operation is $O(1)$ $[O(n) / n]$.

Note: For analysis, refer the *Implementation* section.

Comparing Array Implementation and Linked List Implementation

Array Implementation

- Operations take constant time.
- Expensive doubling operation every once in a while.
- Any sequence of n operations (starting from empty stack) -- "*amortized*" bound takes time proportional to n.

Linked list Implementation

- Grows and shrinks gracefully.
- Every operation takes constant time O(1).
- Every operation uses extra space and time to deal with references.

Problems and Questions with Answers

Question 1: Discuss how stacks can be used for checking balancing of symbols?

Answer: Stacks can be used to check whether the given expression has balanced symbols. This algorithm is very useful in compilers. Each time parser reads one character at a time. If the character is an opening delimiter such as (, {, or [- then it is written to the stack. When a closing delimiter is encountered like), }, or]- is encountered the stack is popped.

The opening and closing delimiters are then compared. If they match, the parsing of the string continues. If they do not match, the parser indicates that there is an error on the line. A linear-time $O(n)$ algorithm based on stack can be given as:

Algorithm:

a) Create a stack.
b) while (end of input is not reached) {
    1) If the character read is not a symbol to be balanced, ignore it.
    2) If the character is an opening symbol like (, [, {, push it onto the stack
    3) If it is a closing symbol like),],}, then if the stack is empty report an error. Otherwise pop the stack.
    4) If the symbol popped is not the corresponding opening symbol, report an error.
   }

c) At end of input, if the stack is not empty report an error

Examples:

Example	Valid?	Description
(A+B)+(C-D)	Yes	The expression is having balanced symbol
((A+B)+(C-D)	No	One closing brace is missing
((A+B)+[C-D])	Yes	Opening and immediate closing braces correspond
((A+B)+[C-D]}	No	The last closing brace does not correspond with the first opening parenthesis

For tracing the algorithm let us assume that the input is: () (() [()])

Input Symbol, A[i]	Operation	Stack	Output
(	Push (	(	
)	Pop (Test if (and A[i] match? YES		
(	Push (	(	
(	Push (	((	
)	Pop (Test if (and A[i] match? YES	(	
[	Push [	([	
(	Push (	([(	
)	Pop (Test if(and A[i] match? YES	([	
]	Pop [Test if [and A[i] match? YES	(	
)	Pop (Test if(and A[i] match? YES		
	Test if stack is Empty? YES		TRUE

Question 2: Discuss infix to postfix conversion algorithm using stack.

Answer: Before discussing the algorithm, first let us see the definitions of infix, prefix and postfix expressions.

Infix: An infix expression is a single letter, or an operator, proceeded by one infix string and followed by another Infix string.

```
A
A+B
(A+B)+ (C-D)
```

Prefix: A prefix expression is a single letter, or an operator, followed by two prefix strings. Every prefix string longer than a single variable contains an operator, first operand and second operand.

```
A
+AB
++AB-CD
```

Postfix: A postfix expression (also called Reverse Polish Notation) is a single letter or an operator, preceded by two postfix strings. Every postfix string longer than a single variable contains first and second operands followed by an operator.

```
A
AB+
AB+CD-+
```

Prefix and postfix notions are methods of writing mathematical expressions without parenthesis. Time to evaluate a postfix and prefix expression is $O(n)$, where n is the number of elements in the array.

Infix	Prefix	Postfix
A+B	+AB	AB+
A+B-C	-+ABC	AB+C-
(A+B)*C-D	-*+ABCD	AB+C*D-

Now, let us focus on the algorithm. In infix expressions, the operator precedence is implicit unless we use parentheses. Therefore, for the infix to postfix conversion algorithm we have to define the operator precedence (or priority) inside the algorithm.

The table shows the precedence and their associatively (order of evaluation) among operators.

Token	Operator	Precedence	Associatively
( ) [ ] → .	function call array element struct or union member	17	left-to-right
-- ++	increment, decrement	16	left-to-right
-- ++ ! - - + & * sizeof	decrement, increment logical not one's complement unary minus or plus address or indirection size (in bytes)	15	right-to-left
(type)	type cast	14	right-to-left
* / %	multiplicative	13	Left-to-right
+ -	binary add or subtract	12	left-to-right
<< >>	shift	11	left-to-right
> >= < <=	relational	10	left-to-right
== !=	equality	9	left-to-right
&	bitwise and	8	left-to-right
^	bitwise exclusive or	7	left-to-right
|	bitwise or	6	left-to-right
&&	logical and	5	left-to-right
| |	logical or	4	left-to-right
?:	conditional	3	right-to-left
= += -= /= *= %= <<= >>= &= ^=	assignment	2	right-to-left
,	Comma	1	left-to-right

Important Properties

- Let us consider the infix expression 2 + 3 * 4 and its postfix equivalent 2 3 4 * +. Notice that between infix and postfix the order of the numbers (or operands) is unchanged. It is 2 3 4 in both cases. But the order of the operators * and + is affected in the two expressions.

- Only one stack is enough to convert an infix expression to postfix expression. The stack that we use in the algorithm will be used to change the order of operators from infix to postfix. The stack we use will only contain operators and the open parentheses symbol '('.
  Postfix expressions do not contain parentheses. We shall not output the parentheses in the postfix output.

Algorithm:

```
a) Create a stack
b) for each character t in the input stream{
       if(t is an operand)
               output t
       else if(t is a right parenthesis){
               Pop and output tokens until a left parenthesis is popped (but not
               output)
       }
       else // t is an operator or left parenthesis{
               pop and output tokens until one of lower priority than t is
               encountered or a left parenthesis is encountered or the stack is
               empty
               Push t
       }
   }
c) pop and output tokens until the stack is empty
```

For better understanding let us trace out some example: A * B- (C + D) + E

Input Character	Operation on Stack	Stack	Postfix Expression
A		Empty	A
*	Push	*	A
B		*	AB
-	Check and Push	-	AB*
(	Push	-(	AB*
C		-(	AB*C
+	Check and Push	-(+	AB*C
D			AB*CD
)	Pop and append to postfix till '('	-	AB*CD+
+	Check and Push	+	AB*CD+-
E		+	AB*CD+-E
End of input	Pop till empty		AB*CD+-E+

Question 3: Discuss postfix evaluation using stacks?

Answer:

Algorithm:

1 Scan the Postfix string from left to right.
2 Initialize an empty stack.
3 Repeat steps 4 and 5 till all the characters are scanned.
4 If the scanned character is an operand, push it onto the stack.
5 If the scanned character is an operator, and if the operator is unary operator then pop an element from the stack. If the operator is binary operator then pop two elements from the stack. After popping the elements, apply the operator to those popped elements. Let the result of this operation be retVal onto the stack.
6 After all characters are scanned, we will have only one element in the stack.

7 Return top of the stack as result.

Example: Let us see how the above-mentioned algorithm works using an example. Assume that the postfix string is 123*+5-.

Initially the stack is empty. Now, the first three characters scanned are 1, 2 and 3, which are operands. They will be pushed into the stack in that order.

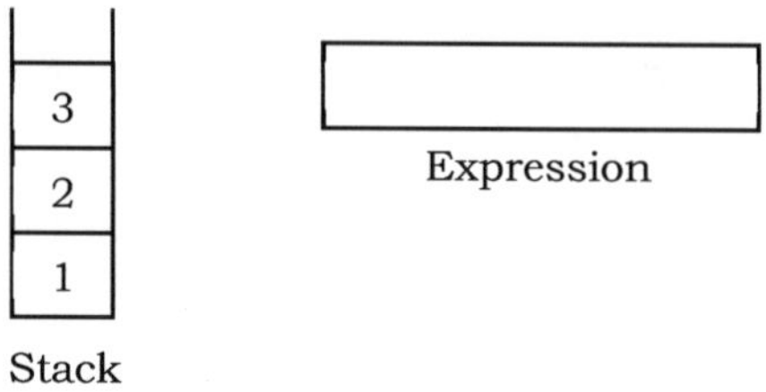

Next character scanned is "*", which is an operator. Thus, we pop the top two elements from the stack and perform the "*" operation with the two operands. The second operand will be the first element that is popped.

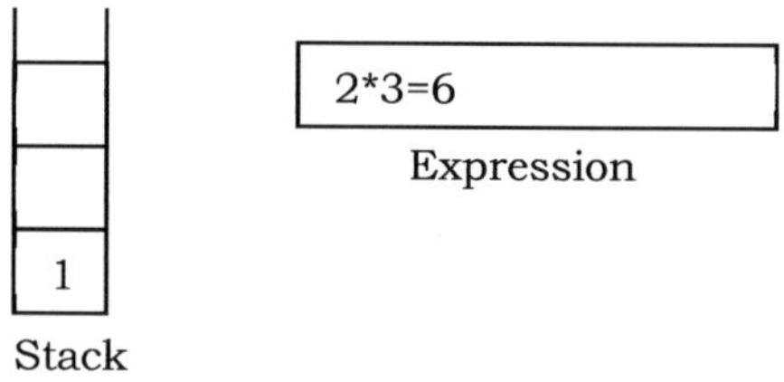

The value of the expression (2*3) that has been evaluated (6) is pushed into the stack.

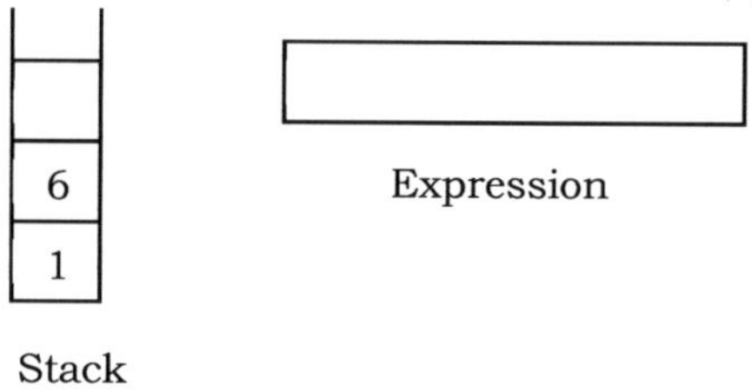

Next character scanned is "+", which is an operator. Thus, we pop the top two elements from the stack and perform the "+" operation with the two operands. The second operand will be the first element that is popped.

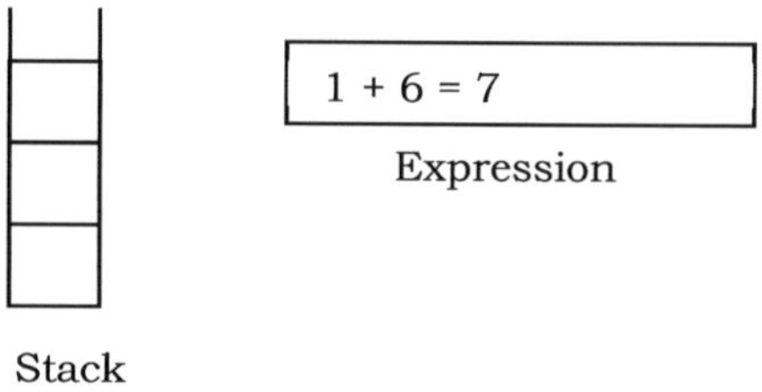

The value of the expression (1+6) that has been evaluated (7) is pushed into the stack.

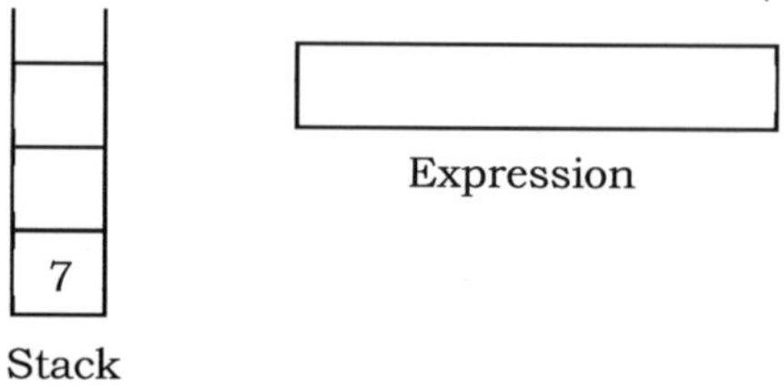

Next character scanned is "5", which is added to the stack.

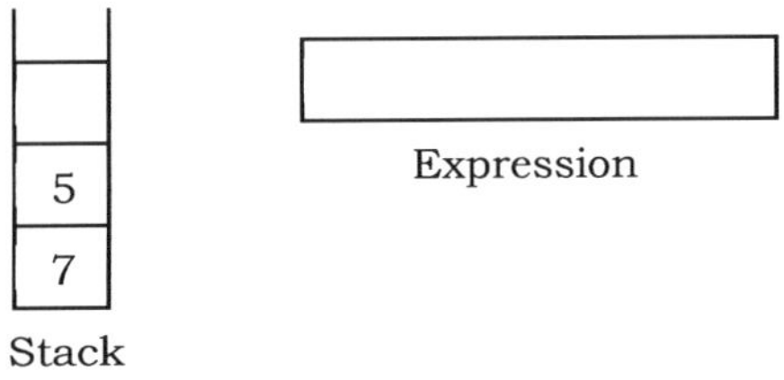

Next character scanned is "-", which is an operator. Thus, we pop the top two elements from the stack and perform the "-" operation with the two operands. The second operand will be the first element that is popped.

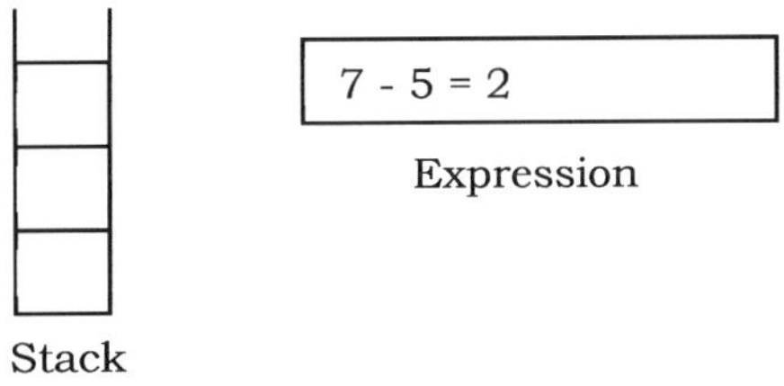

The value of the expression(7-5) that has been evaluated(23) is pushed into the stack.

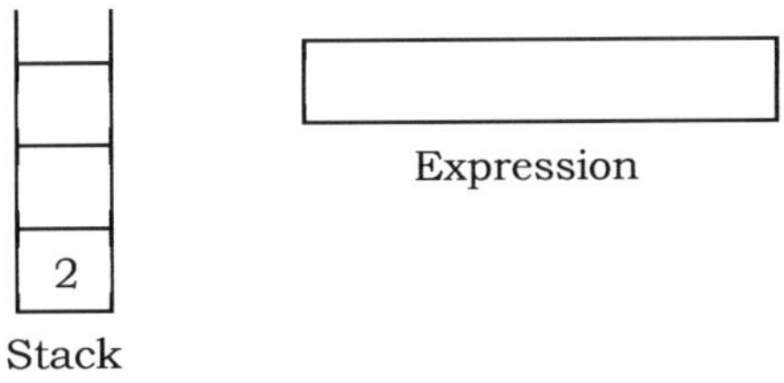

Now, since all the characters are scanned, the remaining element in the stack (there will be only one element in the stack) will be returned. End result:

- Postfix String : 123*+5-
- Result : 2

Question 4: How to design a stack such that GetMinimum( ) should be O(1)?

Answer: Take an auxiliary stack that maintains the minimum of all values in the stack. Also, assume that, each element of the stack is less than its below elements. For simplicity let us call the auxiliary stack as *min stack*. When we *pop* the main stack, *pop* the min stack too. When we push the main stack, push either the new element or the current minimum, whichever is lower. At any point, if we want to get the minimum then we just need to return the top element from the min stack. Let us take some example and trace out. Initially let us assume that we have pushed 2, 6, 4, 1 and 5. Based on above-mentioned algorithm the *min stack* will look like:

Main stack	Min stack
5 → top	1 → top
1	1
4	2
6	2
2	2

After popping twice we get:

Main stack	Min stack
4 -→ top	2 → top
6	2
2	2

Based on the discussion above, now let us code the push, pop and GetMinimum() operations.

```
struct AdvancedStack{
    struct Stack elementStack;
    struct Stack minStack;
};
void Push(struct AdvancedStack *S, int data ){
    Push (S→elementStack, data);
    if(IsEmptyStack(S→minStack) | | Top(S→minStack) >= data)
        Push (S→minStack, data);
    else    Push (S→minStack, Top(S→minStack));
}
int Pop(struct AdvancedStack *S ){
    int temp;
    if(IsEmptyStack(S→elementStack)) return -1;
    temp = Pop (S→elementStack);
    Pop (S→minStack);
    return temp;
}
int GetMinimum(struct AdvancedStack *S){
    return Top(S→minStack);
}
struct AdvancedStack *CreateAdvancedStack(){
    struct AdvancedStack *S = (struct AdvancedStack *)
                                        malloc(sizeof(struct AdvancedStack));
    if(!S) return NULL;
    S→elementStack = CreateStack();
    S→minStack = CreateStack();
    return S;
}
```

Time complexity: O(1). Space complexity: O(n) [for Min stack]. This algorithm has much better space usage if we rarely get a "new minimum or equal".

Question 5: For 0 is it possible to improve the space complexity?

Answer: **Yes**. The main problem of the previous approach is, for each push operation we are pushing the element on to min stack also (either the new element or existing minimum element). That means, we are pushing the duplicate minimum elements on to the stack.

Now, let us change the algorithm to improve the space complexity. We still have the min stack, but we only pop from it when the value we pop from the main stack is equal to the one on the min stack. We only *push* to the min stack when the value being pushed onto the main stack is less than *or equal* to the current min value. In this modified algorithm also, if we want to get the minimum then we just need to return the top element from the min stack. For example, taking the original version and pushing 1 again, we'd get:

Main stack	Min stack
1 → top	
5	
1	
4	1 → top
6	1
2	2

Popping from the above pops from both stacks because 1 == 1, leaving:

Main stack	Min stack
5 → top	
1	
4	
6	1 → top
2	2

Popping again *only* pops from the main stack, because 5 > 1:

Main stack	Min stack
1 → top	
4	
6	1 → top
2	2

Popping again pops both stacks because 1 == 1:

Main stack	Min stack
4 → top	
6	
2	2 → top

Note: The difference is only in push & pop operations.

```
struct AdvancedStack {
    struct Stack elementStack;
    struct Stack minStack;
};
void Push(struct AdvancedStack *S, int data){
    Push (S→elementStack, data);
    if(IsEmptyStack(S→minStack) || Top(S→minStack) >= data)
        Push (S→minStack, data);
}
int Pop(struct AdvancedStack *S ){
    int temp;
    if(IsEmptyStack(S→elementStack)) return -1;
    temp = Top (S→elementStack);
    if(Top(S→ minStack) == Pop(S→elementStack))
        Pop (S→ minStack);
    return temp;
}
int GetMinimum(struct AdvancedStack *S){
    return Top(S→minStack);
}
struct AdvancedStack * AdvancedStack(){
    struct AdvancedStack *S = (struct AdvancedStack)
                                        malloc (sizeof (struct AdvancedStack));
    if(!S) return NULL;
    S→elementStack = CreateStack();
    S→minStack = CreateStack();
    return S;
}
```

Time complexity: O(1). Space complexity: O(n) [for Min stack]. But this algorithm has much better space usage if we rarely get a "new minimum or equal".

Queues

CHAPTER 15

15.1 What is a Queue?

A queue is a data structure used for storing data (similar to Linked Lists and Stacks). In queue, the order in which data arrives is important. In general, a queue is a line of people or things waiting to be served in sequential order starting at the beginning of the line or sequence.

Definition: A *queue* is an ordered list in which insertions are done at one end (*rear*) and deletions are done at other end (*front*). The first element to be inserted is the first one to be deleted. Hence, it is called First in First out (FIFO) or Last in Last out (LILO) list.

Similar to *Stacks*, special names are given to the two changes that can be made to a queue. When an element is inserted in a queue, the concept is called *EnQueue*, and when an element is removed from the queue, the concept is called *DeQueue*.

DeQueueing an empty queue is called *underflow* and *EnQueuing* an element in a full queue is called *overflow*. Generally, we treat them as exceptions. As an example, consider the snapshot of the queue.

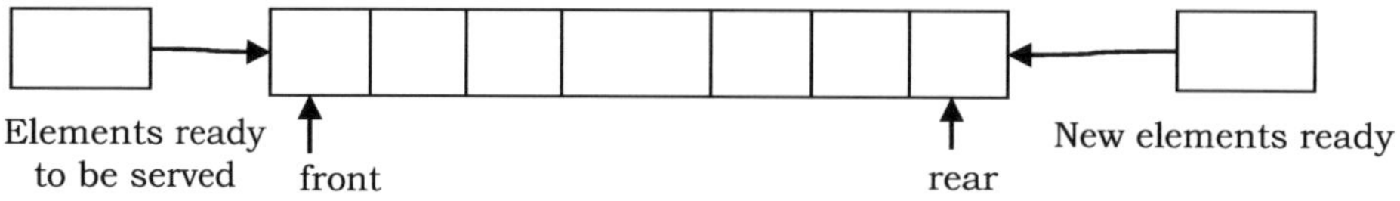

15.2 How are Queues Used?

The concept of a queue can be explained by observing a line at a reservation counter. When we enter the line we stand at the end of the line and the person who is at the front of the line is the one who will be served next. He will exit the queue and be served.

As this happens, the next person will come at head of the line, will exit the queue and will be served. As each person at the head of the line keeps exiting the queue we move towards the head of the line. Finally we will reach head of the line and we will exit the queue and be served. This behavior is very useful in cases where there is a need to maintain the order of arrival.

15.3 Queue ADT

The following operations make a queue an ADT. Insertions and deletions in queue must follow the FIFO scheme. For simplicity we assume the elements are integers.

Main Queue Operations

- EnQueue(int data): Inserts an element at the end of the queue
- int DeQueue(): Removes and returns the element at the front of the queue

Auxiliary Queue Operations

- int Front(): Returns the element at front without removing it
- int QueueSize(): Returns the number of elements stored in the queue
- int IsEmptyQueue(): Indicates whether no elements are stored in the queue or not

15.4 Exceptions

Similar to other ADTs, executing *DeQueue* on an empty queue throws an *"Empty Queue Exception"* and executing *EnQueue* on a full queue throws an *"Full Queue Exception"*.

15.5 Applications

Following are the some of the applications that are using queues.

Direct Applications

- Operating systems schedule jobs (with equal priority) in the order of arrival (e.g., a print queue).
- Simulation of real-world queues such as lines at a ticket counter or any other first-come first-served scenario requires a queue.
- Multiprogramming.
- Asynchronous data transfer (file IO, pipes, sockets).
- Waiting times of customers at call center.
- Determining number of cashiers to have at a supermarket.

Indirect Applications

- Auxiliary data structure for algorithms
- Component of other data structures

15.6 Implementation

There are many ways (similar to Stacks) of implementing queue operations and some of the commonly used methods are listed below.

- Simple circular array based implementation
- Dynamic circular array based implementation
- Linked list implementation

Why Circular Arrays?

First, let us see whether we can use simple arrays for implementing queues as we have done for stacks. We know that, in queues, the insertions are performed at one end and deletions are performed at other end. After performing some insertions and deletions the process becomes easy to understand.

In the example shown below, it can be seen clearly that the initial slots of the array are getting wasted. So, simple array implementation for queue is not efficient. To solve this problem we assume the arrays as circular arrays. That means, we treat last element and first array elements as contiguous. With this representation, if there are any free slots at the beginning, the rear pointer can easily go to its next free slot.

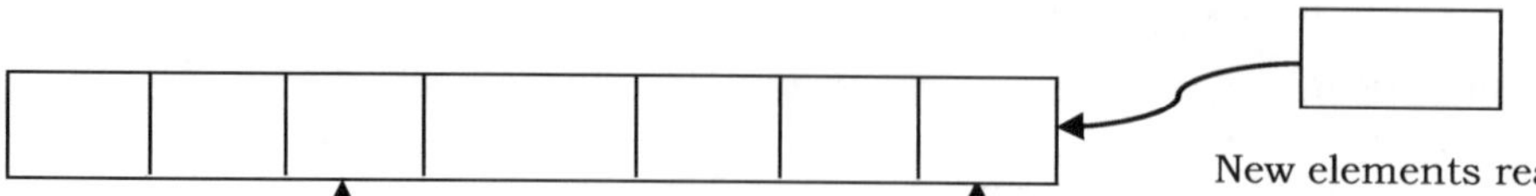

Note: The simple circular array and dynamic circular array implementations are very similar to stack array implementations. Refer *Stacks* chapter for analysis of these implementations.

Simple Circular Array Implementation

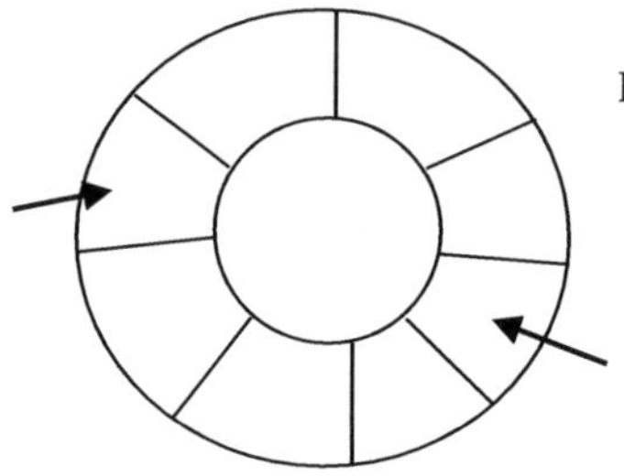

This simple implementation of Queue ADT uses an array. In the array, we add elements circularly and use two variables to keep track of start element and end element. Generally, *front* is used to indicate the start element and *rear* is used to indicate the end element in the queue.

The array storing the queue elements may become full. An *EnQueue* operation will then throw a *full queue exception*. Similarly, if we try deleting an element from empty queue then it will throw *empty queue exception*.

Note: Initially, both front and rear points to -1 which indicates that the queue is empty.

```
struct ArrayQueue {
    int front, rear;
    int capacity;
    int *array;
};
struct ArrayQueue *Queue(int size) {
    struct ArrayQueue *Q = malloc(sizeof(struct ArrayQueue));
    if(!Q)
        return NULL;
    Q→capacity = size;
    Q→front = Q→rear = -1;
    Q→array= malloc(Q→capacity * sizeof(int));
    if(!Q→array)
        return NULL;
    return Q;
}
int IsEmptyQueue(struct ArrayQueue *Q) {
    // if the condition is true then 1 is returned else 0 is returned
    return (Q→front == -1);
}
int IsFullQueue(struct ArrayQueue *Q) {
    //if the condition is true then 1 is returned else 0 is returned
```

```
    return ((Q→rear +1) % Q→capacity == Q→front);
}
int QueueSize() {
    return (Q→capacity - Q→front + Q→rear + 1)% Q→capacity;
}
void EnQueue(struct ArrayQueue *Q, int data) {
    if(IsFullQueue(Q))
        printf("Queue Overflow");
    else {
        Q→rear = (Q→rear+1) % Q→capacity;
        Q→ array[Q→rear]= data;
        if(Q→front == -1)
            Q→front = Q→rear;
    }
}
int DeQueue(struct ArrayQueue *Q) {
    int data = 0;//or element which does not exist in Queue
    if(IsEmptyQueue(Q)) {
        printf("Queue is Empty");
        return 0;
    }
    else {
        data = Q→array[Q→front];
        if(Q→front == Q→rear)
            Q→front = Q→rear = -1;
        else Q→front = (Q→front+1) % Q→capacity;
    }
    return data;
}
void DeleteQueue(struct ArrayQueue *Q) {
    if(Q) {
        if(Q→array)
            free(Q→array);
        free(Q);
    }
}
```

Performance and Limitations

Performance: Let *n* be the number of elements in the queue:

Space Complexity (for *n* EnQueue operations)	O(*n*)
Time Complexity of EnQueue()	O(1)
Time Complexity of DeQueue()	O(1)
Time Complexity of IsEmptyQueue()	O(1)
Time Complexity of IsFullQueue()	O(1)
Time Complexity of QueueSize()	O(1)
Time Complexity of DeleteQueue()	O(1)

Limitations: The maximum size of the queue must be defined a prior and cannot be changed. Trying to *EnQueue* a new element into a full queue causes an implementation-specific exception.

Dynamic Circular Array Implementation

```
struct DynArrayQueue {
    int front, rear;
    int capacity;
    int *array;
};
struct DynArrayQueue *CreateDynQueue() {
    struct DynArrayQueue *Q = malloc(sizeof(struct DynArrayQueue));
    if(!Q)
        return NULL;
    Q→capacity = 1;
    Q→front = Q→rear = -1;
    Q→array = malloc(Q→capacity * sizeof(int));
    if(!Q→array)
        return NULL;
    return Q;
}
int IsEmptyQueue(struct DynArrayQueue *Q) {
    // if the condition is true then 1 is returned else 0 is returned
    return (Q→front == -1);
}
int IsFullQueue(struct DynArrayQueue *Q) {
    //if the condition is true then 1 is returned else 0 is returned
    return ((Q→rear +1) % Q→capacity == Q→front);
}
int QueueSize() {
    return (Q→capacity - Q→front + Q→rear + 1)% Q→capacity;
}
void EnQueue(struct DynArrayQueue *Q, int data) {
    if(IsFullQueue(Q))
        ResizeQueue(Q);
    Q→rear = (Q→rear+1)% Q→capacity;
    Q→ array[Q→rear]= data;
    if(Q→front == -1)
        Q→front = Q→rear;
}
void ResizeQueue(struct DynArrayQueue *Q) {
        int size = Q→capacity;
        Q→capacity = Q→capacity*2;
        Q→array = realloc (Q→array, Q→capacity);
        if(!Q→array) {
            printf("Memory Error");
            return;
        }
        if(Q→front > Q→rear ) {
            for(int i=0; i < Q→front; i++) {
                Q→array[i+size] =Q→array[i];
            }
        Q→rear = Q→rear + size;
    }
}
int DeQueue(struct DynArrayQueue *Q) {
```

```
    int data = 0;//or element which does not exist in Queue
    if(IsEmptyQueue(Q)) {
        printf("Queue is Empty");
        return 0;
    }
   else {
        data = Q→array[Q→front];
        if(Q→front== Q→rear)
            Q→front= Q→rear = -1;
        else
            Q→front = (Q→front+1) % Q→capacity;
    }
    return data;
}
void DeleteQueue(struct DynArrayQueue *Q) {
    if(Q) {
        if(Q→array)
              free(Q→array);
        free(Q→array);
    }
}
```

Performance

Let n be the number of elements in the queue.

Space Complexity (for n EnQueue operations)	$O(n)$
Time Complexity of EnQueue()	O(1) (Average)
Time Complexity of DeQueue()	O(1)
Time Complexity of QueueSize()	O(1)
Time Complexity of IsEmptyQueue()	O(1)
Time Complexity of IsFullQueue()	O(1)
Time Complexity of QueueSize()	O(1)
Time Complexity of DeleteQueue()	O(1)

Linked List Implementation

Another way of implementing queues is by using Linked lists. *EnQueue* operation is implemented by inserting element at the ending of the list. *DeQueue* operation is implemented by deleting an element from the beginning of the list.

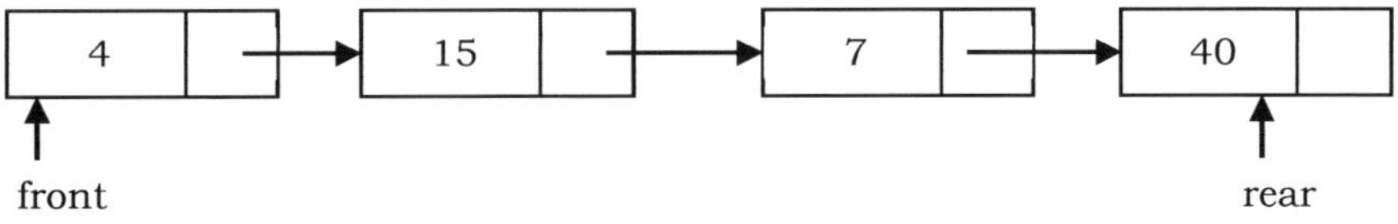


```
    struct ListNode {
        int data;
        struct ListNode *next;
    };
```

```
    struct Queue {
        struct ListNode *front;
        struct ListNode *rear;
    };
```

```
struct Queue *CreateQueue() {
    struct Queue *Q;
    struct ListNode *temp;
    Q = malloc(sizeof(struct Queue));
    if(!Q)
        return NULL;
```

```
    temp = malloc(sizeof(struct ListNode));
    Q→front = Q→rear = NULL;
    return Q;
}
int IsEmptyQueue(struct Queue *Q) {
    // if the condition is true then 1 is returned else 0 is returned
    return (Q→front == NULL);
}
void EnQueue(struct Queue *Q, int data) {
    struct ListNode *newNode;
    newNode = malloc(sizeof(struct ListNode));
    if(!newNode)
        return NULL;
    newNode→data = data;
    newNode→next = NULL;
    Q→rear→next = newNode;
    Q→rear = newNode;
    if(Q→front == NULL)
        Q→front = Q→rear;
}
int DeQueue(struct Queue *Q) {
    int data = 0;     //or element which does not exist in Queue
    struct ListNode *temp;
    if(IsEmptyQueue(Q)) {
        printf("Queue is empty");
        return 0;
    }
    else {
        temp = Q→front;
        data = Q→front→data;
        Q→front== Q→front→next;
        free(temp);
    }
    return data;
}
void DeleteQueue(struct Queue *Q) {
    struct ListNode *temp;
    while(Q) {
        temp = Q;
        Q = Q→next;
        free(temp);
    }
    free(Q);
}
```

Performance

Let n be the number of elements in the queue, then

Space Complexity (for n EnQueue operations)	$O(n)$
Time Complexity of EnQueue()	O(1) (Average)
Time Complexity of DeQueue()	O(1)
Time Complexity of IsEmptyQueue()	O(1)
Time Complexity of DeleteQueue()	O(1)

Problems and Questions with Answers

Question 1: Give an algorithm for reversing a queue Q. To access the queue, we are only allowed to use the methods of queue ADT.

Answer:

```
void ReverseQueue(struct Queue *Q) {
   struct Stack *S = CreateStack();
   while (!IsEmptyQueue(Q))
      Push(S, DeQueue(Q));
   while (!IsEmptyStack(S))
      EnQueue(Q, Pop(S));
}
```

Question 2: How can you implement a queue using two stacks?

Answer: Let S1 and S2 be the two stacks to be used in the implementation of queue. All we have to do is to define the EnQueue and DeQueue operations for the queue.

```
struct Queue {
   struct Stack *S1; // for EnQueue
   struct Stack *S2; // for DeQueue
}
```

EnQueue Algorithm

- Just push on to stack S1

```
void EnQueue(struct Queue *Q, int data) {
   Push(Q→S1, data);
}
```

DeQueue Algorithm

- If stack S2 is not empty then pop from S2 and return that element.
- If stack is empty, then transfer all elements from S1 to S2 and pop the top element from S2 and return that popped element [we can optimize the code little by transferring only $n-1$ elements from S1 to S2 and pop the nth element from S1 and return that popped element].
- If stack S1 is also empty then throw error.

```
int DeQueue(struct Queue *Q) {
   if(!IsEmptyStack(Q→S2))
      return Pop(Q→S2);
   else {
      while(!IsEmptyStack(Q→S1))
         Push(Q→S2, Pop(Q→S1));
      return Pop(Q→S2);
   }
}
```

Question 3: Show how can you efficiently implement one stack using two queues. Analyze the running time of the stack operations.

Answer: Let Q1 and Q2 be the two queues to be used in the implementation of stack. All we have to do is to define the push and pop operations for the stack.

```
struct Stack {
   struct Queue *Q1;
   struct Queue *Q2;
```

```
}
```

In the algorithms below, we make sure that one queue is always empty.

Push Operation Algorithm: Insert the element in whichever queue is not empty.

- Check whether queue Q1 is empty or not. If Q1 is empty then Enqueue the element into Q2.
- Otherwise EnQueue the element into Q1.

```
Push(struct Stack *S, int data) {
    if(IsEmptyQueue(S→Q1))
        EnQueue(S→Q2, data);
        else EnQueue(S→Q1, data);
}
```

Time Complexity: O(1).

Pop Operation Algorithm: Transfer $n - 1$ elements to the other queue and delete last from queue for performing pop operation.

- If queue Q1 is not empty then transfer $n - 1$ elements from Q1 to Q2 and then, DeQueue the last element of Q1 and return it.
- If queue Q2 is not empty then transfer $n - 1$ elements from Q2 to Q1 and then, DeQueue the last element of Q2 and return it.

```
int Pop(struct Stack *S) {
    int i, size;
    if(IsEmptyQueue(S→Q2)) {
        size = size(S→Q1);
        i = 0;
        while(i < size-1) {
            EnQueue(S→Q2, DeQueue(S→Q1));
            i++;
        }
        return DeQueue(S→Q1);
    }
    else {
        size =  size(S→Q2);
        while(i < size-1) {
            EnQueue(S→Q1, DeQueue(S→Q2));
            i++;
        }
        return DeQueue(S→Q2);
    }
}
```

CHAPTER

Trees 16

16.1 What is a Tree?

A *tree* is a data structure similar to a linked list but instead of each node pointing simply to the next node in a linear fashion, each node points to a number of nodes. Tree is an example of non-linear data structures. A *tree* structure is a way of representing the hierarchical nature of a structure in a graphical form.

In trees ADT (Abstract Data Type), order of the elements is not important. If we need ordering information linear data structures like linked lists, stacks, queues, etc. can be used.

16.2 Glossary

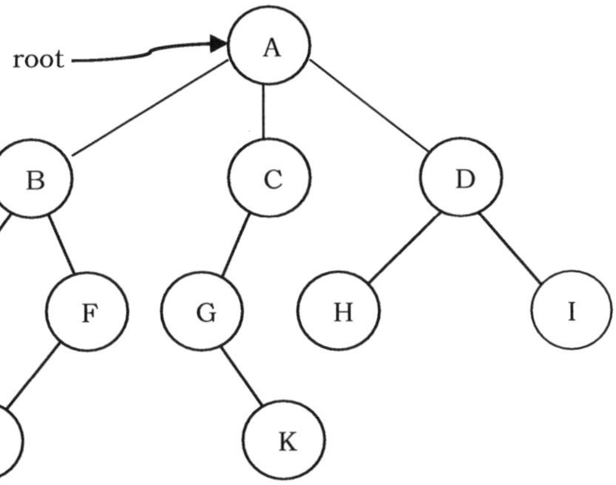

- The *root* of a tree is the node with no parents. There can be at most one root node in a tree (node A in the above example).
- An *edge* refers to the link from parent to child (all links in the figure).
- A node with no children is called *leaf* node (E, J, K, H and I).
- Children of same parent are called *siblings* (B, C, D are siblings of A and E, F are the siblings of B).
- A node p is an *ancestor* of node q if there exists a path from *root* to q and p appears on the path. The node q is called a *descendant* of p. For example, A, C and G are the ancestors of K.
- Set of all nodes at a given depth is called *level* of the tree (B, C and D are same level). The root node is at level zero.

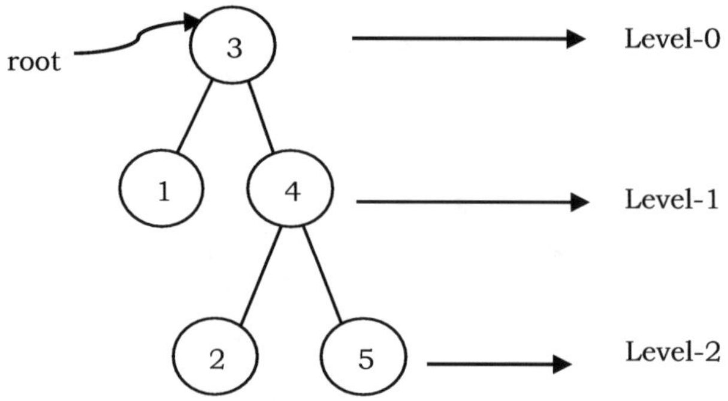

- The *depth* of a node is the length of the path from the root to the node (depth of G is 2, $A - C - G$).
- The *height* of a node is the length of the path from that node to the deepest node. The height of a tree is the length of the path from the root to the deepest node in the tree. A (rooted) tree with only one node (the root) has a height of zero. In the previous example, height of B is 2 $(B - F - J)$.
- *Height of the tree* is the maximum height among all the nodes in the tree and *depth of the tree* is the maximum depth among all the nodes in the tree. For a given tree depth and height returns the same value. But for individual nodes we may get different results.
- Size of a node is the number of descendants it has including itself (size of the subtree C is 3).
- If every node in a tree has only one child (except leaf nodes) then we call such trees *skew trees*. If every node has only left child then we call them as *left skew trees*. Similarly, if every node has only right child then we call them *right skew trees*.

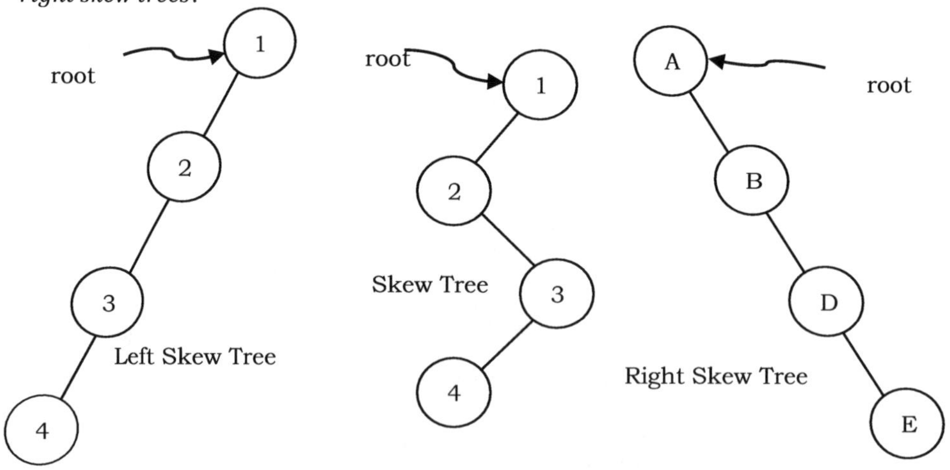

16.3 Binary Trees

A tree is called *binary tree* if each node has zero child, one child or two children. Empty tree is also a valid binary tree.

We can visualize a binary tree as consisting of a root and two disjoint binary trees, called the left and right subtrees of the root.

Generic Binary Tree

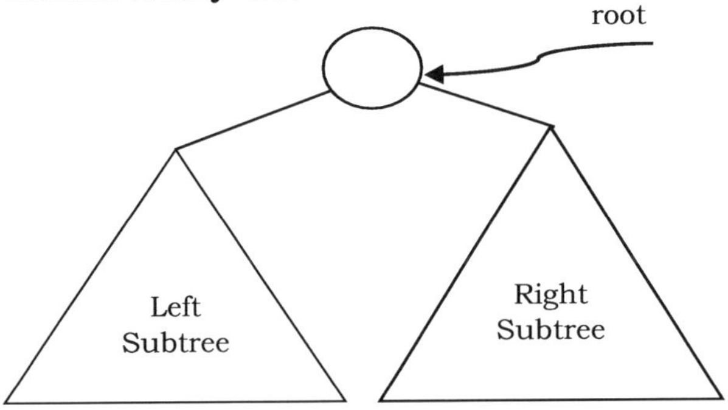

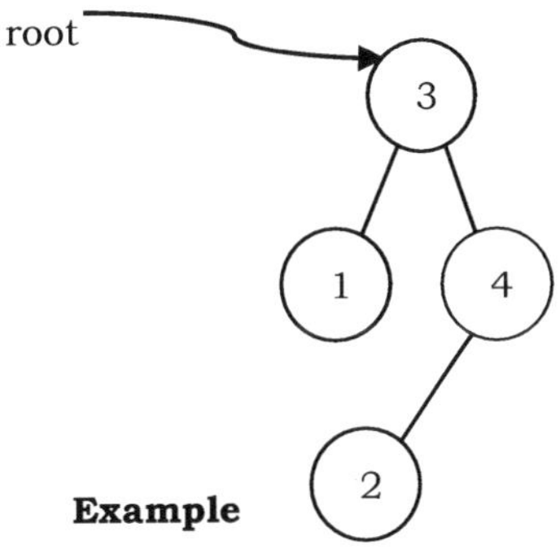

Example

16.4 Types of Binary Trees

Strict Binary Tree: A binary tree is called *strict binary tree* if each node has exactly two children or no children.

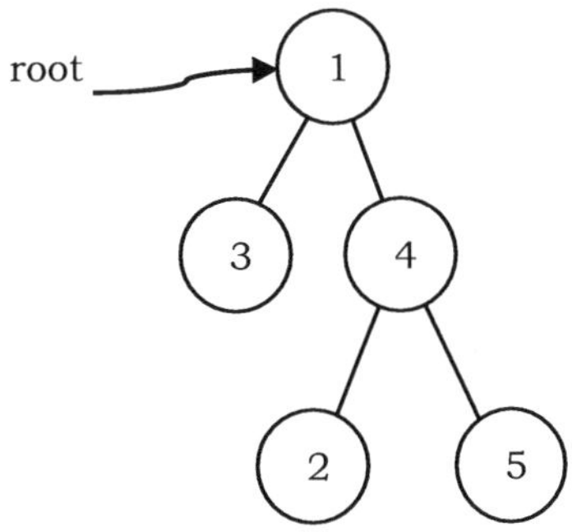

Full Binary Tree: A binary tree is called *full binary tree* if each node has exactly two children and all leaf nodes are at same level.

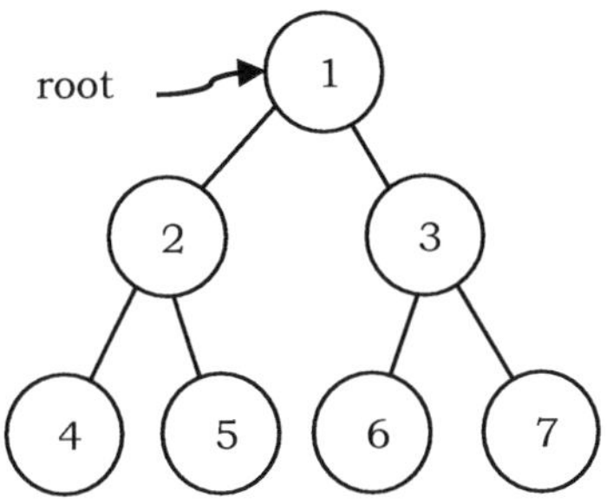

Complete Binary Tree: Before defining the *complete binary tree,* let us assume that the height of the binary tree is *h*.

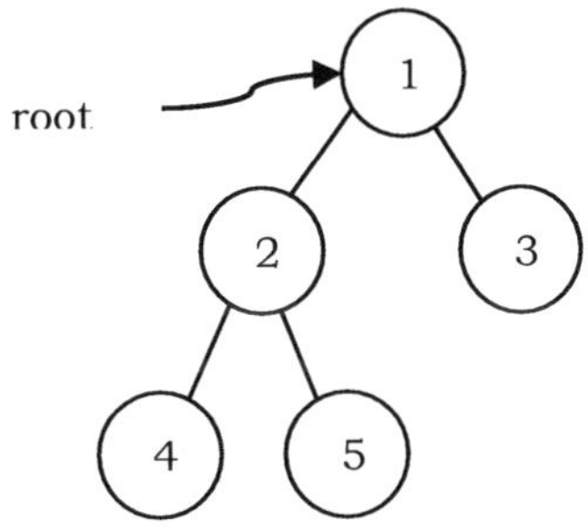

In complete binary trees, if we give numbering for the nodes by starting at root (let us say the root node has 1) then we get a complete sequence from 1 to number of nodes in the tree. While traversing we should give numbering for NULL pointers also. A binary tree is called *complete binary tree* if all leaf nodes are at height h or $h-1$ and also without any missing number in the sequence.

16.5 Properties of Binary Trees

For the following properties, let us assume that the height of the tree is h. Also, assume that root node is at height zero.

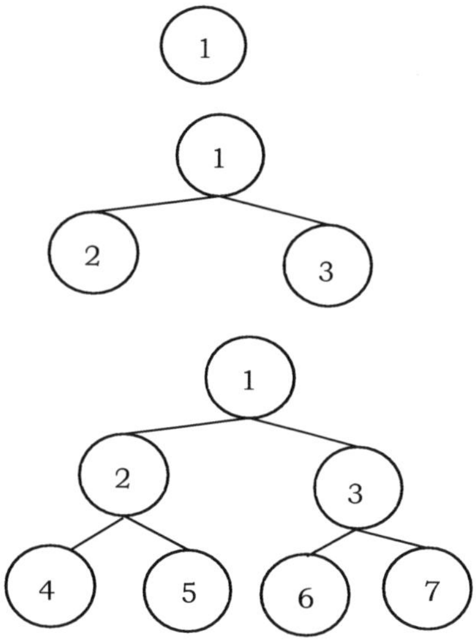

Height	Number of nodes at level $\boldsymbol{h}$
$h = 0$	$2^0 = 1$
$h = 1$	$2^1 = 2$
$h = 2$	$2^2 = 4$

From the diagram we can infer the following properties:

- The number of nodes n in a full binary tree is $2^{h+1} - 1$. Since, there are h levels we need to add all nodes at each level $[2^0 + 2^1 + 2^2 + \cdots + 2^h = 2^{h+1} - 1]$.
- The number of nodes n in a complete binary tree is between 2^h (minimum) and $2^{h+1} - 1$ (maximum). For more information on this, refer *Priority Queues* chapter.
- The number of leaf nodes in a full binary tree is 2^h.
- The number of NULL links (wasted pointers) in a complete binary tree of n nodes is $n + 1$.

Structure of Binary Trees

Now let us define structure of the binary tree. For simplicity, assume that the data of the nodes are integers. One way to represent a node (which contains data) is to have two links which points to left and right children along with data fields as shown below:

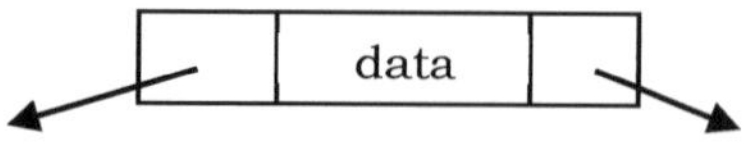

Or

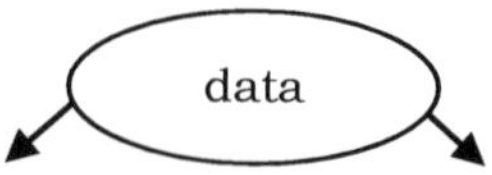


```
struct BinaryTreeNode {
   int data;
   struct BinaryTreeNode *left;
   struct BinaryTreeNode *right;
};
```

Note: In trees, the default flow is from parent to children and it is not mandatory to show directed branches. For our discussion, we assume both the representations shown below are same.

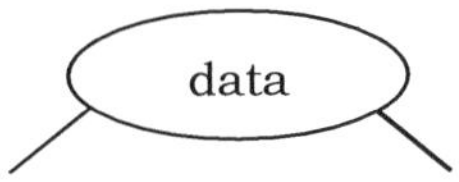

Operations on Binary Trees

Basic Operations

- Inserting an element into a tree
- Deleting an element from a tree
- Searching for an element
- Traversing the tree

Auxiliary Operations

- Finding size of the tree
- Finding height of the tree
- Finding the level which has maximum sum
- Finding least common ancestor (LCA) for a given pair of nodes and many more.

Applications of Binary Trees

Following are the some of the applications where *binary trees* play important role:

- Expression trees are used in compilers.
- Huffman coding trees that are used in data compression algorithms.
- Binary Search Tree (BST), which supports search, insertion and deletion on a collection of items in $O(logn)$ (average).
- Priority Queues (PQ), which supports search and deletion of minimum(or maximum) on a collection of items in logarithmic time (in worst case).

16.6 Binary Tree Traversals

In order to process trees, we need a mechanism for traversing them and that forms the subject of this section. The process of visiting all nodes of a tree is called *tree traversal.* Each node is processed only once but it may be visited more than once. As seen in linear data structures (like linked lists, stacks, queues, etc.), the elements are visited in sequential order. But, in tree structures there are many different ways.

Tree traversal is like searching the tree except that in traversal the goal is to move through the tree in a particular order. In addition, all nodes are processed in the *traversal by searching* stops when the required node is found.

Traversal Possibilities

Starting at the root of a binary tree, there are three main steps that can be performed and the order in which they are performed defines the traversal type. These steps are: performing an action on the current node (referred to as "visiting" the node and denoted with "*D*"), traversing to the left child node (denoted with "*L*"), and traversing to the right child node (denoted with "*R*"). This process can be easily described through recursion. Based on the above definition there are 6 possibilities:

1. *LDR*: Process left subtree, process the current node data and then process right subtree
2. *LRD*: Process left subtree, process right subtree and then process the current node data

3. *DLR*: Process the current node data, process left subtree and then process right subtree
4. *DRL*: Process the current node data, process right subtree and then process left subtree
5. *RDL*: Process right subtree, process the current node data and then process left subtree
6. *RLD*: Process right subtree, process left subtree and then process the current node data

Classifying the Traversals

The sequence in which these entities (nodes) processed defines a particular traversal method. The classification is based on the order in which current node is processed. That means, if we are classifying based on current node (D) and if D comes in the middle then it does not matter whether L is on left side of D or R is on left side of D.

Similarly, it does not matter whether L is on right side of D or R is on right side of D. Due to this, the total 6 possibilities are reduced to 3 and these are:

Preorder (*DLR*) Traversal	Inorder (*LDR*) Traversal	Postorder (*LRD*) Traversal

There is another traversal method which does not depend on above orders and it is:

- Level Order Traversal: This method is inspired from Breadth First Traversal (BFS of Graph algorithms).

Let us use the diagram below for remaining discussion.

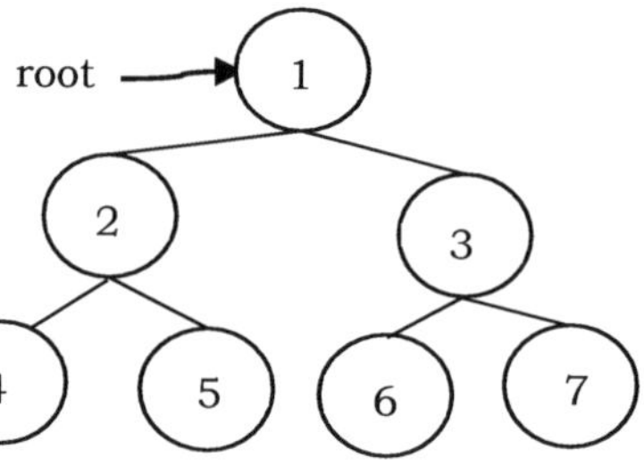

PreOrder Traversal

In pre-order traversal, each node is processed before (pre) either of its sub-trees. This is the simplest traversal to understand. However, even though each node is processed before the subtrees, it still requires that some information must be maintained while moving down the tree. In the example above, 1 is processed first, then the left sub-tree, and this is followed by the right subtree.

Therefore, processing must return to the right sub-tree after finishing the processing of the left subtree. To move to right subtree after processing left subtree, we must maintain the root information. The obvious ADT for such information is a stack. Because of its LIFO structure, it is possible to get the information about the right subtrees back in the reverse order.

Preorder traversal is defined as follows:

- Visit the root.
- Traverse the left subtree in Preorder.
- Traverse the right subtree in Preorder.

The nodes of tree would be visited in the order: 1 2 4 5 3 6 7

```
void PreOrder(struct BinaryTreeNode *root){
    if(root) {
        printf("%d",root→data);
```

```
        PreOrder(root→left);
        PreOrder (root→right);
    }
}
```

Non-Recursive Preorder Traversal

In recursive version a stack is required as we need to remember the current node so that after completing the left subtree we can go to right subtree. To simulate the same, first we process the current node and before going to left subtree, we store the current node on stack.

After completing the left subtree processing, *pop* the element and go to its right subtree. Continue this process until stack is nonempty.

```
void PreOrderNonRecursive(struct BinaryTreeNode *root){
    struct Stack *S = CreateStack();
    while(1) {
        while(root) {
            //Process current node
            printf("%d",root→data);

            Push(S,root);

            //If left subtree exists, add to stack
            root = root→left;
        }
        if(IsEmptyStack(S))
            break;

        root = Pop(S);

        // Indicates completion of left subtree and current node,
        // now go to right subtree
        root = root→right;
    }
    DeleteStack(S);
}
```

InOrder Traversal

In Inorder traversal the root is visited between the subtrees. Inorder traversal is defined as follows:

- Traverse the left subtree in Inorder.
- Visit the root.
- Traverse the right subtree in Inorder.

The nodes of tree would be visited in the order: 4 2 5 1 6 3 7

```
void InOrder(struct BinaryTreeNode *root){
    if(root) {
        InOrder(root→left);
        printf("%d",root→data);
        InOrder(root→right);
    }
}
```

Non-Recursive Inorder Traversal

Non-recursive version of Inorder traversal is similar to Preorder. The only change is, instead of processing the node before going to left subtree, process it after popping (which indicates after completion of left subtree processing).

```
void InOrderNonRecursive(struct BinaryTreeNode *root){
    struct Stack *S = CreateStack();
    while(1) {
        while(root) {
            Push(S,root);
            //Got left subtree and keep on adding to stack
            root = root→left;
        }
        if(IsEmptyStack(S))
            break;
        root = Pop(S);
        printf("%d", root→data);  //After popping, process the current node
        // Indicates completion of left subtree and current node,
        // now go to right subtree
        root = root→right;
    }
    DeleteStack(S);
}
```

PostOrder Traversal

In postorder traversal, the root is visited after both subtrees. Postorder traversal is defined as follows:

- Traverse the left subtree in Postorder.
- Traverse the right subtree in Postorder.
- Visit the root.

The nodes of tree would be visited in the order: 4 5 2 6 7 3 1

```
void PostOrder(struct BinaryTreeNode *root){
    if(root)   {
        PostOrder(root→left);
        PostOrder(root→right);
        printf("%d",root→data);
    }
}
```

Non-Recursive Postorder Traversal

In preorder and inorder traversals, after popping the stack element we do not need to visit the same vertex again. But in postorder traversal, each node is visited twice. That means, after processing left subtree we will visit the current node and after processing the right subtree we will visit the same current node. But we should be processing the node during the second visit. Here the problem is how to differentiate whether we are returning from left subtree or right subtree?

Trick to solving this problem is that after popping an element from stack, check whether that element and right of top of the stack are same or not. If they are same then we have completed the process of left subtree and right subtree. In this case we just need to pop the stack one more time and print its data.

```
void PostOrderNonRecursive(struct BinaryTreeNode *root){
    struct Stack *S = CreateStack();
    while (1) {
        if (root) {
            Push(S,root);
            root=root→left;
        }
```

```
        else {
            if(IsEmptyStack(S)) {
                printf("Stack is Empty");
                return;
            }
            else if(Top(S)→right == NULL) {
                root = Pop(S);
                printf("%d",root→data);
                if(root == Top(S)→right) {
                    printf("%d",Top(S)→data);
                    Pop(S);
                }
            }
            if(!IsEmptyStack(S))
                root=Top(S)→right;
            else
                root=NULL;
        }
    }
    DeleteStack(S);
}
```

Level Order Traversal

Level order traversal is defined as follows:

- Visit the root.
- While traversing level l, keep all the elements at level $l + 1$ in queue.
- Go to the next level and visit all the nodes at that level.
- Repeat this until all levels are completed.

The nodes of tree would be visited in the order: 1 2 3 4 5 6 7

```
void LevelOrder(struct BinaryTreeNode *root){
    struct BinaryTreeNode *temp;
    struct Queue *Q = CreateQueue();
    if(!root)
        return;
    EnQueue(Q,root);
    while(!IsEmptyQueue(Q)) {
        temp = DeQueue(Q);
        //Process current node
        printf("%d", temp→data);
        if(temp→left)
            EnQueue(Q, temp→left);
        if(temp→right)
            EnQueue(Q, temp→right);
    }
    DeleteQueue(Q);
}
```

Problems and Questions with Answers

Question 1: Give an algorithm for finding maximum element in binary tree.

Answer: One simple way of solving this problem is: find the maximum element in left subtree, find maximum element in right sub tree, compare them with root data and select the one which is giving the maximum value. This approach can be easily implemented with recursion.

```
int FindMax(struct BinaryTreeNode  *root) {
    int root_val, left, right, max = INT_MIN;
    if(root !=NULL) {
        root_val = root→data;
        left = FindMax(root→left);
        right = FindMax(root→right);
        // Find the largest of the three values.
        if(left > right)
            max = left;
        else max = right;
        if(root_val > max)
            max = root_val;
    }
    return max;
}
```

Question 2: Give an algorithm for finding maximum element in binary tree without recursion.

Answer: Using level order traversal: just observe the elements data while deleting.

```
int FindMaxUsingLevelOrder(struct BinaryTreeNode *root){
    struct BinaryTreeNode *temp;
    int max = INT_MIN;
    struct Queue *Q = CreateQueue();
    EnQueue(Q,root);
    while(!IsEmptyQueue(Q)) {
        temp = DeQueue(Q);
        // largest of the three values
        if(max < temp→data)
            max =  temp→data;
        if(temp→left)
            EnQueue (Q, temp→left);
        if(temp→right)
            EnQueue (Q, temp→right);
    }
    DeleteQueue(Q);
    return max;
}
```

Question 3: Give an algorithm for searching an element in binary tree.

Answer: Given a binary tree, return true if a node with data is found in the tree. Recurse down the tree, choose the left or right branch by comparing data with each nodes data.

```
int FindInBinaryTreeUsingRecursion(struct BinaryTreeNode *root, int data) {
    int temp;
    // Base case == empty tree, in that case, the data is not found so return false
    if(root == NULL)
        return 0;
    else {
        //see if found here
        if(data == root→data)
          return 1;
```

```
        else {
          // otherwise recur down the correct subtree
          temp = FindInBinaryTreeUsingRecursion (root→left, data)
          if(temp != 0)
            return temp;
          else return(FindInBinaryTreeUsingRecursion(root→right, data));
        }
    }
    return 0;
}
```

Question 4: Give an algorithm for searching an element in binary tree without recursion.

Answer: We can use level order traversal for solving this problem. The only change required in level order traversal is, instead of printing the data we just need to check whether the root data is equal to the element we want to search.

```
int SearchUsingLevelOrder(struct BinaryTreeNode *root, int data){
    struct BinaryTreeNode *temp;
    struct Queue *Q;
    if(!root)
        return -1;

    Q = CreateQueue();
    EnQueue(Q,root);

    while(!IsEmptyQueue(Q)) {
        temp = DeQueue(Q);
        //see if found here
        if(data == root→data)
          return 1;
        if(temp→left)
            EnQueue (Q, temp→left);
        if(temp→right)
            EnQueue (Q, temp→right);
    }
    DeleteQueue(Q);
    return 0;
}
```

Question 5: Give an algorithm for inserting an element into binary tree.

Answer: Since the given tree is a binary tree, we can insert the element wherever we want. To insert an element, we can use the level order traversal and insert the element wherever we found the node whose left or right child is NULL.

```
void InsertInBinaryTree(struct BinaryTreeNode *root, int data){
    struct Queue *Q;
    struct BinaryTreeNode *temp;
    struct BinaryTreeNode *newNode;

    newNode = (struct BinaryTreeNode *) malloc(sizeof(struct BinaryTreeNode));
    newNode→left = newNode→right = NULL;

    if(!newNode) {
        printf("Memory Error");
        return;
    }
    if(!root) {
        root = newNode;
```

```
            return;
        }
        Q = CreateQueue();
        EnQueue(Q,root);
        while(!IsEmptyQueue(Q)) {
            temp = DeQueue(Q);
          if(temp→left)
                EnQueue(Q, temp→left);
            else {
                temp→left=newNode;
                DeleteQueue(Q);
                return;
            }
            if(temp→right)
                EnQueue(Q, temp→right);
            else {
                temp→right=newNode;
                DeleteQueue(Q);
                return;
            }
        }
        DeleteQueue(Q);
}
```

Question 6: Give an algorithm for finding the size of binary tree.

Answer: Calculate the size of left and right subtrees recursively, add 1 (current node) and return to its parent.

```
// Compute the number of nodes in a tree.
int SizeOfBinaryTree(struct BinaryTreeNode *root) {
    if(root==NULL)
        return 0;
    else return(SizeOfBinaryTree(root→left) + 1 +
                    SizeOfBinaryTree(root→right));
}
```

Question 7: Can we solve Question 6: without recursion?

Answer: Yes, using level order traversal.

```
int SizeofBTUsingLevelOrder(struct BinaryTreeNode *root){
    struct BinaryTreeNode *temp;
    struct Queue *Q;
    int count = 0;
    if(!root)
        return 0;
    Q = CreateQueue();
    EnQueue(Q,root);
    while(!IsEmptyQueue(Q)) {
        temp = DeQueue(Q);
        count++;
        if(temp→left)
            EnQueue (Q, temp→left);
        if(temp→right)
            EnQueue (Q, temp→right);
```

```
    }
    DeleteQueue(Q);
    return count;
}
```

Question 8: Give an algorithm for deleting the tree.

Answer: To delete a tree we must traverse all the nodes of the tree and delete them one by one. So which traversal should we use Inorder, Preorder, Postorder or Level order Traversal?

Before deleting the parent node we should delete its children nodes first. We can use postorder traversal as it does the work without storing anything. We can delete tree with other traversals also with extra space complexity. For the following tree nodes are deleted in order – 4, 5, 2, 3, 1.

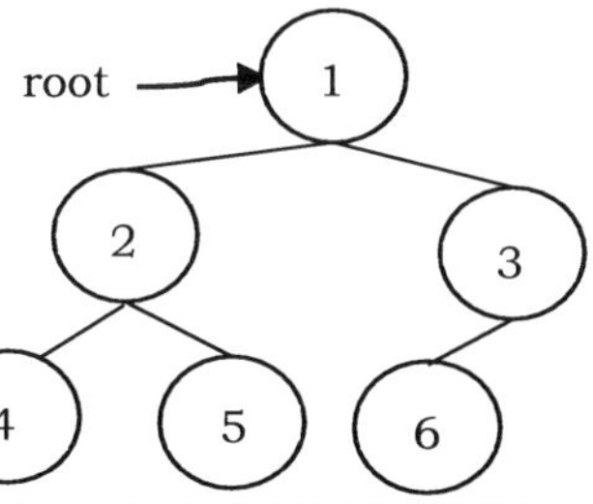


```
void DeleteBinaryTree(struct BinaryTreeNode *root){
    if(root == NULL)
        return;
    /* first delete both subtrees */
    DeleteBinaryTree(root→left);
    DeleteBinaryTree(root→right);
    //Delete current node only after deleting subtrees
    free(root);
}
```

Question 9: Give an algorithm for finding the height (or depth) of the binary tree.

Answer: Recursively calculate height of left and right subtrees of a node and assign height to the node as max of the heights of two children plus 1. This is similar to *PreOrder* tree traversal (and *DFS* of Graph algorithms).

```
int HeightOfBinaryTree(struct BinaryTreeNode   *root){
    int leftheight, rightheight;
    if(root == NULL)
        return 0;
    else {
        /* compute the depth of each subtree */
        leftheight = HeightOfBinaryTree(root→left);
        rightheight = HeightOfBinaryTree(root→right);
        if(leftheight > rightheight)
            return(leftheight + 1);
        else
            return(rightheight + 1);
    }
}
```

Question 10: Can we solve Question 9: without recursion?

Answer: Yes, using level order traversal. This is similar to *BFS* of Graph algorithms. End of level is identified with NULL.

```
int FindHeightofBinaryTree(struct BinaryTreeNode *root){
    int level=1;
    struct Queue *Q;
    if(!root)
            return 0;
    Q = CreateQueue();
    EnQueue(Q,root);
    // End of first level
    EnQueue(Q,NULL);
    while(!IsEmptyQueue(Q)) {
        root=DeQueue(Q);
        // Completion of current level.
        if(root==NULL) {
            //Put another marker for next level.
            if(!IsEmptyQueue(Q))
                EnQueue(Q,NULL);
            level++;
        }
        else {
            if(root→left)
                EnQueue(Q, root→left);
            if(root→right)
                EnQueue(Q, root→right);
        }
    }
    return level;
}
```

Question 11: Give an algorithm for finding the deepest node of the binary tree.

Answer:

```
struct BinaryTreeNode *DeepestNodeinBinaryTree(struct BinaryTreeNode *root){
    struct BinaryTreeNode *temp;
    struct Queue *Q;
    if(!root)
        return NULL;
    Q = CreateQueue();
    EnQueue(Q,root);
    while(!IsEmptyQueue(Q)) {
        temp = DeQueue(Q);
        if(temp→left)
            EnQueue(Q, temp→left);
        if(temp→right)
            EnQueue(Q, temp→right);
    }
    DeleteQueue(Q);
    return temp;
}
```

Question 12: Give an algorithm for deleting an element (assuming data is given) from binary tree.

Answer: The deletion of a node in binary tree can be implemented as

- Starting at root, find the node which we want to delete.
- Find the deepest node in the tree.
- Replace the deepest nodes data with node to be deleted.
- Then delete the deepest node.

Question 13: Give an algorithm for finding the number of leaves in the binary tree without using recursion.

Answer: The set of nodes whose both left and right children are NULL are called leaf nodes.

```
int NumberOfLeavesInBTusingLevelOrder(struct BinaryTreeNode *root){
    struct BinaryTreeNode *temp;
    struct Queue *Q;
    int count = 0;
    if(!root)
        return 0;
    Q = CreateQueue();
    EnQueue(Q,root);
    while(!IsEmptyQueue(Q)) {
        temp = DeQueue(Q);
        if(!temp→left && !temp→right)
            count++;
        else {
            if(temp→left)
                EnQueue(Q, temp→left);
            if(temp→right)
                EnQueue(Q, temp→right);
        }
    }
    DeleteQueue(Q);
    return count;
}
```

Question 14: Give an algorithm for finding the number of full nodes in the binary tree without using recursion.

Answer: The set of all nodes with both left and right children are called full nodes.

```
int NumberOfFullNodesInBTusingLevelOrder(struct BinaryTreeNode *root){
    struct BinaryTreeNode *temp;
    struct Queue *Q;
    int count = 0;
    if(!root)
        return 0;
    Q = CreateQueue();
    EnQueue(Q,root);
    while(!IsEmptyQueue(Q)) {
        temp = DeQueue(Q);
        if(temp→left && temp→right)
            count++;
        if(temp→left)
            EnQueue (Q, temp→left);
        if(temp→right)
            EnQueue (Q, temp→right);
    }
    DeleteQueue(Q);
    return count;
}
```

Question 15: Give an algorithm for finding the number of half nodes (nodes with only one child) in the binary tree without using recursion.

Answer: The set of all nodes with either left or either right child (but not both) are called half nodes.

```
int NumberOfHalfNodesInBTusingLevelOrder(struct BinaryTreeNode *root){
    struct BinaryTreeNode *temp;
    struct Queue *Q;
    int count = 0;
    if(!root)
        return 0;
    Q = CreateQueue();
    EnQueue(Q,root);
    while(!IsEmptyQueue(Q)) {
        temp = DeQueue(Q);
        //we can use this condition also instead of two temp→left ^ temp→right
        if(!temp→left && temp→right || temp→left && !temp→right)
            count++;
        if(temp→left)
            EnQueue (Q, temp→left);
        if(temp→right)
            EnQueue (Q, temp→right);
    }
    DeleteQueue(Q);
    return count;
}
```

Question 16: Given two binary trees, return true if they are structurally identical.

Answer:

Algorithm:

- If both trees are NULL then return true.
- If both trees are not NULL, then compare data and recursively check left and right subtree structures.

```
//Return true if they are structurally identical.
int AreStructurullySameTrees(struct BinaryTreeNode *root1,
                                        struct BinaryTreeNode *root2) {
    // both empty→1
    if(root1==NULL && root2==NULL)
        return 1;
    if(root1==NULL || root2==NULL)
        return 0;
    // both non-empty→compare them
    return(root1→data == root2→data &&
                    AreStructurullySameTrees(root1→left, root2→left) &&
                    AreStructurullySameTrees(root1→right, root2→right));
}
```

Question 17: Give an algorithm for finding the diameter of the binary tree. The diameter of a tree (sometimes called the *width*) is the number of nodes on the longest path between two leaves in the tree.

Answer: To find the diameter of a tree, first calculate the diameter of left subtree and right sub trees recursively. Among these two values, we need to send maximum value along with current level (+1).

```
int DiameterOfTree(struct BinaryTreeNode *root, int *ptr){
    int left, right;
    if(!root)
```

```
        return 0;
    left = DiameterOfTree(root→left, ptr);
    right = DiameterOfTree(root→right, ptr);
    if(left + right > *ptr)
        *ptr = left + right;
    return Max(left, right)+1;
}
```

Question 18: Give an algorithm for finding the level that has the maximum sum in the binary tree.

Answer: The logic is very much similar to finding number of levels. The only change is, we need to keep track of sums as well.

```
int FindLevelwithMaxSum(struct BinaryTreeNode *root){
    struct BinaryTreeNode *temp;
    int level=0, maxLevel=0;
    struct Queue *Q;
    int currentSum = 0, maxSum = 0;
    if(!root)
        return 0;
    Q=CreateQueue();
    EnQueue(Q,root);
    EnQueue(Q,NULL);                //End of first level.
    while(!IsEmptyQueue(Q)) {
        temp =DeQueue(Q);
        // If the current level is completed then compare sums
        if(temp == NULL) {
            if(currentSum> maxSum) {
                maxSum = currentSum;
                maxLevel = level;
            }
        currentSum = 0;
        //place the indicator for end of next level at the end of queue
        if(!IsEmptyQueue(Q))
            EnQueue(Q,NULL);
            level++;
        }
        else {
            currentSum   += temp→data;
            if(temp→left)
                EnQueue(temp, temp→left);
            if(root→right)
                EnQueue(temp, temp→right);
        }
    }
    return maxLevel;
}
```

Question 19: Given a binary tree, print out all its root-to-leaf paths.

Answer: Refer comments in functions.

```
void PrintPathsRecur(struct BinaryTreeNode *root, int path[], int pathLen) {
    if(root ==NULL)
        return;
    // append this node to the path array
```

```
    path[pathLen] = root→data;
    pathLen++;
    // it's a leaf, so print the path that led to here
    if(root→left==NULL && root→right==NULL)
        PrintArray(path, pathLen);
    else {
        // otherwise try both subtrees
        PrintPathsRecur(root→left, path, pathLen);
        PrintPathsRecur(root→right, path, pathLen);
    }
}
// Function that prints out an array on a line.
void PrintArray(int ints[], int len) {
    for (int i=0; i<len; i++)
        printf("%d",ints[i]);
}
```

Question 20: Give an algorithm for finding the sum of all elements in binary tree.

Answer: Recursively, call left subtree sum, right subtree sum and add their values to current nodes data.

```
int Add(struct BinaryTreeNode  *root) {
    if(root == NULL)
        return 0;
    else
        return (root→data + Add(root→left) +  Add(root→right));
}
```

Question 21: Can we solve Question 20: without recursion?

Answer: We can use level order traversal with simple change. Every time after deleting an element from queue, add the nodes data value to *sum* variable.

```
int SumofBTusingLevelOrder(struct BinaryTreeNode *root){
    struct BinaryTreeNode *temp;
    struct Queue *Q;
    int sum = 0;
    if(!root)
        return 0;
    Q = CreateQueue();
    EnQueue(Q,root);
    while(!IsEmptyQueue(Q)) {
        temp = DeQueue(Q);
        sum += temp→data;
        if(temp→left)
          EnQueue (Q, temp→left);
        if(temp→right)
          EnQueue (Q, temp→right);
    }
    DeleteQueue(Q);
    return sum;
}
```

Question 22: Give an algorithm for converting a tree to its mirror. Mirror of a tree is another tree with left and right children of all non-leaf nodes interchanged. The trees below are mirrors to each other.

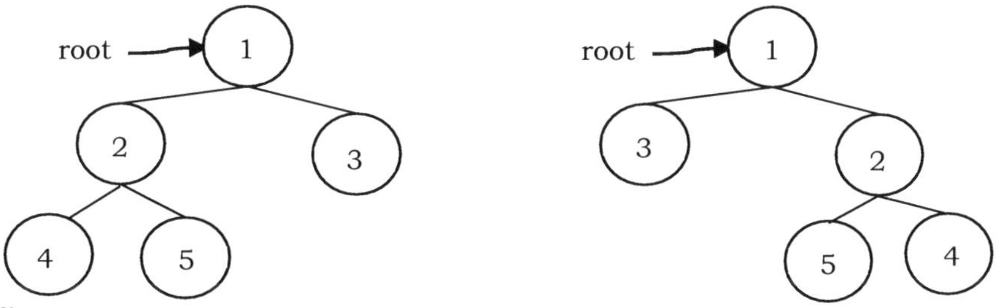

Answer:

```
struct BinaryTreeNode *MirrorOfBinaryTree(struct BinaryTreeNode *root){
    struct BinaryTreeNode * temp;
    if(root) {
        MirrorOfBinaryTree(root→left);
        MirrorOfBinaryTree(root→right);
        /* swap the pointers in this node */
        temp  = root→left;
        root→left  = root→right;
        root→right = temp;
    }
        return root;
}
```

Question 23: Given two trees, give an algorithm for checking whether they are mirrors of each other.

Answer:

```
int AreMirrors(struct BinaryTreeNode  * root1, struct BinaryTreeNode  * root2) {
    if(root1 == NULL && root2 == NULL)
        return 1;
    if(root1 == NULL || root2 == NULL)
        return 0;
    if(root1→data != root2→data)
        return 0;
    else return AreMirrors(root1→left, root2→right) &&
                                                AreMirrors(root1→right, root2→left);
}
```

Question 24: Give an algorithm for finding LCA (Least Common Ancestor) of two nodes in a Binary Tree.

Answer:

```
struct BinaryTreeNode *LCA(struct BinaryTreeNode *root,
                                    struct BinaryTreeNode *á,
                                    struct BinaryTreeNode *â){
    struct BinaryTreeNode *left, *right;
    if(root == NULL)
        return root;
    if(root == á || root == â)
        return root;
    left = LCA (root→left, á, â );
        right = LCA (root→right, á, â );
        if(left && right)
            return root;
    else    return (left? left: right)
}
```

Question 25: Give an algorithm for constructing binary tree from given Inorder and Preorder traversals.

Answer: Let us consider the traversals below:

```
Inorder sequence:  D B E A F C
Preorder sequence: A B D E C F
```

In a Preorder sequence, leftmost element denotes the root of the tree. So we know *'A'* is root for given sequences. By searching *'A'* in Inorder sequence we can find out all elements on left side of *'A'*, which come under left subtree and elements right side of *'A'*, which come under right subtree. So we get the structure as given below.

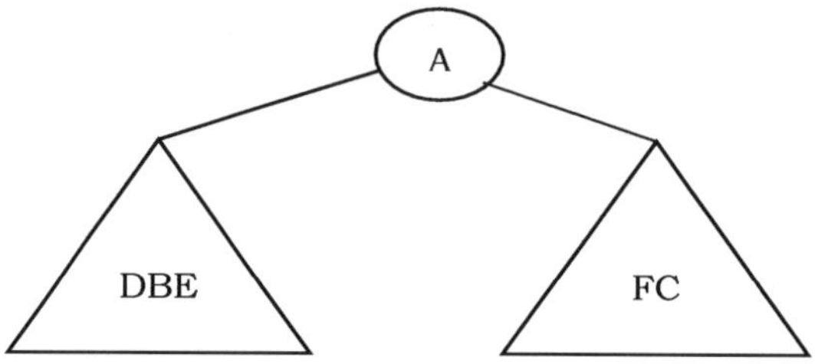

We recursively follow above steps and get the following tree.

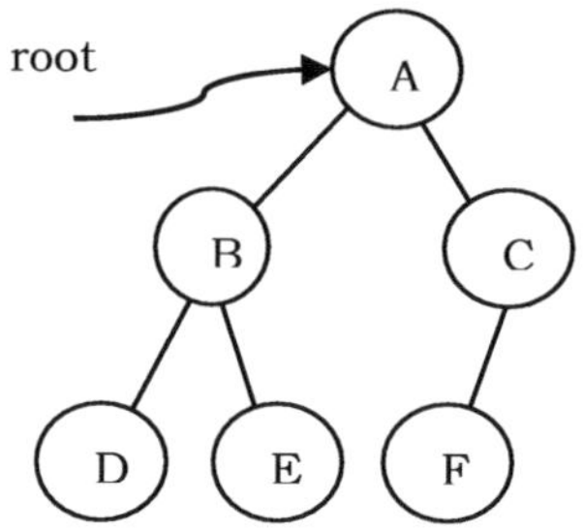

Algorithm: BuildTree()

1 Select an element from Preorder. Increment a Preorder index variable (preIndex in below code) to pick next element in next recursive call.
2 Create a new tree node (newNode) with the data as selected element.
3 Find the selected elements index in Inorder. Let the index be inIndex.
4 Call BuildBinaryTree for elements before inIndex and make the built tree as left subtree of newNode.
5 Call BuildBinaryTree for elements after inIndex and make the built tree as right subtree of newNode.
6 return newNode.

```
struct BinaryTreeNode *BuildBinaryTree(int inOrder[], int preOrder[], int inStrt, int inEnd){
    static int preIndex = 0;
    struct BinaryTreeNode *newNode;
    if(inStrt > inEnd)
        return NULL;
    newNode = (struct BinaryTreeNode *) malloc (sizeof(struct BinaryTreeNode));
    if(!newNode) {
          printf("Memory Error");
          return NULL;
    }
```

```
    // Select current node from Preorder traversal using preIndex
    newNode→data = preOrder[preIndex];
    preIndex++;
    if(inStrt == inEnd)              //if this node has no children then return
        return newNode;
    // else find the index of this node in Inorder traversal
    int inIndex = Search(inOrder, inStrt, inEnd, newNode→data);
    //Using index in Inorder traversal, construct left and right subtress
    newNode→left = BuildBinaryTree(inOrder, preOrder, inStrt, inIndex-1);
    newNode→right = BuildBinaryTree(inOrder, preOrder, inIndex+1, inEnd);
    return newNode;
}
```

Question 26: If we are given two traversal sequences, can we construct the binary tree uniquely?

Answer: It depends on what traversals are given. If one of the traversal methods is *Inorder* then the tree can be constructed uniquely, otherwise not.

Therefore, following combination can uniquely identify a tree:

- Inorder and Preorder
- Inorder and Postorder
- Inorder and Level-order

The following combinations do not uniquely identify a tree.

- Postorder and Preorder
- Preorder and Level-order
- Postorder and Level-order

For example, Preorder, Level-order and Postorder traversals are same for above trees:

Preorder Traversal = AB Postorder Traversal = BA Level-order Traversal = AB

So, even if three of them (PreOrder, Level-Order and PostOrder) are given, the tree cannot be constructed uniquely.

Question 27: How many different binary trees are possible with n nodes?

Answer: For example, consider a tree with 3 nodes ($n = 3$). It will have the maximum combination of 5 different (i.e., $2^3 - 3 = 5$) trees.

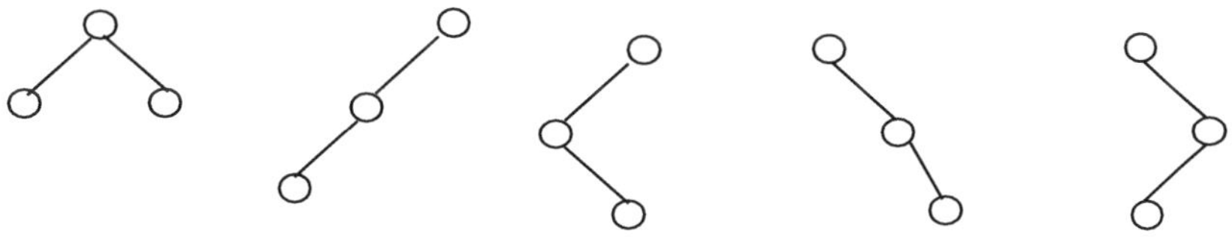

In general, if there are n nodes, there exist $2^n - n$ different trees.

16.7 Generic Trees (N-ary Trees)

In the previous section we discussed binary trees where each node can have maximum of two children and these are represented easily with two pointers.

But suppose if we have a tree with many children at every node and also if we do not know how many children a node can have, how do we represent them? For example, consider the tree shown below.

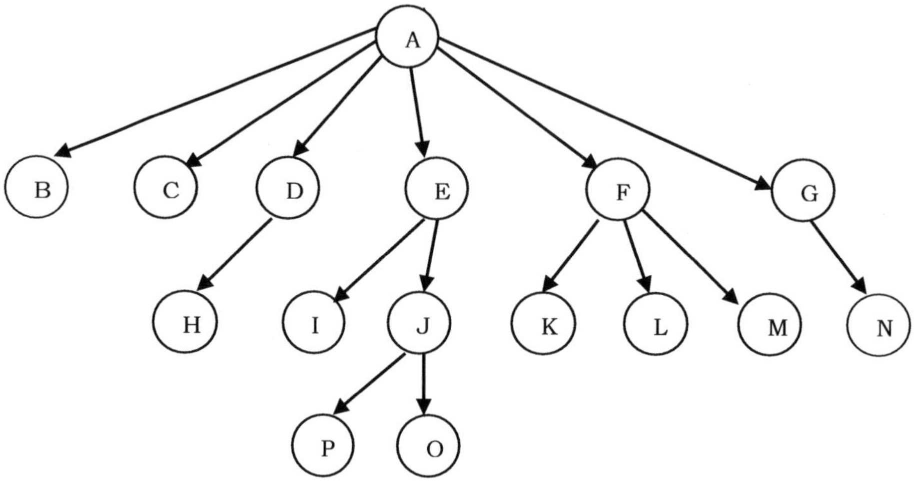

How do we represent the tree?

In the above tree, there are nodes with 6 children, with 3 children, 2 children, with 1 child, and with zero children (leaves). To present this tree we have to consider the worst case (6 children) and allocate those many child pointers for each node. Based on this, the node representation can be given as:

```
struct TreeNode{
    int data;
    struct TreeNode *firstChild;
    struct TreeNode *secondChild;
    struct TreeNode *thirdChild;
    struct TreeNode *fourthChild;
    struct TreeNode *fifthChild;
    struct TreeNode *sixthChild;
};
```

Since we are not using all the pointers in all the cases there is a lot of memory wastage. Also, another problem is that, in advance we do not know the number of children for each node.

In order to solve this problem we need a representation that minimizes the wastage and also accept nodes with any number of children.

Representation of Generic Trees

Since our objective is to reach all nodes of the tree, a possible solution to this is as follows:

- At each node link children of same parent (siblings) from left to right.
- Remove the links from parent to all children except the first child.

What these above statements say is if we have a link between children then we do not need extra links from parent to all children. This is because we can traverse all the elements by starting at the first child of the parent.

So if we have link between parent and first child and also links between all children of same parent then it solves our problem. This representation is sometimes called first child/next sibling representation.

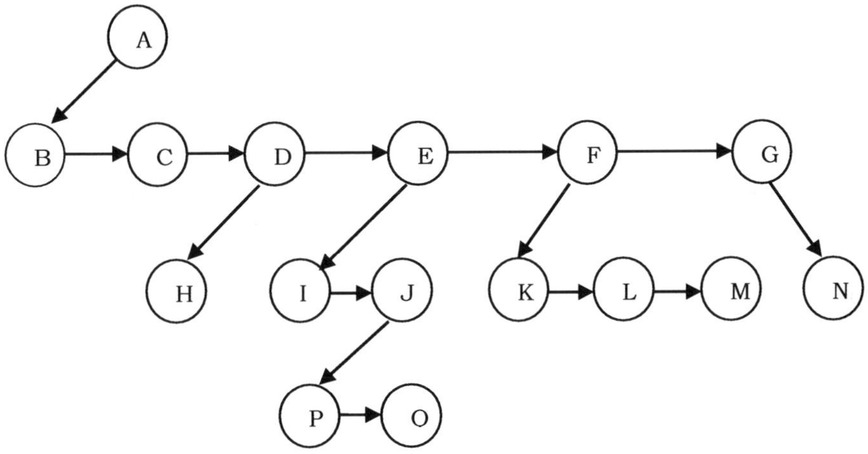

First child/next sibling representation of the generic tree is shown above. The actual representation for this tree is:

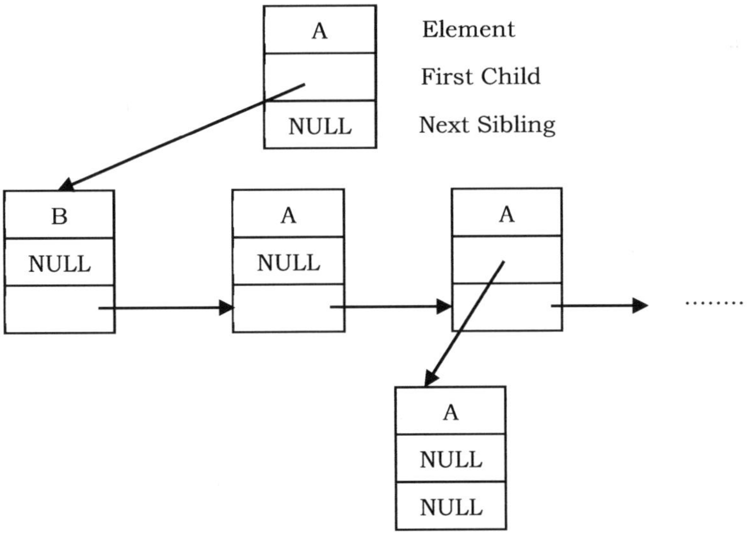

Based on this discussion, the tree node declaration for general tree can be given as:

```
struct TreeNode {
    int data;
    struct TreeNode *firstChild;
    struct TreeNode *nextSibling;
};
```

Note: Since we are able to represent any generic tree with binary representation, in practice we use only binary tree.

Problems and Questions with Answers

Question 28: Given a tree, give an algorithm for finding the sum of all the elements of the tree.

Answer: The solution is similar to what we have done for simple binary trees. That means, traverse the complete list and keep on adding the values. We can either use level order traversal or simple recursion.

```
int FindSum(struct TreeNode *root){
    if(!root)
        return 0;
    return root→data + FindSum(root→firstChild) + FindSum(root→nextSibling);
}
```

Note: All problems which we have discussed for binary trees are applicable for generic trees also. Instead of left and right pointers we just need to use firstChild and nextSibling.

Question 29: For a 4-ary tree (each node can contain maximum of 4 children), what is the maximum possible height with 100 nodes? Assume height of a single node is 0.

Answer: In 4-ary tree each node can contain 0 to 4 children and to get maximum height, we need to keep only one child for each parent. With 100 nodes the maximum possible height we can get is 99.

If we have a restriction that at least one node has 4 children, then we keep one node with 4 children and remaining nodes with 1 child. In this case, the maximum possible height is 96. Similarly, with n nodes the maximum possible height is $n - 4$.

Question 30: For a 4-ary tree (each node can contain maximum of 4 children), what is the minimum possible height with n nodes?

Answer: Similar to above discussion, if we want to get minimum height, then we need to fill all nodes with maximum children (in this case 4). Now let's see the following table, which indicates the maximum number of nodes for a given height.

Height, h	Maximum Nodes at height, $h = 4^h$	Total Nodes height $h = \frac{4^{h+1}-1}{3}$
0	1	1
1	4	1+4
2	4 × 4	1+ 4 × 4
3	4 × 4 × 4	1+ 4 × 4 + 4 × 4 × 4

For a given height h the maximum possible nodes are: $\frac{4^{h+1}-1}{3}$. To get minimum height, take logarithm on both sides:

$$n = \frac{4^{h+1}-1}{3} \Rightarrow 4^{h+1} = 3n + 1 \Rightarrow (h + 1)log4 = \log(3n + 1) \Rightarrow h + 1 = \log_4(3n + 1) \Rightarrow h = \log_4(3n + 1) - 1$$

16.8 Threaded Binary Tree Traversals

In earlier sections we have seen that, *preorder, inorder and postorder* binary tree traversals used stacks and *level order* traversal used queues as an auxiliary data structure. In this section we will discuss new traversal algorithms which do not need both stacks and queues and such traversal algorithms are called *threaded binary tree traversals* or *stack/queue less traversals*.

Issues with Regular Binary Tree Traversals

- The storage space required for the stack and queue is large.

- The majority of pointers in any binary tree are NULL. For example, a binary tree with n nodes has $n+ 1$ NULL pointers and these were wasted.

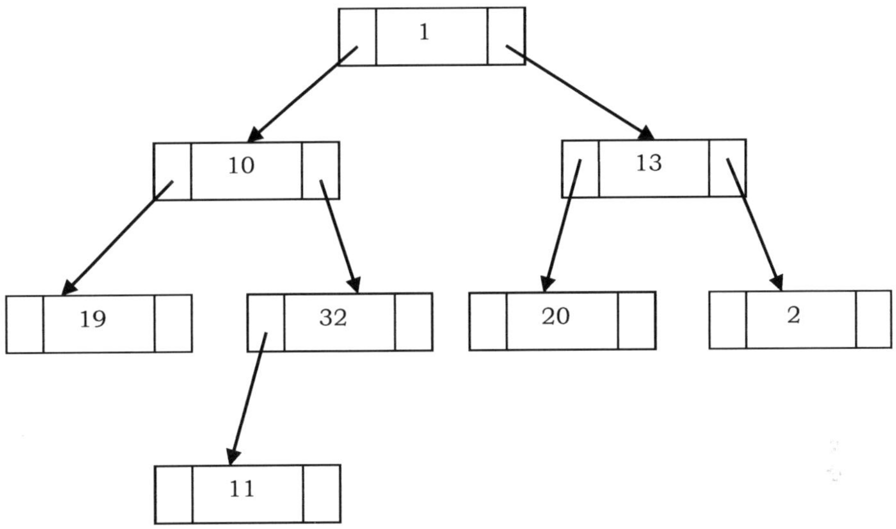

- It is difficult to find successor node (preorder, inorder and postorder successors) for a given node.

Motivation for Threaded Binary Trees

To solve these problems, one idea is to store some useful information in NULL pointers. If we observe previous traversals carefully, stack/queue is required because we have to record the current position in order to move to right subtree after processing the left subtree. If we store the useful information in NULL pointers, then we don't have to store such information in stack/queue.

The binary trees which store such information in NULL pointers are called *threaded binary trees*. From the above discussion, let us assume that we want to store some useful information in NULL pointers. The next question is what to store?

The common convention is to put predecessor/successor information. That means, if we are dealing with preorder traversals then for a given node, NULL left pointer will contain preorder predecessor information and NULL right pointer will contain preorder successor information. These special pointers are called *threads*.

Classifying Threaded Binary Trees

The classification is based on whether we are storing useful information in both NULL pointers or only in one of them.

- If we store predecessor information in NULL left pointers only then we can call such binary trees *left threaded binary trees*.
- If we store successor information in NULL right pointers only then we can call such binary trees *right threaded binary trees*.
- If we store predecessor information in NULL left pointers only then we can call such binary trees *fully threaded binary trees* or simply *threaded binary trees*.

Note: For the remaining discussion we consider only (*fully*) *threaded binary trees*.

Types of Threaded Binary Trees

Based on above discussion we get three representations for threaded binary trees.

- *Preorder Threaded Binary Trees*: NULL left pointer will contain PreOrder predecessor information and NULL right pointer will contain PreOrder successor information
- *Inorder Threaded Binary Trees*: NULL left pointer will contain InOrder predecessor information and NULL right pointer will contain InOrder successor information
- *Postorder Threaded Binary Trees*: NULL left pointer will contain PostOrder predecessor information and NULL right pointer will contain PostOrder successor information

Note: As the representations are similar, for the remaining discussion, we will use InOrder threaded binary trees.

Threaded Binary Tree structure

Any program examining the tree must be able to differentiate between a regular *left/right* pointer and a *thread*. To do this, we use two additional fields into each node giving us, for threaded trees, nodes of the following form:

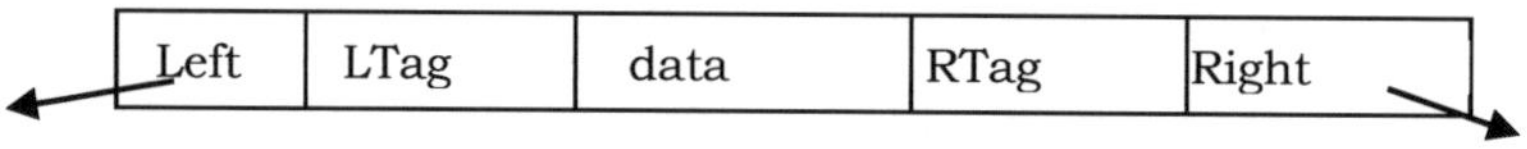


```
struct ThreadedBinaryTreeNode{
    struct ThreadedBinaryTreeNode *left;
    int LTag;
    int data;
    int RTag;
    struct ThreadedBinaryTreeNode *right;
};
```

Binary Tree Versus Threaded Binary Tree Structures

	Regular Binary Trees	Threaded Binary Trees
if LTag == 0	NULL	left points to the in-order predecessor
if LTag == 1	left points to the left child	left points to left child
if RTag == 0	NULL	right points to the in-order successor
if RTag == 1	right points to the right child	right points to the right child

Note: Similarly, we can define for preorder/postorder differences as well.

As an example, let us try representing a tree in inorder threaded binary tree form. The tree below shows what an inorder threaded binary tree will look like. The dotted arrows indicate the threads.

Observing carefully, the left pointer of left most node (2) and right pointer of right most node (31) are hanging.

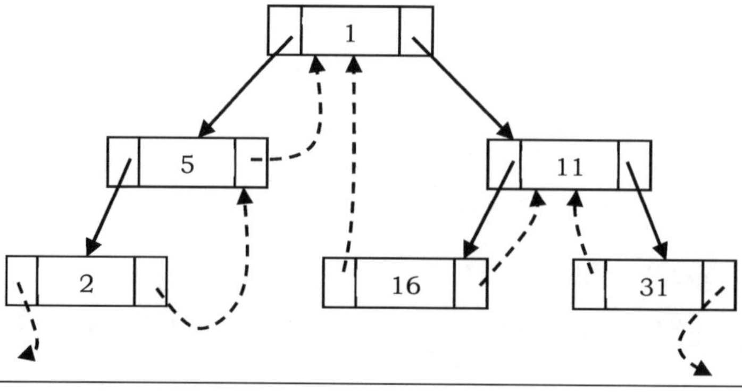

What should leftmost and rightmost pointers point to?

In the representation of a threaded binary tree, it is convenient to use a special node *Dummy* which is always present even for an empty tree. Note that right tag of dummy node is 1 and its right child points to itself.

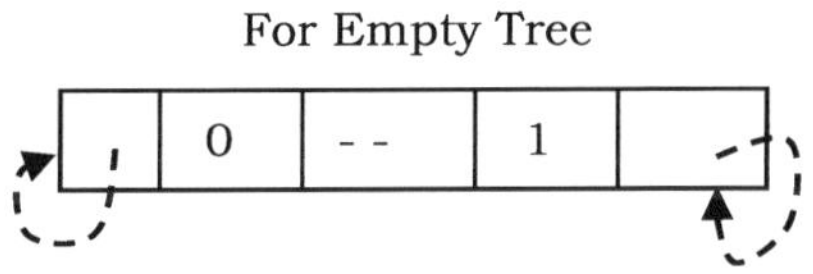

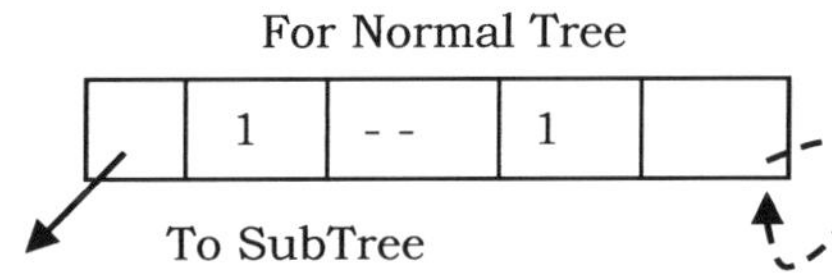

With this convention the above tree can be represented as:

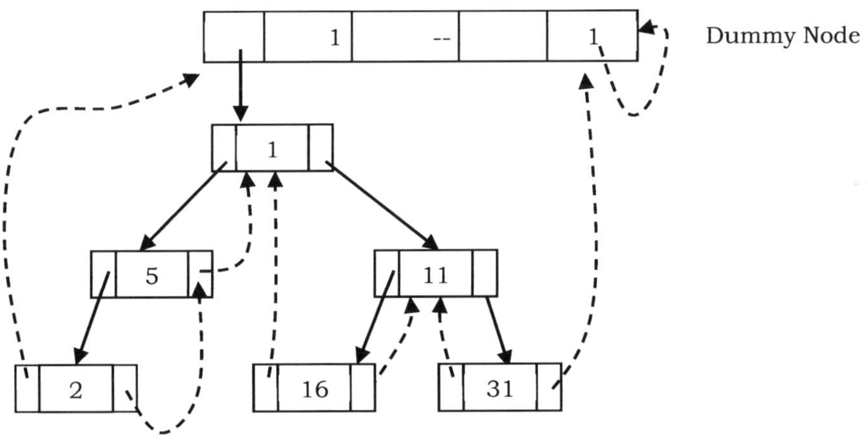

Finding Inorder Successor in Inorder Threaded Binary Tree

To find inorder successor of a given node without using a stack, assume that the node for which we want to find the inorder successor is *P*.

Strategy: If *P* has a no right subtree, then return the right child of *P*. If *P* has right subtree, then return the left of the nearest node whose left subtree contains *P*.

```
struct ThreadedBinaryTreeNode* InorderSuccessor(
                                        struct ThreadedBinaryTreeNode *P){
    struct ThreadedBinaryTreeNode *Position;
    if(P→RTag == 0)
        return P→right;
    else {
        Position = P→right;
        while(Position→LTag == 1)
            Position = Position→left;
        return Position;
    }
}
```

Inorder Traversal in Inorder Threaded Binary Tree

We can start with *dummy* node and call InorderSuccessor() to visit each node until we reach *dummy* node.

```
void InorderTraversal(struct ThreadedBinaryTreeNode *root){
    struct ThreadedBinaryTreeNode *P = InorderSuccessor(root);
    while(P != root) {
```

```
        P = InorderSuccessor(P);
        printf("%d",P→data);
    }
}
```

Other way of coding:

```
void InorderTraversal(struct ThreadedBinaryTreeNode *root){
    struct ThreadedBinaryTreeNode *P = root;
    while(1) {
        P = InorderSuccessor(P);
        if(P == root)
            return;
        printf("%d",P→data);
    }
}
```

Finding PreOrder Successor in InOrder Threaded Binary Tree

Strategy: If *P* has a left subtree, then return the left child of *P*. If *P* has no left subtree, then return the right child of the nearest node whose right subtree contains *P*.

```
struct ThreadedBinaryTreeNode* PreorderSuccessor(
                                        struct ThreadedBinaryTreeNode *P){
        struct ThreadedBinaryTreeNode *Position;
        if(P→LTag == 1)
                return P→left;
        else {
                Position = P;
                while(Position→RTag == 0)
                    Position = Position→right;
                return Position→right;
        }
}
```

PreOrder Traversal of InOrder Threaded Binary Tree

As in inorder traversal, start with *dummy* node and call PreorderSuccessor() to visit each node until we get *dummy* node again.

```
void PreorderTraversal(struct ThreadedBinaryTreeNode *root){
    struct ThreadedBinaryTreeNode *P;
    P = PreorderSuccessor(root);
    while(P != root) {
        P = PreorderSuccessor(P);
        printf("%d",P→data);
    }
}
```

Other way of coding:

```
void PreorderTraversal(struct ThreadedBinaryTreeNode *root) {
    struct ThreadedBinaryTreeNode *P = root;
    while(1){
        P = PreorderSuccessor(P);
            if(P == root)
             return;
```

```
        printf("%d",P→data);
    }
}
```

Note: From the above discussion, it should be clear that inorder and preorder successor finding is easy with threaded binary trees. But finding postorder successor is very difficult if we do not use stack.

Insertion of Nodes in InOrder Threaded Binary Trees

For simplicity, let us assume that there are two nodes *P* and *Q* and we want to attach *Q* to right of *P*. For this we will have two cases.

- Node *P* does not have right child: In this case we just need to attach *Q* to *P* and change its left and right pointers.

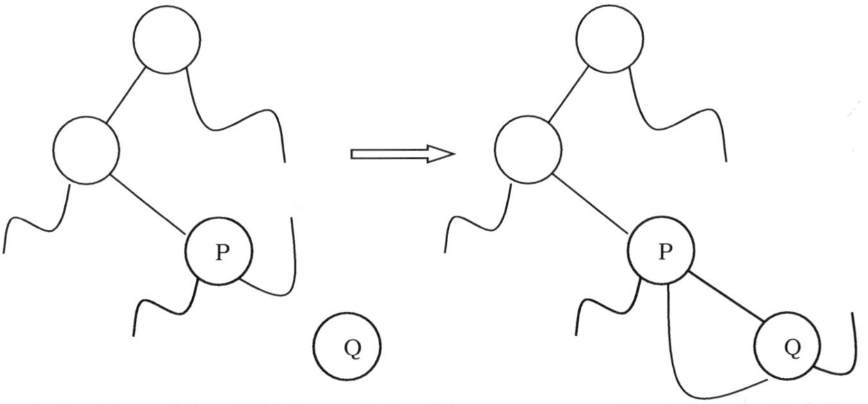

- Node *P* has right child (say, *R*): In this case we need to traverse *R's* left subtree and find the left most node and then update the left and right pointer of that node (as shown below).

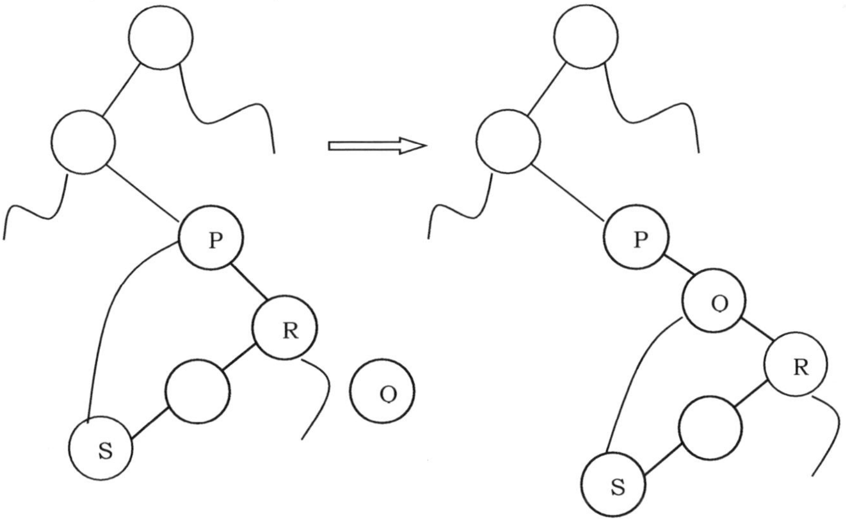


```
void InsertRightInInorderTBT(struct ThreadedBinaryTreeNode *P,
                             struct ThreadedBinaryTreeNode *Q){
    struct ThreadedBinaryTreeNode *Temp;
    Q→right = P→right;
    Q→RTag = P→RTag;
    Q→left = P;
```

```
    Q→LTag = 0;
    P→right = Q;
    P→RTag = 1;
    if(Q→RTag == 1) {              //Case-2
        Temp = Q→right;
        while(Temp→LTag)
            Temp = Temp→left;
        Temp→left = Q;
    }
}
```

Problems and Questions with Answers

Question 31: For a given binary tree (not threaded) how do we find the preorder successor?

Answer: For solving this problem, we need to use an auxiliary stack *S*. On the first call, the parameter node is a pointer to the head of the tree, thereafter its value is NULL. Since we are simply asking for the successor of the node we got last time we called the function.

It is necessary that the contents of the stack *S* and the pointer *P* to the last node *visited* are preserved from one call of the function to the next; they are defined as static variables.

```
// pre-order successor for an unthreaded binary tree
struct BinaryTreeNode *PreorderSuccssor(struct BinaryTreeNode *node){
    static struct BinaryTreeNode *P;
    static Stack *S = CreateStack();
    if(node != NULL)
        P = node;
    if(P→left != NULL) {
        Push(S,P);
        P = P→left;
    }
    else {
        while (P→right == NULL)
            P = Pop(S);
        P = P→right;
    }
    return P;
}
```

Question 32: For a given binary tree (not threaded) how do we find the inorder successor?

Answer: Similar to above discussion, we can find the inorder successor of a node as:

```
// In-order successor for an unthreaded binary tree
struct BinaryTreeNode *InorderSuccssor(struct BinaryTreeNode *node){
    static struct BinaryTreeNode *P;
    static Stack *S = CreateStack();
    if(node != NULL)
        P = node;
    if(P→right == NULL)
        P = Pop(S);
    else {
        P = P→right;
        while (P→left != NULL)
            Push(S, P);
```

```
        P = P→left;
    }
    return P;
}
```

16.9 Binary Search Trees (BSTs)

Why Binary Search Trees?

In previous sections we have discussed different tree representations and in all of them we did not impose any restriction on the nodes data. As a result, to search for an element we need to check both in left subtree and in right subtree. Due to this, the worst case complexity of search operation is $O(n)$.

In this section, we will discuss another variant of binary trees: Binary Search Trees (BSTs). As the name suggests, the main use of this representation is for *searching*. In this representation we impose restriction on the kind of data a node can contain. As a result, it reduces the worst case average search operation to $O(logn)$.

Binary Search Tree Property

In binary search trees, all the left subtree elements should be less than root data and all the right subtree elements should be greater than root data. This is called binary search tree property. Note that, this property should be satisfied at every node in the tree.

- The left subtree of a node contains only nodes with keys less than the nodes key.
- The right subtree of a node contains only nodes with keys greater than the nodes key.
- Both the left and right subtrees must also be binary search trees.

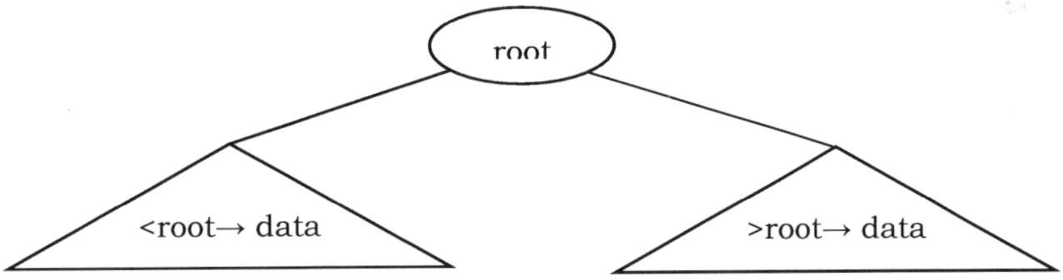

Example: The left tree is a binary search tree and right tree is not binary search tree (at node 6 it's not satisfying the binary search tree property).

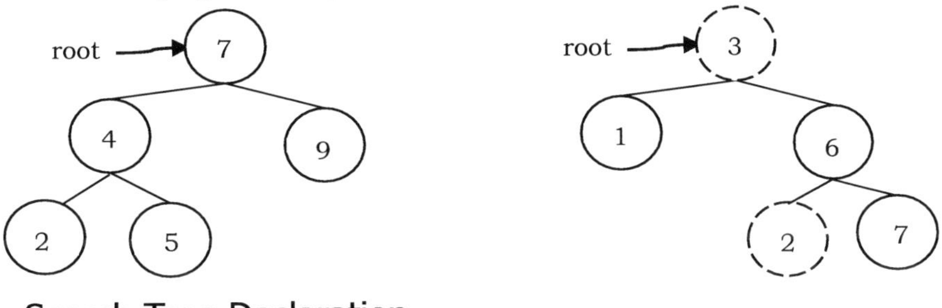

Binary Search Tree Declaration

There is no difference between regular binary tree declaration and binary search tree declaration. The difference is only in data but not in structure. But for our convenience we change the structure name as:

```
struct BinarySearchTreeNode{
    int data;
    struct BinarySearchTreeNode *left;
    struct BinarySearchTreeNode *right;
};
```

Operations on Binary Search Trees

Main operations: Following are the main operations that are supported by binary search trees:

- Find/ Find Minimum / Find Maximum element in binary search trees
- Inserting an element in binary search trees
- Deleting an element from binary search trees

Auxiliary operations:

- Checking whether the given tree is a binary search tree or not
- Finding k^{th}-smallest element in tree
- Sorting the elements of binary search tree and many more

Important Notes on Binary Search Trees

- Since root data is always between left subtree data and right subtree data, performing inorder traversal on binary search tree produces a sorted list.
- While solving problems on binary search trees, first we process left subtree, then root data and finally we process right subtree. This means, depending on the problem only the intermediate step (processing root data) changes and we do not touch the first and third steps.
- If we are searching for an element and if the left subtree roots data is less than the element we want to search then skip it. Same is the case with right subtree.. Because of this binary search trees take less time for searching an element than regular binary trees. In other words, the binary search trees consider either left or right subtrees for searching an element but not both.

Finding an Element in Binary Search Trees

Find operation is straightforward in a BST. Start with the root and keep moving left or right using the BST property. If the data we are searching is same as nodes data then we return current node.

If the data we are searching is less than nodes data then search left subtree of current node; otherwise search right subtree of current node. If the data is not present, we end up in a NULL link.

```
struct BinarySearchTreeNode *Find(struct BinarySearchTreeNode *root, int data ){
    if( root == NULL )
        return NULL;
    if( data < root→data )
        return Find(root→left, data);
    else if( data > root→data )
          return( Find( root→right, data );
    return root;
}
```

Non recursive version of the above algorithm can be given as:

```
struct BinarySearchTreeNode *Find(struct BinarySearchTreeNode *root, int data ){
    if( root == NULL )
        return NULL;
```

```
    while (root) {
        if(data == root→data)
            return root;
        else if(data > root→data)
            root = root→right;
        else root = root→left;
    }
    return NULL;
}
```

Finding Minimum Element in Binary Search Trees

In BSTs, the minimum element is the left-most node, which does not has left child. In the BST below, the minimum element is **4**.

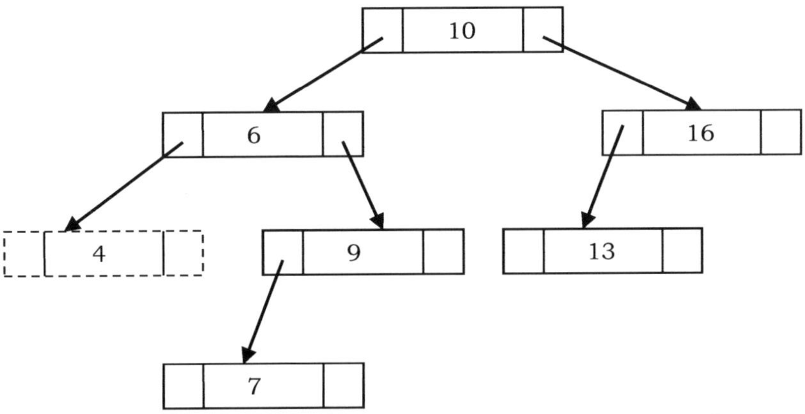


```
struct BinarySearchTreeNode *FindMin(struct BinarySearchTreeNode *root){
    if(root == NULL)
        return NULL;
    else   if( root→left == NULL )
        return root;
    else
        return FindMin( root→left );
}
```

Non recursive version of the above algorithm can be given as:

```
struct BinarySearchTreeNode *FindMin(struct BinarySearchTreeNode * root ) {
    if( root == NULL )
        return NULL;
    while( root→left != NULL )
        root = root→left;
    return root;
}
```

Finding Maximum Element in Binary Search Trees

In BSTs, the maximum element is the right-most node, which does not have right child. In the BST below, the maximum element is **16**.

```
struct BinarySearchTreeNode *FindMax(struct BinarySearchTreeNode *root) {
    if(root == NULL)
        return NULL;
    else if( root→right == NULL )
        return root;
```

```
    else return FindMax( root→right );
}
```

Non recursive version of the above algorithm can be given as:

```
struct BinarySearchTreeNode *FindMax(struct BinarySearchTreeNode * root ) {
    if( root == NULL )
        return NULL;
    while( root→right != NULL )
        root = root→right;
    return root;
}
```

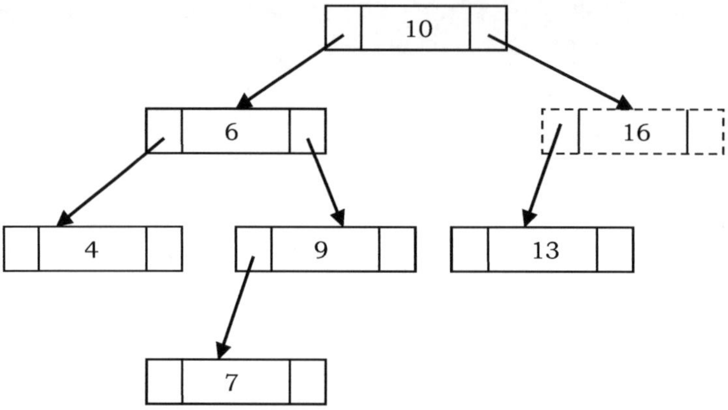

Where is Inorder Predecessor and Successor?

Where is the inorder predecessor and successor of node *X* in a binary search tree assuming all keys are distinct?

If *X* has two children then its inorder predecessor is the maximum value in its left subtree and its inorder successor the minimum value in its right subtree.

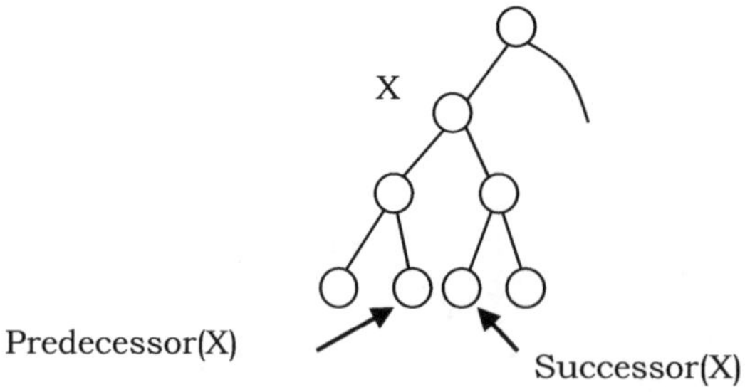

If it does not have a left child a nodes inorder predecessor is its first left ancestor.

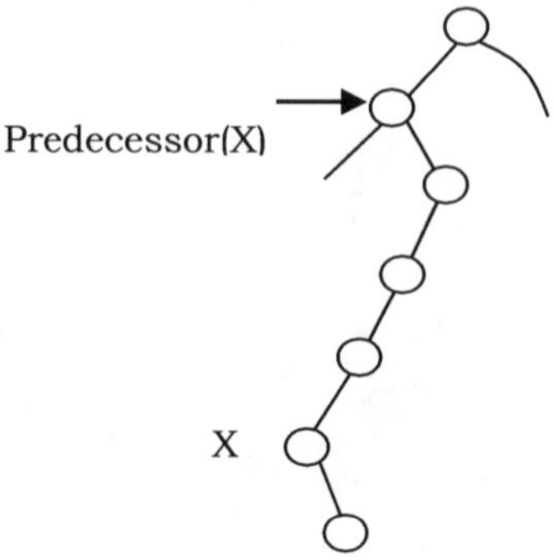

Inserting an Element from Binary Search Tree

To insert *data* into binary search tree, first we need to find the location for that element. We can find the location of insertion by following the same mechanism as that of *find* operation. While finding the location if the *data* is already there then we can simply neglect and come out. Otherwise, insert *data* at the last location on the path traversed.

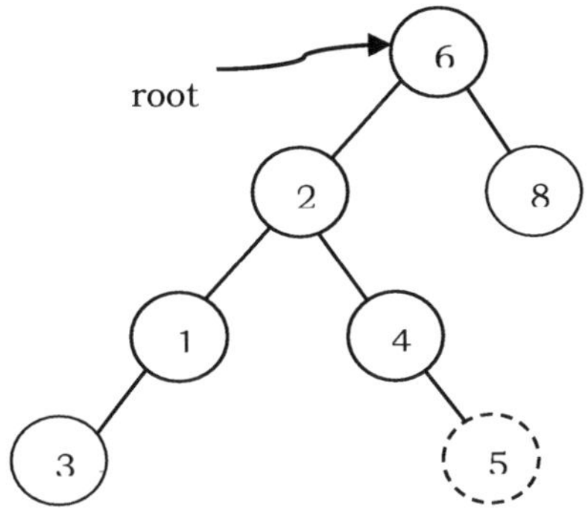

As an example let us consider the following tree. The dotted node indicates the element (5) to be inserted. To insert 5, traverse the tree as using *find* function. At node with key 4, we need to go right, but there is no subtree, so 5 is not in the tree, and this is the correct location for insertion.

```
struct BinarySearchTreeNode *Insert(struct BinarySearchTreeNode *root, int data) {
    if( root == NULL ) {
        root = (struct BinarySearchTreeNode *) malloc(sizeof(
                                                    struct BinarySearchTreeNode));
        if( root == NULL ) {
            printf("Memory Error");
            return;
        }
        else {
            root→data = data;
            root→left = root→right = NULL;
        }
    }
    else {
        if( data < root→data )
            root→left = Insert(root→left, data);
        else if( data > root→data )
            root→right = Insert(root→right, data);
    }
    return root;
}
```

Note: In the above code, after inserting an element in subtrees, the tree is returned to its parent. As a result, the complete tree will get updated.

Deleting an Element from Binary Search Tree

The delete operation is more complicated than other operations. This is because the element to be deleted may not be the leaf node. In this operation also, first we need to find the location of the element which we want to delete.

Once we have found the node to be deleted, consider the following cases:

- If the element to be deleted is a leaf node: return NULL to its parent. That means make the corresponding child pointer NULL. In the tree below to delete 5, set NULL to its parent node 2.

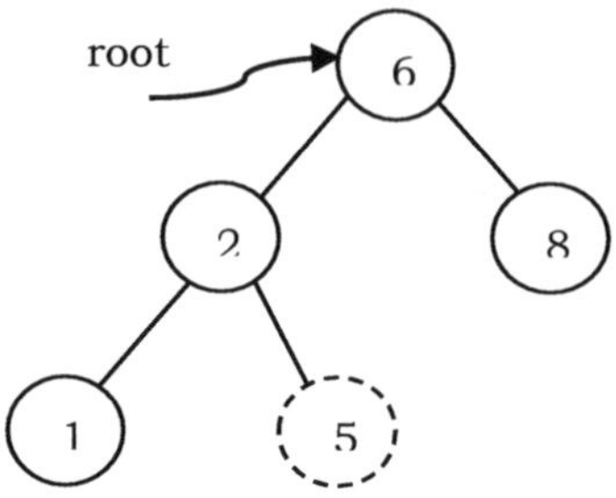

- If the element to be deleted has one child: In this case we just need to send the current nodes child to its parent. In the tree below, to delete 4, 4 left subtree is set to its parent node 2.

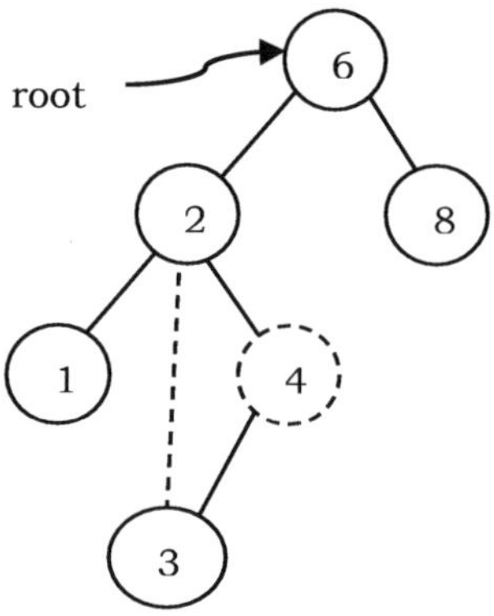

- If the element to be deleted has both children: The general strategy is to replace the key of this node with the largest element of the left subtree and recursively delete that node (which is now empty). The largest node in the left subtree cannot have a right child, the second *delete* is an easy one. As an example, let us consider the following tree. In the tree below, to delete 8, it is the right child of root. The key value is 8. It is replaced with the largest key in its left subtree (7), and then that node is deleted as before (second case).

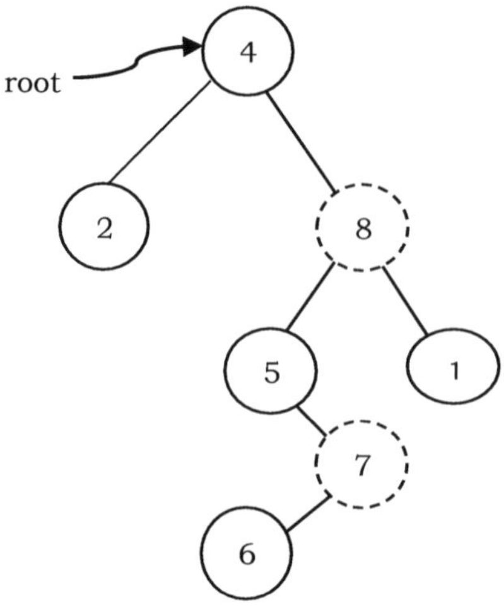

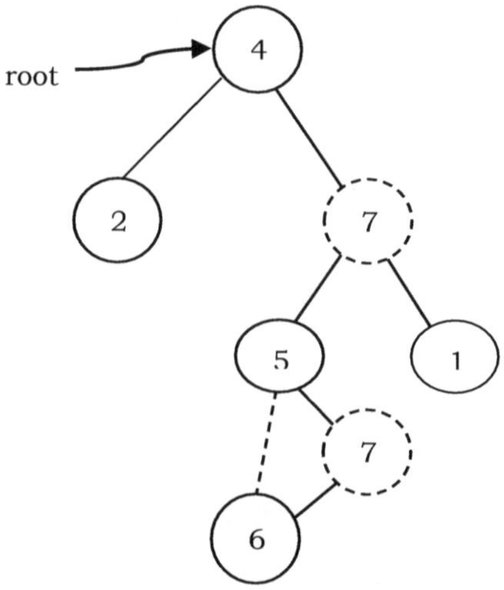

Note: We can replace with minimum element in right subtree also.

```
struct BinarySearchTreeNode *Delete(struct BinarySearchTreeNode *root, int data) {
    struct BinarySearchTreeNode *temp;
    if( root == NULL )
        printf("Element not there in tree");
    else if(data < root→data)
        root→left = Delete(root→left, data);
    else if(data > root→data )
        root→right = Delete(root→right, data);
    else {
        //Found element
        if( root→left && root→right ) {
            /* Replace with largest in left subtree */
                temp = FindMax( root→left );
                root→data = temp→data;
                root→left = Delete(root→left, root→data);
        }
        else {
                /* One child */
                temp = root;
                if( root→left == NULL )
                    root = root→right;
                if( root→right == NULL )
                    root = root→left;
                free( temp );
        }
    }
    return root;
}
```

Problems and Questions with Answers

Question 33: Given pointers to two nodes in a binary search tree, find lowest common ancestor (*LCA*). Assume that both values already exist in the tree.

Answer:

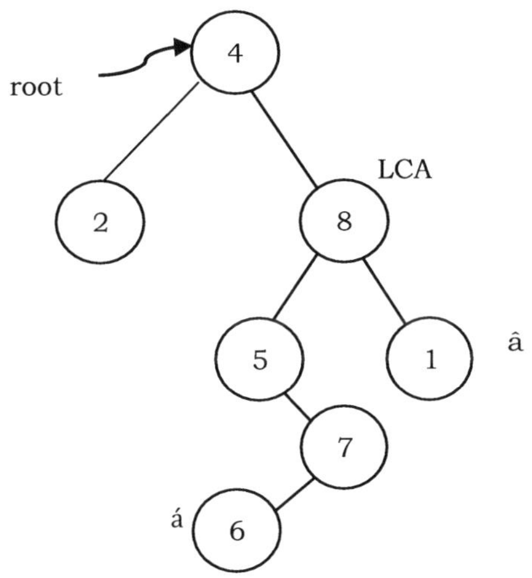

The main idea of the solution is: while traversing BST from root to bottom, the first node we encounter with value between á and â, i.e., á < *node → data* < â is the Least Common Ancestor(LCA) of á and â (where á < â). So just traverse the BST in pre-order, if we find a node with value in between á and â, then that node is the LCA.

If its value is greater than both á and â then LCA lies on left side of the node and if its value is smaller than both á and â then LCA lies on right side.

```
struct BinarySearchTreeNode *FindLCA(struct BinarySearchTreeNode *root,
struct BinarySearchTreeNode *á,
struct BinarySearchTreeNode * â) {
    while(1) {
        if((á→data < root→data && â→data > root→data) | |
                                    (á→data > root→data && â→data < root→data))
            return root;
        if(á→data < root→data)
            root = root→left;
        else root = root→right;
    }
}
```

Question 34: Give an algorithm for finding the shortest path between two nodes in a BST.

Answer: It's nothing but finding the LCA of two nodes in BST.

Question 35: Give an algorithm to check whether the given binary tree is a BST or not.

Answer: Consider the following simple program. For each node, check if node on its left is smaller and check if the node on its right is greater. This approach is wrong as this will return true for binary tree below. Checking only at current node is not enough.

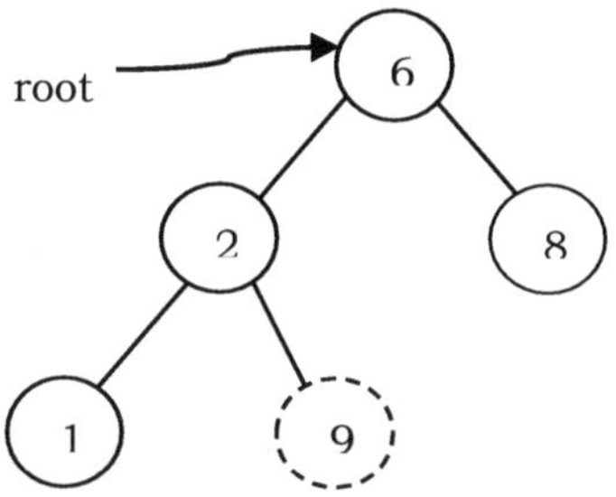


```
int IsBST(struct BinaryTreeNode* root) {
    if(root == NULL)
            return 1;
    /* false if left is > than root */
    if(root→left != NULL && root→left→data > root→data)
            return 0;
    /* false if right is < than root */
    if(root→right != NULL && root→right→data < root→data)
            return 0;
    /* false if, recursively, the left or right is not a BST */
    if(!IsBST(root→left) | | !IsBST(root→right))
            return 0;
```

```
    /* passing all that, it's a BST */
    return 1;
}
```

Question 36: Can we think of getting the correct algorithm?

Answer: For each node, check if max value in left subtree is smaller than the current node data and min value in right subtree greater than the node data. It is assumed that we have helper functions *FindMin*() and *FindMax*() that return the min or max integer value from a non-empty tree.

```
/* Returns true if a binary tree is a binary search tree */
int IsBST(struct BinaryTreeNode* root) {
    if(root == NULL)
            return 1;
    /* false if the max of the left is > than root */
    if(root→left != NULL && FindMax(root→left) > root→data)
            return 0;
    /* false if the min of the right is <= than root */
    if(root→right != NULL && FindMin(root→right) < root→data)
            return 0;
    /* false if, recursively, the left or right is not a BST */
    if(!IsBST(root→left) || !IsBST(root→right))
            return 0;
    /* passing all that, it's a BST */
    return 1;
}
```

Question 37: Can we improve the performance of Question 36?

Answer: Yes. A better solution looks at each node only once. The trick is to write a utility helper function IsBSTUtil(struct BinaryTreeNode* root, int min, int max) that traverses down the tree keeping track of the narrowing min and max allowed values as it goes, looking at each node only once. The initial values for min and max should be INT_MIN and INT_MAX — they narrow from there.

```
Initial call: IsBST(root, INT_MIN, INT_MAX);
int IsBST(struct BinaryTreeNode *root, int min, int max) {
        if(!root)
          return 1;
        return (root→data >min && root→data < max &&
                 IsBSTUtil(root→left, min, root→data) &&
                 IsBSTUtil(root→right, root→data, max));
}
```

Question 38: Can we further improve the performance of Question 36?

Answer: Yes, by using inorder traversal. The idea behind this solution is that, inorder traversal of BST produces sorted lists. While traversing the BST in inorder, at each node check the condition that its key value should be greater than the key value of its previous visited node. Also, we need to initialize the prev with possible minimum integer value (say, INT_MIN).

```
int prev = INT_MIN;
int IsBST(struct BinaryTreeNode *root, int *prev) {
        if(!root)
           return 1;
        if(!IsBST(root→left, prev))
                  return 0;
        if(root→data < *prev)
```

```
                return 0;
        *prev = root→data;
        return IsBST(root→right, prev);
}
```

Question 39: Give an algorithm for converting BST to circular DLL.

Answer: Convert left and right subtrees to DLLs and maintain end of those lists. Then, adjust the pointers.

```
struct BinarySearchTreeNode *BST2DLL(struct BinarySearchTreeNode *root,
struct BinarySearchTreeNode **Ltail) {
    struct BinarySearchTreeNode *left, *ltail, *right, *rtail;
    if(!root) {
        * ltail = NULL;
        return NULL;
    }
    left = BST2DLL(root→left, &ltail);
    right = BST2DLL(root→right, &rtail);
    root→left = ltail;
    root→right = right;

    if(!right)
          * ltail = root;
    else {
         right→left = root;
        * ltail = rtail;
    }
    if(!left)
          return root;
    else {
        ltail→right = root;
        return left;
    }
}
```

Question 40: For Question 39, is there any other way of solving?

Answer: Yes. There is an alternative solution based on divide and conquer method which is quite neat.

```
struct BinarySearchTreeNode  *Append(struct BinarySearchTreeNode  *a,
                                                struct BinarySearchTreeNode  *b) {
            struct BinarySearchTreeNode   *aLast, *bLast;
   if (a==NULL)
          return b;
   if (b==NULL)
          return a;
   aLast = a→left;
   bLast = b→left;
   aLast→right = b;
   b→left = aLast;
   bLast→right = a;
   a→left = bLast;
   return a;
}
struct BinarySearchTreeNode* TreeToList(struct BinarySearchTreeNode  *root) {
```

```
    struct BinarySearchTreeNode  *aList, *bList;
    if (root==NULL)
            return NULL;
    aList = TreeToList(root→left);
    bList = TreeToList(root→right);
    root→left = root;
    root→right = root;
    aList = Append(aList, root);
    aList = Append(aList, bList);
    return(aList);
}
```

Question 41: Given a sorted doubly linked list, give an algorithm for converting it into balanced binary search tree.

Answer: Find the middle node and adjust the pointers.

```
struct DLLNode  * DLLtoBalancedBST(struct DLLNode  *head) {
    struct DLLNode  *temp, *p, *q;
    if( !head || !head→next)
          return head;
    temp = FindMiddleNode(head);
    p = head;
    while(p→next != temp)
        p = p→next;
    p→next = NULL;
    q = temp→next;
    temp→next = NULL;
    temp→prev = DLLtoBalancedBST(head);
    temp→next = DLLtoBalancedBST(q);
    return temp;
}
```

Note: For *FindMiddleNode* function refer *Linked Lists* chapter.

Question 42: Given a sorted array, give an algorithm for converting the array to BST.

Answer: If we have to choose an array element to be the root of a balanced BST, which element should we pick? The root of a balanced BST should be the middle element from the sorted array. We would pick the middle element from the sorted array in each iteration. We then create a node in the tree initialized with this element. After the element is chosen, what is left? Could you identify the sub-problems within the problem?

There are two arrays left — The one on its left and the one on its right. These two arrays are the sub-problems of the original problem, since both of them are sorted. Furthermore, they are subtrees of the current node's left and right child.

The code below creates a balanced BST from the sorted array in O(n) time (n is the number of elements in the array). Compare how similar the code is to a binary search algorithm. Both are using the divide and conquer methodology.

```
struct BinaryTreeNode  *BuildBST(int A[], int left, int right) {
    struct BinaryTreeNode  *newNode;
    int mid;
    if(left > right)
          return NULL;
    newNode = (struct BinaryTreeNode  *)malloc(sizeof(struct BinaryTreeNode));
    if(!newNode) {
```

```
        printf("Memory Error");
        return;
    }
    if(left == right) {
        newNode→data = A[left];
        newNode→left = newNode→right = NULL;
    }
    else {
        mid = left + (right-left)/ 2;
        newNode→data = A[mid];
        newNode→left = BuildBST(A, left, mid - 1);
        newNode→right = BuildBST(A, mid + 1, right);
    }
    return newNode;
}
```

Question 43: Give an algorithm for finding the kth smallest element in BST.

Answer: The idea behind this solution is that, inorder traversal of BST produces sorted lists. While traversing the BST in inorder, keep track of the number of elements visited.

```
struct BinarySearchTreeNode *kthSmallestInBST(struct BinarySearchTreeNode *root,
int k, int *count){
    if(!root)
        return NULL;
    struct BinarySearchTreeNode *left = kthSmallestInBST(root→left, k, count);
    if( left )
        return left;
    if(++count == k)
        return root;
    return kthSmallestInBST(root→right, k, count);
}
```

Question 44: Given a *BST* and two numbers $K1$ and $K2$, give an algorithm for printing all the elements of *BST* in the range $K1$ and $K2$.

Answer:

```
void RangePrinter(struct BinarySearchTreeNode *root, int K1, int K2) {
    if(root == NULL)
        return;
    if(root→data >= K1)
        RangePrinter(root→left, K1, K2);
    if(root→data >= K1 && root→data <= K2)
        printf("%d", root→data);
    if(root→data <= K2)
        RangePrinter(root→right, K1, K2);
}
```

16.10 Balanced Binary Search Trees

In earlier sections we have seen different trees whose worst case complexity is $O(n)$, where n is the number of nodes in the tree. This happens when the trees are skew trees. In this section we will try to reduce this worst case complexity to $O(logn)$ by imposing restrictions on the heights. In general, the height balanced trees are represented with $HB(k)$, where k is the difference between left subtree height and right subtree height. Sometimes k is called balance factor.

Full Balanced Binary Search Trees

In $HB(k)$, if $k = 0$ (if balance factor is zero), then we call such binary search trees as *full* balanced binary search trees. That means, in $HB(0)$ binary search tree, the difference between left subtree height and right subtree height should be at most zero. This ensures that the tree is a full binary tree. For example,

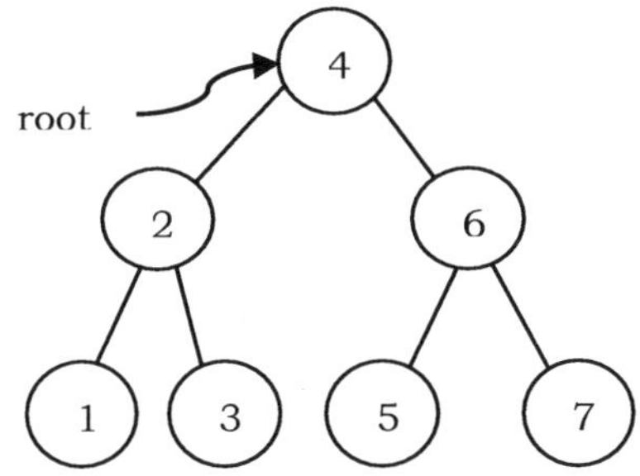

Note: For constructing $HB(0)$ tree refer problems section.

16.11 AVL (Adelson-Velskii and Landis) Trees

In $HB(k)$, if $k = 1$ (if balance factor is one), such binary search tree is called an AVL tree. That means an AVL tree is a binary search tree with a *balance* condition: the difference between left subtree height and right subtree height is at most 1.

Properties of AVL Trees

A binary tree is said to be an AVL tree, if:

- It is a binary search tree, and
- For any node X, the height of left subtree of X and height of right subtree of X differ by at most 1.

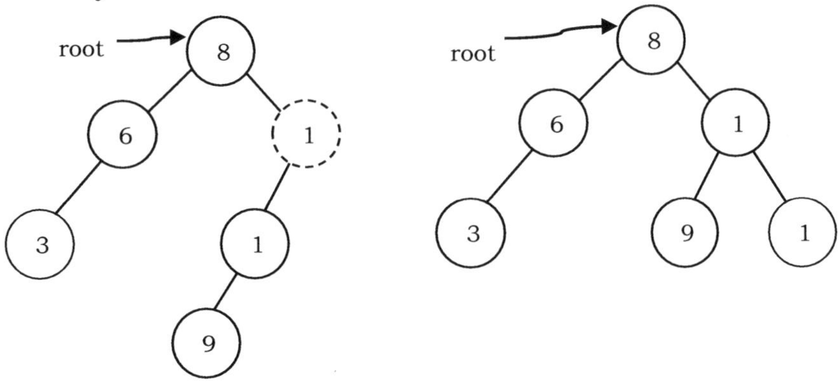

As an example among the above binary search trees, the left one is not an AVL tree, whereas the right binary search tree is an AVL tree.

Minimum/Maximum Number of Nodes in AVL Tree

For simplicity let us assume that the height of an AVL tree is h and $N(h)$ indicates the number of nodes in AVL tree with height h. To get minimum number of nodes with height h, we should fill the tree with as minimum nodes as possible. That means if we fill the left subtree with height $h-1$ then we should fill the right subtree with height $h-2$. As a result, the minimum number of nodes with height h is:

$$N(h) = N(h-1) + N(h-2) + 1$$

In the above equation:

- $N(h-1)$ indicates the minimum number of nodes with height $h-1$.
- $N(h-2)$ indicates the minimum number of nodes with height $h-2$.
- In the above expression, "1" indicates the current node.

We can give $N(h-1)$ either for left subtree or right subtree. Solving the above recurrence gives:

$$N(h) = O(1.618^h) \Rightarrow h = 1.44logn \approx O(logn)$$

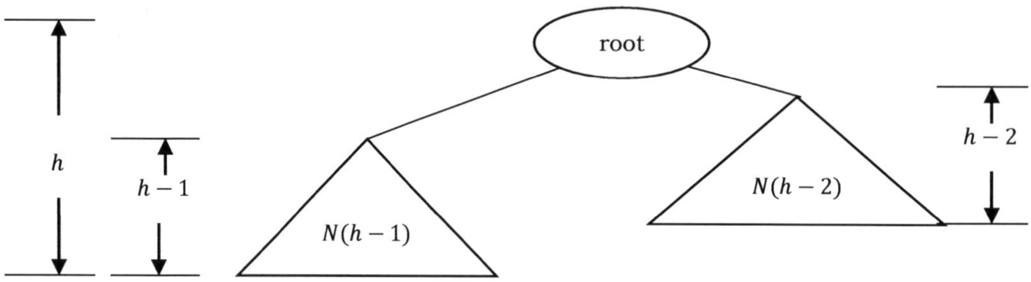

Where n is the number of nodes in AVL tree. Also, the above derivation says that the maximum height in AVL trees is $O(logn)$. Similarly, to get maximum number of nodes, we need to fill both left and right subtrees with height $h-1$. As a result, we get

$$N(h) = N(h-1) + N(h-1) + 1 = 2N(h-1) + 1$$

The above expression defines the case of full binary tree. Solving the recurrence we get:

$$N(h) = O(2^h) \Rightarrow h = logn \approx O(logn)$$

$\therefore$ In both the cases, AVL tree property is ensuring that the height of an AVL tree with n nodes is $O(logn)$.

AVL Tree Declaration

Since AVL tree is a BST, the declaration of AVL is similar to that of BST. But just to simplify the operations, we include the height also as part of declaration.

```
struct AVLTreeNode{
    struct AVLTreeNode *left;
    int data;
    struct AVLTreeNode *right;
    int height;
};
```

Finding Height of an AVL tree

```
int Height(struct AVLTreeNode *root ){
    if( !root)
        return -1;
    else return root→height;
}
```

Rotations

When the tree structure changes (e.g., with insertion or deletion), we need to modify the tree to restore the AVL tree property. This can be done using single rotations or double rotations. Since an insertion/deletion involves adding/deleting a single node, this can only increase/decrease the height of some subtree by 1.

So, if the AVL tree property is violated at a node X, it means that the heights of left(X) and right(X) differ by exactly 2. This is because, if we balance the AVL tree every time, then at any point, the difference in heights of left(X) and right(X) differ by exactly 2. Rotations is the technique used for restoring the AVL tree property. This means, we need to apply the rotations for the node X.

Observation: One important observation is that, after an insertion, only nodes that are on the path from the insertion point to the root might have their balances altered because only those nodes have their subtrees altered. To restore the AVL tree property, we start at the insertion point and keep going to root of the tree.

While moving to root, we need to consider the first node whichever is not satisfying the AVL property. From that node onwards every node on the path to root will have the issue.

Also, if we fix the issue for that first node, then all other nodes on the path to root will automatically satisfy the AVL tree property. That means we always need to care for the first node whichever is not satisfying the AVL property on the path from insertion point to root and fix it.

Types of Violations

Let us assume the node that must be rebalanced is X. Since any node has at most two children, and a height imbalance requires that $X's$ two subtree heights differ by two, we can observe that a violation might occur in four cases:

1. An insertion into the left subtree of the left child of X.
2. An insertion into the right subtree of the left child of X.
3. An insertion into the left subtree of the right child of X.
4. An insertion into the right subtree of the right child of X.

Cases 1 and 4 are symmetric and easily solved with single rotations. Similarly, cases 2 and 3 are also symmetric and can be solved with double rotations (needs two single rotations).

Single Rotations

Left Left Rotation (LL Rotation) [Case-1]: In the case below, at node X, the AVL tree property is not satisfying. As discussed earlier, rotation does not have to be done at the root of a tree.

In general, we start at the node inserted and travel up the tree, updating the balance information at every node on the path.

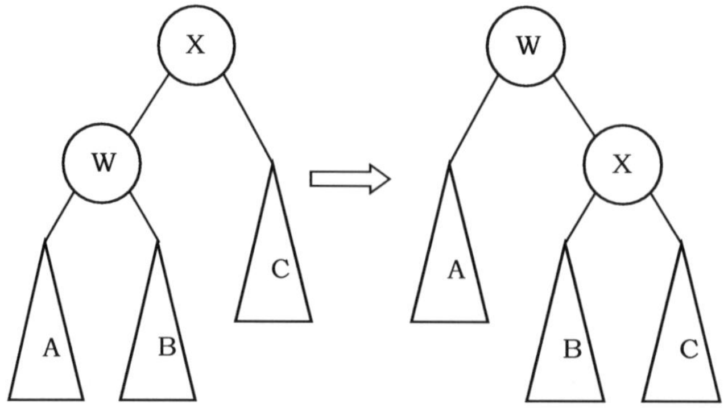

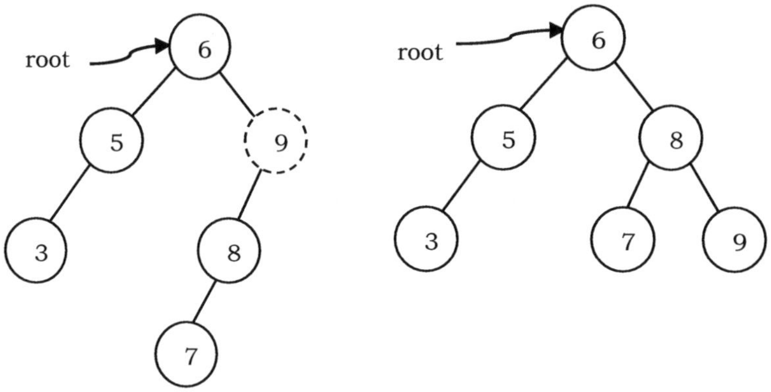

For example, in the figure above, after the insertion of 7 in the original AVL tree on the left, node 9 becomes unbalanced. So, we do a single left-left rotation at 9. As a result we get the tree on the right.

```
struct AVLTreeNode *SingleRotateLeft(struct AVLTreeNode *X ){
    struct AVLTreeNode *W = X→left;
    X→left = W→right;
    W→right = X;
    X→height = max( Height(X→left), Height(X→right) ) + 1;
    W→height = max( Height(W→left), X→height ) + 1;
    return W;  /* New root */
}
```

Right Right Rotation (RR Rotation) [Case-4]: In this case, the node *X* is not satisfying the AVL tree property.

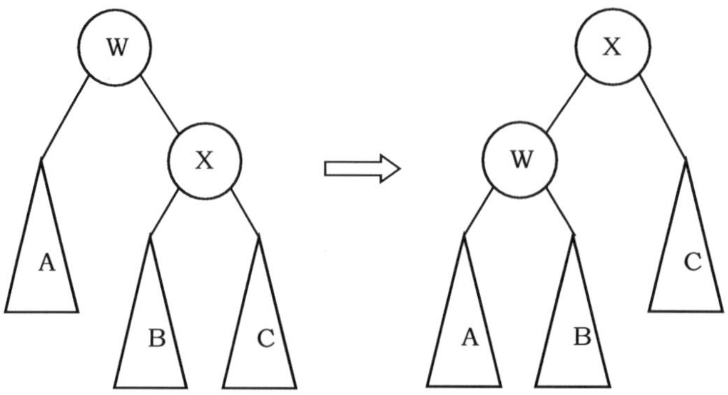

For example, in above figure, after the insertion of 29 in the original AVL tree on the left, node 15 becomes unbalanced. So, we do a single right-right rotation at 15. As a result we get the tree on the right.

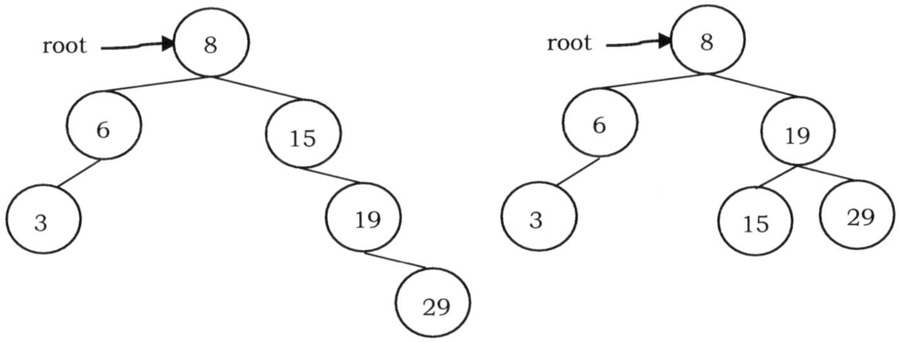


```
struct AVLTreeNode *SingleRotateRight(struct AVLTreeNode *W ) {
    struct AVLTreeNode *X  = W→right;
    W→right = X→left;
    X→left = W;
    W→height = max( Height(W→right), Height(W→left) ) + 1;
    X→height = max( Height(X→right), W→height) + 1;
    return X;
}
```

Double Rotations

Left Right Rotation (LR Rotation) [Case-2]: For case-2 and case-3 single rotation does not fix the problem. We need to perform two rotations.

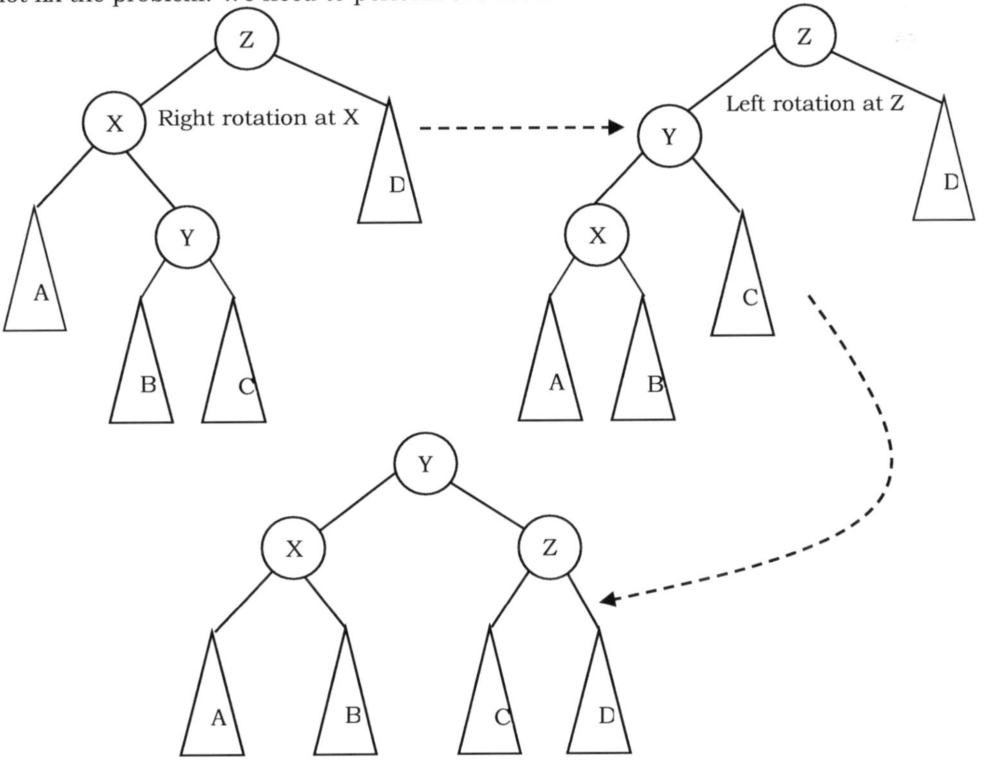

As an example, let us consider the following tree: Insertion of 7 is creating the case-2 scenario and right side tree is the one after double rotation.

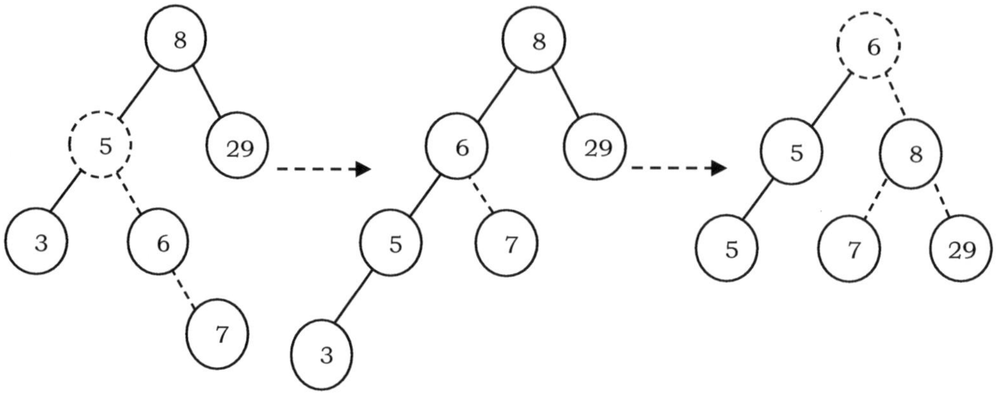

Code for left-right double rotation can be given as:

```
struct AVLTreeNode *DoubleRotatewithLeft( struct AVLTreeNode *Z ){
    Z→left = SingleRotateRight( Z→left );

    return SingleRotateLeft(Z);
}
```

Right Left Rotation (RL Rotation) [Case-3]: Similar to case-2, we need to perform two rotations for fixing this scenario.

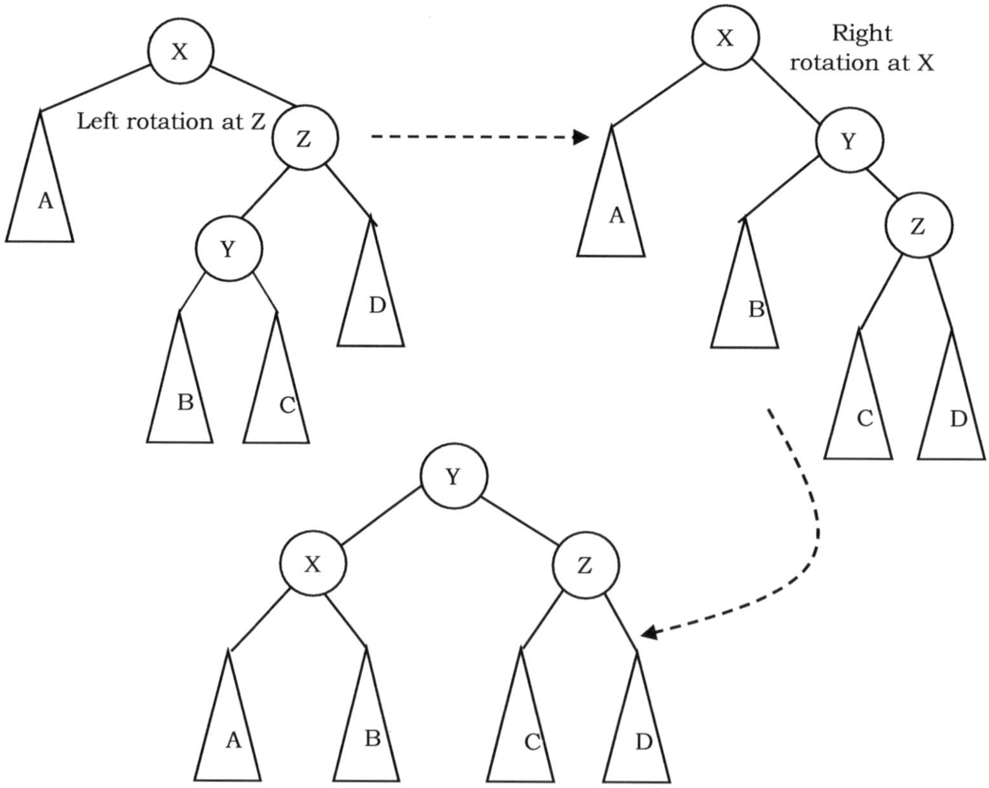

As an example, let us consider the following tree: Insertion of 6 is creating the case-3 scenario and right side tree is the one after double rotation.

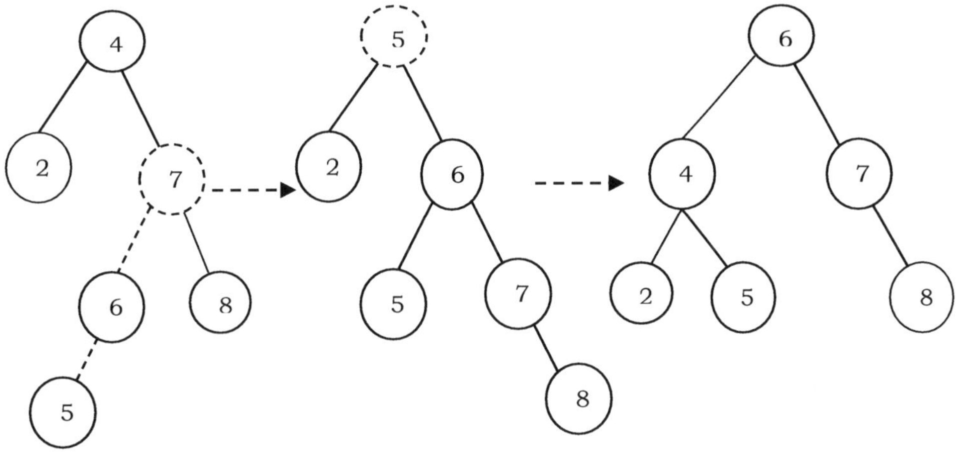

Insertion into an AVL tree

Insertion in AVL tree is similar to BST insertion. After inserting the element, we just need to check whether there is any height imbalance. If there is any imbalance, call the appropriate rotation functions.

```
struct AVLTreeNode *Insert( struct AVLTreeNode *root, struct AVLTreeNode *parent, int
data){
    if( !root) {
        root = (struct AVLTreeNode*) malloc(sizeof (struct AVLTreeNode*) );
          if(!root) {
               printf("Memory Error"); return NULL;
          }
        else {
           root→data = data;
           root→height = 0;
           root→left = root→right = NULL;
        }
    }
    else if( data < root→data ) {
        root→left = Insert( root→left, root, data );
        if( ( Height( root→left ) - Height( root→right ) ) == 2 ) {
           if( data < root→left→data )
               root = SingleRotateLeft( root );
           else    root = DoubleRotateLeft( root );
        }
    }
    else if( data > root→data ) {
        root→right = Insert( root→right, root, data );
        if( ( Height( root→right ) - Height( root→left ) ) == 2 ) {
           if( data < root→right→data )
               root = SingleRotateRight( root );
           else    root = DoubleRotateRight( root );
        }
    }
    /* Else data is in the tree already. We'll do nothing */
    root→height = max( Height(root→left), Height(root→right) ) + 1;
    return root;
}
```

Time Complexity: $O(n)$. Space Complexity: $O(logn)$.

Problems and Questions with Answers

Question 45: Given a height h, give an algorithm for generating the $HB(0)$.

Answer: As we have discussed, $HB(0)$ is nothing but generating full binary tree. In full binary tree the number of nodes with height h are: $2^{h+1} - 1$ (let us assume that the height of a tree with one node is 0). As a result the nodes can be numbered as: 1 to $2^{h+1} - 1$.

```
struct BinarySearchTreeNode *BuildHB0(int h){
    struct BinarySearchTreeNode *temp;
    if(h == 0)
        return NULL;
    temp = (struct BinarySearchTreeNode *) malloc (sizeof(
                                        struct BinarySearchTreeNode));
    temp→left = BuildHB0 (h-1);
    temp→data = count++;      //assume count is a global variable
    temp→right = BuildHB0 (h-1);
    return temp;
}
```

Question 46: Is there any alternative way of solving Question 45?

Answer: Yes, we can solve following Mergesort logic. That means, instead of working with height, we can take the range. With this approach we do not need any global counter to be maintained.

```
struct BinarySearchTreeNode *BuildHB0(int l, int r){
    struct BinarySearchTreeNode *temp;
    int mid = l + (r-l)/2;
    if( l > r)
       return NULL;
    temp = (struct BinarySearchTreeNode *) malloc (sizeof(
                                        struct BinarySearchTreeNode));
    temp→data = mid;
    temp→left = BuildHB0(l, mid-1);
    temp→right = BuildHB0(mid+1, r);
    return temp;
}
```

The initial call to *BuildHB0* function could be: $BuildHB0(1,\ 1 \ll h)$. $1 \ll h$ does the shift operation for calculating the $2^{h+1} - 1$.

Time Complexity: $O(n)$. Space Complexity: $O(logn)$. Where $logn$ indicates maximum stack size which is equal to height of the tree.

Question 47: Construct minimal AVL trees of height $0, 1, 2, 3, 4,$ and 5. What is the number of nodes in a minimal AVL tree of height 6?

Answer: Let $N(h)$ be the number of nodes in a minimal AVL tree with height h.

$$N(0) = 1$$

$$N(1) = 2$$

$$N(h) = 1 + N(h-1) + N(h-2)$$

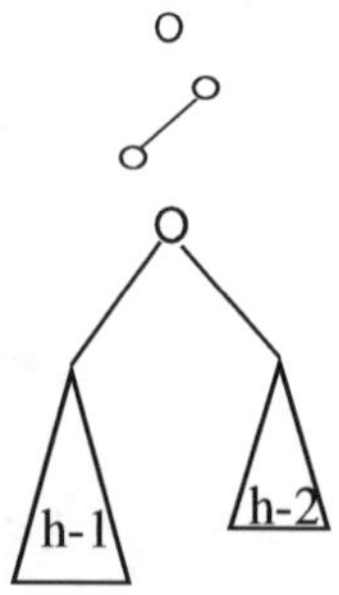

$$N(2) = 1 + N(1) + N(0)$$
$$= 1 + 2 + 1 = 4$$

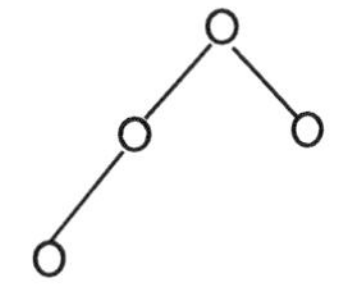

$$N(3) = 1 + N(2) + N(1)$$
$$= 1 + 4 + 2 = 7$$

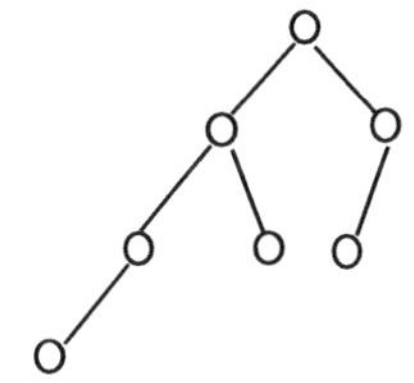

$$N(4) = 1 + N(3) + N(2)$$
$$= 1 + 7 + 4 = 12$$

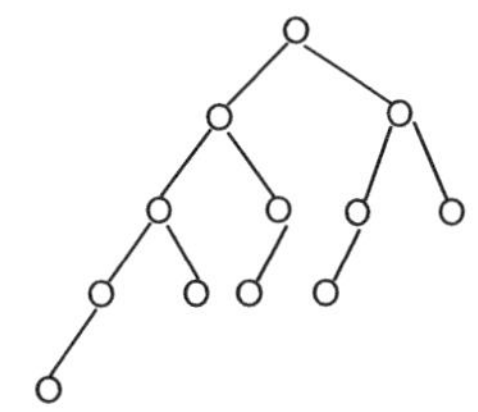

$$N(5) = 1 + N(4) + N(3)$$
$$= 1 + 12 + 7 = 20$$

...

Question 48: For Question 47, how many different shapes can there be of a minimal AVL tree of height?

Answer: Let $NS(h)$ be the number of different shapes of a minimal AVL tree of height h.

$$NS(0) = 1$$

$$NS(1) = 2$$

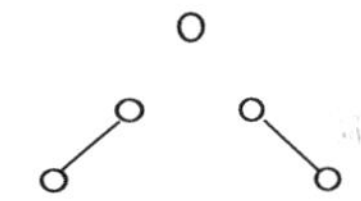

$$NS(2) = 2 * NS(1) * NS(0)$$
$$= 2 * 2 * 1 = 4$$

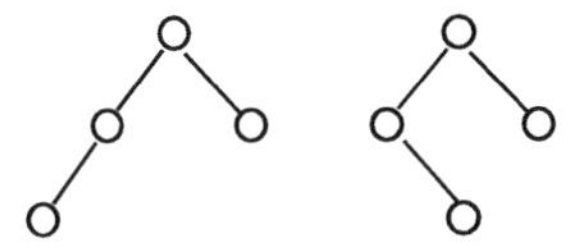

$$NS(3) = 2 * NS(2) * NS(1)$$
$$= 2 * 4 * 1 = 8$$

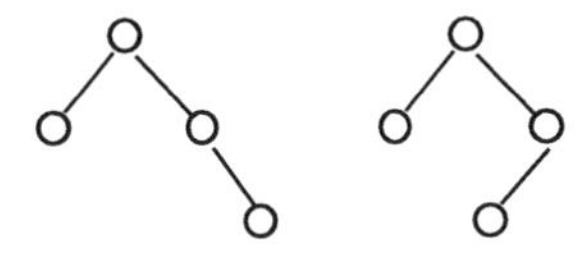

...

$$NS(h) = 2 * NS(h-1) * NS(h-2)$$

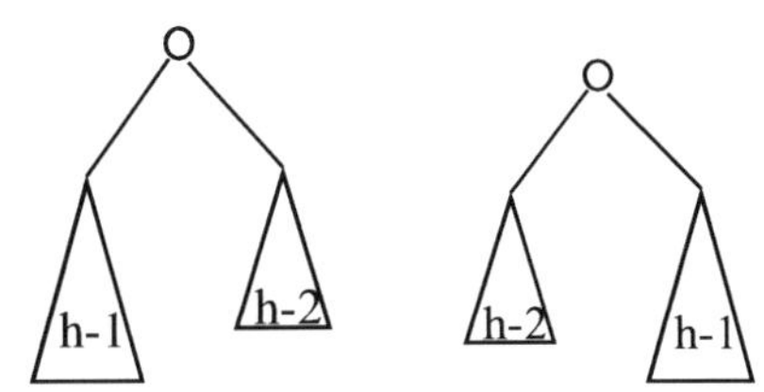

Question 49: Given a binary search tree check whether it is an AVL tree or not?

Answer: Let us assume that *IsAVL* is the function which checks whether the given binary search tree is an AVL tree or not. *IsAVL* returns −1 if the tree is not an AVL tree. During the checks each node sends height of it to their parent.

```
int IsAVL(struct BinarySearchTreeNode *root){
    int left, right;
    if(!root)
```

```
        return 0;
    left = IsAVL(root→left);
    if(left == -1)
        return left;
    right = IsAVL(root→right);
    if(right == -1)
        return right;
    if(abs(left-right)>1)
        return -1;
    return Max(left, right)+1;
}
```

Question 50: Given a height *h*, give an algorithm to generate an AVL tree with min number of nodes.

Answer: To get minimum number of nodes, fill one level with $h-1$ and other with $h-2$.

```
struct AVLTreeNode *GenerateAVLTree(int h){
    struct AVLTreeNode *temp;
    if(h == 0)
        return NULL;
    temp = (struct AVLTreeNode *)malloc (sizeof(struct AVLTreeNode));
    temp→left = GenerateAVLTree(h-1);
    temp→data = count++; //assume count is a global variable
    temp→right = GenerateAVLTree(h-2);
    temp→height = temp→left→height+1; // or temp→height = h;
    return temp;
}
```

CHAPTER 17

Priority Queues and Heaps

17.1 What is a Priority Queue?

In some situations we may need to find the minimum/maximum element among a collection of elements. We can do this with the help of Priority Queue ADT.A priority queue ADT is a data structure that supports the operations *Insert* and *DeleteMin* (which returns and removes the minimum element) or *DeleteMax* (which returns and removes the maximum element).

These operations are equivalent to *EnQueue* and *DeQueue* operations of a queue. The difference is that, in priority queues, the order in which the elements enter the queue may not be the same in which they were processed. An example application of a priority queue is job scheduling, which is prioritized instead of serving in first come first serve.

A priority queue is called an *ascending – priority* queue, if the item with smallest key has the highest priority (that means, delete smallest element always).

Similarly, a priority queue is said to be a *descending – priority* queue if the item with largest key has the highest priority (delete maximum element always). Since these two types are symmetric we will be concentrating on one of them, say, ascending-priority queue.

17.2 Priority Queue ADT

The following operations make priority queues an ADT.

Main Priority Queues Operations

A priority queue is a container of elements, each having an associated key.

- Insert(key, data): Inserts data with *key* to the priority queue. Elements are ordered based on key.
- DeleteMin/DeleteMax: Remove and return the element with the smallest/largest key.
- GetMinimum/GetMaximum: Return the element with the smallest/largest key without deleting it.

Auxiliary Priority Queues Operations

- k^{th} –Smallest/k^{th} –Largest: Returns the kth –Smallest/k^{th} –Largest key in priority queue.
- Size: Returns number of elements in priority queue.
- Heap Sort: Sorts the elements in the priority queue based on priority (key).

17.3 Priority Queue Applications

Priority queues have many applications and few of them are listed below:

- Data compression: Huffman Coding algorithm
- Shortest path algorithms: Dijkstra's algorithm
- Minimum spanning tree algorithms: Prim's algorithm
- Event-driven simulation: customers in a line
- Selection problem: Finding k^{th}-smallest element

17.4 Heaps and Binary Heap

Priority queues can be efficiently implemented with binary heaps.

What is a Heap?

A heap is a tree with some special properties. The basic requirement of a heap is that the value of a node must be $\geq$ (or $\leq$) to the values of its children. This is called *heap property*. A heap also has the additional property that all leaves should be at h or $h - 1$ levels (where h is the height of the tree) for some $h > 0$ (*complete binary trees*). That means heap should form a *complete binary tree* (as shown below).

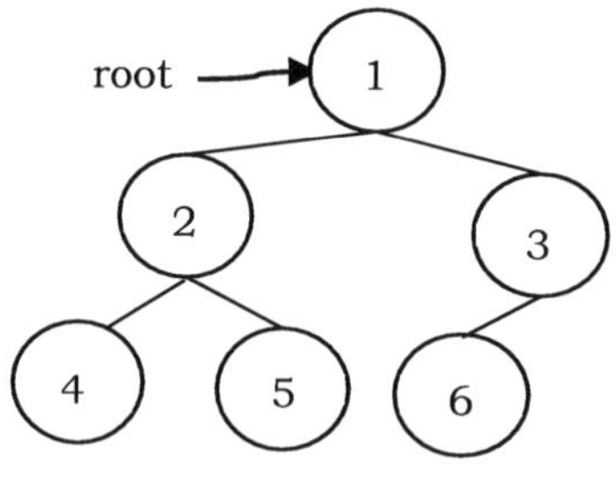

In the examples below, the left tree is a heap (each element is greater than its children) and right tree is not a heap (since, 11 is greater than 22).

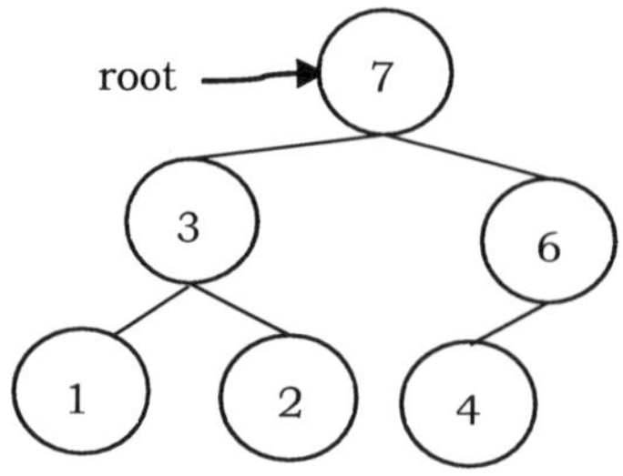

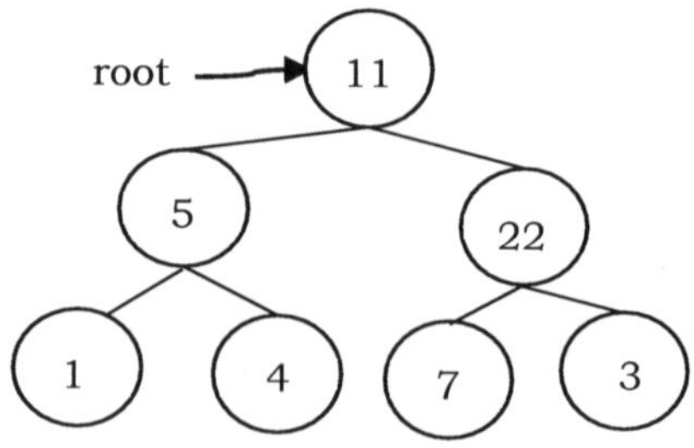

Types of Heaps?

Based on the property of a heap we can classify heaps into two types:

- **Min heap:** The value of a node must be less than or equal to the values of its children

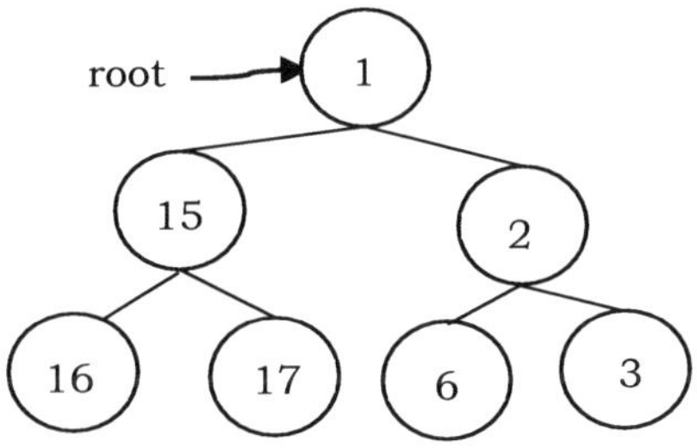

- **Max heap:** The value of a node must be greater than or equal to the values of its children

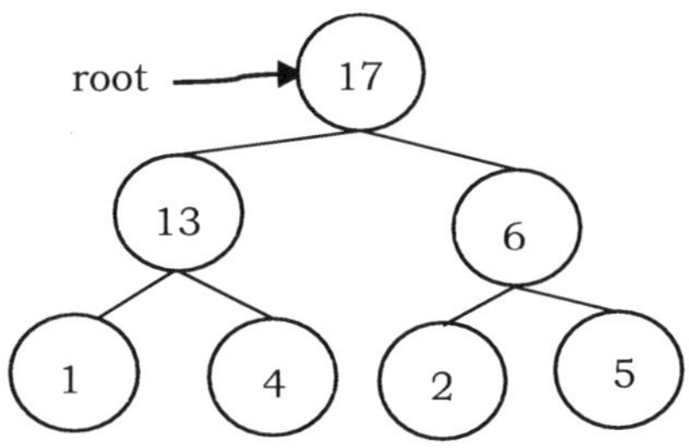

17.5 Binary Heaps

In binary heap each node may have up to two children. In practice, binary heaps are enough and we concentrate on binary min heaps and binary max heaps for remaining discussion.

Representing Heaps: Before looking at heap operations, let us see how heaps can be represented. One possibility is using arrays. Since heaps are forming complete binary trees, there will not be any wastage of locations. For the discussion below let us assume that elements are stored in arrays, which starts at index 0. The previous max heap can be represented as:

17	13	6	1	4	2	5
0	1	2	3	4	5	6

Note: For the remaining discussion let us assume that we are doing manipulations in max heap.

Declaration of Heap

```
struct Heap {
    int *array;
    int count;       // Number of elements in Heap
    int capacity;    // Size of the heap
    int heap_type;   // Min Heap or Max Heap
};
```

Creating Heap

```
struct Heap * CreateHeap(int capacity, int heap_type) {
    struct Heap * h = (struct Heap *)malloc(sizeof(struct Heap));
    if(h == NULL) {
            printf("Memory Error");
           return;
    }
    h→heap_type = heap_type;
```

```
    h→count = 0;
    h→capacity = capacity;
    h→array = (int *) malloc(sizeof(int) * h→capacity);
    if(h→array == NULL) {
        printf("Memory Error");  return;
    }
    return h;
}
```

Parent of a Node

For a node at i^{th} location, its parent is at $\frac{i-1}{2}$ location. In the previous example, the element 6 is at second location and its parent is at 0th location.

```
int Parent (struct Heap * h, int i) {
    if(i <= 0 || i >= h→count)
        return -1;
    return i-1/2;
}
```

Children of a Node

Similar to above discussion for a node at i^{th} location, its children are at $2*i+1$ and $2*i+2$ locations. For example, in the above tree the element 6 is at second location and its children 2 and 5 are at 5 $(2*i+1 = 2*2+1)$ and 6 $(2*i+2 = 2*2+2)$ locations.

```
int LeftChild(struct Heap *h, int i) {
    int left = 2 * i + 1;
    if(left >= h→count)
        return -1;
    return left;
}
```

```
int RightChild(struct Heap *h, int i) {
    int right = 2 * i + 2;
    if(right >= h→count)
        return -1;
    return right;
}
```

Getting the Maximum Element

Since the maximum element in max heap is always at root, it will be stored at h→array[0].

```
int GetMaximum(Heap * h) {
    if(h→count == 0)
        return -1;
    return h→array[0];
}
```

Heapifying an Element

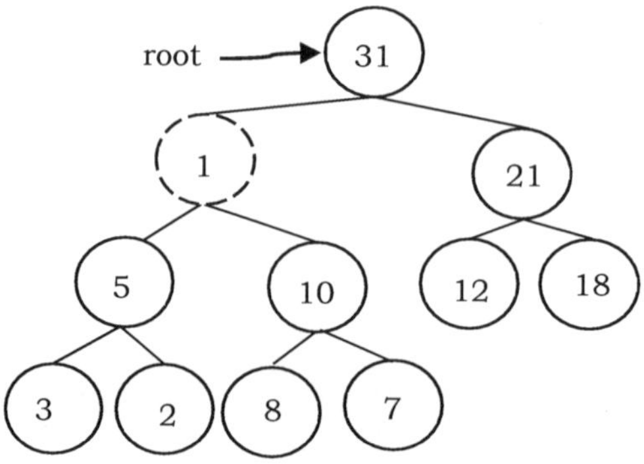

After inserting an element into heap, it may not satisfy the heap property. In that case we need to adjust the locations of the heap to make it heap again. This process is called *heapifying*. In max-heap, to heapify an element, we have to find the maximum of its children and swap it with the current element and continue this process until the heap property is satisfied at every node.

Observation: One important property of heap is that, if an element is not satisfying the heap property then all the elements from that element to root will also have the same problem. In the example below, element 1 is not satisfying the heap property and its parent 31 is also having the issue.

Similarly, if we heapify an element then all the elements from that element to root will also satisfy the heap property automatically. Let us go through an example. In the above heap, the element 1 is not satisfying the heap property. Let us try heapifying this element.

To heapify 1, find maximum of its children and swap with that.

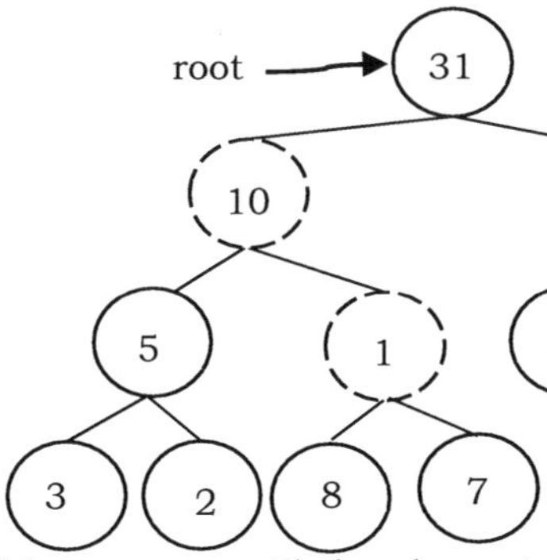

We need to continue this process until the element satisfies the heap properties. Now, swap 1 with 8.

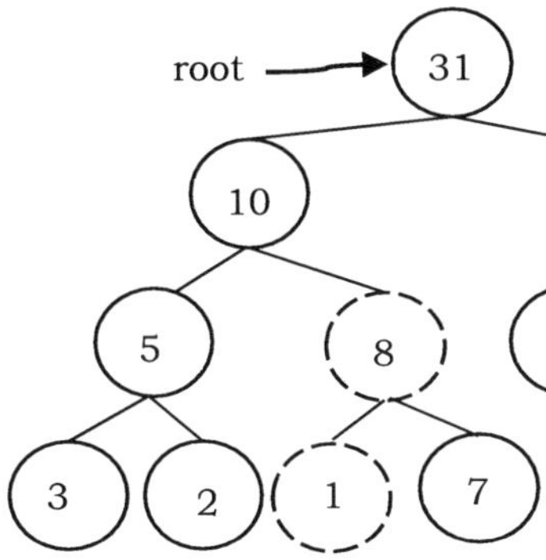

Now the tree is satisfying the heap property. In the above heapifying process, since we are moving from top to bottom, this process is sometimes called *percolate down*.

```
//Heapifying the element at location i.
void PercolateDown(struct Heap *h, int i) {
    int l, r, max, temp;
    l = LeftChild(h, i);
    r = RightChild(h, i);

    if(l != -1 && h→array[l] > h→array[i])
        max = l;
    else
        max = i;

    if(r != -1&& h→array[r] > h→array[max])
        max = r;
```

```
    if(max != i) {
        //Swap h→array[i] and  h→array[max];
        temp = h→array[i];
        h→array[i] = h→array[max];
        h→array[max] = temp;
    }
    PercolateDown(h, max);
}
```

Deleting an Element

To delete an element from heap, we just need to delete the element from root. This is the only operation (maximum element) supported by standard heap. After deleting the root element, copy the last element of the heap (tree) and delete that last element.

After replacing the last element the tree may not satisfy the heap property. To make it heap again, call *PercolateDown* function.

- Copy the first element into some variable
- Copy the last element into first element location
- *PercolateDown* the first element

```
int DeleteMax(struct Heap *h) {
    int data;
    if(h→count == 0)
        return -1;
    data = h→array[0];
    h→array[0] = h→array[h→count-1];
    h→count--; //reducing the heap size

    PercolateDown(h, 0);
    return data;
}
```

Note: Deleting an element uses *percolate down.*

Inserting an Element

Insertion of an element is similar to heapify and deletion process.

- Increase the heap size
- Keep the new element at the end of the heap (tree)
- Heapify the element from bottom to top (root)

Before going through code, let us look at an example. We have inserted the element 19 at end of the heap and this is not satisfying the heap property.

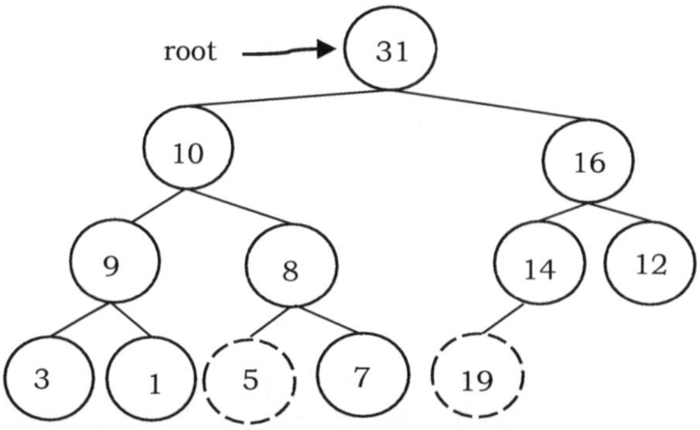

In-order to heapify this element (19), we need to compare it with its parent and adjust them. Swapping 19 and 14 gives:

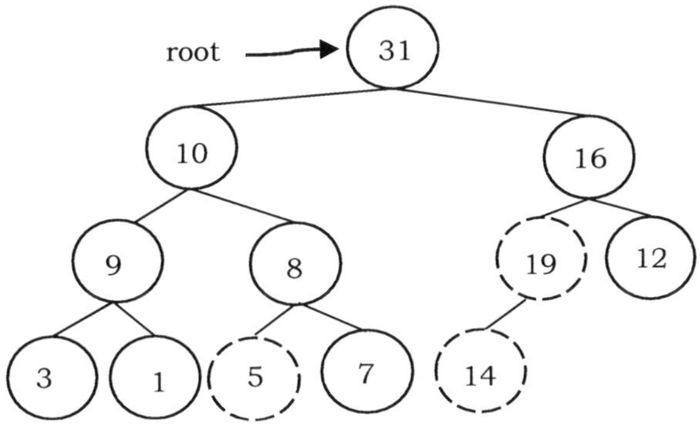

Again, swap 19 and16:

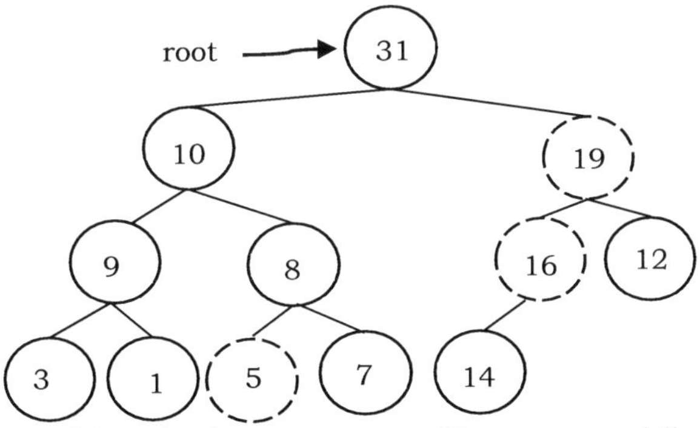

Now the tree is satisfying the heap property. Since we are following the bottom-up approach we sometimes call this process is *percolate up*.

```
int Insert(struct Heap *h, int data) {
    int i;
    if(h→count == h→capacity)
        ResizeHeap(h);
    h→count++;      //increasing the heap size to hold this new item
    i = h→count-1;
    while(i>=0 && data > h→array[(i-1)/2]) {
        h→array[i] = h→array[(i-1)/2];
        i = i-1/2;
    }
    h→array[i] = data;
}
void ResizeHeap(struct Heap * h) {
    int *array_old = h→array;
    h→array = (int *) malloc(sizeof(int) * h→capacity * 2);
    if(h→array == NULL) {
        printf("Memory Error");
        return;
    }
    for (int i = 0; i < h→capacity; i ++)
        h→array[i] = array_old[i];
    h→capacity *= 2;
    free(array_old);
}
```

Destroying Heap

```
void DestroyHeap (struct Heap *h) {
    if(h == NULL)
```

```
        return;
    free(h→array);
    free(h);
    h = NULL;
}
```

Heapifying the Array

One simple approach for building the heap is, take n input items and place them into an empty heap. This can be done with n successive inserts and takes $O(nlogn)$ in the worst case. This is due to the fact that each insert operation takes $O(logn)$.

Observation: Leaf nodes always satisfy the heap property and do not need to care for them. The leaf elements are always at the end and to heapify the given array it should be enough if we heapify the non-leaf nodes. Now let us concentrate on finding the first non-leaf node. The last element of the heap is at location $h \rightarrow count - 1$, and to find the first non-leaf node it is enough to find the parent of last element.

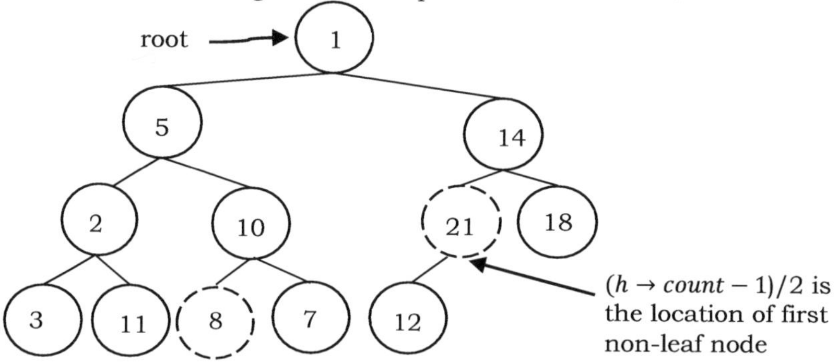


```
void BuildHeap(struct Heap *h, int A[], int n) {
    if(h == NULL)
        return;
    while (n > h→capacity)
        ResizeHeap(h);
    for (int i = 0; i < n; i ++)
        h→array[i] = A[i];
    h→count = n;
    for (int i = (n-1)/2; i >=0; i --)
        PercolateDown(h, i);
}
```

17.6 Heapsort

One main application of heap ADT is sorting (heap sort). Heap sort algorithm inserts all elements (from an unsorted array) into a heap, then removes them from the root of a heap until the heap is empty. Note that heap sort can be done in place with the array to be sorted.

Instead of deleting an element, exchange the first element (maximum) with the last element and reduce the heap size (array size). Then, we heapify the first element. Continue this process until the number of remaining elements is one.

```
void Heapsort(int A[], in n) {
    struct Heap *h = CreateHeap(n);
    int old_size, i, temp;
    BuildHeap(h, A, n);
    old_size = h→count;
```

```
    for(i = n-1; i > 0; i--) {
        //h→array [0] is the largest element
        temp = h→array[0];
        h→array[0] = h→array[h→count-1];
        h→array[0] = temp;
        h→count--;
        PercolateDown(h, i);
    }
    h→count = old_size;
}
```

Problems and Questions with Answers

Question 1: What are the minimum and maximum number of elements in a heap of height h?

Answer: Since heap is a complete binary tree (all levels contain full nodes except possibly the lowest level), it has at most $2^{h+1} - 1$ elements (if it is complete). This is because, to get maximum nodes, we need to fill all the h levels completely and the maximum number of nodes is nothing but sum of all nodes at all h levels.

To get minimum nodes, we should fill the $h - 1$ levels fully and last level with only one element. As a result, the minimum number of nodes is nothing but sum of all nodes from $h - 1$ levels plus 1 (for last level) and we get $2^h - 1 + 1 = 2^h$ elements (if the lowest level has just 1 element and all the other levels are complete).

Question 2: Is there a min-heap with seven distinct elements so that, the preorder traversal of it gives the elements in sorted order?

Answer: **Yes**. For the tree below, preorder traversal produces ascending order.

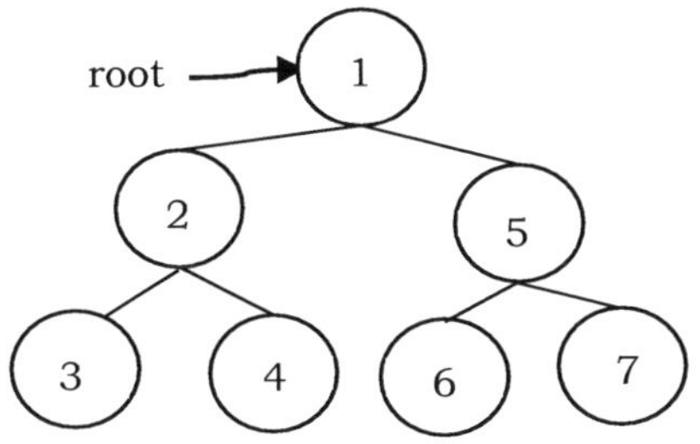

Question 3: Is there a max-heap with seven distinct elements so that, the preorder traversal of it gives the elements in sorted order?

Answer: **Yes**. For the tree below, preorder traversal produces descending order.

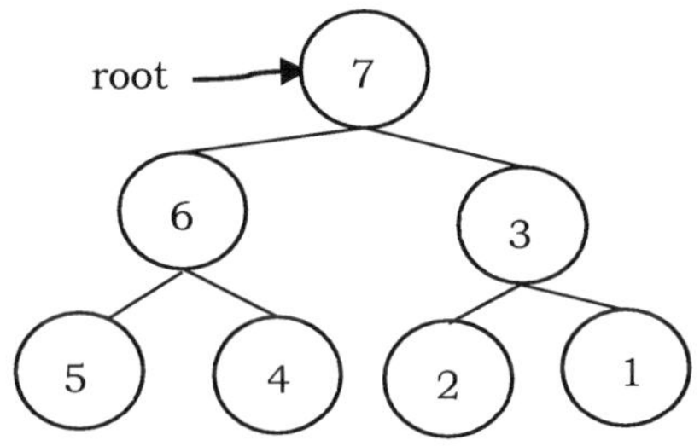

Question 4: Is there a min-heap/max-heap with seven distinct elements so that, the inorder traversal of it gives the elements in sorted order?

Answer: **No**, since a heap must be either a min-heap or a max-heap, the root will hold the smallest element or the largest. An inorder traversal will visit the root of tree as its second step, which is not the appropriate place if trees root contains the smallest or largest element.

Question 5: Is there a min-heap/max-heap with seven distinct elements so that, the postorder traversal of it gives the elements in sorted order?

Answer: **Yes**, if tree is a max-heap and we want descending order (below left), or if tree is a min-heap and we want ascending order (below right).

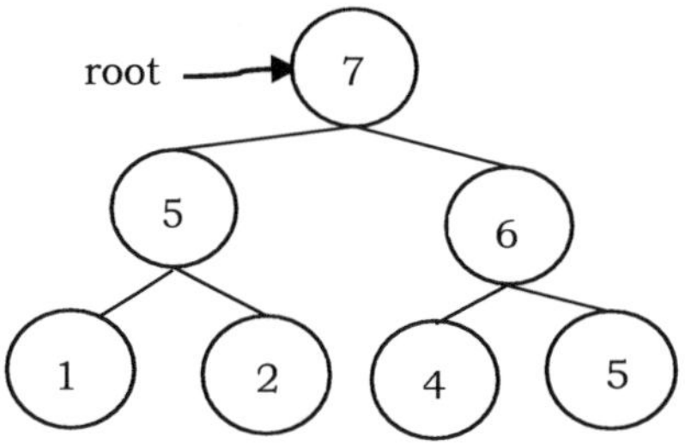

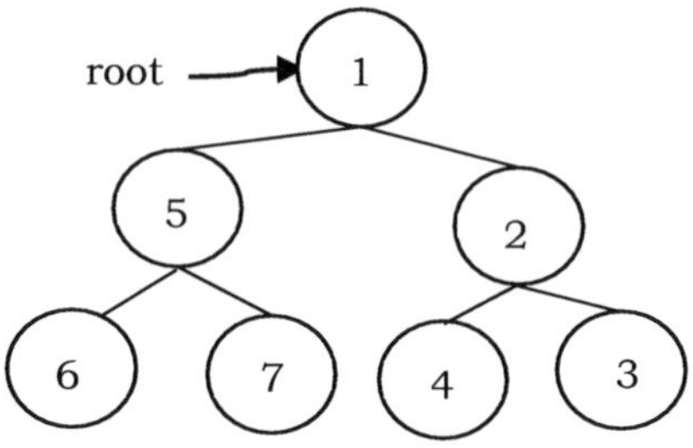

Question 6: Show that the height of a heap with n elements is $logn$?

Answer: A heap is a complete binary tree. All the levels, except the lowest, are completely full. A heap has at least 2^h element and atmost elements. $2^h \leq n \leq 2^{h+1} - 1$. This implies, $h \leq logn \leq h + 1$. Since h is integer, $h = logn$.

Question 7: Given a min-heap, give an algorithm for finding the maximum element.

Answer: For a given min heap the maximum element will always be at leaf only. Now, the next question is how to find the leaf nodes in tree.

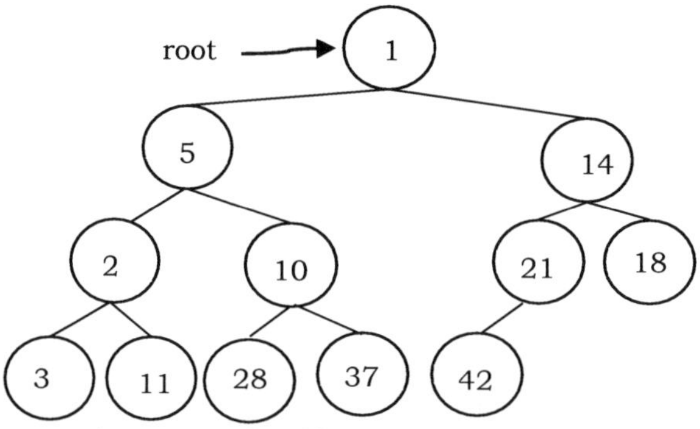

If we carefully observe, the next node of last elements parent is the first leaf node. Since the last element is always at $h \to count - 1^{th}$ location, the next node of its parent (parent at location $\frac{h \to count - 1}{2}$) can be calculated as:

$$\frac{h \to count - 1}{2} + 1 \approx \frac{h \to count + 1}{2}$$

Now, the only step remaining is scanning the leaf nodes and finding the maximum among them.

```
int FindMaxInMinHeap(struct Heap *h) {
    int Max = -1;
        for(int i = (h→count+1)/2; i < h→count; i++)
            if(h→array[i] > Max)
                Max = h→array[i];
}
```

Graph Algorithms

CHAPTER 18

18.1 Introduction

In real world, many problems are represented in terms of objects and connections between them.

For example, in an airline route map, we might be interested in questions like: "What's the fastest way to go from Hyderabad to New York?" *or* "What is the cheapest way to go from Hyderabad to New York?" To answer these questions we need information about connections (airline routes) between objects (towns). Graphs are data structures used for solving these kinds of problems.

18.2 Glossary

Graph: A graph is a pair (*V*, *E*), where *V* is a set of nodes, called *vertices* and *E* is a collection of pairs of vertices, called *edges*.

- *Vertices* and *edges* are positions and store elements
- Definitions that we use:
  - *Directed edge*:
  - ordered pair of vertices (u, v)
  - first vertex u is the origin
  - second vertex v is the destination
  - Example: One-way road traffic

  - *Undirected edge*:
  - unordered pair of vertices (u, v)
  - Example: Railway lines

  - *Directed graph*:
  - all the edges are directed
  - Example: route network

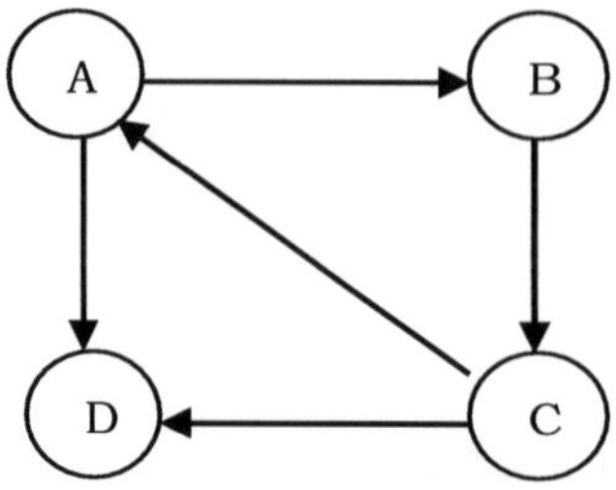

- o *Undirected graph*:
- o all the edges are undirected. Example: flight network

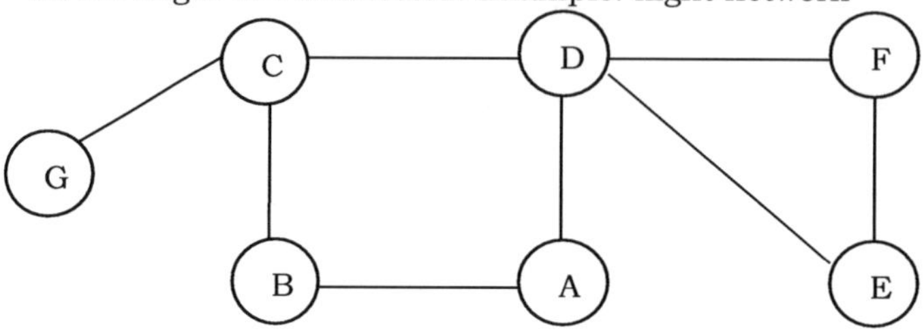

- When an edge connects two vertices, the vertices are said to be adjacent to each other and that the edge is incident on both vertices.
- A graph with no cycles is called a *tree*. A tree is an acyclic connected graph.

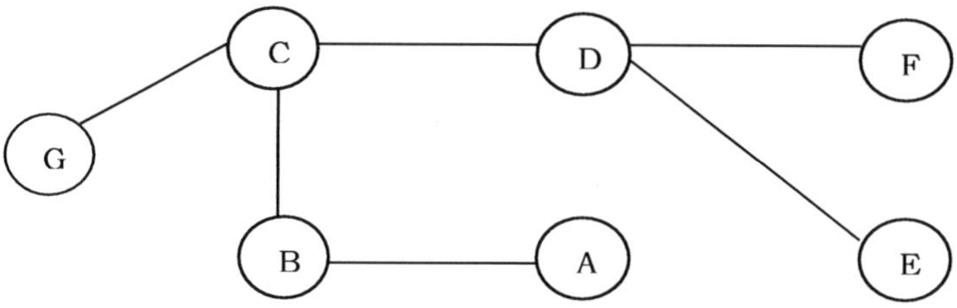

- A self loop is an edge that connects a vertex to itself.

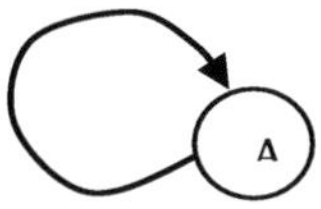

- Two edges are parallel if they connect the same pair of vertices.

- *D*egree of a vertex is the number of edges incident on it.
- A subgraph is a subset of a graphs edges (with associated vertices) that forms a graph.
- A path in a graph is a sequence of adjacent vertices. *S*imple path is a path with no repeated vertices. In the graph below, dotted lines represent a path from G to E.

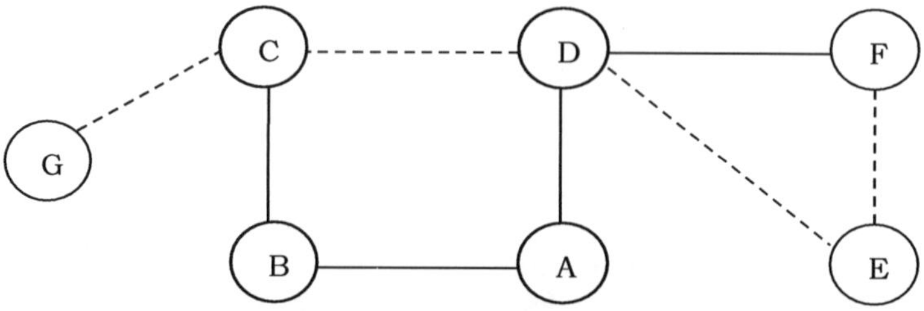

- A cycle is a path where first and last vertices are the same. A simple cycle is a cycle with no repeated vertices or edges (except the first and last vertices).

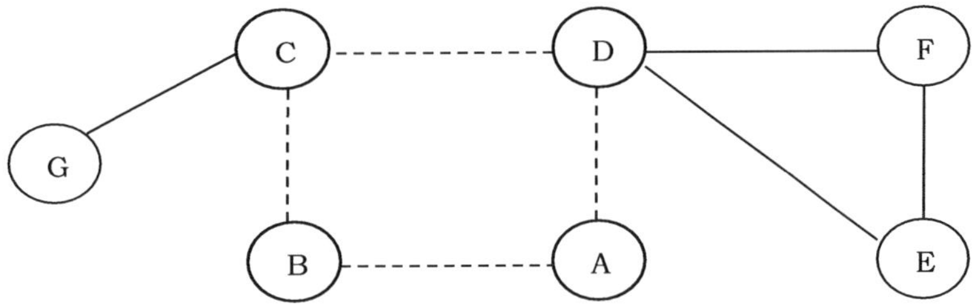

- We say that one vertex is connected to another if there is a path that contains both of them.
- A graph is connected if there is a path from *every* vertex to every other vertex.
- If a graph is not connected then it consists of a set of connected components.

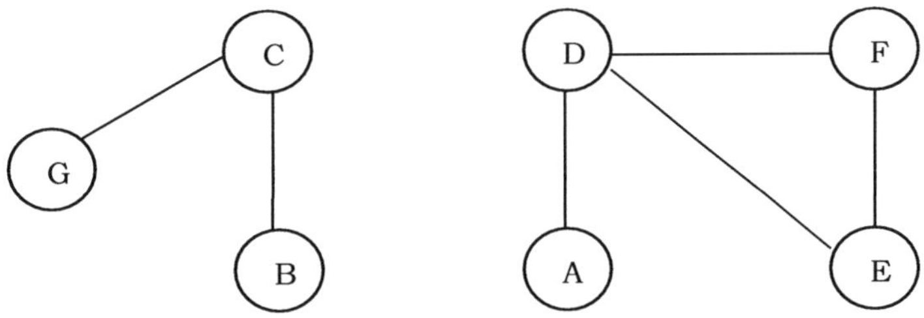

- A *directed* acyclic graph [DAG] is a directed graph with no cycles.

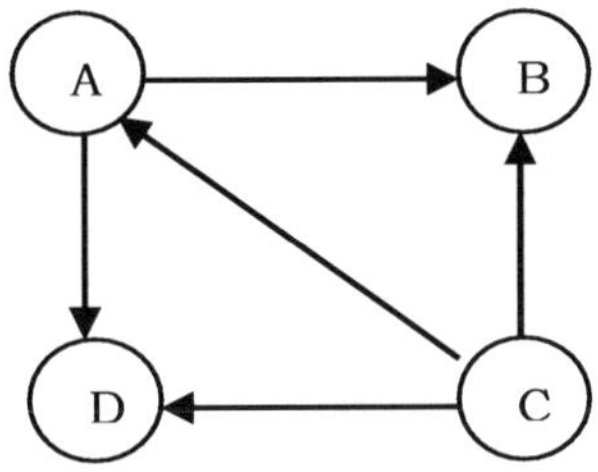

- A forest is a disjoint set of trees.
- A spanning tree of a connected graph is a subgraph that contains all of that graph's vertices and is a single tree. A spanning forest of a graph is the union of spanning trees of its connected components.
- A bipartite graph is a graph whose vertices can be divided into two sets such that all edges connect a vertex in one set with a vertex in the other set.

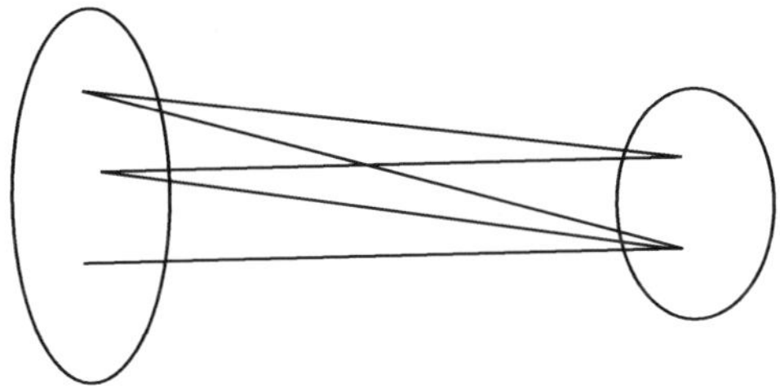

- In *weighted graphs* integers *(weights)* are assigned to each edge to represent (distances or costs).

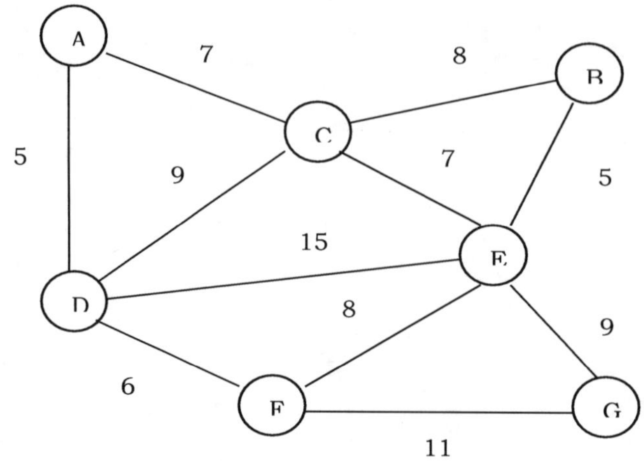

- Graphs with all edges present are called *complete* graphs.

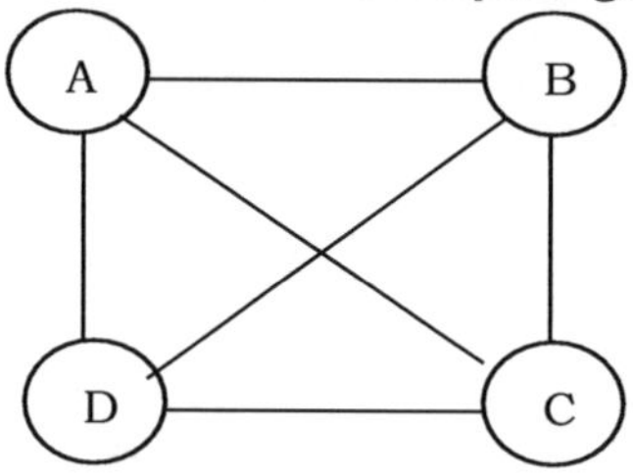

- Graphs with relatively few edges (generally if it edges $< |V| \log |V|$) are called *sparse graphs*.
- Graphs with relatively few of the possible edges missing are called *dense*.
- Directed weighted graphs are sometimes called *network*.
- We will denote the number of vertices in a given graph by $|V|$, the number of edges by $|E|$. Note that E can range anywhere from 0 to $|V|(|V| - 1)/2$ (in undirected graph). This is because each node can connect to every other node.

18.3 Applications of Graphs

- Representing relationships between components in electronic circuits
- Transportation networks: Highway network, Flight network
- Computer networks: Local area network, Internet, Web
- Databases: For representing ER (Entity Relationship) diagrams in databases, for representing dependency of tables in databases

18.4 Graph Representation

As in other ADTs, to manipulate graphs we need to represent them in some useful form. Basically, there are three ways of doing this:

- Adjacency Matrix
- Adjacency List
- Adjacency Set

Adjacency Matrix

Graph Declaration for Adjacency Matrix

First, let us see the components of the graph data structure. To represent graphs, we need number of vertices, number of edges and also their interconnections. So, the graph can be declared as:

```
struct Graph {
    int V;
    int E;
    int **Adj; //Since we need two dimensional matrix
};
```

Description

In this method, we use a matrix with size $V \times V$. The values of matrix are boolean. Let us assume the matrix is Adj. The value $Adj[u,v]$ set to 1 if there is an edge from vertex u to vertex v and 0 otherwise.

In the matrix, each edge is represented by two bits for undirected graphs. That means, an edge from u to v is represented by 1 values in both $Adj[\text{u},\text{v}]$ and $Adj[u,v]$. To save time, we can process only half of this symmetric matrix. Also, we can assume that there is an "edge" from each vertex to itself. So, $Adj[\text{u},\text{u}]$ is set to 1 *for all* vertices.

If the graph is a directed graph then we need to mark only one entry in the adjacency matrix. As an example, consider the directed graph below.

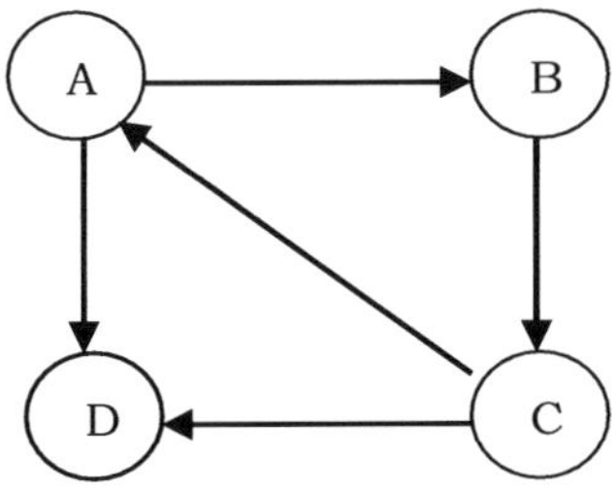

Adjacency matrix for this graph can be given as:

	A	B	C	D
A	0	1	0	1
B	0	0	1	0
C	1	0	0	1
D	0	0	0	0

Now, let us concentrate on the implementation. To read a graph, one way is to first read the vertex names and then read pairs of vertex names (edges). The code below reads an undirected graph.

The adjacency matrix representation is good if the graphs are dense. The matrix requires $O(V^2)$ bits of storage and $O(V^2)$ time for initialization. If the number of edges is proportional to V^2, then there is no problem because V^2 steps are required to read the edges. If the graph is sparse, since initializing the matrix takes V^2 and it dominates the running time of algorithm.

Adjacency List

Graph Declaration for Adjacency List

In this representation all the vertices connected to a vertex v are listed on an adjacency list for that vertex v. This can be easily implemented with linked lists. That means, for each vertex v we use a linked list and list nodes represents the connections between v and other vertices to which v has an edge.

Description

Considering the same example as that of adjacency matrix, the adjacency list representation can be given as:

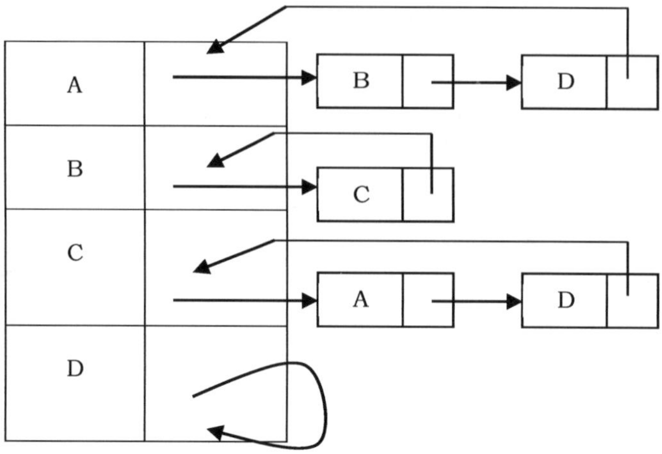

Since vertex A has an edge for B and D, we have added them in the adjacency list for A. Same is the case with other vertices as well.

For this representation, the order of edges in the input is *important*. This is because they determine the order of the vertices on the adjacency lists. Same graph can be represented in many different ways in an adjacency list. The order in which edges appear on the adjacency list affects the order in which edges are processed by algorithms.

Disadvantages of Adjacency Lists

Using adjacency list representation we cannot perform some operations efficiently. As an example, consider the case of deleting a node. In adjacency list representation, if we delete a node from the adjacency list then that is enough. For each node on the adjacency list of that node specifies another vertex.

We need to search other nodes linked list also for deleting it. This problem can be solved by linking the two list nodes which correspond to a particular edge and make the adjacency lists doubly linked. But all these extra links are risky to process.

Adjacency Set

It is very much similar to adjacency list but instead of using Linked lists, Disjoint Sets [Union-Find] are used. For more details refer *Disjoint Sets ADT* chapter.

Comparison of Graph Representations

Directed and undirected graphs are represented with same structures. For directed graphs, everything is the same, except that each edge is represented just once, an edge from x to y is represented by a 1 value in $Adj[x][y]$ in the adjacency matrix or by adding y on x's adjacency list. For weighted graphs, everything is same except that fill the adjacency matrix with weights instead of boolean values.

Representation	Space	Checking edge between v and w?	Iterate over edges incident to v?
List of edges	E	E	E
Adj Matrix	V^2	1	V
Adj List	$E + V$	$Degree(v)$	$Degree(v)$
Adj Set	$E + V$	$log(Degree(v))$	$Degree(v)$

18.5 Graph Traversals

To solve problems on graphs, we need a mechanism for traversing the graphs. Graph traversal algorithms are also called as *graph search* algorithms. Like trees traversal algorithms (Inorder, Preorder, Postorder and Level-Order traversals), graph search algorithms can be thought of as starting at some source vertex in a graph, and "search" the graph by going through the edges and marking the vertices.

Now, we will discuss two such algorithms for traversing the graphs.

- Depth First Search [DFS]
- Breadth First Search [BFS]

Depth First Search [DFS]

DFS algorithm works in a manner similar to preorder traversal of the trees. Like preorder traversal, internally this algorithm also uses stack.

The time complexity of DFS is $O(V + E)$, if we use adjacency lists for representing the graphs. This is because we are starting at a vertex and processing the adjacent nodes only if they are not visited.

Similarly, if an adjacency matrix is used for a graph representation, then all edges adjacent to a vertex can't be found efficiently, this gives $O(V^2)$ complexity.

Applications of DFS

- Topological sorting
- Finding connected components
- Finding articulation points (cut vertices) of the graph
- Finding strongly connected components
- Solving puzzles such as mazes

For algorithms refer *Problems Section*.

Breadth First Search [BFS]

BFS algorithm works similar to $level - order$ traversal of the trees. Like $level - order$ traversal BFS also uses queues. In fact, $level - order$ traversal got inspired from BFS. BFS works level by level. Initially, BFS starts at a given vertex, which is at level 0. In the first stage it visits all vertices at level 1 (that means, vertices whose distance is 1 from start vertex of the graph).

In the second stage, it visits all vertices at second level. These new vertices are the one which are adjacent to level 1 vertices. BFS continues this process until all the levels of the graph are completed. Generally *queue* data structure is used for storing the vertices of a level.

As similar to DFS, assume that initially all vertices are marked *unvisited* ($false$). Vertices that have been processed and removed from the queue are marked *visited* ($true$). We use a queue to represent the visited set as it will keep the vertices in order of when they were first visited.

The implementation for the above discussion can be given as:

```
void BFS(struct Graph *G, int u) {
    int v;
    struct Queue *Q = CreateQueue();

    EnQueue(Q, u);
    while(!IsEmptyQueue(Q)) {
```

```
        u = DeQueue(Q);
        Process u; //For example, print
        Visited[s]=1;
        /* For example, if the adjacency matrix is used for representing the  graph,
        then the condition be used for finding unvisited adjacent vertex of u  is:
        if( !Visited[v] && G→Adj[u][v] ) */
        for each unvisited adjacent node v of u {
            EnQueue(Q, v);
        }
    }
}
void BFSTraversal(struct Graph *G) {
    for (int i = 0; i< G→V;i++)
        Visited[i]=0;
    //This loop is required if the graph has more than one component
    for (int i = 0; i< G→V;i++)
        if(!Visited[i])
            BFS(G, i);
}
```

As an example, let us consider the same graph as that of DFS example. The BFS traversal can be shown as:

Starting vertex *A* is marked unvisited. Assume this is at level 0.

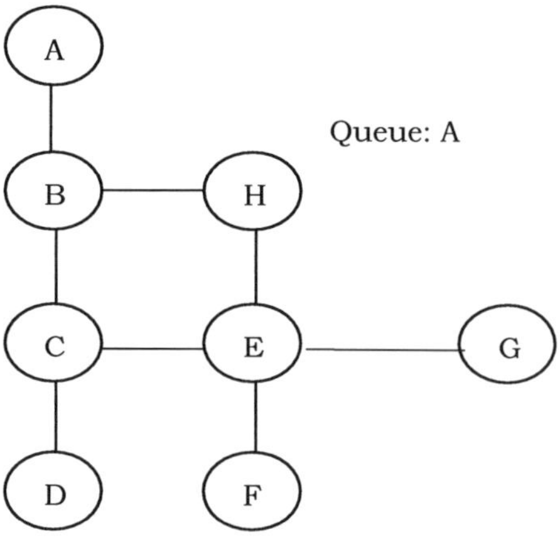

Visited Table

0	0	0	0	0	0	0

Vertex *A* is completed. Circled part is level 1 and added to Queue.

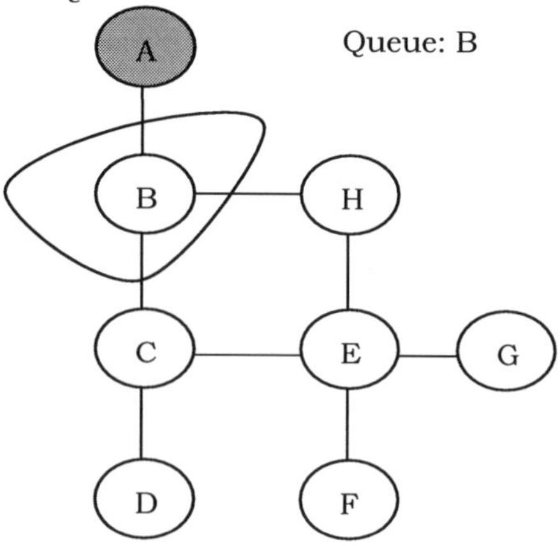

Visited Table

1	0	0	0	0	0	0

B is completed. Selected part is level 2 (add to Queue).

Queue: C, H

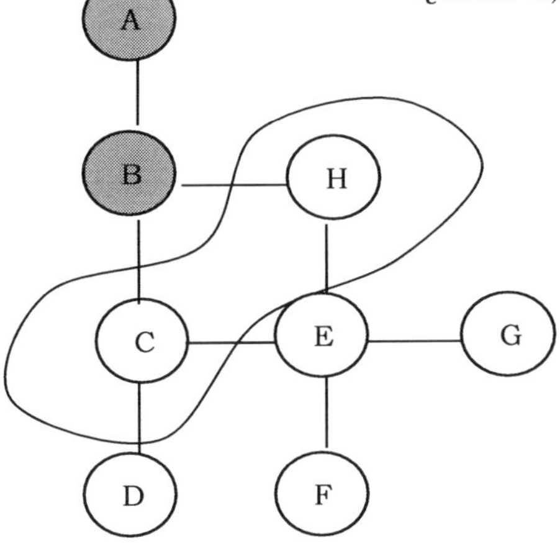

Visited Table

1	1	0	0	0	0	0

Vertices C and H are completed. Circled part is level 3 (add to Queue).

Queue: D, E

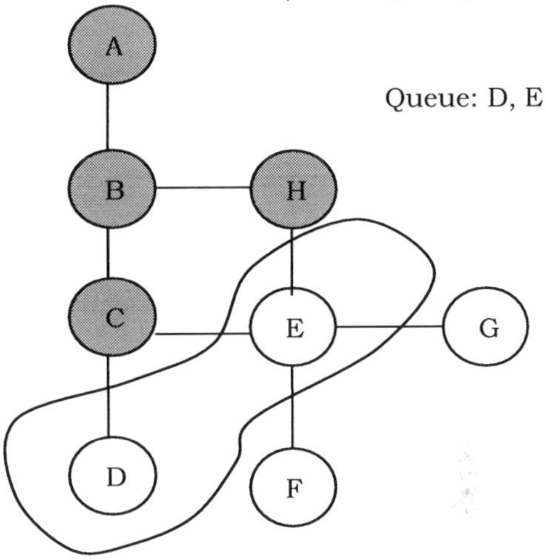

Visited Table

1	1	0	0	0	0	1

D and E are completed. F and G are marked with gray color (next level).

Queue: F, G

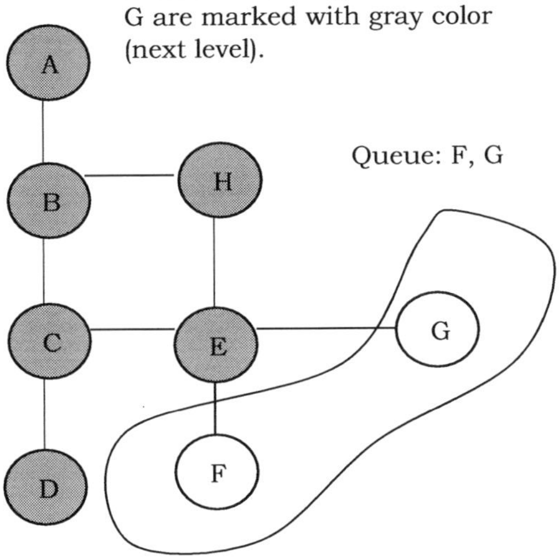

Visited Table

1	1	1	1	0	0	1

All vertices completed and Queue is empty.

Queue: Empty

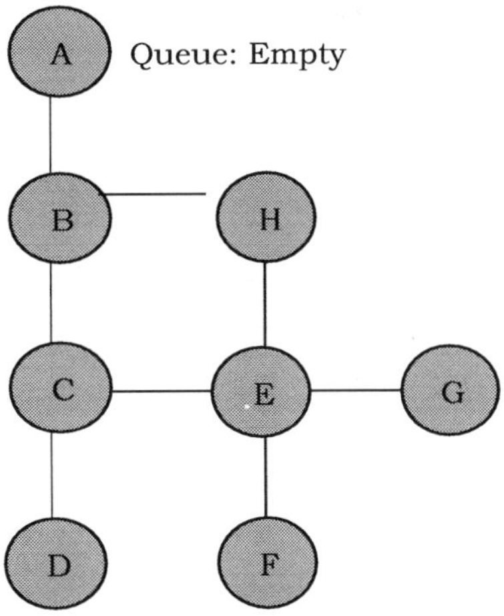

Visited Table

1	1	1	1	1	1	1

Time complexity of BFS is $O(V + E)$, if we use adjacency lists for representing the graphs and $O(V^2)$ for adjacency matrix representation.

Applications of BFS

- Finding all connected components in a graph
- Finding all nodes within one connected component
- Finding the shortest path between two nodes
- Testing a graph for bipartiteness

Comparing DFS and BFS

Comparing BFS and DFS, the big advantage of DFS is that it has much lower memory requirements than BFS, because it's not required to store all of the child pointers at each level. Depending on the data and what we are looking for, either DFS or BFS could be advantageous. For example, in a family tree if we are looking for someone who's still alive and if we assume that person would be at bottom of the tree then DFS is a better choice. BFS would take a very long time to reach that last level.

DFS algorithm finds the goal faster. Now, if we were looking for a family member who died a very long time ago, then that person would be closer to the top of the tree. In this case, BFS finds faster than DFS. So, the advantages of either vary depending on the data and what we are looking for.

DFS is related to preorder traversal of a tree. Like *preorder* traversal simply DFS visits each node before its children. BFS algorithm works similar to *level – order* traversal of the trees.

If someone asks whether DFS is better or BFS is better? The answer depends on the type of the problem that we are trying to solve. BFS visits each level one at a time, and if we know the solution we are searching for is at a low depth then BFS is good. DFS is better choice if the solution is at maximum depth. Below table shows the differences between DFS and BFS in terms of their applications.

Applications	DFS	BFS
Spanning forest, connected components, paths, cycles	Yes	Yes
Shortest paths		Yes
Minimal use of memory space	Yes	

18.6 Shortest Path Algorithms

Let us consider the other important problem of graph. Given a graph $G = (V, E)$ and a distinguished vertex s, we need to find the shortest path from s to every other vertex in G. There are variations in the shortest path algorithms which depend on the type of the input graph and are given below.

Variations of Shortest Path Algorithms

Shortest path in unweighted graph
Shortest path in weighted graph [Dijkstra Algorithm]
Shortest path in weighted graph with negative edges [Bellman Ford Algorithm]

Applications of Shortest Path Algorithms

- Finding fastest way to go from one place to another
- Finding cheapest way to fly/send data from one city to another

CHAPTER

Sorting

19

19.1 What is Sorting?

Sorting is an algorithm that arranges the elements of a list in a certain order [either *ascending* or *descending*]. The output is a permutation or reordering of the input.

19.2 Why is Sorting necessary?

Sorting is one of the important categories of algorithms in computer science. Sometimes sorting significantly reduces the complexity of the problem. We can use sorting as a technique to reduce the search complexity.

Great research went into this category of algorithms because of its importance. These algorithms are used in many computer algorithms [for example, searching elements], database algorithms and many more.

19.3 Classification of Sorting Algorithms

Sorting algorithms are generally categorized based on the following parameters.

By Number of Comparisons

In this method, sorting algorithms are classified based on the number of comparisons. For comparison based sorting algorithms best case behavior is O($nlogn$) and worst case behavior is O(n^2). Comparison-based sorting algorithms evaluate the elements of the list by key comparison operation and need at least O($nlogn$) comparisons for most inputs.

Later in this chapter we will discuss few *non – comparison* (*linear*) sorting algorithms like Counting sort, Bucket sort, and Radix sort, etc. Linear Sorting algorithms impose few restrictions on the inputs to improve the complexity.

By Number of Swaps

In this method, sorting algorithms are categorized by number of *swaps* (also called *inversions*).

By Memory Usage

Some sorting algorithms are "*in place*" and they need O(1) or O($logn$) memory to create auxiliary locations for sorting the data temporarily.

By Recursion

Sorting algorithms are either recursive [quick sort] or non-recursive [selection sort, and insertion sort]. There are some algorithms which use both (merge sort).

By Stability

Sorting algorithm is *stable* if for all indices i and j such that the key $A[i]$ equals key $A[j]$, if record $R[i]$ precedes record $R[j]$ in the original file, record $R[i]$ precedes record $R[j]$ in the sorted list. Few sorting algorithms maintain the relative order of elements with equal keys (equivalent elements retain their relative positions even after sorting).

By Adaptability

Few sorting algorithms complexity changes based on pre-sortedness [quick sort]: pre-sortedness of the input affects the running time. Algorithms that take this into account are known to be adaptive.

19.4 Other Classifications

Another method of classifying sorting algorithms is:

- Internal Sort
- External Sort

Internal Sort

Sort algorithms that use main memory exclusively during the sort are called *internal* sorting algorithms. This kind of algorithm assumes high-speed random access to all memory.

External Sort

Sorting algorithms that use external memory, such as tape or disk, during the sort come under this category.

19.5 Bubble sort

Bubble sort is the simplest sorting algorithm. It works by iterating the input array from the first element to last, comparing each pair of elements and swapping them if needed. Bubble sort continues its iterations until no more swaps are needed. The algorithm gets its name from the way smaller elements "*bubble*" to the top of the list. Generally, insertion sort has better performance than bubble sort. Some researchers suggest that we should not teach bubble sort because of its simplicity and complexity.

The only significant advantage that bubble sort has over other implementations is that it can detect whether the input list is already sorted or not.

Implementation

```
void BubbleSort(int A[], int n) {
    for (int pass = n - 1; pass >= 0; pass--){
        for (int i = 0; i < pass - 1 ; i++)    {
            if(A[i] > A[i+1]) {
                // swap elements
                int temp = A[i];
                A[i] = A[i+1];
                A[i+1] = temp;
```

```
            }
        }
    }
}
```

Algorithm takes $O(n^2)$ (even in best case). We can improve it by using one extra flag. No more swaps indicate the completion of sorting. If the list is already sorted, we can use this flag to skip the remaining passes.

```
void BubbleSortImproved(int A[], int n) {
    int pass, i, temp, swapped = 1;
    for (pass = n - 1; pass >= 0 && swapped; pass--) {
        swapped = 0;
        for (i = 0; i < pass - 1 ; i++) {
            if(A[i] > A[i+1]) {
                // swap elements
                temp = A[i];
                A[i] = A[i+1];
                A[i+1] = temp;
                swapped = 1;
            }
        }
    }
}
```

This modified version improves the best case of bubble sort to $O(n)$.

Performance

Worst case complexity : $O(n^2)$
Best case complexity (Improved version) : $O(n)$
Average case complexity (Basic version) : $O(n^2)$
Worst case space complexity : $O(1)$ auxiliary

19.6 Selection Sort

Selection sort is an in-place sorting algorithm. Selection sort works well for small files. It is used for sorting the files with very large values and small keys. This is because selection is made based on keys and swaps are made only when required.

Advantages

- Easy to implement
- In-place sort (requires no additional storage space)

Disadvantages

- Doesn't scale well: $O(n^2)$

Algorithm

1. Find the minimum value in the list
2. Swap it with the value in the current position
3. Repeat this process for all the elements until the entire array is sorted

This algorithm is called *selection sort* since it repeatedly *selects* the smallest element.

Implementation

```
void Selection(int A [], int n) {
    int i, j, min, temp;
    for (i = 0; i < n - 1; i++) {
        min = i;
        for (j = i+1; j < n; j++) {
            if(A [j] < A [min])
                min = j;
        }
        // swap elements
        temp = A[min];
        A[min] = A[i];
        A[i] = temp;
    }
}
```

Performance

Worst case complexity : $O(n^2)$
Best case complexity : $O(n)$
Average case complexity : $O(n^2)$
Worst case space complexity: O(1) auxiliary

19.7 Insertion sort

Insertion sort is a simple and efficient comparison sort. In this algorithm each iteration removes an element from the input data and inserts it into the correct position in the list being sorted. The choice of the element being removed from the input is random and this process is repeated until all input elements have gone through.

Advantages

- Simple implementation
- Efficient for small data
- Adaptive: If the input list is presorted [may not be completely] then insertions sort takes $O(n + d)$, where d is the number of inversions
- Practically more efficient than selection and bubble sorts even though all of them have $O(n^2)$ worst case complexity
- Stable: Maintains relative order of input data if the keys are same
- In-place: It requires only a constant amount O(1) of additional memory space
- Online: Insertion sort can sort the list as it receives it

Algorithm

Sorted partial result Unsorted elements

$\leq x$	$> x$	x	...

Sorted partial result Unsorted elements

becomes

$\leq x$	x	$> x$	...

Every repetition of insertion sort removes an element from the input data, inserts it into the correct position in the already-sorted list until no input elements remain. Sorting is typically done in-place. The resulting array after k iterations has the property where the first $k + 1$ entries are sorted.

Each element greater than x copied to the right as it is compared against x.

Implementation

```
void InsertionSort(int A[], int n) {
    int i, j, v;
    for (i = 2; i <= n - 1; i++) {
        v = A[i];
        j = i;
        while (A[j-1] > v && j >= 1) {
            A[j] = A[j-1];
            j--;
        }
        A[j] = v;
    }
}
```

Example

Given an array: 6 8 1 4 5 3 7 2 and the goal is to put them in ascending order.

6 8 1 4 5 3 7 2 (Consider index 0)
6 8 1 4 5 3 7 2 (Consider indices 0 - 1)
1 6 8 4 5 3 7 2 (Consider indices 0 - 2: insertion places 1 in front of 6 and 8)
1 4 6 8 5 3 7 2 (Process same as above is repeated until array is sorted)
1 4 5 6 8 3 7 2
1 3 4 5 6 7 8 2
1 2 3 4 5 6 7 8 (The array is sorted!)

Analysis

Worst case analysis

Worst case occurs when for every i the inner loop has to move all elements $A[1], \ldots,$ $A[i-1]$ (which happens when $A[i]$ = key is smaller than all of them), that takes $\Theta(i-1)$ time.

$$T(n) = \Theta(1) + \Theta(2) + \Theta(2) + \ldots\ldots + \Theta(n-1)$$
$$= \Theta(1 + 2 + 3 + \ldots\ldots + n - 1) = \Theta(\frac{n(n-1)}{2}) \approx \Theta(n^2)$$

Average case analysis

For the average case, the inner loop will insert $A[i]$ in the middle of $A[1], \ldots, A[i-1]$. This takes $\Theta(i/2)$ time.

$$T(n) = \sum_{i=1}^{n} \Theta(i/2) \approx \Theta(n^2)$$

Performance

Worst case complexity : $O(n^2)$
Best case complexity : $O(n^2)$
Average case complexity : Î(n^2)
Worst case space complexity: $O(n^2)$ total, $O(1)$ auxiliary

Comparisons to Other Sorting Algorithms

Insertion sort is one of the elementary sorting algorithms with $O(n^2)$ worst-case time. Insertion sort is used when the data is nearly sorted (due to its adaptiveness) or when the input size is small (due to its low overhead). For these reasons and due to its stability, insertion sort is used as the recursive base case (when the problem size is small) for higher overhead divide-and-conquer sorting algorithms, such as merge sort or quick sort.

Notes:

- Bubble sort takes $\frac{n^2}{2}$ comparisons and $\frac{n^2}{2}$ swaps (inversions) in both average case and in worst case.
- Selection sort takes $\frac{n^2}{2}$ comparisons and n swaps.
- Insertion sort takes $\frac{n^2}{4}$ comparisons and $\frac{n^2}{8}$ swaps in average case and in the worst case they are double.
- Insertion sort is almost linear for partially sorted input.
- Selection sort is best suits for elements with bigger values and small keys.

19.8 Shell sort

Shell sort (also called *diminishing increment sort*) was invented by *Donald Shell*. This sorting algorithm is a generalization of insertion sort. Insertion sort works efficiently on input that is already almost sorted.

In insertion sort, comparisons are made between the adjacent elements. At most 1 inversion is eliminated for each comparison done with insertion sort. The variation used in shell sort is to avoid comparing adjacent elements until the last step of the algorithm. So, the last step of shell sort is effectively the insertion sort algorithm.

It improves insertion sort by allowing the comparison and exchange of elements that are far away. This is the first algorithm which got less than quadratic complexity among comparison sort algorithms.

Shell sort uses a sequence $h1, h2, \ldots, ht$ called the *increment sequence*. Any increment sequence is fine as long as $h1 = 1$ and some choices are better than others. Shell sort makes multiple passes through input list and sorts a number of equally sized sets using the insertion sort. Shell sort improves the efficiency of insertion sort by *quickly* shifting values to their destination.

Implementation

```
void ShellSort(int A[], int array_size) {
    int i, j, h, v;
    for (h = 1; h = array_size/9; h = 3*h+1);
    for ( ; h > 0; h = h/3) {
        for (i = h+1; i = array_size; i += 1) {
            v = A[i];
            j = i;
            while (j > h && A[j-h] > v) {
                A[j] = A[j-h];
                j -= h;
            }
            A[j] = v;
        }
    }
}
```

Note that when $h == 1$, the algorithm makes a pass over the entire list, comparing adjacent elements, but doing very few element exchanges. For $h == 1$, shell sort works just like insertion sort, except the number of inversions that have to be eliminated is greatly reduced by the previous steps of the algorithm with $h > 1$.

Analysis

Shell sort is efficient for medium size lists. For bigger lists, the algorithm is not the best choice. It is the fastest of all $O(n^2)$ sorting algorithms.

The disadvantage of Shell sort is that it is a complex algorithm and not nearly as efficient as the merge, heap, and quick sorts. Shell sort is significantly slower than the merge, heap, and quick sorts, but is a relatively simple algorithm, which makes it a good choice for sorting lists of less than 5000 items unless speed is important. It is also a good choice for repetitive sorting of smaller lists.

The best case in Shell sort is when the array is already sorted in the right order. The number of comparisons is less. Running time of Shell sort depends on the choice of increment sequence.

Performance

Worst case complexity depends on gap sequence. Best known: $O(nlog^2n)$
Best case complexity: $O(n)$
Average case complexity depends on gap sequence
Worst case space complexity: $O(n)$

19.9 Merge sort

Merge sort is an example of the divide and conquer.

Important Notes

- *Merging* is the process of combining two sorted files to make one bigger sorted file.
- *Selection* is the process of dividing a file into two parts: k smallest elements and $n - k$ largest elements.
- Selection and merging are opposite operations
    - selection splits a list into two lists
    - merging joins two files to make one file
- Merge sort is Quick sorts complement
- Merge sort accesses the data in a sequential manner
- This algorithm is used for sorting a linked list
- Merge sort is insensitive to the initial order of its input
- In Quick sort most of the work is done before the recursive calls. Quick sort starts with the largest subfile and finishes with the small ones and as a result it needs stack. Moreover, this algorithm is not stable. Merge sort divides the list into two parts; then each part is conquered individually. Merge sort starts with the small subfiles and finishes with the largest one. As a result it doesn't need stack. This algorithm is stable.

Implementation

```
void Mergesort(int A[], int temp[], int left, int right) {
    int mid;
    if(right > left) {
        mid = (right + left) / 2;
        Mergesort(A, temp, left, mid);
```

```
        Mergesort(A, temp, mid+1, right);
        Merge(A, temp, left, mid+1, right);
    }
}
void Merge(int A[], int temp[], int left, int mid, int right) {
    int i, left_end, size, temp_pos;
    left_end = mid - 1;
    temp_pos = left;
    size = right - left + 1;
    while ((left <= left_end) && (mid <= right)) {
        if(A[left] <= A[mid]) {
            temp[temp_pos] = A[left];
            temp_pos = temp_pos + 1;
            left = left +1;
        }
        else {
            temp[temp_pos] = A[mid];
            temp_pos = temp_pos + 1;
            mid = mid + 1;
        }
    }
    while (left <= left_end) {
        temp[temp_pos] = A[left];
        left = left + 1;
        temp_pos = temp_pos + 1;
    }
    while (mid <= right) {
        temp[temp_pos] = A[mid];
        mid = mid + 1;
        temp_pos = temp_pos + 1;
    }
    for (i = 0; i <= size; i++) {
        A[right] = temp[right];
        right = right - 1;
    }
}
```

Analysis

In Merge sort the input list is divided into two parts and these are solved recursively. After solving the sub problems they are merged by scanning the resultant sub problems. Let us assume $T(n)$ is the complexity of Merge sort with n elements. The recurrence for the Merge Sort can be defined as:

Recurrence for Mergesort is $T(n) = 2T(\frac{n}{2}) + \Theta(n)$.
Using Master theorem, we get, $T(n) = \Theta(nlogn)$.

Note: For more details, refer *Divide and Conquer* chapter.

Performance

Worst case complexity : $\Theta(nlogn)$
Best case complexity : $\Theta(nlogn)$
Average case complexity : $\Theta(nlogn)$
Worst case space complexity: $\Theta(n)$ auxiliary

19.10 Heapsort

Heapsort is a comparison-based sorting algorithm and is part of the selection sort family. Although somewhat slower in practice on most machines than a good implementation of Quick sort, it has the advantage of a more favorable worst-case È($nlogn$) runtime. Heapsort is an in-place algorithm but is not a stable sort.

Performance

Worst case performance: $\Theta(nlogn)$
Best case performance: $\Theta(nlogn)$
Average case performance: $\Theta(nlogn)$
Worst case space complexity: $\Theta(n)$ total, $\Theta(1)$ auxiliary

For other details on Heapsort refer *Priority Queues* chapter.

19.11 Quicksort

Quick sort is an example of divide-and-conquer algorithmic technique. It is also called *partition exchange sort*. It uses recursive calls for sorting the elements. It is one of famous algorithms among comparison-based sorting algorithms.

Divide: The array $A[low \dots high]$ is partitioned into two non-empty sub arrays $A[low \dots q]$ and $A[q+1 \dots high]$, such that each element of $A[low \dots high]$ is less than or equal to each element of $A[q+1 \dots high]$. The index q is computed as part of this partitioning procedure.

Conquer: The two sub arrays $A[low \dots q]$ and $A[q+1 \dots high]$ are sorted by recursive calls to Quick sort.

Algorithm

The recursive algorithm consists of four steps:

1) If there are one or no elements in the array to be sorted, return.
2) Pick an element in the array to serve as "*pivot*" point. (Usually the left-most element in the array is used.)
3) Split the array into two parts - one with elements larger than the pivot and the other with elements smaller than the pivot.
4) Recursively repeat the algorithm for both halves of the original array.

Implementation

```
Quicksort( int A[], int low, int high ) {
    int pivot;
    /* Termination condition! */
    if( high > low ) {
        pivot = Partition( A, low, high );
        Quicksort( A, low, pivot-1 );
        Quicksort( A, pivot+1, high );
    }
}
int Partition( int A, int low, int high ) {
    int left, right, pivot_item = A[low];
    left = low;
    right = high;
    while ( left < right ) {
        /* Move left while item < pivot */
```

```
        while( A[left] <= pivot_item )
            left++;
        /* Move right while item > pivot */
        while( A[right] > pivot_item )
            right--;
        if( left < right )
            swap(A,left,right);
    }
    /* right is final position for the pivot */
    A[low] = A[right];
    A[right] = pivot_item;
    return right;
}
```

Analysis

Let us assume that T(n) be the complexity of Quick sort and also assume that all elements are distinct. Recurrence for $T(n)$ depends on two subproblem sizes which depend on partition element. If pivot is i^{th} smallest element then exactly $(i - 1)$ items will be in left part and $(n - i)$ in right part. Let us call it as i −split. Since each element has equal probability of selecting it as pivot the probability of selecting i^{th} element is $\frac{1}{n}$.

Best Case: Each partition splits array in halves and gives

$$T(n) = 2T(n/2) + \Theta(n) = \Theta(nlogn), \text{[using } \textit{Divide and Conquer} \text{ master theorem]}$$

Worst Case: Each partition gives unbalanced splits and we get

$$T(n) = T(n - 1) + \Theta(n) = \Theta(n^2)[using\ Subtraction\ and\ Conquer\ master\ theorem]$$

The worst-case occurs when the list is already sorted and last element chosen as pivot.

Average Case: In the average case of Quick sort, we do not know where the split happens. For this reason, we take all possible values of split locations, add all their complexities and divide with n to get the average case complexity.

$$T(n) = \sum_{i=1}^{n} \frac{1}{n}(runtime\ with\ i - split) + n + 1$$

$$= \frac{1}{n}\sum_{i=1}^{N}\left(T(i-1) + T(n-i)\right) + n + 1$$

//since we are dealing with best case we can assume
// $T(n-i)$ and $T(i-1)$ are equal

$$= \frac{2}{n}\sum_{i=1}^{n} T(i-1) + n + 1$$

$$= \frac{2}{n}\sum_{i=0}^{n-1} T(i) + n + 1$$

Multiply both sides by n.

$$nT(n) = 2\sum_{i=0}^{n-1} T(i) + n^2 + n$$

Same formula for $n - 1$.

$$(n-1)T(n-1) = 2\sum_{i=0}^{n-2} T(i) + (n-1)^2 + (n-1)$$

Subtract the n − 1 formula from n.

$$nT(n) - (n-1)T(n-1) = 2\sum_{i=0}^{n-1} T(i) + n^2 + n - (2\sum_{i=0}^{n-2} T(i) + (n-1)^2 + (n-1))$$

$$nT(n) - (n-1)T(n-1) = 2T(n-1) + 2n$$
$$nT(n) = (n+1)T(n-1) + 2n$$

Divide with $n(n+1)$.

$$\frac{T(n)}{n+1} = \frac{T(n-1)}{n} + \frac{2}{n+1}$$
$$= \frac{T(n-2)}{n-1} + \frac{2}{n} + \frac{2}{n+1}$$

.

.

$$= O(1) + 2\sum_{i=3}^{n} \frac{1}{i}$$
$$= O(1) + O(2logn)$$
$$\frac{T(n)}{n+1} = O(logn)$$
$$T(n) = O((n+1)\,logn) = O(nlogn)$$

Time Complexity, $T(n) = O(nlogn)$.

Performance

Worst case Complexity: $O(n^2)$
Best case Complexity: $O(nlogn)$
Average case Complexity: $O(nlogn)$
Worst case space Complexity: $O(1)$

Randomized Quick sort

In average-case behavior of Quicksort, we assumed that all permutations of the input numbers are equally likely. However, we cannot always expect it to hold. We can add randomization to an algorithm in order to reduce the probability of getting worst case in Quick sort.

There are two ways of adding randomization in Quick sort: either by randomly placing the input data in the array or by randomly choosing an element in the input data for pivot. The second choice is easier to analyze and implement. The change will only be done at the Partition algorithm.

In normal Quicksort, *pivot* element was always the leftmost element in the list to be sorted. Instead of always using $A[low]$ as *pivot*, we will use a randomly chosen element from the subarray $A[low..high]$ in the randomized version of Quicksort. It is done by exchanging element $A[low]$ with an element chosen at random from $A[low..high]$. This ensures that the *pivot* element is equally likely to be any of the $high - low + 1$ elements in the subarray.

Since the pivot element is randomly chosen, we can expect the split of the input array to be reasonably well balanced on average. This can help in preventing the worst-case behavior of quick sort which occurs in unbalanced partitioning.

Even though, randomized version improves the worst case complexity, its worst case complexity is still $O(n^2)$. One way to improve *Randomized – QuickSort* is to choose the pivot for partitioning more carefully than by picking a random element from the array. One common approach is to choose the pivot as the median of a set of 3 elements randomly selected from the array.

19.12 Tree Sort

Tree sort uses a binary search tree. It involves scanning each element of the input and placing it into its proper position in a binary search tree. This has two phases:

- First phase is creating a binary search tree using the given array elements.
- Second phase is traversing the given binary search tree in inorder, thus resulting in a sorted array.

Performance

The average number of comparisons for this method is $O(nlogn)$. But in worst case, number of comparisons is reduced by $O(n^2)$, a case which arises when the sort tree is skew tree.

19.13 Comparison of Sorting Algorithms

Name	Average Case	Worst Case	Auxiliary Memory	Is Stable?	Other Notes
Bubble	$O(n^2)$	$O(n^2)$	1	yes	Small code
Selection	$O(n^2)$	$O(n^2)$	1	no	Stability depends on the implementation.
Insertion	$O(n^2)$	$O(n^2)$	1	yes	Average case is also $O(n + d)$, where d is the number of inversions
Shell	-	$O(nlog^2n)$	1	no	
Merge	$O(nlogn)$	$O(nlogn)$	depends	yes	
Heap	$O(nlogn)$	$O(nlogn)$	1	no	
Quick Sort	$O(nlogn)$	$O(n^2)$	$O(logn)$	depends	Can be implemented as a stable sort depending on how the pivot is handled.
Tree sort	$O(nlogn)$	$O(n^2)$	$O(n)$	depends	Can be implemented as a stable sort.

Note: n denotes the number of elements in the input.

19.14 Linear Sorting Algorithms

In earlier sections, we have seen many examples on comparison-based sorting algorithms. Among them, the best comparison-based sorting can has the complexity $O(nlogn)$. In this section, we will discuss other types of algorithms: Linear Sorting Algorithms. To improve the time complexity of sorting these algorithms, make some assumptions about the input. Few examples of Linear Sorting Algorithms are:

- Counting Sort
- Bucket Sort
- Radix Sort

19.15 Counting Sort

Counting sort is not a comparison sort algorithm and gives $O(n)$ complexity for sorting. To achieve $O(n)$ complexity, Counting sort assumes that each of the elements is an integer in the range 1 to K, for some integer K. When $K = O(n)$, the Counting-sort runs in $O(n)$ time. The basic idea of Counting sort is to determine, for each input element X, the number of elements less than X. This information can be used to place directly into its correct position. For example, if 10 elements are less than X, then X belongs to position 11 in output.

In the code below, $A[0..n-1]$ is the input array with length n. In counting sort we need two more arrays: let us assume array $B[0..n-1]$ contains the sorted output and the array $C[0..K-1]$ provides temporary storage.

```
void CountingSort (int A[], int n, int B[], int K) {
    int C[K], i, j;
    //Complexity: O(K)
    for (i =0 ; i<K; i++)
        C[i] = 0;

    //Complexity: O(n)
    for (j =0 ; j<n; j++)
        C[A[j]] = C[A[j]] + 1;

    //C[i] now contains the number of elements equal to i
    //Complexity: O(K)
    for (i =1 ; i<K; i++)
        C[i] = C[i] + C[i-1];

    // C[i] now contains the number of elements ≤ i
    //Complexity: O(n)
    for (j = n-1; j>=0; j--) {
        B[C[A[j]]] = A[j];
        C[A[j]] = C[A[j]] - 1;
    }
}
```

Total Complexity: $O(K) + O(n) + O(K) + O(n) = O(n)$ if $K = O(n)$.
Space Complexity: $O(n)$ if $K = O(n)$.

Note: Counting works well if $K = O(n)$. Otherwise, the complexity will be more.

19.16 Bucket sort [or Bin Sort]

Like to *Counting* sort, *Bucket* sort also imposes restrictions on the input to improve the performance. In other words, Bucket sort works well if the input is drawn from fixed set. *Bucket* sort is the generalization of *Counting* Sort. For example, suppose that all the input elements from $\{0, 1, \ldots, K-1\}$, i.e., the set of integers in the interval $[0, K-1]$. That means, K is the number of distant elements in the input. *Bucket* sort uses K counters. The ith counter keeps track of the number of occurrences of the ith element. Bucket sort with two buckets is effectively a version of Quick sort with two buckets.

```
#define BUCKETS 10
void BucketSort(int A[], int array_size) {
    int i, j, k;
    int buckets[BUCKETS];
    for(j =0; j < BUCKETS; j++)
        buckets[j] = 0;
    for(i =0; i < array_size; i++)
        ++ buckets[A[i]];
    for(i =0, j=0; j < BUCKETS; j++)
        for(k = buckets[j];k > 0; --k)
            A[i++] = j;
}
```

Time Complexity: $O(n)$.
Space Complexity: $O(n)$.

19.17 Radix sort

Similar to *Counting* sort and *Bucket* sort, this sorting algorithm also assumes some kind of information about the input elements. Suppose that the input values to be sorted are from base d. That means all numbers are d-digit numbers.

In radix sort, first sort the elements based on last digit [least significant digit]. These results were again sorted by second digit [next to least significant digits]. Continue this process for all digits until we reach most significant digits. Use some stable sort to sort them by last digit. Then stable sort them by the second least significant digit, then by the third, etc. If we use counting sort as the stable sort, the total time is $O(nd) \approx O(n)$.

Algorithm:

1) Take the least significant digit of each element.
2) Sort the list of elements based on that digit, but keep the order of elements with the same digit (this is the definition of a stable sort).
3) Repeat the sort with each more significant digit.

The speed of Radix sort depends on the inner basic operations. If the operations are not efficient enough, Radix sort can be slower than other algorithms such as Quick sort and Merge sort. These operations include the insert and delete functions of the sub-lists and the process of isolating the digit we want. If the numbers were not of equal length then a test is needed to check for additional digits that need sorting. This can be one of the slowest parts of Radix sort and also one of the hardest to make efficient.

Since Radix sort depends on the digits or letters, it is less flexible than other sorts. For every different type of data, Radix sort needs to be rewritten and if the sorting order changes, the sort needs to be rewritten again. In short, Radix sort takes more time to write, and it is very difficult to write a general purpose Radix sort that can handle all kinds of data.

For many programs that need a fast sort, Radix sort is a good choice. Still, there are faster sorts, which is one reason why Radix sort is not used as much as some other sorts.

Time Complexity: $O(nd) \approx O(n)$, if d is small.

19.18 External Sorting

External sorting is a generic term for a class of sorting algorithms that can handle massive amounts of data. These External sorting algorithms are useful when the files are too big and cannot fit into main memory.

Like internal sorting algorithms, there are number for algorithms for external sorting also. One such algorithm is External Mergesort. In practice these external sorting algorithms are being supplemented by internal sorts.

Simple External Mergesort

A number of records from each tape would be read into main memory and sorted using an internal sort and then output to the tape. For the sake of clarity, let us assume that 900 megabytes of data needs to be sorted using only 100 megabytes of RAM.

1) Read 100MB of the data into main memory and sort by some conventional method (let us say Quick sort).
2) Write the sorted data to disk.
3) Repeat steps 1 and 2 until all of the data is sorted in chunks of 100MB. Now we need to merge them into one single sorted output file.

4) Read the first 10MB of each sorted chunk (call them input buffers) in main memory (90MB total) and allocate the remaining 10MB for output buffer.

Perform a 9-way Mergesort and store the result in the output buffer. If the output buffer is full, write it to the final sorted file. If any of the 9 input buffers gets empty, fill it with the next 10MB of its associated 100MB sorted chunk or otherwise mark it as exhausted if there is no more data in the sorted chunk and do not use it for merging.

The above algorithm can be generalized by assuming that the amount of data to be sorted exceeds the available memory by a factor of K. Then, K chunks of data need to be sorted and a K -way merge has to be completed.

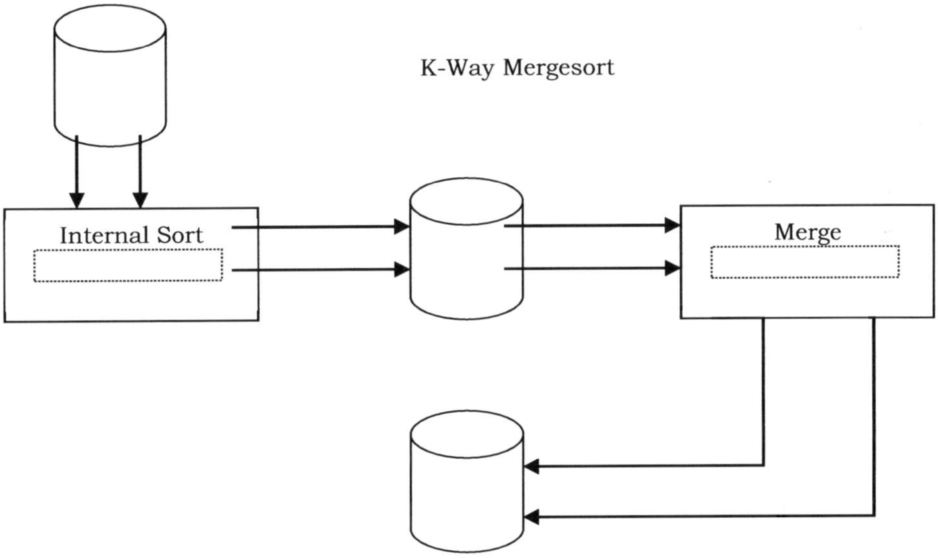

If X is the amount of main memory available, there will be K input buffers and 1 output buffer of size $X/(K+1)$ each. Depending on various factors (how fast is the hard drive?) better performance can be achieved if the output buffer is made larger (for example, twice as large as one input buffer).

Complexity of the 2-way External Merge sort: In each pass we read + write each page in file. Let us assume that there are n pages in file. That means we need $\lceil logn \rceil + 1$ number of passes. The total cost is $2n(\lceil logn \rceil + 1)$.

Problems and Questions with Answers

Question 1: Given an array $A[0 \dots n-1]$ of n numbers containing repetition of some number. Give an algorithm for checking whether there are repeated elements or not. Assume that we are not allowed to use additional space (i.e., we can use a few temporary variables, O(1) storage).

Answer: Since we are not allowed to use any extra space, one simple way is to scan the elements one by one and for each element check whether that elements appears in the remaining elements. If we find a match we return true.

```
int CheckDuplicatesInArray(in A[], int n) {
    for (int i = 0; i < n; i++)
        for (int j = i + 1; j < n; j++)
            if(A[i]==A[j])
                reutrn true;
    return false;
}
```

Each iteration of the inner, j-indexed loop uses O(1) space, and for a fixed value of i, the j loop executes $n-i$ times. The outer loop executes $n-1$ times, so the entire function uses time proportional to

$$\sum_{i=1}^{n-1} n-i = n(n-1) - \sum_{i=1}^{n-1} i = n(n-1) - \frac{n(n-1)}{2} = \frac{n(n-1)}{2} = O(n^2)$$

Time Complexity: O(n^2). Space Complexity: O(1).

Question 2: Can we improve the time complexity of Question 1:?

Answer: **Yes**, using sorting technique.

```
int CheckDuplicatesInArray(in A[], int n) {
    //for heap sort algorithm refer Priority Queues chapter
    Heapsort( A, n );
    for (int i = 0; i < n-1; i++)
        if(A[i]==A[i+1])
            reutrn true;
    return false;
}
```

Heapsort function takes O($nlogn$) time, and requires O(1) space. The scan clearly takes for $n - 1$ iterations, each iteration using O(1) time. The overall time is O($nlogn + n$) = O($nlogn$).

Time Complexity: O($nlogn$). Space Complexity: O(1).

Note: For variations of this problem, refer *Searching* chapter.

Question 3: Given an array $A[0 \dots n-1]$, where each element of the array represents a vote in the election. Assume that each vote is given as an integer representing the ID of the chosen candidate. Give an algorithm for determining who wins the election.

Answer: For this problem, we need to find the element which repeated maximum number of times. Solution is similar to Question 1: with a *counter* for tracking frequencies.

```
int CheckWhoWinsTheElection(in A[], int n) {
    int i, j, counter = 0, maxCounter = 0, candidate;
    candidate = A[0];
    for (i = 0; i < n; i++) {
        candidate = A[i];
        counter = 0;
        for (j = i + 1; j < n; j++) {
            if(A[i]==A[j]) counter++;
        }
        if(counter > maxCounter) {
            maxCounter = counter;
            candidate = A[i];

        }
    }
    return candidate;
}
```

Time Complexity: O(n^2). Space Complexity: O(1).

Note: For variations of this problem, refer *Searching* chapter.

Question 4: Can we improve the time complexity of Question 3:? Assume we don't have any extra space.

Answer: **Yes.** The approach is to sort the votes based on candidate ID, then scan the sorted array and count up which candidate so far has the most votes. We only have to remember the winner, so we don't need a clever data structure. We can use heapsort as it is an in-place sorting algorithm.

```
int CheckWhoWinsTheElection(in A[], int n) {
    int i, j, currentCounter = 1, maxCounter = 1;
    int currentCandidate, maxCandidate;
    currentCandidate = maxCandidate= A[0];
    //for heap sort algorithm refer Priority Queues Chapter
    Heapsort( A, n );
    for (int i  =  1; i <= n; i++) {
        if( A[i] == currentCandidate)
            currentCounter ++;
        else {
            currentCandidate = A[i];
            currentCounter = 1;
        }
        if(currentCounter > maxCounter)
            maxCounter = currentCounter;
        else {
            maxCandidate = currentCandidate;
            maxCounter = currentCounter;
        }
    }
    return candidate;
}
```

Since Heapsort time complexity is $O(nlogn)$ and in-place, so it only uses an additional $O(1)$ of storage in addition to the input array. The scan of the sorted array does a constant-time conditional $n - 1$ times, thus using $O(n)$ time. The overall time bound is $O(nlogn)$.

Question 5: Can we further improve the time complexity of Question 3:?

Answer: In the given problem, number of candidates is less but the number of votes is significantly large. For this problem we can use counting sort.

Time Complexity: $O(n)$, n is the number of votes (elements) in array.
Space Complexity: $O(k)$, k is the number of candidates participated in election.

Question 6: Given an array A of n elements, each of which is an integer in the range $[1, n^2]$. How do we sort the array in $O(n)$ time?

Answer: If we subtract each number by 1 then we get the range $[0, n^2 - 1]$. If we consider all number as 2 –digit base n. Each digit ranges from 0 to n^2 - 1. Sort this using radix sort. This uses only two calls to counting sort. Finally, add 1 to all the numbers. Since there are 2 calls, the complexity is $O(2n) \approx O(n)$.

Question 7: For the Question 6:, what if the range is $[1 \ldots n^3]$?

Answer: If we subtract each number by 1 then we get the range $[0, n^3 - 1]$. Considering all number as *3*-digit base n: each digit ranges from 0 to n^3 - 1. Sort this using radix sort. This uses only three calls to counting sort. Finally, add 1 to all the numbers. Since there are 3 calls, the complexity is $O(3n) \approx O(n)$.

Question 8: Given an array with n integers each of value less than n^{100}, can it be sorted in linear time?

Answer: **Yes.** Reasoning is same as in of Question 6: and Question 7:.

Question 9: Let A and B be two arrays of n elements, each. Given a number K, give an $O(nlogn)$ time algorithm for determining whether there exists a ∈ A and b ∈ B such that $a + b = K$.

Answer: Since we need $O(nlogn)$, it gives us a pointer that we need sorting. So, we will do that.

```
int Find( int A[], int B[], int n, K ) {
    int i, c;
    Heapsort( A, n );                 //O(nlogn)
    for (i =0; i< n; i++) {           //O(n)
        c = k-B[i];                   //O(1)
        if(BinarySearch(A, c))        //O(logn)
            return 1;
    }
    return 0;
}
```

Note: For variations of this problem, refer *Searching* chapter.

Question 10: Let A, B and C are three arrays of n elements, each. Given a number K, give an $O(nlogn)$ time algorithm for determining whether there exists $a \in A$, $b \in B$ and $c \in C$ such that $a + b + c = K$.

Answer: Refer *Searching* chapter.

Question 11: Given an array of n elements, can we output in sorted order the K elements following the median in sorted order in time $O(n + KlogK)$.

Answer: **Yes**. Find the median and partition about the median. With this we can find all the elements greater than it. Now find the Kth largest element in this set and partition about it; and get all the elements less than it. Output the sorted list of final set of elements. Clearly, this operation takes $O(n + KlogK)$ time.

Question 12: Consider the sorting algorithms: Bubble Sort, Insertion Sort, Selection Sort, Merge Sort, Heap Sort, and Quick Sort. Which of these are stable?

Answer: Let us assume that A is the array to be sorted. Also, let us say R and S have the same key and R appears earlier in the array than S. That means, R is at $A[i]$ and S is at $A[j]$, with $i < j$. To show any stable algorithm, in the sorted output R must precede S.

Bubble sort: Yes. Elements change order only when a smaller record follows a larger. Since S is not smaller than R it cannot precede it.

Selection sort: No. It divides the array into sorted and unsorted portions and iteratively finds the minimum values in the unsorted portion. After finding a minimum x, if the algorithm moves x into the sorted portion of the array by means of a swap then the element swapped could be R which then could be moved behind S. This would invert the positions of R and S, so in general it is not stable. If swapping is avoided, it could be made stable but the cost in time would probably be very significant.

Insertion sort: Yes. As presented, when S is to be inserted into sorted subarray $A[1..j-1]$, only records larger than S are shifted. Thus R would not be shifted during $S's$ insertion and hence would always precede it.

Merge sort: Yes, In the case of records with equal keys, the record in the left subarray gets preference. Those are the records that came first in the unsorted array. As a result, they will precede later records with the same key.

Heap sort: No. Suppose $i = 1$ and R and S happen to be the two records with the largest keys in the input. Then R will remain in location 1 after the array is heapified, and will be placed in location n in the first iteration of Heapsort. Thus S will precede R in the output.

Quick sort: No. The partitioning step can swap the location of records many times, and thus two records with equal keys could swap position in the final output.

Question 13: Consider the same sorting algorithms as that of Question 12:. Which of them are in-place?

Answer:

Bubble sort: Yes, because only two integers are required.

Insertion sort: Yes, since we need to store two integers and a record.

Selection sort: Yes. This algorithm would likely need space for two integers and one record.

Merge sort: No. Arrays need to perform the merge. (If the data is in the form of a linked list, the sorting can be done in-place, but this is a nontrivial modification.)

Heap sort: Yes, since the heap and partially-sorted array occupy opposite ends of the input array.

Quicksort: No, since it is recursive and stores $O(logn)$ activation records on the stack. Modifying it to be non-recursive is feasible but nontrivial.

Question 14: Among, Quick sort, Insertion sort, Selection sort, Heap sort algorithms, which one needs the minimum number of swaps?

Answer: Selected sort, it needs n swaps only (refer theory section).

Question 15: What is the minimum number of comparisons required to determine if an integer appears more than $n/2$ times in a sorted array of n integers?

Answer: Refer *Searching* chapter.

Question 16: **Sort an array of 0's, 1's and 2's:** Given an array A[] consisting $0's$, $1's$ and $2's$, give an algorithm for sorting $A[]$. The algorithm should put all $0's$ first, then all $1's$ and all $2's$ in last.
Example: Input = {0,1,1,0,1,2,1,2,0,0,0,1}, Output = $\{0,0,0,0,0,1,1,1,1,1,2,2\}$

Answer: Use Counting Sort. Since there are only three elements and the maximum value is 2, we need a temporary array with 3 elements.

Time Complexity: $O(n)$. Space Complexity: $O(1)$.

Note: For variations of this problem, refer *Searching* chapter.

Question 17: Is there any other way of solving Question 15:?

Answer: Using Quick Sort. Since we know that there are only 3 elements $0, 1$ and 2 in the array, we can select 1 as a pivot element for Quick Sort. Quick Sort finds the correct place for 1 by moving all 0's to the left of 1 and all 2's to the right of 1. For doing this it uses only one scan.

Time Complexity: $O(n)$. Space Complexity: $O(1)$.

Note: For efficient algorithm, refer *Searching* chapter.

Question 18: How do we find the number which appeared the maximum number of times in an array?

Answer: One simple approach is to sort the given array and scan the sorted array. While scanning, keep track of the elements that occur the maximum number of times.

Algorithm:

```
QuickSort(A, n);
int i, j, count=1, Number=A[0], j=0;
for(i=0;i<n;i++) {
```

```
            if(A[j]==A) {
                count++;
                Number=A[j];
            }
            j=i;
    }
    printf("Number:%d, count:%d", Number, count);
```

Time Complexity = Time for Sorting + Time for Scan = $O(nlogn)$ +$O(n)$ = $O(nlogn)$.
Space Complexity: $O(1)$.

Note: For variations of this problem, refer *Searching* chapter.

Question 19: Is there any other way of solving the Question 18:?

Answer: **Using Binary Tree.** Create a binary tree with an extra field *count* which indicates the number of times an element appeared in the input. Let us say we have created a Binary Search Tree [BST]. Now, do the In-Order of the tree. In-Order traversal of BST produces sorted list. While doing In-Order traversal keep track of maximum element.

Time Complexity: $O(n)$ +$O(n)$ ≈$O(n)$. First parameter is for constructing the BST and the second parameter is for Inorder Traversal. Space Complexity: $O(2n)$ ≈$O(n)$, since every node in BST needs two extra pointers.

Question 20: Is there yet other way of solving the Question 18:?

Answer: **Using Hash Table:** For each element of the given array we use a counter and for each occurrence of the element we increment the corresponding counter. At the end we can just return the element which has the maximum counter.

Time Complexity: $O(n)$. Space Complexity: $O(n)$. For constructing hash table we need $O(n)$.

Note: For efficient algorithm, refer *Searching* chapter.

Question 21: Given a 2 GB file with one string per line, which sorting algorithm would we use to sort the file and why?

Answer: When we have a size limit of 2GB, it means that we cannot bring all the data into main memory.

Algorithm: How much memory do we have available? Let's assume we have X MB of memory available. Divide the file into K chunks, where $X * K 2 GB$.

- Bring each chunk into memory and sort the lines as usual (any $O(nlogn)$ algorithm).
- Save the lines back to the file.
- Now bring next chunk into memory and sort.
- Once we're done, merge them one by one; in case of one set finish bring more data from concerned chunk.

The above algorithm is also known as external sort. Step 3 – 4 is known as K-way merge. The idea behind going for external sort is the size of data. Since data is huge and we can't bring it to the memory, we need to go for a disk based sorting algorithm.

Question 22: **Nearly sorted:** Given an array of n elements, each which is at most K positions from its target position, devise an algorithm that sorts in $O(n\ logK)$ time.

Answer: Divide the elements into n/K groups of size K, and sort each piece in $O(KlogK)$ time, say using Mergesort. This preserves the property that no element is more than K elements out of position. Now, merge each block of K elements with the block to its left.

Question 23: Which sorting method is better for Linked Lists?

Answer: Merge Sort is a better choice. At a first appearance, merge sort may not be a good selection since the middle node is required to subdivide the given list into two sub-lists of equal length. We can easily solve this problem by moving the nodes alternatively to two lists would also solve this problem (refer *Linked Lists* chapter). Then, sorting these two lists recursively and merging the results into a single list will sort the given one.

```
typedef struct ListNode {
    int data;
    struct ListNode *next;
};
struct ListNode * LinkedListMergeSort(struct ListNode * first) {
    struct ListNode * list1HEAD = NULL;
    struct ListNode * list1TAIL = NULL;
    struct ListNode * list2HEAD = NULL;
    struct ListNode * list2TAIL = NULL;
    if(first==NULL || first→next==NULL)
        return first;
    while (first != NULL) {
        Append(first, list1HEAD, list1TAIL);
        if(first != NULL)
            Append(first, list2HEAD, list2TAIL);
    }
    list1HEAD = LinkedListMergeSort(list1HEAD);
    list2HEAD = LinkedListMergeSort(list2HEAD);
    return Merge(list1HEAD, list2HEAD);
}
```

Note: Append() appends the first argument to the tail of a singly linked list whose head and tail are defined by the second and third arguments.

All external sorting algorithms can be used for sorting linked lists since each involved file can be considered as a linked list that can only be accessed sequentially. We can sort a doubly linked list using its next fields as if it is a singly linked one and reconstruct the prev fields after sorting with an additional scan.

Question 24: Can we implement Linked Lists Sorting with Quick Sort?

Answer: Original Quick Sort cannot be used for sorting the Singly Linked Lists. This is because we cannot move backward in Singly Linked Lists. We can modify the original Quick Sort and make it work for Singly Linked Lists.

Let us consider the following modified Quick Sort implementation. The first node of the input list is considered as a *pivot* and is moved to *equal*. The value of each node is compared with the *pivot* and moved *to less* (respectively, *equal* or *larger*) if the nodes value is smaller than (respectively, *equal* to or *larger* than) the *pivot*. Then, *less* and *larger* are sorted recursively. Finally, joining *less*, *equal* and *larger* into a single list yields a sorted one.

Append() appends the first argument to the tail of a singly linked list whose head and tail are defined by the second and third arguments. On return, the first argument will be modified so that it *equal* points to the next node of the list. *Join*() appends the list whose head and tail are defined by the third and fourth arguments to the list whose head and tail are defined by the first and second arguments. For simplicity, the first and fourth arguments become the head and tail of the resulting list.

```
typedef struct ListNode {
    int data;
    struct ListNode *next;
};
void Qsort(struct ListNode *first, struct ListNode * last) {
    struct ListNode *lesHEAD=NULL, lesTAIL=NULL;
```

```
    struct ListNode *equHEAD=NULL, equTAIL=NULL;
    struct ListNode *larHEAD=NULL, larTAIL=NULL;
    struct ListNode *current = *first;
    int pivot, info;
    if(current == NULL)
        return;
    pivot = current→data;
    Append(current, equHEAD, equTAIL);
    while (current != NULL) {
        info = current→data;
        if(info < pivot)
            Append(current, lesHEAD, lesTAIL)
        else if(info > pivot)
            Append(current, larHEAD, larTAIL)
        else
            Append(current, equHEAD, equTAIL);
    }
    Quicksort(&lesHEAD, &lesTAIL);
    Quicksort(&larHEAD, &larTAIL);
    Join(lesHEAD, lesTAIL,equHEAD, equTAIL);
    Join(lesHEAD, equTAIL,larHEAD, larTAIL);
    *first = lesHEAD;
    *last = larTAIL;
}
```

Question 25: Given an array of $1,00,000$ pixel color values, each of which is an integer in the range [0,255]. Which sorting algorithm is preferable for sorting them?

Answer: Counting Sort. There are only 256 key values, so the auxiliary array would only be of size 256, and there would be only two passes through the data which would be very efficient in both time and space.

Question 26: Similar to Question 25:, if we have a telephone directory with $1,00,000$ entries, which sorting algorithm is best?

Answer: Bucket sort. In Bucket sort the buckets are defined by the last 7 digits. This requires an auxiliary array of size 10 million, and has the advantage of requiring only one pass through the data on disk. Each bucket contains all telephone numbers with the same last 7 digits but different area codes. The buckets can then be sorted on area code by selection or insertion sort; there are only a handful of area codes.

Question 27: Give an algorithm for merging K-sorted lists.

Answer: Refer *Priority Queues* chapter.

Question 28: Given a big file containing billions of numbers. Find maximum 10 numbers from those file.

Answer: Refer *Priority Queues* chapter.

Question 29: There are two sorted arrays A and B. First one is of size $m + n$ containing only m elements. Another one is of size n and contains n elements. Merge these two arrays into the first array of size $m + n$ such that the output is sorted.

Answer: The trick for this problem is to start filling the destination array from the back with the largest elements. We will end up with a merged and sorted destination array.

```
void Merge(int[] A[], int m, int B[], int n) {
    int count = m;
    int i = n – 1, j = count – 1, k = m - 1;
    for(;k>=0;k--) {
        if(B[i] > A[j] | | j < 0) {
```

```
            A[k] =B[i];
            i--;
            if(i<0)
                break;
        }
        else {
            A[k] = A[j];
            j--;
        }
    }
}
```

Time Complexity: $O(m + n)$. Space Complexity: $O(1)$.

Question 30: **Nuts and Bolts Problem:** Given a set of n nuts of different sizes and n bolts such that there is a one-to-one correspondence between the nuts and the bolts, find for each nut its corresponding bolt. Assume that we can only compare nuts to bolts: we cannot compare nuts to nuts and bolts to bolts.

Other way of framing the question: We are given a box which contains bolts and nuts. Assume there are n nuts and n bolts and that each nut matches exactly one bolt (and vice versa). By trying to match a bolt and a nut we can see which one is bigger, but we cannot compare two bolts or two nuts directly. Design an efficient algorithm for matching the nuts and bolts.

Answer: **Brute Force Approach:** Start with the first bolt and compare it with each nut until we find a match. In the worst case, we require n comparisons. Repeat this for successive bolts on all remaining gives $O(n^2)$ complexity.

Question 31: For Question 30:, can we improve the complexity?

Answer: In Question 30:, we got $O(n^2)$ complexity in the worst case (if bolts are in ascending order and nuts are in descending order). Its analysis is same as that of quick sort. The improvement is also on same line.

To reduce the worst case complexity, instead of selecting the first bold every time, we can select some random bolt and match it with nuts. This randomized selection reduces the probability of getting the worst case but still the worst case is $O(n^2)$ only.

Question 32: For Question 30:, can we further improve the complexity?

Answer: We can use a divide-and-conquer technique for solving this problem and the solution is very similar to randomized Quicksort. For simplicity let us assume that bolts and nuts are represented in two arrays B and N.

The algorithm first performs a partition operation as follows: pick a random bolt $B[i]$. Using this bolt, rearrange the array of nuts into three groups of elements:

- First the nuts smaller than $B[i]$
- Nut that matches $B[i]$, and
- Finally, the nuts larger than $B[i]$.

Next, using the nut that matches $B[i]$, perform a similar partition on the array of bolts. This pair of partitioning operations can easily implemented in $O(n)$ time, and it leaves the bolts and nuts nicely partitioned so that the "*pivot*" bolt and nut are aligned with each-other and all other bolts and nuts are on the correct side of these pivots -- smaller nuts and bolts precede the pivots, and larger nuts and bolts follow the pivots. Our algorithm then completes by recursively applying itself to the subarray to the left and right of the pivot position to match these remaining bolts and nuts. We can assume by induction on n that these recursive calls will properly match the remaining bolts.

To analyze the running time of our algorithm, we can use the same analysis as that of randomized Quicksort. Therefore, applying the analysis from Quicksort, the time complexity of our algorithm is $O(nlogn)$.

Alternative Analysis: We can solve this problem by making little change to quick sort. Let us assume that we pick the last element as pivot, say it is a nut. Compare the nut with only bolts as we walk down the array. This will partition the array for the bolts. Every bolt less than the partition nut will be on the left. And every bolt greater than the partition nut will be on the right.

While traversing down the list, the matching bolt for the partition nut will have been found. Now we do the partition again using the matching bolt. As a result, all the nuts less than the matching bolt will be on the left side and all the nuts greater than the matching bolt will be on the right side. Recursively call on the left and right arrays.

The time complexity is O(2nlogn) ≈O(nlogn).

Question 33: Given a binary tree, can we print its elements in sorted order in $O(n)$ time by performing an In-order tree traversal?

Answer: Yes, if the tree is a Binary Search Tree [BST]. For more details refer *Trees* chapter.

CHAPTER

Searching 20

20.1 What is Searching?

In computer science, *searching* is the process of finding an item with specified properties from a collection of items. The items may be stored as records in a database, simple data elements in arrays, text in files, nodes in trees, vertices and edges in graphs, or may be elements of other search space.

20.2 Why do we need Searching?

Searching is one of core computer science algorithms. We know that today's computers store a lot of information. To retrieve this information proficiently we need very efficient searching algorithms.

There are certain ways of organizing the data which improves the searching process. That means, if we keep the data in a proper order, it is easy to search the required element. Sorting is one of the techniques for making the elements ordered. In this chapter we will see different searching algorithms.

20.3 Types of Searching

Following are the types of searches which we will be discussing in this book.

- Unordered Linear Search
- Sorted/Ordered Linear Search
- Binary Search
- Symbol Tables and Hashing
- String Searching Algorithms: Tries, Ternary Search and Suffix Trees

20.4 Unordered Linear Search

Let us assume that given an array whose elements order is not known. That means the elements of the array are not sorted. In this case if we want to search for an element then we have to scan the complete array and see if the element is there in the given list or not.

```
int UnsorteddLinearSearch (int A[], int n, int data) {
    for (int i  = 0; i < n; i++) {
        if(A[i] == data)
            return i;
    }
    return -1;
}
```

Time complexity: O(n), in the worst case we need to scan the complete array.
Space complexity: O(1).

20.5 Sorted/Ordered Linear Search

If the elements of the array are already sorted then in many cases we don't have to scan the complete array to see if the element is there in the given array or not. In the algorithm below, it can be seen that, at any point if the value at $A[i]$ is greater than *data* to be searched then we just return -1 without searching the remaining array.

```
int SortedLinearSearch(int A[], int n, int data) {
    for (int i  = 0; i < n; i++) {
        if(A[i] == data)
            return i;
        else if(A[i] > data)
            return -1;
    }
    return -1;
}
```

Time complexity of this algorithm is O(n). This is because in the worst case we need to scan the complete array. But in the average case it reduces the complexity even though the growth rate is same. Space complexity: O(1).

Note: For the above algorithm we can make further improvement by incrementing the index at faster rate (say, 2). This will reduce the number of comparisons for searching in the sorted list.

20.6 Binary Search

Let us consider the problem of searching a word in a dictionary. Typically, we directly go to some approximate page [say, middle page] start searching from that point. If the *name* that we are searching is same then the search is complete. If the page is before the selected pages then apply the same process for the first half otherwise apply the same process to the second half. Binary search also works in the same way. The algorithm applying such a strategy is referred to as *binary search* algorithm.

```
//Iterative Binary Search Algorithm
int BinarySearchIterative[int A[], int n, int data) {
    int low =  0;
    int high = n-1;
    while (low <= high) {
        mid  = low + (high-low)/2; //To avoid overflow
        if(A[mid] == data)
            return mid;
        else if(A[mid] < data)
            low =  mid + 1;
        else high =  mid - 1;
    }
    return -1;
}

//Recursive Binary Search Algorithm
int BinarySearchRecursive[int A[], int low, int high, int data) {
    int mid  = low + (high-low)/2; //To avoid overflow
    if(A[mid] == data)
        return mid;
    else if(A[mid] < data)
        return BinarySearchRecursive (A, mid + 1, high, data);
    else    return BinarySearchRecursive (A, low, mid - 1 , data);
```

```
    return -1;
}
```

Recurrence for binary search is $T(n) = T(\frac{n}{2})$ +È(1). This is because we are always considering only half of the input list and throwing out the other half. Using *Divide and Conquer* master theorem, we get, $T(n$ =O($logn$).

Time Complexity: O($logn$). Space Complexity: O(1) [for iterative algorithm].

20.7 Comparing Basic Searching Algorithms

Implementation	Search-Worst Case	Search-Avg. Case
Unordered Array	n	$n/2$
Ordered Array (Binary Search)	$logn$	$logn$
Unordered List	n	$n/2$
Ordered List	n	$n/2$
Binary Search Trees (for skew trees)	n	$logn$

Note: For discussion on binary search trees refer *Trees* chapter.

Problems and Questions with Answers

Question 1: Given an array of n numbers, give an algorithm for checking whether there are any duplicate elements in the array or not?

Answer: This is one of the simplest problems. One obvious answer to this is, exhaustively searching for duplicates in the array. That means, for each input element check whether there is any element with same value. This we can solve just by using two simple *for* loops. The code for this solution can be given as:

```
void CheckDuplicatesBruteForce(int A[], int n) {
    for(int i = 0; i < n; i++) {
        for(int j = i+1; j < n; j++) {
            if(A[i] == A[j])    {
                printf("Duplicates exist: %d", A[i]);
                return;
            }
        }
    }
    printf("No duplicates in given array.");
}
```

Time Complexity: O(n^2), for two nested *for* loops. Space Complexity: O(1).

Question 2: Can we improve the complexity of Question 1:'s solution?

Answer: **Yes.** Sort the given array. After sorting all the elements with equal values come adjacent. Now, just do another scan on this sorted array and see if there are elements with same value and adjacent.

```
void CheckDuplicatesSorting(int A[], int n) {
    Sort(A, n);           //sort the array
    for(int i = 0; i < n-1; i++) {
        if(A[i] == A[i+1]) {
            printf("Duplicates exist: %d", A[i]);
            return;
        }
    }
    printf("No duplicates in given array.");
```

```
}
```

Time Complexity: $O(nlogn)$, for sorting. Space Complexity: $O(1)$.

Question 3: Is there any other way of solving Question-1?

Answer: **Yes**, using hash table. Hash tables are a simple and effective method used to implement dictionaries. *Average* time to search for an element is $O(1)$, while worst-case time is $O(n)$. Refer *Hashing* chapter for more details on hashing algorithms. As an example, consider the array, $A = \{3, 2, 1, 2, 2, 3\}$. Scan the input array and insert the elements into the hash. For each inserted element, keep the *counter* as 1 (assume initially all entires are filled with zeros). This indicates that the corresponding element has occurred already. For the given array, the hash table will look like (after inserting first three elements 3, 2 and 1):

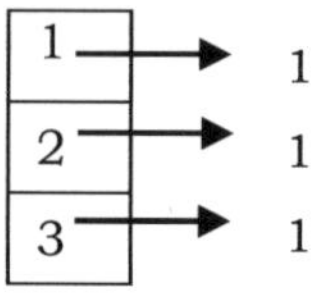

Now if we try inserting 2, since counter value of 2 is already 1, we can say the element has appeared twice.

Time Complexity: $O(n)$. Space Complexity: $O(n)$.

Question 4: Can we further improve the complexity of Question 1: solution?

Answer: Let us assume that the array elements are positive numbers and also all the elements are in the range 0 to $n - 1$. For each element $A[i]$, go to the array element whose index is $A[i]$. That means select $A[A[i]]$ and mark - $A[A[i]]$ (negate the value at $A[A[i]]$). Continue this process until we encounter the element whose value is already negated. If one such element exists then we say duplicate elements exist in the given array. As an example, consider the array, $A = \{3, 2, 1, 2, 2, 3\}$.

Initially,

3	2	1	2	2	3
0	1	2	3	4	5

At step-1, negate A[abs(A[0])],

3	2	1	-2	2	3
0	1	2	3	4	5

At step-2, negate A[abs(A[1])],

3	2	-1	-2	2	3
0	1	2	3	4	5

At step-3, negate A[abs(A[2])],

3	-2	- 1	-2	2	3
0	1	2	3	4	5

At step-4, negate A[abs(A[3])],

3	-2	- 1	-2	2	3
0	1	2	3	4	5

At step-4, observe that $A[abs(A[3])]$ is already negative. That means we have encountered the same value twice.

```
void CheckDuplicates(int A[], int n) {
    for(int i = 0; i < n; i++) {
        if(A[abs(A[i])] < 0) {
            printf("Duplicates exist:%d", A[i]);
            return;
```

```
        }
        else  A[A[i]] = - A[A[i]];
    }
    printf("No duplicates in given array.");
}
```

Time Complexity: $O(n)$. Since, only one scan is required. Space Complexity: $O(1)$.

Notes:

- This solution does not work if the given array is read only.
- This solution will work only if all the array elements are positive.
- If the elements range is not in 0 to $n-1$ then it may give exceptions.

Question 5: Given an array of n numbers. Give an algorithm for finding the element which appears maximum number of times in the array?

Brute Force Solution: One simple solution to this is, for each input element check whether there is any element with same value and for each such occurrence, increment the counter. Each time, check the current counter with the max counter and update it if this value is greater than max counter. This we can solve just by using two simple *for* loops.

```
int CheckDuplicatesBruteForce(int A[], int n) {
    int counter =0, max=0;
    for(int i = 0; i < n; i++) {
        counter=0;
        for(int j = 0; j < n; j++) {
            if(A[i] == A[j])
                counter++;
        }
        if(counter > max) max = counter;
    }
    return max;
}
```

Time Complexity: $O(n^2)$, for two nested *for* loops. Space Complexity: $O(1)$.

Question 6: Can we improve the complexity of Question 5: solution?

Answer: **Yes.** Sort the given array. After sorting all the elements with equal values come adjacent. Now, just do another scan on this sorted array and see which element is appearing maximum number of times.

Time Complexity: $O(nlogn)$. (for sorting). Space Complexity: $O(1)$.

Question 7: Is there any other way of solving Question 5:?

Answer: **Yes,** using hash table. For each element of the input keep track of how many times that element appeared in the input. That means the counter value represents the number of occurrences for that element.

Time Complexity: $O(n)$. Space Complexity: $O(n)$.

Question 8: For Question 5:, can we improve the time complexity? Assume that the elements range is 0 to $n-1$. That means all the elements are within this range only.

Answer: **Yes.** We can solve this problem in two scans. We *cannot* use the negation technique of Question 3: for this problem because of number of repetitions. In the first scan, instead of negating add the value n. That means for each of occurrence of an element add the array size to that element. In the second scan, check the element value by dividing it with n and return the element whichever gives the maximum value. The code based on this method is given below.

```
void MaxRepititions(int A[], int n) {
```

```
    int i =  0, max = 0, maxIndex;
    for(i = 0; i < n; i++)
        A[A[i]%n] +=n;

    for(i = 0; i < n; i++)
        if(A[i]/n > max) {
            max = A[i]/n;
            maxIndex =i;
        }
    return maxIndex;
}
```

Notes:

- This solution does not work if the given array is read only.
- This solution will work only if the array elements are positive.
- If the elements range is not in 0 to $n-1$ then it may give exceptions.

Time Complexity: O(n). Since no nested *for* loops are required. Space Complexity: O(1).

Question 9: Given an array of n numbers, give an algorithm for finding the first element in the array which is repeated. For example, in the array, $A = \{3, 2, 1, 2, 2, 3\}$ the first repeated number is 3 (not 2). That means, we need to return the first element among the repeated elements.

Answer: We can use the brute force solution that we used for Question 1:. For each element since it checks whether there is a duplicate for that element or not, whichever element duplicates first will be returned.

Question 10: For Question 9:, can we use sorting technique?

Answer: **No**. For proving the failed case, let us consider the following array. For example, $A = \{3, 2, 1, 2, 2, 3\}$. After sorting we get $A = \{1, 2, 2, 2, 3, 3\}$. In this sorted array the first repeated element is 2 but the actual answer is 3.

Question 11: For Question 9:, can we use hashing technique?

Answer: **Yes.** But the simple hashing technique which we used for Question 3: will not work. For example, if we consider the input array as A = {3, 2, 1, 2, 3}, then first repeated element is 3 but using our simple hashing technique we get the answer as 2. This is because 2 is coming twice before 3. Now let us change the hashing table behavior so that we get the first repeated element.

Let us say, instead of storing 1 value, initially we store the position of the element in the array. As a result the hash table will look like (after inserting 3, 2 and 1):

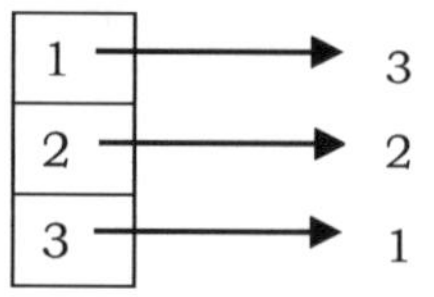

Now, if we see 2 again, we just negate the current value of 2 in the hash table. That means, we make its counter value as −2. The negative value in the hash table indicates that we have seen the same element two times. Similarly, for 3 (next element in input) also, we negate the current value of hash table and finally the hash table will look like:

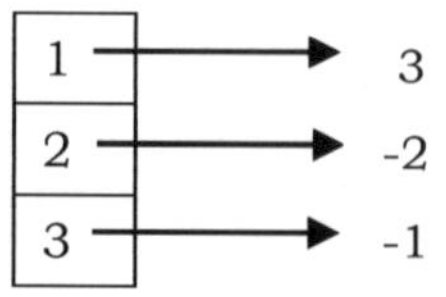

After processing the complete input array, scan the hash table and return the highest negative indexed value from it (i.e., −1 in our case). The highest negative value indicates that we have seen that element first (among repeated elements) and also repeating.

What if the element is repeated more than twice? In this case, just skip the element if the corresponding value i already negative.

Question 12: For Question 9:, can we use the technique that we used for Question 3: (negation technique)?

Answer: **No.** As a contradiction example, for the array $A = \{3,2,1,2,2,3\}$ the first repeated element is 3. But with negation technique the result is 2.

Question 13: Finding the Missing Number: We are given a list of $n-1$ integers and these integers are in the range of 1 to n. There are no duplicates in list. One of the integers is missing in the list. Given an algorithm to find the missing integer. **Example**: I/P: [1,2,4,6,3,7,8] O/P: 5

Brute Force Solution: One simple solution to this is, for each number in 1 to n check whether that number is in the given array or not.

```
int FindMissingNumber(int A[], int n) {
    int i, j, found=0;
    for (i = 1; i < =n; i ++) {
        found = 0;
        for (j = 0; j < n; j ++)
            if(A[j]==i)
                found = 1;
            if(!found) return i;
    }
    return -1;
}
```

Time Complexity: $O(n^2)$. Space Complexity: O(1).

Question 14: For Question 13:, can we use sorting technique?

Answer: **Yes.** Sorting the list will give the elements in increasing order and with another scan we can find the missing number.

Time Complexity: $O(nlogn)$, for sorting. Space Complexity: O(1).

Question 15: For Question 13:, can we use hashing technique?

Answer: **Yes.** Scan the input array and insert elements into the hash. For inserted element keep *counter* as 1 (assume initially all entires are filled with zeros). This indicates that the corresponding element has occurred already. Now, scan the hash table and return the element which has counter value zero.

Time Complexity: $O(n)$. Space Complexity: $O(n)$.

Question 16: For Question 13:, can we improve the complexity?

Answer: Using summation formula

1) Get the sum of numbers, $sum = n * (n + 1)/2$.
2) Subtract all the numbers from sum and you will get the missing number.

Time Complexity: $O(n)$, for scanning the complete array.

Question 17: In Question 13:, if the sum of the numbers goes beyond maximum allowed integer, then there can be integer overflow and we may not get correct answer. Can we solve this problem?

Answer:

1) XOR all the array elements, let the result of XOR be X.
2) XOR all numbers from 1 to n, let XOR be Y.
3) XOR of X and Y gives the missing number.

```
int FindMissingNumber(int A[], int n) {
    int i, X, Y;
    for (i = 0; i < n; i ++)
        X ^= A[i];
    for (i = 1; i <= n; i ++)
        Y ^= i;
    //In fact, one variable is enough.
    return X ^ Y;
}
```

Time Complexity: O(n), for scanning the complete array. Space Complexity: O(1).

Question 18: **Find the Number Occurring Odd Number of Times:** Given an array of positive integers, all numbers occurs even number of times except one number which occurs odd number of times. Find the number in O(n) time & constant space. **Example**: I/P = [1, 2, 3, 2, 3, 1, 3] O/P = 3

Answer: Do a bitwise XOR of all the elements. We get the number which has odd occurrences. This is because, $A\ XOR\ A = 0$.

Time Complexity: O(n). Space Complexity: O(1).

Question 19: **Find the two repeating elements in a given array:** Given an array with $n+2$ elements, all elements of the array are in range 1 to n and also all elements occur only once except two numbers which occur twice. Find those two repeating numbers. For example: if the array is 4, 2, 4, 5, 2, 3, 1 with $n = 5$. This input has $n + 2 = 7$ elements with all elements occurring once except 2 and 4 which occur twice. So the output should be 4 2.

Answer: One simple way is to scan the complete array for each element of the input elements. That means use two loops. In the outer loop, select elements one by one and count the number of occurrences of the selected element in the inner loop. For the code below assume that *PrintRepeatedElements* is called with $n + 2$ to indicate the size.

```
void PrintRepeatedElements(int A[], int n) {
    for(int i = 0; i < n; i++)
        for(int j = i+1; j <n; j++)
            if(A[i] == A[j])
                printf("%d", A[i]);
}
```

Time Complexity: O(n^2). Space Complexity: O(1).

Question 20: For Question 19:, can we improve the time complexity?

Answer: Sort the array using any comparison sorting algorithm and see if there are any elements which contiguous with same value.

Time Complexity: O($nlogn$). Space Complexity: O(1).

Question 21: For Question 19:, can we improve the time complexity?

Answer: Use Count Array. This solution is like using a hash table. For simplicity we can use array for storing the counts. Traverse the array once and keep track of count of all elements in the array using a temp array *count*[] of size n. When we see an element whose count is already set, print it as duplicate. For the code below assume that *PrintRepeatedElements* is called with $n + 2$ to indicate the size.

```
void PrintRepeatedElements(int A[], int n) {
    int *count = (int *)calloc(sizeof(int), (n - 2));
```

```
    for(int i = 0; i < size; i++) {
        count[A[i]]++;
        if(count[A[i]] == 2)
            printf("%d", A[i]);
    }
}
```

Time Complexity: O(n). Space Complexity: O(n).

Question 22: Consider Question 19:. Let us assume that the numbers are in the range 1 to n. Is there any other way of solving the problem?

Answer: **Yes by using XOR Operation.** Let the repeating numbers be X and Y, if we XOR all the elements in the array and also all integers from 1 to n, then the result will be $X\ XOR\ Y$. The 1's in binary representation of $X\ XOR\ Y$ correspond to the different bits between X and Y. If the kth bit of $X\ XOR\ Y$ is 1, we can XOR all the elements in the array and also all integers from 1 to n, whose k^{th} bits are 1. The result will be one of X and Y.

```
void PrintRepeatedElements (int A[], int size) {
    int XOR = A[0];
    int i, right_most_set_bit_no, X= 0, Y = 0;
    for(i = 1; i < size; i++)                /* Compute XOR of all elements in A[]*/
        XOR ^= A[i];
    for(i = 1; i <= n; i++)                  /* Compute XOR of all elements {1, 2 ..n} */
        XOR ^= i;
    right_most_set_bit_no = XOR & ~( XOR -1);
    for(i = 0; i < size; i++) {
        if(A[i] & right_most_set_bit_no)
            X = X^ A[i];            /*XOR of first set in A[] */
        else    Y = Y ^ A[i];       /*XOR of second set inA[] */
    }
    for(i = 1; i <= n; i++) {
        if(i & right_most_set_bit_no)
            X = X ^ i;              /*XOR of first set in A[] and {1, 2, ...n }*/
        else    Y = Y ^ i;          /*XOR of second set in A[] and {1, 2, ...n } */
    }
    printf("%d and %d",X, Y);
}
```

Time Complexity: O(n). Space Complexity: O(1).

Question 23: Consider Question 19:. Let us assume that the numbers are in the range 1 to n. Is there yet other way of solving the problem?

Answer: We can solve this by creating two simple mathematical equations. Let us assume that two numbers which we are going to find are X and Y. We know the sum of n numbers is $n(n+1)/2$ and product is $n!$. Make two equations using these sum and product formulae, and get values of two unknowns using the two equations. Let the summation of all numbers in array be S and product be P and the numbers which are being repeated are X and Y.

$$X + Y = \frac{n(n+1)}{2} - S$$

$$XY = n!/P$$

Using above two equations, we can find out X and Y. There can be addition and multiplication overflow problem with this approach.

Time Complexity: O(n). Space Complexity: O(1).

Question 24: Similar to Question 19:, let us assume that the numbers are in the range 1 to n. Also, $n-1$ elements are repeating thrice and remaining element repeated twice. Find the element which repeated twice.

Answer: If we XOR all the elements in the array and all integers from 1 to n, then all the elements which are thrice will become zero. This is because, since the element is repeating thrice and XOR with another time from range makes that element appearing four times. As a result, output of $a\, XOR\, a\, XOR\, a\, XOR\, a = 0$. Same is case with all elements which repeated three times.

With the same logic, for the element which repeated twice, if we XOR the input elements and also the range, then the total number of appearances for that element are 3. As a result, output of $a\, XOR\, a\, XOR\, a = a$. Finally, we get the element which repeated twice.

Time Complexity: O(n). Space Complexity: O(1).

Question 25: Given an array of n elements. Find two elements in the array such that their sum is equal to given element K.

Brute Force Solution: One simple solution to this is, for each input element check whether there is any element whose sum is K. This we can solve just by using two simple for loops. The code for this solution can be given as:

```
void BruteForceSearch[int A[], int n, int K) {
    for (int i = 0; i < n; i++) {
        for(int j = i; j < n; j++) {
            if(A[i]+A[j] == K) {
                printf("Items Found:%d %d", i, j);
                return;
            }
        }
    }
    printf("Items not found: No such elements");
}
```

Time Complexity: O(n^2). This is because of two nested *for* loops. Space Complexity: O(1).

Question 26: For Question 25:, can we improve the time complexity?

Answer: **Yes.** Let us assume that we have sorted the given array. This operation takes O($nlogn$). On the sorted array, maintain indices $loIndex = 0$ and hiIndex $= n-1$ and compute $A[loIndex] + A[hiIndex]$. If the sum equals K, then we are done with the solution. If the sum is less than K, decrement *hiIndex*, if the sum is greater than K, increment *loIndex*.

```
void Search[int A[], int n, int K) {
    int i, j, temp;
    Sort(A, n);
    for(i = 0, j = n-1; i < j) {
        temp = A[i] + A[j];
        if(temp == K) {
            printf("Elements Found: %d %d", i, j);
            return;
        }
        else if(temp < K)
            i = i + 1;
        else j = j - 1;
    }
    return;
}
```

Time Complexity: O($nlogn$). If the given array is already sorted then the complexity is O(n).
Space Complexity: O(1).

Question 27: Does the solution of Question 25: work even if the array is not sorted?

Answer: **Yes.** Since we are checking all possibilities, the algorithm ensures that we get the pair of numbers if they exist.

Question 28: Is there any other way of solving Question 25:?

Answer: **Yes,** using hash table. Since our objective is to find two indexes of the array whose sum is K. Let us say those indexes are X and Y. That means, $A[X] + A[Y] = K$.

What we need is, for each element of the input array $A[X]$, check whether $K - A[X]$ also exists in input array. Now, let us simplify that searching with hash table.

Algorithm:

- For each element of the input array, insert into the hash table. Let us say the current element is $A[X]$.
- Before proceeding to the next element we check whether K - $A[X]$ also exists in hash table or not.
- Existence of such number indicates that we are able to find the indexes.
- Otherwise proceed to the next input element.

Time Complexity: O(n). Space Complexity: O(n).

Question 29: Given an array A of n elements. Find three indices, i, j & k such that $A[i]^2 + A[j]^2 = A[k]^2$?

Answer:

Algorithm:

- Sort the given array in-place.
- For each array index i compute $A[i]^2$ and store in array.
- Search for 2 numbers in array from 0 to $i-1$ which adds to $A[i]$ similar to Question 25:. This will give us the result in O(n) time. If we find such sum return true otherwise continue.

```
Sort(A); // Sort the input array
for (int i=0; i < n; i++)
    A[i] = A[i]*A[i];
for (i=n; i > 0; i--) {
    res = false;
    if(res) {
        //Question-11/12 Solution
    }
}
```

Time Complexity: Time for sorting + $n \times$ (Time for finding the sum) =O($nlogn$) + $n \times$O(n)= n^2.
Space Complexity: O(1).

Question 30: **Two elements whose sum is closest to zero:** Given an array with both positive and negative numbers, find the two elements such that their sum is closest to zero. For the below array, algorithm should give −80 and 85. Example: 1 60 − 10 70 − 80 85

Brute Force Solution: For each element, find the sum with every other element in the array and compare sums. Finally, return the minimum sum.

```
void TwoElementsWithMinSum(int A[], int n) {
    int i, j, min_sum, sum, min_i, min_j, inv_count = 0;
```

```
    if(n < 2) {
        printf("Invalid Input");
        return;
    }
    min_i = 0;
    min_j = 1;
    min_sum = A[0] + A[1];
    for(i= 0; i < n - 1; i ++) {
        for(j = i + 1; j < n; j++) {
            sum = A[i] + A[j];
            if(abs(min_sum) > abs(sum)) {
                min_sum = sum;
                min_i = i;
                min_j = j;
            }
        }
    }
    printf(" The two elements are %d and %d", arr[min_i], arr[min_j]);
}
```

Time complexity: O(n^2). Space Complexity: O(1).

Question 31: Can we improve the time complexity of Question 30:?

Answer: Use Sorting.

Algorithm:

1. Sort all the elements of the given input array.
2. Maintain two indexes one at the beginning ($i = 0$) and other at the ending ($j = n - 1$). Also, maintina two variables to keep track of smallest positive sum closest to zero and smallest negative sum closest to zero.
3. While $i < j$:
    a. If the current pair sum is > zero and < postiveClosest then update the postiveClosest. Decrement j.
    b. If the current pair sum is < zero and > negativeClosest then update the negativeClosest. Increment i.
    c. Else, print the pair

```
void TwoElementsWithMinSum(int A[], int n) {
    int i = 0, j = n-1, temp, postiveClosest = INT_MAX, negativeClosest = INT_MIN;
    Sort(A, n);
    while(i < j) {
        temp = A[i] + A[j];
        if(temp > 0) {
            if (temp < postiveClosest)
                postiveClosest = temp;
            j--;
        }
        else if (temp < 0) {
            if (temp > negativeClosest)
                negativeClosest = temp;
            i++;
        }
        else printf("Closest Sum: %d ", A[i] + A[j]);
    }
    return (abs(negativeClosest)> postiveClosest: postiveClosest: negativeClosest);
}
```

Time Complexity: O($nlogn$), for sorting. Space Complexity: O(1).

Question 32: Given an array of n elements. Find three elements in the array such that their sum is equal to given element K?

Brute Force Solution: The default solution to this is, for each pair of input elements check whether there is any element whose sum is K. This we can solve just by using three simple for loops. The code for this solution can be given as:

```
void BruteForceSearch[int A[], int n, int data) {
  for (int i = 0; i < n; i++) {
    for(int j = i+1; j < n; j++) {
      for(int k = j+1; k < n; k++)    {
        if(A[i] + A[j] + A[k]== data) {
          printf("Items Found:%d %d %d", i, j, k);
          return;
        }
      }
    }
  }
  printf("Items not found: No such elements");
}
```

Time Complexity: $O(n^3)$, for three nested *for* loops. Space Complexity: O(1).

Question 33: Does the solution of Question 32: work even if the array is not sorted?

Answer: **Yes.** Since we are checking all possibilities, the algorithm ensures that we can find three numbers whose sum is K if they exist.

Question 34: Can we use sorting technique for solving Question 32:?

Answer: **Yes.**

```
void Search[int A[], int n, int data) {
  Sort(A, n);
  for(int k = 0; k < n; k++) {
    for(int i =  k + 1, j = n-1; i < j;  ) {
      if(A[k] + A[i] + A[j]  == data) {
        printf("Items Found:%d %d %d", i, j, k);
        return;
  }
      else if(A[k] + A[i] + A[j]  < data)
        i = i + 1;
      else   j = j - 1;
    }
  }
  return;
}
```

Time Complexity: Time for sorting + Time for searching in sorted list $= O(nlogn) + O(n^2) \approx O(n^2)$. This is because of two nested *for* loops. Space Complexity: O(1).

Question 35: Can we use hashing technique for solving Question 32:?

Answer: **Yes.** Since our objective is to find three indexes of the array whose sum is K. Let us say those indexes are X, Y and Z. That means, $A[X] + A[Y] + A[Z] = K$.

Let us assume that we have kept all possible sums along with their pairs in hash table. That means the key to hash table is $K - A[X]$ and values for $K - A[X]$ are all possible pairs of input whose sum is $K - A[X]$.

Algorithm:

- Before starting the searching, insert all possible sums with pairs of elements into the hash table.

- For each element of the input array, insert into the hash table. Let us say the current element is $A[X]$.
- Check whether there exists a hash entry in the table with key: $K - A[X]$.
- If such element exists then scan the element pairs of $K - A[X]$ and return all possible pairs by including $A[X]$ also.
- If no such element exists (with $K - A[X]$ as key) then go to next element.

Time Complexity: Time for storing all possible pairs in Hash table + searching = $O(n^2) + O(n^2) \approx O(n^2)$.
Space Complexity: $O(n)$.

Question 36: Given an array of n integers, the $3 - sum\ problem$ is to find three integers whose sum is closest to *zero*.

Answer: This is same as that of Question 32: with K value is zero.

Question 37: Let A be an array of n distinct integers. Suppose A has the following property: there exists an index $1 \le k \le n$ such that $A[1],\ldots,A[k]$ is an increasing sequence and $A[k+1],\ldots,A[n]$ is a decreasing sequence. Design and analyze an efficient algorithm for finding k.
Similar question: Let us assume that the given array is sorted but starts with negative numbers and ends with positive numbers [such functions are called monotonically increasing function]. In this array find the starting index of the positive numbers. Assume that we know the length of the input array. Design a $O(logn)$ algorithm.

Answer: Let us use a variant of the binary search.

```
int Search (int A[], int n, int first, int last) {
    int mid, first = 0, last = n-1;
    while(first <= last) {
        // if the current array has size 1
        if(first == last)
            return A[first];
        // if the current array has size 2
        else if(first == last-1)
            return max(A[first], A[last]);
        // if the current array has size 3 or more
        else {
            mid = first + (last-first)/2;
            if(A[mid-1] < A[mid] && A[mid] > A[mid+1])
                return A[mid];
            else if(A[mid-1] < A[mid] && A[mid] < A[mid+1])
                first = mid+1;
            else if(A[mid-1] > A[mid] && A[mid] > A[mid+1])
                last = mid-1;
        else    return INT_MIN ;
        }
    }
}
```

The recursion equation is $T(n) = 2T(n/2) + c$. Using master theorem, we get $O(logn)$.

Question 38: If we don't know n, how do we solve the Question 37:?

Answer: Repeatedly compute $A[1], A[2], A[4], A[8], A[16]$, and so on until we find a value of n such that $A[n] > 0$.

Time Complexity: $O(logn)$, since we are moving at the rate of 2. Refer *Introduction to Analysis of Algorithms* chapter for details on this.

Question 39: Given an input array of size unknown with all $1's$ in the beginning and $0's$ in the end. Find the index in the array from where $0's$ start. Consider there are millions of $1's$ and $0's$ in the array. E.g. array contents 1111111.......1100000.........0000000.

Answer: This problem is almost similar to Question 38:. Check the bits at the rate of $2^K$where $k = 0, 1, 2 ....$ Since we are moving at the rate of 2, the complexity is $O(logn)$.

Question 40: Given a sorted array of n integers that has been rotated an unknown number of times, give a $O(logn)$ algorithm that finds an element in the array. **Example**: Find 5 in array (15 16 19 20 25 1 3 4 5 7 10 14) **Output**: 8 (the index of 5 in the array)

Answer: Let us assume that the given array is $A[]$and use the solution of Question 37: with extension. The function below *FindPivot* returns the k value (let us assume that this function return the index instead of value). Find the pivot point, divide the array into two sub-arrays and call binary search.

The main idea for finding pivot is – for a sorted (in increasing order) and pivoted array, pivot element is the only element for which next element to it is smaller than it. Using above criteria and binary search methodology we can get pivot element in $O(logn)$ time.

Algorithm:

1) Find out pivot point and divide the array in two sub-arrays.
2) Now call binary search for one of the two sub-arrays.
   a. if element is greater than first element then search in left subarray
   b. else search in right subarray
3) If element is found in selected sub-array then return index *else* return −1.

```
int FindPivot(int A[], int start, int finish) {
    if(finish - start == 0)
        return start;
    else if(start == finish - 1) {
        if(A[start] >= A[finish])
            return start;
        else    return finish;
    }
    else {
        mid = start + (finish-start)/2;
        if(A[start] >= A[mid])
            return FindPivot(A, start, mid);
        else    return FindPivot(A, mid, finish);
    }
}
int Search(int A[], int n, int x) {
    int pivot = FindPivot(A, 0, n-1);
    if(A[pivot] == x)
        return pivot;
    if(A[pivot] <= x)
        return BinarySearch(A, 0, pivot-1, x);
    else    return BinarySearch(A, pivot+1, n-1, x);
}
int BinarySearch(int A[], int low, int high, int x) {
    if(high >= low)  {
        int mid = low + (high - low)/2;
        if(x == A[mid])
            return mid;
        if(x > A[mid])
            return BinarySearch(A, (mid + 1), high, x);
```

```
        else    return BinarySearch(A, low, (mid -1), x);
    }
    return -1;          /*Return -1 if element is not found*/
}
```

Time complexity:O($logn$).

Question 41: For Question 40:, can we solve in one scan?

Answer: **Yes.**

```
int BinarySearchRotated(int A[], int start, int finish, int data) {
    int mid = start + (finish - start) / 2;
    if(start > finish)
        return -1;
    if(data == A[mid])
        return mid;
    else if(A[start] <= A[mid]) {     // start half is in sorted order.
        if(data >= A[start] && data < A[mid])
            return BinarySearchRotated(A, start, mid - 1, data);
        else    return BinarySearchRotated(A, mid + 1, finish, data);
    }
    else {  // A[mid] <= A[finish], finish half is in sorted order.
        if(data > A[mid] && data <= A[finish])
            return BinarySearchRotated(A, mid + 1, finish, data);
        else    return BinarySearchRotated(A, start, mid - 1, data);
    }
}
```

Time complexity:O($logn$).

Question 42: **Bitonic search:** An array is *bitonic* if it is comprised of an increasing sequence of integers followed immediately by a decreasing sequence of integers. Given a bitonic array A of n distinct integers, describe how to determine whether a given integer is in the array in O($logn$) steps.

Answer: The solution is the same as that for Question 37:.

Question 43: Yet, other way of framing Question 37:.
Let $A[]$ be an array that starts out increasing, reaches a maximum, and then decreases. Design an O($logn$) algorithm to find the index of the maximum value.

Question 44: Give an O($nlogn$) algorithm for computing the median of a sequence of n integers.

Answer: Sort and return element at $\frac{n}{2}$.

Question 45: Given two sorted lists of size m and n, find median of all elements in O($log\ (m+n)$) time.

Answer: Refer *Divide and Conquer* chapter.

Question 46: Given a sorted array A of n elements, possibly with duplicates, find the index of the first occurrence of a number in O($logn$) time.

Answer: To find the first occurrence of a number we need to check for the following condition. Return the position if any one of the following is true:

```
        mid == low && A[mid] == data  ||  A[mid] == data && A[mid-1] < data
```

```
int BinarySearchFirstOccurrence(int A[], int low, int high, int data) {
    int mid;
    if(high >= low) {
        mid = low + (high-low) / 2;
```

```
        if((mid == low && A[mid] == data) || (A[mid] == data && A[mid - 1] < data))
            return mid;
        // Give preference to left half of the array
        else if(A[mid] >= data)
            return BinarySearchFirstOccurrence (A, low, mid - 1, data);
        else    return BinarySearchFirstOccurrence (A, mid + 1, high, data);
    }
    return -1;
}
```

Time Complexity: $O(logn)$.

Question 47: Given a sorted array A of n elements, possibly with duplicates. Find the index of the last occurrence of a number in $O(logn)$ time.

Answer: To find the last occurrence of a number we need to check for the following condition. Return the position if any one of the following is true:

```
    mid == high && A[mid] == data  ||  A[mid] == data && A[mid+1] > data
```

```
int BinarySearchLastOccurrence(int A[], int low, int high, int data) {
    int mid;
    if(high >= low) {
        mid = low + (high-low) / 2;
        if((mid == high && A[mid] == data) || (A[mid] == data && A[mid + 1] > data))
            return mid;
        // Give preference to right half of the array
        else if(A[mid] <= data)
            return BinarySearchLastOccurrence (A, mid + 1, high, data);
        else    return BinarySearchLastOccurrence (A, low, mod - 1, data);
    }
    return -1;
}
```

Time Complexity: $O(logn)$.

Question 48: Given a sorted array of n elements, possibly with duplicates. Find the number of occurrences of a number.

Brute Force Solution: Do a linear search over the array and increment count as and when we find the element data in the array.

```
int LinearSearchCount(int A[], int n, int data) {
    int count = 0;
    for (int i = 0; i < n; i++)
        if(A[i] == k)
            count++;
    return count;
}
```

Time Complexity: $O(n)$.

Question 49: Can we improve the time complexity of Question 48:?

Answer: **Yes.** We can solve this by using one binary search call followed by another small scan.

Algorithm:

- Do a binary search for the *data* in the array. Let us assume its position is K.
- Now traverse towards left from K and count the number of occurrences of *data*. Let this count be $leftCount$.

- Similarly, traverse towards right and count the number of occurrences of *data*. Let this count be *rightCount*.
- Total number of occurrences = $leftCount + 1 + rightCount$

Time Complexity – $O(logn + S)$ where S is the number of occurrences of *data*.

Question 50: Is there any alternative way of solving Question 48:?

Answer:

Algorithm:

- Find first occurrence of *data* and call its index as *firstOccurrence* (for algorithm refer Question 46:)
- Find last occurrence of *data* and call its index as *lastOccurrence* (for algorithm refer Question 47:)
- Return $lastOccurrence - firstOccurrence + 1$

Time Complexity = $O(logn + logn)$ =$O(logn)$.

Question 51: What is the next number in the sequence 1, 11, 21 and why?

Answer: Read the given number loudly. This is just a fun problem.

```
One One
Two Ones
One two, one one→ 1211
```

So answer is, the next number is the representation of previous number by reading it loudly.

Question 52: Finding second smallest number efficiently.

Answer: We can construct a heap of the given elements using up just less than n comparisons (Refer *Priority Queues* chapter for algorithm). Then we find the second smallest using $logn$ comparisons for the GetMax() operation. Overall, we get $n + logn + constant$.

Question 53: Is there any other solution for Question 52:?

Answer: Alternatively, split the n numbers into groups of 2, perform $n/2$ comparisons successively to find the largest using a tournament-like method. The first round will yield the maximum in $n - 1$ comparisons. The second round will be performed on the winners of the first round and the ones the maximum popped. This will yield $logn - 1$ comparisons for a total of $n + logn - 2$.

The above solution is called *tournament problem*.

Question 54: An element is a majority if it appears more than $n/2$ times. Give an algorithm takes an array of n element as argument and identifies a majority (if it exists).

Answer: The basic solution is to have two loops and keep track of maximum count for all different elements. If maximum count becomes greater than $n/2$ then break the loops and return the element having maximum count. If maximum count doesn't become more than $n/2$ then majority element doesn't exist.

Time Complexity: $O(n^2)$. Space Complexity: $O(1)$.

Question 55: Can we improve Question 54: time complexity to $O(nlogn)$?

Answer: Using binary search we can achieve this. Node of the Binary Search Tree (used in this approach) will be as follows.

```
struct TreeNode {
    int element;
```

```
    int count;
    struct TreeNode *left;
        struct TreeNode *right;
} BST;
```

Insert elements in BST one by one and if an element is already present then increment the count of the node. At any stage, if count of a node becomes more than $n/2$ then return. The method works well for the cases where $n/2+1$ occurrences of the majority element is present in the starting of the array, for example $\{1,1,1,1,1,2,3, \text{and } 4\}$.

Time Complexity: If a binary search tree is used then worst time complexity will be $O(n^2)$. If a balanced-binary-search tree is used then $O(nlogn)$. Space Complexity: $O(n)$.

Question 56: Is there any other of achieving $O(nlogn)$ complexity for Question 54:?

Answer: Sort the input array and scan the sorted array to find the majority element.

Time Complexity: $O(nlogn)$. Space Complexity: $O(1)$.

Question 57: Can we improve the complexity for Question 54:?

Answer: If an element occurs more than $n/2$ times in A then it must be the median of A. But, the reverse is not true, so once the median is found, we must check to see how many times it occurs in A. We can use linear selection which takes $O(n)$ time (for algorithm refer *Selection Algorithms* chapter).

int CheckMajority(int A[], in n) {

1) Use linear selection to find the median m of A.
2) Do one more pass through A and count the number of occurrences of m.
    a. If m occurs more than $n/2$ times then return true;
    b. Otherwise return false.

}

Question 58: Is there any other way of solving Question 54:?

Answer: Since only one element is repeating, we can use simple scan of the input array by keeping track of count for the elements. If the count is 0 then we can assume that the element is coming first time otherwise that the resultant element.

```
int MajorityNum(int[] A, int n) {
    int count = 0, element = -1;
    for(int i = 0; i < n; i++) {
        // If the counter is 0 then set the current candidate to majority num
        //  and set the counter to 1.
        if(count == 0) {
            element = A[i];
            count = 1;
        }
        else if(element == A[i]) {
            // Increment counter If the counter is not 0 and
            //element is same as current candidate.
            count++;
        }
        else {
            // Decrement counter If the counter is not 0 and
            // element is different from current candidate.
            count--;
        }
    }
```

```
    return element;
}
```

Time Complexity: O(n). Space Complexity: O(1).

Question 59: Given an array of $2n$ elements of which n elements are same and the remaining n elements are all different. Find the majority element.

Answer: The repeated elements will occupy half the array. No matter what arrangement it is, only one of the below will be true,

- All duplicate elements will be at a relative distance of 2 from each other. Ex: n, *1*, n, *100*, n, *54*, n ...
- At least two duplicate elements will be next to each other
  Ex: $n, n, 1, 100, n, 54, n, \ldots$
  $n, 1, n, n, n, 54, 100 \ldots$
  $1, 100, 54, n, n, n, n \ldots$

In worst case, we will need two passes over the array,

- First Pass: compare $A[i]$ and $A[i+1]$
- Second Pass: compare $A[i]$ and $A[i+2]$

Something will match and that's your element. This will cost O(n) in time and O(1) in space.

Question 60: Given an array with $2n+1$ integer elements, n elements appear twice in arbitrary places in the array and a single integer appears only once somewhere inside. Find the lonely integer with O(n) operations and O(1) extra memory.

Answer: Except one element all other elements are repeated. We know that $A\ XOR\ A = 0$. Based on this if we XOR all the input elements then we get the remaining element.

```
int Solution(int* A) {
    int i, res;
    for (i = res = 0; i < 2n+1; i++)
          res = res ^ A[i];
    return res;
}
```

Time Complexity: O(n). Space Complexity: O(1).

Question 61: **Local minimum of an array:** Given an array A of n distinct integers, design an O($logn$) algorithm to find a *local minimum*: an index i such that $A[i-1] < A[i] < A[i+1]$.

Answer: Check the middle value $A[n/2]$, and two neighbors $A[n/2 - 1]$ and $A[n/2 + 1]$. If $A[n/2]$ is local minimum, stop; otherwise search in half with smaller neighbor.

Question 62: Give an $n \times n$ array of elements such that each row is in ascending order and each column is in ascending order, devise an O(n) algorithm to determine if a given element x in the array. You may assume all elements in the $n \times n$ array are distinct.

Answer: Let us assume that the given matrix is $A[n][n]$. Start with the last row, first column [or first row - last column]. If the element we are searching for is greater than the element at $A[1][n]$, then the column 1 can be eliminated. If the search element is less than the element at $A[1][n]$, then the last row can be completely eliminated.

Once the first column or the last row is eliminated, start over the process again with left-bottom end of the remaining array. In this algorithm, there would be maximum n elements that the search element would be compared with.

Time Complexity: O(n). This is because we will traverse at most $2n$ points. Space Complexity: O(1).

Question 63: Given an $n \times n$ array a of n^2 numbers, give an O(n) algorithm to find a pair of indices i and j such that $A[i][j] < A[i+1][j], A[i][j] < A[i][j+1], A[i][j] < A[i-1][j]$, and $A[i][j] < A[i][j-1]$.

Answer: This problem is same as Question 62:.

Question 64: Given $n \times n$ matrix, and in each row all 1's are followed 0's. Find row with maximum number of 0's.

Answer: Start with first row, last column. If the element is 0 then move to the previous column in the same row and at the same time increase the counter to indicate the maximum number of 0's. If the element is 1 then move to next row in the same column. Repeat this process until we reach last row, first column.

Time Complexity: O($2n$) ≈O(n) (similar to Question 62:).

Question 65: **Separate Even and Odd numbers:** Given an array $A[\,]$, write a function that segregates even and odd numbers. The functions should put all even numbers first, and then odd numbers. **Example**: Input = $\{12, 34, 45, 9, 8, 90, 3\}$ Output = $\{12, 34, 90, 8, 9, 45, 3\}$

Note: In the output, order of numbers can be changed, i.e., in the above example 34 can come before 12 and 3 can come before 9.

Answer: The problem is very similar to *Separate* 0's *and* 1's (Question 66:) in an array, and both problems are variations of the famous *Dutch national flag problem.*

Algorithm: Logic is similar to Quick sort.

1) Initialize two index variables left and right: $left = 0$, $right = n - 1$
2) Keep incrementing left index until we see an odd number.
3) Keep decrementing right index until we see an even number.
4) If $left < right$ then swap $A[left]$ and $A[right]$

```
void DutchNationalFlag(int A[], int n) {
    int left = 0, right = n-1;
    while(left < right) {
        // Increment left index while we see 0 at left
        while(A[left]%2 == 0 && left < right)
            left++;
        // Decrement right index while we see 1 at right
        while(A[right]%2 == 1 && left < right)
            right--;
        if(left < right) {
            /* Swap A[left] and A[right]*/
            swap(&A[left], &A[right]);
            left++;
            right--;
        }
    }
}
```

Time Complexity: O(n).

Question 66: The following is another way of structuring Question 65:, but with little difference.

Separate 0's and 1's in an array: We are given an array of 0's and 1's in random order. Separate 0's on left side and 1's on right side of the array. Traverse array only once.

Input array = $[0, 1, 0, 1, 0, 0, 1, 1, 1, 0]$ **Output array** = $[0, 0, 0, 0, 0, 1, 1, 1, 1, 1]$

Answer: Counting 0's or 1's

1. Count the number of $0's$. Let count be C.
2. Once we have count, put C 0's at the beginning and $1's$ at the remaining $n - C$ positions in array.

Time Complexity: O(n). This solution scans the array two times.

Question 67: Can we solve Question 66: in one scan?

Answer: **Yes.** Use two indexes to traverse: Maintain two indexes. Initialize first index left as 0 and second index right as $n - 1$. Do following while $left < right$:

1) Keep incrementing index left while there are 0s at it
2) Keep decrementing index right while there are 1s at it
3) If left < right then exchange $A[left]$ and $A[right]$

```
// Function to put all 0s on left and all 1s on right
void Separate0and1(int A[], int n) {
    int left = 0, right = n-1;
    while(left < right) {
        // Increment left index while we see 0 at left
        while(A[left] == 0 && left < right)
            left++;
        //Decrement right index while we see 1 at right
        while(A[right] == 1 && left < right)
            right–;
        /* If left is smaller than right then there is a 1 at left
        and a 0 at right.  Swap A[left] and A[right]*/
        if(left < right) {
            A[left] = 0;
            A[right] = 1;
            left++;
            right–;
        }
    }
}
```

Time Complexity: O(n). Space Complexity: O(1).

Question 68: **Sort an array of 0's, 1's and 2's [or R's, G's and B's]:** Given an array A[] consisting $0's$, $1's$ and $2's$, give an algorithm for sorting $A[]$.The algorithm should put all $0's$ first, then all $1's$ and finally all the $2's$ at the end. **Example Input** = {0,1,1,0,1,2,1,2,0,0,0,1}, **Output** = {0, 0, 0, 0, 0, 1, 1, 1, 1, 1, 2, 2}

Answer:

```
void Sorting012sDutchFlagProblem(int A[],int n){
    int low=0,mid=0,high=n-1;
    while(mid <=high){
        switch(A[mid]){
            case 0:
                swap(A[low],A[mid]);
                low++;mid++;
                break;
            case 1:
                mid++;
                break;
            case 2:
                swap(A[mid],A[high]);
                high--;
                break;
        }
```

```
    }
}
```

Time Complexity: O(n). Space Complexity: O(1).

Question 69: Given an array of 101 elements. Out of them 25 elements are repeated twice, 12 elements are repeated 4 times and one element is repeated 3 times. Find the element which repeated 3 times in O(1).

Answer: Before solving this problem let us consider the following XOR operation property: $a \, XOR \, a = 0$. That means, if we apply the XOR on same elements then the result is 0.

Algorithm:

- XOR all the elements of the given array and assume the result is A.
- After this operation, 2 occurrences of number which appeared 3 times becomes 0 and one occurrence remains the same.
- The 12 elements that are appearing 4 times become 0.
- The 25 elements that are appearing 2 times become 0.
- So just $XOR'ing$ all the elements give the result.

Time Complexity: O(n), because we are doing only one scan. Space Complexity: O(1).

Question 70: Given a number n, give an algorithm for finding the number of trailing zeros in $n!$.

Answer:

```
int NumberOfTrailingZerosInNumber(int n) {
    int i, count = 0;
    if(n < 0) return -1;
    for (i = 5; n / i > 0; i *= 5)
        count += n / i;
    return count;
}
```

Time Complexity: O($logn$).

Question 71: Given an array of $2n$ integers in the following format $a1\ a2\ a3 \ldots an\ b1\ b2\ b3 \ldots bn$. Shuffle the array to $a1\ b1\ a2\ b2\ a3\ b3 \ldots an\ bn$ without any extra memory.

Answer: A brute force solution involves two nested loops to rotate the elements in the second half of the array to the left. The first loop runs n times to cover all elements in the second half of the array. The second loop rotates the elements to the left. Note that the start index in the second loop depends on which element we are rotating and the end index depends on how many positions we need to move to the left.

```
void ShuffleArray() {
    int n = 4;
    int A[] = {1,3,5,7,2,4,6,8};
    for (int i = 0, q =1, k = n; i < n; i++, k++, q++) {
        for (int j = k; j > i + q; j--) {
            int tmp = A[j-1];
            A[j-1] = A[j];
            A[j] = tmp;
        }
    }
    for (int i = 0; i  < 2*n; i++)
        printf("%d", A[i]);
}
```

Time Complexity: O(n^2).

Question 72: Can we improve Question 71: solution?

Answer: Refer Divide and Concur chapter. A better solution of time complexity O($nlogn$) can be achieved using *Divide and Concur* technique. Let us take an example

1. Start with the array: $a1\ a2\ a3\ a4\ b1\ b2\ b3\ b4$
2. Split the array into two halves: $a1\ a2\ a3\ a4\ :\ b1\ b2\ b3\ b4$
3. Exchange elements around the center: exchange $a3\ a4$ with $b1\ b2$ you get: $a1\ a2\ b1\ b2\ a3\ a4\ b3\ b4$
4. Split $a1\ a2\ b1\ b2$ into $a1\ a2\ :\ b1\ b2$ then split $a3\ a4\ b3\ b4$ into $a3\ a4\ :\ b3\ b4$
5. Exchange elements around the center for each subarray you get: $a1\ b1\ a2\ b2$ and $a3\ b3\ a4\ b4$

Note that this solution only handles the case when $n = 2^i$ where $i = 0,1,2,3$ etc. In our example $n = 2^2 = 4$ which makes it easy to recursively split the array into two halves. The basic idea behind swapping elements around the center before calling the recursive function is to produce smaller size problems. A solution with linear time complexity may be achieved if the elements are of specific nature. For example, if you can calculate the new position of the element using the value of the element itself. This is nothing but a hashing technique.

Question 73: Given an Aay A[], find the maximum j – i such that A[j] > A[i]. For example, Input: {34, 8, 10, 3, 2, 80, 30, 33, 1} and Output: 6 (j = 7, i = 1).

Answer: **Brute Force Approach:** Run two loops. In the outer loop, pick elements one by one from left. In the inner loop, compare the picked element with the elements starting from right side. Stop the inner loop when you see an element greater than the picked element and keep updating the maximum j-i so far.

```
int maxIndexDiff(int A[], int n){
   int maxDiff = -1;
   int i, j;
    for (i = 0; i < n; ++i){
       for (j = n-1; j > i; --j){
          if(A[j] > A[i] && maxDiff < (j - i))
              maxDiff = j - i;
       }
   }
   return maxDiff;
}
```

Time Complexity: O(n^2). Space Complexity: O(1).

Question 74: Can we improve the complexity of Question 73:?

Answer: To solve this problem, we need to get two optimum indexes of A[]: left index i and right index j. For an element A[i], we do not need to consider A[i] for left index if there is an element smaller than A[i] on left side of A[i]. Similarly, if there is a greater element on right side of A[j] then we do not need to consider this j for right index.

So we construct two auxiliary arrays LeftMins[] and RightMaxs[] such that LeftMins[i] holds the smallest element on left side of A[i] including A[i], and RightMaxs[j] holds the greatest element on right side of A[j] including A[j]. After constructing these two auxiliary arrays, we traverse both these arrays from left to right.

While traversing LeftMins[] and RightMaxs[] if we see that LeftMins[i] is greater than RightMaxs[j], then we must move ahead in LeftMins[] (or do i++) because all elements on left of LeftMins[i] are greater than or equal to LeftMins[i]. Otherwise we must move ahead in RightMaxs[j] to look for a greater $j - i$ value.

```
int maxIndexDiff(int A[], int n){
   int maxDiff;
```

```
    int i, j;
    int *LeftMins = (int *)malloc(sizeof(int)*n);
    int *RightMaxs = (int *)malloc(sizeof(int)*n);
    LeftMins[0] = A[0];
    for (i = 1; i < n; ++i)
        LeftMins[i] = min(A[i], LeftMins[i-1]);
    RightMaxs[n-1] = A[n-1];
    for (j = n-2; j >= 0; --j)
        RightMaxs[j] = max(A[j], RightMaxs[j+1]);
    i = 0, j = 0, maxDiff = -1;
    while (j < n && i < n){
        if (LeftMins[i] < RightMaxs[j]){
            maxDiff = max(maxDiff, j-i);
            j = j + 1;
        }
        else
            i = i+1;
    }
    return maxDiff;
}
```

Time Complexity: O(n). Space Complexity: O(n).

Question 75: Given an array of elements, how do you check whether the list is pairwise sorted or not? A list is considered pairwise sorted if each successive pair of numbers is in sorted (non-decreasing) order.

Answer:

```
int checkPairwiseSorted(int A[], int n) {
  if (n == 0 || n == 1)
    return 1;
  for (int i = 0; i < n - 1; i += 2){
    if (A[i] > A[i+1])
      return 0;
  }
  return 1;
}
```

Time Complexity: O(n). Space Complexity: O(1).

CHAPTER

Hashing

21

21.1 What is Hashing?

Hashing is a technique used for storing and retrieving information as fast as possible. It is used to perform optimal search and is useful in implementing symbol tables.

21.2 Why Hashing?

In *Trees* chapter we have seen that balanced binary search trees support operations such as *insert*, *delete* and *search* in O(*logn*) time. In applications if we need these operations in O(1), then hashing provides a way. Remember that worst case complexity of hashing is still O(n), but it gives O(1) on the average.

21.3 HashTable ADT

The common operations on hash table are:

- CreatHashTable: Creates a new hash table
- HashSearch: Searches the key in hash table
- HashInsert: Inserts a new key into hash table
- HashDelete: Deletes a key from hash table
- DeleteHashTable: Deletes the hash table

21.4 Understanding Hashing

In simple terms we can treat *array* as a hash table. For understanding the use of hash tables, let us consider the following example: Give an algorithm for printing the first repeated character if there are duplicated elements in it. Let us think about the possible solutions. The simple and brute force way of solving is: given a string, for each character check whether that character is repeated or not. Time complexity of this approach is O(n^2) with O(1) space complexity.

Now, let us find the better solution for this problem. Since our objective is to find the first repeated character, what if we remember the previous characters in some array?

We know that the number of possible characters is 256 (for simplicity assume *ASCII* characters only). Create an array of size 256 and initialize it with all zeros. For each of the input characters go to the corresponding position and increment its count. Since we are using arrays, it takes constant time for reaching any location. While scanning the input, if we get a character whose counter is already 1 then we can say that the character is the one which is repeating first time.

```
char FirstRepeatedChar ( char *str ) {
    int i, len=strlen(str);
    int count[256]; //additional array
    for(i=0; i<256; ++i)
      count[i] = 0;
    for(i=0; i<len; ++i) {
      if(count[str[i]]==1) {
          printf("%c", str[i]);
          break;
      }
      else   count[str[i]]++;
    }
    if(i==len)
      printf("No Repeated Characters");
    return 0;
}
```

Why not Arrays?

In the previous problem, we have used an array of size 256 because we know the number of different possible characters [256] in advance. Now, let us consider a slight variant of the same problem. Suppose the given array has numbers instead of characters then how do we solve the problem?

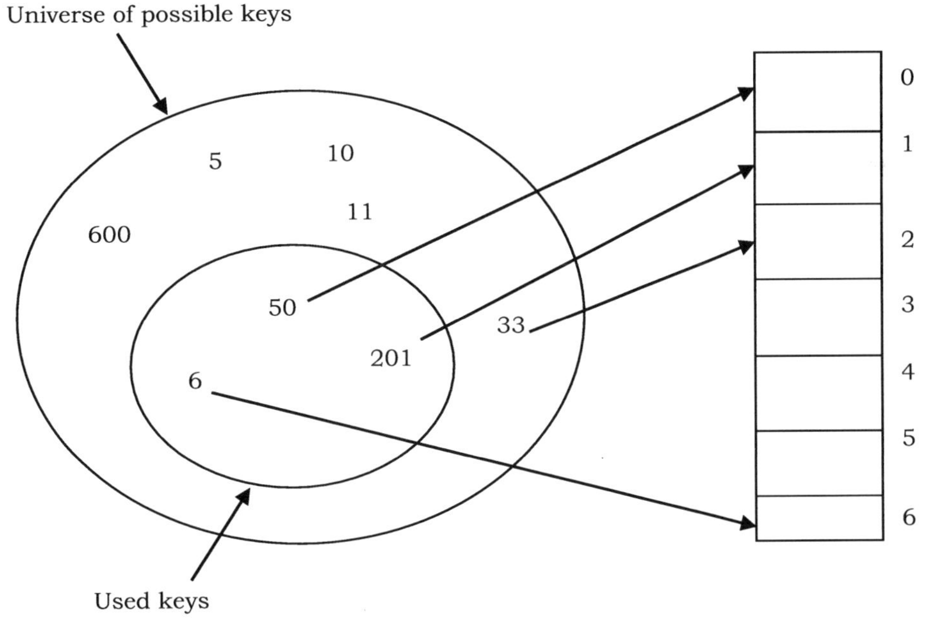

In this case the set of possible values is infinity (or at least very big). Creating a huge array and storing the counters is not possible. That means there are a set of universal keys and limited locations in the memory. If we want to solve this problem we need to somehow map all these possible keys to the possible memory locations.

From the above discussion and diagram it can be seen that we need a mapping of possible keys to one of the available locations. As a result using simple arrays is not the correct choice for solving the problems whose possible keys are very big. The process of mapping the keys to locations is called *hashing*.

Note: For now, do not worry about how the keys are mapped to locations. That depends on the function used for conversions. One such simple function is *key % table size*.

21.5 Components of Hashing

Hashing has four key components:

1) Hash Table
2) Hash Functions
3) Collisions
4) Collision Resolution Techniques

21.6 Hash Table

Hash table is a generalization of array. With an array, we store the element whose key is k at a position k of the array. That means, given a key k, we find the element whose key is k by just looking in the kth position of the array. This is called *direct addressing*.

Direct addressing is applicable when we can afford to allocate an array with one position for every possible key. Suppose we do not have enough space to allocate a location for each possible key then we need a mechanism to handle this case. Other way of defining the scenario is, if we have less locations and more possible keys then simple array implementation is not enough.

In these cases one option is to use hash tables. Hash table or hash map is a data structure that stores the keys and their associated values. Hash table uses a hash function to map keys to their associated values. General convention is that we use a hash table when the number of keys actually stored is small relative to the number of possible keys.

21.7 Hash Function

The hash function is used to transform the key into the index. Ideally, the hash function should map each possible key to a unique slot index, but it is difficult to achieve in practice.

How to Choose Hash Function?

The basic problems associated with the creation of hash tables are:

- An efficient hash function should be designed so that it distributes the index values of inserted objects uniformly across the table.
- An efficient collision resolution algorithm should be designed so that it computes an alternative index for a key whose hash index corresponds to a location previously inserted in the hash table.
- We must choose a hash function which can be calculated quickly, returns values within the range of locations in our table, and minimizes collisions.

Characteristics of Good Hash Functions

A good hash function should have the following characteristics:

- Minimize collision
- Be easy and quick to compute
- Distribute key values evenly in the hash table
- Use all the information provided in the key
- Have a high load factor for a given set of keys

21.8 Load Factor

The load factor of a non-empty hash table is the number of items stored in the table divided by the size of the table. This is the decision parameter used when we want to rehash *or* expand the existing hash table entries. This also helps us in determining the efficiency of the hashing function. That means, it tells whether the hash function is distributing the keys uniformly or not.

$$Load\ factor = \frac{Number\ of\ elements\ in\ hash\ table}{Hash\ Table\ size}$$

21.9 Collisions

Hash functions are used to map each key to different address space but practically it is not possible to create such a hash function and the problem is called *collision*. Collision is the condition where two records are stored in the same location.

21.10 Collision Resolution Techniques

The process of finding an alternate location is called *collision resolution*. Even though hash tables are having collision problem, they are more efficient in many cases comparative to all other data structures like search trees.

There are a number of collision resolution techniques, and the most popular are open addressing and chaining.

- **Direct Chaining:** An array of linked list application
  - Separate chaining
- **Open Addressing:** Array based implementation
  - Linear probing (linear search)
  - Quadratic probing (nonlinear search)
  - Double hashing (use two hash functions)

21.11 Separate Chaining

Collision resolution by chaining combines linked representation with hash table. When two or more records hash to the same location, these records are constituted into a singly-linked list called a *chain*.

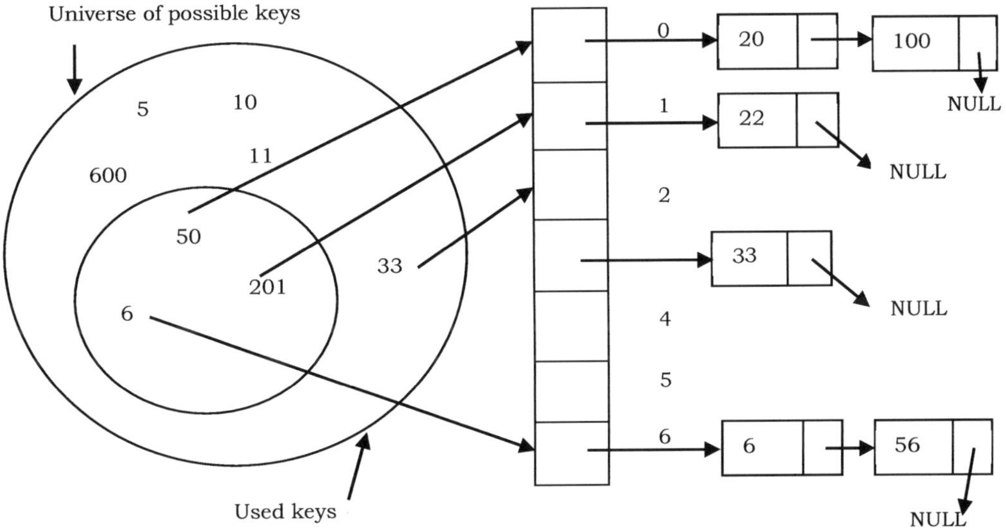

21.12 Open Addressing

In open addressing all keys are stored in the hash table itself. This approach is also known as *closed hashing*. This procedure is based on probing. A collision is resolved by probing.

Linear Probing

Interval between probes is fixed at 1. In linear probing, we search the hash table sequentially starting from the original hash location. If a location is occupied, we check the next location. We wrap around from the last table location to the first table location if necessary. The function for rehashing is the following:

$$rehash(key) = (n + 1)\%\ tablesize$$

One of the problems with linear probing is that table items tend to cluster together in the hash table. This means that table contains groups of consecutively occupied locations that are called *clustering*.

Clusters can get close to one another, and merge into a larger cluster. Thus, the one part of the table might be quite dense, even though another part has relatively few items. Clustering causes long probe searches and therefore decreases the overall efficiency.

The next location to be probed is determined by the step-size, where other step-sizes (than one) are possible. The step-size should be relatively prime to the table size, i.e. their greatest common divisor should be equal to 1. If we choose the table size to be a prime number, then any step-size is relatively prime to the table size. Clustering cannot be avoided by larger step-sizes.

Quadratic Probing

Interval between probes increases proportional to the hash value (the interval thus increasing linearly and the indices are described by a quadratic function). The problem of Clustering can be eliminated if we use quadratic probing method.

In quadratic probing, we start from the original hash location i. If a location is occupied, we check the locations $i + 1^2$, $i + 2^2$, $i + 3^2$, $i + 4^2$...We wrap around from the last table location to the first table location if necessary. The function for rehashing is the following:

$$rehash(key) = (n + k^2)\%\ tablesize$$

Even though clustering is avoided by quadratic probing, still there are chances of clustering. Clustering is caused by multiple search keys mapped to the same hash key.

Thus, the probing sequence for such search keys is prolonged by repeated conflicts along the probing sequence. Both linear and quadratic probing use a probing sequence that is independent of the search key.

Double Hashing

Interval between probes is computed by another hash function. Double hashing reduces clustering in a better way. The increments for the probing sequence are computed by using a second hash function. The second hash function $h2$ should be:

$$h2(key) \neq 0 \text{ and } h2 \neq h1$$

We first probe the location $h1(key)$. If the location is occupied, we probe the location $h1(key) + h2(key)$, $h1(key) + 2 * h2(key)$, ...

21.13 Comparison of Collision Resolution Techniques

Comparisons: Linear Probing vs. Double Hashing

The choice between linear probing and double hashing depends on the cost of computing the hash function and on the load factor [number of elements per slot] of the table. Both use few probes but double hashing take more time because it hashes to compare two hash functions for long keys.

Comparisons: Open Addressing vs. Separate Chaining

It is somewhat complicated because we have to account for the memory usage. Separate chaining uses extra memory for links. Open addressing needs extra memory implicitly within the table to terminate probe sequence. Open-addressed hash tables cannot be used if the data does not have unique keys. An alternative is to use separate chained hash tables.

Comparisons: Open Addressing methods

Linear Probing	Quadratic Probing	Double hashing
Fastest among three	Easiest to implement and deploy	Makes more efficient use of memory
Uses few probes	Uses extra memory for links and it does not probe all locations in the table	Use few probes but take more time
A problem occurs known as primary clustering	A problem occurs known as secondary clustering	More complicated to implement
Interval between probes is fixed - often at 1.	Interval between probes increases proportional to the hash value	Interval between probes is computed by another hash function

21.14 How Hashing Gets O(1) Complexity?

From the previous discussion, one doubts how hashing gets O(1) if multiple elements map to the same location?

The answer to this problem is simple. By using load factor we make sure that each block (for example linked list in separate chaining approach) on the average stores maximum number of elements less than $load\ factor$. Also, in practice this load factor is a constant (generally, 10 or 20). As a result, searching in 20 elements or 10 elements becomes constant.

If the average number of elements in a block is greater than load factor then we rehash the elements with bigger hash table size. One thing we should remember is that we consider average occupancy (total number of elements in the hash table divided by table size) while deciding the rehash.

The access time of table depends on the load factor which in turn depends on the hash function. This is because hash function distributes the elements to hash table. For this reason, we say hash table gives O(1) complexity on the average. Also, we generally use hash tables in cases where searches are more than insertion and deletion operations.

21.15 Hashing Techniques

There are two types of hashing techniques: static hashing and dynamic hashing

Static Hashing

If the data is fixed then static hashing is useful. The set of keys is kept fixed and given in advance in static hashing. In static hashing the number of primary pages in the directory are kept fixed.

Dynamic Hashing

If data is not fixed static hashing can give bad performance and dynamic hashing is the alternative for such types of data. The set of keys can change dynamically in this.

21.16 Problems for which Hash Tables are not suitable

- Problems for which data ordering is required.
- Problems having multidimensional data.
- Prefix searching especially if the keys are long and of variable-lengths.
- Problems that have dynamic data
- Problems in which the data does not have unique keys.

CHAPTER

String Algorithms 22

22.1 Introduction

To understand the importance of string algorithms let us consider the case of entering the URL (Uniform Resource Locator) in any browser (say, Internet Explorer, Firefox, or Google Chrome). You will observe that after typing the prefix of the URL, a list of all possible URLs is displayed. That means, the browsers are doing some internal processing and giving us the list of matching URLs. This technique is sometimes called *auto − completion*.

Similarly, consider the case of entering the directory name in command line interface (in both *Windows* and *UNIX*). After typing the prefix of the directory name if we press *tab* button, then we get a list of all matched directory names available. This is another example of auto completion.

In order to support these kind of operations, we need a data structure, which stores the sting data efficiently. In this chapter, we will look at the data structures that are useful for implementing string algorithms.

We start our discussion with the basic problem of strings: given a string, how do we search a substring (pattern)? This is called *string matching* problem. After discussing various string matching algorithms, we will see different data structures for storing strings.

22.2 String Matching Algorithms

In this section, we concentrate on checking whether a pattern P is a substring of another string T (T stands for text) or not. Since we are trying to check a fixed string P, sometimes these algorithms are called *exact string matching* algorithms.

To simplify our discussion let us assume that the length of given text T is n and the length of the pattern P which we are trying to match has the length m. That means, T has the characters from 0 to $n-1$ ($T[0 \dots n-1]$) and P has the characters from 0 to $m-1$ ($P[0 \dots m-1]$). This algorithm is implemented in $C++$ as $strstr()$.

In the subsequent sections, we start with brute force method and gradually move towards better algorithms.

- Brute Force Method
- Robin-Karp String Matching Algorithm
- KMP Algorithm
- Boyce-Moore Algorithm

22.3 Brute Force Method

In this method, for each possible position in the text T we check whether the pattern P matches or not. Since the length of T is n, we have $n-m+1$ possible choices for comparisons. This is because we do not need to check last $m-1$ locations of T as the pattern length is m.

The following algorithm searches for the first occurrence of a pattern string P in a text string T.

Algorithm

```
int BruteForceStringMatch (int T[], int n,  int P[], int m) {
    for (int i  = 0; i <=n - m; i++) {
        int j  = 0;
        while (j < m && P[j] == T[i + j])
            j  = j + 1;
        if(j == m )
            return i;
    }
    return -1;
}
```

Time Complexity: $O((n-m+1) \times m) \approx O(n \times m)$. Space Complexity: O(1).

22.4 Robin-Karp String Matching Algorithm

In this method, we will use the hashing technique and instead of checking for each possible position in T, we check only if the hashing of P and hashing of m characters of T gives the same result.

Initially, apply hash function to first m characters of T and check whether this result and P's hashing result is same or not. If they are not same then go to the next character of T and again apply hash function to m characters (by starting at second character). If they are same then we compare those m characters of T with P.

Selecting Hash Function

At each step, since we are finding the hash of m characters of T, we need an efficient hash function. If the hash function takes $O(m)$ complexity in every step then the total complexity is $O(n \times m)$. This is worse than brute force method because first we are applying the hash function and also comparing.

Our objective is to select a hash function which takes O(1) complexity for finding the hash of m characters of T every time. Then only we can reduce the total complexity of the algorithm.

If the hash function is not good (worst case), then the complexity of Robin-Karp algorithm complexity is $O(n-m+1) \times m) \approx O(n \times m)$. If we select a good hash function then the complexity of Robin-Karp algorithm complexity is $O(m+n)$. Now let us see how to select a hash function which can compute the hash of m characters of T at each step in O(1).

For simplicity, let's assume that the characters used in string T are only integers. That means, all characters in $T \in \{0, 1, 2, \ldots, 9\}$. Since all of them are integers, we can view a string of m consecutive characters as decimal numbers. For example, string "61815" corresponds to the number 61815.

With the above assumption, the pattern P is also a decimal value and let us assume that decimal value of P is p. For the given text $T[0..n-1]$, let $t(i)$ denote the decimal value of length$-m$ substring $T[i..i+m-1]$ for $i = 0,1,\ldots,n-m-1$. So, $t(i) == p$ if and only if $T[i..i+m-1] == P[0..m-1]$.

We can compute p in $O(m)$ time using Horner's Rule as:

$$p = P[m-1] + 10(P[m-2] + 10(P[m-3] + \ldots + 10\,(P[1] + 10\,P[0])\ldots))$$

Code for above assumption is:

```
value = 0;
for (int i = 0; i < m-1; i++) {
   value = value * 10;
   value = value + P[i];
}
```

We can compute all $t(i)$, for $i = 0,1,\ldots,n-m-1$ values in a total of $O(n)$ time. The value of $t(0)$ can be similarly computed from $T[0..m-1]$ in $O(m)$ time. To compute the remaining values $t(0), t(1),\ldots, t(n-m-1)$, understand that $t(i+1)$ can be computed from $t(i)$ in constant time.

$$t(i+1) = 10 * (t(i) - 10^{m-1} * T[i]) + T[i+m-1]$$

For example, if T = "123456" and $m = 3$

$$t(0) = 123$$
$$t(1) = 10 * (123 - 100 * 1) + 4 = 234$$

Step by Step explanation

First : remove the first digit : $123 - 100 * 1 = 23$

Second: Multiply by 10 to shift it : $23 * 10 = 230$

Third: Add last digit : $230 + 4 = 234$

The algorithm runs by comparing, $t(i)$ with p. When $t(i) == p$, then we have found the substring P in T, starting from position i.

22.5 KMP Algorithm

As before, let us assume that T is the string to be searched and P is the pattern to be matched. This algorithm was given by Knuth, Morris and Pratt. It takes $O(n)$ time complexity for searching a pattern.

To get $O(n)$ time complexity, it avoids the comparisons with elements of T that were previously involved in comparison with some element of the pattern P.

The algorithm uses a table and in general we call it as *prefix function* or *prefix table* or *fail function* F. First we will see how to fill this table and later how to search for a pattern using this table. The prefix function, F for a pattern stores the knowledge about how the pattern matches against shifts of itself. This information can be used to avoid useless shifts of the pattern P. It means that, this table can be used for avoiding backtracking on the string T.

Prefix Table

```
int F[]; //assume F is a global array
void Prefix-Table(int P[], int m) {
   int i=1,j=0, F[0]=0;
   while(i<m) {
      if(P[i]==P[j]) {
         F[i]=j+1;
         i++;
         j++;
      }
        else if(j>0)
         j=F[j-1];
      else {
         F[i]=0;
         i++;
      }
```

```
    }
}
```

As an example, assume that $P = a\ b\ a\ b\ a\ c\ a$. For this pattern, les us follow the step-by-step instructions for filling the prefix table F. Initially: $m = length[P] = 7, F[0] = 0$ and $F[1] = 0$.

Step 1: $i = 1, j = 0, \mathrm{F}[1] = 0$

	0	1	2	3	4	5	6
P	a	b	a	b	a	c	a
F	0	0					

Step 2: $i = 2, j = 0, \mathrm{F}[2] = 1$

	0	1	2	3	4	5	6
P	a	b	a	b	a	c	a
F	0	0	1				

Step 3: $i = 3, j = 1, \mathrm{F}[3] = 2$

	0	1	2	3	4	5	6
P	a	b	a	b	a	c	a
F	0	0	1	2			

Step 4: $i = 4, j = 2, \mathrm{F}[4] = 3$

	0	1	2	3	4	5	6
P	a	b	a	b	a	c	a
F	0	0	1	2	3		

Step 5: $i = 5, j = 3, \mathrm{F}[5] = 1$

	0	1	2	3	4	5	6
P	a	b	a	b	a	c	a
F	0	0	1	2	3	0	

Step 6: $i = 6, j = 1, \mathrm{F}[6] = 1$

	0	1	2	3	4	5	6
P	a	b	a	b	a	c	a
F	0	0	1	2	3	0	1

At this step filling of prefix table is complete.

Matching Algorithm

The KMP algorithm takes pattern P, string T and prefix function F as input, finds a match of P in T.

```
int KMP(char T[], int n, int P[], int m) {
    int i=0,j=0;
    Prefix-Table(P,m);
    while(i<n) {
        if(T[i]==P[j]) {
            if(j==m-1)
                return i-j;
            else {
                i++;
                j++;
            }
        }
        else if(j>0)
            j=F[j-1];
        else i++;
    }
    return -1;
}
```

Time Complexity: $O(m + n)$, where m is the length of the pattern and n is the length of the text to be searched. Space Complexity: $O(m)$.

Now, to understand the process let us go through an example. Assume that $T = b\,a\,c\,b\,a\,b\,a\,b\,a\,b\,a\,c\,a\,c\,a$ & $P = a\,b\,a\,b\,a\,c\,a$. Since we have already filled the prefix table, let us use it and go to the matching algorithm. Initially: $n = size\ of\ T = 15$; $m = size\ of\ P = 7$.

Step 1: $i = 0$, $j = 0$, comparing $P[0]$ with $T[0]$. $P[0]$ does not match with $T[0]$. P will be shifted one position to the right.

T	b	a	c	b	a	b	a	b	a	b	a	c	a	c	a
P	a	b	a	b	a	c	a								

Step 2: $i = 1$, $j = 0$, comparing $P[0]$ with $T[1]$. $P[0]$ matches with $T[1]$. Since there is a match, P is not shifted.

T	b	a	c	b	a	b	a	b	a	b	a	c	a	c	a
P		a	b	a	b	a	c	a							

Step 3: $i = 2$, $j = 1$, comparing $P[1]$ with $T[2]$. $P[1]$ does not match with $T[2]$. Backtracking on P, comparing $P[0]$ and $T[2]$.

T	b	a	c	b	a	b	a	b	a	b	a	c	a	c	a
P		a	b	a	b	a	c	a							

Step 4: $i = 3$, $j = 0$, comparing $P[0]$ with $T[3]$. $P[0]$ does not match with $T[3]$.

T	b	a	c	b	a	b	a	b	a	b	a	c	a	c	a
P				a	b	a	b	a	c	a					

Step 5: $i = 4$, $j = 0$, comparing $P[0]$ with $T[4]$. $P[0]$ matches with $T[4]$.

T	b	a	c	b	a	b	a	b	a	b	a	c	a	c	a
P					a	b	a	b	a	c	a				

Step 6: $i = 5$, $j = 1$, comparing $P[1]$ with $T[5]$. $P[1]$ matches with T[5].

T	b	a	c	b	a	b	a	b	a	b	a	c	a	c	a
P					a	b	a	b	a	c	a				

Step 7: $i = 6$, $j = 2$, comparing $P[2]$ with $T[6]$. $P[2]$ matches with $T[6]$.

T	b	a	c	b	a	b	a	b	a	b	a	c	a	c	a
P					a	b	a	b	a	c	a				

Step 8: $i = 7$, $j = 3$, comparing $P[3]$ with $T[7]$. $P[3]$ matches with $T[7]$.

T	b	a	c	b	a	b	a	b	a	b	a	c	a	c	a
P					a	b	a	b	a	c	a				

Step 9: $i = 8$, $j = 4$, comparing $P[4]$ with $T[8]$. $P[4]$ matches with $T[8]$.

T	b	a	c	b	a	b	a	b	a	b	a	c	a	c	a
P					a	b	a	b	a	c	a				

Step 10: $i = 9$, $j = 5$, comparing $P[5]$ with $T[9]$. $P[5]$ does not matches with $T[9]$. Backtracking on P, comparing $P[4]$ with $T[9]$ because after mismatch $j = F[4] = 3$.

T	b	a	c	b	a	b	a	b	a	b	a	c	a	c	a
P					a	b	a	b	a	c	a				

Comparing $P[3]$ with $T[9]$.

T	b	a	c	b	a	b	a	b	a	b	a	c	a	c	a
P							a	b	a	b	a	c	a		

Step 11: $i = 10$, $j = 4$, comparing $P[4]$ with $T[10]$. $P[4]$ matches with $T[10]$.

T	b	a	c	b	a	b	a	b	a	b	a	c	a	c	a
P							a	b	a	b	a	c	a		

Step 12: $i = 11$, $j = 5$, comparing $P[5]$ with $T[11]$. $P[5]$ matches with $T[11]$.

T	b	a	c	b	a	b	a	b	a	b	a	c	a	c	a
P							a	b	a	b	a	c	a		

Step 13: $i = 12$, $j = 6$, comparing $P[6]$ with $T[12]$. $P[6]$ matches with $T[12]$.

T	b	a	c	b	a	b	a	b	a	b	a	c	a	c	a
P							a	b	a	b	a	c	a		

Pattern P has been found to completely occur in string T. The total number of shifts that took place for the match to be found are: $i - m = 13 - 7 = 6$ shifts.

Problems and Questions with Answers

Question 1: Implement strstr() to find a substring in a string.

Answer: Objective of this question is to write C code to implement the strstr (Search for a substring) function without using any system library such as strlen.

The strstr function locates a specified substring within a source string. Strstr returns a pointer to the first occurrence of the substring in the source. If the substring is not found, strstr returns a null pointer.

Of course, you can demonstrate to your interviewer that this problem can be solved using known efficient algorithms such as Rabin-Karp algorithm, KMP algorithm, and the Boyer-Moore algorithm. Since these algorithms are usually studied in advanced algorithms class, for an interview it is sufficient to solve it using the most direct method — The brute force method.

```
char* StrStr(const char *str, const char *destination) {
  if (!*destination) return str;
  char *ptr1 = (char*)str;
  while (*ptr1) {
    char *ptr1Begin = ptr1, *ptr2 = (char*)destination;
    while (*ptr1 && *ptr2 && *ptr1 == *ptr2) {
      ptr1++;
      ptr2++;
    }
    if (!*ptr2)
      return ptr1Begin;
    ptr1 = ptr1Begin + 1;
  }
  return NULL;
}
```

CHAPTER

Algorithms Design Techniques

23

23.1 Introduction

In the previous chapters, we have seen many algorithms for solving different kinds of problems. Before solving a new problem, the general tendency is to look for the similarity of current problem with other problems for which we have solutions. This helps us in getting the solution easily.

In this chapter, we will see different ways of classifying the algorithms and in subsequent chapters we will focus on a few of them (say, Greedy, Divide and Conquer and Dynamic Programming).

23.2 Classification

There are many ways of classifying algorithms and few of them are shown below:

- Implementation Method
- Design Method
- Other Classifications

23.3 Classification by Implementation Method

Recursion or Iteration

A *recursive* algorithm is one that calls itself repeatedly until a base condition is satisfied. It is a common method used in functional programming languages like $C, C++$, etc..

Iterative algorithms use constructs like loops and sometimes other data structures like stacks and queues to solve the problems.

Some problems are suited for recursive and other suited for iterative. For example, *Towers of Hanoi* problem can be easily understood in recursive implementation. Every recursive version has an iterative version, and vice versa.

Procedural or Declarative (Non-Procedural)

In *Declarative* programming languages, we say what we want without having to say how to do it. With *procedural* programming, we have to specify exact steps to get the result. For example, SQL is more declarative than procedural, because the queries don't specify steps to produce the result. Examples for procedural languages include: C, PHP, PERL, etc..

Serial or Parallel or Distributed

In general, while discussing the algorithms we assume that computers execute one instruction at a time. These are called *serial* algorithms.

Parallel algorithms take advantage of computer architectures to process several instructions at a time. They divide the problem into subproblems and serve them to several processors or threads. Iterative algorithms are generally parallelizable.

If the parallel algorithms are distributed on to different machines then we call such algorithms as *distributed* algorithms.

Deterministic or Non-Deterministic

Deterministic algorithms solve the problem with a predefined process whereas *non – deterministic* algorithms guess the best solution at each step through the use of heuristics.

Exact or Approximate

As we have seen, for many problems we are not able to find the optimal solutions. That means, the algorithms for which we are able to find the optimal solutions are called *exact* algorithms. In computer science, if we do not have optimal solution, then we give approximation algorithms.

Approximation algorithms are generally associated with NP-hard problems (refer *Complexity Classes* chapter for more details).

23.4 Classification by Design Method

Another way of classifying algorithms is by their design method.

Greedy Method

Greedy algorithms work in stages. In each stage, a decision is made that is good at that point, without bothering about the future consequences. Generally, this means that some *local best* is chosen. It assumes that local good selection makes the *global* optimal solution.

Divide and Conquer

The D & C strategy solves a problem by:

1) Divide: Breaking the problem into sub problems that are themselves smaller instances of the same type of problem.
2) Recursion: Recursively solving these sub problems.
3) Conquer: Appropriately combining their answers.

Examples: merge sort and binary search algorithms.

Dynamic Programming

Dynamic programming (DP) and memoization work together. The difference between DP and divide and conquer is that incase of the latter there is no dependency among the sub problems, whereas in DP there will be overlap of sub problems. By using memoization [maintaining a table for already solved sub problems], DP reduces the exponential complexity to polynomial complexity (O(n^2), O(n^3), etc.) for many problems.

The difference between dynamic programming and recursion is in memoization of recursive calls. When sub problems are independent and if there is no repetition, memoization does not help, hence dynamic programming is not a solution for all problems.

By using memoization [maintaining a table of sub problems already solved], dynamic programming reduces the complexity from exponential to polynomial.

Linear Programming

In linear programming, there are inequalities in terms of inputs and *maximize* (or *minimize*) some linear function of the inputs. Many problems (example: maximum flow for directed graphs) can be discussed using linear programming.

Reduction [Transform and Conquer]

In this method we solve the difficult problem by transforming it into a known problem for which we have asymptotically optimal algorithms. In this method, the goal is to find a reducing algorithm whose complexity is not dominated by the resulting reduced algorithms. For example, selection algorithm for finding the median in a list involves first sorting the list and then finding out the middle element in the sorted list. These techniques are also called *transform and conquer*.

23.5 Other Classifications

Classification by Research Area

In computer science each field has its own problems and needs efficient algorithms. Examples: search algorithms, sorting algorithms, merge algorithms, numerical algorithms, graph algorithms, string algorithms, geometric algorithms, combinatorial algorithms, machine learning, cryptography, parallel algorithms, data compression algorithms and parsing techniques and more.

Classification by Complexity

In this classification, algorithms are classified by the time they take to find a solution based on their input size. Some algorithms take linear time complexity ($O(n)$) and others may take exponential time, and some never halt. Note that some problems may have multiple algorithms with different complexities.

Randomized Algorithms

Few algorithms make choices randomly. For some problems the fastest solutions must involve randomness. Example: Quick sort.

Branch and Bound Enumeration and Backtracking

These were used in Artificial Intelligence and we do not need to explore these fully. For backtracking method refer *Recusion and Backtracking* chapter.

Note: In the next few chapters we discuss these [greedy, divide and conquer and dynamic programming] design techniques. Importance is given to these techniques as the number of problems solved with these techniques is more as compared to others.

Greedy Algorithms

CHAPTER 24

24.1 Introduction

Let us start our discussion with simple theory which will give us an idea about the greedy technique. In the game of *Chess*, every time we make a decision about a move, we have to think about the future consequences as well. Whereas, in the game of *Tennis* (or *Volley Ball*), our action is based on current situation, which looks right at that moment, without bothering about the future consequences.

This means that in some cases making a decision which looks right at that moment gives the best solution (*Greedy*) and for others it's not. Greedy technique is best suited for the second class of problems.

24.2 Does Greedy Always Work?

Making locally optimal choices does not always work. Hence, greedy algorithms will not always give best solutions. We will see such examples in *Problems* section and in *Dynamic Programming* chapter.

24.3 Advantages and Disadvantages of Greedy Method

The main advantage of greedy method is that it is straightforward, easy to understand and easy to code. In greedy algorithms, once we make a decision, we do not have to spend time in re-examining already computed values.

Its main disadvantage is that for many problems there is no greedy algorithm. That means, in many cases there is no guarantee that making locally optimal improvements in a locally optimal solution gives the optimal global solution.

24.4 Greedy Applications

- Sorting: Selection sort, Topological sort
- Priority Queues: Heap sort
- Huffman coding compression algorithm
- Prim's and Kruskal's algorithms
- Coin change problem
- Fractional Knapsack problem
- Disjoint sets-UNION by size and UNION by height (or rank)
- Job scheduling algorithm
- Greedy techniques can be used as approximation algorithm for complex problems

24.5 Understanding Greedy Technique

For better understanding let us go through an example. For more details, refer the topics of *Greedy* applications.

Huffman Coding Algorithm

Definition

Given a set of n characters from the alphabet A [each character c ∈ A] and their associated frequency *freq(c)*, find a binary code for each character c ∈ A, such that $\sum_{c \in A} \text{freq}(c)|\text{binarycode}(c)|$ is minimum, where $|\text{binarycode}(c)|$ represents the length of binary code of character c. That means sum of lengths of all character codes should be minimum [sum of each characters frequency multiplied by number of bits in the representation].

The basic idea behind Huffman coding algorithm is to use fewer bits for more frequently occurring characters. Huffman coding algorithm compresses the storage of data using variable length codes. We know that each character takes 8 bits for representation. But in general, we do not use all of them. Also, we use some characters more frequently than others.

When reading a file, generally system reads 8 bits at a time to read a single character. But this coding scheme is inefficient. The reason for this is that some characters are more frequently used than other characters. Let's say that the character *'e'* is used 10 times more frequently than the character *'q'*. It would then be advantageous for us to use a 7 bit code for e and a 9 bit code for *q* instead because that could reduce our overall message length.

On average, using Huffman coding on standard files can reduce them anywhere from 10% to 30% depending to the character frequencies. The idea behind the character coding is to give longer binary codes for less frequent characters and groups of characters. Also, the character coding is constructed in such a way that no two character codes are prefixes of each other.

An Example

Let's assume that after scanning a file we found the following character frequencies:

Character	Frequency
a	12
b	2
c	7
d	13
e	14
f	85

In this, create a binary tree for each character that also stores the frequency with which it occurs (as shown below).

b-2 c-7 a-12 d-13 e-14 f-85

The algorithm works as follows: Find the two binary trees in the list that store minimum frequencies at their nodes.

Connect these two nodes at a newly created common node that will store no character but will store the sum of the frequencies of all the nodes connected below it. So our picture looks like follows:

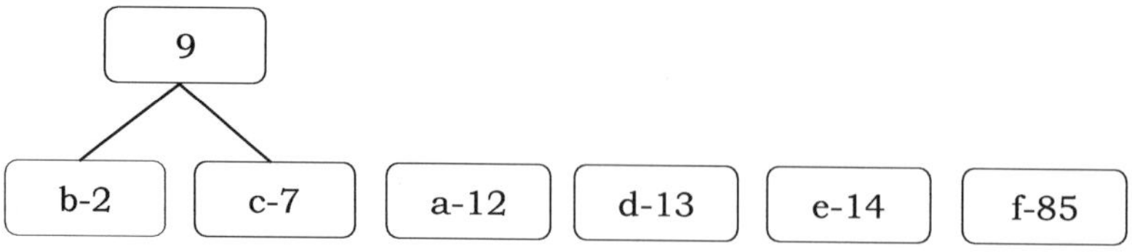

Repeat this process until only one tree is left:

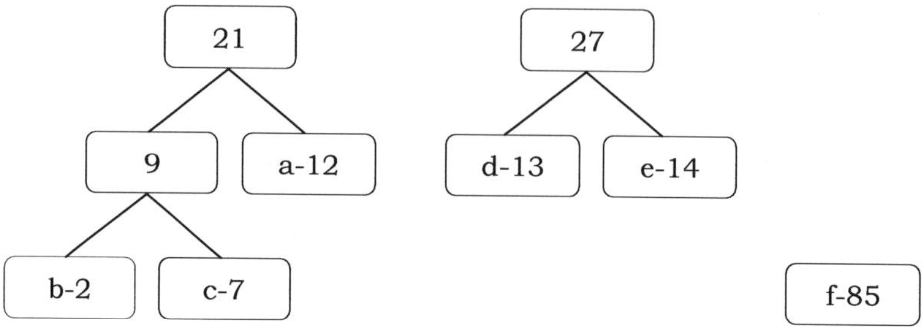

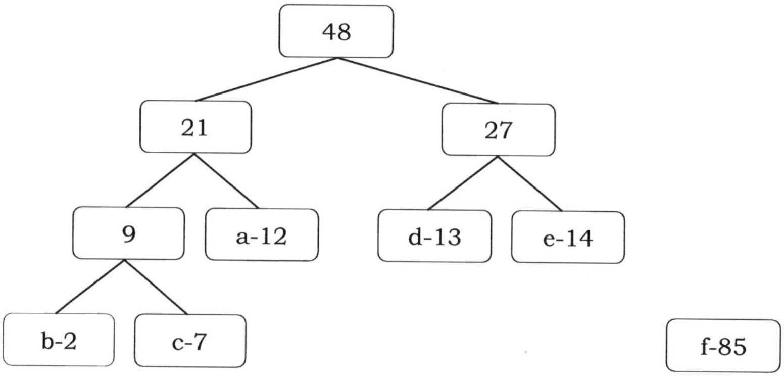

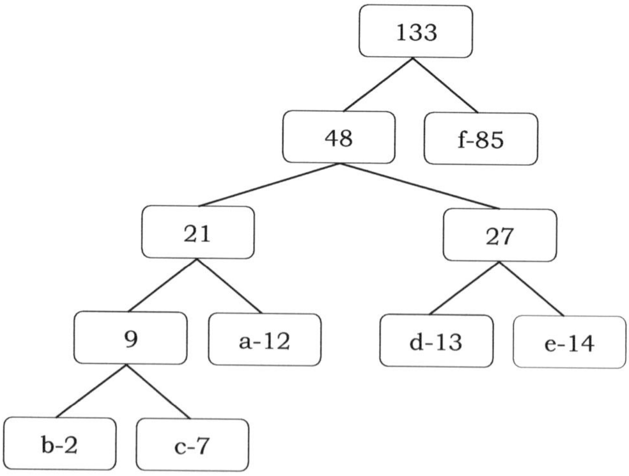

Once the tree is built, each leaf node corresponds to a letter with a code. To determine the code for a particular node, traverse from the root to the leaf node. For each move to the left, append a 0 to the code and for each move right append a 1. As a result for the above generated tree, we get the following codes:

Letter	Code
a	001

b	0000
c	0001
d	010
e	011
f	1

Calculating Bits Saved

Now, let us see how many bits that Huffman coding algorithm is saving. All we need to do for this calculation is see how many bits are originally used to store the data and subtract from that how many bits are used to store the data using the Huffman code.

In the above example, since we have six characters, let's assume each character is stored with a three bit code. Since there are 133 such characters (multiply total frequencies with 3), the total number of bits used is $3 * 133 = 399$. Using the Huffman coding frequencies we can calculate the new total number of bits used:

Letter	Code	Frequency	Total Bits
a	001	12	36
b	0000	2	8
c	0001	7	28
d	010	13	39
e	011	14	42
f	1	85	85
Total			238

Thus, we saved $399 - 238 = 161$ bits, or nearly 40% storage space.

Divide and Conquer Algorithms

CHAPTER 25

25.1 Introduction

In *Greedy* chapter, we have seen that for many problems Greedy strategy failed to provide optimal solutions. Among those problems, there are some that can be easily solved by using *Divide and Conquer* (*D* & *C*) technique. Divide and Conquer is an important algorithm design technique based on recursion.

The *D* & *C* algorithm works by recursively breaking down a problem into two or more sub problems of the same type, until they become simple enough to be solved directly. The solutions to the sub problems are then combined to give a solution to the original problem.

25.2 What is Divide and Conquer Strategy?

The D & C strategy solves a problem by:

1) *Divide*: Breaking the problem into sub problems that are themselves smaller instances of the same type of problem.
2) *Recursion*: Recursively solving these sub problems.
3) *Conquer*: Appropriately combining their answers.

25.3 Does Divide and Conquer Always Work?

It's not possible to solve all the problems with Divide & Conquer technique. As per the definition of D & C the recursion solves the subproblems which are of same type. For all problems it is not possible to find the subproblems which are same size and *D* & *C* is not a choice for all problems.

25.4 Divide and Conquer Visualization

For better understanding, consider the following visualization. Assume that n is the size of original problem. As described above, we can see that the problem is divided into sub problems with each of size n/b (for some constant b). We solve the sub problems recursively and combine their solutions to get the solution for the original problem.

```
DivideAndConquer ( P ) {
   if( small ( P ) )
        // P is very small so that a solution is obvious
        return solution ( n );
        divide the problem P into k sub problems P1, P2, ..., Pk;
        return (
```

```
            Combine (
            DivideAndConquer ( P1 ),
            DivideAndConquer ( P2 ),
            ...
            DivideAndConquer ( Pk )
            )
    );
}
```

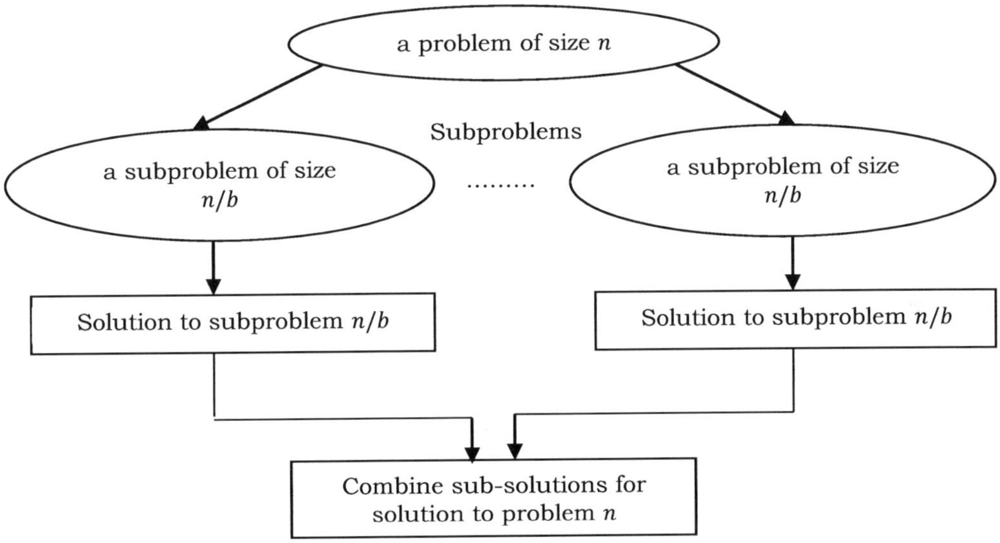

25.5 Understanding Divide and Conquer

For clear understanding of $D \& C$, let us consider a story. There was an old man who was a rich farmer and had seven sons. He was afraid that when he died, his land and his possessions would be divided among his seven sons, and that they would quarrel with one another.

So he gathered them together and showed them seven sticks that he had tied together and told them that anyone who could break the bundle would inherit everything. They all tried, but no one could break the bundle. Then the old man untied the bundle and broke the sticks one by one. The brothers decided that they should stay together and work together and succeed together. The moral for problem solvers is different. If we can't solve the problem, divide it into parts, and solve one part at a time.

In earlier chapters we have already solved many problems based on $D \& C$ strategy: like Binary Search, Merge Sort, Quick Sort, etc.... Refer those topics to get an idea of how $D \& C$ works. Below are few other real-time problems which can easily be solved with $D \& C$ strategy. For all these problems we can find the subproblems which are similar to original problem.

- Looking for a name in a phone book: We have a phone book with names in alphabetical order. Given a name, how do we find whether that name is there in the phone book or not?
- Breaking a stone into dust: We want to convert a stone into dust (very small stones).
- Finding the exit in a hotel: We are at the end of a very long hotel lobby with a long series of doors, with one door next to you. We are looking for the door that leads to the exit.
- Finding our car in a parking lot.

25.6 Advantages of Divide and Conquer

Solving difficult problems: *D & C* is a powerful method for solving difficult problems. As an example, consider Tower of Hanoi problem. This requires breaking the problem into subproblems, solving the trivial cases and combining subproblems to solve the original problem. Dividing the problem into subproblems so that subproblems can be combined again is a major difficulty in designing a new algorithm. For many such problems D & C provides simple solution.

Parallelism: Since *D & C* allows us to solve the subproblems independently, they allow execution in multi-processor machines, especially shared-memory systems where the communication of data between processors does not need to be planned in advance, because different subproblems can be executed on different processors.

Memory access: *D & C* algorithms naturally tend to make efficient use of memory caches. This is because once a subproblem is small, all its subproblems can be solved within the cache, without accessing the slower main memory.

25.7 Disadvantages of Divide and Conquer

One disadvantage of *D & C* approach is that recursion is slow. This is because of the overhead of the repeated subproblem calls. Also, *D & C* approach needs stack for storing the calls (the state at each point in the recursion). Actually this depends upon the implementation style. With large enough recursive base cases, the overhead of recursion can become negligible for many problems.

Another problem with *D & C* is that, for some problems, it may be more complicated than an iterative approach. For example, to add n numbers, a simple loop to add them up in sequence is much easier than a divide-and-conquer approach that breaks the set of numbers into two halves, adds them recursively, and then adds the sums.

25.8 Divide and Conquer Applications

- Binary Search
- Merge Sort and Quick Sort [Best-case]
- Median Finding
- Min and Max Finding
- Matrix Multiplication
- Closest Pair problem

CHAPTER

Dynamic Programming 26

26.1 Introduction

In this chapter we will try to solve the problems for which we failed to get the optimal solutions using other techniques (say, *Divide & Conquer* and *Greedy* methods). Dynamic Programming (DP) is a simple technique but it can be difficult to master. One easy way to identify and solve DP problems is by solving as many problems as possible. The term *Programming* is not related to coding but it is from literature, and means filling tables (similar to *Linear Programming*).

26.2 What is Dynamic Programming Strategy?

Dynamic programming and memoization work together. The main difference between dynamic programming and divide and conquer is that in-case of the latter, sub problems are independent, whereas in DP there can be an overlap of sub problems. By using memoization [maintaining a table of sub problems already solved], dynamic programming reduces the exponential complexity to polynomial complexity ($O(n^2)$, $O(n^3)$, etc.) for many problems. The major components of DP are:

- Recursion: Solves sub problems recursively.
- Memoization: Stores already computed values in table (*Memoization* means caching).

Dynamic Programming = Recursion + Memoization

26.3 Can Dynamic Programming Solve All Problems?

Like Greedy and Divide and Conquer techniques, DP cannot solve every problem. There are problems which cannot be solved by any algorithmic technique [Greedy, Divide and Conquer and Dynamic Programming].

The difference between Dynamic Programming and straightforward recursion is in memoization of recursive calls. If the sub problems are independent and there is no repetition then memoization does not help, so dynamic programming is not a solution for all problems.

26.4 Examples of Dynamic Programming Algorithms

- Many string algorithms including longest common subsequence, longest increasing subsequence, longest common substring, edit distance.
- Algorithms on graphs can be solved efficiently: Bellman-Ford algorithm for finding the shortest distance in a graph, Floyd's All-Pairs shortest path algorithm etc...
- Chain matrix multiplication

- Subset Sum
- 0/1 Knapsack
- Travelling salesman problem and many more

26.5 Understanding Dynamic Programming

Before going to problems, let us understand how DP works through examples.

Fibonacci Series

In Fibonacci series, the current number is the sum of previous two numbers. The Fibonacci series is defined as follows:

$$
\begin{aligned}
Fib(n) &= 0, \quad for\ n = 0 \\
&= 1, for\ n = 1 \\
&= Fib(n-1) + Fib(n-2), for\ n > 1
\end{aligned}
$$

The recursive implementation can be given as:

```
int RecursiveFibonacci(int n) {
    if(n == 0) return 0;
    if(n == 1) return 1;
    return RecursiveFibonacci(n -1) + RecursiveFibonacci(n -2);
}
```

Solving the above recurrence gives,

$$T(n) = T(n-1) + T(n-2) + 1 \approx \left(\frac{1+\sqrt{5}}{2}\right)^n \approx 2^n = O(2^n)$$

Note: For proof, refer *Introduction* chapter.

How does Memoization help?

Calling $fib(5)$ produces a call tree that calls the function on the same value many times:

$$
\begin{gathered}
fib(5) \\
fib(4) + fib(3) \\
(fib(3) + fib(2)) + (fib(2) + fib(1)) \\
((fib(2) + fib(1)) + (fib(1) + fib(0))) + ((fib(1) + fib(0)) + fib(1)) \\
(((fib(1) + fib(0)) + fib(1)) + (fib(1) + fib(0))) + ((fib(1) + fib(0)) + fib(1))
\end{gathered}
$$

In the above example, $fib(2)$ was calculated three times (overlapping of subproblems). If n is big then many more values of fib (sub problems) are recalculated, which leads to an exponential time algorithm. Instead of solving the same sub problems again and again we can store the previous calculated values and reduce the complexity.

Memorization works like this: Start with a recursive function and add a table that maps the functions parameter values to the results computed by the function. Then if this function is called twice with the same parameters, we simply look up the answer in the table.

Improving: Now, we see how DP reduces this problem complexity from exponential to polynomial. As discussed earlier, there are two ways of doing this. One approach is bottom-up: these methods starts with lower values of input and keep building the solutions for higher values.

```
int fib[n];
int fib(int n) {
    // Check for base cases
    if(n == 0 || n == 1) return 1;
    fib[0] = 1;
    fib[1] = 1;
```

```
    for (int i = 2; i < n; i++)
        fib[i] = fib[i - 1] + fib[i - 2];
    return fib[n - 1];
}
```

Other approach is top-down. In this method, we preserve the recursive calls and use the values if they are already computed. The implementation for this is given as:

```
int fib[n];
int fibonacci( int n ) {
    if(n == 1) return 1;
    if(n == 2) return 1;
    if( fib[n] != 0) return fib[n] ;
    return fib[n] = fibonacci(n-1) + fibonacci(n -2) ;
}
```

Note: For all problems, it may not be possible to find both top-down and bottom-up programming solutions.

Both the versions of Fibonacci series implementations clearly reduce the problem complexity to $O(n)$. This is because if a value is already computed then we are not calling the subproblems again. Instead, we are directly taking its value from table.

Time Complexity: $O(n)$. Space Complexity: $O(n)$, for table.

Further Improving: One more observation from the Fibonacci series is: The current value is the sum of previous two calculations only. This indicates that we don't have to store all the previous values. Instead if we store just the last two values, we can calculate the current value. Implementation for this is given below:

```
int fibonacci(int n) {
    int a = 0, b = 1, sum, i;
    for (i=0;i < n;i++) {
        sum = a + b;
        a = b;
        b = sum;
    }
    return sum;
}
```

Time Complexity: $O(n)$. Space Complexity: $O(1)$.

Note: This method may not be applicable (available) for all problems.

Observations

While solving the problems using DP, try to figure out the following:

- See how problems are defined in terms of subproblems recursively.
- See if we can use some table [memoization] to avoid the repeated calculations.

Factorial of a Number

As another example consider the factorial problem: $n!$ is the product of all integers between n and 1. Definition of recursive factorial can be given as:

$$n! = n * (n-1)!$$
$$1! = 1$$
$$0! = 1$$

This definition can easily be converted to implementation. Here the problem is finding the value of $n!$, and sub problem is finding the value of $(n-l)!$. In the recursive case, when n is greater than 1, function calls itself to find the value of $(n - l)!$ and multiplies that with n. In the base case, when n is 0 or 1, the function simply returns 1.

```
int fact(int n) {
    if(n == 1) return 1;
    else if(n == 0) return 1;
    else      // recursive case: multiply n by (n -1) factorial
        return n *fact(n -1);
}
```

The recurrence for the above implementation can be given as: $T(n) = n \times T(n - 1) \approx O(n)$

Time Complexity: $O(n)$. Space Complexity: $O(n)$, recursive calls need a stack of size n.

In the above recurrence relation and implementation, for any n value, there are no repetitive calculations (*no* overlapping of sub problems) and the factorial function is not getting any benefits with dynamic programming. Now, let us say we want to compute a series of $m!$ for some arbitrary value m. Using the above algorithm, for each such call we can compute it in $O(m)$. For example, to find both $n!$ and $m!$ we can use the above approach, wherein the total complexity for finding $n!$ and $m!$ is $O(m + n)$.

Time Complexity: $O(n + m)$.
Space Complexity: $O(\max(m, n))$, recursive calls need a stack of size equal to the maximum of m and n.

Improving: Now let us see how DP reduces the complexity. From the above recursive definition it can be seen that $fact(n)$ is calculated from $fact(n\ \text{-}1)$ and n and nothing else. Instead of calling $fact(n)$ every time, we can store the previous calculated values in a table and use these values to calculate a new value. This implementation can be given as:

```
int facto[n];
int fact(int n) {
    if(n == 1) return 1;
    else if(n == 0) return 1;
    //Already calculated case
    else if(facto[n]!=0) return facto[n];
    else      // recursive case: multiply n by (n -1) factorial
    return facto[n]= n *fact(n -1);
}
```

For simplicity, let us assume that we have already calculated $n!$ and want to find $m!$. For finding $m!$, we just need to see the table and use the existing entries if they are already computed. If $m < n$ then we do not have to recalculate $m!$. If $m > n$ then we can use $n!$ and call the factorial on remaining numbers only.

The above implementation clearly reduces the complexity to $O(max(m, n))$. This is because if the $fact$(n) is already there then we are not recalculating the value again. If we fill these newly computed values then the subsequent calls further reduces the complexity.

Longest Common Subsequence

Given two strings: string X of length m $[X(1..m)]$, and string Y of length n $[Y(1..n)]$, find longest common subsequence: the longest sequence of characters that appear left-to-right (but not necessarily in a contiguous block) in both strings. For example, if X = "ABCBDAB" and Y = "BDCABA", the LCS(X, Y) = {"BCBA", "BDAB", "BCAB"}. As we can see there are several optimal solutions.

Brute Force Approach: One simple idea is to check every subsequence of $X[1..m]$ (m is the length of sequence X) to see if it is also a subsequence of $Y[1..n]$ (n is the length of sequence Y). Checking takes O(n) time, and there are 2^m subsequences of X. The running time thus is exponential $O(n.2^m)$ and is not good for large sequences.

Recursive Solution: Before going to DP solution, let us form the recursive solution for this and later we can add memoization to reduce the complexity. Let's start with some simple observations about the LCS problem. If we have two strings, say "ABCBDAB" and "BDCABA", if we draw lines from the letters in the first string to the corresponding letters in the second, no two lines cross:

```
A  B    C    B D A B
   |    |    |     |
   B D  C A  B     A
```

From the above observation, we can see that current characters of X and Y may or may not match. That means, suppose that the two first characters differ. Then it is not possible for both of them to be part of a common subsequence - one or the other (or maybe both) will have to be removed. Finally, observe that once we have decided what to do with the first characters of the strings, the remaining sub problem is again a LCS problem, on two shorter strings. Therefore we can solve it recursively.

Solution to LCS should find two sequences in X and Y and let us say the starting index of sequence in X is i and starting index of sequence in T is j. Also, assume that $X[i \dots m]$ is a substring of X starting at character i and going until the end of X and $Y[j \dots n]$ is a substring of Y starting at character j and going until the end of Y.

Based on the above discussion, here we get the possibilities as described below:

1) If $X[i] == Y[j]$: $1 + LCS(i+1, j+1)$
2) If $X[i] \neq Y[j]$: $LCS(i, j+1)$ // skipping j^{th} character of Y
3) If $X[i] \neq Y[j]$: $LCS(i+1, j)$ // skipping i^{th} character of X

In the first case, if $X[i]$ is equal to $Y[j]$, we get a matching pair and can count it towards the total length of the LCS. Otherwise, we need to skip either i^{th} character of X or j^{th} character of Y and find the longest common subsequence. Now, $LCS(i, j)$ can be defined as:

$$LCS(i,j) = \begin{cases} 0, & \text{if } i = m \text{ or } j = n \\ Max\{LCS(i, j+1), LCS(i+1, j)\}, & \text{if } X[i] \neq Y[j] \\ 1 + LCS[i+1, j+1], & \text{if } X[i] == Y[j] \end{cases}$$

LCS has many applications. In web searching, if we find the smallest number of changes that are needed to change one word into another. A *change* here is an insertion, deletion or replacement of a single character.

```
//Initial Call: LCSLength(X, 0, m-1, Y, 0, n-1);
int LCSLength( int X[], int i, int m, int Y[], int j, int n) {
    if (i == m || j == n)
        return 0;
    else if (X[i] == Y[j]) return 1 + LCSLength(X, i+1, m, Y, j+1, n);
    else return max( LCSLength(X, i+1, m, Y, j, n),  LCSLength(X, i, m, Y, j+1, n));
}
```

This is a correct solution but it is very time consuming. For example, if the two strings have no matching characters, so the last line always gets executed which give (if $m == n$) are close to $O(2^n)$.

DP Solution: Adding Memoization: The problem with the recursive solution is that the same subproblems get called many different times. A subproblem consists of a call to LCSLength, with the arguments being two suffixes of X and Y, so there are exactly $(i +$

1)($j+1$) possible subproblems (a relatively small number). If there are nearly 2^n recursive calls, some of these subproblems must be being solved over and over.

The DP solution is to check whenever we want to solve a sub problem, whether we've already done it before. So we look up the solution instead of solving it again. Implemented in the most direct way, we just add some code to our recursive solution. To do this, look up the code. This can be given as:

```
int LCS[1024][1024];
int LCSLength( int X[], int m, int Y[], int n) {
    for( int i = 0; i <= m; i++ )
        LCS[i][n] = 0;
    for( int j = 0; j <= n; j++ )
        LCS[m][j] = 0;
    for( int i = m - 1; i >= 0; i) {
        for( int j = n - 1; j >= 0; j) {
            LCS[i][j] = LCS[i + 1][j + 1]; // matching X[i] to Y[j]

            if( X[i] == Y[j] )
                LCS[i][j]++; // we get a matching pair
            // the other two cases - inserting a gap
            if(LCS[i][j + 1] > LCS[i][j] )
                LCS[i][j] = LCS[i][j + 1];
            if(LCS[i + 1][j] > LCS[i][j] )
                LCS[i][j] = LCS[i + 1][j];
        }
    }
    return LCS[0][0];
}
```

First, take care of the base cases. We have created LCS table with one row and one column larger than the lengths of the two strings. Then run the iterative DP loops to fill each cell in the table. This is like doing recursion backwards, or bottom up.

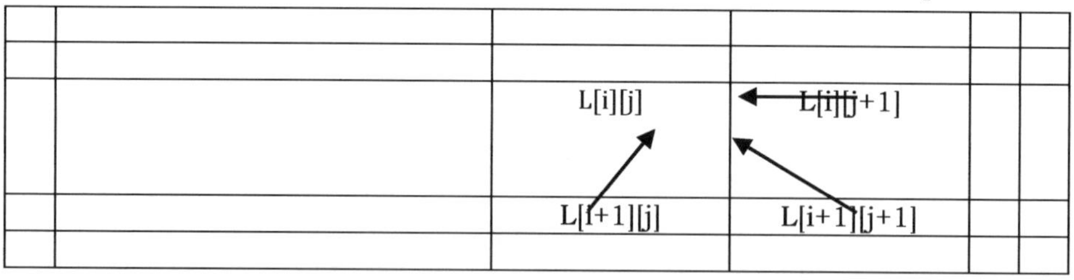

The value of $LCS[i][j]$ depends on 3 other values ($LCS[i+1][j+1]$, $LCS[i][j+1]$ and $LCS[i+1][j]$), all of which have larger values of i or j. They go through the table in the order of decreasing i and j values. This will guarantee that when we need to fill in the value of $LCS[i][j]$, we already know the values of all of the cells on which it depends.

Time Complexity: O(mn), since i takes values from 1 to m and and j takes values from 1 to n.
Space Complexity: O(mn).

Note: In the above discussion, we have assumed $LCS(i,j)$ is the length of the LCS with $X[i \dots m]$ and $Y[j \dots n]$. We can solve the problem by changing the definition as $LCS(i,j)$ is the length of the LCS with $X[1 \dots i]$ and $Y[1 \dots j]$.

Printing the subsequence: Above algorithm can find the length of the longest common subsequence but cannot give the actual longest subsequence. To get the sequence, we trace it through the table. Start at cell $(0,0)$. We know that the value of $LCS[0][0]$ was the maximum of 3 values of the neighboring cells. So we simply recompute $LCS[0][0]$ and note which cell gave the maximum value. Then we move to that cell (it will be one of $(1,1)$, $(0,1)$ or $(1,0)$) and repeat this until we hit the boundary of the table. Every time we pass through a cell (i,j) where $X[i] == Y[j]$, we have a matching pair and print $X[i]$. At the end, we will have printed the longest common subsequence in $O(mn)$ time.

An alternative way of getting path is to keep a separate table, for each cell. This will tell us which direction we came from when computing the value of that cell. At the end, we again start at cell $(0,0)$ and follow these directions until the opposite corner of the table.

From the above examples, I hope you understood the idea behind DP. Now let us see more problems which can be easily solved using DP technique.

Note: As we have seen above, in DP the main component is recursion. If we know the recurrence then converting that to code is a minimal task. For the problems below, we concentrate on getting recurrence.

CHAPTER

Basics of Design Patterns

27

A design pattern is a *defined*, *used* and *tested* solution for a known problem. Design patterns got popularity after the evolution of object oriented programming. Object oriented programming and design patterns became inseparable. In software engineering, a *design pattern* is a general reusable solution to a commonly occurring problem within a given context in software design. A design pattern is *not* a finished design that can be transformed directly into code. It is a *description* for how to solve a problem that can be used in many different situations.

27.1 Brief History Of Design Patterns

Patterns originated as an *architectural* concept by *Christopher Alexander* who is a *civil* engineer. In 1987, Kent Beck and Ward Cunningham began experimenting with the idea of applying patterns to *programming* and presented their results at a conference that year. In the following years, Beck, Cunningham and others followed up on this work.

Design patterns gained popularity in computer science after the *book* Design Patterns: Elements of Reusable Object-Oriented Software was published in 1994 by the so-called *Gang of Four* (*GoF*).

27.2 Why Design Patterns?

Design patterns can speed up the development process by providing tested, proven development paradigms. Good software design requires considering issues that may not become visible until later in the implementation. Reusing design patterns helps to prevent issues that can cause major problems, and it also improves code readability.

- Experienced designers reuse solutions that have worked in the past.
- Knowledge of the patterns that have worked in the past allows a designer to be more productive and the resulting designs to be more flexible and reusable.

27.3 Categories Of Design Patterns

There are many types of design patterns. Lot of research is going to codify design patterns in particular domains, including use of existing design patterns as well as domain specific design patterns. Examples include:

- User interface design patterns
- Secure usability patterns
- Web design patterns
- Business model design patterns
- Information visualization design patterns
- Secure design patterns

This chapter deals with fundamental design patterns given by *GoF*. *GoF* gave 23 design patterns and they were categorized into to *three* types as given below.

- Creational design patterns
- Structural design patterns
- Behavioral design patterns

Creational patterns: Creational design patterns are used to instantiate objects. Instead of instantiating objects directly, depending on scenario either *X* or *Y* object can be instantiated. This will give flexibility for instantiation in high complex business logic situations.

Creational design patterns (based on *GoF*):

- Abstract Factory Design Pattern
- Builder Design Pattern
- Factory Method Design Pattern
- Prototype Design Pattern
- Singleton Design Pattern

Structural patterns: Structural design patterns are used to organize our program into groups. This segregation will provide us clarity and gives us easier maintainability.

Structural design patterns (based on *GoF*):

- Adapter Design Pattern
- Bridge Design Pattern
- Composite Design Pattern
- Decorator Design Pattern
- Facade Design Pattern
- Flyweight Design Pattern
- Proxy Design Pattern

Behavioral patterns: Behavioral design patterns are used to define the communication and control flow between objects. Most of these design patterns are specifically concerned with communication between objects.

Behavioral design patterns (based on *GoF*):

- Chain of Responsibility Design Pattern
- Command Design Pattern
- Interpreter Design Pattern
- Iterator Design Pattern
- Mediator Design Pattern
- Memento Design Pattern
- Observer Design Pattern
- Strategy Design Pattern
- State Design Pattern
- Template Method Design Pattern
- Visitor Design Pattern

27.4 What To Observe For A Design Pattern?

For each of the design pattern understand the following:

- What is the name of the pattern?
- What is the type of the pattern? Whether it is a Structural, Creational or Behavioral pattern.
- What is the goal (also called *intent*) of the pattern?
- What are the other names for the pattern?
- When to use the pattern?
- What are the examples for the pattern?

- What is the UML diagram (also called *Structure*) for the pattern? A graphical representation of the pattern. Class diagrams and Interaction diagrams are used for this purpose.
- Who are the participants in the pattern? A listing of the classes and objects used in the pattern and their roles in the design.
- How classes and objects used in the pattern interact with each other.
- A description of the results, side effects, and tradeoffs (Consequences) caused by using the pattern.
- How to Implement the pattern?
- What are the related Patterns? Other patterns that have some relationship with the pattern; discussion of the differences between the pattern and similar patterns.

27.5 Using Patterns To Gain Experience

An important step in designing object-oriented system is discovering the objects. There are various techniques that help discovering the objects (for example, use cases and collaboration diagrams). Discovering the objects is the difficult step for inexperienced designers.

Lack of experience can lead to too many objects with too many interactions and therefore dependencies and that creates a system which is hard to maintain and impossible to reuse. This spoils the goal of object-oriented design.

Design patterns help overcome this problem because they teach the lessons distilled from experience by experts: patterns document expertise.

Also, patterns not only describe how software is structured, but also tell how classes and objects interact, especially at run time. Taking these interactions and their into account leads to more flexible and reusable software.

27.6 Can We Use Design Patterns Always?

Using design patterns properly gives reusable code, the consequences generally include some costs as well as benefits. Reusability is often obtained by introducing encapsulation, or indirection, which can decrease performance and increase complexity.

We should *not* try to *force* the code into a specific pattern, rather notice which patterns start to crystalize out of your code and help them along a bit. That means, writing a program that does *X* using pattern *Y* is *not* a *good idea*. It might work for hello world class programs (small programs) fit for demonstrating the code constructs for patterns, but not much more.

The main concern is that people often have a tendency to wrong design patterns. After learning a few, see the usefulness of them, and without realizing it turn those few patterns into a kind of golden hammer which they then apply to everything.

The key isn't necessarily to learn the patterns themselves. The key is to learn to identify the scenarios and problems which the patterns are meant to address. Then applying the pattern is simply a matter of using the right tool for the job. It's the job that must be identified and understood before the tool can be chosen.

The question is when did you start doing everything using patterns? Not all solutions fit neatly into an existing design pattern and adopting a pattern may mean that you muddy the cleanness of your solution. You may find that rather than the design pattern solving your problem you generate a further problem by trying to force your solution to fit a design pattern.

We should not overuse the patterns in projects where they are really not necessary. The key is *try* to keep the code clean, modular and readable and make sure the classes aren't tightly coupled.

27.7 Design Patterns vs. Frameworks

Software frameworks can be confused with design patterns. They are closely related.

Design Patterns	Frameworks
Design patterns are recurring solutions to problems that arise during the life of an application in a particular context.	A framework is a group of components that cooperate with each other to provide a reusable architecture for applications with a given domain.
The primary goal is to help improve the quality of the software in terms of the software being reusable, maintainable, extensible, etc...	The primary goal is to help improve the quality of the software in terms of the software being reusable, maintainable, extensible, etc...
Patterns are logical in nature.	Frameworks are more physical in nature, as they exist in the form of some software.
Pattern descriptions are independent of programming language.	Since frameworks exist in the form of some software, they dependent of programming language.
Patterns are more generic in nature and can be used in any kind of application.	Frameworks provide domain-specific functionality.
Patterns provide a way to do *good* design and are used to help design frameworks.	Design patterns may be used in the design and implementation of a framework.

27.8 Creational Design Patterns

This design category is all about the class instantiation. Creational design deal with object creation methods. These design patterns tries to create objects in a manner suitable to the situation. If we do not follow creational patterns, the basic form of object creation may create design problems and adds complexity to the design. Creational design patterns solve this problem by controlling this object creation.

27.8.1 Categories Of Creational Design Patterns

Creational design patterns are sub-categorized into:

- *Object-Creational* patterns: Deals with Object creation and defer part of its object creation to another object. These patterns use delegation to get the job done.
- *Class-Creational* patterns: Deals with Class-instantiation and defer its object creation to subclasses. These patterns use inheritance effectively in the instantiation process.

Creational design patterns (5 Design Patterns):

- *Abstract Factory* pattern: Provides an interface for creating related or dependent objects without specifying the objects' concrete classes.
- *Builder* pattern: It separates the construction of a complex object from its representation so that the same construction process can create different representation.
- *Factory Method* pattern: Allows a class to defer instantiation to subclasses.
- *Prototype* pattern: Specifies the kind of object to create using a prototypical instance, and creates new objects by cloning this prototype.
- *Singleton* pattern: Ensures that a class only has one instance, and provides a global point of access to it.

Object-Creational patterns	Class-Creational patterns
Abstract Factory Builder Prototype Singleton	Factory Method

27.9 Singleton Design Pattern

Singleton pattern is the most commonly used design pattern. This is one of favorite interview questions and has lots of interesting follow-up to dig into details. This not only check the knowledge of design pattern but also check coding, multithreading concepts which are very important while working for a real life application.

The singleton design pattern is used when only one instance of an object is needed throughout the lifetime of an application. The singleton class is instantiated at the time of first access and the same instance is used thereafter till the application quits.

There are only two points in the definition of a singleton design pattern,

- There should be only one instance allowed for a class and
- We should allow global point of access to that single instance.

In singleton pattern, trickier part is implementation and management of that single instance.

Strategy for Singleton instance creation: We suppress the constructor (by making it *private*) and *don't* allow even a single instance for the class. But we *declare* an *attribute* for that *same* class inside, create instance for that and return it.

27.9.1 UML Diagram For Singleton Design Pattern

UML diagram for the same is given below. This implementation provides global access to the object through static method *getInstance*.

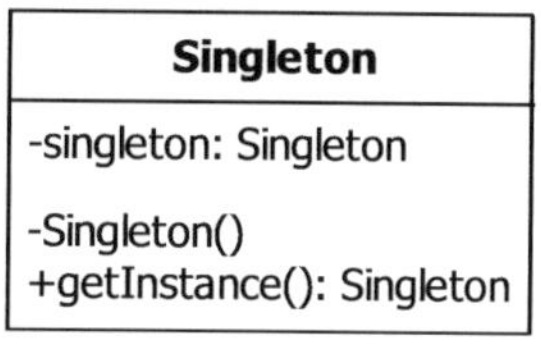

27.9.2 Singleton Design Pattern Implementation

```
public class Singleton {
    private static Singleton instance;
    private Singleton() { }
    public static Singleton getInstance() {
        if (instance == null) {
            instance = new Singleton();
        }
        return instance;
    }
}
```

The singleton implemented above is easy to understand. The Singleton class maintains a *static* reference to the lone singleton *instance* and returns that reference from the static *getInstance*() method. There are several interesting points concerning the *Singleton* class. First, *Singleton* employs a technique known as *lazy instantiation* to create the singleton. As a result, the singleton instance is not created until the *getInstance*() method is called for the first time. This technique ensures that singleton instances are created only when needed.

We need to be careful with multiple threads. In a single-threaded environment, this works fine. If we don't synchronize the method which is going to return the instance, there is a possibility of allowing multiple instances in a multi-threaded scenario.

If two threads (say, *Thread* 1 and *Thread* 2) call *getInstance*() at the same time, two Singleton instances can be created if *Thread* 1 is preempted just after it enters the *if* block and control is subsequently given to *Thread* 2. Making the classic *Singleton* implementation thread safe is easy. Just *synchronize* the *getInstance*() method.

```
public class Singleton {
   private static Singleton instance;
   private Singleton() { }
   public synchronized static Singleton getInstance() {
      if (instance == null) {
         instance = new Singleton();
      }
      return instance;
   }
}
```

The problem with this solution is that it may be expensive. Each access to the *Singleton* requires acquisition of a lock, but in reality, we need a lock only when initializing *instance*. That should occur only the first time instance is called. If *instance* is called *n* times during the course of a program run, we need the lock only for the first call. To solve this problem, instead of synchronizing the entire method, the below code only synchronizes the *critical* code.

```
public class Singleton {
   private static Singleton instance;
   private Singleton() { }
   public static Singleton getInstance() {
      if (instance == null) {
         synchronized(Singleton.class) {
            instance = new Singleton();
         }
      }
      return instance;
   }
}
```

27.9.3 Double-Checked Locking

However, the above code is not thread-safe. Consider the following scenario: *Thread* 1 enters the synchronized block, and, before it can assign the singleton member variable, the thread is preempted. Subsequently, another thread can enter the if block. The second thread will wait for the first thread to finish, but we will still wind up with two distinct singleton instances.

To solve this problem, we generally go for *double-checked locking* mechanism. Double-checked locking is a technique that, at first glance, appears to make *lazy* instantiation thread-safe. What happens if two threads simultaneously access *getInstance*()? Assume *Thread* 1 enters the synchronized block and is preempted. Subsequently, a second thread enters the *if* block.

When *Thread* 1 exits the synchronized block, *Thread* 2 makes a second check to see if the singleton instance is still null. Since *Thread* 1 set the singleton member variable, *Thread* 2's second check will fail, and a second singleton will not be created.

```
public class Singleton {
   private static Singleton instance;
   private Singleton() { }
   public synchronized static Singleton getInstance() {
      if (instance == null) {
         synchronized(Singleton.class) {
               if (instance == null) {
            instance = new Singleton();
```

```
                }
            }
        }
        return instance;
    }
}
```

27.9.4 Early and Lazy Instantiation In Singleton Pattern

The above example code is a sample for *lazy* instantiation for singleton design pattern. The single instance will be created at the time of first call of the *getInstance*() method. We can also implement the same singleton design pattern in a simpler way but that would instantiate the single instance early at the time of loading the class (*early* instantiation). Following example code describes how we can instantiate early. It also takes care of the multithreading scenario.

```
public class Singleton {
    private static Singleton instance = new Singleton();
    private Singleton() {}
    public static Singleton getInstance() {
        return instance;
    }
}
```

Question: Given a large program how can we find Singletons in it?

Answer: In a large, complex program it may not be simple to discover where in the code a Singleton has been instantiated. Remember that in Java, global variables do not really exist, so we can't save these Singletons in a single place.

One solution is to create such singletons at the beginning of the program and pass them as arguments to the major classes that might need to use them.

```
instance = Singleton.getInstance();
Processor p = new Processor(instance);    //some class which uses Singleton
instance
```

Question: Are there any other consequences of the Singleton Pattern?

Answer:

- It can be difficult to subclass a Singleton, since this works only if the base Singleton class has not yet been instantiated.
- We can easily change a Singleton to allow a small number of instances where this is allowable and meaningful.

Question: Given an online book store, can you think of classes where we can use Singleton?

Answer: The following code fragment shows a Catalog class which could be part of an online book store. It collaborates with a servlet, which shows the customer the entire catalog. Every shop can only have one catalogue it makes sense to design the catalogue class as Singleton. Doing it this way it is more save because the Singleton guarantees that every client sees the same catalogue.

```
public class Catalog {
    private static Singleton catalog = null;
    private ArrayList catalogList;
    private Catalog() { }
    public static Catalog getInstance() {
        if (catalog == null) {
         catalog = new Catalog();
        }
        return catalog;
```

```
    }
    ....
}
```

This example shows a possible design for a Singleton class in Java. The static variable catalog holds the single existing object of the class. To get it another class cannot access the constructor as it is set to private. It must call the public method *getInstance*() which returns the object. Inside *getInstance*() it is first checked if the variable catalog was already instantiated and has a reference; if not the constructor is called – which may only happen once.

27.10 Structural Design Patterns

Structural Patterns describe how objects and classes can be combined to form larger structures. In software engineering, structural design patterns are design patterns that help the design by identifying a simple way to realize relationships between entities.

Structural design patterns are used to organize our program into groups. This segregation will provide us clarity and gives us easier maintainability. Structural design patterns are used for structuring code and objects.

27.10.1 Categories Of Structural Design Patterns

Structural design patterns are used to organize our program into groups. This segregation will provide us clarity and gives us easier maintainability. Structural design patterns are sub-categorized into:

- Object-Structural patterns: Deals with how objects can be associated and composed to form larger, more complex structures.
- Class-Structural patterns: Deals with abstraction using inheritance and describe how it can be used to provide more useful program interface.

Structural design patterns (7 Design Patterns):

- *Adapter* pattern: Allows us to provide a new interface for a class that already exists, allowing reuse of a class where our client requires a different interface.
- *Bridge* pattern: Allows us to decouple a class from its interface. This allows the class and its interface to be changed independently over time which can lead to more reuse and less future shock. It also allows us to dynamically switch between implementations at runtime allowing more runtime flexibility.
- *Composite* pattern: It allows the client to deal with complex and flexible tree structures. The trees can be built from various types of containers or leaf nodes, and its depth or composition can be adjusted or determined at runtime.
- *Decorator* pattern: Allows us to dynamically modify an object at runtime by attaching new behaviors, or by modifying existing ones.
- *Facade* pattern: This pattern allows us to simplify the client by creating a simplified interface for a subsystem.
- *Flyweight* pattern: This pattern optimizes memory use when we need a design a class with which our client will need to create huge number runtime of objects.
- *Proxy* pattern: This pattern provides a surrogate object that controls access to some other object. The aim of this pattern is to simplify the client when it needs to use an object that has complications.

Object-Structural patterns	Class-Structural patterns
Bridge Composite Decorator Facade Flyweight Object Adapter Proxy	Class Adapter

27.11 Behavioral Design Patterns

Behavioral patterns are those patterns which are specifically concerned with communication (interaction) between the objects. The interactions between the objects should be such that they are talking to each other and still are loosely coupled.

Tight coupling occurs when a group of classes are highly dependent on one another. In object oriented design, the amount of coupling refers to how much the design of one class depends on the design of another class. In other words, how often do changes in one class force related changes in other classes class?

Loose coupling is the key for architectures. In behavioral patterns, the implementations and the client which uses them should be loosely coupled in order to avoid hard-coding and dependencies. Behavioral design patterns deals with relationships among communications using different objects. They find common communication patterns and provide a well-known solution to implement this communication giving more flexibility.

27.11.1 Categories Of Behavioral Design Patterns

Behavioral patterns describe not just patterns of objects or classes but also the patterns of communication between them. Behavioral patterns are used to avoid hard-coding and dependencies. Behavioral design patterns are sub-categorized into:

- Object-Behavioral patterns: Behavioral object patterns use object composition rather than inheritance. Describes how a group of objects collaborate to perform some task that no single object can perform alone.
- Class-Behavioral patterns: Behavioral class patterns uses *inheritance* rather than inheritance to describe algorithms and flow of control.

Behavioral design patterns (11 Design Patterns):

- *Chain* of *Responsibility* Pattern (CoR): A way of passing a request between a chain of objects.
- *Command* Pattern: The *Command* pattern is used when there is a need to issue requests to objects without knowing anything about the operation being requested or the receiver of the request.
- *Interpreter* Pattern: *Interpreter* provides way to include language elements in a program. Interpreter pattern is a design pattern that specifies how to evaluate sentences in a language.
- *Iterator* Pattern: Iterators are used to access elements of an aggregate (collection) object sequentially without exposing its underlying representation.
- *Mediator* Pattern: Defines simplified communication between classes.
- *Momento* Pattern: Capture and restore an object's internal state.
- *Observer* Pattern: A way of notifying change to a number of classes.
- *State* Pattern: Changes an object's behavior when its state changes.
- *Strategy* Pattern: Encapsulates an algorithm inside a class.
- *Template Method* Pattern: Defer the exact steps of an algorithm to a subclass.
- *Visitor* Pattern: Defines a new operation to a class without change.

Object-Behavioral Patterns	Class-Behavioral Patterns
Chain of Responsibility Command Iterator Mediator Memento Observer State Strategy Visitor	Interpreter Template Method

CHAPTER

Non-Technical Help

28

28.1 Tips

- Arrive 5-10 minutes before the interview. Never arrive too late or too early. If you are running late due to some unavoidable situation, call ahead and make sure that the interviewers know your situation. Also, be apologetic for arriving late due to unfortunate situation.
- *First impressions* are everything: Firm handshake, maintain eye contact, smile, watch your body language, be pleasant, dress neatly and know the names of your interviewers and thank them by their names for the opportunity.
- Try, *not* to show that you are *nervous*. Everybody is nervous for interviews but try not to show it. [Hint: Just think that even if you do not get the job, it is a good learning experience and you would do better in your next interview and appreciate yourself for getting this far. You can always learn from your mistakes and do better at your next interview.]
- It is good to be confident but *do not* make up your answer or try to *bluff*. If you put something in your resume then better be prepared to back it up. Be honest to answer technical questions because you are not expected to remember everything (for example, you might know a few design patterns but not all of them etc.). If you have not used a design pattern in question, request the interviewer, if you could describe a different design pattern. Also, try to provide brief answers, which means not too long and not too short like yes or no. Give examples of times you performed that particular task. If you would like to expand on your answer, ask the interviewer if you could elaborate or go on. It is okay to verify your answers every now and then but avoid verifying or validating your answers too often because the interviewer might think that you lack self-confidence or you cannot work independently. But if you do not know the answer to a particular question and keen to know the answer, you could politely request for an answer but should not request for answers too often. If you think you could find the answer(s) readily on the internet then try to remember the question and find the answer(s) soon after your interview.
- You should also *ask questions* to make an impression on the interviewer. Write out specific questions you want to ask and then look for opportunities to ask them during the interview. Many interviewers end with a request to the applicant as to whether they have anything they wish to add. This is an opportunity for you to end on a positive note by making succinct statements about why you are the best person for the job.
- Try to be yourself. Have a good sense of humor, a smile and a positive outlook. Be friendly but you should not tell the sagas of your personal life. If you cross your boundaries then the interviewer might feel that your personal life will interfere with your work.

- *Be confident*. I have addressed many of the popular technical questions in this book and it should improve your confidence. If you come across a question relating to a new piece of technology you have no experience, then you can mention that you have a very basic understanding and demonstrate that you are a quick learner by reflecting back on your past job where you had to quickly learn a new piece of a technology or a framework. Also, you can mention that you keep a good rapport with a network of talented *Java/J2EE* developers or mentors to discuss any design alternatives or work a rounds to a pressing problem.
- Unless asked, do *not talk about money*. Leave this topic until the interviewer brings it up or you can negotiate this with your agent once you have been offered the position. At the interview you should try to sell or promote your technical skills, business skills, ability to adapt to changes, and interpersonal skills. Prior to the interview find out what skills are required by thoroughly reading the job description or talking to your agent for the specific job and be prepared to promote those skills (Sometimes you would be asked why you are the best person for the job?). You should come across as you are more keen on technical challenges, learning a new piece of technology, improving your business skills etc. as opposed to coming across as you are only interested in money.
- Speak *clearly*, *firmly* and with *confidence* but should not be aggressive and egoistical. You should act interested in the company and the job and make all comments in a positive manner. Should not speak negatively about past colleagues or employers. Should not excuse yourself halfway through the interview, even if you have to use the bathroom. Should not ask for refreshments or coffee but accept it if offered.
- At the end of the interview, thank the interviewers by their names for their time with a *firm handshake*, maintain eye contact and ask them about the next steps if not already mentioned to know where you are at the process and show that you are interested.
- Try to find out the needs of the project in which you will be working and the needs of the people within the project.
- 80% of the interview questions are based on your *own resume*.
- Where possible briefly demonstrate how you applied your skills/knowledge in the key areas [design concepts, transactional issues, performance issues, memory leaks etc.], business skills, and interpersonal skills as described in this book. Find the right time to raise questions and answer those questions to show your strength.
- Be honest to answer technical questions, you are not expected to remember everything (for example you might know a few design patterns but not all of them etc.). If you have not used a design pattern in question, request the interviewer, if you could describe a different design pattern.
- Do not be critical, focus on what you can do. Also try to be humorous to show your smartness.
- Do not act superior.

Questions with Answers

Question 1: Why are you leaving your current position?

Sample Answer: Do not criticize your previous employer or co-workers or sound too opportunistic. It is fine to mention a major problem like a buyout, budget constraints or merger. You may also say that your chance to make a contribution is very low due to companywide changes or looking for a more challenging senior or designer role.

Question 2: What do you like and/or dislike most about your current and/or last position?

Sample Answer: The interviewer is trying to find the compatibility with the open position. So, do not say anything like:

- You dislike overtime.

- You dislike management or co-workers etc.

It is safe to say:

- You like challenges.
- Opportunity to grow into design, architecture, performance tuning etc.
- Opportunity to learn and/or mentor junior developers..
- You dislike frustrating situations like identifying a memory leak problem or a complex transactional or a concurrency issue. You want to get on top of it as soon as possible.

Question 3: How do you handle pressure? Do you like or dislike these situations?

Sample Answer: These questions could mean that the open position is pressure-packed and may be out of control. Know what you are getting into. If you do perform well under stress then give a descriptive example. High achievers tend to perform well in pressure situations.

Question 4: What are your strengths and weaknesses?

Sample Answer: *Strengths*:

- Taking initiatives and being pro-active: You can illustrate how you took initiative to fix a transactional issue, a performance problem or a memory leak problem.
- Design skills: You can illustrate how you designed a particular application using OO concepts.
- Problem solving skills: Explain how you will break a complex problem into more manageable sub-sections and then apply brain storming and analytical skills to solve the complex problem. Illustrate how you went about identifying a scalability issue or a memory leak problem.
- Communication skills: Illustrate that you can communicate effectively with all the team members, business analysts, users, testers, stake holders etc.
- Ability to work in a team environment as well as independently: Illustrate that you are technically sound to work independently as well as have the interpersonal skills to fit into any team environment.
- Hardworking, honest, and conscientious etc. are the adjectives to describe you.

Weaknesses: Select a trait and come up with a solution to overcome your weakness. Stay away from personal qualities and concentrate more on professional traits for example:

- I pride myself on being an attention to detail guy but sometimes miss small details. So I am working on applying the 80/20 principle to manage time and details. Spend 80% of my effort and time on 20% of the tasks, which are critical and important to the task at hand.
- Some times when there is a technical issue or a problem I tend to work continuously until I fix it without having a break. But what I have noticed and am trying to practice is that taking a break away from the problem and thinking outside the square will assist you in identifying the root cause of the problem sooner.

Question 5: What are your career goals? Where do you see yourself in 5-10 years?

Sample Answer: Be realistic. For example:

- Next 2-3 years to become a senior developer or a team lead.
- Next 3-5 years to become a solution designer or an architect.

Question 6: Give me an example of a time when you set a goal and were able to achieve it? Give me an example of a time you showed initiative and took the lead? Tell me about a difficult decision you made in the last year? Give me an example of a time you motivated others? Tell me about a most complex project you were involved in?

Sample Answer: This is a behavioral testing question.

Situation: When you were working for the *CareerMonk* Corporation, the overnight batch process called the "Data Packager" was developed for a large fast food chain which has over 100 stores. This overnight batch process is responsible for performing a very database intensive search and compute changes like cost of ingredients, selling price, new menu item etc. made in various retail stores and package those changes into XML files and send those XML data to the respective stores where they get uploaded into their point of sale registers to reflect the changes. This batch process had been used for the past two years, but since then the number of stores had increased and so did the size of the data in the database. The batch process, which used to take 6-8 hours to complete, had increased to 14-16 hours, which obviously started to adversely affect the daily operations of these stores. The management assigned you with the task of improving the performance of the batch process to 5-6 hours (i.e. suppose to be an overnight process).

Action: After having analyzed the existing design and code for the "Data Packager", you had to take the difficult decision to let the management know that this batch process needed to be re-designed and re-written as opposed to modifying the existing code, since it was poorly designed. It is hard to extend, maintain (i.e. making a change in one place can break the code somewhere else and so on) and had no object reuse through caching (makes too many unnecessary network trips to the database) etc. The management was not too impressed with this approach and concerned about the time required to rewrite this batch process since the management had promised the retail stores to provide a solution within 8-12 weeks. You took the initiative and used your persuasive skills to convince the management that you would be able to provide a re-designed and re-written solution within the 8-12 weeks with the assistance of 2-3 additional developers and two testers.

You were entrusted with the task to rewrite the batch process and you set your goal to complete the task in 8 weeks. You decided to build the software iteratively by building individual vertical slices as opposed to the big bang waterfall. You redesigned and wrote the code for a typical use case from end to end (i.e. full vertical slice) within 2 weeks and subsequently carried out functional and integration testing to iron out any unforeseen errors or issues. Once the first iteration is stable, you effectively communicated the architecture to the management and to your fellow developers. Motivated and mentored your fellow developers to build the other iterations, based on the first iteration. At the end of iteration, it was tested by the testers, while the developers moved on to the next iteration.

Results: After having enthusiastically worked to your plan with hard work, dedication and teamwork, you were able to have the 90% of the functionality completed in 9 weeks and spent the next 3 weeks fixing bugs, tuning performance and coding rest of the functionality. The fully functional data packager was completed in 12 weeks and took only 3-4 hours to package *XML* data for all the stores. The team was under pressure at times but you made them believe that it is more of a challenge as opposed to think of it as a stressful situation. The newly designed data packager was also easier to maintain and extend. The management was impressed with the outcome and rewarded the team with an outstanding achievement award. The performance of the newly developed data packager was further improved by 20% by tuning the database (i.e. partitioning the tables, indexing etc.).

Question 7: Describe a time when you were faced with a stressful situation that demonstrated your coping skills? Give me an example of a time when you used your fact finding skills to solve a problem? Describe a time when you applied your analytical and/or problem solving skills?

Sample Answer: This is also a behavioral testing question.
Situation: When you were working for the Life insurance corporation, you were responsible for the migration of an online insurance application (i.e. external website) to a newer version of application server (i.e. the current version is no longer supported by the vendor). The migration happened smoothly and after a couple of days of going live,

you started to experience "OutOfMemoryError", which forced you to restart the application server every day. This raised a red alert and the immediate and the senior management were very concerned and consequently constantly calling for meetings and updates on the progress of identifying the root cause of this issue. This has created a stressful situation.

Action: You were able to have a positive outlook by believing that this is more of a challenge as opposed to think of it as a stressful situation. You needed to be composed to get your analytical and problem solving skills to get to work. You spent some time finding facts relating to "OutOfMemoryError". You were tempted to increase the heap space as suggested by fellow developers but the profiling and monitoring did not indicate that was the case. The memory usage drastically increased during and after certain user operations like generating PDF reports. The generation of reports used some third party libraries, which dynamically generated classes from your templates. So you decided to increase the area of the memory known as the "perm", which sits next to the heap. This "perm" space is consumed when the classes are dynamically generated from templates during the report generation.

```
java -XX:PermSize=256M -XX:MaxPermSize=256M
```

Results: After you have increased the "perm" size, the "OutOfMemoryError" has disappeared. You kept monitoring it for a week and everything worked well. The management was impressed with your problem solving, fact finding and analytical skills, which had contributed to the identification of the not so prevalent root cause and the effective communication with the other teams like infrastructure, production support, senior management, etc. The management also identified your ability to cope under stress and offered you a promotion to lead a small team of 4 developers.

Question 8: Describe a time when you had to work with others in the organization to accomplish the organizational goals? Describe a situation where others you worked on a project disagreed with your ideas, and what did you do? Describe a situation in which you had to collect information by asking many questions of several people? What has been your experience in giving presentations to small or large groups? How do you show considerations for others?

Sample Answer: This is also a behavioral testing question.
Situation: You were working for *CareerMonk* Pvt. Ltd financial services organization. You were part of a development team responsible for enhancing an existing online web application, which enables investors and advisors view and manage their financial portfolios. The websites of the financial services organizations are periodically surveyed and rated by an independent organization for their ease of use, navigability, content, search functionality etc. Your organization was ranked 21st among 23 websites reviewed. Your chief information officer was very disappointed with this poor rating and wanted the business analysts, business owners (i.e. within the organization) and the technical staff to improve on the ratings before the next ratings, which would be done in 3 months.

Action: The business analysts and the business owners quickly got into work and came up with a requirements list of 35 items in consultation with the external business users such as advisors, investors etc. You were assigned the task of working with the business analysts, business owners (i.e. internal), and project managers to provide a technical input in terms of feasibility study, time estimates, impact analysis etc. The business owners had a preconceived notion of how they would like things done. You had to analyze the outcome from both the business owners' perspective and technology perspective. There were times you had to use your persuasive skills to convince the business owners and analysts to take an alternative approach, which would provide a more robust solution. You managed to convince the business owners and analysts by providing visual mock-up screen shots of your proposed solution, presentation skills, ability to communicate without any technical jargons, and listening carefully to business needs and discussing your ideas with your fellow developers (i.e. being a good listener, respecting others' views and having the right attitude even if you know that you are right). You also strongly believe that good technical skills must be complemented with good interpersonal skills and the right attitude. After 2-3 weeks of constant interaction with the business owners, analysts and fellow developers, you had helped the business users to finalize the list of requirements. You also took the initiative to apply the agile development methodology to improve communication and cooperation between business owners and the developers.

Results: You and your fellow developers were not only able to effectively communicate and collaborate with the business users and analysts but also provided progressive feedback to each other due to iterative approach. The team work and hard work had resulted in a much improved

Question 9: What past accomplishments gave you satisfaction? What makes you want to work hard?

Sample Answer:

- Material rewards such as salary, perks, benefits etc. naturally come into play but focus on your achievements or accomplishments than on rewards.
- Explain how you took pride in fixing a complex performance issue or a concurrency issue. You could substantiate your answer with a past experience. For example while you were working for Bips telecom, you pro-actively identified a performance issue due to database connection resource leak. You subsequently took the initiative to notify your team leader and volunteered to fix it by adding finally {} blocks to close the resources.
- If you are being interviewed for a position, which requires your design skills then you could explain that in your previous job with an insurance company you had to design and develop a sub-system, which gave you complete satisfaction. You were responsible for designing the data model using entity relationship diagrams (E-R diagrams) and the software model using the component diagrams, class diagrams, sequence diagrams etc.
- If you are being interviewed for a position where you have to learn new pieces of technology/framework then you can explain with examples from your past experience where you were not only motivated to acquire new skills/knowledge but also proved that you are a quick and a pro-active learner.
- If the job you are being interviewed for requires production support from time to time, then you could explain that it gives you satisfaction because you would like to interact with the business users and/or customers to develop your business and communication skills by getting an opportunity to understand a system from the users perspective and also gives you an opportunity to sharpen your technical and problem solving skills. If you are a type of person who enjoys more development work then you can be honest about it and indicate that you would like to have a balance between development work and support work, where you can develop different aspects of your skills/knowledge. You could also reflect an experience from a past job, where each developer was assigned a weekly roster to provide support.
- You could say that, you generally would like to work hard but would like to work even harder when there are challenges.

CHAPTER 29

Quantitative Aptitude Concepts

Every placement test paper on quantitative aptitude will contain at least 30% of questions on numbers and series. Aptitude questions on numbers form the backbone for placement preparation. You can score easily on quantitative aptitude section if you understand the basics of number system. Since the questions are simple, importance lies in acquiring the right skills to tackle these problems with speed. Below is the list of important formulae and tips to help you understand and prepare for the quantitative aptitude section.

29.1 Formulas on Number Series

Sum of first n numbers: $1 + 2 + 3 + 4 + 5 + \ldots + n$	=	$\frac{n(n+1)}{2}$
Sum of squares of first n numbers: $1^2 + 2^2 + 3^2 + \ldots.. + n^2$	=	$\frac{n(n+1)(2n+1)}{6}$
Sum of cubes of first n numbers: $1^3 + 2^3 + 3^3 + \ldots.. + n^3$	=	$\left(\frac{n(n+1)}{2}\right)^2$
Sum of first n odd numbers	=	n^2
Sum of first n even numbers	=	$n(n + 1)$

29.2 Tips on Divisibility Checks

- A number is divisible by 2, if its *last* digit (also called *unit's digit*) is any of 0, 2, 4, 6, and 8.
- A number is divisible by 3, if the sum of its digits is divisible by 3.
- A number is divisible by 4, if the number formed by the last two digits is divisible by 4.
- A number is divisible by 5, if its unit's digit is either 0 or 5.
- A number is divisible by 6, if it is divisible by both 2 and 3.
- A number is divisible by 8, if the number formed by the last three digits of the given number is divisible by 8.
- A number is divisible by 9, if the sum of its digits is divisible by 9.
- A number is divisible by 10, if it ends with 0.
- A number is divisible by 11, if the difference of the sum of its digits at odd places and the sum of its digits at even places is either 0 or a number divisible by 11.
- A number is divisible by 12, if it is divisible by both 4 and 3.
- A number is divisible by 14, if it is divisible by 2 as well as 7.
- Two numbers are said to be co-primes if their HCF is 1. To find if a number, say y is divisible by x, find m and n such that $m \times n = x$ and m and n are co-prime numbers. If y is divisible by both m and n then it is divisible by x.
- Product of two numbers = Their LCM × Their HCF.

29.3 Mathematical Formulas

- $(a + b)(a - b) = (a^2 - b^2)$
- $(a + b)^2 = (a^2 + b^2 + 2ab)$
- $(a - b)^2 = (a^2 + b^2 - 2ab)$
- $(a + b + c)^2 = a^2 + b^2 + c^2 + 2(ab + bc + ca)$
- $(a^3 + b^3) = (a + b)(a^2 - ab + b^2)$
- $(a^3 - b^3) = (a - b)(a^2 + ab + b^2)$
- $(a^3 + b^3 + c^3 - 3abc) = (a + b + c)(a^2 + b^2 + c^2 - ab - bc - ac)$
- When $a + b + c = 0$, then $a^3 + b^3 + c^3 = 3abc$

29.4 Ratios and Proportions

The ratio of two quantities of the same units is a fraction that one quantity is of the other. The ratio $a{:}b$ represents a fraction. The first term of a ratio is called *antecedent* while the second term is called *consequent*. So, the ratio 3:7 represents $\frac{3}{7}$ with antecedent 3 and consequent 7. The multiplication or division of each term of a ratio by a same non-zero number does not affect the ratio. Thus, 3:7 = 6:14 = 9:21 = 12:28 = $\frac{3}{7}$:1 etc.

The equality of two ratios is called proportion. If a:b = c:d, we write, a:b :: c:d and we say that a, b, c, d are in proportion. In a proportion, the first and fourth terms are known as extremes, while second and third terms are known as means.

- Product of *Means* = Product of *Extremes*
- Mean production between a and b is $\sqrt{ab}$
- Compounded Ratio: The compounded ratio of the ratios (a : b), (c : d), (e : f) is (ace : bdf)
- $a^2 : b^2$ is called the *duplicate* ratio of a: b
- $\sqrt{a} : \sqrt{b}$ is called the *sub – duplicate* ratio of a: b
- $a^3 : b^3$ is called the *triplicate ratio* of a: b
- $\sqrt[3]{a} : \sqrt[3]{b}$ is called the *sub – triplicate* ratio of a: b
- If $\frac{a}{b} = \frac{c}{d}$, then, $\frac{a+b}{b} = \frac{c+d}{d}$, which is called the *componendo*
- If $\frac{a}{b} = \frac{c}{d}$, then, $\frac{a-b}{b} = \frac{c-d}{d}$, which is called the *dividend*
- If $\frac{a}{b} = \frac{c}{d}$, then, $\frac{a+b}{a-b} = \frac{c+d}{c-d}$, which is called the *componendo and dividend*
- *Variation*: We say that a is directly proportional to b if $a = k \times b$ for some constant k and we write, $a \propto b$
- Also, we say that x is inversely proportional to if $a = \frac{k}{b}$ for some constant k and we write $a \propto \frac{1}{b}$

29.5 Percentage

Percent means for every 100. So, when percent is calculated for any value, it means that we calculate the value for every 100 of the reference value. Percent is denoted by the symbol %. For example, x percent is denoted by x%. In simple terms we can conclude that percentage symbol % means 1/100. In case we are having a fraction and we have to calculate its percentage then we will multiply it by 100. That is,

$$\frac{x}{y} = \left(\frac{x}{y} \times 100\right)\%$$

So if we get a question like 1 is what percent of 4, then we will solve it as,

$$\frac{1}{4}\times 100 = 25\%$$

Similarly,

$$\frac{3}{5}\times 100 = 25\%$$

- If the price of an item increases by R%, the reduction in consumption so as not to increase the expenditure = $\left[\frac{R}{100+R}\times 100\right]\%$
- If the price of an item decreases by R%, the increase in consumption so as not to decrease the expenditure = $\left[\frac{R}{100-R}\times 100\right]\%$
- If the population of a town = P and it increases at the rate of R% per annum, then Population after n years = $P\left[1+\frac{R}{100}\right]^n$
- If the population of a town = P and it increases at the rate of R% per annum, then Population before n years = $\frac{P}{\left[1+\frac{R}{100}\right]^n}$
- If the present value of a machine = P and it depreciates at the rate of R% per annum, Then Value of the machine after n years = $P\left[1-\frac{R}{100}\right]^n$
- If the present value of a machine = P and it depreciates at the rate of R% per annum, Then Value of the machine before n years = $\frac{P}{\left[1-\frac{R}{100}\right]^n}$

29.6 Profit and Loss

Profit	=	Selling Price - Cost Price
Selling Price	=	Cost Price + Profit
Cost Price	=	Selling Price - Profit
Loss	=	Cost Price - Selling Price
Selling Price	=	Cost Price - Loss
Cost Price	=	Selling Price + Loss
Percentage profit / loss are always calculated on cost price unless otherwise stated.		
Profit Percentage	=	$\frac{\text{Profit x 100}}{\textit{Cost Price}}$
Loss Percentage	=	$\frac{\textit{Loss} \times \textit{Cost Price}}{\textit{Cost Price}}$
Selling Price	=	$\frac{(100+\textit{Gain}\,\%)\times \textit{Cost Price}}{100}$
Selling Price	=	$\frac{(100-\text{Loss}\,\%)\times \text{Cost Price}}{100}$
Cost Price	=	$\frac{\text{100 x Selling Price}}{100+\textit{Gain}\,\%}$

29.7 Volumes and Surface Areas

29.7.1 Cuboid

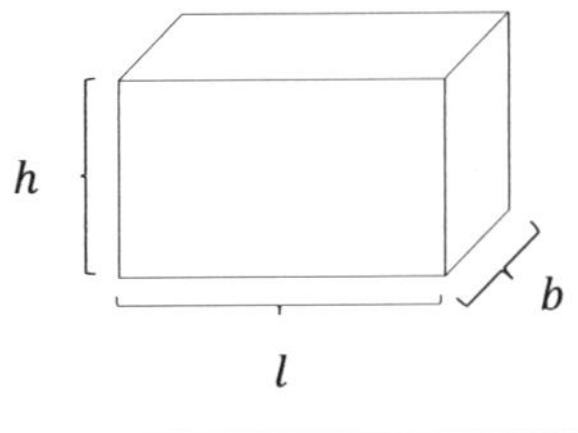

Let l be length, b be breadth and h be height units. Then,

Volume	=	$(l\times b\times h)$ cubic units
Surface Area	=	$2(lb+bh+hl)$ square units
Diagonal	=	$\sqrt{l^2+b^2+h^2}$ units

29.7.2 Cube

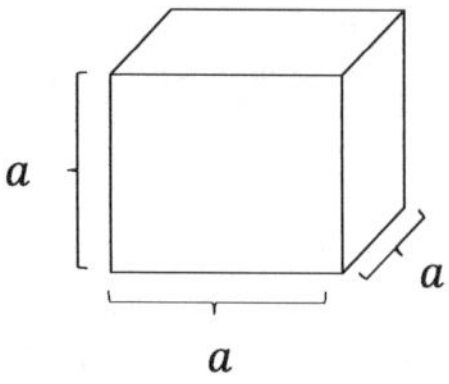

Let each edge of a cube be of length a. Then,

Volume	=	a^3 cubic units
Surface Area	=	$6a^2$ square units
Diagonal	=	$\sqrt{3}a$ units

29.7.3 Cylinder

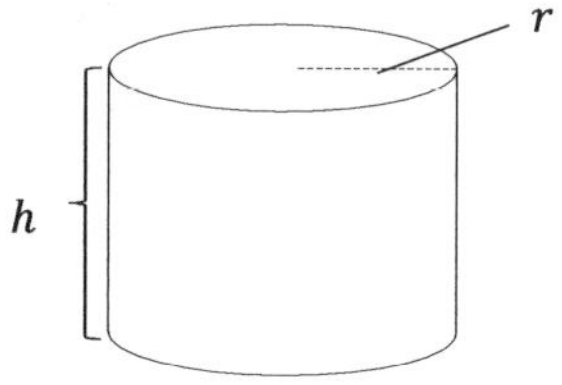

Volume	=	$\pi r^2 h$ cubic units
Curved Surface Area	=	$2\pi rh$ square units
Total Surface Area	=	$2\pi r(h+r)$ square units

29.7.4 Cone

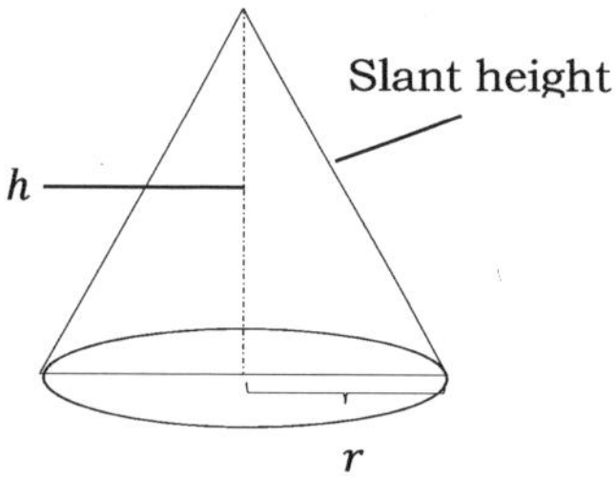

Let radius of base = r and height = h. Then,

Slant height, l	=	$\sqrt{r^2+h^2}$ units
Volume	=	$\frac{1}{3}\pi r^2 h$ cubic units
Curved Surface Area	=	πrl square units
Total Surface Area	=	$\pi rl + \pi r^2$ square units

29.7.5 Sphere

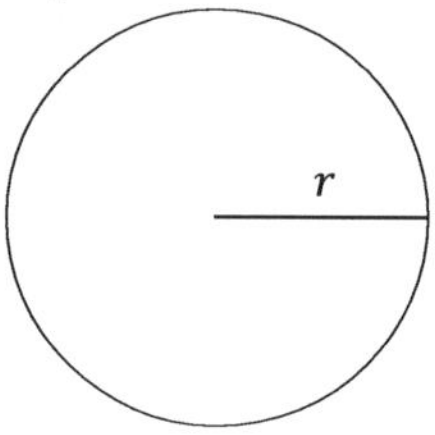

Let radius = r. Then,

Volume	=	$\frac{4}{3}\pi r^3$ cubic units
Surface Area	=	$4\pi r^2$ square units

29.7.6 Hemisphere

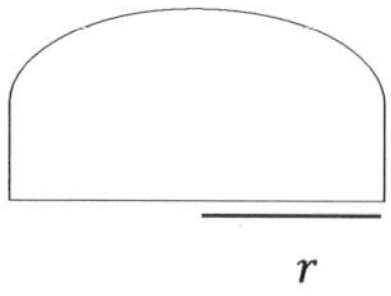

Let radius = r. Then,

Volume	=	$\frac{2}{3}\pi r^3$ cubic units
Curved Surface Area	=	$\frac{2}{\pi}r^2$ square units
Total Surface Area	=	$3\pi r^2$ square units

29.8 Logarithms

$log\, x^y = y\, log\, x$	$logn = log^n_{10}$
$log\, xy = logx + logy$	$log^k n = (logn)^k$
$log\, logn = log(logn)$	$log\frac{x}{y} = logx - logy$
$a^{log^x_b} = x^{log^a_b}$	$log^x_b = \frac{log^x_a}{log^b_a}$

29.9 Formulae for Trains Problems

1. Speed = $\frac{Distance}{Time}$
2. Velocity = $\frac{Displacement}{Time}$
3. Converting km/hr to m/s,

$$x\frac{km}{hr} = x \times \frac{5}{18}\frac{m}{sec}$$

4. Conversion from m/s to km/hr,

$$x\frac{m}{sec} = x \times \frac{18}{5}\frac{km}{hr}$$

5. Time taken by a train of length l metres to pass a pole or standing man or a signal post is equal to the time taken by the train to cover l metres.
6. Time taken by a train of length l metres to pass a stationery object of length b metres is the time taken by the train to cover $(l + b)$ metres.
7. Suppose two trains or two objects bodies are moving in the same direction at u m/s and v m/s, where $u > v$, then their relative speed is = $(u - v)$ m/s.
8. Suppose two trains or two objects bodies are moving in opposite directions at u m/s and v m/s, then their relative speed is = $(u + v)$ m/s.
9. If two trains of length a metres and b metres are moving in opposite directions at u m/s and v m/s, then the time taken by the trains to cross each other

$$\frac{a+b}{u+v} sec$$

Please note this is just formula of time which is distance upon speed. We are just adding two distances and two speeds.

10. If two trains of length a metres and b metres are moving in the same direction at u m/s and v m/s, then the time taken by the faster train to cross the slower train

$$\frac{a+b}{u-v} sec$$

Please note as trains are moving in the same directions so we used $(u - v)$.

11. If two trains (or bodies) start at the same time from points A and B towards each other and after crossing they take a and b sec in reaching B and A respectively, then:

(A's Speed):(B's Speed)=$\sqrt{b}:\sqrt{a}$

29.10 Indices

$a^m \times a^n = a^{m+n}$	$\frac{a^m}{a^n} = a^{m-n}$
$(a^m)^n = a^{mn}$	$a^0 = 1$
$\left(\frac{a}{b}\right) = \frac{a^{mn}}{b^n}$	$(a^b)^n = a^n b^n$

29.11 Surds

If we can't simplify a number to remove a square root (or cube root etc.) then it is a surd. For example $\sqrt{2}$ can't be simplified further so it is a surd and $\sqrt{4}$ can be simplified (to 2), so it is not a surd!

$\sqrt[n]{a} = a^{\frac{1}{n}}$	$\sqrt[n]{ab} = \sqrt[n]{a} \times \sqrt[n]{b}$
$\sqrt[n]{\frac{a}{b}} = \frac{\sqrt[n]{a}}{\sqrt[n]{b}}$	$(a^{1/n})^n = a$
$\sqrt[mn]{a} = \sqrt[m]{\sqrt[n]{a}}$	$(a^{1/n})^m = \sqrt[n]{a^m}$

29.12 Clock

- *Minute Spaces*: The face or dial of clock is a circle whose circumference is divided into 60 equal parts, named minute spaces.
- *Hour hand and minute hand*: A clock has two hands. The smaller hand is called the *hour* hand or *short* hand and the larger one is called *minute* hand or *long* hand.
- 55 min spaces are gained by minute hand (with respect to hour hand) in 60 min. In 60 minutes, hour hand will move 5 min spaces while the minute hand will move 60 min spaces. In effect the space gain of minute hand with respect to hour hand will be $60 - 5 = 55$ minutes.
- Both the hands of a clock coincide once in every hour.
- The hands of a clock are in the same straight line when they are coincident or opposite to each other.
- When the two hands of a clock are at right angles, they are 15 minute spaces apart.
- When the hands of a clock are in opposite directions, they are 30 minute spaces apart.
- Angle traced by hour hand in 12 hrs = 360°.
- Angle traced by minute hand in 60 min. = 360°.
- If a watch or a clock indicates 9.15, when the correct time is 9, it is said to be 15 minutes too fast.
- If a watch or a clock indicates 8.45, when the correct time is 9, it is said to be 15 minutes too slow.
- The hands of a clock will be in straight line but opposite in direction, 22 times in a day.
- The hands of a clock coincide 22 times in a day.
- The hands of a clock are straight 44 times in a day.
- The hands of a clock are at right angles 44 times in a day.
- The two hands of a clock will be together between H and $(H+1)$o' clock at $\frac{60H}{11}$ minutes past Ho' clock.
- The two hands of a clock will be in the same straight line but not together between H and $(H + 1)$ o' clock at

$$\begin{cases} (5H - 30)\frac{12}{11} \text{ minutes past H, if H} > 6 \\ (5H + 30)\frac{12}{11} \text{ minutes past H, if H} < 6 \end{cases}$$

- Angle between Hands of a clock
    - When the minute hand is behind the hour hand, the angle between the two hands at M minutes past H'o clock $= 30\left(H - \frac{M}{5}\right) + \frac{M}{2}$ degree
    - When the minute hand is ahead of the hour hand, the angle between the two hands at M minutes past H'o clock $= 30\left(\frac{M}{5} - H\right) - \frac{M}{2}$ degree
- The two hands of the clock will be at right angles between H and (H + 1)o' clock at $(5H \pm 15)\frac{12}{11}$ minutes past H'o clock.
- The minute hand of a clock overtakes the hour hand at intervals of M minutes of correct time. The clock gains or losses in a day by $= (\frac{720}{11}\text{-M})(\frac{60\times24}{M})$ minutes.
- Between H and $(H + 1)$o' clock, the two hands of a clock are M minutes apart at $(5H \pm M)\frac{12}{11}$ minutes past H'o clock.

29.13 Blood Relations Tricks

Mother's or father's son	Brother
Mother's or father's daughter	Sister

Mother's or father's brother	Uncle
Mother's or father's sister	Aunt
Mother's or father's father	Grandfather
Mother's or father's mother	Grandmother
Son's wife	Daughter-in-law
Daughter's husband	Son-in-law
Husband's or wife's sister	Sister-in-law
Husband's or wife's brother	Brother-in-law
Brother's son	Nephew
Brother's daughter	Niece
Uncle or aunt's son or daughter	Cousin
Sister's husband	Brother-in-law
Brother's wife	Sister-in-law
Grandson's or Granddaughter's daughter Great	Grand daughter

29.14 Probability

This is a basic overview of the basic concepts of probability theory.

29.14.1 Events

An event is defined as any outcome that can occur. There are two main categories of events: Deterministic and Probabilistic. A deterministic event always has the same outcome and is predictable 100% of the time.

- Distance traveled = time x velocity
- The speed of light
- The sun rising in the east
- Rajnikanth winning the fight without a scratch

A probabilistic event is an event for which the exact outcome is not predictable 100% of the time.

- The number of heads in ten tosses of a coin
- The number of games played in a World Series
- The number of defects in a batch of product

In a cricket match there may be three possible events. (There could be more depending on the question asked.)

- Team A wins
- Team B wins
- Draw

29.14.1.1 Basic Types of Events

Mutually Exclusive Events: These are events that cannot occur at the same time. The cause of mutually exclusive events could be a force of nature or a manmade law. Being twenty-five years old and also becoming president of the United States are mutually exclusive events because by law these two events cannot occur at the same time.

Complementary Events: These are events that have two possible outcomes. The probability of event A plus the probability of $\bar{A}$ equals one. $P(A) + P(\bar{A}) = 1$. Any event A and its complementary event $\bar{A}$ are mutually exclusive. Heads or tails in one toss of a coin are complementary events.

Independent Events: These are two or more events for which the outcome of one does not affect the other. They are events that are not dependent on what occurred previously. Each toss of a fair coin is an independent event.

Conditional Events: These are events that are dependent on what occurred previously. If five cards are drawn from a deck of fifty-two cards, the likelihood of the fifth card being an ace is dependent on the outcome of the first four cards.

29.14.2 Probability

Probability is defined as the chance that an event will happen or the likelihood that an event will happen. The definition of probability is

$$Probability = \frac{Number\ of\ Favourable\ Events}{Total\ Number\ of\ Events}$$

The favourable events are the events of interest. They are the events that the question is addressing. The total events are all possible events that can occur relevant to the question asked. In this definition, favourable has nothing to do with something being defective or non-defective.

What is the probability of a head occurring in one toss of a coin?

The number of favourable events is 1 (one head) and the number of total events is 2 (head or tail). In this case, the probability formula verifies what is obvious.

Probability numbers always range from 0 to 1 in decimals or from 0 to 100 in percentages.

29.14.2.1 Notation for Probability Questions

Instead of writing out the complete question, the following notation is used.

- What is the probability of event A occurring? = Probability (A) = P(A)
- What is the probability of events A and B occurring? = P(A and B) = P(A) and P(B)
- What is the probability of events A or B occurring? = P(A or B) = P(A) or P(B)

29.14.2.2 Probability in Terms of Areas

Probability may also be defined in terms of areas rather than the number of events.

$$Probability = \frac{Favourable\ Area}{Total\ Area}$$

29.14.3 Methods to Determine Probability Values

There are three major methods used to determine probability values.

- *Subjective Probability*: This is a probability value based on the best available knowledge or maybe an educated guess. Examples are betting on horse races, selecting stocks or making product-marketing decisions.
- *Priori Probability*: This is a probability value that can be determined prior to any experimentation or trial. For example, the probability of obtaining a tail in tossing a coin once is fifty percent. The coin is not actually tossed to determine this probability. It is simply observed that there are two faces to the coin, one of which is tails and that heads and tails are equally likely.
- *Empirical Probability*: This is a probability value that is determined by experimentation. An example of this is a manufacturing process where after checking one hundred parts, five are found defective. If the sample of one hundred parts was representative of the total population, then the probability of finding a defective part is .05 (5/100). The question may be asked: How is it known that this sample is representative of the total population? If repeated trials average .05 defective, with little variation between trials, then it can be said that the empirical probability of a defective part is .05.

29.14.4 Multiplication Theorem

The multiplication theorem is used to answer the following questions:

- What is the probability of two or more events occurring either simultaneously or in succession?
- For two events A and B: What is the probability of event A and event B occurring?

The individual probability values are simply multiplied to arrive at the answer. The word "*and*" is the key word that indicates multiplication of the individual probabilities. The multiplication theorem is applicable only if the events are independent. It is not valid when dealing with conditional events. The product of two or more probability values yields the intersection or common area of the probabilities. The intersection is illustrated by the Venn diagrams in next section. Mutually exclusive events do not have an intersection or common area. The probability of two or more mutually exclusive events is always zero.

- For mutually exclusive events: P(A) and P(B) = 0
- For independent events: Probability (A and B) = P(A) and P(B) = P(A) X P(B)
- For multiple independent events, the multiplication formula is extended. The probability that five events A, B, C, D and E occur is

P(A) and P(B) and P(C) and P(D) and P(E) = P(A) x P(B) x P(C) x P(D) x P(E)

29.14.5 Addition Theorem

The addition theorem is used to answer the following questions:

- What is the probability of one event or another event or both events occurring?
- What is the probability of event A or event B occurring?

The word "*or*" indicates addition of the individual probabilities. The answers to the above questions are different depending on whether the events are mutually exclusive or independent.

Mutually exclusive events do not have an intersection or common area. The individual probabilities are simply added to arrive at the answer. For mutually exclusive events:

P(A or B) = P(A) or P(B) = P(A) + P(B)
P(A or B or C or D) = P(A) + P(B) + P(C) + P(D)

For two independent events, the intersecting or common area must be subtracted or it will be included twice.

Probability (A or B) = P(A) or P(B) = P(A) + P(B) – P(A X B)
For three independent events: P(A or B or C) = P(A) + P(B) + P(C) – P(A X B) – P(A X C)

29.14.6 Permutations and Combinations

Permutations and combinations are mathematical tools used for counting. In many cases, it may be difficult to count the number of favorable events or the number of total events when solving probability problems. Permutations and combinations help simplify the task.

29.14.6.1 Permutations

A permutation is an arrangement of things, objects or events where the order is important. Telephone numbers are special permutations of the numerals 0 to 9 where each numeral may be used more than once. The order defines each unique telephone number. In the following example, it is assumed that each object is unique and cannot be used more than once. The letters A, B, and C may be arranged in the following ways:

ABC BAC CAB

ACB BCA CBA

This is an ordered arrangement, because ABC is different than BCA. Since the order of the letters makes a difference, each arrangement is a permutation. From the above example, It is concluded that there are six permutations that can be made from three objects. The general formula for permutations is

$$n_{p_r} = \frac{n!}{(n-r)!}$$

n = The total objects to arrange
r = Number of objects taken from the total to be used in the arrangements

By definition: 0! = 1 and 1! = 1

29.14.6.2 Combinations

A combination is a grouping or arrangement of objects where the order does not make a difference. The arrangement of the letters ABC is the same as BCA. The number of combinations that can be made by using three letters, three at a time, is one. This can be expanded to state that the number of combinations that can be made by using n letters, *n* at a time, is one.

A hand of five cards consisting of a Jack, a Queen, a King, and two Aces is the same as a Queen, two Aces, a Jack and a King. The order in which the cards were received makes no difference. There is only one combination that can be made by using five cards, five at a time.

The formula for combinations is

$$n_{c_r} = \frac{n_{p_r}}{r!} = \frac{n!}{(n-r!)r!}$$

n = Total objects to arrange
r = Number of objects taken from the total to be used in the arrangements

The symbol for number of combinations is often shown as $\binom{n}{r}$. When the symbol appears in a formula, the number of combinations is to be computed using the combination formula.

$$\binom{n}{r} = \frac{n!}{(n-r!)r!}$$

The permutation and combination formulas are very useful tools in evaluating and solving probability problems. It is often necessary to count the number of favorable and total events that can occur. Without these counting techniques, this would be a very cumbersome and sometimes impossible task.

29.14.7 Conditional Probability

Conditional probability is defined as the probability of an event occurring if another has occurred or has been specified to occur simultaneously, and the outcome of the first event affects the probability of the second event. Conditional events are not independent.

The probability of B occurring given that A has already occurred is stated as P(B/A), where the symbol / means "given that". The formulas for conditional probability are shown below. These are known as Bayes Formulas.

$$P\left(\frac{B}{A}\right) = \frac{P(A\&B)}{P(A)}$$

$$P\left(\frac{A}{B}\right) = \frac{P(A\&B)}{P(B)}$$

Since the two formulas have a common term P(A & B), they may be used together to solve many problems involving conditional probability. Conditional events are not independent so P(A & B) is not equal to P(A) X P(B). From Bayes formulas:

$$P(A \,\&\, B) = P\left(\frac{B}{A}\right)P(A)$$
$$P(A \,\&\, B) = P\left(\frac{B}{A}\right)P(B)$$

29.15 Banker's Discount

Let F = Face Value of the Bill, TD = True Discount, BD = Bankers Discount, BG = Banker's Gain, R = Rate of Interest, PW = True Present Worth and T = Time in Years

BD	=	Simple Interest on the face value of the bill for unexpired time = $\frac{FTR}{100}$
PW	=	$\frac{F}{1+T\left(\frac{R}{100}\right)}$
TD	=	Simple Interest on the present value for unexpired time = $\frac{PW \times TR}{100} = \frac{FTR}{100+TR}$
TD	=	$\frac{BD \times 100}{100 + TR}$
PW	=	F - TD
F	=	$\frac{BD \times TD}{BD - TD}$
BG	=	BD – TD = Simple Interest on TD = $\frac{TD^2}{PW}$
TD	=	$\sqrt{PW \times BG}$
TD	=	$\frac{BG \times 100}{TR}$

29.16 Simple Interest

- *Principal*: The money borrowed or lent out for a certain period is called the principal or the sum.
- *Interest*: Extra money paid for using other's money is called interest.
- *Simple Interest*: If the interest on a sum borrowed for certain period is reckoned uniformly, then it is called simple interest.
- Simple Interest Formula: Let Principal = P, Rate = R% per annum and Time = n years. Then,

$$\text{Simple Interest (SI)} = \frac{P \times R \times n}{100}$$

- We can also calculate Principal, Rate and Time using above formula as,

$$P = \frac{100 \times SI}{R \times n}$$
$$\text{Rate} = \frac{100 \times SI}{P \times n}$$
$$\text{Time} = \frac{100 \times SI}{P \times R}$$

29.17 Compound Interest

Let Principal = P, Rate = R % per annum and Time = n years.

- Annual Compound Interest Formula:

$$\text{Amount} = P\left(1 + \frac{R}{100}\right)^n$$

- Half Yearly Compound Interest: When interest is compounded half yearly, then

$$\text{Amount} = P\left(1+\frac{\frac{R}{2}}{100}\right)^{2n}$$

- Quarterly Compound Interest: When interest is compounded Quarterly, then

$$\text{Amount} = P\left(1+\frac{\frac{R}{4}}{100}\right)^{4n}$$

- When interest is compounded Annually but time is in fraction, say $5\frac{2}{7}$ years, then Amount will be,

$$\text{Amount} = P\left(1+\frac{R}{100}\right)^{5} \times \left(1+\frac{\left(\frac{2}{7}\right)R}{100}\right)$$

- When Rates are different for different years, say R1%, R2%, R3% for first, second and third year respectively. Then Amount will be,

$$\text{Amount} = P\left(1+\frac{R1}{100}\right)\left(1+\frac{R2}{100}\right)\left(1+\frac{R3}{100}\right)$$

- Present worth of Rs. x due n years hence will be:

$$\text{Present Worth} = \frac{x}{1+\left(\frac{R}{100}\right)^{n}}$$

29.18 Pipes

- A pipe connected with a tank or a cistern or a reservoir, that fills it, is called an *inlet*.
- A pipe connected with a tank or cistern or reservoir, emptying it, is called an *outlet*.
- If a pipe can fill a tank in x hours, then part filled in 1 hour = $\frac{1}{x}$.
- If a pipe can empty a tank in x hours, then part emptied in 1 hour = $\frac{1}{x}$.
- If a pipe can fill a tank in x hours and another pipe can empty the full tank in y hours (where $y > x$), then on opening both the pipes, then the net part filled in 1 hour $= \frac{1}{x} - \frac{1}{y}$.
- If a pipe can fill a tank in x hours and another pipe can empty the full tank in y hours (where $x > y$), then on opening both the pipes, the net part filled in 1 hour $= \frac{1}{y} - \frac{1}{x}$..
- If two pipes A and B can fill a tank in x hours and y hours respectively. If both the pipes are opened simultaneously, part filled by $A + B$ in 1 hour $= \frac{1}{x} + \frac{1}{y}$.
- Time for emptying (emptying pipe is bigger in size), E = $\frac{f \times e}{f-e}$

Where, E represents total time taken to empty the tank
F represents total time taken to fill the tank
e represents time taken to empty the tank
f represents time taken to fill the tank

- Time for filling (filling pipe is bigger in size), F = $\frac{f \times e}{e-f}$.

29.19 Stocks and Shares

- *Stock Capital* is the total amount of money needed to run the company.
- The whole capital is divided into small units, called *shares* or *stock*. For each investment, the company issues a 'share-certificate', showing the value of each share and the number of shares held by a person. The person who subscribes in shares or stock is called a *shareholder* or *stock holder*.
- The annual profit distributed among shareholders is called *dividend*. Dividend is paid annually as per share or as a percentage.

- The value of a share or stock printed on the share-certificate is called its Face Value or Nominal Value or Par Value.
- *Market Value*: The stock of different companies are sold and bought in the open market through brokers at stock-exchanges. A share or stock is said to be:
    - At premium or above par, if its market value is more than its face value.
    - At par, if its market value is the same as its face value.
    - At discount or below par, if its market value is less than its face value.

Thus, if a Rs. 200 stock is quoted at premium of 32, then market value of the stock = Rs.(200 + 32) = Rs. 232. Similarly, if a Rs. 200 stock is quoted at a discount of 7, then market value of the stock = Rs. (200 -7) = 186.

- Brokerage: The broker's charge is called *brokerage*.
    - When stock is purchased, brokerage is added to the cost price.
    - When stock is sold, brokerage is subtracted from the selling price.
    - The face value of a share always remains the same.
    - The market value of a share changes from time to time.
    - Dividend is always paid on the face value of a share.
    - Number of shares held by a person
    $$= \frac{Total\ Investment}{Investment\ in\ 1\ share} = \frac{Total\ Income}{Income\ from\ 1\ share} = \frac{Total\ Face\ Value}{Face\ Value\ of\ 1\ Share}$$
- Thus, by a Rs. 100, 9% stock at 120, we mean that:
    - Face Value of stock = Rs. 100.
    - Market Value (M.V) of stock = Rs. 120.
    - Annual dividend on 1 share = 9% of face value = 9% of Rs. 100 = Rs. 9.
    - An investment of Rs. 120 gives an annual income of Rs. 9.
    - Rate of interest per anum = Annual income from an investment of Rs. 100 = $\left(\frac{9}{12C} \times 100\right)\% = 7\frac{1}{2}\%$.

CHAPTER 30

Basics of Cloud Computing

Cloud Computing is a new concept which was recently came popular in computer industry. The main idea of cloud computing is the sharing of computing recourses among a community of users.

Cloud computing is a term you can see being used a lot, but there is a lack of clarity about what cloud computing is. However, most of us are probably making use of the cloud without realizing that this is the case; whenever we access our Gmail, Hotmail, or Yahoo mail accounts, or upload a photo to Facebook, we are using the cloud. The potential benefits and risks, however, are more apparent. In this chapter, we will try to shed some focus on defining cloud computing and other latest buzz words.

30.1 What is Cloud Computing?

Broadly, the cloud can be described as on-demand computing, for anyone with a network connection. Accessing applications and data anywhere, anytime, from any device is the potential outcome. The end user-level cloud is a good starting point for this – websites like Picasa, Flickr, and Facebook act as digital repositories for data and we can access this data from any internet-enabled device, from our smartphones to our desktop computers. In the case of Flickr and the like, storage of our digital images is, from the consumer point of view, somewhere in the cloud. We don't need to know where specifically, we just need our Flickr login credentials and a web connection. We can see this model as evident in web-based email too.

Cloud computing is a computing model, where resources such as computing power, storage, network and software are abstracted and provided as services on the internet in a remotely accessible fashion.

In simple terms, cloud computing is the delivery of *computing services* over the Internet. Whether they realize it or not, many people use cloud computing services for their own personal needs. For example, many people use *Google docs* or *Drop Box*, and these are cloud services. Photographs that people once kept on their own computers are now being stored on servers owned by third parties. These are also examples of cloud services.

Finally, we would say cloud computing is a means of delivery computing as a service rather than as a product.

30.2 Organizations are interested in Cloud Computing

Cloud computing can reduces the cost and complexity of owning and operating computers and networks. If an organization uses a cloud provider, it does not need to spend money on information technology infrastructure, or buy hardware or software licenses. Cloud services can often be customized and flexible to use, and providers can offer advanced services that an individual and small company might not have the money or expertise to develop.

30.3 Evolution of Cloud Computing

There are multiple factors that led to the evolution of Cloud Computing. One of the key factors is the way Internet Service Providers (ISP) matured over a period of time.

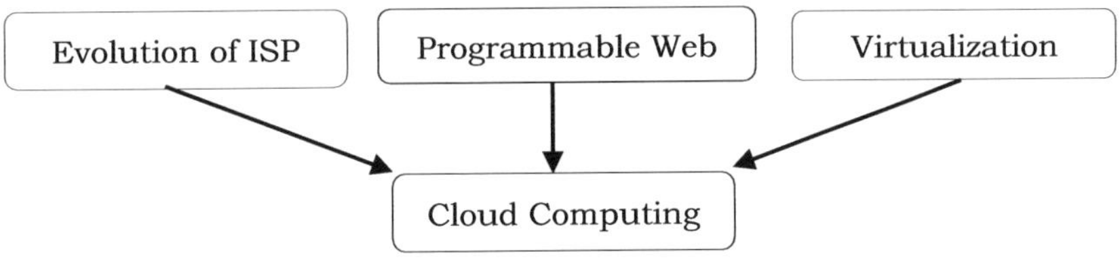

30.3.1 Evolution of ISP

From the initial days of offering basic Internet connectivity to offering Software as a Service (SaaS), the ISPs have come a long way. ISP 1.0 was all about providing Internet access to their customers. ISP 2.0 was the phase where ISPs offered hosting capabilities. The next step was co-location through which the ISPs started leasing out the rack space and bandwidth.

By this, companies could host their servers running custom, Line of Business (LoB) applications that could be accessed over the public internet by its employees, trading partners and customers. ISP 3.0 was offering applications on subscription resulting in the Application Service Provider (ASP) model. The latest trend of Software as a Service is a mature ASP model. The next logical step for ISPs would be to embrace the Cloud.

30.3.2 The Programmable Web

Web Services made the web programmable. They enabled the developers to look at the Internet as a class library or an object model. Protocols like Simple Object Access Protocol (SOAP), Representational State Transfer (REST), JavaScript Object Notation (JSON) and Plain Old XML (POX) fueled the growth of APIs on the web. Today every popular search engine (say Google, Bing), social networking sites (say, Facebook, Twitter, g+) have exposed APIs exposed to developers.

30.3.3 Virtualization

Virtualization is a hot topic in IT circles right now, but it's often misunderstood by many. Virtualization is the creation of a virtual (rather than actual) version of something, such as an operating system, a server, a storage device or network resources. In other words, it's defined as a method of decoupling an application and the resources required to run it — processor, memory, operating system, storage and network access — from the underlying hardware host.

Note; In subsequent sections we will have detailed discussion on virtualization.

Though the evolution of ISP, programmable web and virtualization are independent trends, they contribute to the evolution of Cloud Computing.

30.4 Cloud Deployment Models

Cloud computing model can be deployed in several ways. Based on the characteristics of those models we can classify them into four different deployment models: public, community, private, and hybrid. Each model has advantages and disadvantages.

30.4.1 Private Cloud

Private clouds are accessible only by a single, typically a company or an organization. This allows for maximum security and privacy. However, since only one group is allowed access to a private cloud, there is dispute as to whether using the cloud model is feasible at all because many feel that private clouds lack the economic model that makes cloud computing such an intriguing concept in the first place.

In other words, the cloud infrastructure has been deployed, and is maintained and operated for a specific organization. The operation may be in-house or with a third party on the premises.

30.4.2 Community Cloud

A community cloud offers cloud services that are shared with various organizations and companies. Shared costs and convenient interplay between groups are the main advantages. Similar privacy and security threats are applicable to community clouds as public clouds, as a substantial amount of information is reachable to others as well as the possibility of alteration or even deletion at the hand of the service provider.

That means, in this model, the cloud infrastructure is shared among a number of organizations with similar interests and requirements. This may help reducing the capital expenditure costs for its establishment as the costs are shared among the organizations.

30.4.3 Public Cloud

A public cloud is accessible to the general public. The provider (who offers the service) allows for accessibility to resources over the Internet and can either offer it free of charge or on a pay-to-use basis. Of course, using a public cloud service can pose some privacy and security issues. Being open to the public, a public cloud system can create easy access for anyone to the data, resources, or services offered by it.

The cloud infrastructure is available to the public on a commercial basis by a cloud service provider. This enables a consumer to develop and deploy a service in the cloud with very little financial outlay compared to the capital.

30.4.4 Hybrid Cloud

The cloud infrastructure consists of a number of clouds of any type, but the clouds have the ability (through their interfaces) to allow data and/or applications to be moved from one cloud to another. This can be a combination of private and public clouds that support the requirement to retain some data in an organization, and also the need to offer services in the cloud.

Hybrid clouds are a mix of any two or more services and take advantage of what each of those services has to offer. Companies get fault tolerance combined with locally immediate usability without dependency on Internet connectivity. Basically this means that if part of the system were to fail, it would continue to run though on a reduced level and have no reliance on Internet signal strength or connection whatsoever.

30.5 Types of Cloud Computing Services

There are mainly three types of Cloud Computing Services:

- SaaS [Software as a Service]
- PaaS [Platform as a Service]
- IaaS [Infrastructure as a Service]

30.5.1 SaaS [Software as a Service]

SaaS is the most widely known and widely used form of Cloud Computing. SaaS provides all the functions of a sophisticated traditional application, but through a Web browser, not a locally-installed application.

SaaS eliminates worries about application servers, storage, application development and related updates, common concerns of IT. Examples are Salesforce.com, Google's Gmail and Apps, instant messaging from AOL, Yahoo and Google, and VoIP from Vonage and Skype.

30.5.2 PaaS [Platform as a Service]

The consumer uses a hosted environment for their own applications. The consumer controls the applications that run in the environment (and possibly has some control over the hosting environment), but does not control the operating system, hardware or network infrastructure on which they are running. The platform is typically an application framework.

30.5.3 IaaS [Infrastructure as a Service]

The consumer uses "fundamental computing resources" such as grids or clusters or virtualized servers, networks, storage and system software designed to augment or replace the functions of an entire data center.

Examples are IBM's Smart Cloud Entry and PowerVC, Amazon's Elastic Compute Cloud [EC2] and Simple Storage Service, Microsoft's Azure etc...

30.6 Advantages of Cloud Computing

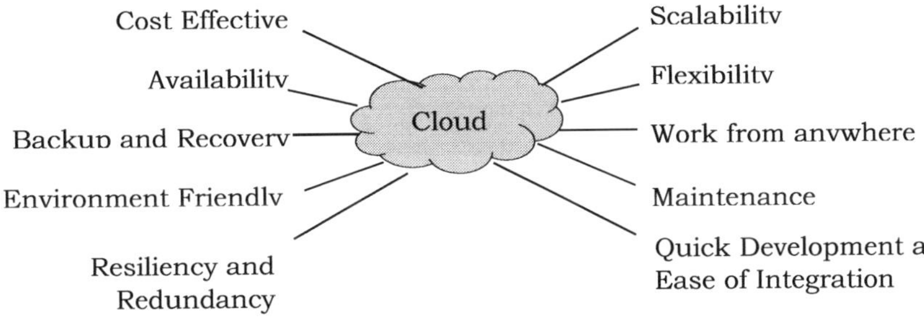

Cloud computing offers many advantages both to end users and organizations of all sizes. The main advantage is that organization's not have to support the infrastructure or have the knowledge necessary to develop and maintain the infrastructure, development environment or application, as were things up until recently.

The burden has been lifted and someone else is taking care of all that. Business is now able to focus on their core business by outsourcing all the hassle of IT infrastructure. Let us look at *ten* most important advantages of cloud computing.

30.6.1 Cost Efficiency

This is the biggest advantage of cloud computing, achieved by the elimination of the investment in stand-alone software or servers. By leveraging cloud's capabilities, companies can save on licensing fees and at the same time eliminate overhead charges such as the cost of data storage, software updates, management etc.

The cloud is in general available at much cheaper rates than traditional approaches and can significantly lower the overall IT expenses. At the same time, convenient and scalable charging models have emerged (such as one-time-payment and pay-as-you-go), making the cloud even more attractive.

30.6.2 Convenience and Continuous Availability

Public clouds offer services that are available wherever the end user might be located. This approach enables easy access to information and accommodates the needs of users in different time zones and geographic locations. As a side benefit, collaboration booms since it is now easier than ever to access, view and modify shared documents and files.

Moreover, service uptime is in most cases guaranteed, providing in that way continuous availability of resources. The various cloud vendors typically use multiple servers for maximum redundancy. In case of *system failure*, alternative instances are automatically spawned on other machines.

30.6.3 Backup and Recovery

The process of backing up and recovering data is simplified since those now reside on the cloud and not on a physical device. The various cloud providers offer reliable and flexible backup/recovery solutions.

In some cases, the cloud itself is used solely as a backup repository of the data located in local computers.

30.6.4 Cloud is Environmentally Friendly

The cloud is in general more efficient than the typical IT infrastructure and it takes fewer resources to compute, thus saving energy. For example, when servers are not used, the infrastructure normally scales down, freeing up resources and consuming less power.

At any moment, only the resources that are truly needed are consumed by the system.

30.6.5 Resiliency and Redundancy

A cloud deployment is usually built on a robust architecture thus providing resiliency and redundancy to its users. The cloud offers automatic failover between hardware platforms out of the box, while disaster recovery services are also often included.

30.6.6 Scalability and Performance

Scalability is a built-in feature for cloud deployments. Cloud instances are deployed automatically only when needed and as a result, you pay only for the applications and data storage you need.

Regarding performance, the systems utilize distributed architectures which offer excellent speed of computations. Again, it is the provider's responsibility to ensure that your services run on cutting edge machinery.

Instances can be added instantly for improved performance and customers have access to the total resources of the cloud's core hardware via their dashboards.

30.6.7 Quick Deployment and Ease of Integration

A cloud system can be up and running in a very short period, making quick deployment a key benefit. On the same aspect, the introduction of a new user in the system happens instantaneously, eliminating waiting periods.

Furthermore, software integration occurs automatically and organically in cloud installations. A business is allowed to choose the services and applications that best suit their preferences, while there is minimum effort in customizing and integrating those applications.

30.6.8 Increased Storage Capacity

The cloud can accommodate and store much more data compared to a personal computer and in a way offers almost unlimited storage capacity. It eliminates worries about running out of storage space and at the same time It spares businesses the need to upgrade their computer hardware, further reducing the overall IT cost.

30.6.9 Device Diversity and Location Independence

Cloud computing services can be accessed via many electronic devices that are able to have access to the Internet. These devices include not only the traditional PCs, but also smartphones, tablets etc.

An end-user might decide not only which device to use, but also where to access the service from. There is no limitation of place and medium. We can access our applications and data anywhere in the world, making this method very attractive to people. Cloud computing is in that way especially appealing to international companies as it offers the flexibility for its employees to access company files wherever they are.

30.6.10 Smaller Learning Curve

Cloud applications usually entail smaller learning curves since people are quietly used to them. Users find it easier to adopt them and come up to speed much faster. Main examples of this are applications like Gmail and Google Docs.

30.7 Clustering

Connecting two or more computers together in such a way that they behave like a single computer. Clustering is used for parallel processing, load balancing and fault tolerance.

Clustering, in the context of databases, refers to the ability of several servers or instances to connect to a single database. An instance is the collection of memory and processes that interacts with a database, which is the set of physical files that actually store data.

Clustering offers two main advantages, especially in database environments:

- *Fault tolerance*: Because there is more than one server or instance for users to connect to, clustering offers an alternative, in the event of individual server failure.
- *Load balancing*: The clustering feature is usually set up to allow users to be automatically allocated to the server with the least load.

Clustering takes different forms, depending on how the data is stored and allocated resources. The first type is known as the shared-nothing architecture. In this clustering mode, each node/server is fully independent, so there is no single point of contention. An example of this would be when a company has multiple data centers for a single website. With many servers across the globe, no single server is a *master*. Shared-nothing is also called *database sharding*."

Contrast this with shared-disk architecture, in which all data is stored centrally and then accessed via instances stored on different servers or nodes.

The distinction between the two types has become blurred recently with the introduction of grid computing or distributed caching. In this setup, data is still centrally managed but controlled by a powerful *virtual server* that is comprised of many servers that work together as one.

30.8 Grid Computing

At its most basic level, grid computing is a computer network in which each computer's resources are shared with every other computer in the system. In other words, grid Computing is a technique in which the idle systems in the network and their *wasted* CPU cycles can be efficiently used by uniting pools of servers, storage systems and networks into a single large virtual system for resource sharing dynamically at runtime. These systems can be distributed across the globe; they're heterogeneous (some PCs, some servers, maybe mainframes and supercomputers); somewhat autonomous (a Grid can potentially access resources in different organizations). IBM is one of the biggest exploiters of grid computing.

The grid computing concept isn't a new one. It's a special kind of distributed computing. In distributed computing, different computers within the same network share one or more resources. In the ideal grid computing system, every resource is shared, turning a computer network into a powerful supercomputer. With the right user interface, accessing a grid computing system would look no different than accessing a local machine's resources. Every authorized computer would have access to enormous processing power and storage capacity.

Though the concept isn't new, it's also not yet perfected. Computer scientists, programmers and engineers are still working on creating, establishing and implementing standards and protocols. Right now, many existing grid computer systems rely on proprietary software and tools. Once people agree upon a reliable set of standards and protocols, it will be easier and more efficient for organizations to adopt the grid computing model.

Grid computing systems work on the principle of pooled resources. Let's say you and a couple of friends decide to go on a camping trip. You own a large tent, so you've volunteered to share it with the others. One of your friends offers to bring food and another says he'll drive the whole group up in his car. Once on the trip, the three of you share your knowledge and skills to make the trip fun and comfortable. If you had made the trip on your own, you would need more time to assemble the resources you'd need and you probably would have had to work a lot harder on the trip itself.

A grid computing system uses that same concept: share the load across multiple computers to complete tasks more efficiently and quickly. Before going too much further, let's take a quick look at a computer's resources:

Central processing unit (CPU): A CPU is a microprocessor that performs mathematical operations and directs data to different memory locations. Computers can have more than one CPU.

- Memory: In general, a computer's memory is a kind of temporary electronic storage. Memory keeps relevant data close at hand for the microprocessor. Without memory, the microprocessor would have to search and retrieve data from a more permanent storage device such as a hard disk drive.
- Storage: In grid computing terms, storage refers to permanent data storage devices like hard disk drives or databases.

Normally, a computer can only operate within the limitations of its own resources. There's an upper limit to how fast it can complete an operation or how much information it can store. Most computers are upgradeable, which means it's possible to add more power or capacity to a single computer, but that's still just an incremental increase in performance.

Grid computing systems link computer resources together in a way that lets someone use one computer to access and leverage the collected power of all the computers in the system. To the individual user, it's as if the user's computer has transformed into a supercomputer.

30.9 Virtualization

The term virtualization broadly describes the separation of a resource or request for a service from the underlying physical delivery of that service. With virtual memory, for example, computer software gains access to more memory than is physically installed, via the background swapping of data to disk storage. Similarly, virtualization techniques can be applied to other IT infrastructure layers including networks, storage, laptop or server hardware, operating systems and applications.

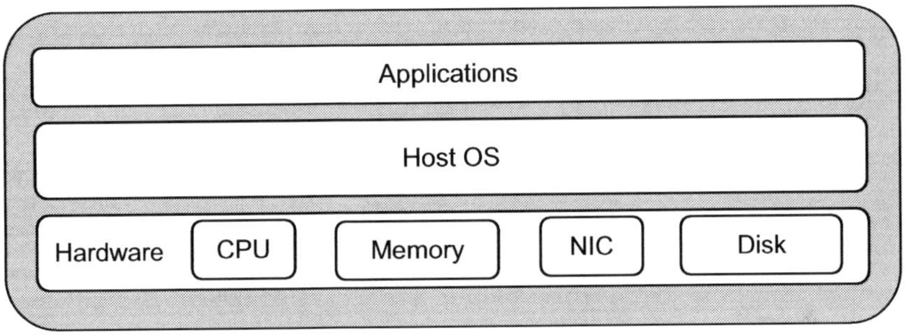

Virtualization is typically defined as the ability to run more than one application or operating system in an isolated and secure environment on a single physical system.

This blend of virtualization technologies or virtual infrastructure provides a layer of abstraction between computing, storage and networking hardware, and the applications running on it. The deployment of virtual infrastructure is non-disruptive, since the user experiences are largely unchanged. However, virtual infrastructure gives administrators the advantage of managing pooled resources across the enterprise, allowing IT managers to be more responsive to dynamic organizational needs and to better leverage infrastructure investments.

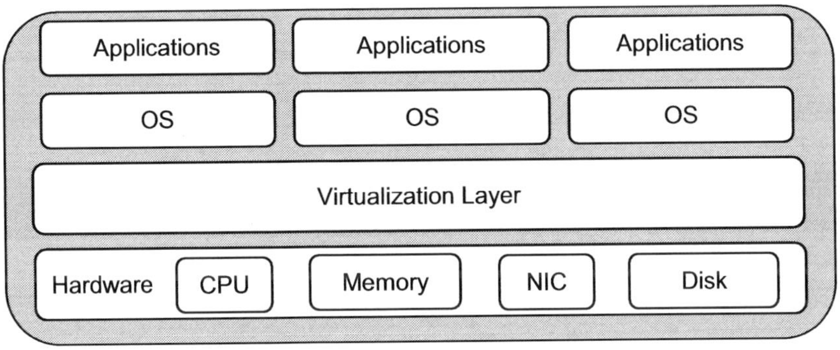

Virtualization is a hot topic in IT circles right now, but it's often misunderstood by many. Virtualization is the creation of a virtual (rather than actual) version of something, such as an operating system, a server, a storage device or network resources. In other words, it is defined as a method of decoupling an application and the resources required to run it — processor, memory, operating system, storage and network access — from the underlying hardware host.

Virtualization allows multiple operating system instances to run concurrently on a single computer; it is a means of *separating* hardware from a single operating system. Each "guest" OS is managed by a *Virtual Machine Monitor* (VMM), also known as a *hypervisor*. Because the virtualization system sits between the guest and the hardware, it can control the guests' use of CPU, memory, and storage, even allowing a guest OS to migrate from one machine to another.

30.9.1 Virtualization Approaches

While virtualization has been a part of the IT landscape for decades, it is only recently (in 1998) that VMware delivered the benefits of virtualization to industry-standard x86-based platforms, which now form the majority of desktop, laptop and server shipments. A key benefit of virtualization is the ability to run multiple operating systems on a single physical system and share the underlying hardware resources called *partitioning*.

Basically, there are three virtualization approaches:

- Hosted Virtualization
- Hypervisor Virtualization
- Application Virtualization

30.9.1.1 Hosted Virtualization

A hosted approach provides partitioning services on top of a standard operating system and supports the broadest range of hardware configurations.

This is the simplest type of virtualization to set up for a new user or for testing and development. This is often the starting point for most IT organizations looking to get into virtualization on a large scale. Hosted virtualization resides on top of a host operating system (Windows, Linux, UNIX etc.) and all I/O is dependent on the hosting operating system.

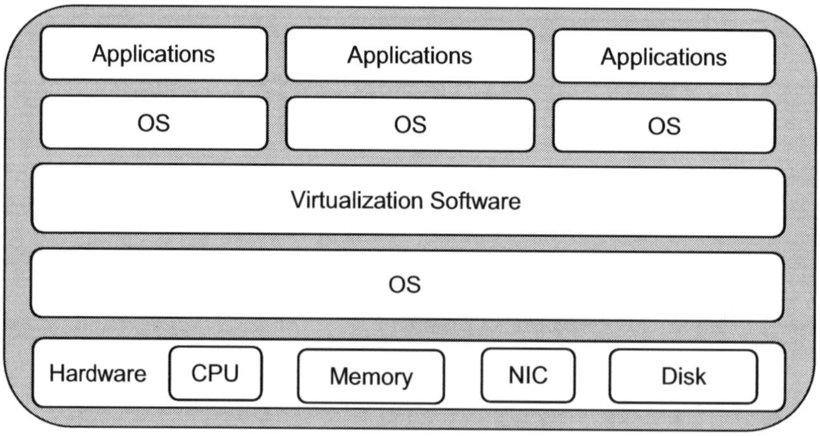

This is the same as before, but a couple additional layers have been added. First there is the layer of the host operating system. All virtualization is dependent on this operating system, if maintenance needs to be done then all virtual machines running on top of it will be impacted. The next layer is the virtualization software itself. This layer cannot be avoided in most methods of virtualization (hardware virtualization being the exception). It is safe to assume that there will most likely be some sort of software doing the coordination of the I/O and hardware access. The only difference in this case is that this software is dependent on the domain0 operating system's drivers for interaction with the hardware. This approach is acceptable for development environments or very small deployments where maximized uptime is not a requirement.

30.9.1.2 Hypervisor Virtualization

A hypervisor virtualization is the first layer of software installed on a clean operating system (hence it is often referred to as a *"bare metal"* approach). Since it has direct access to the hardware resources, a hypervisor is more efficient than hosted architectures, enabling greater scalability, robustness and performance. Hypervisor virtualization is where the true power in virtualization comes from. This approach takes away the host operating system and virtualization software and replaces it with another piece of software called a *hypervisor*.

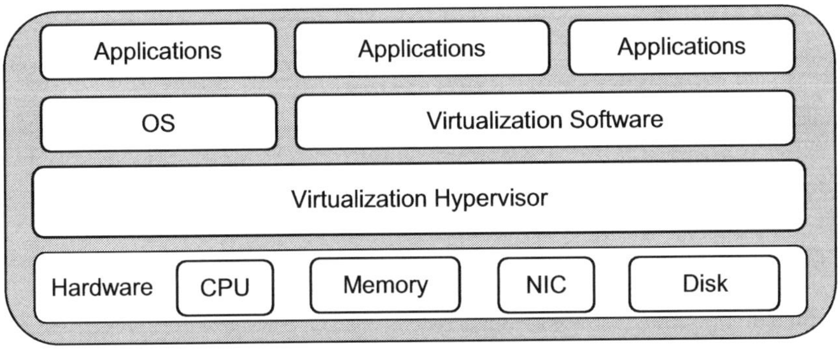

This hypervisor software plays the role of a traffic cop, controlling access to hardware resources on the physical machine. It also keeps the resources for virtual machines separate and secure. Also, because the hypervisor has total control over the hardware there are far more possibilities for optimization. For example, VMware ESX has the ability to share memory pages between similar virtual machines. This means is that when the first Windows virtual machine is booted, Windows is loaded into memory. Then when subsequent machines are booted memory pointers are created to duplicate memory pages.

30.9.1.3 Application Virtualization

This is sort of a different topic, but still relates here. The idea here is to extend some of the benefits of server virtualization down to the application layer. Application virtualization technology isolates applications from the underlying operating system and from other applications to increase compatibility and manageability.

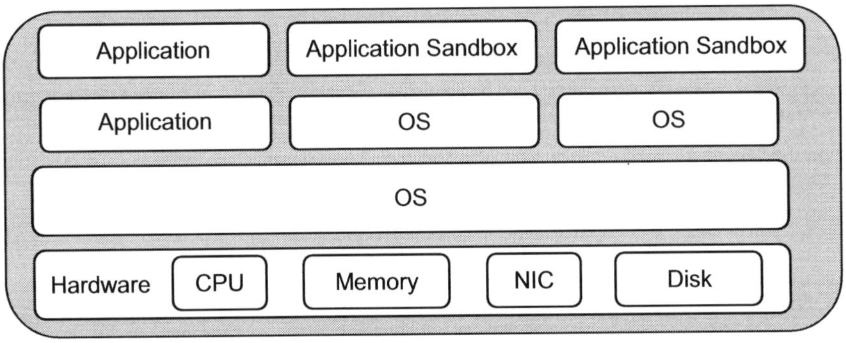

Applications can be placed in a *sealed sandbox* where they do not have the ability to affect the underlying operating system components directly. This can be extremely useful for running multiple conflicting versions of the same software on the same system. Keep in mind that this technology can be combined with other virtualization technology to achieve even higher levels of control. This is also a way to prevent applications from contaminating a clean operating system image on a client computer or server. In this, application files, configuration, and settings are copied to the target device and the application execution at run time is controlled by the application virtualization layer.

30.9.2 Virtualization versus Cloud Computing

While these two IT terms are often substituted for one another, there is a very big difference.

Virtualization software makes it possible to run multiple operating systems and multiple applications on the same server at the same time. At its most basic level, *Cloud* treats computing as a utility rather than a specific product or technology. Virtualization is part of a physical infrastructure, while cloud computing is a service.

There is also a significant cost difference: Those who use virtualization encounter high upfront costs but save money in the long run; those who opt for cloud computing typically pay a subscription fee based on how much they use. If your user base grows, or consumers eat up more resources, your fees could increase over time.

Another important distinction is that virtualization can be a method for delivering a private cloud, but it doesn't work the other way around. Every cloud is composed of virtual infrastructure but not every virtual infrastructure is part of a cloud."

Finally, what we can say is cloud computing is a broad area which includes virtualization as a component.

30.9.3 Categories of Virtualization

Virtualization is an umbrella term for many different types of computing:

30.9.3.1 Hardware Virtualization

This allows one server to run multiple operating systems at the same time, decreasing the number of servers needed to power a workforce. This is the simplest type of virtualization to set up for a new user or for testing and development. This is often the starting point for most IT organizations looking to get into virtualization on a large scale. Hosted virtualization resides on top of a host operating system (Windows, Linux, AIX etc.) and all I/O is dependent on the hosting operating system.

30.9.3.2 Software Virtualization

If you've ever booted your Mac in Windows, or vice versa, you were virtualizing your software. This typically happens on individual computers, not entire networks.

30.9.3.3 Desktop Virtualization

VMware calls this VDI, and although that is their proprietary system, the concept of desktop virtualization is not limited to any single company. In this scenario, each computer's preferences, OS, application and files are hosted somewhere other than the local machine. This has a number of benefits, both for end users and for IT departments.

.3.4 Storage Virtualization

This is the consolidation of data in a central location, where multiple users can access it. It allows for the reduction in duplicated data and potentially fewer servers.

30.10 Big Data

Let us take a look at another latest buzz word *Big Data*.

30.10.1 What is big data?

Every day, we create 2.5 quintillion (*one* followed by 30 zeros 10^{30}) bytes of data. Also, 90% of the data in the world today has been created in the last two years alone. This data comes from everywhere: sensors used to gather climate information, posts to social media sites, digital pictures and videos, purchase transaction records, and cell phone GPS signals to name a few. This data is *big data*.

In defining big data, it's also important to understand the mix of *unstructured* and *multi – structured* data that comprises the volume of information.

Unstructured data comes from information that is not organized or easily interpreted by traditional databases or data models, and typically, it's text-heavy. Metadata, Twitter tweets, and other social media posts are good examples of unstructured data.

Multi – structured data refers to a variety of data formats and types and can be derived from interactions between people and machines, such as web applications or social networks. A good example is web log data, which includes a combination of *text* and *images* along with structured data like *form* or *transactional* information.

30.10.2 Characteristics of big data

Big data is data that exceeds the processing capacity of conventional database systems. The data is too big, moves too fast, or doesn't fit the strictures of your database architectures. To gain value from this data, you must choose an alternative way to process it.

The main characteristics of big data are:

1. Volume
2. Variety
3. Velocity
4. Variability
5. Complexity

30.10.2.1 Volume

The quantity of data that is generated is very important in this context. It is the size of the data which determines the value and potential of the data under consideration and whether it can actually be considered as big data or not. The name big data itself contains a term which is related to size and hence the characteristic.

30.10.2.2 Variety

The next aspect of big data is its *variety*. This means that the category to which big data belongs to is also a very essential fact that needs to be known by the data analysts. This helps the people, who are closely analyzing the data and are associated with it, to effectively use the data to their advantage and thus upholding the importance of the big data.

30.10.2.3 Velocity

The term *velocity* in this context refers to the speed of generation of data or how fast the data is generated and processed to meet the demands and the challenges which lie ahead in the path of growth and development.

30.10.2.4 Variability

This is a factor which can be a problem for those who are analysing the data. This refers to the inconsistency which can be shown by the data at times, thus hampering the process of being able to handle and manage the data effectively.

30.10.2.5 Complexity

Data management can become a very complex process, especially when large volumes of data come from multiple sources. These data need to be linked, connected and correlated in order to be able to grasp the information that is supposed to be conveyed by these data. This situation, is therefore, termed as the *complexity* of big data. As discussed above, big data comes mainly in structured and unstructured data.

30.10.3 Big Data in Markets

Big data has increased the demand of information management specialists. Specially, IBM, Oracle Corporation, Microsoft, SAP, EMC, HP and Dell have spent more than $15 billion on software firms only specializing in data management and analytics.

Major big data software's are:

- Hadoop - Apache Foundation
- MongoDB - MongoDB, Inc
- Splunk - Splunk Inc

30.10.4 Architecture

In 2004, Google published a paper on a process called MapReduce that used such architecture. MapReduce framework provides a parallel processing model and associated implementation to process huge amount of data. With MapReduce, queries are split and distributed across parallel nodes and processed in parallel (the Map step). The results are then gathered and delivered (the Reduce step). The framework was incredibly successful, so others wanted to replicate the algorithm. Therefore, an implementation of MapReduce framework was adopted by an *Apache* open source project named *Hadoop*.

Apache Hadoop is an open source software project that enables the distributed processing of large data sets across clusters of servers. It is designed to scale up from a single server to thousands of machines. It provides a very high degree of fault tolerance. Rather than depending on high-end hardware, the resiliency of these clusters comes from the software's ability to detect and handle failures at the application layer.

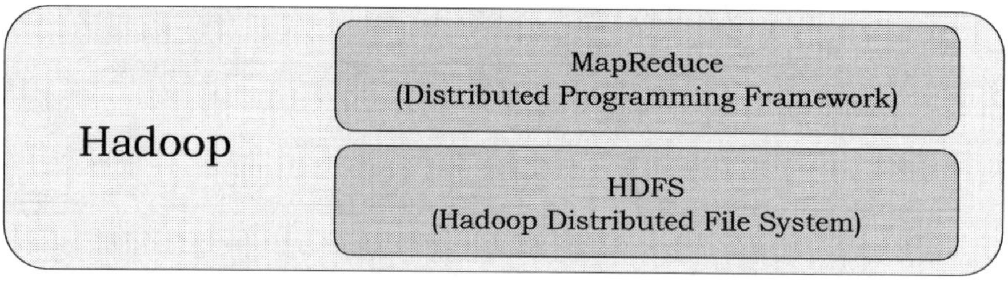

Apache Hadoop has two main subprojects:

- *MapReduce*
- *Hadoop Distributed File System* (HDFS)

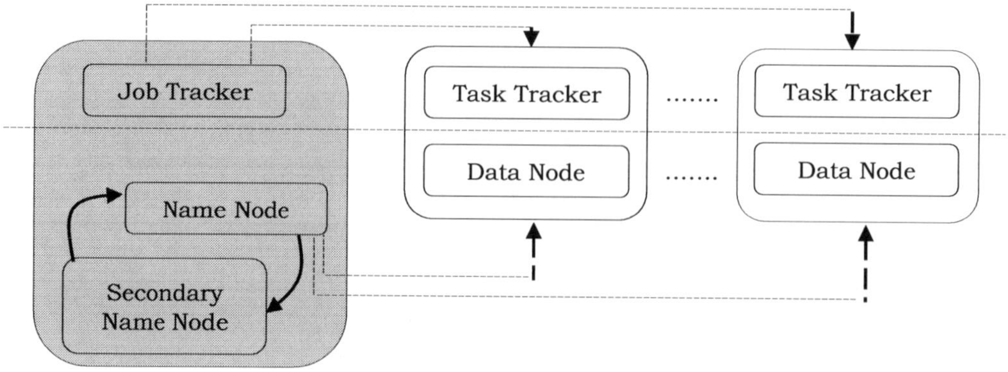

30.10.4.1 MapReduce

MapReduce is the distributed programming framework that understands and assigns work to the nodes in a cluster. MapReduce is the base component of a Hadoop framework. It manages the data processing part on the Hadoop cluster. A cluster runs MapReduce jobs written in Java or any other language (Python, Ruby, R, etc.) via streaming.

A single job may consist of multiple tasks. The number of tasks that can run on a data node is decided by the amount of memory installed. It is recommended to have more memory installed on each data node for better cluster performance. Based on the application workload that is going to run on the cluster, a data node may require high compute power, high disk I/O or additional memory.

The job execution process is handled by the *Job Tracker* and *Task Tracker* services. The type of job scheduler chosen for a cluster depends on the application workload. If the cluster will be running short running jobs, then FIFO scheduler will serve the purpose. For a much more balanced cluster, one can choose to use Fair Scheduler. In *MapReduce version* 1.0, there's no high availability (HA) for the JobTracker service.

If the node running Job Tracker service fails, all jobs submitted in the cluster will be discontinued and must be resubmitted once the node is recovered or another node is made available. This issue has been fixed in the newer release — i.e., *MapReduce version* 2.0, also called yet another resource negotiator (YARN).

The *Secondary Name Node* plays the vital role of check-pointing. It is this node that off-loads the work of metadata image creation and updating on a regular basis. It is recommended to keep the machine configuration the same as *Name Node* so that in the case of an emergency

30.10.4.2 Hadoop Distributed File System (HDFS)

Hadoop distributed file system (HDFS) is a base component of the Hadoop framework that manages the data storage. It stores data in the form of data blocks (default size: 64MB) on the local hard disk. The input data size defines the block size to be used in the cluster. A block size of 128MB for a large file set is a good choice.

Keeping large block sizes means a small number of blocks can be stored, thereby minimizing the memory requirement on the master node (commonly known as *Name Node*) for storing the metadata information. Block size also impacts the job execution time, and thereby cluster performance. A file can be stored in HDFS with a different block size during the upload process. For file sizes smaller than the block size, the Hadoop cluster may not perform optimally.

HDFS is a file system that spans all the nodes in a Hadoop cluster for data storage. It links together the file systems on many local nodes to make them into one big file system. HDFS assumes nodes will fail, so it achieves reliability by replicating data across multiple nodes.

30.10.4.2.1 Examples of HDFS

Think of a file that contains the phone numbers for everyone in the India; the people with a last name starting with A might be stored on server 1, B on server 2, and so on. In a Hadoop world, pieces of this phonebook would be stored across the cluster, and to reconstruct the entire phonebook, your program would need the blocks from every server in the cluster. To achieve availability as components fail, HDFS replicates these smaller pieces onto two additional servers by default.

This redundancy can be increased or decreased on a per-file basis or for a whole environment; for example, a development Hadoop cluster typically doesn't need any data redundancy. This redundancy offers multiple benefits, the most obvious being higher availability.

Also, this redundancy allows the Hadoop cluster to break work up into smaller chunks and run those jobs on all the servers in the cluster for better scalability. Finally, you get the benefit of data locality, which is critical when working with large data sets.

HDFS has built-in fault tolerance capability, thereby eliminating the need for setting up a redundant array of inexpensive disks (RAID) on the data nodes. The data blocks stored in HDFS automatically get replicated across multiple data nodes based on the replication factor (default: 3). The replication factor determines the number of copies of a data block to be created and distributed across other data nodes. The larger the replication factor, the better the read performance of the cluster. On the other hand, it requires more time to replicate the data blocks and more storage for replicated copies.

For example, storing a file size of 1GB requires around 4GB of storage space, due to a replication factor of 3 and an additional 20% to 30% of space required during data processing.

Both block size and replication factor impact Hadoop cluster performance. The value for both the parameters depends on the input data type and the application workload to run on this cluster. In a development environment, the replication factor can be set to a smaller number — say, 1 or 2 — but it is advisable to set this value to a higher factor, if the data available on the cluster is crucial. Keeping a default replication factor of 3 is a good choice from a data redundancy and cluster performance perspective.

CHAPTER

Miscellaneous Concepts 31

31.1 Basics of HTML and CSS

HTML is short for *HyperText Markup Language*.

- Hypertext is simply a piece of text that works as a link.
- Markup Language is a way of writing layout information within documents.

Basically an HTML document is a plain text file that contains text and nothing else. When a browser opens an HTML file, the browser will look for HTML codes in the text and use them to change the layout, insert images, or create links to other pages. Since HTML documents are just text files they can be written in even the simplest text editor. A more popular choice is to use a special HTML editor - maybe even one that puts focus on the visual result rather than the codes - a so-called WYSIWYG editor ("What You See Is What You Get").

31.1.1 HTML File

HTML is a format that tells a web browser how to display a web page. The documents themselves are plain text files with special "tags" or codes that a web browser uses to interpret and display information.

An HTML file is a text file containing small markup tags and the markup tags tell the Web browser how to display the page. HTML files have an htm or html file extension.

31.1.2 Example

Open your text editor and type the following text:

```
<html>
    <head>
        <title>My First Webpage</title>
    </head>
    <body>
        This is my homepage. <b>This text is bold</b>
    </body>
</html>
```

Save the file as TestPage.html. Start your Internet browser (say, Google Chrome). Select Open (or Open Page) in the File menu of your browser. A dialog box will appear. Select Browse (or Choose File) and locate the html file you just created - TestPage.html - select it and click Open. Now you should see an address in the dialog box, for example C:\Test\TestPage.html. Click OK, and the browser will display the page.

What we just made is a skeleton html document. This is the minimum required information for a web document and all web documents should contain these basic components. The first tag in our html document is <html>. This tag tells the browser that this is the start of an html document. The last tag in our document is </html>. This tag tells the browser that this is the end of the html document.

The text between the <head> tag and the </head> tag is header information. Header information is not displayed in the browser window. The text between the <title> tags is the title of our document. The <title> tag is used to uniquely identify each document and is also displayed in the title bar of the browser window. The text between the <body> tags is the text that will be displayed in the browser. The text between the <b> and </b> tags will be displayed in a bold font.

31.1.3 Viewing HTML Source

A good way to learn HTML is to look at how other people have coded their html pages. To find out, simply click on the View option in your browsers toolbar and select Source or Page Source. This will open a window that shows you the actual HTML of the page.

31.1.4 Structure of a HTML Document

The tags below must appear in the order that they are shown here

<HTML>	Means the start of the document
<HEAD>	This is where you will put in key words so that search engines will find your page when people do a search on a subject area
<TITLE>	Here you type the title you want the page to have. It will appear in the Title Bar of your browser
</TITLE>	Defines end of title area
</HEAD>	Defines end of head area
<BODY>	Here you put the text, pictures, etc. that you want on your web page. This is what the viewer to your website will see on the screen
</BODY>	defines the end of what you will see in the browser window
</HTML>	

Everything that is seen on your web page in the Browser is between the <body> and </body> tags!!!!!! Notice that all the tags are closed in the opposite order to that in which they are opened.

Note: HTML is not a case-sensitive language. Hence, we can use either uppercase or lower case tags.

31.1.5 Elements, Attributes and Values

The ELEMENTS (Body, Font, Table, Align, Center etc.) are formatting that we use to define how the text looks in your web pages. The name of the element is always enclosed in the brackets e.g. <BODY> or <FONT> or <Center>. Note that it does not matter whether you use capital letters or not. It is a good idea to be consistent with whichever you use.

Elements are used in pairs with an opening and closing TAG (a word used to describe the elements) for each element ie

```
<FONT FACE="Comic Sans MS">
    This sentence is in Comic Sans MS
</FONT>
```

We can define the attributes of the element we want to apply such as

```
<BODY BGCOLOR="yellow"> or <Align="right">
```

Here is an example – the FONT element can have the attributes SIZE, COLOR and FACE

```
<FONT FACE="Verdana" SIZE="15", COLOR="red">
```

There are a few exceptions to the use of closing tags but it is best practice to use both at all times. When you close the tag the formatting of the text ends.

31.1.6 The Page Title

```
<Title>My First Test Web Page</Title>
```

This is what is seen in the Title Bar of the browser. This should be relevant to the topic of the page. It is also used by Search Engines to categorize your web page/site.

31.1.7 The Body

This contains everything that will appear on the browser screen which can be seen on the WWW. You need to enclose everything that you want inside the tags <body> .....</body> otherwise it will not be seen.

31.1.8 Text/Font Size

It is important to display text attractively and to use headings and space to make it easier to read. Variation in text size can be done using the following tags:

31.1.9 Using The HEADING element

```
<H1>... largest heading size. </H1>
<H2>....</H2> is smaller
<H6> ....</H6> is the smallest heading size. This is even smaller than normal sized text
<Hx>(where x is a figure from 1 to 6)...text..../Hx>
```

31.1.10 Using The FONT element

```
<FONT SIZE="x">...text...</FONT> (where x is a figure from 1 to 7)
   or
<FONT SIZE="+x">...text...</FONT> (x can be 1 to 6)
   or
<FONT SIZE="-x">...text...</FONT> (x can be 1 to 6)
```

31.1.11 What is Normal Text?

If we key in text between the two body tags and do not format it in any way it will be displayed across the width of the screen and will wrap when it reaches the screen edge. It will be normal size and default font or typeface (normal size is size 3 and default is whatever the user has set their browser to display – often Times New Roman!). It will be left-aligned on screen.

31.1.12 Other Formatting of Text

Text can be made to stand out from its surroundings by using some of the following tags:

- To center text across the screen use <CENTER> .....</CENTER>

- To darken text use <STRONG> ......</STRONG> will darken anything between the 2 tags
- To bold text use <B> ....</B> all between the tags will appear bold
- To underline text use <U> ....</U>
- Another way to create emphasis is <EM>....</EM> which usually puts text in italics
- To use italics use <I> ....</I>
- The <ALIGN> tag determines the alignment of text and can be <ALIGN=”right”> or <ALIGN=”left”> or <ALIGN=”center”>

31.1.13 Using Tags Together in Groups

```
<EM><STRONG><CENTER> ............. .....</EM></STRONG></CENTER>
```

and everything in between will be in bold, emphasized in some way (italic or underlined) and centered. Note the closing of tags opposite to order of opening.

31.1.14 Use Horizontal Rule

It is a line that is used to break up text. A line is drawn across the page and the tag used is <HR> no closing tag! You can define the length, height, colour and alignment of the line as follows:

```
<HR ALIGN=center COLOR=blue SIZE=20 width=500>
```

SIZE is defined as a number of pixels and determines the vertical height of the line WIDTH can be defined as a number of pixels or as a percentage of the screen width (often safer). A further attribute is NOSHADE which means that the line will not be displayed as 3D.

31.1.15 Line Spacing

By default text is in single-line spacing.

31.1.16 Begin a New Line

To start a new line without leaving a blank line and before the normal word wrapping would come into plan use
 (Note the <BR> tag does not really need to be closed!)

31.1.17 Start a New Paragraph

To start a new paragraph and leave one blank line between paragraphs

```
<p> .......</p>
```

For a series of paragraphs we can do this

```
<p> .....text
<p> ...text...... </p> </p> (notice we had to close the two paragraph commands)
```

31.1.18 Create White Space/Margins/Indents

To indent text from the sides of the screen <BLOCKQUOTE> ....</BLOCKQUOTE> is used. Each blockquote indents the text from both sides by half an inch.

```
<BLOCKQUOTE><BLOCKQUOTE><BLOCKQUOTE>........text............</BLOCKQUOTE>
```

Note that closing the BLOCKQUOTE will only bring you back half an inch from the current indent. If you want to go back to the original margin then you need 3 closing tags.

31.1.19 Create Character Spacing

HTML only recognizes ONE space between words and after full stops even if you key in more. To put in extra spaces we have to use the special code * * which puts in an extra character space. There are no brackets around these special characters.

31.1.20 Use Preformatted Text

If you want the text you type to be displayed on the screen EXACTLY as you typed it put the following tags around it and whatever spaces, indents, enters etc. that you type will be reflected in the browser.

```
<PRE> ....</PRE>
```

31.1.21 Use Basefont

Basefont is a tag that can be used to determine the font for a complete document. It is put inside the HEAD tag:

```
<HEAD>
    <BASEFONT FACE="Verdana">
</HEAD>
```

31.1.22 Inline Font Changes

Anything that happens between the two <BODY> tags this is called *in – line* formatting and will take precedence over any settings in the <HEAD> section.

- To change typeface, use <FONT FACE = "Verdana">......</FONT>
- To change type colour, use <FONT COLOR="green">......</FONT>
- To change type size, use <FONT SIZE="5">.......</FONT>
- To simplify these can be put together as follows:
  <FONT FACE="Verdana" COLOR="green" SIZE="5">.........</FONT>

31.1.23 Change Text Alignment

DIV stands for a section of the document that you want to format in a particular way as seen below and is often used with the ALIGN tag as shown here

```
<DIV ALIGN="Right"> ....</DIV>
<DIV ALIGN="Justify"> ....</DIV>
<DIV ALIGN="Centre"> ....</DIV>
```

When you close the tag the text reverts to the original format

31.1.24 Creating Lists

31.1.24.1 A Definition List

This list gives you a headline on the first line and then indents the remaining lines that are contained between the <DD> <DD> tags.

The HTML code is:

```
<DL> Defines the list
    <DT> This is the highest order line (appears to left of others)
        <DD> List item one </DD>
        <DD> List item two </DD>
        <DD> List item three</DD>
    </DT>
```

```
</DL> Ends the list
```

<DD>...</DD> is where you put the items in the list and you can put as many items as you wish as long as you keep repeating <DD> and </DD>

31.1.24.2 An Ordered List

An ordered list lists items in order of priority. It displays numbers ie 1, 2, 3 or (i), (ii), (iii) etc.

```
<OL> List begins
    <LI> List items go here </LI>
    <LI> and here </LI>
</OL> List ends
```

31.1.24.3 An Unordered List

An unordered list means that every item in the list has the same importance. A bulleted list is an unordered list
Displays bullets in front of each line

```
<UL>
    <LI> </LI>
    <LI> </LI>
</UL>
```

31.1.25 Use Page Backgrounds - Colour

To use a background colour

```
<BODY BGCOLOR="choose your colour">
```

We can check the Hexadecimal colour chart to choose a suitable colour.

31.1.26 Use Page Backgrounds - Images

To use a graphic as the background to the page

```
<BODY BACKGROUND ="imagename.gif">
```

For this the graphic needs to be in the same folder as the html document. If the image file is not in the same folder make sure you put in the full path name in your code

```
<BODY BACKGROUND ="path/imagename.gif">
```

The graphic does not have to be the same size as your screen. When the browser displays the image, it 'tiles' it across and down to fill the page. It is important NOT to use a very 'busy' image that will take away from the text or other elements of the page. It should not be annoying or make the page hard to read.

31.1.27 Use In-Line Images

These are pictures that are part of your web page in order to complement the message you are attempting to get across. Again we have the same considerations regarding where the image files are stored (path names important).

For an image that is the *same folder* as the current web page use

```
<IMG SRC="imagename.gif">
```

For an image that is in a *subfolder* of the current folder use

```
<img src="folder name/imagename.gif">
```

We can also determine the height, width and whether to use a border or not around the image.

```
<IMG SRC="imagename.gif" HEIGHT=100 WIDTH=120 BORDER="1">
```

All the figures above are *pixels*. Measurements can also be used

```
<IMG SRC="imagename.gif" HEIGHT=1.5" WIDTH=1.7" BORDER="0.2"">
```

If something is wrong and the picture does not display on the screen you should always have some alternate text to tell the viewer that there should be a picture there and what it is meant to be for example into the tag you would also add the following

```
<IMG SRC="myself.jpg" HEIGHT=1.5" WIDTH=1.7" BORDER="0.2"
                                        ALT = "Photo of myself" >
```

If BORDER is set equal to 0 then there will be no border

31.1.28 Link your Pages to form a Web!

To link the current web page to another page on the WWW:

```
<A HREF=http//www.page address> This text here forms the link </A>
```

A link to another page in the same website (in the same folder as the current one)

```
<A HREF="filename.htm">Go to</A> the next page
```

To link your page to another file that is not in the same folder eg a picture file

```
<A HREF="images/graphicname.jpg">Click here to see the picture</A>
```

31.1.29 Link Colours

Web pages are all about links. The links are usually coloured differently from the surrounding text in order to make them stand out and draw the viewer's attention. Consistency is very important in this. To change the screen background colour, the text colour and the colour of the links you will use

```
<body bgcolor= "Aqua" TEXT="black" LINK="blue" VLINK="Red" ALINK = "Grey">
```

LINK defines the colour of a link as shown when the page is first displayed in the browser

- VLINK is the colour a link and will change to after it has been clicked
- ALINK is the colour of the active link

Email Link

```
<A HREF=mailto:"email address">Contact me by email</A>
```

31.1.30 Tables

A table is used to help format your page as you have definite areas (cells) on the page where you can place information. Tables are used to present text in columns or to break up a screen into cells to contain data.

The table feature begins and ends with the <TABLE> and </TABLE> tags but there are many other things involved such as the width of the table, its alignment, the number of columns, the number of rows and the alignment of text within cells. The following is the basic code for a table that has 2 rows and 2 columns

```
<TABLE>
    <TR>
        <TD> </TD>
```

```
        <TD> </TD>
    </TR>
    <TR>
        <TD </TD>
        <TD> </TD>
    </TR>
</TABLE>
```

31.1.31 Difference between - Font, Basefont and Text

The <FONT> tag allows us to control the appearance of text with the attributes FACE, COLOR and SIZE and can be used anywhere within the BODY area of an HTML document. It is an inline formatting element

```
<FONT FACE="Verdana" COLOR="green" SIZE="4">.......</FONT>
```

The <BASEFONT> tag is a special tag which must go inside the HEAD area of your HTML document and with it we can also define FACE, COLOR and SIZE of text for an entire document.

```
<HEAD><BASEFONT FACE=x " COLOR=x " SIZE=x ">.......</HEAD>
```

Finally TEXT is an attribute of the <BODY> tag which sets only the colour of the text for the document.

```
<BODY BGCOLOR="Aqua" TEXT="red"> ......</BODY>
```

31.2 Javascript

Javascript is a scripting language that will allow us to add real programming to webpages. We can create small application type processes with javascript, like a calculator or a primitive game of some sort.

Below are uses of javascript:

- *Browser Detection*: Detecting the browser used by a visitor at a webpage. Depending on the browser, another page specifically designed for that browser can then be loaded.
- *Cookies*: Storing information on the visitor's computer and then retrieving this information automatically next time the user visits webpage. This technique is called *cookies*.
- *Control Browsers*: Opening pages in customized windows, where we specify if the browser's buttons, menu line, status line or whatever should be present.
- *Validate Forms*: Validating inputs to fields before submitting a form. An example would be validating the entered email address to see if it has an @ in it, since if not, it's not a valid address.

Since javascript isn't HTML, we will need to let the browser know in advance when we enter javascript to an HTML page. This is done using the <script> tag. The browser will use the *<script> type="text/javascript">* and *</script >* to tell where javascript starts and ends.

Consider this example:

```
<html>
    <head>
        <title>My Javascript WebPage</title>
    </head>
    <body>
        <script type="text/javascript">
            alert("Welcome to my Webpage!!!");
```

```
        </script>
    </body>
</html>
```

The word alert is a standard javascript command that will cause an alert box to pop up on the screen. The visitor will need to click the "OK" button in the alert box to proceed.

By entering the alert command between the < *script type* = "*text/javascript*" > and </*script* > tags, the browser will recognize it as a javascript command. If we had not entered the <script> tags, the browser would simply recognize it as pure text, and just write it on the screen.

We can enter javascript in both the < *head* > and < *body* > sections of the document. In general however, it is advisable to keep as much as possible in the < *head* > section.

Now consider this example: Instead of having javascript write something in a popup box we could have it write directly into the document.

```
<html>
    <head>
        <title>My Javascript WebPage</title>
    </head>
    <body>
        <script>
            document.write("Welcome to my WebPage!!!");
        </script>
    </body>
</html>
```

The *document.write* is a javascript command telling the browser that what follows within the parentheses is to be written into the document.

Note: When entering text in javascript you need to include it in " ". The script in the example would produce this output on webpage:

```
Welcome to my WebPage!!!
```

31.3 TeX and LaTeX

TeX is a computer program for typesetting documents, created by *Donald Knuth*. It takes a suitably prepared computer file and converts it to a form which may be printed on many kinds of printers, including dot-matrix printers, laser printers and high-resolution typesetting machines.

LaTeX is an open source document preparation system and document markup language. LaTeX is a set of macros for TeX that aims at reducing the user's task to the role of writing the content, LaTeX taking care of all the formatting process. LaTeX uses the TeX typesetting program for formatting its output, and written in the TeX macro language. LaTeX is not the name of a particular editing program, but refers to the encoding or tagging conventions that are used in LaTeX documents.

LaTeX is widely used in academia. It is also used as the primary method of displaying formulas on Wikipedia. Like TeX, LaTeX started as a writing tool for mathematicians and computer scientists. But from early in its development it was also taken up by research scholars who needed to write documents that included complex non-Latin scripts, such as Arabic, Sanskrit and Chinese.

Examples

LaTeX Formula	Output
`$x=\frac{1+y}{1+2z^2}$`	$x = \frac{1+y}{1+2z^2}$

\begin{eqnarray*} x&=&\sin \alpha = \cos \beta\\ &=&\cos(\pi-\alpha) = \sin(\pi-\beta) \end{eqnarray*}	$x = sin\alpha = cos\beta$ $= \cos(\pi - \alpha) = \sin(\pi - \beta)$
$$ \frac{1}{\displaystyle 1+ \frac{1}{\displaystyle 2+ \frac{1}{\displaystyle 3+y}}} + \frac{1}{1+\frac{1}{2+\frac{1}{3+x}}} $$	$\frac{1}{1+\frac{1}{2+\frac{1}{3+y}}} + \frac{1}{1+\frac{1}{2+\frac{1}{3+x}}}$

31.4 Ruby on Rails

Ruby on Rails is a web framework built on Ruby language. Ruby on Rails, often simply *Rails*, is an open source web application. Ruby on Rails uses the model–view–controller (MVC) pattern to organize application programming.

Like Java or the C language, Ruby is a general-purpose programming language, though it is best known for its use in web programming.

Rails combines the Ruby programming language with HTML, CSS, and JavaScript to create a web application that runs on a web server. Because it runs on a web server, Rails is considered a server-side, or “back end,” web application development platform (the web browser is the “front end”).

Rails establishes conventions for easier collaboration and maintenance.

31.5 Google Search Tips

Google search is a very powerful search tool. Using the tips outlined below, you can find anything and everything you could ever need on the World Wide Web.

31.5.1 Use the Tabs

The first tip is to use the tabs in Google search. On the top of every search are a number of tabs. Usually you'll see Web, Image, News, and More. Using these tabs, you can help define what kind of search you need to do. If you need images, use the Image tab. If you are looking for a recent news article, use the News tab. They can cut search times dramatically if utilized properly.

31.5.2 Use Quotes

When searching for something specific, try using quotes to minimize the guesswork for Google search. When you put your search parameters in quotes, it tells the search engine to search for the whole phrase.

For instance, if you search for Marketing Techniques, the engine will search for content that contains those two words in any order. However, if you search “Marketing Techniques”, it will search for that phrase exactly as you typed it. This can help locate specific information that may be buried under other content if not sorted out correctly.

31.5.3 Use a hyphen to exclude words

Sometimes you may find yourself searching for a word with an ambiguous meaning. An example is Safari. When you Google search for Safari, you may get results for both the car made by Tata or the Safari books online store. If you want to cut one out, use the hyphen to tell the engine to ignore content with one of the other. See the example below.

Safari -cars

This tells the search engine to search for Safari but to remove any results that have the word “car” in it. It can be wildly helpful when finding information about something without getting information about something else.

31.5.3 Use a colon to search specific sites

There may be an instance where you need to Google search for articles or content on a certain website. The syntax is very simple and we'll show you below.

31.5.4 Interview Questions site:CareerMonk.com

This will search for all content about Interview Questions, but only on CareerMonk.com. All other search results will be removed. If you need to find specific content on a particular site, this is the shortcut you can use.

31.5.5 Find a page that links to another page

This Google search tip is a little obscure. Instead of searching for a specific page, you're searching for a page that links to a specific page. Think about it this way. If you want to see who cited a CareerMonk on their site, you would use this trick to find all the sites that link to it. The syntax is below.

link:CareerMonk.com

That will return all pages that link to the CareerMonk official website. The URL on the right side can be practically anything. Be aware, though, that the more specific it is, the fewer results you'll get. We know not a lot of people will likely use this Google search trick, but it could be very useful for some.

31.5.6 Use the asterisk wildcard

The asterisk wildcard is one of the most useful ones on the list. Here's how it works. When you use an asterisk in a search term on Google search, it will leave a placeholder that may be automatically filled by the search engine later. This is a brilliant way to find song lyrics if you don't know all the words. Let's look at the syntax.

“Come * right now * me”

In general, it may look like nonsense. However, Google search will search for that phrase knowing that the asterisks can be any word. More often than not, you'll find they are lyrics to The Beatles song “Come Together” and that's what the search will tell you.

31.5.7 Find sites that are similar to other sites

This is a unique one that could be used by practically everyone if they knew it existed. Let's say you have a favorite website. It can be anything. However, that website is getting a little bit boring and you want to find other websites like it. You would use this trick. Below is the syntax.

related:amazon.com

If you search the above, you won't find a link to Amazon. Instead, you'll find links to online stores like Amazon. Sites like Flipkart, Barnes & Noble, Best Buy, and others that sell physical items online. It's a powerful Google search tool that can help you find new sites to browse.

31.5.8 Use Google search to do math

Google search can actually do math for you. This is a rather complex one to describe because it can be used in so many ways. You can ask it basic questions or some more difficult ones. It is important to note that it won't solve all math problems, but it will solve a good number of them. Here are a couple of examples of the syntax.

```
8 * 5 + 5
```

If you search the first one, it'll return 45. It will also show a calculator that you can use to find answers to more questions. This is handy if you need to do some quick math but don't want to do it in your head.

31.5.9 Search for multiple words at once

Google search is flexible. It knows you may not find what you want by searching only a single word or phrase. Thus, it lets you search for multiples. By using this trick, you can search for one word or phrase along with a second word or phrase. This can help narrow down your search to help you find exactly what you're looking for. Here is the syntax.

```
"Best ways to prepare for a job interview" OR "How to prepare for a job interview"
```

By searching that, you will search both phrases. Remember the quotes tip above? It's being used here as well. In this instance, these two exact phrases will be searched. It can be done by word too, like the example below.

```
Chocolate OR white chocolate
```

This will search for pages that have either chocolate or white chocolate!

31.5.10 Search a range of numbers

Searching for a range of numbers is another tip we don't anticipate a lot of people using. The people that do use it, though, will probably use it quite a bit. People interested in money or statistics will find this tip particularly useful. Essentially, you use two dots and a number to let Google search know you're looking for a specific range of numbers. Like the syntax below.

```
What teams have won the Cricket World Cup ..2011
31..33
```

In the first instance, the search will toss back the team that won the Cricket World Cup in 2011. The two dots with only one number will tell the search that you don't need anything before or after 2004. This can help narrow down searches to a specific number to improve search results. In the second, Google will search for the numbers 31, 32, and 33. It is obscure, but wildly useful if you happen to need to search for numbers like this.

31.5.11 Keep it simple

Now we're getting into the general tips. Google search knows how to search for a lot of things. What this means is you don't need to be too specific. If you need a pizza place nearby, use this to search.

```
Pizza places nearby
```

Google search will grab your location and deliver a variety of results about pizza places that are near you.

31.5.12 Gradually add search terms

There will come a time when Google search doesn't shovel out the results you expect. In this instance, keeping it simple may not be the best option. As Google itself suggests, the best method is to start with something simple then gradually get more complicated. See the example below.

First try: fresher job interviews
Second try: prepare for fresher job interviews
Third try: how to prepare for a fresher job interview

This will gradually refine the search to bring you fewer, more targeted terms. The reason you don't go straight from the first try to the third try is because you may miss what you're looking for by skipping the second step. Millions of websites phrase the same information in a number of different ways; using this technique lets you search as many of them as possible to find the best info.

31.5.13 Use words that websites would use

This is a very important one. When people use Google search to hunt the web, they generally search for things using the same language that they would use for speaking. Unfortunately, websites don't say things the way people do; instead, they try to use language that sounds professional. Let's look at some examples.

"I have a flat tire" could be replaced by "repair a flat tire."
"My head hurts" could be replaced by "headache relief."

The list goes on and on. When searching, try to use terminology you would find on a professional website. This will help you get more reliable results.

31.5.14 Use important words only

The way Google search works is to take what you search for and match it with keywords in online content. When you search for too many words, it may limit your results. That means it may actually take you longer to find what you're looking for. Thus, it is apropos to use only the important words when searching for something. Let's see an example.

Don't use: Where can I find a Indian restaurant that delivers.
Instead try: Indian restaurants nearby.
Or: Indian restaurants near me.

Doing this can help Google find what you need without the clutter. So remember, keep it simple and use important words only.

31.5.15 Google search has shortcuts

A number of commands can be entered to give you instantaneous results. Like the math example above, Google can immediately give you the information you need that is displayed right at the top of the search results. This can save time and effort so you don't have to click a bunch of bothersome links. Here are a few examples of some commands you can enter into Google.

Weather *zip code* – This will show you the weather in the given zip code. You can also use town and city names instead of area codes, but it may not be as accurate if there are multiple area codes in the city.

What is the definition of *word* or Define: *word* – This will display the definition of a word.

Time *place* – This will display the time in whatever place you type in.

You can check any stock by typing its ticker name into Google. If you search for GOOG, it will check the stock prices for Google.

These quick commands can take a web search that is usually multiple clicks and condense it into a single search. This is very helpful for information you need repeatedly.

31.5.16 Spelling doesn't necessarily matter

Google search has gotten a lot smarter over the years. These days, you don't even need to spell words correctly. As long as it's pretty close, Google can usually figure out what it means. Here are some examples.

If you search "Nver Gna Gve Yo Up" Google will automatically assume you mean to search for "Never Gonna Give You Up." If by chance your misspelling was intentional, Google gives you the option to search for the misspelled term instead.

This trick is great if you happen to forget how to spell something or are not altogether sure how something is spelled. It can also be helpful when searching for obscure words. This applies to capitalization and grammar as well.

31.5.17 Use descriptive words

Pretty much everything can be described in multiple ways. Take our namesake, the "life hack." The terminology "hack" refers to a computer programmer breaking security on a network or system. However, when used in conjunction with the word "life", it alters the meaning to tips and tricks people can use to improve their lives.

If you have trouble finding what you're searching for, keep in mind that people may search or define what you need in a different way than you do.

You may search "How to install drivers in AIX OS?"
When you really mean "Troubleshoot driver problems AIX OS."

There really isn't a good specific example for this one. If you search for something and you can't find an answer, try asking the same question using different words and see if that helps the results.

31.5.18 Find a specific file

An often forgotten feature of Google search is the ability to search for a specific file or file type. This can be infinitely useful if you need a specific PDF or PowerPoint file that you previously viewed or need to use for another project. The syntax is quite simple.

Search term here filetype:doc

In the above example, you simply replace the search term with whatever you're searching for. Then use the filetype command and enter the extension of any file type you can think of. This can mostly be useful for scholarly purposes, but business presentations and other assorted presentations can benefit from this kind of search as well.

31.5.19 Money and unit conversions

Google search can quickly and accurately convert both measurement units and currency value. There are a variety of uses for this, like checking to see the conversion rate between two currencies. If you happen to be a math student, you can use it to convert from feet to meters or from ounces to liters. Here's how to do it.

miles to km – This will convert miles to kilometers. You can put numbers in front to convert a certain number. Like "10 miles to km" will show you how many kilometers are in 10 miles.

USD to INR – This will convert a US dollar to Indian Rupees. Like the measurements above, you can add numbers to find exact conversions for a certain amount of money.

It's true that this tip is geared toward math students and international business people. However, you'd be surprised how often these tips are used by regular people.

31.5.20 Track your packages

Our last trick is to use Google search to find out where your packages are. You can enter any UPS, USPS, or Fedex tracking number directly into the Google search bar, and it'll show you the tracking information about your package. This is much easier than going to the specific sites, waiting for them to load, then searching for your packages there. No examples are really needed for this one. Just type your tracking number in and see where your package is.

31.6 Web Crawling

A web crawler (also called a web spider or web robot) is a program or automated script which browses the World Wide Web in a systematic, automated manner. This process is called *Web crawling* or *spidering*.

Many sites, in particular search engines such as Google, use spidering as a means of providing latest data. Web crawlers are mainly used to create a copy of all the visited webpages for later processing by a search engine that will index the downloaded pages to provide fast searches. Crawlers can also be used for automating maintenance tasks on a Web site, such as checking links or validating HTML code. Also, crawlers can be used to gather specific types of information from Web pages, such as harvesting e-mail addresses (usually for spam).

In general, it starts with a list of URLs to visit, called the *seeds*. As the crawler visits these URLs, it identifies all the hyperlinks in the page and adds them to the list of URLs to visit, called the *crawl* frontier. URLs from the frontier are recursively visited according to a set of policies.

31.6.1 Characteristics of Crawlers

There are important characteristics of the Web that make crawling very difficult:

- Large volume
- Fast rate of change
- Dynamic page generation

The large volume indicates that the crawler can only download a fraction of the Web pages within a given time, so it needs to prioritize downloads. The high rate of change implies that by the time the crawler is downloading the last pages from a site, it is very likely that new pages have been added to the site, or that pages have already been updated or even deleted.

31.6.2 Crawling Policies

The behavior of a Web crawler is dependent on a list of policies:

- A selection policy that states which pages to download,
- A re-visit policy that states when to check for changes to the pages,
- A politeness policy that states how to avoid overloading Web sites, and
- A parallelization policy that states how to coordinate distributed Web crawlers.

31.6.3 Web Crawler Architectures

A crawler must not only have a good crawling strategy but it should also have a good architecture. While it is fairly easy to build a slow crawler that downloads a few pages per second for a short period of time, building a high-performance system that can download hundreds of millions of pages over several weeks presents a number of challenges in system design, I/O and network efficiency, and robustness and manageability.

Web crawlers are a central part of search engines, and details on their algorithms and architecture are kept as business secrets. When crawler designs are published, there is often an important lack of detail that prevents others from reproducing the work.

There are also emerging concerns about "search engine spamming", which prevent major search engines from publishing their ranking algorithms.

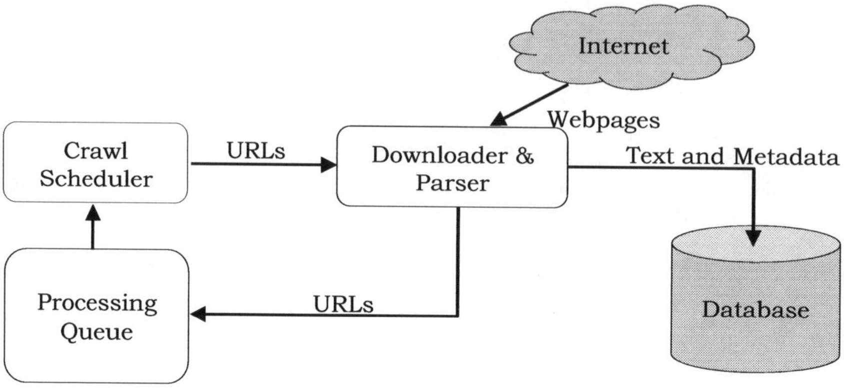

31.6.4 Normalization of URLs

Crawlers usually perform some type of URL normalization in order to avoid crawling the same resource more than once. *URL normalization* is also called URL *canonicalization*, refers to the process of modifying and standardizing a URL in a consistent manner.

There are several types of normalization that may be performed including conversion of URLs to lowercase, removal of "." and ".." segments, and adding trailing slashes to the non-empty path component.

31.6.5 Examples of Web crawlers

The following is a list of published crawler architectures for general-purpose crawlers (excluding focused web crawlers), with a brief description that includes the names given to the different components and outstanding features:

- Yahoo Crawler (Slurp) is the name of the Yahoo Search crawler.
- Google Crawler is based in C++ and Python. The crawler was integrated with the indexing process, because text parsing was done for full-text indexing and also for URL extraction. There is a URL server that sends lists of URLs to be fetched by several crawling processes. During parsing, the URLs found were passed to a URL server that checked if the URL has been previously seen. If not, the URL was added to the queue of the URL server.

Note: There are open source web crawlers as well. Examples include mnoGoSearch, GRUB etc..

31.7 Google's Page Ranking Algorithm

The Google's most important feature is arguably the Page Ranking Algorithm, a patented automated process that determines where each search result appears on Google's search engine return page.

Most users tend to concentrate on the first few search results, so getting a spot at the top of the list usually means more user traffic. So how does Google determine search results standings? Many people have tried to figure out the exact formula, but Google keeps the official algorithm a secret.

What we do know is this:

- It assigns a rank or score to every search result. The higher the page's score, the further up the search results list it will appear.
- Scores are partially determined by the number of other Web pages that link to the target page. Each link is counted as a vote for the target. The logic behind this is that pages with high quality content will be linked to more often than mediocre pages.
- Not all votes are equal. Votes from a high-ranking Web page count more than votes from low-ranking sites. You can't really boost one Web page's rank by making a bunch of empty Web sites linking back to the target page.
- The more links a Web page sends out, the more diluted its voting power becomes. In other words, if a high-ranking page links to hundreds of other pages, each individual vote won't count as much as it would if the page only linked to a few sites.
- Other factors that might affect scoring include the how long the site has been around, the strength of the domain name, how and where the keywords appear on the site and the age of the links going to and from the site. Google tends to place more value on sites that have been around for a while.
- Some people claim that Google uses a group of human testers to evaluate search returns, manually sorting through results to hand pick the best links. Google denies this and says that while it does employ a network of people to test updated search formulas, it doesn't rely on human beings to sort and rank search results.
- Google's strategy works well. By focusing on the links going to and from a Web page, the search engine can organize results in a useful way. While there are a few tricks webmasters can use to improve Google standings, the best way to get a top spot is to consistently provide top quality content, which gives other people the incentive to link back to their pages.

31.8 Basics of XML

Extensible Markup Language (XML) is an abbreviated version of Standard Generalized Markup Language (SGML). It is used for the exchange of structured documents over the Internet. Unlike HTML, XML readily enables the definition, transmission, validation, and interpretation of data. XML permits people in a specialized field, such as chemistry, finance, or environmental data collection, to develop XML schema that define the markup language for the exchange of specialized data unique to their fields.

XML is extensible, meaning a developer can extend the language by devising new tags to describe and share data in any specialized way desired as long as the new tags follow the XML syntax defined by the W3C XML specification. XML is very useful for organizations that do not share but need to develop a common data exchange format.

Its extensibility provides flexibility in developing exchange formats in XML schema, provided all partners agree on the data format and definitions of the data it contains.

31.8.1 How does XML work?

XML is not a programming language like C++ or Java, but a markup specification language. A browser or other application must read the XML document in order to make it do something.

Development of XML documents begins with the identification and definition of the data elements that will be displayed or exchanged. The data elements are defined using tags that indicate what a data element represents. For example, in the simplest explanation, a person's name might contain three tags:

```
<Name>
    <First>Aryan</First>
    <MiddleInitial>Babu</MiddleInitial>
```

```
    <Last>K</Last>
</Name>
```

Developers create a schema that contains the tag name, their data formats, and the relationships to one another.

31.8.2 Building XML

XML files will consist of content plus markup. You place much of your content in elements by surrounding your content with tags. For example, suppose you need to create an XML cookbook. You have a recipe named Ice Cream Vanilla to prepare in XML. To mark up the recipe name, you enclose that text in your element by placing the beginning tag before your text and the ending tag after your text.

You might call the element recipename. To mark the beginning tag of the element, place the element's name inside angle brackets (<>) like this: <recipename>. Then, type your text Ice Cream Sundae.

After the text, enter the element's ending tag, which is the element's name inside angle brackets plus an ending forward slash (/) before the element's name, like this: </recipename>. These tags form an element, into which you can enter content or even other elements.

31.8.3 Start your XML file

The first line of your XML document might be an XML declaration. This optional part of the file identifies it as an XML file, which can help tools and humans identify the file as XML rather than SGML or some other markup. The declaration can be written simply as <?xml?> or include the XML version (<?xml version="1.0"?>) or even the character encoding, such as <?xml version="1.0" encoding="utf-8"?> for Unicode.

Because this declaration must be first in the file, if you plan to combine smaller XML files into a larger file, you might want to omit this optional information.

31.8.4 Create your root element

The root element's beginning and end tags surround your XML document's content. Only one root element is in the file, and you need this "wrapper" to contain it all. We use here with a root element named <recipe>.

```
<?xml version="1.0" encoding="UTF-8"?>
<recipe>
</recipe>
```

As you build your document, your content and additional tags will go between <recipe> and </rccipc>.

31.8.5 Name your elements

So far, you have <recipe> as your root element. With XML, you choose the names for your elements, then define the corresponding DTD or schema based on those names. The names you create can contain alphabetic characters, numbers, and special characters such as underscores (_). Here are a few things to note about your naming: Spaces are not allowed in the element names.

Names must begin with an alphabetic character, not a number or symbol. (After this first character, you can use any combination of letters, numbers and the allowed symbols.) Case does not matter, but be consistent to avoid confusion.

Building on the prior example, if you add an element named <recipename>, it will have a beginning tag <recipename> and a corresponding end tag </recipename>.

```
<?xml version="1.0" encoding="UTF-8"?>
<recipe>
<recipename>Ice Cream Vanilla</recipename>
<preptime>5 minutes</preptime>
</recipe>
```

An XML document can have some empty tags that do not have anything inside and can be expressed as a single tag instead of as a set of beginning and end tags. To use an HTML-like example, you might have <img src="image.gif"> as a stand-alone element. It doesn't contain any child elements or text, so it is an empty element and you can express it as <img src="image.gif" /> (finished off with a space and the familiar ending slash).

31.8.6 Nest the elements

Nesting is the placement of elements inside other elements. These new elements are called child elements, and the elements that enclose them are their parent elements. Several elements are nested inside the <recipe> root element. These nested child items include <recipename>, <ingredlist>, and <preptime>. Inside the <ingredlist> element are multiple occurrences of its own child element, <listitem>. Nesting can be many levels deep in an XML document.

A common syntax error is improper nesting of parent and child elements. Any child element must be completely enclosed between the starting and end tags of its parent element. Sibling elements must each end before the next sibling begins.

The tags begin and end without intermingling with other tags.

```
<?xml version="1.0" encoding="UTF-8"?>
<recipe>
<recipename>Ice Cream Vanilla</recipename>
<ingredlist>
<listitem>
<quantity>3</quantity>
<itemdescription>chocolate syrup</itemdescription>
</listitem>
<listitem>
<quantity>1</quantity>
<itemdescription>nuts</itemdescription>
</listitem>
<listitem>
<quantity>1</quantity>
<itemdescription>cherry</itemdescription>
</listitem>
</ingredlist>
<preptime>5 minutes</preptime>
</recipe>
```

31.8.7 Add attributes

Attributes are sometimes added to elements. Attributes consist of a name-value pair, with the value in double quotation marks ("), thus: type="dessert". Attributes provide a way to store additional information each time you use an element, varying the attribute value as needed from one instance of an element to another within the same document.

You type the attribute—or even multiple attributes—within the starting tag of an element: <recipe type="dessert">. If you add multiple attributes, separate them with spaces: <recipename cuisine="indian" servings="1">.

```
<?xml version="1.0" encoding="UTF-8"?>
```

```
<recipe type="dessert">
<recipename cuisine="indian" servings="1">Ice Cream Vanilla</recipename>
<preptime>5 minutes</preptime>
</recipe>
```

You can use as few or as many attributes as you feel you need. Consider the details you might add to your documents. Attributes are especially helpful if documents will be sorted—for example, by type of recipe. Attribute names can include the same characters as element names, with similar rules for omitting spaces and starting names with alphabetic characters.

31.8.8 What is an XML schema?

An XML schema is a single file or collection of files that serve as the framework for defining the data content, format and structure of an XML document. A well written schema expresses agreed upon vocabularies and allows computers to validate the data against the rules written to describe the data. It provides a means for defining the structure and content of XML documents.

While a schema describes the content and structure of an XML document, an XML instance document contains the actual data. The schema and instance document are always separate, and the instance document is frequently validated against the schema to ensure the contents and structure are correct. XML schema can be combined and reused, so that one schema can reference another. When creating schema for new data flows, schema developers should look for existing schema that may describe a portion of their data flow.

31.8.9 Valid and Well-Formed XML

If you follow the rules outlined in your structure, you can easily produce well-formed XML. Well-formed XML is XML that follows all the rules of XML: proper element naming, nesting, attribute naming, and so on.

Depending on what you do with your XML, you might work with well-formed XML. But consider the aforementioned example of sorting by recipe type. You need to ensure that every <recipe> element contains the type attribute in order to sort recipes. Being able to properly validate and ensure that this attribute's value is always present can be invaluable (no pun intended).

Validation is checking your document's structure against rules for your elements and how you defined child elements for each parent element. You define these rules in a Document Type Definition (DTD) or in a schema. This validation requires you to create your DTD or schema, and then reference the DTD or schema file within your XML files.

To enable validation, you include the document type (DOCTYPE) in your XML documents near the top. This line refers to the DTD or schema (your list of elements and rules) to be used to validate that document.

```
<!DOCTYPE MyDocs SYSTEM "filename.dtd">
```

This example assumes that your element list file is named filename.dtd and resides on your computer

Note: Many languages have support for processing XML.

CHAPTER

Career Options 32

You must have asked yourself this question a lot of times at some or the other point in your life. The society is more concerned about the job and pay you get after education and not the intellectual property you have earned. Don't leave an option straight forward because it is too mediocre. You don't need to follow others but to follow your heart. It's okay if a million other people like you are preparing for an entrance exam, including your friends! If you believe you can crack the exam, trust me YOU CAN. Do whatever you want with 100% dedication.

Below are the list of options that you can explore.

32.1 Campus Placement

Usually, all colleges has a separate *Career Development* and *Placement Cell* which is an integral part of the institute. It ensures and takes care to provide the best arrangements for placing its students in premier companies. It also conducts training programs for the students to enable them to face interviews. These programmes include workshops on self-esteem, presentation skills, communication skills and mock personal interviews etc. If your college does not hold this, ask your principal and it is the bare minimal thing. In other words, do not prefer colleges which do not care for this.

The *placement cell* remains in constant touch with the prospective employers to intimate their human resource (HR) requirement. On learning the requirements, a placement mutually agreeable date is fixed for holding interview at the college campus and the candidates are guided and trained for the demonstrations and interviews.

Already bored of studying? Then getting selected in a decent company visiting your campus seems a good option. If you don't have any intentions of studying further, or at least immediately after B. Tech, you can opt for a job. This is considered to be a safer option where you get time to decide which field you want to stick to technical or you want to shift your core interest area from technical to management or some other stream.

32.2 Going for M. Tech./M.S. in India

If you studied engineering out of passion and not because you were forced by your parents or just for sake of doing it, then *M.Tech.* (Master of Technology) or *M.S.* (Master of Science) is a good option. You can opt for the field of study you aspire to expertise in. For this, you need to prepare well for the entrance exams to get into a good college. GATE (Graduate Aptitude Test in Engineering) is a national exam conducted in India which can fetch you admission in IITs, IISC or NITs and many others. . The pattern and syllabus are usually based on a candidate's *B.Tech.* (Bachelor of Technology) *or B.E.* (Bachelor of Engineering) syllabus.

If you feel, you have less technical capabilities then give less preference to this. Securing good rank in GATE is pretty tough if you do not put 100% effort in preparation.

32.3 Going for M.S. in Foreign Countries

It is also a very good option to explore. If you choose to study abroad, you will get a lot of exposure and learning along with the education part. You might also be able to get a job at international locations if you have plans to settle abroad permanently in the future.

You can also explore integrated opportunities abroad. Along with options of MS you may explore options of MS+PhD and other research oriented courses. In addition, you could look at the various fellowships in research and development category available that may fascinate you too. You can also apply for the various scholarships which will fund your education partially or completely.

GRE: The Graduate Record Examination or GRE is a standardized test that is an admissions requirement for many graduate schools in English speaking countries. It is created and administered by the Educational Testing Service and is similar in format and content to the SAT. It is a computer based Online test. The percentile scored in this exam will decide your future in doing M.S in foreign nations.

TOEFL: The Test of English as a Foreign Language (or TOEFL®, pronounced "toe-full" or sometimes "toffle") evaluates the potential success of an individual to use and understand Standard American English at a college level. It is required for non-native applicants at many English-speaking colleges and universities. A TOEFL score is valid for two years and then is deleted from the official database.

Students with less technical capabilities and who could not get good rank in GATE can prefer this option. Of course, it does need financial support. If you get good score, many foreign universities are giving full scholarship with living expenses. It would be helpful if you meet your seniors who already got good score in GRE for their suggestions in preparation. Also along with good GRE/TOEFL score, references from *professors* who has contacts in foreign universities helps you in getting scholarship.

For financial help, I saw cases where few people put required amount in bank accounts for the period of 3 months on interest basis. So if one cannot get financial help can think of this option. Once they go for M.S. they can give back this money and try for scholarship seriously.

Big Note: It is not worthy for anyone doing P.G in some college other than Foreign/Indian University Colleges, and Premier Private Engineering Colleges.

32.4 Going for MBA

Don't feel you are the technical guy your parents wanted you to be? Always felt like you are a manager and want to see yourself in a business suit in some MNC? Probably you have a fascination for MBA (Master of Business Administration) too. Don't get diverted by the thoughts that everyone is doing an MBA right now and its value has decreased. If you want to make a career in the management sector, hold managerial positions, then MBA is the right choice.

You may specialize in your area of interest which may be the all-time popular fields like HR, Marketing, Sales or the new growing domains like Digital Marketing, International Relations etc. In India, there are various entrance examinations that will help you get into the top 30 MBA colleges. CAT (Common Admission Test) serves as a gateway for an MBA at the IIMs and many other leading institutes. Some other popular exams are XAT (Xaviers), NMAT, SNAP, CMAT, TISS, IRMA etc.

32.5 Entrepreneurship-Start your venture

Do you have dreams of being an employer? Always wanted to be your own boss? Then, starting something of your own is a great option. But before you think about it you need to be sure about your options. Start-up is trending more as a fashion than a career option. Being your own boss does not mean you can ignore work and life would be easy.

Starting your venture and making it success would be the toughest of all the things you can do. It will have ups and downs every new day. Maybe you would not get any client for the whole year. Be ready for the challenges and immense learning if you are determined to be an entrepreneur. This is the road less traveled.

I suggest you to get some experience before venturing your own. Meet few entrepreneurs to get suggestions.

32.6 Trying for Government Jobs and Civil Services

Even though corporate jobs may offer the best of salaries and perks, a majority of youngsters and their parents still crave entry to the prestigious Indian Civil Services held by the UPSC. The very fact that a big share of every year's top posts in the civil services exams are bagged by professionals from various streams, shows that the IAS is still the dream job for many.

Graduate Aptitude Test in Engineering (GATE) is now attracting several engineering students as a number of Public Sector Units (PSUs) are taking the test score as benchmark for recruitment in their companies. As has been the trend since 2013, recruitment by the Public Sector Undertakings (PSUs) through GATE has already started. All GATE aspirants must apply within the specified dates for each PSU.

All candidates interested must note that only GATE qualified candidates will be considered. Many Public Sector Undertakings (PSUs) are increasingly conducting their recruitment through Graduate Aptitude Test in Engineering (GATE).

The big PSUs which will use GATE scores for recruitment include Indian Oil, NTPC, BHEL and DVC. A total of 14 PSUs consider GATE scores for recruitment and these companies pay their employees as per the recommendation of the sixth pay commission.

32.7 Final Notes

- For M.Tech./M.S. in India prefer IITs, NITs, IIITs, and other colleges which have good placements. Just for the sake of degree do not go for post-graduation.
- If you hold M.Tech./M.S. from good college in India and if you plan further studies (like Ph.D.: Doctor of Philosophy), prefer foreign universities.
- If you cannot get good GATE rank (below 500 or 600), prefer PSUs.
- If you are not technically sound and have financial support, go for M.S. in foreign countries.
- Never try things in parallel. For example, preparing for GATE while working. It rarely works. But, you can try GRE while working as the competition is not too high.

32.8 Tips to Become Successful in Your Career

Career planning is not an activity that should be done once and then left behind as we move forward in our jobs and careers. Rather, career planning is an activity that is best done on a regular basis; especially given the data that the average worker will change careers (not jobs) multiple times over his or her lifetime. And it's never too soon or too late to start your career planning.

Know Your Values

The place to start building career success is with yourself. First, zero in on your values. Values are the core principles that run your life. The more your career aligns with and honors your values, the deeper the sense of satisfaction you will derive from what you do.

Play to Your Strengths

Second, find your strengths. It is easier and a lot more fun to play to your strengths than to compensate for weaknesses.

Be Willing to Work Hard

You want to make yourself indispensable and known as the reliable person who's willing to go the extra mile.

Be Positive and Proactive

Introduce yourself to everyone in the office as well as new hires. Find ways to get noticed in a positive light. Smile and cultivate a can-do attitude. Have a sense of humor. Everyone loves working with a positive, energized person.

Get Along with the Boss

Strive to cultivate positive relationships with those in charge of your fate at the company. Show appropriate respect and connect on a genuine level where you have shared common interests and opinions.

Get Control on What You are Doing

During your initial days of the role, spend more hours; understand the project concepts, set-up (configurations), current issues and make yourself comfortable in doing job without so much dependency with team members. Seeking help from team members too frequently for smaller things might give bad impression about your capabilities. This not only give more control on what you are doing, but also, gets you more honour from your squad members.

Be a Team Player

A team player inspires others and is willing to set aside their ego for the greater good of the project or company goal.

Have Specialized Skills

Having specialized skills that are valuable and relevant to your company can set you apart. You'll get noticed and become indispensable to the company.

Own Up to Mistakes and Learn from Them

If you made a mistake admit it. Find the lesson and resolve not to make the same mistake again.

Be Flexible

There are probably a number of different areas that you could see yourself working in. Experiment and see what you like best! Strive to be fluid and open to change, never rigid. Most companies are continually looking for new and better ways to do business and increase profits. Be ready to adjust and change as the company grows and evolves.

Seek out Mentors

Mentors can be invaluable in your career path and growth. Seek out those who have excelled in your career and glean insights and wisdom from them.

Plan Something Which Others Cannot

In a competitive IT environment it is important to prove yourself contiguously and stand unique among your team members. For example, along with regular job you can plan a journal, book, on-line articles, filing patents, taking sessions for team members, etc..

Network

Stay connected with others in your field. Watch for new opportunities and be willing to give referrals as appropriate. Share knowledge and resources with others.

Here's the real secret of career building: the best jobs come up because someone who knows you thinks that you would be the right person for the job. So networking is a critical piece of career success. Yet many people are afraid to network, thinking that it is somehow impolite to ask others for help. Even worse, they may wonder why would anyone want to spend time with someone new to the field.

Networking does not have to be scary. Think of networking as connecting with another person so that the two of you are in sync and are relevant to each other. People are always looking for talent and those big executives/stars were once beginners just like you.

Get support

Seek out people who understand your situation or are a positive influence. Join a support group or create your own with like-minded friends.

Never Stop Learning and Improving

Lastly, never stop growing. Take classes and seminars related to your field. Challenge yourself and set new goals each year. If your performance and productivity continue to rise, so will your value as an asset to the company.

Keep an Eye on Current Job Trends

Everyone makes his or her own job and career opportunities, so that even if your career is shrinking, if you have excellent skills and know how to market yourself, you should be able to find a new job. However, having information about current job trends is important to long-term career planning success.

A career path that is expanding today could easily shrink tomorrow or next year. It's important to see where job growth is expected, especially in the career fields that most interest you. Besides knowledge of these trends, the other advantage of conducting this research is the power it gives you to adjust and strengthen your position, your unique selling proposition. One of the keys to job and career success is having a unique set of accomplishments, skills, and education that make you better than all others in your career.

References

[1] W. Stallings. Local and Metropolitan Area Networks. Prentice Hall, Upper Saddle River, NJ, sixth edition, 2000.
[2] W. Stallings. Cryptography and Network Security. Prentice Hall, Upper Saddle River, NJ, third edition, 2003.
[3] W. Stallings. Data and Computer Communications. Prentice Hall, Upper Saddle River, NJ, eighth edition, 2007.
[4] A. S. Tanenbaum. Modern Operating Systems. Prentice Hall, Upper Saddle River, NJ, second edition, 2001.
[5] A. S. Tanenbaum. Computer Networks. Prentice Hall, Upper Saddle River, NJ, fourth edition, 2003.
[6] csee.usf.edu
[7] Data Structures and Algorithms Made Easy by Narasimha Karumanchi, Second Edition, CareerMonk Publications
[8] Data Structures and Algorithms Made Easy in Java by Narasimha Karumanchi, Second Edition, CareerMonk Publications
[9] Peeling Design Patterns by Narasimha Karumanchi, Dr. Meda Sreenivasa Rao, CareerMonk Publications
[10] Elements of Computer Networking by Narasimha Karumanchi, Meda Sreenivasa Rao, Dr. A. Damodaram, CareerMonk Publications
[11] T. V. Lakshman and D. Stiliadis. "High-Speed Policy-Based Packet Forwarding Using Efficient Multidimensional Range Matching." Proceedings of the SIGCOMM '98 Symposium, pp. 203–214, September 1998.
[12] W. Leland, M. Taqqu, W. Willinger, and D. Wilson. "On the Self-Similar Nature of Ethernet Traffic." IEEE/ACM Transactions on Networking, 2:1–15, February 1994.
[13] J. Mashey. "RISC, MIPS, and the Motion of Complexity." UniForum 1986 Conference Proceedings, pp. 116–124, 1986.
[14] J.Mogul and S. Deering. "Path MTU Discovery." Request for Comments 1191, November 1990.
[15] National Research Council, Computer Science and Telecommunications Board. Realizing the Information Future: The Internet and Beyond. National Academy Press, Washington, DC, 1994.
[16] National Research Council. Looking Over the Fence at Networks. National Academy Press, Washington DC, 2001.
[17] T. R. N. Rao and E. Fujiwara. Error-Control Coding for Computer Systems. Prentice Hall, Englewood Cliffs, NJ, 1989.
[18] K. Ramakrishnan, S. Floyd, and D. Black. "The Addition of Explicit Congestion Notification (ECN) to IP." Request for Comments 3168, September 2001.
[19] R. Rejaie, M.Handley, and D. Estrin. "RAP: An End-to-End Rate-Based Congestion ControlMechanism for Realtime Streams in the Internet." INFOCOM (3), pp. 1337–1345, 1999.
[20] D. Ritchie. "A Stream Input-Output System." AT&T Bell Laboratories Technical Journal, 63(8):311–324, October 1984.
[21] Y. Rekhter, T. Li, and S. Hares. "A Border Gateway Protocol 4 (BGP-4)." Request for Comments 4271, January 2006.
[22] T. G. Robertazzi, editor. Performance Evaluation of High-Speed Switching Fabrics and Networks: ATM, Broadband ISDN, and MAN Technology. IEEE Press, Piscataway, NJ, 1993.

31638468R20314

Made in the USA
Middletown, DE
06 May 2016